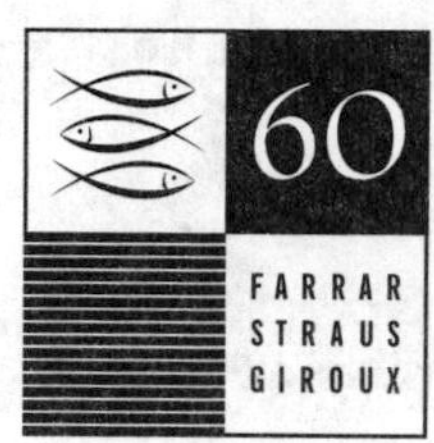
60
FARRAR
STRAUS
GIROUX

ALSO BY DAVID FRIEND

The Meaning of Life: Reflections in Words and Pictures of Why We Are Here

More Reflections on the Meaning of Life

With Graydon Carter

Vanity Fair's *Hollywood*

Oscar Night

WATCHING THE WORLD CHANGE

WATCHING THE WORLD CHANGE

THE STORIES BEHIND THE IMAGES OF 9/11

David Friend

FARRAR, STRAUS AND GIROUX

NEW YORK

Farrar, Straus and Giroux
19 Union Square West, New York 10003

Distributed in Canada by Douglas & McIntyre Ltd.
Printed in the United States of America
First edition, 2006

Owing to limitations of space, all acknowledgments for permission to reprint previously published material appear on page 437.

Library of Congress Cataloging-in-Publication Data
Friend, David, 1955–
Watching the world change : the stories behind the images of 9/11 / David Friend.— 1st ed.
p. cm.
Includes bibliographical references.
ISBN-13: 978-0-374-29933-0 (hardcover : alk. paper)
ISBN-10: 0-374-29933-1 (hardcover : alk. paper)
1. September 11 Terrorist Attacks, 2001. 2. September 11 Terrorist Attacks, 2001—Pictorial works. 3. World Trade Center (New York, N.Y.)—Pictorial works. 4. Terrorism—New York (State)—New York—Pictorial works. 5. Documentary photography. I. Title.

HV6432.7.F75 2006
974.7'1004—dc22

2005036158

Designed by Cassandra J. Pappas

www.fsgbooks.com

1 3 5 7 9 10 8 6 4 2

For my mother and father

and for Harry Benson

In memory of those who perished

in the September 11 attacks,

including New Yorkers working in

photography and television that day:

Bill Biggart, Gerard Coppola, Donald J. DiFranco,

Steven Jacobson, Robert Edward Pattison,

Glen Pettit, Isaias Rivera,

and William Steckman

CONTENTS

INTRODUCTION

The eyes were everywhere.

Witnesses were observing, and photographing, the deadliest terrorist strike in American history even before they realized it. At 8:46 a.m. on September 11, 2001, at least three different photographers (one in Manhattan, two in Brooklyn) happened to have their video cameras rolling. Then, within the span of a few seconds—no more—they found themselves chronicling The Event. A plane was suddenly colliding with one of the towers of the World Trade Center.

As the minutes elapsed, and people took to the streets, Manhattan seemed alive with cameras. There was the father who had brought along a Handycam, intending to tape his son's first morning at nursery school, only to turn his lens on clouds dark as coal. There was the deli owner who dispensed disposable cameras to customers, for free. There was the man who videotaped through the window of an elevated Q train as it rumbled across the Manhattan Bridge, the smoking towers bobbing through his LED screen.

Bucky Turco, an arts editor and gallery owner, shot footage with a two-hundred-dollar camcorder, shuttling from place to place on Rollerblades. Computer programmer Mike Cunga secured a video camera onto his bicycle handlebars, aimed it behind him, then filmed as he sped away from the collapsing structure, streaks of brown soot coating his lens. Photojournalist Carolina Salguero hopped into her powerboat in Brooklyn and cruised west, encountering what she calls "this wall of impenetrable black smoke" above Battery Park City. "I prayed while photographing," says Salguero, who has covered conflicts in Bosnia and Romania, Peru (where she was wounded in a bomb blast) and South Africa (where she was abducted at gunpoint). "I've never done that before."

Jenny Merot Mannerheim, a graphic designer from Stockholm, made her way toward the site to pitch in, and ended up staying twelve days, shooting roll after roll with her husband, Ronan, while handing out food to emergency personnel at a downtown Burger King. TV producer Mark Obenhaus, video camera in hand, traversed the streets with his son Sam, still camera in hand; the father had decided, on impulse, to tape an ABC News segment about his own fifteen-year-old, and together they watched scenes unfold through eyes that had become somehow wise beyond their years: volunteers in Foley Square preparing plywood stretchers for the wounded; the word CHAOS finger-painted in the ash on a car's windshield; a truck stacked with empty body bags. Journalist Jacques Menasche, who had been downtown dropping off his six-year-old son, Emanuel, at school, would recall "one young woman, face puffed into a red ball, [who] walked about dazed with a Leica, taking photos and crying at the same time. Weirdly, I had the sudden vision of her as a surreal advertisement—'Leica: Our Photographers Cry.' "

It would be a matter of hours before they—we—would learn the whole truth: that four commercial airliners, hijacked by members of an extremist Islamist faction, al-Qaeda, had been rerouted and sent on suicide missions. Two of the aircraft had deliberately veered into the twin towers, claiming 2,749 victims; one plane had struck the Pentagon, taking 184 lives; and a final jet had crashed in a field in Shanksville, Pennsylvania, killing 40, when a group of courageous passengers chose to head for the cockpit, intent on overwhelming the hijackers.

Amid the horror, New Yorkers by the tens of thousands had committed millions of moments to film and video. They recorded the conflagration and implosion, the panic of pedestrians, the human toll of the worst terrorist attack, ever, on U.S. soil. They then went on to document the waves of response—entreaties for the missing, the emergency teams, the rescue effort, each frame dispensing its own ripples of compassion, sorrow, and valor.

What had mesmerized every one of these men and women with cameras, surely, was the gravity of sudden death, in numbers of such magnitude. But they were also gripped by the pure visual spectacle—by the sense that this irreconcilably infernal scene was somehow *meant* to be seen. Skyscrapers, along with the hundreds and hundreds of lives within them, were being ravaged, with passenger planes, *in order that* the violence be witnessed. Terrorism, by definition, demanded frightened eyes. It required that the media be present to acknowledge, process, and then fan the fury. These targets had been selected precisely because they were icons of America's economic preeminence, and because they were perfectly situated for riveting multitudes. The goal was to enact scenes of unprecedented violence on a world stage while gaining maximum exposure (with all that the term implied—politically, psychologically, photographically).

The terrorists' motive was so warped, their method so pyrotechnic, the result so profoundly painful that the horror literally had to be seen, and seen again, to be believed. So inconceivable was the event that viewers doubted not their television screens, but their eyes. The scene called to mind a passage from Edgar Allan Poe. "My very senses," says one of his horrified characters, "reject their own evidence." People with cameras understood immediately: only rendering this act visually would confirm its reality; only images, not words, would suffice.

In fact, this was not the first coordinated series of terrorist acts in recent memory aimed at multiple American targets. Simultaneous attacks on U.S. and French military compounds in Beirut, for example, had killed three hundred in October 1983; simultaneous attacks on U.S. embassies in Kenya and Tanzania, in August 1998, killed 224 and wounded more than five thousand. But even as those bloody assaults brought America and the world to a standstill, they were enacted in the shadows, as it were; their primary intention was to inflict massive casualties, not to entice a mass audience across twenty-four time zones. This attack was of a different order. This was terror enacted as sadistic, global reality show.

Many eyewitnesses on September 11 immediately compared the atrocity to one of similar tenor and national moment—the assassination of President John F. Kennedy, gunned down while riding in a motorcade through Dallas. But there was a striking contrast between perceptions of the events of November 1963 and those of September 2001. For decades after the Dallas shooting, Americans would ask one another, "Where were you when you heard the news?" And each would have a private recollection of that first alert: "An announcement came over the intercom" . . . "I heard it on the radio" . . . "Our teacher told us, trying to remain calm. I remember a few kids were crying."

In contrast, when recalling that instant of recognition on the eleventh of September, many tend to pose a slightly different question: "Where were you when you saw it?" The "where" remains constant; we crave the details of how others coped with their shock and anguish because we too want to revisit how we shared in their experience of historic, if tragic, proportions. The "when" stays the same, as well: most of us learned of the event that morning, between 8:46 and 10:28, Eastern Daylight Time (a span of 102 minutes, marked by the first plane's impact with the north tower, Tower One, of the Trade Center, and the collapse of that structure, the second to fall). What has changed, obviously, is the verb. And the reason for this shift has to do with a shift in how the world communicates.

At the start of the new millennium, news organizations phased in a pair of relatively new technologies that would prove transformative. These two advances, just coming of age in the 1990s, enabled the events of September 2001 to be the first such acts witnessed in "real time," in virtually identical fashion, by an overwhelming share of the world's inhabitants.

The first breakthrough was satellite newsgathering (via digital video cameras, space-based satellites, and fiber optics), linked to a matrix of local TV stations, and national and international networks (both broadcast and cable). The second development was the rapid transmission of digital news pictures, allowing instantaneous electronic posting and more timely publication of still photographs. Together, these two new visual platforms—24/7 television news and digital photography, both in league with the Internet—helped alter the world's media landscape.

Suddenly the purveyors and consumers of news belonged to a community of image hunters, image gatherers, and image seekers—a loose amalgam of professional and civilian picture providers (thanks to a new arsenal of digital camcorders and still cameras in the public's hands) sending eyewitness accounts to a single, vast, if ultimately fractured audience. On 9/11, we were one world taking in the same scene and connected by the same horrifying picture story.

In the days that followed, photography itself, like some potent virus, would permeate the crisis. Pictures would sustain the memory of loved ones. Pictures would comfort those in mourning. Pictures would preserve the sequence and dread of the day, as if trapping wisps of history in amber. Images of all kinds would connect cultures and ricochet across government networks, allowing law enforcement agents to identify hijackers and military planners to later plot their bomb runs in Afghanistan and, in time, Iraq.

All through that tragic week in September the photograph did its work. And the city, the nation, and the human race looked on as one unblinking eye.

For my entire professional life I have been bewitched by photographs and befriended by photographers. My first full-time job was as a reporter for *Life* magazine, traveling the world in pursuit of picture stories with some of the best photojournalists in the business. For much of the 1990s I served as *Life*'s director of photography, then was recruited by editor Graydon Carter to join *Vanity Fair*, where I have often worked on visual projects—several of which have addressed the events of September 11. I helped edit the magazine's special edition "One Week in September," devoted to New Yorkers affected by the tragedy, wrote two *V.F.* articles on photographic aspects of the attacks, and served as an executive producer of the CBS television documentary *9/11*, which aired in more than 140 countries.

I believe, in short, in the power of pictures. I believe that the digital age, as no period before it, has turned ours into a world awash in visual information. I believe that in this era of political spin, agitprop, Photoshop, and made-for-TV reality, we still regard photographs—even those suspected of having been manipulated—as conveying a kernel of truth. And I believe that deep in our psyches we are constructed like cameras: we observe, remember, and relive events, faces, and places, not in the blur of motion pictures, but in discrete, photolike "stills."

I believe that pictures, in a sense, are the sociological equivalent of carbon dating. Take a week, any week, and one can glean much of its meaning through the pictures that it generates.

Take the week of September 4, 2001, for example—the seven days *prior* to 9/11.

All week long, families, back from their summer vacations, dropped off rolls of film at their local photo stores or uploaded digital shots onto their computer hard drives. Museums and galleries in most major cities began mounting their fall photo exhibitions. Photographers and picture editors convened and caroused at the annual Visa pour l'Image, the premier international photojournalism festival, in Perpignan, France. Political candidates across America, vying in September 11 primaries, flooded channels with TV spots, trying to etch their platforms, and their images, in voters' minds. Television audiences around the globe planned their days and nights around the World Cup soccer qualification rounds.

In New York City, more than five hundred photographers were accredited to cover the runways, parties, and events of Fashion Week. Fifteen photojournalists from Magnum, the esteemed picture cooperative, had come to town for the agency's bimonthly meeting. Some sixty photographers flocked to town for Sunday's MTV Video Music Awards.

In and around Washington, D.C., photo hobbyists took pictures of a curious streak of light above the North Atlantic seaboard, the result of a Soviet-era spacecraft breaking up as it returned and bruised Earth's atmosphere. At a science conference, astronomers announced they had acquired the first convincing X-ray evidence of a massive black hole gobbling up light in our very own galaxy. And the administration of President George W. Bush held its first-ever cabinet-level meeting devoted to addressing the threat from the al-Qaeda chief Osama bin Laden. Attendees debated, and rejected, a plan for flying an armed, unmanned, camera-equipped drone to spy on and attack bin Laden and his operatives in Afghanistan.

Also making news that week: *Popular Mechanics* touted VideoRay (a roving underwater camera that skulks across the ocean floor, transmitting pictures to the surface), *Wired* plugged the Casio WQV3D-8 (a new Dick Tracy–style wristwatch digicam set to grace showcases that September), and cover girl Carolyn Murphy was introduced as the new "face" of the cosmetics giant Estée Lauder in many upcoming ads.

The week before September 11 began with the death, at age eighty-two, of Pauline Kael. As one of America's longest-reigning movie critics, Kael had probably taken in as much visual data as any cineaste who ever lived. And as the week ended, the Afghan opposition leader Ahmad Shah Massoud was killed in a mountain hideout—assassinated by two suicide bombers, supposedly on orders from Osama bin Laden. The assailants, disguised as TV journalists, had hidden their explosives in their video equipment. Massoud, possibly the most storied warrior in recent Afghan history, had been done in by a camera retrofitted as a bomb and intended to shoot its subject, quite literally, as it passed within its proverbial crosshairs.

Watching the World Change, then, takes a similar assay of a thin wedge of time. It examines, in effect, a week in the life of the photograph. It is an attempt to chart the role of imagery over the course of a single seven-day period: September 11 through 17, 2001—arguably the most historic and horrific week, from America's perspective, since the end of World War II. This book will reveal how digital photography and electronic newsgathering came of age that week and made their marks on society and the world at large. More important, this book will attempt to come to grips with how photographs, that September and thereafter, have helped shape our understanding of the week's events, and have helped us mourn, connect, communicate, and respond.

My intention is to focus on New York City. I pay scant attention to the attacks on Washington, D.C., and Pennsylvania because I believe that an examination of the role pictures played in those locales is best left to others with direct knowledge of those events, and because New York was the locus, the crux, the horror of horrors. What's more, I was here, not there.

In addition, this book is less about the tragic and deadly consequences of September 11—discussed eloquently and exhaustively in many other accounts—than it is about pixels and videoclips, photographers and camera operators, and about our *responses* to images of the events. As a result, the interwoven stories, the dissection of particular pictures, and the discussions of the personalities behind them can seem somewhat distant, even heartless. My motivation, however, is neither to offend readers nor to violate the memory of the lost by minimizing the horror of the events through their objectification. This volume, instead, is meant to explore our collective visual memory in the digital era.

It may seem blasphemous to talk of Photography with a capital *P* when so many lives were extinguished so brutally. Such a discussion seems of narrow focus at best, a symptom of the woeful self-regard of the photographic act—and of this writer's marginal preoccupations. But the weeks, nonetheless, have receded into months, into seasons, into years. Their passing has provided perspective. And we have come to realize that for much of the world it is pictures that have served as the only reliable vessels of the experience of that day. We remain beholden to photographs—and to the photographers of September 11, witnesses who happened to be possessed of hands and eyes steady enough to stand their ground and make pictures of the otherwise unfathomable. Through images we ached, mourned, and gained our footing. Through images, we retained our memory, conscience, and resolve. And it is through this seven-day trove of photographs that we can begin to discern the historical essence of that week, and the impact and potency of photography in the modern age.

Like most people, I saw it first in photographs.

Entering the vast bowl of Times Square on my way to work that morning, I was confronted with a wall of pictures. All around me, splashed across three vaulting video screens, were images of the World Trade Center spewing huge plumes of smoke.

There was a crowd, transfixed, in the street. Everyone seemed to be taking it in as I was, in triplicate. The twin towers soared as six crippled pillars: one pair appeared on the monitor beside *Good Morning America*'s third-floor studio, another on the huge cylindrical facade of the NASDAQ Building, a third on NBC's Jumbotron at the fulcrum of Times Square. The middle screen, eight stories tall, bore a small caption: "Moments Ago" or "Earlier." Then it showed a plane, the towers, a fireball. I could taste a sour sting coming up from my gullet.

In the crowd, some gasped. Others lurched forward, then rushed off. Many were on cell phones, several were in tears. Most were silent, still processing it all: the magnitude of the attack, the bracing strangeness, the clarity and certainty of death, so near, on such a scale.

On morbid impulse, I rapidly tallied the carnage. Two buildings, ten blackened stories each, hundreds dead. Clearly, this was a terrorist act.

I steadied myself against the wall of the bank behind me. I thought of my wife, working a dozen blocks from the Trade Center. Without success, I peered south, trying to spot smoke, or the structures themselves, several miles downtown.

In front of me spread an odd tableau—part George Orwell, part Fritz Langian kabuki. I saw row upon motionless row of the backs of heads tilted up toward the monitors. Above those heads were photographs of smoldering buildings, projected onto the sides of buildings. Curiously amplified on the cathode canvas of Times Square, and replicated in a sort of fractured panorama on screen after screen, the scene seemed all the more sinister for its format, as if televised terror had suddenly supplanted the steel and stone of the city.

Involuntarily, I found myself reacting to some of the morning's events in photographic terms. For an instant, the glint of an old picture crossed my mind's eye. I recalled a 1963 shot by a photographer who later became a close friend, Carl Mydans of *Life*, which showed commuters on a train the day Kennedy was killed. In the photo, the passengers, their faces hidden in their newspapers, ride in silence to their suburban homes. Their papers bear bold black headlines: PRESIDENT DEAD . . . PRESIDENT SHOT DEAD . . . PRESIDENT DEAD, SHOT BY ASSASSIN. Times Square, right then, seemed suspended in that same communal stasis—a frieze of crisis, dire and universal, shared among strangers. The hammer blow of reality had tripped a visual response, as if my subconscious, to help me get grounded, had cued a similar picture from the depths of the cortex. Even dire calamity, my fevered mind reasoned, needed a context.

Though I heard sirens on distant avenues, midtown had fallen largely silent. The traffic seemed to have come to a halt, and people with dazed or heartsick expressions passed me in the streets. I moved from the curb, out onto a concrete island in the center of Times Square. A shock of white hair rushed by: Mike Smith, deputy picture editor of *The New York Times*.

"Mike," I called. He turned, incredulous, his jaw slack.

"Can you *believe* this?" he said, his eyes bulging.

Above the hush, we exchanged a few notes of consternation. Then he turned and began to jog toward his office, just around the corner. The two of us, I knew, could feel horror and history in the very air. And right now, for Mike, there were tasks at hand—fielding calls from those already on the scene, assigning new shooters, editing photographs.

In turn, I ascended to the offices of *Vanity Fair*, twenty-two floors above Times Square. With a handful of colleagues, all of us rather numb, I stood at a window in the production department. Facing downtown, we watched the south tower as it spouted more and more smoke, then seemingly disappeared from view. From our obscured sight line, with the north tower eclipsing the south, we believed, or wanted to believe, that both were still standing. But there were too many white billows. The worst *had* to be true.

I recall a surreal and curiously New York sort of moment. At one point I discovered that I was standing next to the actor Billy Baldwin, who happened to be visiting the offices that day. I told him that the south tower had just fallen. "That can't be," he said, peering out the same window as I was. "Do you hear what you're saying?" But the longer we watched, the worse it became, as a new bank of cloud surrounded the space where the towers had stood.

And so I slipped away to a nearby office, alone, to watch the scene on TV for a minute or two. By checking a televised replay of what I had just witnessed from afar, I could gauge the reliability of my own eyes.

WATCHING THE WORLD CHANGE

1 TUESDAY, SEPTEMBER 11

French filmmaker Jules Naudet, shooting downtown, heard the roar of a plane above him. He raised his digital video camera. He aimed a bit ahead of him, to the space in the sky where he thought the plane was headed. His response was uncanny: just in time, and position, to record the impact of the plane as it plunged into the north face of the north tower.

At the same instant, across the East River, a Czech immigrant named Pavel Hlava was sitting in the passenger's seat of an SUV in Brooklyn, video camera in hand. He was accompanied by his brother Josef, in town for a visit and eager to see the sights of Manhattan. As Hlava focused his camcorder on the Trade Center towers in the distance, he caught an indistinct blob moving toward one of the buildings. He continued taping as a puff of white signaled the plane's collision. Hlava's shaky video next captured the fiery gash in the side of the structure, along with the approach, seventeen minutes later, of a second plane as it tipped its wing and tore through the south tower.

Also fixed on the twin towers that morning were two unmanned Webcams, positioned in an apartment window in Williamsburg, Brooklyn. Several days before, Wolfgang Staehle, a German-born Internet-art pioneer, had carefully calibrated the cameras' shutters to trip at four-second intervals, hour after hour, day after day, automatically snapping postcard-style views of lower Manhattan. Staehle's photos would then be transmitted over the World Wide Web to twin film projectors, their beams directed at the wall of a West Side art gallery. In the name of art (Staehle's show was called "2001"), the Webcams silently documented the aircraft's approach, then its concussion, then the explosion *(Image 1)*. The resulting high-resolution triptych—three panoramas shot in the span of twelve seconds—showed the downtown skyline as it degenerated from a placid morning vista into a cityscape under siege.

A French documentary filmmaker, a Czech immigrant, and a German artist—New Yorkers all—each happened to have cameras rolling and focused on the World Trade Center when it was attacked. Moments later, artist Lawrence Heller, who had heard the first jet slam into Tower One (the north tower), picked up his digital video camera. He had just set it down on the window ledge in his Franklin Street loft, taking a short break from shooting video "still lifes" of several wall sculptures he was about to crate up and send off for an exhibition. Over the next few minutes, Heller and his wife, Mi-Kyung Hwang, took turns filming Tower One engulfed in smoke. On the tape, Heller can be heard on the phone with his grandparents: "Hey Grandma. I'll tell you what woke me up. They bombed the World Trade Center . . . I'm looking at it, Mi-Kyung's videotaping it . . . Terrible . . . Grandpa, I saw it. Could have been a plane. But I think it was a bomb, a missile. This could be World War Three . . . I don't know, Grandma . . . How early? Just happened, I don't know, three minutes ago."

And so it went. As the morning crept on, New Yorkers poured into the streets, many to help, many in flight, all of them aghast. Out, too, came their cameras. Men and women by the hundreds, then thousands—bystanders with point-and-shoots, TV news teams, photojournalists by the score—felt compelled to snap history, fiery and cruel against the blue.

People photographed from windows and parapets and landings. They photographed as they fled: in cars, across bridges, up avenues blanketed in drifts of ash and dust. They even photographed the images on their television sets as they watched the world changing, right there on the screen.

Patricia McDonough was jolted from sleep by a shake and then a high-pitched wail outside her window. She lay still a moment, taking in the roar of the sirens. These were the same sounds, and the same rumble, she realized, that she had felt in 1993 when terrorists bombed the World Trade Center, just four blocks away.

McDonough, a professional photographer, jumped from bed and took her Nikon with its fish-eye lens (a bulbous "trick" attachment she happened to have left on the camera) and directed it at the smoking structure outside her picture window *(Image 2)*. The exaggerated curve of the 16-mm lens made her apartment appear to warp and buckle. Her living room, swollen with morning sunshine, seemed set to implode. Out beyond the lamp, the potted plants, the thin tissue of the glass, smoke columns billowed like ink, then milk, then cumulus.

"At first," she says, "when I was taking my pictures, I was doing it as a personal document: This is this morning. This is what happened, to me, in my apartment. Soon, however, thousands of people were there. And ambulances. There were all these photographers." Then downtown Manhattan literally transformed in front of her. And photography, strangely enough, "suddenly seemed superfluous," she says.

"When I saw the first building come down on all these trucks and ambulances, the situation became something else. I felt immediately needed. I have had a lot of Red Cross training, CPR classes. I have preternatural calm in disasters. I thought, This is New York. What good is another photographer—and a million people who *think* they're photographers? What was needed was another person who could help."

McDonough threw on a T-shirt. (She thought it odd, later in the day, when she realized it sported a caricature of a butcher with a mustache and a sneer, holding a butcher's knife.) She loaded her bike bag with disposable gloves and water bottles. She grabbed her heavily stocked first-aid kit. She decided to leave her exposed film and equipment behind, taking along a single camera and a few rolls. Since the building's electricity had gone out, a result of the towers' collapse, she rushed down seventeen flights of stairs in the dark.

"There was an ambulance outside my door," she says, "and I just opened the back and got in. [Inside] were ambulance drivers from Yonkers. They may have been hiding. They were scared. They didn't know what to do. I saw it as a ride to go and help." After a bit of prodding from McDonough, the men gunned the engine and raced with her toward the Trade towers.

That day, McDonough guided people to emergency vehicles and helped set up operating tables at a triage center at Chelsea Piers. Later that week (after a stop to retrieve the film she'd left behind), she assisted rescue workers at hydration stations. Her photos of the view inside and outside her apartment window that Tuesday morning, tightly framed and claustrophobic, would later run in *Esquire*, then other magazines, winning her awards.

Jonathan Torgovnik noticed that his hands were trembling. "I should shoot this at a high shutter speed because I'm shaking," he thought.

Around nine in the morning, Torgovnik had spied the edge of an airplane wing from the kitchen window of his top-floor apartment on Houston Street and Sixth Avenue. He watched the wing disappear as the plane plowed into the south tower. It then registered: one building was spouting smoke; the other had just been hit; terrorist strikes must be under way. Torgovnik, a frequent contributor to *Newsweek*, intuitively shifted into work mode. He opened the refrigerator, where, like many photographers, he stored his film in a temperature-controlled environment, and gathered fifteen rolls of Kodak negative, then packed two Canons, one Hasselblad panoramic, and three lenses. He saw that he was still shaking.

Torgovnik had covered conflicts around the world. As an Israeli citizen he had completed three years of compulsory military duty, serving in Gaza and Lebanon. Yet only once before in his life had he experienced the fear he felt that moment in his kitchen: during the first Gulf War, when Iraq began hurling Scud missiles through the night skies, targeting cities in Israel. "You're looking at your grandmother in a gas mask and she's ninety-two," he says, recounting how they sat in his parents' apartment in Tel Aviv. "She went through World War II and three wars in Israel. And *I'm* trying to keep calm. In both cases, 9/11 and the Gulf War, you're in your home. You're in your protected space. And [suddenly] you've peeled off all your shields of protection."

He bicycled the twenty blocks to the World Trade Center. At one point he turned his camera vertically to capture Tower One, above the glass-roofed Winter Garden, just a stairway and a plaza away from him, to the east. His mind registered that he was in danger because he saw, through his viewfinder, that two businessmen with briefcases were fleeing for their lives, one staring back at the building in free fall. "I saw the top of the tower crumbling," says Torgovnik. "I thought, 'What am I doing? I can die.' But I said to myself, 'I'm here. I *have* to take a picture of this.' " He squeezed off four frames, then thought, "Now I have to run."

Dave Brondolo was a printing plant account manager and aspiring photographer. He hurried downtown from his Nineteenth Street office on the number 1 subway, hoping to use his high-end Nikon to garner his own firsthand view of the scenes he had glimpsed on TV. He caught the last subway train to discharge passengers at Chambers Street, one stop north of the tower, arriving just in time to see the south tower plummet before his lens, the camera's motor drive tripping the shutter in rapid, blurry bursts *(Image 3)*.

"Every time I press the shutter," he says, "the viewfinder closes. And it happens so fast what I'm mostly seeing is black: the shutter, closed. I didn't know what was occurring in front of my eyes. As I'm taking the pictures I heard a sound like cracking spaghetti and just kept firing.

"Then I turned and saw these monstrous smoke clouds coming down the street, straight at me, moving faster than people could run. The ground was shaking. Although it was a horrible sight, my adrenaline was pumping. [I kept shooting. I still] hadn't realized the building had fallen.

"I ducked into Trinity Church," Brondolo remembers, "and I actually thought I was going to die. Objects landed on the roof. I was afraid we'd suffocate from the smoke. Then some security guy tried to evacuate us out the back door *toward* the towers. Two women with babies," he says, his eyes welling with tears, "rushed through the dust and were in a panic to get out. I turned around and went back *into* the church. And just as I did, we heard the second tower come down. And the women and the babies were out there somewhere. They had left their strollers behind."

For eight months, he kept his photographs to himself. "I let them sit on my shelf," explains Brondolo, who lives in Rockville Centre, Long Island, which lost thirty-eight people that day. "I didn't want to exploit the deaths. I thought it would reflect poorly on my community and me. We lost the soccer coach in my son's league. I lost my father's cousin. For a year, my kids, eight and five at the time, didn't know what I went through. But I *had* to go down there. Others were running away. Photographers were *drawn* to it."

Also inside the church on Tuesday was Evan Fairbanks, a videographer who had been helping set up a four-camera teleconference scheduled to include the Anglican Archbishop of Wales, visiting New York at the time. "I was in the right place at the wrong time," Fairbanks says. For a moment, the lights flickered, inexplicably. Soon he heard that there had been an explosion at the twin towers. Intrigued and alarmed, Fairbanks went out in the street with a Panasonic DVC Pro video camera and started shooting.

Seeing hundreds of people streaming away from the Trade Center plaza, he headed against the human tide. "I was kind of drawn to the energy," he says. "I never worked full-time for a news station. But I've always been a big photojournalism fan. I guess like everybody in that business you always are fantasizing about the big story that you're [going to be] Johnny-on-the-spot for." His storyteller's instincts kicked in. As much as his attention became fixed upon the gaping hole in the tower up above, he was determined, he says, not to focus on the building but on the human drama around him. In all, he would record twenty-three minutes of tape. (Though he had shot with the audio turned on, the FBI had impounded his footage as evidence, returning a single copy to him with the sound inexplicably erased.)

His video shows firemen on the march and pedestrians dazed. It shows clusters of employees *inside* the World Trade Center lobby, filing down stalled escalators. (Fairbanks ducked into the complex for a while.) Most memorably, it shows the mayhem in the streets, the scenes made all the more disorienting because the camera gyrates while Fairbanks, still shooting, runs through the crowds or crouches behind a car or swivels his lens to glimpse the sky. Here are tilts and pans of debris-filled streets, there a flurry of paper, or disembodied legs fleeing across the frame. Because the photographer's life appears to be at stake, the viewer feels vulnerable too. The footage is unvarnished and authentic, hallucinatory and hesitant—terror vérité.

At one point, a neat, clean-cut man suddenly appears through the viewfinder, like some Pinter character come to life, "just leaning against his car," as Fairbanks remembers. "On the other side of the hood was this battery-operated multiband radio. [I was taken with] his kind of calm demeanor in the middle of all this . . . confusion. [He had] his hands on his chin, just hangin' out there. It was kind of a freak situation to come across. He was listening to [news reports on] the radio and would occasionally look up to the left, to the buildings. In retrospect it was odd." But Fairbanks, trained in the news photography dictum that a single shot should tell the whole tale, decided to stoop down low to present the man in the shadowy foreground *against* the smoking building, which towered behind him in the bright sunlight *(Image 4)*. To get the right angle, Fairbanks bent over, cradling the camera in his arms. "I was adjusting the focus and exposure," says Fairbanks, "and as soon as I settled the shot and locked it in and steadied it up, I saw this flash in the left corner of my viewfinder."

The nose of a passenger plane came from behind another building, then the entire aircraft disappeared into the skin of the south tower, Tower Two. Fairbanks caught the jet's passage in twelve frames of video. "I was looking down into the viewfinder and pointing the lens *up*," says Fairbanks, describing the posture of videographers in the digital age: heads bowed toward their LED screens, almost in the manner of a person at prayer, as if paying homage to the image, out of deference to, or fear of, the actual. "I essentially saw it on TV, just like everybody else."

"His videotape," Sarah Boxer would later write in *The New York*

Times, recorded "25 stunning, silent minutes [that reveal] the very climate changing minute by minute . . . Over the head of [a man], who clearly does not see what is happening, a plane silently penetrates the . . . tower. The man's head reels out of the frame as he reacts to the crash. His head snaps back in time to watch the aftermath. A black cloud envelops the tower. Debris sprays out like a fountain from the top. The sky goes dark. The traffic stops."

Despite the danger, Fairbanks felt the urge to continue taping, and shot what he calls "shock and awe" in those around him. "I felt a sense of obligation," he now says, having seen no other cameramen in his vicinity. "Since I was the only one down there, I felt, This is something that I have to document." But the debris specks on his lens were getting progressively larger. He took this as a sign that he needed to seek refuge. For cover, he jumped underneath a van and continued to shoot. Through his lens, he saw "groups stream by, panic-stricken. Flailing arms. People running really fast, scared. Total havoc."

Fairbanks senses that he may have been destined to be there with a camera—and to have been spared. "Before that one event," he says, "I would have called it a freak of luck. But I think of the circumstances that forced me down there—I'm in a *church*—and put me on *that* corner. I had been kind of randomly shooting people's reactions, but I suddenly felt compelled to tilt the camera toward the towers at [a] perfect moment. That now makes fate or God certainly seem to me an option. Even though I'm not religious, I have a feeling there's a power that kind of keeps an eye on things. Even if it's not necessarily a guardian angel, I have some kind of a force looking out for me . . . saying to me, Listen, we've kept you here for [a] reason. Leave a mark."

Around 10:15, Fairbanks fell in with two Port Authority officers who wanted a copy of his footage as evidence. He agreed to cooperate, walking with them toward Trinity Church, where he planned to make a duplicate tape in the building's audiovisual facility. At the last moment before heading inside, he decided to turn his camera skyward for a final shot. "I did this very graceful zoom out from the plume of smoke," he remembers, "and put these two people in the foreground," careful to provide human scale. Just as he did, he heard and felt a rumble. He looked up to record the north tower coming down.

"I knew I was going to die," he says. "That's it. There's a one-hundred-and-ten-story building falling and I'm basically across the street. I just remember kind of wishing that I could stop the clock, thinking that I really got greedy. Why didn't I get out of there? I had gotten the shot of a lifetime—the plane going in. What could be more dramatic that day than getting a plane crashing into the World Trade Center? What am I still doing on the scene? It was unfathomable that worse than that could happen."

He recalls the last moments that appear on his tape. "I just turned and ran," he says, "even though I felt almost certain that it was a futile attempt." As he sprinted away, he somehow turned the camera backward under his arm, leaving it on wide angle. His lens absorbed it all. "You saw the cloud come down to the ground, then billowed up over Building 5, came across, and obscured the traffic lights at Vesey Street, just kind of chasing me . . . like a tidal wave down the block. I never once looked behind me. It was the point of no return." Halfway up the block, Fairbanks dove under a rescue-unit fire truck he happened to sprint past, and was able to roll within the three-foot clearance of its chassis. "I curled myself into a ball, put my back to the south. And that's where the video cuts off. It just goes black."

Grant Peterson was in a quiet photo studio near Broome Street and Broadway. His photo assignment: a *Brides* magazine story, "Quintessential Wedding Gifts." Peterson was about to take a few still lifes of ice buckets and vases when he looked out the eighth-floor window and noticed smoke pouring from the upper reaches of the Trade Center. He grabbed his 4×5 view camera.

There was a crater, he recalls, ripped in the tower facade, as large as an airplane hangar. The gash conferred proportion upon a building he had always viewed as remote and monolithic. "It was a very tangible experience," he says. "Everything was close-up and in-your-face. You felt you could barely breathe because of the scale. How many people could be *in* that fire?"

Peterson took sixteen exposures in all, on oversized sheet film, which provided him enough of a canvas to bring the towers into stunning relief. Later, determined to give others a visual sense of the immensity of the inferno out his window, Peterson scanned the shots, creating colossal two-gigabyte files. Next, he retouched them electronically, before locating the largest available print carriage he could find—as tall as a man—and producing enormous, five-by-nine-foot panels, 32,000 pixels across, with almost pristine definition. His work would be displayed at the New-York Historical Society for thousands to see. "My whole goal," Peterson insists, "was to re-create that experience: the first fright. I thought I'd create pictures of the magnitude of the day."

Some of the first news bulletins and police alerts implied that a bomb might have gone off at the World Trade Center, like the one in 1993 that had killed six people and wounded more than a thousand people. Other reports suggested that a private plane or commuter aircraft had crashed into the north tower. In the sketchy, frantic interlude that followed the first attack, enough people had gotten the message (through television, radio, telephone, or the naked eye) that the impact of the second hijacked flight, at 9:03, just seventeen minutes after the first, was "covered" like an elbow-to-elbow photo op, the scene filmed or taped from myriad angles. From downtown Manhattan, Brooklyn, and New Jersey, men and women spotted the distinct outline of a jet speeding toward the tower from the south, then suddenly banking its wings at the last instant before it sheared, diagonally, two-thirds of the way up the building. And they focused their cameras.

Some were pros, many were enterprising amateurs. Most were poised and ready, like sharpshooters. Video sequences of the plane's approach and collision were photographed by the likes of Maurizio Benazzo, Peter DiPilato, Chris Hopewell, and Jennifer Spell, and by others working for video agencies or local, cable, and network outlets. HBO would later show footage of the plane streaking toward Tower Two, and the explosion's fiery corona—from Scott Myers (positioned on John Street), Michael Kovalenko (King Street), Mike Toole (Desbrosses Street), Park Foreman (Brooklyn Heights), and Ronald S. Pordy (Long Island City). The same scene was photographed by dozens, among them: Sean Adair, Tamara Beckwith, Moshe Bursuker, Kathy Cacicedo, Tom Callan, Chao Soi Cheong, Robert Clark, Anthony Cotsifas, Adger Cowans, Robert A. Cumins, Frank J. DeNicola, Dr. Harry Dym, Giovanni Giannoni, Kelly Guenther, Tammy Klein, Ernesto Mora, Spencer Platt, Sara K. Schwittek, James Sullivan, Carmen Taylor, and Steve Ludlum, whose photo of the two towers—one disgorging huge coils of flame, the other jet-black smoke, stunting the Brooklyn Bridge in the foreground—would appear on the front page of the next day's *New York Times (Figure A).*

The power of Ludlum's image, says John Loengard, former director of photography of *Life,* derives from the fact that it "put the event in a context—human habitation, the size of the city—whereas many of the others were focused directly on the towers. It speaks well of the picture that millions of people weren't affected *directly* by the attack. The picture gets across the city as vast, putting it in perspective. This engineering marvel, the Brooklyn Bridge, from another century, is standing perfectly well, untouched, next to the Trade Center."

Bond analyst Will Nuñez had gone to his corner newsstand and bought a $14.99 disposable Kodak, hoping to record the smoking tower out his office window "for history's sake," he says. "I remembered an incident back in the thirties when a plane had hit the Empire State Building, and I was always impressed by photos in encyclopedias." Instead, from his perch on the thirty-second floor of One State Street Plaza, he captured the plane's breathtaking blur out his office window, quite unintentionally. In his shot, a colleague, standing before a vast picture window, looks on in silhouette, next to an innocuous baseball trophy, its tiny batter poised on a two-handled loving cup. The plane had streaked by with such speed, Nuñez had not even realized he had caught it on film until he finally got around to developing the roll a week or two later. (Many people put off having their film processed, some not wanting to face the terror of the day head-on, others not wanting to break the overpowering spell of that week, as horrible as it was.)

Rob Howard was at the window of his apartment on Rector Street and Broadway. A photographer accustomed to shooting travel, lifestyle, and portraiture, with medium and large-format cameras, Howard leaned out over the sill. He shot up at the bold, vaulting lines of the structure with a Pentax 6×7—just as the plane "flew over our building and slammed into the south tower," he says. "It seemed to take forever. Time stood still." He rendered the moment right before impact in finely detailed black-and-white, as if he were on an architecture shoot *(Image 5)*.

Kristen Brochmann, a *New York Times* freelancer, expressed ambivalence about having been on hand to document the same moment. The next day her image of the impact ran above the fold on front pages across the land. "The only way I could sort of reconcile my [journalistic] good fortune," she said in the book *Running Toward Danger*, "is that I was able to take a record of this for everybody else to see. Lots of other horrible things happen [such as] ethnic cleansing, and there's no record. This is what it looked like, and this is what it was."

By the time the south tower collapsed (fifty-six minutes after the second collision) and its twin followed suit (twenty-nine minutes after that), hundreds of photographers were poised and shooting, many unable mentally or emotionally to accept what they were witnessing. Photographer Steve McCurry stood on his rooftop, just north of Washington Square Park, and shot south. "To have them crumble," he said, was "like ripping your heart out . . . You kind of felt like the world was coming unglued." Photo researcher Adam Woodward, who had grabbed his Mamiya and headed toward SoHo, began to feel a "weird tinge of guilt that I was taking pictures," he recalls. In fact, he waited many months before agreeing to publish his arresting photo of the morning, uneasy with the idea of publicly exploiting the picture for what might appear to be commercial gain. In his pin-sharp frame a hundred pedestrians, like extras on a movie soundstage, stand frozen in the crosswalk at the intersection of Prince and Broadway, bathed in sidelight by the morning sun. The photo's hyperclarity, due to its oversized six-by-seven-inch negative, helps conduct the horror and absurdity of a day when cascading buildings and mass murder were set against a model-railroad-set foreground of neat, tree-lined streets and traffic lights blinking red and green.

Astoundingly, dozens of photographers continued to shoot even as they sensed that their own lives were at risk—when clouds of debris, from the falling towers, mushroomed up and down the streets. Suzanne Plunkett was immovable on the sidewalk, composing pictures. In one frame a half-dozen men stampede toward her, away from the swarm; a man in a tie seems to be screaming *(Image 6)*. Doug Kanter photographed pedestrians running from smothering dust balls, as did Tony Fioranelli, Robert Mecca, Allan Tannenbaum, and Magnum's Susan Meiselas, who planted herself in the center of Church Street to confront the rushing wall of white, like some latter-day Mount St. Helens.

Kelly Price, a freelance photo editor, was downtown on a consulting job that morning. After the first plane hit, she ducked into a bodega and bought several disposable cameras. When the first tower fell, she fled for her life down Broadway, but couldn't help looking over her shoulder after a block or two. The sight of the advancing thunderheads was too irresistible an image, so she stopped in her tracks at Pine Street, fired off four or five frames, then resumed her flight. Her sequence—a remarkable achievement given the primitive, throwaway lens she used—shows a lone man with a camera in his right hand, running for his life. The wall of debris is erupting just behind his back and gaining on him *(Jacket Photo)*. Both photographer and subject made it out of the cloud alive, though shaken.

Price's imperiled photographer commands the nexus of the frame, her picture bisected by khaki billows above the horizon line and the littered pavement below. Death seems certain, just steps behind the curtain. The scene incorporates much of the horror evident in images of men dwarfed by nature (Frank Hurley's haunting shots, from 1915, of Ernest Shackleton's Antarctic expedition) or of soldiers enveloped in the fog of war (W. Eugene Smith's 1945 image of a Marine demo squad recoiling from a bomb blast on Iwo Jima). But this figure isn't equipped with a dogsled or a detonator. Like the woman who consigned him forever to a roll of film, he is armed only with a camera.

That man, it turns out, was George Mannes, then a senior writer for TheStreet.com, a financial Web site. It might seem odd that Mannes would undergo a spontaneous metamorphosis as a war reporter. But so he did that day, even bringing a camera along. His was an immediate medium, and his audience, focused on the concerns of Wall Street, urgently needed any information he and his colleagues could provide.

The attacks had come to Mannes's doorstep, quite literally. At 8:47, a minute after the first plane hit, one of the Web site's message boards posted a bulletin about an event at the Trade Center. The fall of the towers would take out the company's offices and take the life of one of its columnists, William J. Meehan, chief market analyst for Cantor Fitzgerald. Mannes, instead of writing about his usual beat—tech stocks—would file an online dispatch that day about fleeing workers and the cloud he saw on Cedar Street: "I tried to outrun it as it chased me south down Broadway, but I lost."

As the sprinting figure in Price's picture, however, George Mannes, at that moment, is Everyman with a Camera. He is alone, vulnerable, a vital witness to an enveloping world. He exemplifies the edict of Robert Capa, who is considered by many to have been history's finest combat photographer: "If your pictures aren't good enough, you're not close enough."

Don Halasy and Bolivar Arellano (both shooting for the *New York Post*) and David Handschuh (a New York *Daily News* staffer) positioned themselves directly *underneath* the Trade Center during the collapse. Shaken, Halasy would file a story Tuesday night describing how "the world caved in" on him. Moments before, he noted, he had lent a roll of film to another photographer, unknown to him, who then suddenly "vanished . . . in a hailstorm of debris." Handschuh, like Halasy, was swept off his feet, likening the experience to "getting hit in the back by a wave . . . of hot, black gravel," as he would recount a month later on *The Digital Journalist*, a photojournalism Web site (to which I contribute occasionally) that featured images from thirty-five photographers who had covered the attacks. Hurled under a parked van, Handschuh came away with a fractured leg.

"Before September 11, all I did was go out to murder scenes and fires," Handschuh would tell *New York* magazine on the second anniversary of the attacks, explaining how he had to take a year off work and undergo extensive rehabilitation before he could walk again. "That was my beat. I photographed things blowing up and falling down." Thereafter he found himself "never, ever wanting to either see or photograph anybody dead or dying again . . . Now, I'm photographing chocolate mousse and doll refurbishing. It's still photojournalism, it's still going out and making great pictures, it's still meeting people I've never met before. Just without the blood, without the gore.

"It continues to be a long haul," he says. And memories of his experience under the towers remain seared in his psyche. So, too, do his mental images of his fellow photographers. Just prior to the collapse, Handschuh had encountered Glen Pettit, a video cameraman for the New York Police Department. Pettit told Handschuh that he had "unbelievable footage." Handschuh responded, "Be careful." They embraced. Then Pettit took off to shoot some more. He was last seen by a fellow officer who remembers him running toward the Trade Center.

Bill Biggart was an intense, impetuous, and driven photographer. "He was Type A-plus-plus," says his wife, Wendy Doremus. "You either loved him or you hated him. He got arrested at Wounded Knee [the Native American protest site, in 1973], got tear-gassed [and] arrested in the first Intifada [Palestinian uprising] in 1987. He had his press pass taken away covering squatters in New York. He was beaten up by the British police for being a little too close covering the twentieth anniversary of the reoccupation of Northern Ireland. He's Catholic, Irish, the second oldest of twelve."

Born in Berlin, the son of a U.S. Army officer, Biggart, according to Doremus, had anticipated the fall of the Berlin Wall by several months, then headed over to cover the celebrations at the Brandenburg Gate that marked the end of the division of Germany in 1989. But no matter the story, he liked to push the limits. "He always ended up too close," she says. "He'd always get behind the blockades to get inside . . . He was a pacifist and his family was very much in the Army, so this was his way of compensating . . . He always took the contrary position. He took the

Palestinian side. He was a sailor too. If Palestine ever became a state, he wanted to be one of the first to sail into Gaza harbor, which is mined."

Biggart, fifty-four, was an old-school freelancer who shot self-assigned stories, concentrating on socially relevant subjects that he considered politically or personally significant. The Impact Visuals photo agency would then sell his images and photo essays to publications such as *The Village Voice* and *The New York Times*. Before rushing off to cover the disaster downtown on September 11, he didn't wait to get a "guarantee" from an editor; he just went. Here was a story that encompassed many of his abiding themes—the Middle East conflict, post–cold war issues, New York City, and fire (two of his siblings had perished in a house fire).

True to form, Biggart got as close as, if not closer than, any other journalist that day. *New York Post* photographer Bolivar Arellano remembers seeing Biggart directly beneath Tower Two. Though he had been repeatedly kicked out of the area by police, Arellano had slipped past the security cordon and hunkered down, hiding behind a fence so that he could continue shooting, but from a more protected position. He spotted Biggart thirty yards *in front of him*, and thought, "He's going to get killed. This guy is too close. He has a telephoto lens . . . What's he doing there? I was in the same spot a few minutes before. I was insulting him [in my mind], but I was insulting myself too. A few minutes after that, that tower collapsed."

Biggart *survived* that first downfall, however, moving to safer ground, then pressing on through the dust. He had assumed that by sticking with the authorities in charge—the firefighters—he would be assured some measure of protection.

Doremus learned as much when she finally reached him by cell phone. She had walked downtown, hoping to find him somehow. "Everything had stopped," she says, "all the taxis had their doors opened, [like a scene from] *The Day the Earth Stood Still*. I got through to him after the first tower went down. I said, 'This is an attack. Bill, this is dangerous.' But he was just dismissing me." He was composed enough to arrange to meet her twenty minutes later, telling her, "I'm safe. I'm with the firemen."

And that was how they found him. On Saturday, Doremus says, she was informed that her husband's body had been recovered near the remains of several firefighters. On a follow-up trip to the morgue, she says she was ushered in and told, " 'Come this way.' There were all his cameras, the film, his keys, his ring, twenty-six dollars, and some cents. In a wet police bag."

Doremus and a friend, photographer Chip East, pored over the equipment *(Image 14)*. Biggart's three cameras were thoroughly battered. One roll of color-negative film, showing the first collapse, was intact. One hundred and fifty other shots, on six rolls of 24-exposure Fuji transparency film, survived, though some were streaked with light leaks. Next, they opened his digital camera, a Canon EOS D30, and removed a 256 MB CompactFlash memory card. They dumped the card's contents onto a computer and could see that Biggart had taken 154 digital photographs—from 9:09.51 a.m. until 10:28.24, according to the time code on the frames—all perfectly intact.

Biggart's pictures present a step-by-step chronicle of the disaster, literally in the shadows of the towers. A lone bird flies away as Two World Trade Center (the south tower, Tower Two) spews fire. Clots of smoke and cloud stream out as the tower crashes to earth. Debris-cobbled streets suddenly seem desolate as snowdrifts. Storefronts have the gray pallor of corpses. Men in hard hats and helmets, like Arctic explorers caked by hoarfrost, appear imperiled by the elements conspiring around them.

Biggart's last image, of the splintered stalk of Tower Two, obscured by smoke, was framed just six seconds before the other tower crumbled above him at 10:28 and 31 seconds.

Wendy Doremus feels that her husband, on his last day of shooting, symbolized nothing less than the photo community at a crossroads. "He was at the cusp of photography," she says. "He took three hundred pictures. Half the film Bill carried that day was digital, half color-negatives and slides. September 11 became the watershed day. After that, [almost all] photographers went digital."

Doremus claims that she doesn't linger too often over his September 11 take. "It's painful for me," she says, "like looking through his brain, looking through his eyes the last hour and a half of his life." And yet without any prompting from a visitor, she gravitates to the computer to rummage anyway, four years after that day. She opens the file she keeps on the Mac's desktop and proceeds to scroll through every last frame. Clicking the mouse, she runs through the sequence, stopping to explain certain moments, to point out certain faces. "He loved crowds," she observes. "He loved the crossfire. The only thing you can say is: If you gotta go, you might as well go doing what you love the most."

One of her husband's last exposures shows a nameless police officer, daubed in dust, with a vexed expression. He is looking up at the lone, remaining tower. "One thing he always taught me," Biggart's photographer friend Tom McKitterick would tell *Newsweek*'s Jerry Adler, "was that sometimes the picture is behind you, in the faces of the people watching." Shooting the firemen, the exiting workers, the figures cloaked in mysterious gray powder, Biggart was an eyewitness to other eyewitnesses. "In his own way," Adler would write, "Biggart was a hero as well. He rescued faces."

The Smithsonian Institution would contact Doremus soon after the attacks. She would agree to loan her husband's pulverized digital camera.

"I think it was the most photographed event of our time, if not in history," says curator and writer Michael Shulan.

"It was a photogenic event to an almost unparalleled degree. It had beauty—terrible beauty. It was violent and visually heightened, with an emotional intensity [evident] in every face in the street. If it wasn't in the frame, the humanity of it hovered around the edges of every picture, just out of view. It [also] coincided with the revolution of digital photography, which was beginning at that moment. This event really ushered in or propelled that revolution. Since then, everything that [has] happened in Afghanistan and Iraq, [along with] the development of the equipment, has made it easier [to photograph]. Digital cameras are used now as visual note-taking devices. Storage is easy now. A still image is a memory bank, if not a memory."

But on September 11 there was another force at work as well. "It felt so surreal," insists Shulan, that people "had to photograph it and then look at it in order to validate that it actually happened. You had to record it in order to register that you were there. The photograph as 'the mediator' fell away, and you felt you were seeing the event itself when, instead, you were seeing and [then] remembering the photograph."

Some of the most agonizing images taken that day captured knots of incredulous pedestrians peering up at the towers. There were the two bereaved African American women, shot in extreme close-up, one with her hand to her mouth, the other shielding her eyes, photographed by Angel Franco of *The New York Times (Image 7)*. Their body language spoke volumes: the view outside the frame was too horrifying for words, for sight itself. Then there was the woman with a Canon around her neck, who leaned against a car as she tearfully described the scene to someone on her mobile phone, photographed by Cynthia Colwell, a retired administrator for the Museum of Modern Art, who reluctantly brought her Olympus Stylus with her when she saw neighbors and strangers taking pictures out on Fifth Avenue *(Image 8)*.

Patrick Witty, standing at Park Row and Beekman Street, was five blocks from the site when he turned his lens on a wedge of bystanders, ten of whom stood with mouths agape, several with their heads tilted back or their eyes bulging *(Image 9)*. Shooting in stark black-and-white, the freelance photographer chose to show heads and shoulders only, by stepping up on a curb to get a slightly higher angle on the sweep of the crowd. "The thought process took microseconds," says Witty, now a picture editor at *The New York Times*. "How do I *not* shoot the obvious—the buildings—and shoot my own shock? I saw this cross section of races [and types]: this guy with a suit, this dude, a bike messenger, all together, these faces—this one guy looking disdainful and kind of irritated, this other guy looks kind of euphoric. And the timing of it was serendipity. As I took the picture, Tower Two [the south tower] came down behind me, literally right then." Witty's image gives the impression that he has happened upon an utterly spellbound audience, one he might have encountered had he been perched in front of the first row at a horror movie.

Witty, like many photojournalists, would become covered in crust from the fallen rubble, having outrun the domes of debris. He would take pictures of similarly bedecked men and women trudging through the otherworldly swirl. "After emerging from the cloud," he would write in *Double Take* magazine, "I photographed one woman who had a huge smile, happy as Christmas morning, covered in dust. She stared right into my lens [and asked], 'Can I get an eight-by-ten glossy?' " Witty's reaction today: "She actually asked me it, that way. I thought, That's so inappropriate and crazy and insane of her to ask me that. But she was in shock." He believes that her odd delight came from the endorphin rush of having survived a near-death experience and from seeing a photographer magically appear who might allow her to bring home an honest-to-God trophy: Jane Doe—To Hell and Back. "What *would* she say?" he asks. "She'd survived the worst day in the history of New York."

Scores of photographers chose to focus on the wounded or on the emergency personnel who rushed to their aid. Susan Watts, of the New York *Daily News*, was taken with the sight of a businessman cradling a prostrate woman—a total stranger—who appeared to be stroking or grabbing at his chest. Shannon Stapleton, of Reuters, caught the dust-caked figures of five men, materializing as if from a mist *(Image 10)*. Using a metal chair as a makeshift stretcher, they comprise a sort of urban Pietà, carrying the body of Father Mychal Judge, the revered New York Fire Department chaplain, on their way to St. Peter's Church to set him in the sanctuary there. (A victim of the collapse of the south tower—whose body was listed at the morgue as Victim No. 00001—Father Judge had been blessing the deceased only minutes before.) There were other photographs too layered with misery and meaning to explore just yet. Among them: the images of those who fell from the towers' windows, many leaping to their deaths to escape the inferno inside. And at day's end: the picture of three firefighters unfurling the Stars and Stripes above the ruins that would come to be called Ground Zero—among the few truly hopeful images shot on September 11, 2001.

"Hopeful" is a relative term. Dozens of people that day had the impulse to photograph their loved ones or their neighbors or the unknown companions who happened to be watching the trauma with them. Unconsciously, they were making a choice. They thought it important to treat other witnesses—not the catastrophe—as the subject of their photos. They were not merely standing back and observing the events passively, but were rendering, unconsciously, *why* the calamity mattered.

With the towers belching white smoke behind her, Isabel Daser, a German-born, New York–based architect (and amateur pilot) requested that a coworker photograph her—eight months pregnant with her daughter, Amelia (born three weeks later and named after Amelia Earhart). Daser, in rotund profile, stares at the camera with an inscrutable Mona Lisa expression, standing near Twenty-third Street on Sixth Avenue *(Image 11)*. "At this moment we didn't realize that it was a terror act," she explains in an e-mail from her new home in Zurich. "I flew around 'the twins' myself in a Cessna several times before. So I asked my colleague to take this picture. You can tell by my face that I didn't want to smile, as you normally do in pictures. I know that many hobby pilots take pictures while being on the commands at the same time. So I could imagine one 'tourist pilot' having an accident. We didn't know the truth yet."

Artist Michelle Chojecki stood on her roof with a camera and keyed her lens on the confusion in the face of her neighbor's sixteen-month-old son, Zion, letting the towers behind him go out of focus. "I was wondering what the baby might be thinking about all the commotion," Chojecki now says. Instead of shooting the event, which she calls "too huge to conceive," she grounded herself by peering into the eyes of a child being embraced by its mother.

In the moments after both towers had fallen, photographer Alex Webb noticed Jenna Piccirillo and her three-month-old son, Vaughan, on a roof in Brooklyn Heights, the baby wincing in sunlight in his portable infant seat. Behind him loomed a skyline bathed in gray *(Image 12)*.

Each face had been set against a monstrous backdrop, as if the photographers had felt compelled to shoot the terror in context—in relation to the innocents it had been intended to terrify. They were studies of mothers and children, not urban grotesqueries. And many, in their way, projected the innocent act of getting on with one's existence. The portraits were implying not fragility or defeat, but an affirmation of the cycle of human life, a hint of reassurance. Webb says that his image of Jenna and Vaughan—"a tender moment between mother and child, and Manhattan in the distance, wreathed in smoke—[captures] a kind of incongruity which I often feel exists in situations of strife and which is often ignored: life continues in the face of disaster . . . despite the horrors we inflict on one another. [The picture] also provide[s] some questions: What kind of world is this child being born into? What does the future hold?"

And then there was Jerry Spagnoli. For months, he had been engaged in a photo documentation project, recording modern New York landmarks by using a photographic tool introduced in 1839: the daguerreotype. That Tuesday, upon seeing the disaster from his window, Spagnoli, an expert in nineteenth-century photographic processes, decided to lug a giant wooden view camera to his Chelsea rooftop. He also brought along a daguerreotype plate. On that morning, he left the camera's shutter open for three full seconds, and on a bulky sheet of silver-plated copper he etched a vista in black-and-white (actually in silver crystals on a mirror-finished sheet of polished silver). The image had a haunting, almost tactile sharpness: quiet streets, two old water towers, One World Trade Center raked with smoke on the horizon as the south tower disappeared in a squall of white *(Image 13)*. Spagnoli had recorded the September attacks by employing the same medium that men seven generations before him had used to capture the battlefield dead during the Civil War.

Viewers can behold Spagnoli's faux-vintage image and unconsciously process the destruction as part of a continuum of conflict. "Seen in isolation," he says, "the event is too awful. But it's inherently empowering to know that, given human history, incredibly awful things *do* occur, and then we go on." Spagnoli himself finds a certain solace in having rendered the horror through an antiquated technology. "I used a material which visually alludes to previous events," he explains. "You see it and you think, 'Civil War, the San Francisco earthquake.' The manner in which the photograph is made, and then experienced, provides the viewer with a context for the scene. The daguerreotype compresses the precedents."

While photographers rushed toward the towers, the rest of us rushed to our television sets. "The events of September 11 were shaped largely through their visual representation," University of Pennsylvania communication professor Barbie Zelizer has noted. "As the planes hit the World Trade Center, people ran to their television sets and stayed there for hours on end, watching an endless loop of reruns of the actual attack [which, after a while,] began to look more like still photographs than moving images."

"We couldn't take our eyes off the buildings coming down," says digital-media expert George Kindel, of the University of Richmond, Virginia. "If one station didn't show them, we'd switch to a channel that did. Or we'd log on to the Internet to see the Quick Time movie. Because we *had* to see it and visualize the details—what happened first and when did which tower fall and what did it look like?—until we understood it. That first week we didn't *get* it yet. Usually we watch television as moving pictures. We're on the run or switching channels. The story's changing. That day, [we stopped]. We were in the eye of the hurricane."

The sequences of the towers collapsing (and many of the still photos that we now consider the key images of the event) did not enter the public consciousness like other historical moments caught on film or tape. These were not pictorial watersheds that accrued acceptance with the years—the three-year-old son of an assassinated president saluting his father's casket in 1963; a lone protester staring down a tank in Beijing's Tiananmen Square in 1989. Instead, these were news clips that gained traction in the public skull through hourly repetition in an accelerated and emotionally supercharged time span—a single week. The life cycle from news clip to video icon was compressed to days, not decades.

The initial televised footage of the attacks of September 11, 2001, came from WNYW-TV—the local FOX 5 station—during its morning program *Good Day New York*. Correspondent Dick Oliver had just completed an on-air segment about the primary elections, and was standing near a polling center in lower Manhattan, using the towers as a backdrop for his shot. "He went off the air," recalls that morning's FOX 5 assignment editor, Joe Farrington, who, back at the station, was still watching the view through the crew's camera, even during the commercial. "In between the break, we heard a boom. Dick yelled, 'Studio, studio, come to me, come to me. Something's going on.' You saw the smoke on a television monitor in the newsroom—not live on the air [yet]. At that point, we yelled at the control room, and they prepared to come *out* of the commercial break into Dick Oliver with the smoke behind him. So we broke this to New York City."

Cable News Network, in turn, would be the first to inform the country—and the world. At exactly 8:49:36, the network was up and running with its own view of the towers, from an unmanned, stationary camera on the West Side. CNN's shot showed smoke emanating from Tower One and displayed an "8:49a ET" time code in the lower right-hand corner of the screen, under a CNN LIVE logo *(Image 16)*.

"You are looking at obviously a very disturbing live shot there," came anchor Carol Lin's commentary. "We have unconfirmed reports this morning that a plane has crashed into one of the towers . . ."

That footage was seen "broadly, nationally, first on CNN," according to Karen Curry, the network's vice president and northeast regional bureau chief at the time. (Her account is corroborated by sources at the Newseum, the nonpartisan museum that places news coverage in historical context.) In short order, CNN executives, realizing the global significance of the attack, decided to blanket the planet with identical coverage, running its domestic feed, says CNN's Carolyn Disbrow, across "CNN International and our other CNN networks, wall to wall."

According to Steve Pair, then WNBC's director of engineering, each of the city's stations went "almost instantaneously to their weathercams or beautycams or citycams." NBC had about a dozen fixed cameras around town (on bridges, buildings, Times Square, at the airports), used for covering traffic, storms, crowds, parades, marathons. These were quickly trained on the towers and put up on air. "The minute it happened, we could *see* it," says Pair. "Then helicopters became airborne," and other camera teams were scrambled. Within minutes, according to Jeffrey Schneider, vice president of ABC News, his network cut into *Good Morning America*'s local and national news break, switching to a stationary weather camera from Brooklyn, shooting across the river, and cutting over to a helicopter team that had just finished its last traffic report of the morning.

CBS had a fixed camera on the top of the Empire State Building, with a clear shot south. The station also kept its backup transmitter there, *not* on Tower One, which proved a boon. "For the first five minutes, as I recall," Pair says, "everybody [with antennae] at the World Trade Center was still on the air." Then One World Trade Center underwent a massive power outage. Since its roof bore a 300-plus-foot boom—with the primary transmitters for most New York stations—those channels, says Pair, "went dark." Though televisions with dish and cable service continued to receive signals, antenna-dependent TVs did not. CBS, unlike other stations, was able to soldier on, switching from its downtown to its midtown transmitter and continuing its regional broadcast unimpeded.

Due to the location of the transmitters and the need to man those antennae around the clock, six TV engineers (stationed in offices on the 104th and 110th floors of Tower One) did not survive that day: Gerard Coppola, Donald J. DiFranco, Steven Jacobson, Robert Edward Pattison, Isaias Rivera, and William Steckman. "Almost all of us lost employees and friends down there," says Pair. "I happened to be on the phone with Bill [Steckman], our transmitter supervisor . . . when the plane hit. I remember Bill saying, 'Something just happened.' Then he came back and he said, 'There's some smoke in the room.' And pretty soon the phone just went dead."

"I have never been in a control room where everyone who was working was crying," FOX News executive producer Bill Shine would remark. "I will never forget that."

Still, the event demanded firsthand reporting, so producers pressed on. "For the first forty-five minutes to an hour," says CBS news-service executive John Frazee, only a handful of nonstationary cameras televised real-time imagery. Soon, he notes, "there were crews with cameras and people running around with small consumer cameras. Then there were ENG [electronic newsgathering] trucks that had been sent down there, told to set up microwave signals. As time went on, people were able to get trucks out of their Jersey bureaus and park them along the Palisades and do live shots. There was a lot of tape-ferrying and hand-carrying back to broadcast headquarters."

On-screen, the coverage was lightning-paced, the hard facts coming in scattershot fashion. Harrowing reports from field correspondents sometimes seemed at odds with the composure of the anchors, who tried to remain reassuring amid the chaos. Ashleigh Banfield, of MSNBC, seemed visibly distraught, having survived salvos of debris swarms. NY1's Kristin Shaughnessy, on air as the south tower fell, followed the advice of a nearby FBI agent who told her to sprint for her life. "I took off my high heels and ran," she recalled, "like I was outrunning a tornado." Carol Marin, of CBS News, was pinned against a wall by an anonymous fireman intent on saving her life. "I felt him cover me, and I could feel the pounding of his heart against my backbone," she would recount. "There were things in the air—it was ash, it was granules, it was the atomized parts of desks and sinks and people, I realized later."

While some stations found it difficult to separate rumor from reality ("It looked like a propeller plane . . ."), ABC seemed especially sagacious. The network provided a stream of consistently credible eyewitnesses ("It looked like a normal plane going over the city, and then, all of a sudden, a turn to the left, and it slammed right into the World Trade Center"), even fielding a phone call from a man trapped in the north tower. "I'm stuck on the eighty-sixth floor," he said, about forty-five minutes into the ordeal. "Tower Number One, on the east side. I heard a noise, felt the whole building shake, and the glass on my floor was blown from the inside out, and the interior core of part of the building collapsed." Early on, ABC went to correspondent John Miller, who had interviewed Osama bin Laden in 1998. While the towers were streaming with dark gray smoke, Miller reminded viewers: "[T]he suspects [in the 1993 bombing] later told federal authorities [the attacks] were intended to take the building down . . . And U.S. intelligence, FBI people, for years have heard that they've always wanted to try and finish that job off, to take the buildings out."*

* NBC's Andrea Mitchell, roughly a half hour into the event, mentioned that the "best-known suspect is Osama bin Laden . . . in Afghanistan." Likewise, Jim Stewart of CBS commented that officials "specifically believe this is the work of Osama bin Laden."

Behind the scenes, news teams improvised. Because of the dangers on the ground and the difficulty of transmitting signals from downtown, most footage had to be somehow shuttled back to broadcast centers before being shown on air. The dawn of multiple live-video feeds from a war's front lines had not yet broken.

But despite these limitations, cameramen and producers by the score tried to get as close as they could. Joseph McCarthy, a freelance videographer and director of photography working for ARD, the German television network, was scheduled for a morning shoot at the United Nations. His assignment, of all things: the ringing of a peace bell at a ceremony for the establishment of an international cease-fire day. But when he saw TV coverage of the north tower's precarious state, he shot down the FDR Drive instead, flashed his press credentials, and settled in with emergency workers under the pedestrian bridge at Liberty Street. Soon, he watched as people trapped in the towers began falling from the sky. Onlookers clutched hands to mouths in horror.

McCarthy videotaped it all, shooting directly up at the south tower just as he heard the building churning above him. He turned, bolted, and slammed into the wall of One World Financial Center. Then the morning went black around him. Trapped with others in an alcove, McCarthy heard three gunshots. "It took a cop, Tim McGinn," McCarthy says, "to shoot out this huge, thick, plate-glass window with his pistol, and the whole thing opened up, and we got out." To rush his footage to the East Side offices of ARD-TV, McCarthy decided to walk over to Eleventh Avenue, he says, "and for the first time in my life, I successfully hitchhiked in New York City." He stuck out his thumb and marveled as the first car stopped to pick him up—"a beautiful, white Lexus, with a leather interior," he says. "I got in with glass all over me."

Joe Scurto often responds to fires by listening to FDNY frequencies on a radio scanner, videotapes the blazes, then licenses his footage to television producers, corporations, and public-service outlets. That morning, he took his Sony Hi-8 video camera to the scene. Standing on West Street, he shot the collapse of the south tower (tripping his camera's "on" button the moment he heard what he calls "this chattering-type scream-roar") and its twin to the north.

"I photographed somebody jumping," he recalls, "but then as I was ready to hit 'stop,' it was almost like divine intervention, like somebody held my thumb, and the north tower fell as I was rolling video. On one or two floors, every window belched fire and you could see the initiation of the implosion." For two hours Scurto felt himself "shooting through this sensory overload by running on automatic. It was the only way: keep focused and go from one scene to the next. I saw at least a hundred people jumping. They were coming down like rain." He left only when he couldn't shoot anymore, not because he had run out of film but because a silvery black particle of molten metal had become lodged in his left eyelid—the one that was not affixed to his camera's eyepiece.

Tom Flynn and his wife, Nan Reardon, were sitting on the back deck of their West Village duplex that morning. Flynn, a CBS News producer at the time, recalls that as he read his morning paper, "a plane went over the trees in my garden. It was low, it was loud, and it was determined. It was not right. It seemed to be revving up. Then there was a pop, like the sound of a softball hitting a glove." Almost immediately, his neighbor in the garden next door relayed the radio's traffic-copter report: a small plane had just collided with the World Trade Center. Flynn, a veteran of numerous conflicts in Africa, Asia, and elsewhere, would have none of it. He turned to his wife and said, "We're under attack."

Flynn hopped on his bicycle and sped south. But instead of bringing along his own video gear, Flynn, a natural-born producer, decided he would improvise. The city would undoubtedly be overrun with camcorders, he reasoned; he'd merely hunt around for a few amateurs and "assign" them on the spot. Sure enough, at the foot of the Trade Center, he ran into a man shooting tape—proof positive that the age of the universal lensman had arrived.

"His name was Eddie Remy," Flynn says, "and he told me he worked for Merrill Lynch. He was the audiovisual guy. I said, 'I'm Tom Flynn, CBS, and you're now working for us.' " They exchanged business cards so as to reconnect if they became separated. Remy shot rare footage of evacuees *inside* the complex, documenting some of the thousands who were saved by the coordinated and disciplined efforts of a tide of first responders. Remy "mainly stayed rolling on the north tower, then swish-panned over" to what Flynn was watching: the collapse of the upper floors of the south tower, which, from Flynn's perspective, seemed to "belly out, almost like jello, after an internal mini-explosion around the ninetieth floor. It was liquidy. A concrete building seemed to be melting with this deep-throated, rumbling roar." (Flynn survived by running into an underground garage to escape what he calls "the crash, which came like a hot sirocco of deep, reddish dust and ash.")

Remy also exposed tape of scenes that, according to Flynn, CBS decided not to air. "There were people leaning out of the windows, waving at us below, waving for help," Flynn says. "Smoke poured out from their backs. When they jumped, they were small. One woman jumped from the north side of the north tower. The wind that morning was brisk and out of the north. It blew her *into* the side of the building about halfway up. It haunts me to this day."

Scores of news teams such as McCarthy's, Scurto's, and Flynn's scrambled into the fray, escaped with their lives, then made their way to their stations. Others stood their ground and covered the story as it played out around them. The first international station credited with having broadcast its own live pictures of the attack was Russia's RTR. Its New York correspondent, Evgeny Piskunov, happened to be on the West Side roof of the CBS Broadcast Center at Fifty-seventh Street, with the Manhattan skyline behind him, shooting a live segment on that week's United Nations children's poverty summit. Nearby, a satellite was set to accept his transmission at 8:45 (one minute and forty seconds, it so happened, before the first plane's impact). Shortly into his broadcast, Amy Wall, a CBS colleague transmitting his shot to Russia via London, got a call on a rooftop phone urging her to look south. She saw billows on the horizon (her view of the towers eclipsed by other buildings) and was told that a commuter plane had hit the north tower. "*This* is your story," Wall told Piskunov. "You're not doing the children's poverty summit anymore." Wall stood off camera, listening to sketchy news briefs over her phone line, then gave cues to Piskunov who, in turn, informed his viewers in Russia.

As the day went on, the CBS roof became a video turnstile, with Wall the gatekeeper, feeding images across the world over four fiber-optic lines. "By five p.m.," says Wall, a coordinating producer for international news, "I had arranged for sixty different special reports among representatives from Belgian, French, German, Russian, British, Spanish, Canadian, Ukrainian, Greek, and Italian stations. Everyone was given ten minutes apiece. Some were bringing up people who had escaped from the World Trade Center [to interview them] from a perspective that allowed a view of the smoke. I didn't leave the building for forty-eight hours."

In America alone, as tabulated by Nielsen Media Research, 80 million prime-time households tuned in to the main national TV news outlets that Tuesday.* Much of that coverage was visually comparable because of a unique arrangement among television executives. "Petty competition vanished," media analysts Cathy Trost and Alicia C. Shepard have noted in their book *Running Toward Danger*. "In an unprecedented move, cable and broadcast presidents quickly hammered out an agreement that morning to share footage for one day." Meanwhile, ABC piped the same live national feed through Disney-owned cable channels: for hours, ESPN, ESPN2, and ESPNews covered not sports, but terrorism. The music networks VH1 and MTV (both part of parent company Viacom, which owns CBS) ran live coverage from CBS News. NBC's cable outlets, CNBC and MSNBC, aired original news programming.

CNN's domestic coverage was beamed throughout the world that day, available in 170 million households in more than two hundred countries. And many homes and businesses that didn't get the network directly were watching content supplied by CNN (through its hundreds of broadcast-TV affiliate stations). Or they were watching CNN's competitors, such as Sky TV or BBC World TV or the Middle East's al-Jazeera (each of these networks able to pull the same footage off a satellite). *Or* they were watching similar content on their local or government stations.

In all, more than two billion people on September 11 watched the attacks in real time or watched that day's news reports about the attacks, according to David Hazinski, head of the broadcast news initiative in the

* By comparison, 85.6 million watched during the first day of the U.S. invasion of Iraq in 1991—an event that had been anticipated for months.

University of Georgia's telecommunications department.* "The 1998 World Cup [final, between France and Brazil]," says Hazinski, "was the marker when we crossed the line—over one billion [viewers watching one event]." The increase in global audience since that benchmark has been enormous, as national governments have given up their monopoly of the screen.

"Up until very recently," says Hazinski, who advises many overseas TV launches, "the predominant television [offering] in many countries was governmental TV. But as technological breakthroughs offered new revenue streams to governments and businesses, new channels surged, including news and information programming. There has been this huge bloom in new channels in Asia, the Indian subcontinent, the Middle East. This penetration happened around 2000 and it continues, year in and year out."

A number as unwieldy as two billion, of course, is impossible to verify. In a world peopled by more than six billion, there are an estimated one and a half billion television sets in operation. But there is no methodology for quantifying viewership. (Even in the United States, the ratings system merely offers estimates, based on audience samples.) As a result, hyperbole eclipses accuracy. Carl Bialik, a respected statistical gadfly who analyzes such numbers for *The Wall Street Journal Online*, refutes past claims that 2.5 billion watched the funeral of Britain's Princess Diana or that a billion more tuned into the 2004 Olympic Games. It is certainly safe to assert, however, that "hundreds of millions" were watching television news throughout the day on September 11, says Nigel Pritchard, CNN International's vice president of public relations. This unprecedented breaking story, told in pictures more than words, blazed and crackled across a common, planetwide hearth.

"With 9/11, we were all able to watch the same thing at the same time," says Pritchard. "People turned the TV on and saw the pictures of the smoking Trade Center. Through television sets, one image connected the world. Those pictures, taken from our camera on top of the

* When men first landed on the Moon, in 1969, 40 million American households tuned in, a number equivalent to today's annual U.S. audience for the Academy Awards. The Super Bowl has been known to draw viewers in nearly 150 million American households. Though it is often noted that a billion people, worldwide, watch the Super Bowl or the Oscar ceremony each year, that figure is difficult to calculate reliably.

bureau on Penn Plaza in New York, were shown everywhere, from gyms to street corners to bars. It was nine in the morning in Manhattan, but nine at *night* in Hong Kong."

"It's probably the only period in a day when the whole world *could* actually watch the same event at the same time," says Robert Pledge, head of the photo agency Contact Press Images. "Between nine and ten in the morning [Eastern Daylight Time], it's still not yet nighttime in Europe, Africa, and Asia. It never happens with the Olympics or the World Cup. It never happens when wars start because they usually start under cover of night. During all major events in the recent past—Tiananmen Square, the Gulf War, the Iraq invasion—there's always a part of the world that's in the dark. But this could be seen at once, anywhere, in both hemispheres, any latitude, any culture, throughout the world, live—something that we've never had happen before."

What distinguished most of the video coverage from its still-photo counterpart was its uniformity. While photojournalists moved from point to point as they covered the story, much of the TV footage (due to the perils of on-the-spot coverage and the hurdles of transmission) was stationary, caught from afar, often from fixed positions. Television felt pulled back, panoramic, offering the big picture. And a big picture it was. A vast array of electronic scaffolding, interlinked by unseen satellites, was channeling virtually identical sequences to virtually every TV set. The result was that humanity was observing the same catastrophe at the same time in basically the same format—a wide-angle cityscape. And that one wide picture served to unify, or at least align, the passions and fears of the world's wide viewership. Through the common visual denominator of television, the globe, as never before, shared a tangle of complex, concurrent emotions: outrage and awe and empathy.

The synchronicity of the TV imagery was complemented, in a curious way, by its immobility. In the hour and a half after the first plane's assault, the television audience, by and large, watched a static scene: two buildings consumed in fire and smoke, their stasis an unsettling counterpoint to the riot of death raging inside those structures. As far as TV was concerned, the stricken towers were recorded almost exclusively by remote cameras set up blocks or even miles from the Trade Center. As a result, the televised image acquired many of the characteristics of a still photograph. The video, like a photo, took a dynamic, shifting scene (people were battling raging fires, people were fleeing, people were rushing in to save the trapped and the wounded) and froze it in time and space into objects observed—two immobile towers suddenly made vulnerable. The video became a canvas for absorbing a viewer's private fear, confusion, disbelief. (What *was* this sight that the TV anchors were struggling to place in a meaningful context?) The perpetual motion of reality had assumed the eerie stillness of the surreal; the heat of the instant had been chilled in what the communications-and-culture critic Marshall McLuhan called the "cool medium" of television. The event, like the viewer, had been petrified by the format—the detached stare of fixed cameras having superimposed an appropriately unnerving overlay.

As the event progressed, however, and the enormity of the death toll became clear, and the fulminating towers were no longer there to observe, television, as it always does, sought a way to mediate the moment passed, to reduce the infinite complexity to a single sight-and-sound bite. TV resorted to the instant replay and the neatly spliced videoclip. On air, the second plane struck the south tower again and again, in flashback. The buildings disappeared in a blossom of gray, repeatedly, as a recurrent nightmare might haunt a trauma victim. In the ensuing days the clip would become the signature of the event: the streaking plane, the smoking towers, the death clouds attending the towers' collapse.

Photographs, in contrast, would provide not a single iconic representation of the day (since no individual shot could encapsulate it), but visual diversity—innumerable perspectives. Still pictures would offer the multiplicity of points of view that are typically required for journalistic objectivity. Still pictures would convey thousands of instants, each horrific in its own way.

The video image would show mass murder; the still image would hint at split seconds when a man or a woman had been taken from this earth.

Analog tape, digital video, live feed. Daguerreotype, digital, disposable. Thousands of cameras provided optical confirmation of the unbelievable. September 11, simply put, was the most widely observed and photographed breaking news event in human history. And it occurred, aptly enough, at a time when image reigned supreme in world culture due to a number of factors: the primacy of marketing in a global economy; the modern era's fascination with around-the-clock news and anything rendered real-time; the culture's addiction to speed and immediate gratification; and the rise of various digital technologies, including digital photography, cable and satellite television, and the Internet. The CBS anchor Dan Rather, covering the story that morning, described it in these terms: "If you didn't know better," he remarked, "you'd say it must be from a horror movie. It's horrible. It isn't a movie."

For many people the world over, however, on 9/11 the image, the footage, the movie *was* the event. For most of us, the picture was all we had, and ever will have, to signify it.

A neighbor of mine, Geraldine Davie, of New Rochelle, New York, knew her daughter Amy O'Doherty had been put at risk by the attacks. Amy, twenty-three, was working as a broker's assistant for Cantor Fitzgerald on the 104th floor of Tower One. The last time Davie and her daughter had spoken was over dinner a week before. They discussed rather mundane topics, Davie says, but she recalls being pleasantly surprised by Amy's manner. "The way she ordered was very specific, worldly, with a flair," she says. "I remember thinking, She's really grown."

On the evening of September 11, Amy's close friends picked out a snapshot—taken a year before, at Melissa Della Donna's engagement party—and used it as the centerpiece of a "missing" poster. Below the photo, they printed Davie's phone numbers, hoping that anyone who knew Amy's whereabouts would quickly get in touch. The friends made several hundred copies, and the next day they set out for the streets of Manhattan to affix paper to glass and stone.

As they went about their rounds, Edward Ornelas, a *San Antonio Express-News* photographer, took a picture of two of them: Claudia Trevor, her back to the camera, clutching Liz Gallello, in tears while grasping a flyer in each hand. At that stage, says Davie, "There was no information. We were searching hospitals." Also visible in the news photo, below Amy's beaming smile, was a list of distinguishing physical markers ("Brunette w/ Blond Highlights, 5′4″, 135 lbs, Hazel/Green Eyes . . . Freckles, Large Chest, Diamond Stud Earrings") and her mother's contact numbers.

Liz's face, and Amy's, would run across the newswires. Soon, strangers were phoning Davie from as far away as Brazil, Sweden, Hawaii, the Philippines, New Zealand. "We were getting condolence calls for months," she says. "Usually at night, because of the time differences. They were sharing the grief. That one photograph traveled around the world."

Four years later, Davie continues to discover new truths about Amy through pictures that her daughter's friends send her. "Without photography, the memory of how many things this child did in her life may not have been as clear," she says. "*I* didn't know she took golf lessons. Or went *rock climbing*. The photographs and the stories behind them [have] sustained me. I'm constantly searching for photos of [Amy] because I'm trying to put together a life. I'm also trying to put *her* back together again. I have a lot of remains. I got the first call in December 2001, another call a year later. We had buried the first group of remains. Then two weeks ago they identified her left foot. It's horribly difficult. In one sense they're trying to piece her together—the medical examiner—and I am too. Eventually, some time this year, we'll put her all together in Virginia, reinter her, so that she's not all scattered around this earth."

The pictures, Davie says, help her in "making that connection to my feelings for her. [Any] new photos [bring] new discoveries. The photos are like a lifeline. In most of the pictures I've seen, she's smiling. There's always camaraderie, always that *glow*. I search for the vision that I hold of the child who used to crawl in my bed, the young adult whose hair I smoothed out."

By dusk, photographs, like a soft rain, would begin pattering Manhattan. Families, friends, and colleagues, with no firm fix on the loved ones who had gone off to the Trade Center area that morning, took the initiative and made "missing persons" posters in the form of paper flyers.

The posters were confined to a single sheet—typing paper, digital-printer stock, white signboard. They contained the lost one's name and age (or date of birth) and listed contact numbers (and occasionally an e-mail address) should a passerby happen to be in a position to contribute "any information." Many offered a plea, sometimes printed in script, bold, or colored type: HELP, CALL, PLEASE CALL, OF HAVE YOU SEEN . . . ? As a rule, the flyers included the missing person's height, weight, hair and eye color, company name, office floor and address (Tower One or Two, or a building nearby), and a description of the clothing that he or she was "last seen wearing" ("Docker pants—grey pullover"), along with identifying features, if any: a birthmark or scar or tattoo, a wedding band, "may be carrying an inhaler."

Each page (often designed on a home or office computer) would be graphically anchored by a photograph of the missing man, woman, or child: a downloaded snapshot or a posed portrait, or one removed from a frame, a photo album, or a refrigerator door and then run through a portable scanner. Then, through a second photographic process, the posters would be reproduced in large quantities. Those designed on a computer were often replicated via color laser or ink-jet printer; those created by hand were sometimes photocopied.

The very first poster, according to Marshall Sella in *The New York Times Magazine*, was dashed off by the daughter of Mark Rasweiler, a beaming, white-bearded risk consultant from New Jersey. She produced it in her ad agency firm's art department and had copies out in circulation that afternoon. By nightfall, others were doing the same. Their placards were read by people searching for the lost in the streets downtown. They were videotaped and shown on television news programs and the Internet. Others, in turn, raced to make their own. The template sprang up spontaneously, then spread virally. Hundreds of tech-savvy people across the city had become so adept at handling digital photographs that even when faced with the prospect of having lost a loved one, they had the electronic know-how and graphic sophistication to sit at their desks and make a visually compelling document, down to the minutiae of centering visual and text elements, or choosing headline styles, fonts, the type's point size.

These handbills, created in haste and with heavy heart, were then dispensed throughout the city. The local Kinko's, the office Xerox, the home scanner and printer of every make and model would become samizdat presses for the distraught. By nightfall and into the morning, photomosaics of the missing materialized on shuttered storefronts, plate-glass windows, cyclone fences, construction-site partitions, phone booths, bus shelters. They were lifelines, as Geraldine Davie calls them, frantically cast to the outside world: *Please, please, have you seen this man, this woman? He matters, she matters.*

In those first days, hope was everywhere ascendant. And what erected those walls was the imperative to find one's own, at all costs. The faces of the lost would lap at the city's surfaces as waves lap a shoreline. The posters would stick like barnacles. They would dominate kiosk-style signboards at Grand Central Station and the red-brick edifice of St. Vincent's Hospital. They would paper hundreds of other pedestrian thoroughfares or public spaces where eyes and sympathies might linger *(Image 15)*.

The faces in the photographs were sunny, almost invariably smiling. Most were youthful, hardy, pictured in the proverbial prime of their lives. They were the sign makers' favorite shots (outside the chapel, on a motorbike, with a beer-can collection), the ones that had caught the subject's defining spark. The placards were literally attempts to put a loved one's best face forward. And, except for the occasional lead or closing sentence ("Please Find My Daddy!"), they were certificates of fact, not rhetoric, written with concise newspaper or police-blotter sobriety: "Brooke Jackman, DOB 8/28/78; ht 5′4″; wt 110 lbs.; wearing: tan pants, maroon shirt; brown, shoulder length hair, brown eyes; work: WTC 1, Cantor Fitz, 104th Fl. PLS. CONTACT . . ." In some instances, other details were provided, such as a nickname (in case the missing person was, by chance, found disoriented) or the sign maker's relationship (inadvertently invoking the conventions of obituary notices): "Brenda Conway—Age 40, 1 World Trade Center, Marsh—97th Floor," followed by phone numbers for "Husband," then "Mother," then "Sister." At times there was a solemn "Thank you" meant for those concerned enough to have stopped to read, or there were words of love or encouragement, meant for the missing, or for the eyes of the Divine: "God bless you" or "We love you" or "Keep Holding On."

The majority, however, were devoid of extraneous sentiment. The words served as emergency-response captions. The pictures, in what would soon become a terror-era trope, were "biometric data." The visual and the verbal were to be swiftly processed, and an action prompted. A recollection was to be dislodged from someone's short-term memory (Isn't she the one I saw in the stairwell of Tower One?), then an authority was to be summoned to collect the data, and then a phone number was to be dialed. A voice was then to have intoned, "We've found him. He's shaken up, but he's all right. He's on the fourth floor at Bellevue . . ." These were crisis calling cards.

What impulse drove so many to craft such similar signs in such abundance? The missing posters in those first days were makeshift attempts at cutting through the havoc so as to plead one's case directly, concisely, individually. Loved ones, in the absence of a coherent system for sending information or receiving answers, had to do *something* concrete to broadcast the vital statistics of the missing—*their* missing. Cell-phone networks were overloaded. New York City's 911 lines couldn't handle the call volume. Many of those affected, including agencies offering assistance, were not yet attuned to the Internet's facility for connecting multitudes. Radio and television were one-way media.

Family members just couldn't bear the limbo, the helplessness, or their loved one's silence, which roared above the media's white noise. So, watching others do the same, through news stories presented on television, they concocted their own grassroots medium, collectively: the "missing wall" becoming a hybrid of ID card, spiritual homage, and emergency graffiti. "Amidst the horror," says British television executive Stephen Claypole, four years later, "it was actually quite reassuring that people reverted to a simple, intimate means of communication. They went to their PCs or albums and found a photograph that was the seed of their misfortune, then went as close as they could get to the World Trade Center and put up this impassioned personal appeal."

Another motive behind the posters was the urge to sanctify the lost, through ritual. America, ever since the establishment of Plymouth Colony, has been among the world's most religiously inclined nations. And it has generally been a land of diverse faith and of homespun liturgy and sacrament. According to Paul Elie, an editor and writer whose office abuts Union Square (where street memorials quickly materialized), the philosopher and psychologist William James argued in the nineteenth century that "Americans understand the divine through their own idiosyncratic experiences, not through traditional creeds or institutions. And the novelist Flannery O'Connor, closer to our day, described rural fundamentalism as a 'do-it-yourself religion.' " Yet communal expressions of grief and widespread public "offerings" the week of September 11 seemed of a new and powerful order in an urban American setting. People soon began to treat the missing walls as outdoor shrines.

As Elie recalls, they came with "flyers bearing photos; flags; peace signs; votive candles made out of plastic cups (which they lit in the open air, still smelling of burning ash from the disaster site); laser-printed maxims from the Bible and the Qu'ran, from St. Francis and Walt Whitman; placards blending pictures of the towers with saints and archangels—all of this, emerging overnight, made clear that even in an apparently secular city people still conceive of grief and loss in frankly religious terms, and in terms of their own devising.

"In the week after the catastrophe, downtown Manhattan seemed a scene of unfettered American religiosity, more like Calcutta or Dharmsala than a 'secular city.' And for once this religious home brew didn't seem mawkish or exploitative. It seemed authentic and appropriate."

On Tuesday and Wednesday, for the families of the missing, strands of hope were still entwined with despair, outrage, bewilderment. But by the end of the week (in the minds of the public) and into the following week and sometimes beyond (in the minds of many victims' relatives who still retained expectations of recovery), nerves frayed and prospects waned. Although the efforts of rescue crews were Herculean (survivors *would* be rescued, many believed, because of the indomitable will of the search teams), the rescuers' presumptions, alas, proved Sisyphean. The collapse had just been too devastating to allow for more than a handful of early, miraculous recoveries.

The enormous missing walls would turn into enormous memorial walls, mortared with sorrow. The impulse to create and post the signs became ever more conflicted, as forces of confidence and reliance (and the instinct for rescue) gave way to forces of denial and mourning (and the desire to honor loved ones). The leaflets became outward expressions of inner shock and loss and unbearable grief. But still the walls spread, as *New York Times* correspondent Amy Waldman allowed, "like desperate ivy."

"For the first week, there were still nagging doubts," says my friend Don Johnston, a financial-printing executive from New Rochelle, New York, who lost many friends and colleagues. "Families held on to the belief that the missing were lost, unidentified somewhere in some hospital. And they didn't want to be untrue to their spouses or children—or to themselves—by not holding out some hope. But there was deep despair lurking behind the brave facade. It was in people's eyes. There was a big difference between the ones who kept on believing for five days—each day was like a month—and the ones who went on for two weeks."

Photographer Steve Simon went to the Sixty-ninth Regiment Armory on Lexington and Twenty-sixth Street with the intention of making a visual record of the pictures, the signs, and what he calls the "words of hope and desperation taped to the walls." He encountered a trellis of faces. He remembers that most of those depicted appeared to have been caught at their "proudest moments. Graduation parties, weddings, people with pets and one man standing next to an elephant, a reminder that in a time of pure pain and grief a weird sort of humor is still possible, maybe necessary." Photographer Ken Regan recorded the walls too, roaming the streets. And *Time*'s Christopher Morris. And Jane Barrer, Russell Boyce, John Branch, Phillip Buehler, Betty Hamilton, David Hinder, C. Bronston Jones, Peter Lucas, Nathan Lyons, Melissa Molnar, Margaret Morton, Krista Niles, Jaime Reyes, and many more. Ambreen Qureshi took Polaroids. Nathaniel Welch and Vincent Giordano shot relatives and friends holding up their flyers. Photographers diligently photographed photographs, a tattered, citywide veil of images stitched into place with masking tape and anguish.

The predominant virtue of the walls was that they not only helped assuage the creators of the individual posters, but also were channels of public response and redemption. The walls became a medium for soldering connections between loved ones and the lost, between employers and their missing workers, between neighbors (who felt the posters had become theirs—their missing—on *their* walls) and the anonymous faces, between those wandering the streets and those back home who had made the signs.

The walls became a message board, a sort of metropolitan conscience. Citizens seized the mode of expression that best simulcast their need to identify the missing to the largest audience: pictures on mass-produced posters placed on walls in public spaces. They chose simple, readily available technologies—digital photography, digital scanning and printing, and photocopying—that best addressed the urgency of the crisis. And every step of the way, from the format of the sign to the means of its reproduction to the manner in which it then furnished its message for the viewer, was intrinsically beholden to the photograph and to the photograph's versatility at imparting essential information with swiftness and accuracy (a versatility perhaps matched only by the Internet itself—minus the accuracy).

The walls, in fact, would have been impossible just four or five years earlier. In the summer of 1997, when Princess Diana was killed in a car crash, it seemed as if the city of London had descended en masse on the Buckingham Palace gates to pay their respects in an abundance of objects: bouquets, candles, trinkets, lockets, handwritten notes and poems, and images of Diana ripped from magazines and newspapers or appearing on posters and commemorative items. But few back then had access to devices that might have let them digitally tailor the offerings they would set at the shrines to Diana.

While the walls were still standing, images of the missing would appear at other rituals. Friends and family members would carry pictures at public commemorations, at rock-concert fund-raisers, at memorials or pregame ceremonies where the victims were honored (and where their photographs, it so happened, could be picked up by TV cameras to spread them among even wider audiences). Sometimes the pictures would be held aloft like religious icons, between thumb and forefinger:

wallet photos, laminated school portraits, headshots in news clippings. Some would wear photos, as pendants, on chains of gold or silver, or as pins, upon their hearts. Others would brandish their "missing" posters chest-high as they went about the city. "I'd seen that stance before, that posturing with pictures," says Larry Towell, a Magnum photographer who ran into a Guatemalan woman in the street near Ground Zero and was reminded of "the Mothers of the Disappeared in Guatemala protesting in front of the National Palace on Friday afternoons."

In the otherwise crushing flow of photographs of September 11, the faces of the lost were being placed in reserve, as things apart. Loved ones were taking portraits of the lost *out* of the mainstream media and appropriating them, one by one, for a higher, private purpose. They were displaying the images as sacred objects, as one might display representations of the divine. Many of those in mourning were venerating the missing as children of God, and, in doing so, venerating the Almighty, with whom they believed the missing now resided.

Patty Lampert, a hospital mammographer from Yorktown, New York, knew that her cousin Robert Baierwalter was unaccounted for on Tuesday. But she was, like Bobby, an optimist by nature. She remembers going into the city with confidence undimmed. "We had no doubt," she says. "We thought, He's in a hospital somewhere. We [were] clutching these flyers. We'll find him, no problem." In her mind, as in the minds of thousands of others, it seemed logical to think there would be many more survivors; in violent events like this, there were often twice as many wounded as killed. But early on it was hard to fathom: there had never really been a violent event *like this.*

Bobby Baierwalter was a forty-four-year-old father of three, a Connecticut-based account underwriter, who was attending an 8:30 Trade Center meeting that morning. He was also something of a big-brother figure to Lampert and her sisters. On Tuesday Lampert had watched TV footage of victims' relatives placing photo-laden flyers on the walls of downtown buildings. On Wednesday she had a friend e-mail her an image of Bobby so she could improvise a missing poster of her own. ("I cried when I saw his big, happy, Irish face. But seeing him up on the computer, I knew: There's no way someone so vibrant could be dead.") On Thursday she and Baierwalter's sister, Maureen, decided on a strategy at Maureen's house in Long Island, and on Friday they made their way by train into New York City. On the ride in, the papers in Lampert's lap felt magical—they were tickets, redeemable for Bobby. "We had these bundles of hope," she says. "Great. Now let's get him."

Once downtown, though, the streets seemed surreal, as if the whole town were in a trance. "There was dead silence," she recalls. "This was Manhattan but there wasn't a sound from anywhere. No one spoke to each other. It was eerie, [like] *Night of the Living Dead*. Everything was covered in dust. You passed people, people holding flyers just like you, everyone in a daze. But you were almost afraid to look at them because looking would make it too real, and this was like a dream you were in.

"As I walked I saw one flyer taped on scaffolding. Then another, and another. You read one and then had to walk on. It was too painful to take in more than one at a time. Then we walked and saw papers everywhere . . . One long, unending tunnel of papers. With pictures . . . up and down every street, like Post-it notes.

"It slowly hit me," she says. "There were too many pictures like ours, like Bobby. We weren't going to find him. And we just broke down crying on the street corner—I don't know where.

"We were in a dream but the pictures were what was real. The faces in the pictures were the *only* thing real. I knew then. Bobby's gone and we're never going to see him again."

By Wednesday, the hospitals and trauma centers, amply staffed with medical professionals and volunteers, would be woefully underwhelmed. The injured, it turned out, had largely been treated on Tuesday. There would be few survivors to treat, if any. By late in the week the agony of waiting acquired deeper, darker shades. And the walls, in turn, became expressions not just of those seeking assistance or solace, but of those seeking some spiritual accounting. Many seemed to feel an urgent need to place these faces on a public altar, to enshrine them among others of their kind.

An altar was an apt comparison. The murals of the missing had many of the trappings of religious iconography: an image centered in a frame, faces and torsos confined to that frame, words of simplicity and reverence etched around the border, sometimes on all four sides. Soon, bits of Scripture would appear, typed onto missing posters or written by hand: "Though I walk through the valley of the shadow of death . . ." Stickers with cartoon angels would be affixed to the walls, as would preprinted business cards with the words "Jesus Loves You" set in fleecy clouds. The walls prompted passersby to write their own personal responses in chalk or ink or Magic Marker, prompting further responses, dialogues, a chorus of communion and condolence. "For this was how the language of grief was being passed along," noted Marshall Sella in *The New York Times Magazine*. "Person to person, block by block—then sweeping over the continent on television—then block by block once again. Ritual is transmitted from retina to retina, satellite to satellite."

The walls of the displaced and the lost became a fresco of the World Trade Center diaspora. Textured, layered, and peeling, the walls evoked Rauschenberg panels. Demonstrative, slapdash, full of outcry, the walls evoked the walls of Paris in '68, Berlin in '89, Ramallah and Gaza City at the turn of the millennium. Crammed with tiny, personal messages of mourning, the walls evoked the Western (Wailing) Wall, that remnant of Jerusalem's Second Temple, otherwise left in ruins by the Romans in A.D. 70. The walls evoked Chagall, too, in the spirits that seemed to be hovering above them. From afar, the murals seemed most akin to lost mosaics discovered by archaeologists long after a culture's demise. They were fragmented and cryptic, with huge chunks unaccounted for. And yet, taken as a whole, they maintained a thematic coherence due to the precision and poignancy of the individual tiles.

The walls also rent the tissue between the public and the private. Strangers read about a life (she was a Scorpio . . . she had a two-year-old girl) and the coincidental trivia had the power to reduce them to sobs. "Our insides are now outside," the conceptual artist Gretchen Bender has said about the aches one risks in divulging personal fears through art, typically intended to be displayed on walls, for all to see. Our insides were indeed outside, and this helped to piece us together, right there in the street.

Five years later, what remains most distinct about the walls, in my memory, is the faces that had been streaked by rivulets of ink as the rains came. The weather on Tuesday, and for much of the week, had been unseasonably pristine. Well into the evenings, street shrines had thrived and citizens had gathered in parks and squares, many on their way home from work, lighting candles, leaving flowers, sharing poems, tears, songs of peace. But on Friday, the skies opened. After the downpour, the city enjoyed a respite of five more bone-dry days before the rains swept in again. Many digital photos disintegrated to indistinguishable smudges, just as weathered inscriptions, over years, might fade on timeworn headstones. Looking at an individual sign with its names and numbers streaked, its photograph blurred, was like squinting through one's tears. There was a rush by storeowners to cover walls in plastic. There was a movement by preservationists to save whole panels, intact. (Curator Louis Nevaer, in fact, would amass a collection of 5,200 9/11 flyers.) "In Union Square," wrote Sella, "park workers were verbally accosted as they dismantled [the walls]. At St. Vincent's, there were mass volunteer efforts not just to harvest the leaflets but also to repost them on walls around the neighborhood that would shield them from the weather."

Soon enough, the faces began to take on another cast as well.

For millennia—at least since ancient Egyptians perfected the preservation of human remains—cultures have sanctified the visage of the deceased. Death masks, painted or sculpted, rendered most often in life size, were a way of reclaiming the departed, holding on to them through artistic reanimation. Cemeteries in various corners of the world featured camera-rendered portraits of the deceased, embedded in headstones. The body was ephemeral, but its countenance—the most accessible and human reflection of the soul within—could survive, through art. Part of the urge to post these pictures was the urge to so honor.

In the mid-nineteenth century, Malcolm Daniel has observed, the daguerreotype "offered some small degree of immortality . . . bequeath[ing] to later generations a record of the faces of their ancestors." The ritual of the postmortem photograph became commonplace. A photographer would often be summoned to a deathbed, and the subject would be figuratively laid to rest once again upon the reflective surface of a daguerreotype. Sometimes the images recorded the face alone—perched upon a high collar or framed by a pillow, a bedsheet, and a bonnet's garland.

One hundred and fifty years later, the snapshot, in consort with the digital scanner and printer, would allow for a similar, if more ephemeral, recognition of the dead. The missing walls would become expressions of lives passing, and of souls persisting, the pictorial representing the corporeal, and then some. As with a living cell, the part encapsulated the whole. As with the communion wafer, symbolizing and *incorporating* the body of Christ, the "faithful likeness" was a sacred object, meant not just to embody but also to sanctify and immortalize. The photograph said: This being is no more; long live his image.

Night fell. Scattered clouds moved in. Then the smoke played tricks, as if the sky were thickening with white and gray. Up above the pall, the stars moved toward Wednesday and a new world.

Photographers outside the cemetery gates at St. Paul's Chapel could see the mantle of ash that had settled on the headstones. The flashes of their cameras turned the slabs a ghostly silver.

Nearby, floodlights shone down on a land called Zero, the debris field where the towers had stood. Hundreds of rescuers, laser-focused, raced against the night. In the lamplight, they dug and clawed for survivors, the beacons as bright as a photo studio's.

Throughout the evening and into morning, people took out cameras so as to get their eyes and minds around this new netherworld—television teams, photojournalists, stray citizens (who had managed to penetrate or remain in the zone, now off-limits to outsiders), even search-and-rescue workers, firemen, welders. Given definition by the harsh glare, the twisted beams of steel stood out like the masts of an armada on rocky, nighttime swells. The pools of light served to deepen the shadows. Many searchers would work the night, and nights thereafter, in a setting that suggested sleep deprivation or a waking nightmare: a hallucinogenic landscape with a lunar cast out of Magritte or Delvaux.

Hale Gurland, a sculptor known for his work in steel, bronze, and mixed media—including photography—was one of those who rushed to the scene in what he calls "the confusion of that first afternoon." He came equipped with acetylene torches, volunteering to cut steel beams. He also brought his experience in crisis situations, having been a helicopter pilot who had pitched in on relief missions in Bosnia and Lebanon. Even on September 11, Gurland recalls, he was surprised to find "firemen and cops taking pictures." So when he returned after dark, with more gear, he also toted a Minolta TC1, painted black. He had shoved rolls of black-and-white film in his top jacket pocket. "I paint all my cameras black," he says, "so you don't see me photographing. I'm like Walker Evans, who put a camera in a box and took pictures on the [New York] subway. I take pictures in war zones, [blending into] the background."

Into the early morning, and every night that first week, Gurland cut through tight nests of metal in hopes of finding living men and women within. "They needed guys at night," he says, so that the operation "could run 24 hours, to maybe find people still alive. It's easier to find survivors at night—there's less ambient noise."

He also made stunning photographs. His images, chiseled in deep blacks and grays (some later made into seven-foot blowups), capture the chalky silhouettes of rescuers made minuscule by the ruins. They have a desolate quality, like Apollo moonscapes in which astronauts roam alone on the slopes of a cold, dead world. "It's not iconography," he insists. "I shot what I saw. You're trying to give a smell, the immensity, the power of it. I saw a lot of dead people, but I didn't shoot them." Recognizing that few workers that first week were accomplished artists like Gurland, MaryAnne Golon, the picture editor of *Time*, believes his black-and-white photographs stand apart: "From a historical perspective, some of his pictures are the most important images taken at Ground Zero."

Ira Sapir, a sculptor who works in glass and metal, spent a week alongside Gurland. "We went as welders," says Sapir, "[and] wound up with firefighters, looking for voids, cut[ting] materials. There were a lot of sharp objects coming at you, like shrapnel. Your legs just got chewed up. You'd find a body and cut around it to extract [it]. Somebody would think they heard something [below]. The word would go out. All the equipment would shut down. There'd be a hush—dead quiet for two minutes and everybody would stand, listening. It was eerie as hell. But it was always a false call. Nobody was found alive."

Sapir, like Gurland, decided to take pictures—but didn't dare put his Olympus Stylus to his face. "It was disrespectful," he explains. "You're in this giant morgue." While Gurland's images are epic, showing mortals stunted against the deluge, Sapir's high-speed color-negative photographs, with their grain thick as dust motes, concentrate on the sweat and sacrifice of the men working in the cavernous hollows of "the mound, this pile of spaghetti," he says. "Most of [my] pictures were shot in the holes we were in. You could see the faces of the firemen and their emotion, their humanity. People were worn, spent. You're toast. But you never stopped. Everybody covered everybody's back. You fell a lot, but without fail, mysteriously, this hand would come out to get you [just before] you were going down. You feel that brotherhood in the pictures."

2 WEDNESDAY, SEPTEMBER 12

On Wednesday morning, Detective David Fitzpatrick went up in an NYPD helicopter. A surveillance expert, Fitzpatrick was known in the department as something of an aerial Weegee. In the past, he had shot scores of crime scenes from on high, including the damage caused by the 1993 World Trade Center bombings. On this day, he returned in a Bell Ranger for that same bird's-eye perspective.

Fitzpatrick had been driving to a union meeting the previous morning, in the vicinity of Kennedy Airport, when he heard a radio announcer report the first collision. Never without his Nikon, he gathered his equipment bag and seventy-five rolls of film he had stashed in his trunk, and was airborne within five minutes of the second plane's impact. His was one of a few aircraft allowed to make low passes near the Trade towers that morning.

As he warily scanned the sky, looking out for rogue jets, he fired off frame after frame. The result was a unique set of pictures taken from a perch as high as 6,500 feet. His images of a gigantic pall engulfing lower Manhattan hearken back to pictures of London during the Blitz. The billows are thunderous, apocalyptic. Buildings along the Hudson River, completely draped in banks of cloud, might as well be gravestones swathed in fog.

Fitzpatrick hovered above the crime scene on Wednesday, as he would every day for the next two months, shooting smoke patterns and surveying the damage. His task: to compile evidentiary images of the most deadly murder scene in American history. Fitzpatrick (accomplished as a hostage negotiator as well) confesses to being "a documenter, by nature." In his basement in Rockville Centre, tabletops, boxes, and display cases overflow with helmets, medals, and other relics from the Revolutionary, Indian, and Civil Wars, from both world wars, from Korea and Vietnam. With these latest, grisly additions to his archive, he now has mementos of American wars spread, incredibly, across four centuries.

Orbiting Earth, well above Fitzpatrick's craft, the International Space Station passed some 250 miles above Manhattan. Inside, Commander Frank Culbertson drafted an open letter to friends and family back home.

The day before, Culbertson had been in audio contact with the NASA flight surgeon, who conveyed the first sketchy details of the attacks. "I was flabbergasted, then horrified," he wrote. "[I] glanced at the World Map on the computer . . . and noticed that we were coming southeast out of Canada and would be passing over New England in a few minutes. I zipped around the station until I found a window that would give me a view of NYC and grabbed the nearest camera. It happened to be a video camera."

Culbertson, along with his two fellow passengers, both Russian, clearly made out the trail of gray above lower Manhattan. "The smoke seemed to have an odd bloom to it at the base of the column that was streaming south of the city," he wrote in his mission diary, on September 12. The scar spread across a small patch of the planet, as if a volcano was raging from a fire deep inside. Later he realized he was sweeping past the region shortly after the second tower had collapsed.

"We were about four hundred miles away from New York City when we were coming over Maine," Culbertson remembers, four years later. "When you look at that with your naked eye, you're seeing the entire Northeast. When you look at it through a camera, unzoomed [on] moderate wide-angle, you're seeing New York City and all the surrounding states. When I zoomed in, you see all of Manhattan and probably about half of Long Island. So you could see this big, great blob starting to envelop the southern half of Manhattan."

That week, there was no better perspective than Culbertson's from which to visually place the occurrence within its global context. While Americans could sense that their nation was under attack, Culbertson could actually *see* it. "And I *felt* a nation attacked," he says. "The camera had a pretty decent zoom and you realize, what a horrible situation. A lot of people are suffering down there. Your heart just breaks thinking about what people must be going through, the panic, the pain, the fear. We were going so fast up there, at five miles per second, that New York went over the horizon very quickly, and it takes [an orbit of] ninety minutes to come back around, so it was the longest hour and a half of the flight, because [once we] came back over, I had no idea what else we were going to encounter."

Mission control was not providing immediate updates, so Culbertson, newswise, was figuratively flying blind. "We move about a thousand miles to the west each time we come around," he says, "so the next time, we're coming about over Chicago. I'm looking for evidence there. I can see all the way to Texas, almost to Houston, so I'm looking for smoke on the horizon there, where some of my family was."

Culbertson and his crew photographed New York and Washington, D.C., repeatedly. (They could never find visual evidence of the flight path of United Airlines Flight 93, which had crashed in a field in Pennsylvania, claiming forty passengers and crew members.) The astronauts used Sony digital video cameras and what Culbertson, a photo buff, calls 35-mm Kodak-Nikon digital hybrids—still cameras rigged with the equivalent of 800-mm lenses. Their images, later color-corrected and enhanced, would be released in the days and weeks to come, along with space-based depictions of the devastated city from Landsat and other satellites in orbit at the time *(Image 17)*.

That day, oddly enough, Culbertson had become the twenty-first century's first space-based war photographer. As a space shuttle astronaut, he had filmed the oil-well fires of Kuwait, set ablaze by the Iraqi military during the 1991 Gulf War. Now he was photographing 9/11 and, a month later, the allied invasion of Afghanistan—from a few hundred miles above the battlefield. The Gulf War oil fires, he says, had been dramatic and distressing, but that conflagration seemed largely confined to industrial areas. In contrast, he says, September 11 was an attack on "*my* country, and those were *my* fellow citizens down there, and they [were] huge buildings that were coming down. It seemed more intense."

When the United States and coalition forces responded by sweeping into Afghanistan that fall to unseat the government that had harbored al-Qaeda, Culbertson tried to record as much of the assault as he could. "It's tough to identify cities in that country," he says. "A lot of it happened at night, which is difficult to film, though I could see the explosions of bombs and missiles. You could see strings of bombs going off when the bombers came over."

His reaction, he says, "was somewhat of a perverse sense of satisfaction: that we were actually doing something to retaliate for this. I am 'retired Navy' and I trained to do this kind of stuff, if necessary, and I knew my buddies were down there doing what they were trained to do. And there was a purpose to it. So I hoped it would be successful and short-lived, with minimum casualties . . . But I also felt like this was a clear, visual view of what was happening in response [to 9/11, and I was] trying to record the bomb flashes and explosions . . . the evidence of the combat." (Given the government's strict control of images of the war, it is not surprising that a NASA photo expert says he has no knowledge of the agency's ever having publicly released the crew's nighttime battle footage. Culbertson is careful to point out that the nighttime scenes were tricky to capture and that he probably had better success with the video than the still camera.)

Nothing, of course, could have prepared Culbertson for the sights he would photograph the week of September 11. Though his spacecraft would pass above Washington, D.C., that day, it was difficult to see the smoke-shrouded Pentagon through the haze. On September 12, however, he would be able to isolate the Pentagon "gash," as he calls it, even from that altitude. "I'm a pilot," he says. "It's hard to imagine anybody purposely flying a planeload of people into a building. It's just horrific."

That day he would also learn of the death of one of his Naval Academy classmates—Charles Burlingame. "He was the captain of the American Airlines Flight 77," says Culbertson, "that crashed into the Pentagon. I can't imagine what he must have gone through. He was a great guy at the Academy, always very upbeat about things. I know he took his flying seriously, so it must have been horrible to have people threatening the safety of his passengers. I feel sure he must have fought all he could."

Culbertson recalls that "people on the ground were a little leery of our recording [footage of the disaster sites] and sending it down. I think they were overreacting. Nobody knew how far this was going to go or who was going to retaliate for what. I got a hint from somebody I talked to that they were worried that [my] sending pictures down would make the threat worse for them on the ground. Then one of my friends—this guy really *is* a rocket scientist—did a calculation . . . and sent me an e-mail [while I was up there]: 'You know, with a Scud missile, Frank, they could in fact get one to your orbit, and if they timed it right they could hit you.' "

Culbertson continued to photograph, nonetheless, with a sense of mission. "As we went around and around, you're thinking, I've got to record this because people *need* to see this from this vantage point. I tried to record all I could . . . I took a lot of pictures of New York City at night because for a while you could see a lot of fires burning around and the lights of the rescue effort."

The astronaut witnessed September 11 differently from any American alive—in more ways than one. It took three or four days before his cohorts on Earth would send him images, attached to e-mails. "We weren't getting much [in the way of visual data] from the ground because they were a little preoccupied," he recalls, describing how he was on the receiving end of what others might call a unique form of 9/11 image management. "They weren't sure how much to tell us. They always worry about your psychological well-being." Culbertson says that among the first 9/11-related scenes he saw—with the exception of what he witnessed through his own cameras—were photos of peace and healing. "Some of the first images . . . were pictures of some of the American embassies around the world, where people brought flowers and candles and all. It really got to you to see the outpouring of support for the U.S. One of the [doctors] went around the Houston area taking a digital camera-load of pictures and shipped them up to me: pictures of everyday life, of all the flags on cars . . . people carrying flags or watching TV. [He was] trying to kind of show me how this had impacted people locally. That helped. It was quite a while before we saw any actual pictures of what was happening down there . . . And I didn't see any video of the attacks until I returned [to Earth in December of 2001]."

Even without having seen the attacks directly, Culbertson was nonetheless shaken to the core. He would write in his on-board diary on September 12: "It's difficult to describe how it feels to be the only American completely off the planet at a time such as this. The feeling that I should be there with all of you, dealing with this, helping in some way, is overwhelming . . . Other than the emotional impact of our country being attacked and thousands of our citizens and maybe some friends being killed, the most overwhelming feeling being where I am is one of isolation.

"Tears," he wrote, "don't flow the same in space."

> U.S. ATTACKED . . . DAY OF TERROR . . . IT'S WAR . . .
> UNTHINKABLE . . . HORROR! . . . OUR WORLD IS
> CHANGED

The four-column headlines and the fireball photos leaped off every front page. The morning papers were pried from newsstand stacks, gathered from front lawns at dawn, read ravenously. Online editions were hurriedly checked for updates that might have come in while people slept.

Readers *had* to know: Just how many had died? What about a second wave of attacks? How would the United States respond?

Many were concerned about loved ones and acquaintances. Many were unnerved and confused: How would they get through the day if bridges were closed and planes were not flying? Many just needed to *see*: How on earth did that second plane swoop in, or those towers fall? How had the Pentagon sustained its strike? What had happened in that field in Pennsylvania?

Across the electronic ether, photo agencies and wire services had dispatched thousands of 9/11 pictures to newspapers for Wednesday's papers. The Associated Press, which had gathered news for more than 150 years (dispensing information across the age of the telegraph, the carrier pigeon, and the fiber-optic cable), transmitted 1,200 frames over those first eighteen hours—about seven times the average supply for a breaking story. Pictures showed the building in all manner of implosion, people consoling one another in the street, rescuers clambering around Ground Zero, the outer shell of the north tower reduced to a sliver of honeycomb. (Many photojournalists, newspapers, and photo agencies would donate the proceeds from their picture sales to assist families devastated by the attacks.)

In one especially curious photo op, sent out over the Wednesday wires, the camera-savvy chairman of the Palestine Liberation Organization could be seen donating blood for the counterterror cause. "[Then] came the photograph of Yasir Arafat," journalist Deanne Stillman later observed in *Rolling Stone*, "arm outstretched and primed with a green tourniquet, needle in vein, blood flowing into a vial that would soon be en route to New York City . . . As I studied the image, I wondered about all the buckets of blood he himself had spilled."

And one indelible image showed President George W. Bush.

Among the more widely remembered photos to appear on September 12, it was published on the front page of papers as diverse as *The Miami Herald* and the Indiana University *Daily Student*. Only moments after receiving a bulletin about the first plane's attack, the president had assumed his place in front of a Florida grade-school class, listening as students took turns reading from a children's book entitled *The Pet Goat*. In the picture, the president seems confounded as he listens to his chief of staff, Andrew Card, who is murmuring in the president's ear: "A second plane hit the second tower. America is under attack" *(Image 18)*.

The scene was shot by five photographers in the crowded classroom that day, each from a different angle. As *The Boston Globe*'s David Shribman would later note, the moment proved to be "a portrait . . . of a president undergoing a thorough transformation in the course of two whispered sentences. [T]his photograph . . . has been burned into the retina of the nation's memory."

After receiving Card's warning, the president remained in his seat for at least seven minutes. The children continued reading aloud. He nodded and read along and looked around the room, offering encouragement. He would later say that he observed members of the press, positioned in back of the class, getting alerts from their home offices via cell phones and pagers. He would tell the 9/11 commission that his instinct had been "to project calm, not to have the country see an excited reaction at a moment of crisis."

Video footage of the same scene was famously reprised in excruciating time-lapse fashion in filmmaker Michael Moore's anti-Bush documentary, *Fahrenheit 9/11*. That single clip would take on legendary status as a rebuke of a sitting president, showing him actually *sitting* through a pivotal instant of historic consequence and appearing to pass up an opportunity to exhibit decisiveness under pressure. The tape reduced him, in many viewers' eyes, from commander in chief to caricature: the man of the hour, flummoxed and awkward, stunted by the immensity of the moment. The classroom setting reinforced an unflattering image, and suggested a salient if hackneyed axiom: inside every man resides a lost little boy.

Several days later, the administration decided to release an alternative 9/11 image, this one taken on board Air Force One by the chief White House photographer, Eric Draper. The picture, shot near a window affording dramatic sidelight, showed an "engaged" president, phone to his ear, conferring, as the caption explained, with Vice President Dick Cheney. The following spring, that same image would appear in a GOP mailing intended to solicit funds from would-be donors. Quick to criticize the move as photographic pandering was Bush's political foe Al Gore, who, the year before, had lost to Bush in the contested presidential race. "While most pictures are worth a thousand words," insisted Gore, "a photo that seeks to capitalize on one of the most tragic moments in our nation's history is worth only one—disgraceful."

The Bush team, responding to Gore's broadside, contended that the

Democrats were not in a position to moralize, especially given the fund-raising scandals that had plagued both Gore and President Bill Clinton during their time in the White House. Bush's then press secretary, Ari Fleischer, now says that the motives for releasing that White House image to the public may have had something to do with counteracting the TV commentators who were chastising Bush for his lack of focus that day. "We are part of that punditry in the White House," he says. "We react to it. It was possible that that picture was chosen [for release] to rebut that [impression]."

According to Fleischer, that day's presidential image snafu, if any, was not about dawdling over goats with grade-schoolers. "Nobody until Michael Moore's movie—that I ever heard of, at least—made a controversy of [the president's] staying in the classroom seven minutes," he insists. "The controversy that day was: Did he give a weak first speech [on TV that morning], and then, why didn't he return to Washington earlier? That was the controversy of September 11th." Looking back, Fleischer defends the Air Force One photo wholeheartedly. "On September 11 and [during] the immediate aftermath," he says, "the nation did see—whether it was live on TV for extended periods of time or in the snapshot of a photo—a very determined, strong president. *That* picture caught it. That's one of the reasons that picture resounded so well with the public."

On 9/11, the president took a while to get his public bearings. First, he taped a quick statement (which was fed to the networks after a slight delay, as a counterterror precaution). *Time* columnist Margaret Carlson and others would chide him for his performance, which became a sort of preamble to what Carlson called "two days in which Bush blinked his way through TelePrompTered remarks like a schoolboy reciting his lessons." Then, as Fleischer has pointed out, Bush spent several hours in executive limbo. Key advisers, for security reasons, had insisted on diverting Air Force One to military bases in Louisiana and Nebraska—before the president overruled his deputies and ordered the plane back to the capital. On stopovers, he appeared twice more on television, making brief statements. "His performance was not reassuring," *The Washington Post*'s Bob Woodward would note, in reference to Bush's Louisiana appearance.

"He spoke haltingly, mispronouncing several words as he looked down at his notes. [His] eyes were red-rimmed."

Television, in fact, had kept the administration on top of the unfolding events. The president, monitoring events through dozens of information sources, followed TV coverage intermittently.* The White House national security team was tuned in too, but on a different wavelength. Richard Clarke, the administration's counter-terror czar, chaired a crisis management meeting from the West Wing's Secure Video Conferencing Center. On a series of wall monitors (one always tuned to CNN), he watched as the chiefs or acting deputies of each key government agency (from the CIA and the Pentagon to the FAA and FEMA) appeared on-screen, having positioned themselves in front of cameras in their own remote studios. The president was patched in to the session from an underground facility at Nebraska's Offutt Air Force Base.

Throughout the day, Clarke, via teleconference, coordinated the government's emergency response, the session punctuated by ever more distressing news, while the cameras rolled. (Early on, the Pentagon was hit by American Airlines Flight 77. As Secretary of Defense Donald Rumsfeld appeared, on-screen, he informed Clarke that smoke was beginning to enter his communications studio. The Pentagon chief decamped to an alternate location.)

At 8:30 p.m., President Bush took to the airwaves from the Oval Office and reasserted his authority over his image, through live television. He insisted, without equivocation, that American policy would not distinguish between terrorists and those countries "who harbor them." The president understood, as some of his aides had not, that his country, and the world at large, needed to see and hear him *in Washington*—with all the visual trappings that the occasion and setting demanded. Here was the commander in chief "in command" from the flag-adorned throne room of U.S. power (which, at that time, was thought to have been the likely target of the fourth hijacked plane). The latent message telecast

* Osama bin Laden, in contrast, monitored the attacks via radio; so he claimed in a 2001 video.

that night was that the president would be sleeping in his own bed in the White House, not in some bunker. He would be exposed, should there be a subsequent attack on Washington leaving him as vulnerable as every viewer in every American home.

Over the ensuing days and weeks, Bush, just eight months into his first term, grew enormously and comfortably—and before our very eyes—into his presidential skin. Karen Hughes (counselor to the president and his chief on-message minder), Karl Rove (the president's top political adviser), Fleischer, and their team made sure of that. When Bush's top aides repaired to Camp David to plot their military response, the president, in a down parka, took center stage in the photograph that was soon released to the press: brow knotted, pen in his hands, flanked in his seat by Secretary of State Colin Powell and Cheney, the vice president keenly focused on the man in charge. When the president stood behind his desk on September 13, Fleischer recalls, and "announced that he was going up to Manhattan to go to Ground Zero, he was on the phone with [New York City mayor Rudy] Giuliani and [New York governor George] Pataki. And he started to cry at the end of the call. In that classic way that Bush men do, he started to tear up. And there are some wonderful photographs that captured that tear. The press was in the Oval Office for it."

The following morning, the president spoke at a prayer service at the National Cathedral in Washington, at which a clergyman christened him "our George," as in Saint George—"the designated dragon slayer," so *Newsweek*'s Howard Fineman would observe, "a boyish knight in a helmet of graying hair." Later that day, Bush was a model of the president-as-populist. In a gesture of leadership and of solidarity with the common man—one that would help define his first term—he stood in a windbreaker on the smoking heap at Ground Zero, flag pin on his lapel and bullhorn in his mitt. He embraced Bob Beckwith, a sixty-nine-year-old retired firefighter from Queens, who had immediately headed toward the World Trade Center on Tuesday *(Image 19)*.

"I can hear you," the president bellowed through the bullhorn. "The rest of the world hears you. And the people who knocked these buildings down will hear *all* of us soon." The country, then and there, saw their proxy at the helm, promising retaliation, and standing shoulder to shoulder with a man who represented all first responders, alive or lost. Two men were standing where two towers had been, one embodying sacrifice and valor, one leadership and retribution. That photograph, says Bush's longtime media adviser Mark McKinnon, "will be the most lasting and iconic image of [his] presidency. It is much like President Reagan's call in Berlin to 'Tear down this wall,' except this moment was unscripted and an antecedent to war, which makes it even more powerful."

Ed Kosner, the editor in chief of the New York *Daily News* at the time, also sees the image as capturing an authentic moment. "I think it was unscripted," he says. "They knew they were going down there. But Bush is quite tactile in that way, he's always putting his hands on people."

Not entirely, say some seasoned political observers. "There were genuine reasons for the president to go there and the country *needed* to see him there," says Jonathan Adashek, a strategist who worked on John Kerry's 2004 presidential campaign. "But I thought it was calculated, even if there was a certain air of spontaneity. Any good advance person—and they would have sent their best that day—would have had their eye toward the picture. They would have gone in, pre-positioned the press, and scripted in advance where [Bush] was going to walk, where he was going to end up. Never mind that the Secret Service would have had a say in what 'the principal' was doing, especially in a dangerous location like Ground Zero."

The situation more or less demanded the Ground Zero photo op, contends Luc Sante, the culture critic and photo historian. "People wanted to see him climbing on top of something [down there]," he says. "Even if it had been President Kerry or President Gore, they would have done the exact same thing. Clinton, obviously, would've put his arms around the firefighter. [But] with Bush you *never* get a moment that's not stage-managed . . . Even if the calculation was done five minutes ahead of time, this was calculated. I'm positive of it. [It was] part of an image-management strategy that's characterized this administration from the very beginning."

The image, while retaining its inherent power as a photographic icon, would eventually lose some of its emotional poignancy and, one could even say, its historical purity, once it fell into the hands of political strategists. In March of 2004, as the president prepared to run for reelection, his campaign would recycle the picture in television spots (under a stated theme of "steady leadership in a time of change")—along with shots of firefighters and of flag-draped remains being carried away from Ground Zero. The pictures were redeployed to underscore the Bush candidacy's defining issue in 2004—national security—at a time when his opponent, John Kerry, was questioning Bush's credibility and focusing on the economy, health care, and Kerry's own military service.

While some victims' relatives found the content of the ads entirely appropriate, many expressed misgivings. The International Association of Fire Fighters requested that the Bush team pull the spots. One Queens fireman, in the *Daily News*, compared the commercials to the work of grave robbers, insisting, "It's as sick as people who stole things out of the place. The image of firefighters at Ground Zero should not be used for this stuff, for politics." Kristen Breitweiser, who lost her husband, Ronald, in the attacks, concurred, saying: "After three thousand people were murdered on [Bush's] watch, it seems to me that that takes an awful lot of audacity." (Breitweiser, who helped spur the creation of the official 9/11 commission, would soon be making public appearances on behalf of the Kerry campaign.)

But six months later, at the Republican National Convention, there was the sequence again, front and center, in a short film produced to rally the crowd. Bush was shown in ten shots at Ground Zero, the film's editors having isolated and zoomed in three times on the bullhorn frame. Bush's advisers, shrewdly enough, had selected Manhattan as the backdrop to begin their final leg of the reelection campaign. They had chosen to hold their conclave just two weeks before the third anniversary of the attacks—just fifteen subway stops north of Ground Zero. And they had designated Bush-Beckwith-and-bullhorn as the afterimage that the delegates, and the TV audience, would take away from the convention. With the passage of time, this photograph, iconic and direct, had become politically supercharged. When it appeared on the large screen at Madison Square Garden, the picture prompted not a solemn response, McKinnon remembers, but "a roar."

Careful image crafting would continue to be a central tenet of the Rove-Hughes playbook throughout the war against al-Qaeda and the Taliban, and on through the war in Iraq. Message-marshal Hughes set up a media "war room" next to the White House (with satellite offices in London and Islamabad), where teams would monitor the propaganda offensive from Cairo to Kuala Lumpur, twenty-four hours a day, and quickly dispatch Bush operatives to respond with televised counterattacks or clarifications, or to make new pronouncements.

In late 2001, as the United States and its allies began their campaign against Afghanistan's ruling mullahs, I approached the White House (in my role as a *Vanity Fair* editor) and attempted to persuade insiders, with McKinnon's artful intercession, to pose for a cover story—including a first-ever group photo of Bush and his war council. America was set to retaliate; its citizens, in general, were in favor of a decisive, focused response. The nation needed to stare into the eyes of the men and women who would run this war. (Sentiments against military intervention had not yet splintered, nor had the wider plans of the neoconservatives fully emerged. There was only muted public talk of a possible invasion of Iraq—as punishment for that country's oblique connection, if any, to the attacks, or as possessors of weapons of mass destruction, or as a first step in making the region safe for democracy.)

Hughes and Vice President Cheney's chief communications adviser, Mary Matalin, gave the green light to the *Vanity Fair* story, which was photographed by Annie Leibovitz in early December 2001 just as the Afghan invasion was in full swing. Christopher Buckley (novelist, man of letters, and former speechwriter for George H. W. Bush) was enlisted to pen the homage. Leibovitz, having prepped the set and lighting on a relatively quiet Sunday in the West Wing, summoned the principals to the Cabinet Room bright and early Monday morning. They were, left to right: Powell, Cheney, Bush, national security adviser Condoleezza Rice, White House chief of staff Andrew Card, CIA director George Tenet, and Rumsfeld *(Image 20)*.

The gatefold cover had a warm, gold cast, its composition and setting reminiscent of a painting—a Dutch group portrait: controlled and formal, the subjects harmoniously posed, the background punctuated by a wall sconce, a vase on a mantel, and a stately picture within the stately picture—an 1873 oil showing Ben Franklin and compatriots at the Second Continental Congress, adopting the Declaration of Independence. Through the studied arrangement and accoutrements and the foldout format, the photographic moment would carry its own historic moment, grandeur, bearing.

As the assembled took their places, Powell turned to Leibovitz and said something to the effect of: What should we convey? He was inquiring about the expression that he and his colleagues were to assume, but he was also concerned with the intent of the image itself. How was it meant to be viewed? The photographer had a one-word answer, which did not need further elaboration. "Resolve," she said.

"I was shocked that the photo came off at all," says McKinnon. The fact that the Bush team saw real value in the need to project an image of resolve, he believes, was evident in its granting approval for the shoot in the first place. "To get those people together in the same room at the same time—during war," he says, was an acknowledgment of the power of the "power photograph" when placed in high-profile media real estate such as the glossy cover of *Vanity Fair*.

"And the best part," McKinnon points out, "is you look closely, [with all] the testosterone reeking off that cover . . . and you see a bandage on Rumsfeld's thumb—the detail, the little boo-boo." War, after all, is waged not by nations or machines, but by sometimes courageous, always vulnerable, flesh-and-blood mortals.

Throughout the day on Wednesday, the office of New York's chief medical examiner, on First Avenue and Thirtieth Street, received bundles from fire and law enforcement officials. They contained pictures, dental records, and X-rays of the missing. Over the next three and a half years, these visual markers would be used in identifying the deceased, even as forensics teams would create their own picture database, logging in and photographing the thousands of human remains that the search-and-rescue teams would unearth.

In all, 19,915 body parts would be recovered. From this sample of remains, many of which were no larger than a quarter, 1,592 individuals would be identified (nearly 58 percent of the estimated 2,749 New York victims). Identification was a painstaking procedure. In some cases, more than one victim might be present in a recovered set of remains. At other times, the traces of a single body might appear in dozens of fragments. The identifications were determined by comparing extracts from remains with information gleaned from photographs, fingerprints, X-rays, dental radiographs, personal items (such as bracelets), and personal markings (such as tattoos). But the vast majority came to be known through DNA testing, itself a kind of photographic procedure.

One's DNA fingerprint is actually a genetic snapshot, a tiny swatch of subcellular material etched on X-ray film. Take a single human hair, for example. Within it you can locate cells that contain DNA, the sequence of which is unique to the individual to whom that strand of hair once belonged. A DNA fingerprint—which appears as a patchwork of shadowy gray bands floating against an off-white backdrop of transparent gel—is an image of this unique sequence of units that make up a specific fragment of DNA. "Traditionally," says geneticist Ariel Ruiz i Altaba, "DNA fingerprints are made by using 'radioactively labeled' nucleotides, one of DNA's four component units. As the charged isotope atom [in the nucleotide molecule] decays, it emits beta particles. When these encounter film, a silver-based reaction takes place, creating a trace, whose signature can be seen on the X-ray sheet as a black shadow once the negative is developed. This is similar to writing on photographic paper with a light pen.

"DNA scientists also use fluorochromes," Ruiz i Altaba explains, "which label the nucleotides with 'light markers' that can be detected at different wavelengths and, thus, in different colors." The point, he says, is that genetic snapshots are used "as a method of revealing human identity in a manner not dissimilar to the way in which photographs identify." Without DNA fingerprinting, hundreds of families would never have had any evidence connecting their loved ones to the otherwise undifferentiated remains. Without these murky but distinctive molecular glimpses, lives would literally have been lost without a trace.

In the annals of DNA science, a new chapter was about to be written that second week in September. "We knew what we were facing," recalls Shiya Ribowsky, who would become the chief of identification operations for the World Trade Center site. "This was [going to be] the most significant mass-fatality investigation in the history of modern forensics." On the morning of September 11, while Ribowsky was busy initiating the morgue's response, rumors circulated that the collapse of the south tower had either killed or injured his boss—the chief medical examiner, Charles Hirsch, an inspiring éminence grise in his field. "We were envisioning piles of corpses," Ribowsky says. "We were figuring out how to deal with them and then return them to the families. The difficulty [became] compounded by the [need for] speed, the public scrutiny, and pressure to perform—pressures that are in diametric opposition to doing a good job."

Suddenly, Hirsch appeared, covered in gray ash. "He had lacerations and bruises all over his body," remembers Ribowsky, four years later. "He had dust permeating his clothing and his hair and in his skin. He was going to go home to change, and he put his hand in his pants pocket and he pulled out a handful of change—coins—and dust that had been blown into his pocket—gray particulate matter. And he placed it on his desk, in an ashtray, where it remains to this day—a pile of pulverized concrete. He'd seen people falling [from the buildings]. He said, 'Shiya, it's the most terrible thing I've ever seen.' " (Ten months later, Dan Barry of *The New York Times* would quote Hirsch as saying that he had come to a striking realization at that moment: "If reinforced concrete was rendered into dust, then it wasn't much of a mystery as to what would happen to people.")

"I was never so happy to see somebody in my entire life," says Robert Shaler, the department's chief forensic biologist. "He looked awful. He looked like he'd been in a brawl. But it was still great to see him because you could see in his eyes that he wasn't defeated."

Hirsch and his team proceeded with their painstaking identification protocol. A single DNA extract from each remain would be split into three so-called daughter samples, each of which contained 100 microliters of genetic material (about two eyedrops' worth). The microscopic fragments would then be shipped to different laboratories to see how they statistically measured up against corresponding samples. "Direct matches" would be made, explains Shaler, "by comparing the DNA profile from cellular material left by the victims—on personal possessions such as a hairbrush, pap smear, razor—with the DNA profile of the remains." Indirect identifications were done through "kinship analysis," in which investigators took "Q-Tip–like mouth swabs of biological relatives" of the deceased, then tried to "fit the genetic profile of the remains *into* the genetic structure of the [matching] family."

A camera was always on hand to document each specimen. According to an NYPD detective on morgue detail (who also happened to be a former medical photographer), each set of remains was placed on a piece of disposable gray-blue paper atop a stainless-steel table. The sheet was lined with graduated ruler-style markings, to provide scale, and a handwritten sequence of letters and numbers uniquely identifying the specimen and designating the agency that had recovered it along with the section of the Ground Zero grid from which the remains had been removed. The remains would then be rendered in color Polaroid. "Not film, not digital," says the forensic photographer. "You couldn't take a chance that the film wouldn't come out or that the digital file would be compromised."

Various methods were used to identify the lost. "There were torsos and there would be wallets in the pants," the photographer recalls. "There was one arm that was found that had a very unique tattoo along with [a] wedding ring and a watch with an inscription, but I heard that when they approached the [deceased's] wife"—who was still in denial, thinking her husband might still be alive—"she said, 'Do you think he could still be around?' " During breaks, the photographer, ever the detective, would walk over to hospitals and study the walls covered in missing posters—to uncover clues buried in the descriptions, trying to get a jump on the mounds of evidence in the medical examiner's vast database. "I scoured those pictures, hoping to find something I'd just seen in the morgue. People would write down [things like]: tattoo of a bird on her thigh. I'd go back and look for those little details."

DNA matching, though, predominated. In one dramatic instance, fire captain Brian Hickey was identified, literally, "by the sweat of his brow," according to a New York *Daily News* account, later confirmed by Shaler. In the winter of 2002, never having received any of Hickey's remains, his widow, Donna, was heartened to hear that rescuers had found his white helmet, its numeral 4 denoting his role as commander of the Bronx's Rescue Company 4. Adorned with shamrock decals, the hat was "crushed" and "caked with soot and dirt," writer Michele McPhee would observe. "His perspiration and a few strands of his thinning brown hair found inside the helmet finally provided enough DNA [to determine] that he was wearing it when he died . . . Fire Department officials believe [Hickey] had been in the stairwell of the [south tower] on a high floor and died [with others from Rescue 3, where] he was filling in for a . . . captain who was off that day.

" 'You keep praying, "Anything, anything—give me anything," ' Donna Hickey said. 'God gave me this . . . The helmet is the fireman. It's been through every fire. When you bury the helmet, you bury the man.' "

To identify Hickey, investigators had to settle on a statistical match. But it was actual photographs that would complete the circle. Shaler says that as their cases moved to closure, he and his colleagues would often log on to the office computer system to access photos of the deceased. "We have pictures of the vast majority of people who died," he says. "And whenever we'd make an identification, we would be able to see the person. We would know what they looked like and [this] would give some sort of feeling about the family." Shaler would study the deceased's photo and then read a short biography "to see what they were, where they came from, what they did in life.

"You know it's a tragic event. You know that people are upset, emotionally spent. We were the same way. But [looking at a picture is] humanizing, is one way to put it, takes it from being purely scientific and makes it *real*, makes it real life."

On 9/12, MaryEllen Salamone was going to Manhattan hospitals, door to door. She firmly believed that her husband, John, thirty-seven, a preferred-stock broker at Cantor Fitzgerald, was merely lost in the catastrophe's mayhem—or alive, but trapped in some safe pocket, possibly in the Trade Center concourse. On Thursday she visited a Cantor Fitzgerald command post, then the crisis center that had been set up at the armory. "You had to stand in line forever," says Salamone, an attorney and physical therapist. "They showed you lists of body parts that might be identifiable and descriptions of some John Does in the [area] hospitals. Two weeks later, there was still hope of recovery of survivors [based on] how long they could breathe and how much water [they might need]. The TV broadcasts kept saying the rescuers were working day and night in hopes of finding survivors. So you held out hope—some families . . . till the bitter, bitter end. Your body was in complete denial. For the first month, while I was walking around rationally feeling my husband was dead, emotionally I hadn't processed that."

Salamone, president of the advocacy group Families of September 11, is a fan of pictures. She won a photo contest a few years back. She displays her own artful landscapes and family portraits around her home in Caldwell, New Jersey. A year after "the event," as she calls it, she encouraged her three children (ages six, four, and two when her husband was killed) to go on a nature walk with disposable cameras, armed with an ad hoc assignment: to take pictures of what made them happy and gave them hope. "They came up with pictures of birds, the sky, clouds," she says, but her deeper goal was to tap into the healing effects of photography. "Pictures can be worth a *million* words sometimes, conveying messages that words can't possibly."

Four years after her family's tragedy, her organization began to solicit snapshots for an online "Resiliency Album" that would depict surviving parents and children enjoying positive occasions and rites of passage. "We use the power of photography to foster hope," she says, "showing the process of getting back on your feet: families celebrating birthdays, getting married, graduating from college. Children going to their proms with smiles on their faces, not sobbing. I have a stop-action photo of my middle son, with the old devil look in his eyes, just a millisecond before he pours a bucket of water over my unsuspecting other son's head. That's a huge picture of resiliency."

Salamone also knows the downside of imagery, from the perspective of those in the throes of recovering from loss. She insists—and studies concur—that "graphic news pictures can exacerbate or continue symptoms of post-traumatic stress disorder" (PTSD) when viewed by survivors or relatives of people who have perished in catastrophic circumstances. "Part of the problem with 9/11 families, particularly in children," she says, is that "they are not permitted by today's media and society to go through this 'grief journey' in a normal fashion—analogous to somebody who had lost a family member, even violently, in a car accident or a fire—because they are continually thrust back into 9/11. I don't have a *choice* when the burning buildings are on the cover of *The New York Times* when I stop at ShopRite to go grocery shopping, and that's at the cash register. That's shoved down my throat. That's irresponsible. I shouldn't be required to be subjected to it, like the character in *A Clockwork Orange*, where they held his eyes open and forced him to watch scenes of violence. If it's a picture that you're not already sensitized to, [one] that evokes raw, raw, raw emotion and is particularly horrifying, then [the image] elicits the PTSD . . . all over again.

"What's lost in showing the towers in flames or coming down is that this is the *moment* of death," she says. "They *died* then. My husband's partner was on his cell phone with his wife right up until ten minutes before the buildings came down. A bunch of the jumpers were Cantor people."

Salamone says that one time her family was driving down to the Jersey shore and passed a tour bus emblazoned with "a painting of the Twin Towers, with the fire and the smoke and everything coming all out of it. What am I going to do? Drive off the road? It was right in front of us. It had a slogan, [something like] 'Never forget.' " Another time, she recalls, her sons were watching television's MSG SportsDesk to check the baseball scores. Weaved within the program was "a snippet about an Olympian whose relative had died on 9/11. They showed graphic images of the burning buildings. Pictures of the towers on fire and the smoke—that's my kids' biggest fear point. I heard screams. I came downstairs and my kids were crying on the couch. 'They showed how Daddy died in the fire.' "

This story enrages Salamone's friend Nikki Stern, the former executive director of the Families organization. "I'm wondering why [a sports program] needed the picture of the burning buildings," says Stern, who lost her husband, geologist James Potorti, who had been working at the time as a business analyst for the Marsh & McLennan insurance firm. "That was so tangential to the story. It was gratuitous. But people use these pictures all the time. They just grab them, throw 'em up, and maybe cop an extra visceral reaction in the middle of a boring report."

To limit these sorts of episodes, Salamone, Stern, and others in their circle have tried to promote self-censorship among media organizations. They ask that cautionary messages be placed at the beginning of movie trailers, TV shows, on Web sites, or on the covers of photo books (e.g., "WARNING: This program contains images related to 9/11 that may be upsetting to children and other individuals. Viewer discretion is advised"). Other possible measures include blurring identifiable faces to accommodate the feelings of the bereaved (just as phone numbers of contact people were blurred in many missing-poster photographs), desensationalizing the editorial or theatrical setting of the images (not running blaring headlines or playing opera music when showing a tower falling), and asking editors and news directors to conscientiously weigh the need for showing bodies or other illustrations of death in non-news stories related to 9/11.

"We understand the importance of getting an emotion conveyed with a picture," Salamone says. "However, it has to be the responsibility of these media outlets to consider the damaging effect of the images as well. You could be trying to make a political point, an emotional point, or simply trying to sell newspapers. But if what you are publishing is on a front page or in an unexpected or unrelated television broadcast—venues in which the person does not have a choice whether or not to view it—you should impose upon yourself a higher standard, and run a warning." This concern is especially acute around the time of the anniversary. "August is an incredibly hard month," she says. "It's unpredictable. You always feel like you're tiptoeing. Lurking around the corner [are] these pictures . . . that you're going to try and protect your children from."

Four years on, Nikki Stern, who has a master's degree in political science and has advised or served on several groups studying 9/11 issues, says she doesn't buy editors' arguments that they are still compelled to show particular images "for history's sake" or as a way of emphasizing the point of their story in a graphic manner. "[You don't have to] show death literally in order for people to feel it," she insists. "Piousness comes in when reporters and editors and media types say they can't convey the importance without these pictures. One would hope good journalists could do it in words. Those pictures assaulted us. They still do. You're never free of it. One of the biggest issues for almost anybody who loses someone tragically is: What were they going through? [On 9/11] it was really unknown. To put it bluntly, when you have little or no recovery [of remains], you're left wondering what the last moments were. Nobody knows. It's like losing someone in a traffic accident and you get to watch the car crash every day.

"The question is: What's the truth you're trying to show when you keep trotting out the same pictures? The tower right where the plane smashed in and flames are jumping out. It's easiest to grab that one." Stern remembers one columnist whose piece was illustrated by an image of a man plummeting from one of the towers. "His tie is going up," she says, "and he's falling straight down the building. [But] it wasn't a news story that day. [It was run] to make a point. What [they] really used it for, in my view, is shock value. A cheap shot. Easy way out. That face was pretty clear. I thought, My God, this is someone's husband. Or son."

Mike Rambousek sits in front of his Hewlett-Packard computer, pulling up a chair so that I can join him. He fiddles with a file on the desktop, and says he wants to show me the photograph, the one that is "not a bit pleasant." It shows people standing in the windows a few minutes before their building caves in.

Before he does, though, he stops to tell me about waking up on Wednesday, after the longest day of his life.

On September 12, Mike Rambousek arose, alone, in his Brooklyn apartment. Because of all the security roadblocks, his wife, Jindra, was unable to return to the city, choosing to remain at their summer mobile home in Damascus, Pennsylvania. Lining the walls of Rambousek's small four-room flat were his and Jindra's collections from their native Czechoslovakia: delicate marionettes, antique clocks, and coffee cups, some dating back 150 years. And there, near the far window, were row after row of vinyl records that their son Luke would spin during his off hours as a deejay at a Brooklyn dance club. In the daytime, Luke, twenty-seven, was a computer maintenance temp at eSpeed, a Cantor Fitzgerald subsidiary, working on the 103rd floor of One World Trade Center. The Rambouseks' apartment was quiet that morning, and Luke's bed was empty.

The day before, says Rambousek, "I saw the picture [on the TV] at nine o'clock. People thought, Cessna. I called Luke's office and the phones were ringing. And I thought, He's okay. I'll go pick him up and bring him lunch." Mike believed, naïvely, that the office would dismiss Luke after a plane accident, so Mike packed the usual—pepper steak and diced watermelon—and planned on sharing a meal near the towers, to be followed by a "walkabout," as Mike called it, a ritual stroll around the nearby streets that father and son had enjoyed for years.

Mike and Luke were especially close. Both were enamored of electronics; Mike, now fifty-eight and retired, had been a computer system engineer. Both worked in the World Trade Center—Mike during the 1990s, Luke starting in early 2001. Both revered Mike's father, Ota, a virulent anti-Communist, now in his eighties and living in Prague. Ota, who took part in the Prague uprising against the Nazis in 1945, had been jailed after the war on charges of spying for U.S. Army intelligence. The elder Rambousek would later take part in the reform movement during the Prague Spring of 1968. After the Soviet crackdown that year, he escaped to Italy, then to the United States. (He would later be decorated by President Ronald Reagan "for his outstanding patriotism and desire for world peace.") Having faced down both the Nazis and the Communists, Ota encouraged his son and grandsons, Luke and Martin, to take challenges head-on, and to stand up for their principles.

Only one other period in Mike and Jindra's lives would seem as long or as haunting as that week in September 2001: that stretch in the late 1970s and early '80s when they were stripped of their Czech citizenship, forced onto a plane, and eventually allowed to emigrate to America. "I had a quite decent job as a chemist but they tried to put me into the slammer," he recalls. Neighbors and strangers turned out to be informants, he says; potential promotions were quashed. "Because we were relatives of American spy," he says, "we were on the top of party shit list." His existence in those days had seemed like a passage torn from Kafka or Solzhenitsyn.

On Tuesday, September 11, Rambousek reentered that world of the surreal. On his way into downtown Manhattan, Rambousek became trapped in his subway car. He was disoriented when he looked out the windows to see a station platform (Fulton Street, it turned out) "completely empty," he says. "It was suddenly pitch black. People tried to stay cool, but it was getting hot in the train, smoke was getting in too. People began banging on the driver's door." The darkness, he later calculated, coincided with the collapse of the south tower. Over the next half hour, the passengers in his car managed to exit and make their way toward a turnstile. As they reached the stairway, Rambousek heard a woman yell, "Oh, my God, we're going to die here." The north tower, it turned out, had just collapsed.

"It was like somebody [took] a bucket of ashes and just pour it on me," he says. "If you remember these figures from Pompeii—I thought, that's how we're going to end up." In the black squall of ash, an overwhelming sensation overtook him, he says, his eyes welling up at the memory of it. While crawling up the stairs on his hands and knees, he recalls, "I suddenly got a feeling that Luke's gone. I suddenly knew. There must be particles of him in that stuff we are breathing there."

Rambousek reached into his lunch sack and squeezed the watermelon into his shirt in order to breathe through the wet cloth. He struggled up the stairs, then emerged near a church, hoping to set out again to find Luke, though sensing the search would be futile.

He did not find Luke. Nor did he find out what really happened to Luke until several months later, when he came across an image on the Internet.

In silence, he clicks his mouse and calls up the picture on his computer. It shows some three dozen World Trade Center tenants, having smashed through the glass, standing clustered on windowsills at the highest levels of the north side of the north tower *(Image 21)*. Most are standing and seem to be straining for air. Some have collapsed, possibly dragged to the windows. Others appear to be propped up by their colleagues. A thin ribbon of smoke, blown sideways by the wind, rings the building like a lasso. The long, vertical wall panels that separate the dark window banks give the impression that these hazy figures are clamoring at the bars of a prison. The vague shapes, and the obvious exhaustion and desperation in the faces, suggest a scene out of Dante.

The photo was a revelation—even to the photographer. "I didn't know I had that picture until I blew it up on my computer," says Jeff Christensen, a freelancer for Reuters, who took the shot with a 300-mm lens from six blocks away. "It's only about one-tenth of the original [frame]. In the whole image you can see where the plane went into the building." Christensen estimates that it was taken at a horrendous juncture: fifteen minutes after the south tower had collapsed and fifteen minutes before Luke's building would do the same.

Though Rambousek has no idea how his son met his end that day, he has this remnant of this moment. The picture is extremely grainy, Rambousek having pumped that grain to the limit, using Adobe Photoshop software. He holds up a digital print and points to a blur in one of the precarious, top-floor perches. It shows a man with Luke's dark brown hair, his stocky frame, his bare upper torso. His son, he posits, might have removed his shirt in the extreme heat, or used it to help a colleague handle the smoke. He believes the photo reveals Luke, his arms cradling a woman who is passed out or near death.

Luke, his father says, would not have been the type to jump. Luke was too altruistic a spirit; he had a job to do. "He was holding somebody, so he wouldn't [have] quit," says Mike. Jindra agrees. "He had a gold heart," she says. "He was always like that. He was helping everybody; giving twenty dollars when he got paid to [an old woman] down the street."

She insists the figure is her son's. "He used to lift weights," she says. "He got very big shoulders. Sometimes if I forgot [my house or car] keys, he threw them out on the street without [wearing] a top. So he leaned out the window and he'd throw keys—in [that] same position."

The Rambouseks sound neither irrational nor dogmatic. They just believe what their eyes and hearts tell them. They claim to have tracked down other images and, counting story by story, the figure in Christensen's blowup seems to be located on the 103rd floor, where Luke had reported for work on September 11, an hour earlier than usual.

Such digital detective work was not uncommon. In the absence of any hard information about their loved ones, families tried to contact news photographers, hoping that they might find glimpses of their relatives if they could just get their hands on higher-resolution versions of published pictures, or if they could gain access to frames that were never published. In the spring of 2005, I spoke with Jean Coleman, a real-estate agent from Westport, Connecticut. She had lost two sons, Keith and Scott, both of whom worked on the floor above Luke's. Keith, thirty-four, the father of two young children, had moved back from London to start up Cantor's equities-options operations. Keith ("big man, six-foot-one, big voice, and big heart," his mother says) had enlisted his younger brother, Scott, thirty-one ("the baby, adorable, he had a passion for every sport"), to help set up the department's bookkeeping systems and to eventually make the move to the trading desk. "They loved working together," she recalls. "In a business like that they felt they had an advantage [as brothers]: they had somebody [watching] their back."

Jean Coleman believes she can make out both of them in Christensen's image, which she first came across in 2002. She asks me if I know of a way to reach Christensen, having waited three years to try to contact him. What's her motivation, I ask, for hunting down the answers in these pictures when the process would inevitably cause such pain? She responds, rhetorically, her voice quavering: "Who knew what [we] were looking for? I guess for me it was important to have a sense that they didn't go into oblivion, that the essence of the person you knew was somewhat intact. So many people died and disappeared. That's truly awful. From my point of view, I *wanted* them not to have been nameless and faceless.

"I do a lot of soul-searching," she admits. "Do you think this picture was Scott or do you *want* it to be Scott? [That figure looks like] Keith, sitting back, inside the building, receded into one of the windows. His posture and what you intuit from the picture, spoke to me as Keith. Many pictures speak to people . . . Who knows? They have not found remains of Keith. A portion of one of Scott's ribs was identified."

Mike Rambousek, staring at the same picture, says he has never received even a trace of his son's remains. "*This* is the closest place to him." Despite its gruesome reality, the photo, he says, affords him neither comfort nor closure, but a kind of stark certainty. "Before this picture, he was 'Hi, Bye' in the morning, and just vanished. At least we [now] have some idea. For almost an hour and a half they were surviving and hanging out the windows, waiting, waiting."

Photography, in other ways, has helped Mike Rambousek begin to accept Luke's loss. Soon after 9/11, Rambousek lost his job. He says he struggled to hold on to his rent-stabilized apartment, went on disability, sought treatment for anxiety—due, in part, to his own trauma of having been trapped underground. In the course of his counseling he started to carry around an Olympus D-490, he says, "to keep my mind off things and to keep me busy and to keep my mind *on* things." He created photo files on his computer, photo albums to share with his counselor. "Nine-eleven," he says, "pushed me to *create* something—something people like to look at." But always he came back to memories and photos of Luke, and of the tragedy itself. He would listen to Luke's music and, trawling the Internet, would collect pictures of devastation and regeneration.

Four minutes before Flight 11 hit his building, Luke, a fan of throbbing techno and trance music, had sent an e-mail to a friend about the upcoming Junkfest, an all-night music-and-junk-food party at his parents' place in Pennsylvania, for which he had served as deejay for years. Luke practically lived for the Junkfest; he would often practice two hours a day for it in his home studio, using two turntables and a mixing board.

Rambousek slips in a DVD and double-clicks on a desktop icon. Up springs a music video, edited by Mike himself, and set to a soundtrack from one of his son's favorite trance songs. Pictures skitter along—the twin towers in fleecy cloud, twinkling at night, burnt orange at sunset—playing off the melancholy strains of a techno version of the old standard "Autumn Leaves."

News photos begin to barrel across the monitor. The plane attacks, smoke spills out, bodies plummet. Each frame, plucked from the Web, is pin-sharp, hi-res, technicolor. Tugged taut against an electronic backbeat, one picture pulses up for one to three seconds, then twirls into the next and the next, like a horror-theme thrill ride. The refrain weaves in mournfully, in counterpoint: "But I miss you most of all . . . my darling / When autumn leaves . . . start to fall." And then, interlaced, come subliminal faces in split-second flashes: Osama bin Laden . . . Mohammed Atta . . . Lukas Rambousek. Osama, Mohammed, Luke. Luke's track blaring: "But I miss you most of all . . ." Six minutes and eleven seconds of black clouds and orange flames, terrorist headshots and figures crouched in windows. Then the twin towers in fleecy cloud. Then silence.

Rambousek spent three months making the video. "Days, nights, months," his wife says, with a note of pity in her voice. But what has driven him to burn such visions of violence onto DVD? "I didn't want a shrine," he explains. "I've seen a lot of memorials. Everybody's making shrines, candlelights, and playing 'touchy' music. So I said, 'Let's make it to Luke's music. The music [he played] in all-night 'rave' parties."

At first, one wonders if he hasn't dropped down a hole, obsessively reenvisioning the particulars of Luke's death. Perhaps he is "stuck" in the trauma of the subway car. Instead, the more we talk, the more I see these news photos as his sackcloth and ashes, harsh scenes he must revisit in order to accept them and move on. Luke's music is Mike's blues. "It's my personal view of it," he says of the video. "We better remember it was dirty. It was smelly. Probably a reason for this view is my experience in the subway. Bin Laden is [the] guy we're chasing around, unsuccessfully. The video should remind people he was there in the first place. I get a feeling that officials in government are not crazy about showing these pictures. I think they want people to have idealized memories of it. Everything's clean, [everything's] flags. But people should see how it *really* was."

The blues, said Ralph Ellison, "is an impulse to keep the painful details and episodes of a brutal experience alive in one's aching consciousness, to finger its jagged grain, and to transcend it." Luke's techno blues, and these high-tech pictures, have helped his father conquer his own demons by consuming them. Once he takes it all, digitizes it, paces it, makes it his own, he emerges, empowered, at the other end. This is how Mike's father, Ota, in his prison cell, might have stared this devastation down.

Mike inserts a second disc. This one—a PowerPoint presentation of seventy shots—recounts Luke's life in pictures. Baby photos, first haircut, first trip to the Trade Center. This time the music is transporting, enveloping. Appropriately, Mike has chosen Dvořák's *New World* Symphony. And Luke is beaming in the photographs: Luke at his graduation. Luke on vacation, Luke spinning discs at the Junkfest. With a crescendo comes Luke's death certificate, Luke's ID picture, a hazy figure trapped in a window, cradling a woman's limp frame. We watch and we listen, together, in tears.

On Wednesday, Michael Shulan, a journalist and writer, germinated the idea for a 9/11 photo show and fund-raising effort—right in the window of his writer's studio at 116 Prince Street in SoHo, a few blocks north of where the two towers had stood.

The day before, he had been sitting in the vacant space, a former clothing boutique, when he heard the howl of a jet overhead. He hurried outside and watched the nightmare play out just fifteen blocks south of him. He went downtown to volunteer, then was dispersed when Building 7 was on the verge of collapse. The next day he happened to see a fragment of verse that someone had stuck on the wall of the building next door. The lines, by the ancient Greek dramatist Aeschylus, had been copied out in Magic Marker across a page torn from the September 10 *New York Times* classifieds. The passage, based on Edith Hamilton's translation of the tragic play *Agamemnon*, read: "[Even] in our sleep, pain which cannot forget, falls drop by drop upon the heart until, in our own despair, against our will, comes wisdom through the awful grace of God."

The lines embodied the essence of tragedy: through our despair we find our transcendent salvation. It was a message astutely resurrected during turmoil: the Lord would see to it that, given time, our sorrow would enlighten us. It was the same passage, in fact, that Senator Robert F. Kennedy would cite in April 1968 after civil rights leader Martin Luther King, Jr., was assassinated. (Two months later, Kennedy himself would be gunned down, his assailant intent on bringing global attention to the ongoing conflict in the Middle East, as would be the 9/11 hijackers thirty-three years later.)

Shulan was inspired by the text, and by the directness and anonymity of the medium—one stranger, through graffiti from the ancient Greeks, had touched another. In response, he ferreted through some old files in search of a shard of his own that might serve (to use Robert Frost's characterization of a poem) as "a momentary stay against confusion." Shulan found an old picture of the twin towers that he'd once bought at a flea market. He placed it in the front window of the vacant storefront.

That single photograph, in a street-level window, began to draw a crowd. People congregated, stared, then moved on. Spurred on by the encouragement of a friend, the photographer Gilles Peress, Shulan added more pictures. Other friends then brought him their own images of the towers and the day. Within two weeks the impromptu display was a living, evolving photo exhibition, shot by neighbors and out-of-towners, amateurs and professionals, shaped by Shulan and Peress, along with Alice Rose George and Charles Traub.

They developed a curatorial vision and a set of overriding principles: the pictures that they hung in Shulan's studio would capture New York and its inhabitants as shaped by the events of September 11; no one who submitted an image would be turned away; at least one photograph from every participant would become part of the show. Each image would be scanned into a computer database and offered up for sale (for $25 a photograph, churned out on ink-jet printers) to raise money for the Children's Aid Society, benefiting youngsters-in-need who were among the most severely impacted by the tragedy.

They called their exhibition "here is new york," in deferential lowercase type. The title was taken from an essay by E. B. White about the city's vulnerability after World War II. White, in an oft-quoted passage, had presciently written in 1949: "The city, for the first time in its long history, is destructible. A single flight of planes no bigger than a wedge of geese can quickly end this island fantasy, burn the towers, crumble the bridges, cremate the millions. The intimation of mortality is part of New York now: in the sound of jets overhead, in the black headlines of the latest edition."

The submissions to "here is new york" were placed on the walls, floor to ceiling, and strung on clothesline-style wire, like pennants. The pictures, row after row of them, hung above the room as haunting bunting. Images of flags, shrines, candlelight vigils. Images of messages scrawled on signs and walls and car windows: RIP MANNY; I Miss U Dennis; Welcome To Hell; THE DANGER IS INSIDE OF US; Revenge; NUKE THEM ALL; We Are Not Afraid; You Will Pay Bin Laden; We are all related; NO MORE WAR.

A woman, photographed in her bedroom mirror, watches the immolation on her TV set while she stands, barrette in her mouth, absently gathering her hair into a bun. A couple embraces on their roof, their city blotted out by white cloud. Khaki-colored snow settles on items in shop windows, on lone shoes discarded in the frenzy, on random business memos in the street, curled like autumn leaves, fronds of individual lives—of executives, middle managers, secretaries, neighbors—now only hinted at, through the litter rudely scattered in their wake.

Continually, New Yorkers would walk into the SoHo gallery with their own pictures to contribute. On one occasion a man brought in an image of the burning towers, which he had taken while standing near Worth Street. By coincidence, the stranger standing behind him was bringing in a photo that *he* had taken—of the man in front of him in line, *photographing* the burning towers near Worth Street. Their pictures, and their encounter in the gallery, encapsulated the entire project, and the numbing abundance of imagery generated by that week's events.

Visitors crowded the SoHo space day after day. The mood was cramped but welcoming, urgent but sensitive, frenetic (with so many people, young and old, locals and tourists, waiting in separate lines to buy pictures from twenty-odd volunteers standing in front of donated computer terminals) but anchored by a deeper sense of refuge. People seemed to find solace in the communal act of viewing. The gallery was a crackling village bonfire, of sorts, a setting where visitors were warmed, and sometimes singed, as they shared their grief and confusion. The show promoted common bonds and allowed release—*that's what I saw too . . . others feel as I do*—not in the corner of one's room but in the company of like-souled strangers.

Viewers wanted to connect with others who had been similarly battered by the event—people who had been moved to share their impression of it or their reaction to it through the simple gesture of visual expression. They came to dissipate their confusion, and to transcend it, in a manner, through art. "Part of it was participatory, part of it was to bear witness, part of it was to pause and reflect, which the [fast-paced] media often doesn't allow us to do," says curator and art historian Carol Solomon Kiefer. (In 2004 at Amherst College's Mead Art Museum, Kiefer would set up an exhibition, "The Pain of War"—which included several of the same pictures—surveying the use of imagery to document conflict over the centuries.) "Part of it was also this guilt. We're guilty as we look at the photographs because we recognize ourselves, as members of humanity, and see ourselves in this. That's what humanity has as a part of its nature: this awfulness. And, as with the Holocaust, we put up the pictures and look at them to show the world that this won't happen again. But it does, no matter the [era], from the seventeenth century to Rwanda to Darfur."

The SoHo space was suffused with a spirit that seemed to flow in three waves: a searing but cohesive grief, a charmed energy of community, and a sense of pride that people had succeeded here in Shulan's storefront. In this thicket of pictures, less than a mile away from where the smoke clouds had settled, there had emerged some digital-age version of a silver halide lining. In a short time, the corps of photo assistants pitching in had evolved from students and friends to volunteers from every economic and social stratum. As Shulan said, "They took it upon themselves to scan pictures, color-correct pictures, print pictures, label pictures, hang pictures, sell pictures, ship pictures, and database pictures, as well as to build our website, network our computers, arrange our exhibitions, program our slide shows, do our contracts and tax filings."

In short, the photo project gave off the glow of a shared humanity (the exhibition was subtitled "a democracy of photographs"), as if the converted shop had become a Vermont town meeting hall, where everyone had a voice and a vote. By providing or purchasing an ink-jet print, each participant could touch the life of the photographer, the subject in the photograph, the hundreds lost in the tragedy, and the individual who would receive the funds from the sale of that photograph. The way the images were displayed (without frames, usually without captions) reinforced a sense of a "collective vision," to use Shulan's term, a broader context not dictated by curators or shaped by academics or tainted by media conglomerates.

"Photography," Shulan would write, "was the perfect medium to express what happened on 9/11, since it is democratic by its very nature and infinitely reproducible. The tragedy at Ground Zero struck all New Yorkers equally, leaving none of us immune to shock or grief . . . In order to come to grips with all of the imagery that was haunting us, it was essential, we thought, to reclaim it from the media and stare at it without flinching." In the process, the curators collected more than 7,500 images—"one of the largest photographic archives," says Shulan, "devoted to a single event."

The following spring, the International Center of Photography would give a special prize to the SoHo exhibit. At the annual Infinity Awards ceremony, the historian and writer David Halberstam would declare that "September 11 was, in the most elemental way, a moment of the citizen as photographer." Halberstam expressed gratitude to the many photographers in attendance that evening, characterizing their calling as "astonishingly egalitarian." And he addressed them as one: "You make what happened graven on our collective conscience so that we dare not forget too quickly or too readily. [You] bond us with shared emotions."

The camera and the Trade Center had always had an affinity. Ever since employees first started working in the complex in 1970, the pair of buildings had been among America's most photographed landmarks. They had also *generated* hundreds of images each day, as picture takers gravitated to the south tower's 107th-floor observation deck, 1,300 feet above the city, for Manhattan's most stunning perspective. From that vantage point, a visitor could take in the surrounding flatland from a grand oasis: the harbor, Ellis Island and the Statue of Liberty, Staten Island, Brooklyn, New Jersey, the sweep of Manhattan Island. The vista was soundless, as if the visitor were regarding not a cityscape but a photograph. ("An extraordinary silent-screen overview," one guidebook put it.) And one would be taken aback by the hulking mass of the "twin" just to the northwest, itself a perch for optical dissemination: fourteen TV stations—nine conventional, five digital—beamed programs from its rooftop transmitters.

At the early Windows on the World restaurant (it was later a premier party space and nightclub as well), diners with their cameras at the ready would enjoy an incomparable uptown view. Inside and out, dozens of surveillance cameras were mounted, many placed there in response to the 1993 bombing. The complex even served as a picture warehouse: in a basement bank vault at Five World Trade Center, an estimated 40,000 negatives of one of John F. Kennedy's official photographers, Jacques Lowe, were lost on 9/11. The entire collection is believed to have disintegrated. Lost as well were 30,000 one-of-a-kind images from the Broadway Theatre Archive, mainly of stage performances, and the bulk of the archive of the Port Authority of New York and New Jersey, with its exhaustive photo documentation of the construction of the World Trade Center itself.

Few exploited the picture potential of the World Trade Center to grander effect than Sarah Merians, who may have taken more consistently upbeat photos in the towers than anyone alive. Her firm shot more than one hundred wedding receptions in the buildings, along with countless parties and business functions. "We were the house photographers up at Windows on the World for many corporate and social events," she says. "We had a lot of friends up there."

Photographically, says Merians, the chief appeal of the place was "the most incredible view in the world, [one] that you will never see again. [You had] fiery sunsets, and brides and grooms with champagne glasses with the whole view of Manhattan behind them through the windows." Usually a tripod was required to get the depth of field that would keep both the couple and the midtown buildings in focus—and the interior and exterior light in relative balance. The towers' ever-presence added to their allure. "I photographed weddings every weekend," she says, "and we saw [them] from every view at every place I worked in Manhattan."

Merians claims she would routinely lie on her back in the middle of the street outside the World Financial Center in order to snatch bride and groom, mid-kiss, standing above her, twin titans looming behind them. She created many photos depicting "the fragility of a bride and groom joining and then these two towers joining. They were very male-female. Two tall, long figures, very phallic, one of them had that big, tall, vertical male [spire] sticking out of it. It was very romantic, very intense.

"We had sample albums up there," she says, for people to peruse when planning to book a party. "In the explosion, things were found" dispersed across the city. One photograph, with Merians's name and phone number on the reverse, was discovered in Brooklyn and mailed back to her. It showed a wedding—of a friend of hers, it so happened—the bride and groom standing under the traditional chuppah at a Jewish ceremony. "I almost felt that God had brought [the] picture back to me," she says. "The picture had no fire damage. [It was] not ripped. [But] this place was no more."

Some thirty years ago, during their construction, the twin towers seemed the urban-age equivalent of the pyramids. At 110 stories each, providing some ten million square feet of office space, they were, when officially dedicated in 1973, the tallest man-made entities on earth. They housed 50,000 workers from dozens of countries and, every weekday, served as the thoroughfare for 200,000 more. They weighed 1.5 million tons, were ringed with 43,600 windows, possessed their own twin zip codes. From their loftiest floors, world trade was commanded majestically, as if from on high, and global transactions were conducted like the electronic complements to the passage of ships in the harbors below. The buildings' upper stories were the bastion of "traders," their very name evoking earlier ages when their forebears trafficked in silk and spices, tea and armaments.

The Trade Center's distinguishing feature, of course, was its scale. The towers were architecturally audacious. They were meant to stand for epochs, God willing, like ancient citadels. There were not one, but *two* of them, positioned like sentries. Their vertical defiance implied impregnability, even virility. "They pierced the skyline in arrogant confidence," observed President Vaira Vike-Freiberga, of Latvia, "monuments to American know-how, engineering skill, prosperity and imagination. Like the Tower of Babylon, they defied the gods by reaching up into their domain."

They were also totems of the West's economic supremacy. Both Khalid Sheikh Mohammed (KSM), who hatched the plot to fly hijacked planes into the towers, and his nephew Ramzi Yousef, who helped plan the 1993 Trade Center bombing, saw the towers as the seat of American financial prowess. After his 2003 capture, KSM explained his thinking to interrogators. "KSM reasoned he could best influence U.S. policy by targeting the country's economy," according to *The 9/11 Commission Report*. "[KSM] maintains that he and Yousef began thinking about using aircraft as weapons [and] speculated about striking the World Trade Center . . . as early as 1995"—a full six years before the attacks.

New York is also "the cradle of electronic communications," points out producer and journalism professor George Kindel. "It's the Mother of all media centers. It's reasonable to assume that bin Laden saw the World Trade Center as the most visible symbol in the world's most visible city. The bin Laden family was heavily invested in media, so he realized that, for media exposure, New York was the Super Bowl, 24/7, and the world's news organizations kept offices there. While that may not have been the priority for choosing where to strike, it's difficult to believe that wasn't a consideration. If you did something at *that* site, the whole world would see it and tremble."

In the first hours of 9/11, as the globe's attention converged on the towers, they became less like citadels and more like belfries or minarets: structures beckoning eyes and ears to heed them. They gathered in the world's compassion and sympathy. And they quickly became the focus of a planet's revenge fantasies. Well-heeled diners in Beirut's fashionable Hamra district were reportedly seen "celebrating, laughing, cheering and making jokes" after learning of the attacks. Palestinians in East Jerusalem and elsewhere, according to accounts later verified by Reuters and CNN (despite press and Web reports to the contrary), took to the streets in spontaneous displays of merriment, firing off guns and passing out candies. News pictures and video of the scene were beamed worldwide.

The *New York Times* columnist Nicholas Kristof wrote of six thousand postings by Chinese Web surfers who had flocked to the SINA.com chat room on September 11 to giddily applaud the attacks moments after they occurred. The back-and-forth went like this:

"Just one word: cool!"

"Why not the White House?"

"Excellent!!!!!!!! But the hijacked planes didn't carry a nuclear bomb."

"Serves 'em right."

"I'm waiting for the third plane, the fourth . . ."

Kristof commented: "Not until the 44th message is there a reproach. 'Do you people here have no shame? Do you have no morality?' "

Blogs and chat rooms, then, overflowing with commiseration in so many nations, and with venom in China and elsewhere, became the sluice for the runoff of pity—and pent-up rage. But it was the TV screen that served as the planet's mirror. Television was the beveled looking glass into which the entire world gazed, reflecting or refracting viewers' empathy or enmity.

What, then, was the significance of this communal viewing?

We felt closer to one another because, even though we might have had no *direct* experience of the horror, being separated from it by zip codes or oceans, what we did share was the inclusive experience of viewing the event as it was occurring. We felt closer because we ached upon seeing the images, and we believed that we all ached in the same way. We felt closer because we felt a subliminal proximity, an interdependence with the strangers in the towers whom we could only dimly see—innocents like us, who had undertaken the most common of all social acts: they had gone to work that day.

We watched and the world shrank, in that instant, to a pinpoint. This was the photo as photon, the quantum of quantum mechanics. This was the image as a funnel through which time was siphoned, through which space flattened. This was the dark underside of William Blake's call to see the "world in a grain of sand" and hold "eternity in an hour." The epic scene on the small screen signaled the world's diminishment. The picture conveyed an Earth as delicate as the blue ball we'd seen in photographs from space, even if its fragility no longer possessed a tenderness. This new cloud cover was unnatural, enveloping, and coming our way.

The social fabric was now knit, imperceptibly, with microwaves and fiber-optic cables. In watching, we felt no neighborly embrace. Even the usually reassuring network anchors seemed vulnerable, anguished, brought to our level. In our watching, we felt a chill, not a warmth. In our watching, we shared what many nations' citizens had long shared: a common trepidation and mutual distrust. Our watching turned into an ordeal, a process of hours. The scenes were reprised so often that we could see the towers falling even if we closed our eyes. And yet, after the spleen emptied and the heart filled, we felt vague stirrings of comfort in the collective chill. The world must be seeing and therefore feeling as we felt: sorrowful, fearful, as one. "I froze right to the bone," Bob Dylan had written in his song "Talkin' New York," forty years before. "*New York Times* said it was the coldest winter in seventeen years / I didn't feel so cold then."

Three years after Dylan's weather report, Marshall McLuhan, the quixotic prophet of media culture, forecast the dawn of a "global village." He insisted that television, along with other electronic media, might someday help turn humankind into a single, wired community. By universally linking disparate social groups and by expanding the speed and scope of an individual's abilities to perceive the world beyond his ken, electronics would bring about a profound cohesion within and throughout the race. With this sense of unity would come an acknowledgment of one's obligations to society. McLuhan wrote of this new, wired world: "Electric speed in bringing all social and political functions together in a sudden implosion has heightened human awareness of responsibility to an intense degree. [Minority groups] can no longer be *contained* in the political sense of limited association. They are now *involved* in our lives, as we in theirs, thanks to the electric media."

Given other circumstances, television and the Internet circa 2001 might have been perfect testing grounds for McLuhan's prophesies. Instead, they served to illustrate the limits of media in a divided world. The global village was not yet to be. "We were viewing together," notes photo-agency chief Robert Pledge, "but not in the sense of solidarity and support that McLuhan meant. On the one hand there's this massive amount of information, but on the other hand, it's leading to an unbelievable splintering of our understanding. There are other realities—cultural and ideological differences—that McLuhan couldn't foresee forty years ago. At least at this stage we are in a more divided world—maybe *because* there's more technological access to everything that happens—scientific, economic, political—leading to more opinions, more frustrations. That day there were some amazing disconnects. Due to lack of knowledge of the circumstances, there were reactions of glee in some areas. There were different interpretations by different religious communities, huge pockets of ignorance from many quarters [in which the faithful believed] that God was punishing Western society for all its sins.

"The cultural divides and differences," Pledge cautions, "don't allow necessary debate and simultaneous reflection because of the speed with which everything develops. Television doesn't have time to digest. Being the beast that it is, it gobbles all the information up and vomits it out. And we do too. On 9/11—to turn McLuhan's theory on its head—television connected us in our disconnectedness."

Luc Sante believes we may have been unified in being stupefied. "For the Global Viewing Eye that consumes images on TV," he avers, "this was the biggest super-spectacular that anybody's ever seen . . . There was a feverishness to it. Somebody said it wasn't reminiscent of war; it was reminiscent of science fiction. It was like watching the Martian invasion: beyond all imagining. The fact that it was this huge urban landmark being destroyed, it was like Godzilla stomping on buildings. It also means the visual consumer is that much more jaded and therefore numb and cynical and to a certain extent unshockable in the future."

There were deeper and more disturbing repercussions, geopolitically and, to many, spiritually. "The implications from a television standpoint," says Roger Ailes, chairman of FOX News and FOX Television Stations, "are simply that: When the end of the world comes, we'll be able to cover it live until the last camera goes out. I believe I mean it literally.

If you can witness something like [9/11] by two billion people, live, then there's nothing that can't be covered. And if we get into a world war, with nuclear weapons, I assume we'll be covering it live."

Ailes, recognizing TV's corporeal-world role, as it were, at the right hand of omniscience, speaks with a preacher's assurance and without an iota of irony when pondering the ultimate news story—a real-time *Apocalypse Now*: "It's horrifying to think about. But maybe God set it up that way. You can either figure out how to live in freedom . . . and hope, or you can watch yourselves burn to death. Nine-eleven is a warning shot that says: Look, this can go either way. It's your choice, folks."

In terms of the global social compact, the fact that a large segment of the species was attuned to a single trauma underscored our common humanity. The fact that much of humanity was bearing witness forced upon us certain obligations en masse for assessing these actions and for demanding that they be rebuked (as virtually every world government recognized). The fact that we stopped to look, as one, in unprecedented numbers, made the experience of being human and alive on September 11, 2001, inseparable from the experience of being aware of one's place as a citizen of a wider world.

The world had been able to tune in to a single sight because of a relatively new breakthrough that occurred in the years leading up to 2001: the ability to capture, transmit, and broadcast visual information, whether in moving or still pictures, by digital means.

The implications of this transformation were among the most revolutionary in the history of photography. And the revolution transpired so quickly, and by now has come to seem so commonplace, that we often forget how it all works or came to be.

First, some background, beginning with the still picture.

In the mid- to late 1990s, photojournalists (and much of the consumer photography market) began to migrate to the digital format. Legions of professional shooters—from sports to combat to wedding photographers—started to wean themselves off of traditional film cameras. To obtain pictures with a roll-film apparatus, an image is exposed in a positive or negative format (onto strips, whose emulsion is altered by incoming light when the rolls are spooled past an open aperture), then developed in a darkroom, then either viewed with the aid of a light source (a projector or light box, typically) or reproduced on light-sensitive paper. This process requires time, the tactile handling of materials by trained technicians or artisans, and the consumption of chemicals and other resources.

Around the year 2000, however, digital cameras came into their own. They make pictures electronically rather than chemically. By interacting with light, their sensors cause pixels—groups of transistors—to pick up an electrical charge. Those charges are then processed through the computer brain of the camera and ultimately stored as digital photographic files on memory-storage cards. Digital cameras allow for immediate assessment of a shot (because a picture appears right on the camera back), easy correction of exposure and color, and easy storage in (and retrieval from) the camera's or the computer's memory. Digital photography can be cheaper, too, since there are no developing costs, and because every reproduction is a virtual clone of the original image.

Most critical of all—for photojournalists working on a tight deadline—is the facility and speed with which images can be sent to, and from, any location. Digital photographs are as unfettered as e-mail, downloaded from a camera's memory card (or from a camera-equipped cell phone or handheld device) to a computer's desktop, then transmittable over the Internet. Photographers can take, edit, and archive a photograph in less than a minute, then send it to a potential publishing source in seconds. For a breaking news story, such as 9/11, shot in a dicey or dangerous environment such as downtown Manhattan during a terrorist attack, visual velocity was critical—and largely unavailable in the decade before.

To get breaking stories into print in the 1970s, explains photojournalist Mark Greenberg, "you either went to a news bureau to use their souped-up machines or you developed film in your hotel bathroom sink, creating a darkroom by placing duct-tape over the perimeter of the door and black plastic over the windows to prevent light leaks. Then, to transmit one color news picture to the wires, you had to have 30 uninterrupted minutes on your phone line to transmit three black-and-white facsimiles of the same image, each with a different density in its gray tones representing cyan, magenta, and yellow."

By the 1980s, photographers began to work from suitcase-sized devices that scanned and stored the negatives. By the 1990s, the age of the satellite photo-from-the-field had arrived. Derek Hudson, shooting for *Life* and the Paris-based Sygma photo agency during the Gulf War in 1991, created a traveling photo lab (just as those shooting battlefield daguerreotypes had done in the 1800s). Hudson's portable lab doubled as a ground station from which he could process, print, scan, and transmit his images. Since Hudson was not assigned to a press "pool" slot (embedded with a military unit), he decided to create what he called an FTP operation (as in "Fuck the Pool"), directly transmitting film from the field—and circumventing the military censors.

With a colleague, Hudson bought a Land Rover in Riyadh and outfitted it with camouflage netting and fake antennae to make it look like a British military officer's vehicle. He brought along a seventy-seven-pound satellite phone (with a three-to-four-foot dish), a bulky Hasselblad scanner, and a generator to power the equipment. At the end of a day's shooting in the Kuwaiti desert, he would develop his C-41 color-negative film in the vehicle in a stainless-steel fish cooker in which he had placed several tanks (two developers, one stop bath, one fixer), using a makeshift refrigeration system, thanks to the generator, to keep the developer cool in the heat of the desert. "Then I had to wash [the film]," he says, "and dry the damn thing using the car heater. There was sand everywhere."

He would then struggle to place a satellite phone call to a Hasselblad facility on the outskirts of Paris. "The process took forty-five minutes for one frame," he recalls. "It seemed interminable." That was only the first leg. In this era before JPEGs, the image-transmission system used by Hasselblad, in France, was incompatible with *Life*'s, in New York. So finished pictures had to be printed, handed to a courier, and flown by Concorde across the Atlantic, adding almost a day to the process.

Nonetheless, the first image that Hudson sent—of a famished crowd of Kurdish POWs being tossed meal-ration packs by a U.S. Marine—arrived with such relative dispatch from the war zone (in color, no less) that it sold to *Paris Match*, *Life*, and elsewhere, recouping about $50,000, the cost of all the equipment.

The procedure seems quaint by twenty-first-century standards. "Today," says Greenberg, "modern bureaus are generally spelled S-T-A-R-B-U-C-K-S. The photographer *is* the bureau. All he needs is a camera, a computer, and either a cell phone, sat [satellite] phone, or access to a land line. A photographer, in essence, can be anywhere on earth—the top of Mt. Everest or down at Ice Station Zebra—and send his photos anywhere at any time."

On the morning of September 11, this speed and ease of transmission perfectly aligned the photojournalist's needs for swift image dissemination with the public's desire for instantaneous and accurate news and information. That day, Vin Alabiso, executive photo editor of the Associated Press, had scores of photographers out in the field. His AP staffers and freelancers downloaded their images to their laptops, captioned them, and used cell phones to transmit them to a central desk in midtown New York where editors chose the selects, cropped and toned each image, checked them for caption accuracy, and then sent those photos on again—a process that took roughly fifteen minutes—before the shots were "broadcast" or "pushed"—not "pulled" from the Internet, as is commonly done today—"by a transmission system called PhotoStream," Alabiso explains, providing almost simultaneous "satellite delivery of digital images [to] more than a thousand newspapers in the U.S. and thousands more overseas." When photographers couldn't obtain a mobile phone connection, they ran or biked to the AP's midtown offices, downloaded their caches, then turned around and headed back into the breach.

AP realized, however, that for a story like this one, a fifteen-minute lag time wouldn't do. So they went directly to their television sets and downloaded stills. "That immediacy on 9/11 clearly illustrated an important paradigm shift in photojournalism," Alabiso believes. "The very first images we transmitted that morning were not from traditional film or digital stills but, in fact, were 'frame-grabs' from video—in virtual 'live time' of the attack precisely as it happened."

Like most top-flight newsrooms, AP had a wall of televisions playing around the clock; they also had VHS tape recorders through which they could "lift" key shots and convert them into JPEGs. Instead of "standing there waiting for digital images to come through the system," says Alabiso, picture editors switched digital streams entirely, swiping freeze frames from a sister medium—television—to supply stop-action shots to newspapers, magazines, and Web sites. In this caffeinated, must-see-*now* news world, TV and the Internet could provide real-time access to events, an attribute not yet available to the still camera, which wouldn't become incorporated into the Net-linked cell phone for three years. (" 'Frame-grabbing,' " says Alabiso, had been perfected "during the Clinton impeachment hearings of 1999, when still photographers were not given access to the proceedings. But TV cameras did record the hearings and at AP we monitored three or four televisions simultaneously. We'd capture a 'video-still' right from the screen, process it through PhotoShop, and then transmit it on the uplink.")

On September 11, says Alabiso, "we had dozens shooting that day—staff *and* amateurs—because of the advent of consumers' digital cameras. It was Carmen Taylor, an Arkansas tourist visiting New York, who captured one of the most dramatic images of the hijacked airliner a split second before it slammed into the second tower. Taylor sent the image to a local TV station in Arkansas, which quickly aired her photo. With bureaus in every state, AP's local staff spotted Taylor's picture. She quickly agreed to let AP send it around the world." Taylor's serendipitous snaps, in Alabiso's estimation, were evidence that "almost overnight, the power of spot news photography [had] slipped from the hands of the skilled, passionate photojournalist and into the handbags and pockets of consumers everywhere . . . The amateur who is on the scene becomes the first eye on history."

Transformations like these, obviously, had a profound impact on newsgathering. "On 9/11 we could not have met our deadline and done our bestselling issue in three years," says Regis Le Sommier of the French newsmagazine *Paris Match*, "if there hadn't been digital photography. We had *nine* hours to do the *whole* magazine. Keep your Leicas in the closet!" But the new technology had an even more significant impact on our concept of what we can see, and therefore *know*, in these voyeuristic times.

By 2001, digital images—etched electronically onto what the manufacturer has marvelously dubbed a Memory Stick—had done away with the need for the finished print. The process now *is* the picture. Our ability to witness an occurrence that had been previously observed through a viewfinder is no longer a function of lazy, cryptic chemistry. Instead, the pixel, minutely and immediately, encodes the essential lightning flash of an event for virtually spontaneous reconstitution. Today the eye of the photographer is hardly separated by more than a few blinks from the eye of the beholder.

In fact, the digital picture itself has ceased to be a picture in a traditional sense—a representation of a three-dimensional space, real or imagined, on a flat surface. Now the image, reduced to electronic particles, is largely virtual, more photo than graph. It exists more like a vapor or a dapple of sunlight. While so-called true lovers of photography continue to cherish the tactile experience of "taking in" a picture (discerning the meaning and wonder of a given image by experiencing its confluence of light and shadow in three dimensions—in one's grasp or on a page or on a museum wall), consumption of digital photography, in fairness, cannot yet do without the observational surface. Memory-based images are not absorbed intravenously; they must still be transferred to a camera back, a cell phone, a computer desktop, a laser print. But little by little, just as the electronic book already threatens to replace the printed page—leaving us with only the wonderful story underneath—photography is becoming progressively less physical.

Einstein is instructive here. In 1905, the physicist altered humanity's sense of time and space when he first envisioned light as a particle and not just a wave. Digital photography, a hundred years later, has altered our sense of time and space by channeling and then recording light as a pixel. This new incarnation of an old medium has expanded our potential visual universe while collapsing the time frame between action and audience. By altering how and how quickly we can remotely witness an event, the medium exponentially increases what we think we can see and understand. It has endowed humanity (even in this age of photo manipulators, image handlers, and spinmeisters) with expectations, realistic or not, of a here-and-now, around-the-clock omniscience.

Digital photography has also recast our framework for understanding how to quantify information within space. In the digital realm of the Internet, where pictures travel between transmitters and viewers, all space has become virtual. Quite often, many observers cannot separate a news event from its visual representation. This paradox has persisted for ages: we remember that the *Hindenburg* dirigible collided with a mooring tower and exploded in Lakehurst, New Jersey, in 1937, killing thirty-six, in large part *because* Sam Share was there to record it with his camera and because WLS correspondent Herb Morrison transmitted his alarm—"Oh, the humanity!"—over the radio. Likewise, when remembering September 11, 2001, there is no distinction for two billion–plus people between the observed occurrence and the rewitnessed enactment. Many of us equate the event with the pictures of it, and it is pictures that we most readily retain, the medium becoming our memory.

So too with television in the digital age.

Over the same period, and in many of the same ways, television has evolved in breakneck fashion, cutting its teeth, as it were, during the Vietnam War. "I call it the seven ages of satelliting," says Stephen Claypole, a longtime British TV-news executive, borrowing from Jaques's "Seven Ages of Man" soliloquy in Shakespeare's *As You Like it*:

All the world's a stage,
And all the men and women merely players:
They have their exits and their entrances;
And one man in his time plays many parts,
His acts being seven ages. At first the infant,
Mewling and puking in the nurse's arms.
And then the whining school-boy, with his satchel
And shining morning face, creeping like snail
Unwillingly to school . . .

"We've only reached the fourth stage of television satelliting," Claypole asserts, passing from infant to schoolboy to young lover ("sighing like a furnace," as Shakespeare put it), and now to soldier ("[f]ull of strange oaths . . . / Jealous in honour, sudden and quick in quarrel, / Seeking the bubble reputation / Even in the cannon's mouth").

Claypole explains. "The mewling and puking babe," he says, was "the Vietnam War. All the American and international networks shot everything on film which had to be hand-carried by 'fixers' to Hong Kong—due to the absence of technical facilities in Vietnam—where the film was sped through the chemical soup in back-alley processing laboratories in twenty-five minutes. When the film was blow-dried and ready to be edited, it was laid over soundtrack that had been previously recorded in Vietnam by the correspondents. The finished segment was taken to the cable-and-wireless office and satellited into New York. Then the Americans syndicated it."

The whole process, from battlefield to living room, took about twenty-four to thirty-six hours, considered almost instantaneous in the 1960s (when compared with the two or three days of production time that had been previously required to produce and air news stories). Since TV cameramen were allowed to rove with relative freedom, hopping on a chopper and covering the war at will, they were able to send home unvarnished scenes of combat. Their imagery was accompanied by the field reporting of a regiment of first-rate correspondents who, in helmets and fatigues near the front lines, could relate a more credible and captivating narrative than the sanitized, on-the-verge-of-victory homilies doled out by American officials.

"Contemporaneous war coverage undercut the U.S. mission in Vietnam," says Claypole. "This was unprecedented in television and in visual communication of a conflict. Some U.S. officials took the view that satellite television actually ruined [President] Lyndon Johnson and destroyed American prospects in Southeast Asia. But in hindsight, it was a losing cause from the very start."

Telecommunications professor David Hazinski agrees. "By seeing television images of battle, viewers saw that war wasn't wrapped in a flag. Combat was people killing people. And the immediacy and graphic quality of the imagery contributed to turning [U.S. public opinion] against the war. In Somalia [in 1993], American foreign policy changed *overnight* because of the image of one helicopter pilot's body being dragged through the streets of Mogadishu."

The second—"schoolboy"—stage, Claypole contends, was defined by President Richard Nixon's visit to China in 1972, the great Western, capitalist opening to the Eastern, communist goliath. To cover the event, U.S. networks pooled their resources and gave a relatively mobile satellite ground station to China, a nation with an antiquated television system. "The portable electronic cameras that were used," says Claypole, "sat on people's shoulders, and were known as lead parrots. There are cameramen around today with arthritic backs from carrying these around in 1972." As a result of those cameras, microwaving live images of Nixon at the Great Wall back to that spanking new ground station, then up to a space-based satellite, one world could see two worlds converge. "It was unprecedented," Claypole concludes. "The impact was just huge. The American networks covered Nixon in China in the same way they might have covered him in Chicago. If this gear had existed a decade before, we would have all watched John F. Kennedy assassinated, not on film, but in real time."

The third stage of television satelliting, corresponding to Shakespeare's third age of man, the impassioned lover, coincided with the first Gulf War. By the time Iraq invaded Kuwait in August of 1990, and America and its allies began bombing Baghdad in earnest the following January, television pioneer Ted Turner had blanketed the globe with his Cable News Network, offering twenty-four-hour coverage of events and further compressing the time needed to transmit breaking stories. Peter Arnett and CNN's team were ensconced in a wartime catbird seat—the al-Rashid Hotel, in the heart of Baghdad—when the first U.S. salvos shook the city. Correspondents' dramatic accounts of nearby cloudbursts and explosions were transmitted live over a special phone, relayed by microwave to Amman, Jordan, and on to CNN's Atlanta headquarters via satellite. Viewers heard live CNN audio, accompanied by delayed video images, the hue and texture of pea soup. "The rush of watching all that eerie green night-vision footage . . . had become so intense," wrote Don

DeLillo, the novelist, that once coverage slowed down during the next month "it became hard to honor the fact that the war was still going on, untelevised."

Within two weeks, the network had been allowed to shuttle in a portable, state-of-the-art TV "uplink"—the key breakthrough that allowed CNN to cover the conflict in real time. So dawned the age of satellite newsgathering (SNG), in which, as Claypole puts it, "six large metal suitcases could hold all the bits which, when assembled, gave you the capacity to broadcast up to a satellite." News could be covered *from* virtually anywhere on the earth's surface *to* virtually anywhere on the earth's surface, as long as the receiving end had a power supply, a television set, and a human being to watch it.

"[F]or the first time in history," commented producer Robert Wiener (who, with Arnett and Nic Robertson, helped coordinate CNN's war coverage from Baghdad), journalists were able to broadcast "live pictures to the entire world of a war in progress from behind enemy lines. [CBS's legendary newsman Edward R.] Murrow would have loved it!"

Even as their citizens took it all in, the warriors themselves monitored the conflict over CNN. *Time* magazine reported that when "CIA director William Webster received word via intelligence satellite that an Iraqi Scud missile had been launched [toward Israel], he would tell National Security Adviser Brent Scowcroft, 'Turn on CNN to see where it lands.' " The network had become, in *Time*'s words, "the common frame of reference for the world's power elite."

Not to mention its common platform for spinning information to the masses. "What would have been important to [Iraqi leader] Saddam [Hussein] was 24-hour cable television as a propaganda tool," notes communications professor George Kindel. "The entire Arab world could see Iraq defending itself against this Overpowering Aggressor. And *everyone* could tune in, because the entire planet seemed to be sprouting rooftop dishes. By the '90s you had people in huts in remote corners of the globe watching their MTV." To underscore the indispensable role of global video news, *Time* bestowed the title of 1991 Man of the Year not on the commanders who fought the war but on the man whose network had covered it—Ted Turner, CNN's founder (and eventually vice chairman of what would be called, for a brief while, AOL Time Warner, *Time*'s parent company).

September 11, says Claypole, straddled the third and fourth stages of satelliting—aptly, Shakespeare's warrior period. The run-up to the first Gulf War had spooled out over months. Military, diplomatic, and media players had fine-tuned their roles, parried, then dug in for the denouement. In contrast, 9/11 was a surprise assault, one designed by its planners to make a media stir. The premeditated use of television as a tool to terrorize had already been well honed through high-visibility hostage incidents such as the PLO's Munich Olympics massacre of 1972 and by the various Lebanese factions that orchestrated the Beirut kidnappings of the 1980s. By 2001, TV—and its handmaiden, the Internet—had become tactical components in the terrorists' battle plan, with bin Laden's plotters virtually assured an audience of global dimension.

The reason was clear. Over the intervening decade, the TV-news landscape had shifted. Videotape had become digital, allowing for faster and more versatile transmission of picture data than its analog forerunner. Digital compression and transmission could squeeze more information—now in discrete zeros and ones—into the same or smaller sets of pipes. Video cameras were more portable and compact, allowing a single operator-reporter to transmit his own story and decreasing the need for a full-fledged crew (cameraman, sound man, correspondent, producer). And most significant of all, says Claypole, "international television organizations were switching from satellite to fiber optics, with a belt of cables girdling the earth [across] the ocean floors. For those stations that lost their antennae on 9/11, they were able to find a way into the fiber-optic system. *Since* 9/11, we've now moved into the fourth stage. Everything is on the laptop, everything is miniaturized. You can push the picture through the satellite phone, edit on the screen, and broadcast to any continent."

"Part of the transformation," says Nigel Pritchard of CNN, "was digital newsgathering. You were no longer tied to a piece of cable and a satellite truck. We could go anywhere and broadcast with a battery pack. There were literally more places to broadcast live from." Camera prices had also dropped precipitously, "totally eliminating any barriers of entry or distribution," says television producer Ben Silverman. "This opened the visual floodgates. Anyone in the right place at the right time could become a video journalist." The twenty-first century, indeed, seemed bursting with promise and opportunity for bucking the communications status quo.

By 2001, then, the technology was primed. Given the right set of circumstances—a military campaign, a political upheaval, a terrorist attack—a momentous event could literally play out in real time, for the world to see. Global video-news services and a crosshatched array of cross-border relationships among far-flung networks and stations were now in place. "In the ten years . . . before September 11," says John Frazee, senior vice president of News Services at CBS, his network and its competitors had done their satellite-newsgathering spadework, "through judicious investment in knowledge and people and facilities. We had been exercising those facilities continually, like a muscle. They were ready on 9/11."

"For 9/11," says Pritchard, "you couldn't move close to Ground Zero with a truck, a satellite, a cable lead, and a big hand-held camera. You *could*, [however,] with a satellite phone which contained a video camera—an early prototype of which had been pioneered [two] year[s] before by correspondent Nic Robertson." (When hijackers took an Indian airliner to Kandahar, Afghanistan, on Christmas Day, 1999, Robertson had resorted to covering the story with a rudimentary videophone, since the notoriously photo-averse Taliban weren't exactly enamored of satellite trucks.) "A videophone is very grainy, a bit 'bitty'—its signal breaks up," Pritchard explains. "But correspondent Gary Tuchman was able to [use one and] get close on 9/11. Nic Robertson also used it that day to broadcast live from Afghanistan at the press conference held by the Taliban to say they had had nothing to do with the attacks. Suddenly, this videophone started to come to prominence" (as it would, quite famously, in the Iraq invasion of 2003).

CNN had set the stage in the preceding decade. "CNN built the model," says Kindel. "Countries everywhere in the developing world had stations linked to satellites, with an ability to download signals off other stations' satellites. Any station in any country, theoretically, could air any station's content, whether your local affiliate's or al-Jazeera's."* And with digital video cameras, computers, and wireless Internet connections now available to citizens of almost every nation, governments would be hard pressed to stop the flow. Video news became populist, democratic, and ubiquitous. The world, in effect, had become the long-predicted video village, peopled with image makers and image consumers. (The Internet's impact in the equation will be discussed in chapter six.)

"Prior to 1991," says CNN's Pritchard, "there was limited cable and satellite TV penetration around the world. Less than 10 million households had access to CNN. But the Gulf War came along. Other broadcasters were suddenly picking up our imagery, with the little CNN bug [logo] in the corner, and rebroadcasting it. People *thought* they were seeing CNN. Suddenly this satellite channel . . . had real appeal globally. And there was an explosion in cable and satellite distribution, sort of spurred by the war and by people like [News Corporation's] Rupert Murdoch and others starting to invest. It was slow and expensive. You had to dig up all the roads to put cable in. For satellite networks you had to build the infrastructure and purchase the satellite transponders."

According to Roger Ailes, head of CNN's chief competitor, FOX News, the impetus behind this 1990s boom was not the Gulf War or technology, but capitalism. "The driving force in our society has been, can you make a buck doing it?—and that's not bad," says Ailes. "Somebody figured out how to make money running news twenty-four hours a day: Ted Turner." Others, such as Murdoch, Ailes's boss, reworked Turner's formula, providing their own spin and imprint, and video news proliferated locally, nationally, globally. "Originally," Ailes explains, TV news "was a loss leader: Let's do public affairs and see how much money we can lose." Now, he says, it's a profit center, a multi-channel environment that has "allowed so many people to be watching the news, live, when major events happen."

The whole world, then, was poised come September 2001, with satel-

* Al-Jazeera is the provocative Middle Eastern channel, launched in 1996, that serves a pan-Arab audience of 40 million from its base in Qatar, the Persian Gulf emirate, having recently mobilized an international English-language service. Its influence has grown so widely since the Iraq War that in 2004 it was named the fifth most impactful global brand—after Apple, Google, IKEA, and Starbucks—in Brandchannel.com's Readers' Choice Awards.

lite dishes aimed and with cable and fiber-optic lines open—not to mention dial-up and DSL as well.

"It all comes back to Shakespeare," Claypole concludes. "All the world *is* a stage. And all the men and women merely players."

The framework that emerged went something like this: Digital cameras, linked by phone lines, cables, and the Internet, transmitted pictures to newspapers and magazines, agencies and Web sites. Global TV newsgathering systems, linked by fiber-optic cables (snaking across the oceans' beds) and by satellites (poised 22,300 miles above a patch of blue globe) transmitting real-time feeds to all manner of television stations. In a matter of minutes, then, everyone with a monitor, almost anywhere in the world, was able to access similar footage shot only moments before.

And by and large they seemed to trust what they were seeing. Certainly, there were millions of people who accepted the myth (to be explored later) that the United States, Israel, Saudi Arabia, and/or multinational corporations had somehow acted in collusion to bring about the attacks as a way of fomenting wider conflict. (In 2002, when CNN surveyed respondents in nine Muslim nations, over 60 percent professed that they did not think that Arabs were behind the 9/11 plot.) But practically no one, anywhere on the planet, did not buy the reality of four planes streaking toward their targets, or the reality of two towers spouting fists of smoke, with thousands trapped inside. The unspoken compact among us was that this act was incomparably catastrophic and audacious, and that this image was genuine because we were all viewing the same evidence, undeniably, as certain as the fact that the sun above us was the very one that any beast alive might have glimpsed that day.

This was an act of global theater, conceived by bin Laden as if for the camera. And even if various aspects might have been manipulated—this was, after all, the age of the enhanced image and the spliced-and-diced videotape—the gist was there on the screen, undistorted, elemental. Planes were hitting buildings and Americans were dying, jumping to their deaths, because of the coordinated actions of suicide-hijacker jihadists. The scene was too unbelievable not to be believed.

Photography that day gave the world a single focal point through which to observe the global showdown.

My daughter, Molly, then age thirteen, spent Wednesday evening at our home in the Westchester suburbs. She had heard that John Doherty, the father of her friend Maureen, had not returned from the Trade Center on Tuesday. Maureen's dad, fifty-eight, an Aon vice president, was still missing that day and would be missing the next. His company's offices were located in the south tower.

Over the week that followed, Molly would periodically go to the dining room sideboard, open the left-hand drawer, and take out a framed photo she kept there of nineteen sixth-grade girls from the Ursuline School, including Maureen and Molly, posing in their finest dresses.

Throughout the week, people sought the company of personal photographs. To touch them. To find comfort or memories or answers in the very act of feeling the paper against flesh. To connect with someone lost in the tragedy—or someone who had lost someone—by physically holding his or her image in the hand, the mind, the heart.

At the left of this particular frame, just below where Molly stood, sat her friend Maureen. Her face was beaming, her hair buoyant with light brown ringlets. "She had curled it especially for that night," Molly remembered. The event was the annual father-daughter dance.

Maureen's father was one of 176 employees that Aon would lose that day. Another was Tamitha Freeman, a thirty-five-year-old Brooklynite, the proud mother of a newborn son. She had decided to evacuate Two World Trade Center with her coworkers shortly after the first plane hit the opposite tower. But Freeman suddenly had second thoughts. She turned to a colleague and explained that she needed to go back to her office to get her purse.

"I have my baby's pictures in it," Freeman said.

3 THURSDAY, SEPTEMBER 13

On Thursday, U.S. agencies finalized their roster listing the names of the nineteen hijackers. (Working off passenger manifests, the Customs Service and FBI had determined the names of eighteen "probable" suspects by around noon on the eleventh.)

The images of sixteen, then nineteen, would soon surface. Their faces, laid out in a kind of checkerboard, were published and republished in newspapers around the world, and posted on computer and TV screens *(Figure E)*. The grid of faces was a photographic dragnet, cast across continents. It assisted law enforcement teams here and abroad, while satisfying a worldwide curiosity (marked by revulsion in some quarters, fascination in others) as to the identities of the men who had committed these acts.

On the morning of the attacks, communiqués had been sent out to field offices of the FBI and the Customs and Immigration Services, and to intelligence agencies, including the CIA and NSA. Analysts scoured still photographs in databases, especially on visa application files at the State Department and at consular facilities in nations such as Germany and Saudi Arabia.

"Their entry into the U.S.," says *Newsweek* investigative correspondent Mark Hosenball, a national security expert, "would have been logged by both Customs and Immigration. The CIA had surveillance pictures dating back to January of 2000 of two of the hijackers, Khalid al-Mihdhar and Nawaf al-Hazmi, because they had attended the infamous terrorist summit in Malaysia [in 2000]. The photos were taken by the special branch of the Malaysian political police, then turned over to the CIA. Two weeks before September 11, the CIA ordered up an APB [all points bulletin] for them because they realized that they were in the country, and I'm sure their pictures were circulating. The CIA had pictures of this terrorist summit but they didn't know what it meant. A picture's worth a thousand words—but it isn't worth shit if you don't know what you're looking at." (In response to the APB, the FBI had sought to locate the two men during the summer of 2001, but its search was gnarled in a no-man's-land of missed opportunity and unconscionable paper lag.)

As is usually the case with ID photos, dredged from the bureaucratic slurry, the headshots were unadorned and rather murky—the equivalent of mugshots. Most of the men were in their twenties. Most were modest in build, typically around five feet six. Many had trained in al-Qaeda camps. Thirteen had actually gone through a conditioning regime to be able to subdue airline crews and passengers. Almost to a man, their jaws were set and stern (although three appeared to have volunteered an approximation of a smile). All but two stared dead-on, directly addressing the camera—and the intended viewer. Each subject was clear-eyed and intent.

Individually or arrayed in rows or grouped by hijacking "team," the faces suggested menace, were *meant* to menace. Some of the hijackers had recently had their photos reshot, under instructions from their bosses, to update and legitimize their current IDs. (Intelligence officials determined that among them, the hijackers had sixty-three valid driver's licenses, though they usually traveled and made transactions under their own names.) And each of them, prior to 9/11, had sent off photocopies of their passport pictures to intermediaries, who would forward them to al-Qaeda leaders, ostensibly for dispersal as "martyr" shots. One could read the rebuke in their faces: fear me, fear my God. One could read the appeal, as well, to their fellow jihadists: revere me, revere my God.

That first week, the names, photos, a telephone hotline, and a Web site would help generate 36,000 leads, according to the FBI, resulting in dozens of search warrants and subpoenas. "If we get photographs out there, the public responds," explains the FBI's Joe Valiquette, noting the effectiveness of the agency's Ten Most Wanted List, begun fifty-two years before. "No doubt, by distributing photographs of the hijackers, we've been able to make progress in determining the travel and contacts of some." By the end of September a complete set of headshots would circulate around the world and help provide tens of thousands of additional leads to U.S. agencies, Interpol, and foreign intelligence services.

"Moving pictures" were essential as well. The week of the attacks, FBI evidence-response teams, working with local, state, and federal police, used old-fashioned shoe leather to trace the perpetrators' video footprints across the Northeast corridor. First, the agents scoured through "trash collected from hotel rooms, abandoned rental cars, supermarkets, Wal-Marts, Dunkin' Donuts [shops]," recalls FBI forensic photographer and video specialist John Green, who helped assemble a paper trail of receipts left by the hijackers during the two weeks prior to 9/11. Evidence in tow, agents paid visits to each establishment to procure videotapes from security cameras. "We had one of [hijack ringleader Mohammed] Atta's receipts—for a 9-volt battery adapter from a Wal-Mart in Portland, Maine, to be plugged in a car console or into the cockpit of the plane to turn on his GPS [Global Positioning System] unit. Once at the Wal-Mart, we asked for [any] original tapes."

In all, Green's Boston-based forensic lab amassed 311 cassettes within seven days. Using an Avid Xpress video-editing system, the FBI digitized the tapes onto massive hard-drive arrays. (If a location had multiple security cameras feeding into one master panel, they used special forensic tools to separate each camera's footage into distinct video streams.) Technicians would then output the digitized footage onto DVD or VHS. Finally, teams of police officers, dispatched by their respective agencies, would sit and watch the tapes play out, working twelve-hour shifts and making notations whenever they spotted figures they believed to be the hijackers.

Soon, the FBI had a pictorial time line of the perpetrators in the hours before the attacks. On the night of September 10, an ATM camera in South Portland, Maine, had recorded Atta and a man traveling under the name of Abdulaziz Alomari *(Figure F)*. Over the next forty-five minutes, the pair would be photographed twice more: at a nearby gas station and at a Wal-Mart in Scarborough. The next morning, they would appear on a monitor at Portland International Jetport, under a digital readout: 9-11-01 24H/5:45:15. Fifteen minutes later, they would take off on a Colgan Air commuter flight to Boston.

The videos provided countless leads, says Green. "We were able to interview witnesses and account for all the [hijackers'] actions. We prioritized: Were they meeting [along the way] with anybody who would be alive who we could interrogate? Out of all those tapes and the thousands of hours of watching, we never saw them with anybody but themselves [except for occasional] small-talk."

The hijackers had been videotaped on closed-circuit monitors in Maine (as their counterparts would be at Dulles airport), but there were no surveillance cameras at the corresponding security checkpoints at Newark Airport (through which four hijackers passed before boarding United Airlines Flight 93) or in Boston (where ten hijackers filed in, in two groups of five, to board American Flight 11 and United Flight 175). Had there been security cameras—and, possibly, more throughly trained and vetted screening and security personnel—perhaps the outcome of September 11 would have been different, perhaps not.

According to Dennis Murphy, who was an assistant commissioner for the U.S. Customs Service in Washington, D.C., on 9/11, "Some of the most important images [in terms of deterrence] were those where you see [hijackers] going through security"—and being allowed to pass through, unimpeded. Some of the screeners, says Murphy, "had a minimum amount of training . . . They were just hired help, not necessarily a professional workforce or even [working for] contractors who had professional oversight."

But for Murphy, who later moved to the Department of Homeland Security, the key photographs are the ones he keeps in his office to this day. "I've got the poster, 'The Darkest Page,' " he says, which contains "the front pages of newspapers from around the world on September 12." He also has put up an aerial view of his old office building—the devastated U.S. Customs House, at Six World Trade Center—taken shortly after the attacks. "It's just that constant reminder of why we do what we do: to do whatever we can to prevent it from happening again."

If any single image served to reassure New Yorkers the week of September 11, it was that of a stalwart, ever present mayor: Rudolph Giuliani pausing for pictures, and words of solace, as he shuttled around town, mediating, mourning, and responding to new crises, large and small. On local television during the days after the attacks, footage of the mayor seemed to air almost as frequently as footage of the smoking towers.

These photo ops were really a much-needed photo opiate. In hard hat or windbreaker, often in a tie, always speaking in measured tones, Giuliani recognized the importance of consistently projecting the face of authority, along with the voice of reason, compassion, and solidarity. At his daily press briefings, on the street, at Ground Zero, his image helped becalm a city. One shot, shown repeatedly, depicted Giuliani on a podium with the full complement of authorities at his side, including Governor George Pataki, Police Commissioner Bernard Kerik, Fire Commissioner Thomas Von Essen, and Richard Sheirer, the director of the mayor's Office of Emergency Management. In a community once terrorized, now unified, people needed to look into the eyes of a levelheaded parental presence, and to see the clenched jaw of security.

On Thursday, the mayor and Governor Pataki fielded a call from President Bush, who told them, "I look forward to visiting with you in person tomorrow . . . It will be a chance for all three of us to thank and hug and cry with the citizens of your good area."

In a Washington, D.C., conference room, just forty-eight hours after the attacks, historians from the Smithsonian's National Museum of American History held their first curatorial meeting to discuss the acquisition of September 11 artifacts and images. The session—part professional gathering, part healing encounter—covered, as one museum administrator put it, "How should we be reacting to this? And how soon *could* we react before losing the opportunity to collect something that might be destroyed?" The meeting eventually led to an exhibition, which would open a year later: "September 11th: Bearing Witness to History."

"Within a couple of hours, I started thinking that this was probably going to lead to a collecting effort," recalls Michelle Delaney, who curates the museum's photographic-history collection. "I instinctively thought photojournalists and videographers would rush down there and then they'd rush their film back. Many of them, in fact, thought they were going to die. They went through the push-pull of deciding whether or not to go, how close to get.

"There was an added urgency to their enterprise [that] was profound. The world *had* to see the details. I realized that photojournalism, which seemed for years to be on a downslide, was significant that day. It made the general public feel how important the photographer was in documenting history." Congress would eventually give the Smithsonian $5 million to procure 9/11-related objects, including videotapes and photos.

Since all commercial flights had been immediately suspended across American airspace, atmospheric scientists took special interest in the photographs accumulated on September 12 and 13 by various satellites. As a rule, the atmosphere above North America is a patchwork of contrails—thin stripes of condensation, with the consistency of cirrus clouds, that hundreds of jets issue each day on their hops across the continent. Ever since 1960, when the first weather satellite began surveying storm and climate patterns, this patchy thicket—in effect a field of aircraft wakes—has always obscured the view of Earth's surface as seen from skyborne lenses. But suddenly, here was an unprecedented event: three consecutive contrail-free days. Indeed, important discoveries have already emerged from the visual and meteorological data produced over that short September span.

University of Wisconsin climatologist David Travis compared measurements taken during equivalent periods (prior to 9/11) with those taken during the three days that the planes were grounded. He found that North America's daily temperature swing (the range between the average daytime high and the average nighttime low) widened by an appreciable three to five degrees Fahrenheit. What this suggested to Travis was that contrails, over the years, have tended to tamp down temperatures (a phenomenon called global dimming), possibly hiding what could be even more severe ramifications of global warming.

What are the long-term implications glimpsed through these tea leaves of streaks, stats, and photographs? According to a 2005 BBC report, the "unforeseen climatic effects of 9/11 suggest that if we remove other causes of dimming, the impact on global temperatures could be huge. [Climate and ecosystem expert] Dr. [Peter] Cox now believes the cooling effects of dimming may be the reason that, so far, global warming has been relatively muted, despite the rapid rise in greenhouse gases." Cox's conclusion: in the absence of a concerted effort to reverse harmful emissions, "in the next hundred years temperatures worldwide could rise by as much as ten degrees Celsius, twice as quickly as previously thought and enough to turn tracts of Britain into a desert . . . Unless action is taken swiftly, an unstoppable chain of climatic disasters may be set in motion in just 20 years."

Newsday's Thursday edition carried a photo on its front page of a disconsolate Monica Iken. A former schoolteacher, with a fashion model's poise and presence, Iken was looking off camera, distraught. In one hand she held a snapshot of her husband, Michael Iken, thirty-seven, a bond broker who had been on the eighty-fourth floor of Tower Two. "I was one of the first ones out there the day after, on the 12th," Iken now says, recalling how she made the rounds, trying to display his picture in as many public venues as possible. "Everyone was trying to get their photos to be seen. A name is just a name. You need to put an image [to the name]."

Iken says she thought that the picture would prove catalytic: perhaps it would refresh the memory of a coworker or emergency responder. Through a picture, she hoped, "they would've seen his face and recognized something about him that was distinctive if they were all running out [of the building] together. You'd have an idea of where he might have been, even if he didn't get out. Names didn't mean anything [up in the towers]. People helped each other who didn't know each other."

By getting his name and likeness out in circulation, she insists, she began to gather the sand grains of the last moments of his life. After Tower One was attacked, many of Michael's colleagues began making their descent down Tower Two. But one woman had sought refuge under her desk, refusing to budge. "At the time, she wasn't moving," says Iken, "and she was afraid to go anywhere." Just before they headed out, witnesses recalled, Michael and several coworkers stayed behind to calm her down and persuade her to leave. After Iken's TV appearance, she got a call from a woman who had seen her holding up Michael's photo. The caller, Iken says, told her that one of the good Samaritans who had stayed behind was "this guy Michael from Euro Brokers. She connect[ed] the dots."

The knowledge, though of small comfort, was still better than the hideous chill of ignorance. "Through doing that, I pretty much know where Michael was," she says. Those who had stayed and rallied around their colleague, she believes, probably perished together. "On his side [of the eighty-fourth floor] was where the piece of the wing came in. Those people . . . there were probably killed instantly."

Pictures continue to matter to Monica Iken, perhaps now more than ever. Having served on the World Trade Center Memorial Foundation board and other panels focused on downtown development and memorial design, and having founded September's Mission (which has sought to help establish parameters for the eventual memorial), she has fought to preserve the sanctity of the site. She wants to ensure that it has a private, sacred section to house unidentified remains, and that it displays pictures of the deceased. She argues against a design that might echo the Vietnam Veterans Memorial in Washington, D.C., where row upon row of the names of the dead and missing—58,249 in all—are etched in black granite, speaking volumes to visitors because of their understated eloquence and their multitudes. For September 11, however, Iken says she doesn't think names "say enough about the people that were there: everyday people going to work. A lot of them were young and had families." (The Ikens, married eleven months before 9/11, did not.)

"What keeps me going today is Michael's face in my mind," she insists. "The face is what motivates me to focus on the memorial so much, because that's him there, at that place—not only because I have no remains, which is a big factor as well—[but because] I'm going to honor him *there,* at that space . . . where I can have some peace and quiet and be able to reflect, where his unidentified remains may be."

Though she hasn't yet chosen a particular image for the memorial, she says she'll leave it to site architect Michael Arad to determine how images might be incorporated in the finished design. (As of this writing, the Lower Manhattan Development Corporation had not definitively determined whether photographs would eventually be used in the memorial proper, the area where families would come to mourn and honor loved ones.) "A picture will tell you what that person was about: his smile, his presence, the aura he had, his existence here, the love that we had together. If I could—I always joke—I would put his picture up in Times Square with lights illuminating [it]. If you see his face you see why I do this and what his spirit meant and how it carries through, through other people, through a face."

I know of no one who takes more family photos than my friend Scott Gutterson, an attorney and accountant. At his Long Island home, framed photographs line the entrance hall, the main staircase, the basement walls. Photos are propped up on bookshelves, the piano, the bathroom vanity. The walls of his midtown office bear three hundred pictures arranged in thirty-seven different frames. "Some of these become almost like wallpaper," he says. "My grandfather in a chef's hat, baking. My kids with Aunt Roz. Matthew, my son, at Cooperstown, eating ice cream. There's an energy that pictures give. You don't hang up *negative* photographs. They're absolutely windows to happiness and windows to the past."

On Thursday, Gutterson fielded calls and phoned friends and clients, dreading what he'd hear at the other end of the line. "I probably knew fifty people in the towers at the time," he says of his clients, acquaintances, and friends. "A lot of them got out. A lot of them didn't. My best guess is some thirty-odd people I know didn't get out. Kevin Cleary was a friend of mine. Tom Burke was a friend of mine. Billy Hunt, June of 2000, had a baby. Tommy Cahill—there wasn't a beer this guy wouldn't drink.

"The majority of these people had photographs of their lives on their walls, on their desks, in their cubicles. These young kids, the bond traders sitting in the bullpen, would have taped to their computers, photographs. Billy Hunt, I'm sure had pictures taped to his screen.

"Now that these photographs are all burnt up, it wouldn't surprise me if somebody had the only copy of a particular photograph and therefore the stimulus to resurrect a particular memory is gone. It's almost like dying three times. They were murdered—incinerated for nothing. Their wonderful memories are gone. And the memories that *would have* been spurred by those photographs are gone, absolutely turned to dust."

Security, for the firm of Morgan Stanley, had meant one thing only: getting 2,700 employees out of the building—fast. To that end, perhaps no one during the attacks was directly responsible for saving more individual lives than the company's security chief, Rick Rescorla.

His story, quite simply, can be told in a photograph. Two days after the attacks, Eileen Hillock, a Morgan Stanley vice president, picked up a roll of film from the one-hour developer at her local pharmacy. She liked to keep a camera stowed in a drawer on the fifty-sixth floor of Tower Two. "We always had it in the desk to take pictures at celebrations," she says, "or when the boats came in, the Fourth of July, gorgeous sunsets."

On September 11, Hillock had been shocked when she looked up and saw the building across from her burst into flame. She thought a helicopter must have accidentally rammed into it. "I don't know why," she says, "I grabbed the camera, a Minolta. I took a couple of photographs."

What she hadn't realized was that Rick Rescorla had already sprung into action. Rescorla, Morgan Stanley's British-born Trade Center security chief, had been training for a day like this for virtually his entire adult life. Within moments of the first attack, Rescorla—a decorated platoon leader who had served with the U.S. Army in Vietnam—began mobilizing every last Morgan Stanley employee to begin a mass evacuation. Hillock took a picture or two—one showing Rescorla standing against a wall, barking into a bullhorn. Two of his security aides—Jorge Velazquez and Titus Davidson—stood nearby. Then, following the security team's orders, Hillock, as she had been trained to do in countless drills, complied and headed down the stairs.

Five minutes later, unbeknownst to her, the windows on some of the Morgan Stanley floors blew out as United Flight 175 ripped through the building. As she walked down the stairs with thousands of others, the skyscraper began to rock. How calm and unsuspecting we were, she thought as she studied her photo, fresh from the drugstore: Rescorla, the hero in the hard hat.

"We didn't know it was a terrorist attack," she says. "We thought it was an accident. On the way down, somebody in front of me spilled their coffee and I stopped to wipe it up. Our sense of calm was totally because we knew the drill. We were prepared."

For much of the 1990s, Rick Rescorla had insisted that Morgan Stanley's offices be primed for a violent attack—something he viewed as inevitable. With years of combat experience (he was profiled in the book *We Were Soldiers Once . . . and Young*, later made into a film), and well schooled in the security trade, Rescorla understood, quite keenly, that the World Trade Center was a perfect terror target. He had even warned authorities of the vulnerability of the underground parking facility *prior* to the 1993 attack.

On 9/11, soon after the opposite tower was hit, a building official reportedly phoned Rescorla and urged him to keep his twenty-two floors of employees at their desks. Rescorla swore at him and literally marched his troops to safety. To keep spirits up, he belted out songs from his native Cornwall, England.

For an hour and a half, he trudged up and down Tower Two, between floors ten and seventy-two, shepherding and cajoling and offering encouragement. Just before the building collapsed, Rescorla had begun one last sweep to make certain no stragglers remained. All 2,700 employees, and one thousand more from Five World Trade Center, managed to make it out safely—all but Rescorla, the two security men in Eileen Hillock's picture, and nine others.

Susan Rescorla would soon encourage author James B. Stewart to write a biography of her husband (*Heart of a Soldier*, published a year later). She keeps a poster-size copy of Hillock's photo, framed, in her den in Mendham, New Jersey. "When I first saw [the snapshot]," she says, "I thought I was going to be very emotionally taken over. But it calmed me. I was like, 'He's *so* in charge.' They were not panicked. That's what he was all about: a calming voice through the bullhorn, just like in Vietnam. Only afterwards did I realize he was perspiring profusely. His tie was off. At one stage [I'd heard] he sat on a chair to rest. He even took the time out to call me, about twenty after nine. A half hour later, I saw the building come down.

"I was proud of my husband in life," she says, her voice breaking. "I'm even prouder of him in death. His two in-house people [in the picture] and the guard from an outside service—they're all dead. They would've followed him to kingdom come. They *did*. They've never found [his] remains."

With Americans suddenly more security conscious, the Pew Research Center began conducting a poll on September 13 in which they asked respondents whether or not they would favor a move to introduce photo IDs nationwide. The cards, mandatory for citizens in one hundred other nations, were being proposed as part of planned efforts to curtail illegal alien traffic and "identity theft." In theory they would also be shown on demand to security personnel, police, or federal and state agents. Despite the plan's inherent threats to privacy, the idea appealed to 70 percent of those polled. It was becoming apparent that in the modern material world, the lasting record of one's earthly existence was not just one's name or words or deeds, all of which could be easily forgotten or misremembered. What physically endured was one's skull and bones, one's genes (in one's offspring and their descendants), and, now, one's digital visualization.

Among the initiatives soon put forward for enhancing security for air travelers were many involving photographs: the installation of cockpit video cameras (to allow pilots to observe passengers), the increased use of CAT scan–like bomb detection devices, the upgrading of baggage X-ray systems and of airport body-scanning equipment, and stepped-up federal oversight of the screeners who would interpret the imagery. By 2004, thousands of foreign visitors to the United States would be fingerprinted and digitally photographed before being allowed entry at 115 airport terminals. For visitors from some two dozen nations (whose citizens do not need visas to cross U.S. shores), American officials would insist that their home countries adopt new passport standards that would phase in computer-friendly photo IDs (a system the United States would begin to introduce as well). To thwart visa and passport forgery, some entry points would even have special cameras that would digitally compare the facial characteristics of a passenger with corresponding data coded in his or her travel documents.

Concurrent with these initiatives, city, state, and federal government planners began to encourage research and pilot programs in the area of "biometrics," which sociologist David Lyon has defined as "the use of data extracted from the body, such as an iris scan, digital image, or fingerprint [that helps] verify identities [via] truly unique identifiers." These proposals engendered widespread community support and ample industry fervor, given the profits to be made if and when these innovations were adopted.

One program, with the ominous overtones of a Philip K. Dick science fiction tale, would identify an airline passenger by taking a digital scan of his iris, a feature more distinctive and singular than a fingerprint. Much more pervasive—and insidious—were face-recognition cameras and software programs that could scan crowds in public thoroughfares, attempt to identify individual faces, and then match their features to corresponding file photos of known criminals and suspected terrorists. Even though the concept sounded feasible, the technology was unreliable, the database of potential suspects was incomplete, the potential for "false positives" was enormous, and the chances of finding genuine terrorist "needles" among the "haystack" masses were slim to nil. Nonetheless, random-scanning programs were launched at locales like the waterside terminal in lower Manhattan where visitors would board the ferry bound for the Statue of Liberty (considered a prime terrorist target).

The notion of electronically plucking out the faces of evil from a milling crowd seemed both a misplaced allocation of resources and an altogether unrealistic reliance on technology. The plans soon began to sound like the much-touted space-based antimissile defense shield, announced with much fanfare in the 1980s: an expensive, perpetually escalating, pie-in-the-sky scheme that would enrich manufacturers for years through new technical breakthroughs and countermeasures, or through an open-ended series of test phases that would never fully achieve their promised objectives. What's more, in this time of terror, the needs of the state, in all too many instances, were beginning to co-opt the rights of the individual. And thanks to the camera, which was beginning to evolve into a visual vacuum cleaner for various branches of government and law enforcement, it wasn't much of a leap to imagine twenty-first-century Manhattan as a nascent dystopia akin to the world of hidden cameras and giant telescreens in George Orwell's *1984*.

"It was terribly dangerous," wrote Orwell of Big Brother's Thought Police, "to let your thoughts wander when you were in any public place or within range of a telescreen. The smallest thing could give you away. A nervous tic, an unconscious look of anxiety, a habit of muttering to yourself—anything that carried with it the suggestion of abnormality, of having something to hide. In any case, to wear an improper expression on your face . . . was itself a punishable offence. There was even a word for it in Newspeak: *facecrime*, it was called." How long would it be, one wondered, before every Arabic-looking man or woman out for a stroll might be automatically photographed and vetted by an ice-cold eye on a pole? How far a stretch was this digital racial profiling from Orwell's? One winces to recall *1984*'s "Two Minutes Hate" sessions in which the masses would gather under screens to hurl invective at images of "lean Jewish face[s]" or "expressionless Asiatic faces."

In time, ID pictures themselves became the subject of overly restrictive, and discriminatory, mandates. In the spring of 2005, for example, a Milwaukee-born convert to Islam—Khalid Hakim, formerly Charles

Karolik—was denied permission to renew his merchant marine license because he steadfastly refused to take off his kufi, a religious skullcap, upon posing for his requisite picture. "Yet for nearly three decades," wrote Andrea Elliott in *The New York Times*, "Mr. Hakim's cap had posed no problem with the same New York City office of the Coast Guard."

Civil libertarians objected vociferously to many of these restrictions. *Business Week* would warn in a November 2001 cover story on "Privacy in an Age of Terror":

> Since the forefathers, Americans have been committed to the idea that people have the right to control how much information about their thoughts, feelings, choices, and political beliefs is disclosed. It's a matter, first and foremost, of dignity—creating a boundary that protects people from the prying eyes of the outside world. That, in turn, helps to shield religious minorities, political fringe groups, and other outsiders from persecution by the majority.
>
> By reducing our commitment to privacy, we risk changing what it means to be Americans. To the extent that ID cards, databases, and surveillance cameras help the government track ordinary citizens, they may make people marginally less willing to exercise basic freedoms—to travel, to assemble, to speak their minds.

But as the months accumulated, so too did the rules. Over the next few years, the act of photographing without a permit near certain New York City landmarks, especially bridges and tunnels, became a criminal act—part of an attempt to dissuade those who might want to "case" targets while planning would-be attacks. Signs on bridges read: "Photography prohibited. Strictly enforced." Pictures, literally, could be the baby steps on the long road toward mass murder. (Some months after 9/11, according to photo editor Gary Fong, a woman spotted a photographer with a tripod, focusing on the Golden Gate Bridge in the distance. She quickly contacted authorities, Fong remembers, to say that an "Iraqi-looking man was shooting at the bridge with a cannon." When the police showed up, minutes later, they doubled over in laughter: here was the

San Francisco Chronicle's Carlos Gonzalez, shooting the sunset with a Canon.)

Many of these curbs on photography, like the bridge and tunnel restrictions, were prudent; several were long overdue. But the climate of suspicion that ushered in these limits also fostered some excessive corollaries. On the streets fanning out from Ground Zero, professional photographers were routinely stiff-armed by law enforcement officials, no matter how authentic their press passes or how persuasive their excuses. For weeks, police would grant few exceptions, despite the fact that would-be terror scouts—even if they had been destructively inclined—had little left to attack amid the rubble. Along with such restrictions came plans for a blanket ban against "unauthorized" photography to be instituted across the entire New York subway system.

For generations the subway had been a venue for documentary photography, explored by many of the medium's finest urban chroniclers, from Walker Evans to Bruce Davidson to Camilo José Vergara. Photo blogger and artist Eliot Shepard told Matt Haber of *The Village Voice* that he believed the main motivation behind the edict was not a deterrent to reconnaissance but an attempt "to promote a vague public perception of security." His colleague Mike Epstein concurred: "We have been conditioned to accept ever-greater incursions on our liberties in the name of security. But no one has advanced a coherent argument for how banning photography in public areas of the subway—not tracks and switchrooms mind you, but trains and platforms—has any effect whatsoever on security." Despite the Transit Authority's move to impose the ban, the decision was eventually reversed in May 2005 after protests by photographers, arguments by First Amendment lawyers, and an acknowledgment by New York City police that the directive was too broad to enforce.

Such precautions sometimes amplified rather than relieved anxieties. As late as 2005, I saw a woman in a designer business suit stop amid the lunchtime crowd in Times Square and point to two foreign-looking out-of-towners with pricey 35-mm cameras. She loudly reprimanded them, saying, "No, no," like some Homeland Security schoolmarm, despite the fact that streams of tourists filed past them with point-and-shoot cameras and mobile picture phones. Both men were taken aback; one ignored her and kept on shooting, the other made like he was packing up his gear, rather sheepishly. I could only imagine that this Donna Karan vigilante considered their skin too dark, their lenses too long, or their lingering too shadowy an intrusion on her bright and bustling workday.

Depending on one's perspective, closed-circuit TV (CCTV) cameras have become a reassuring or oppressive presence throughout the land, especially in and around Manhattan. From 1998 to 2004, according to a study by the New York Civil Liberties Union (NYCLU), the number of fixed lenses in Times Square, for example, rose from 98 to 258. (A person out for a walk in the city of London—which bristles with a half million CCTVs, the largest such concentration in the world—is likely to have his or her picture taken three hundred times.) Citizens, over time, have come to accept such spying, considering it part of the price of living in urban society, without realizing that much of the imagery originally intended to protect the domains of landlords, shopkeepers, and employers—along with their residents, customers, and employees—also becomes the province of law enforcement agencies. "The distinction between private and government surveillance blurs," NYCLU chief Donna Lieberman told Jennifer 8. Lee of *The New York Times*. "The government can get access to private videotapes that they would not be able to have taken themselves without a warrant."

Watchdog groups hold that there is little proof to suggest that a network of ubiquitous cameras makes an urban environment any safer. Britain's own National Association for the Care and Resettlement of Offenders noted in a post-9/11 report that "the extent of CCTV coverage and the government's funding of new systems has increased dramatically over the last decade with very little substantive research to suggest that CCTV works." According to *The New York Times*, "the study suggested that low-tech measures, like money for better street lighting, could have a more pronounced effect." Sociologist and surveillance expert David Lyon, of Queen's University, Ontario, has noted that in combating terror better money might be spent not on unmanned cameras but on tried and true human interdiction: the use of agents to infiltrate cells and informers to gather information, and intensive screening by trained professionals at airports and the like. (While closed-circuit monitors helped in the arrest of plotters tied to the London Transit bombings of 2005, the cameras didn't prevent the attacks, nor the deaths of fifty-two civilians, in the first place.) And so-called intelligent video systems—that "remember" and refine facial patterns of repeat passersby—are still in development and, for now, can be evaded by wearing a disguise.

"Traditionally, America has based its counterterror surveillance efforts around forensics," says entrepreneur John Levy, who assesses security companies and prototype systems in the United States and the Middle East. "That has meant a focus on video cameras, which capture things happening in the past. Instead, we need a multi-modal approach that deals with interdiction—things happening *now*. The video realm is fine for such things as setting off alarms when someone crosses into a prohibited zone. And video's recent conversion from analog to digital allows more visual data to be pushed over IP networks so that events can be monitored in real time from multiple locations." But a terrorist with a dirty bomb is best nabbed *before* he strikes, not after.

To that end, Levy insists, it is far wiser to invest in non-optical devices—as New York and other cities, along with key government agencies, have already begun to do—that peer into other regions of the electromagnetic spectrum: from gauges that check public thoroughfares for trace amounts of radiation, explosives, or chemicals to "air-sniffer" instruments that sample open areas for biological agents; from infrared monitors that can spot the heat differential between a human body and a hidden object (a gun or a bomb in a knapsack) to wireless devices that check the seals on some of the millions of cargo containers that arrive in U.S. ports each year (only 4 percent of which are currently screened).

As Lyon has pointed out, it was ironic, certainly, that a televised terrorist incident like 9/11—in which "the many watch[ed] the few"—would embolden a surveillance culture in which cameras increasingly enable "the few [to] watch the many." As with so many inventions in the computer age, humankind had created a passive-aggressive device that was at the same time morally neutral and yet metaphorically divine. The surveillance camera, like the Entity Upstairs, was always *regarding* humanity—*regardless of* humanity. Here was a self-perpetuating instrument of faux omniscience that really didn't delve below the surface, and that really didn't need us. Whether we realized it or not, it went on viewing its world, wide-eyed, on its own terms.

It sees, therefore we are. We are, therefore we are suspect.

In terms of public vigilance, paranoia, and photography, few incidents were more preposterous or tragic than one that took place on a sleepy hillside in upstate Hudson, New York, a month after the attacks. The case of the Catskill snapshot was an absurd conjunction of overcautious officials, surveillance mania, and doctrinaire strictures on picture taking.

On October 9, 2001, a man with a camera had the innocent impulse to pose for a photo in a clearing in the Catskill Mountains, the surrounding trees ablaze in their autumn finery. The photographer was no Ansel Adams, it turned out. He was a Domino Pizza deliveryman in his mid-twenties named Ansar Mahmood, who would often mail pictures of his newly adopted country to relatives in his native Pakistan. Mahmood, as luck would have it, had won a green card in 2000 as part of a highly competitive Pakistani lottery. Once Stateside, he worked twelve-to-fourteen-hour days, sending a healthy portion of his earnings back to his parents and eight siblings in and around the Punjabi town of Gujrat. His monthly remittance had begun to help three of his sisters through school. "It seemed too good to be true," he had remarked to a reporter a year before September 11.

That day in October, recalls Susan Davies, a local arts administrator, Mahmood "saw a rather beautiful view through the window of a pizza customer of his." The customer, Davies says, told him, "Hey, if you go up to the top of the hill, you can get a really nice view." Mahmood now says that he returned to the ridge later that day ("the toppest place in the Hudson area"), bringing along "a simple Kodak disposable camera. It's very beautiful, the Catskill Mountains behind the scene. It was almost sunset."

Mahmood then made an incalculably unfortunate error. He saw a nondescript building nearby—a water treatment station, in fact—and asked one of the guards there to photograph him with the foliage behind him. Little did he know that there was a reservoir beyond the tree line, or that there had been heightened security concerns about plots to poison New York's water supply. (Only three weeks before, the first of several "anthrax" letters—envelopes laced with poison, accompanied by anonymous, threatening messages alluding to terrorism—had arrived at the offices of journalists and legislators. Some two dozen people would become seriously ill, five would die of complications related to "inhalation anthrax," and thousands would be forced to take an intense antibiotic regimen.)

Several men in uniform emerged from the building, and one of them kindly obliged Mahmood. "I ask the permission," he says, " 'Can anybody take my picture?' Then I go back to the parking lot and bring my camera from the car and [one of them] say, 'Move here, move here,' and he take my picture. I said, 'Thank you.' I did not think anything was wrong."

Someone, however, considered Mahmood's request rather out of the ordinary, and alerted the authorities. By the time Mahmood returned to Domino's, after dark, two cops were there to meet him, handcuff him, and transport him to the local police station, where teams of federal investigators grilled him about his motives for photographing near the reservoir.

What brand of surveillance operative, except the most boneheaded saboteur, would actually ask a uniformed security guard to step outside and snap his picture in front of his target? "It's absurd," says Susan Davies. "It's all a question of perception on the part of the guards, along with a level of racism and nervousness. People with cameras—journalists, TV crews—get chased out of [the reservoir area, routinely]. To think that a photograph is so threatening—it's not rational. I've seen pictures of the very same place [that Mahmood photographed] *in* the newspaper. There *are* public pictures of this water treatment plant, a public place. So why couldn't *he* take them?"

In this case, he could have. And he could have gotten off, scot-free, since authorities soon realized he was harmless. But Ansar Mahmood's ordeal had only begun. Officers combing his apartment discovered paperwork indicating that he had helped an immigrant couple obtain an apartment and a car. He was rearrested, this time on felony charges. In short order, he agreed to a guilty plea, setting deportation proceedings in motion. As a result, beginning in January of 2001, he began his stay at the Buffalo Federal Detention Center, in Batavia, New York, consigned to a purgatory of legal technicalities and sheer bum luck.

Neighbors such as Davies began to gather around him, drawing attention to his plight, shuttling to Batavia for jailhouse visits. Their group, Chatham Peace Initiative, conscripted Senators Hillary Clinton and Chuck Schumer to his cause. "Mahmood wanted to be an ideal citizen," Schumer would say, "and he's the kind of person America should embrace. There is no reason he should be deported."

By the end of 2001, the Justice Department, under the auspices of the Patriot Act (adopted that October), would round up more than 1,100 detainees, most without formal charges. Over the next four years, according to the American Civil Liberties Union, immigration advocates would estimate that their ranks would swell to "between three and five thousand, almost entirely Arab, South Asian, or Muslim . . . most [of whom had] been deported or allowed to leave the country. None of the detainees [had] been charged with any terrorism-related crime."*

Mahmood's particular misfortune was partly a result of the national mood, a climate of anti-Arab sentiment that festered in various parts of the country. "In the first nine weeks following the September 11 attacks," as monitored by the American-Arab Anti-Discrimination Committee Research Institute (ADCRI), there were "over 700 violent incidents directed at Arab Americans or those perceived to be Arab Americans"—the majority of these taking place from September 11 through September 18.

* The government would also begin a widespread surveillance campaign aimed at Americans or foreigners on U.S. soil suspected of having contacts with al-Qaeda. In time, the ACLU would contend that the FBI had begun monitoring antiwar, religious, and even environmental organizations, and a *New York Times* probe would report that the National Security Agency—without receiving court warrants or typical congressional consent—had started eavesdropping on thousands of phone calls and Internet exchanges. (In this Orwellian environment, wrote *Times* columnist Maureen Dowd, it was fitting that Google, the Internet search engine that offers satellite or aerial pictures of many American homes, had deliberately obscured its online photo of the residence of Vice President Cheney, whom Dowd is fond of calling Vice or, on occasion, the Grim Peeper. "Vice," said Dowd, "has [already] turned America into a camera obscura, a dark chamber with a lens that turns things upside down.")

These instances of assault and battery, vandalism and arson (to homes, businesses, and mosques), along with five "suspected or confirmed hate-crime murders," were followed in the next few months by reports of "over 800 cases of employment discrimination against Arab Americans."

Through it all, Mahmood kept his faith. "He has a wonderful heart and reaches out to people," says Davies. "He's very spiritual. He sees this great wisdom, the creative force that drives this world, so he always defers to that. No matter how he suffers . . . he feels there's a reason for what happened to him. [He believes that] if you pay attention to that bigger picture outside of yourself, you'll see how your circumstances fit in."

Even so, his hopes were dashed that August. After thirty months behind bars, Mahmood was escorted to a plane and sent home to Pakistan and to his distraught family. "Everybody around [my parents] thinks I have done something wrong," he told reporter Rehan Ansari, a civil liberties expert. "It's not just me in jail. My parents have been in it with me."

Ansar Mahmood is now back in his village of Gujrat, operating a jitney service with his brother and pining for a return. "My dream is not completed," he insists, having had to radically recalibrate his life's expectations. "All my family [thought] things [were] going to change," he says. "My family would go to good schools and colleges. More opportunities, trying to make my living standard high." While his dream has been deferred, he is buoyed by the belief that the nation that disowned him will allow him back in. His American friends, he says, "keep sending me money and stand behind me still . . . It shows me a love, a respect that I never see in all my time in Pakistan. I'm very weak. A lot of cry. They say, 'You're not alone.' Sometimes it's more than blood relations that give you support. They treat me like my brother does. That's my luck."

On Thursday a magazine editor I know remarked on the mixture of revulsion and allure he felt in seeing it all, again and again. There was "something pornographic," he said, in images of the towers' destruction. The day before, New York *Daily News* editor in chief Ed Kosner had decided to run a picture showing a severed hand lying in the street near Ground Zero. The paper was criticized in many quarters. His rationale:

"You can't do the story without doing the story," he told *The New York Times*. "It's no time to be squeamish."

Four years later, he is still adamant that his photo selection was proper and necessary, given the paper's mandate to communicate the news without filter or bias. (Its logo, in fact, has a camera icon separating the words *Daily* and *News*.) "That was the reality," he says. "I felt that it would be dishonest, almost, not to use images like that. It was the situation that was horrible, [not] the 'graphicness' of the pictures. The hand was a perfect hand. It looked like a white glove. There were no ragged edges. There was no injury to it. What made it horrible was that this beautiful picture of a hand was actually the severed hand of some poor victim. What made the pictures compelling was the context. I didn't think these images, [including those of people] jumping out of the buildings, were in and of themselves horrific. The circumstance was."

There had been debate in the *Daily News* editorial meeting as Kosner weighed whether or not to run the images. "There were some people who thought the hand would be too upsetting to people. But I thought: It's an extraordinary story and you have to *tell* it. Stanley Walker, who was the city editor of *The* [*New York*] *Herald Tribune* in the twenties and thirties, had a number of aphorisms and axioms that he lived by and edited by. One was: better to know the truth than not. And that's always struck me as a guiding principle."

Mayor Rudolph Giuliani endorsed this sort of thinking. In HBO's September 11 documentary, *In Memoriam*, for which Giuliani served as narrator, he says: "I think we're going to have to remember September 11th in its reality . . . If you censor it too much, if you try to find too many euphemisms for what happened, then I think you rob people of the ability to actually relive it and therefore motivate them to prevent it from happening in the future."

Attitudes like Kosner's and Giuliani's were hardly universal across U.S. newsrooms. Many editors decided to forgo the harsher realities—body parts, individuals jumping from the Trade Center windows, survivors covered in blood—and, instead, favored images that were more tempered. Whether or not they fully understood it at the time, there was a degree of peer pressure involved. At countless news desks, men and women were dealing with the question: At this dark hour in American history, do we want to be that rare network or newspaper that shows this horror this way?

That attitude has persisted, to some degree. "Nine-eleven changed how newsrooms judged the use of pictures," says Naomi Halperin, director of photography of *The* (Allentown, Pa.) *Morning Call*. "Before, it was: you show the story, you'll show the truth. Now it comes down to: What can the reader bear? Now we ask, Who is going to be directly affected by publishing the picture? Are we being journalistically responsible? Is it accurate? Does the size of the headline change the message of the photo? Are we prepared for our readers' reactions? It's a huge responsibility."

In Halperin's view, it cuts both ways. Some atrocities are so horrific, even in the aftermath of September 11, that they require visualization for the magnitude of the transgression to be proven, processed, understood. Editors felt obligated, for instance, to run the Abu Ghraib prison abuse-and-torture photographs (to be discussed later), though they ran them in various ways—as thumbnail shots, with certain sections blurred, on inside pages, so as not to accost their readers. "Prior to nine-eleven," says Halperin, "a lot of papers had a dead-body policy and a disturbing-image policy or guidelines. Since then, many papers have reexamined their practices. The [Iraq War photo of] American [contractors'] bodies burning on the bridge in Fallujah wouldn't have run [if there hadn't] been a September 11th."

Several weeks after the attacks, I received a call from the culture critic and scholar Susan Sontag, whose book *On Photography* is one of the most incisive appraisals of the role of the camera in modern life. She was writing about 9/11, she said. She seemed interested in one main question during our two conversations: Why did I think the American media had been so reluctant to run these so-called graphic pictures? (By the following spring she would publish *Regarding the Pain of Others*, examining how imagery, throughout history, had influenced our understanding of conflict and violence.)

My first response was a *dayenu* defense, citing the Hebrew word for "It would have been enough" (the refrain of a popular Passover seder song). News directors and editors across the country, it seemed to me, had asked themselves: What journalistic purpose did it serve to show severed limbs and falling bodies when they already had ample images of the thing itself: the real-time nightmare of two 110-story buildings cascading down and taking with them scores of human lives with every floor? Executives at ABC News, I pointed out, had made the conscious decision *not* to broadcast sequences of bodies plummeting. NBC had reportedly aired a single body, once, then showed it no further. "The question is, 'Are we informing,' " ABC News chief David Westin commented in the *Times*, " 'or titillating and causing unnecessary grief?' " Such images, in this context, arguably would have catapulted their coverage beyond the pale.

Self-censorship is a double-edged sword. By declining to run potentially alarming sequences—videotapes presented at war crimes tribunals, for example, or images of POW abuse—news executives run the risk of watering down painful truths that demand the glare of the public eye. On the other hand, some would argue, TV viewers (unlike Internet browsers, who can simply click to another site) are a comparatively captive audience and therefore have the right to assume they will not be visually "assaulted," at least not without some verbal or visual warning. (In 2005 the BBC would formally adopt the practice of placing time delays on certain live news broadcasts in order to avoid airing, in the words of a BBC official, "really distressing, upsetting images" before stations had a chance to vet them or to put them in context.)

Many local stations, in contrast, had for years gone to great lengths to use nightly violence as a ratings enhancer. "If it bleeds, it leads" had long been the unwritten motto of countless local news operations throughout America. This overused dictum took on new meaning once it migrated overseas and then mutated, especially when al-Jazeera, the Qatar-based news network, hit its stride in 2003. When U.S. troops invaded Iraq that year, al-Jazeera consistently aired scenes of carnage with abandon, as a way of doling out what its editors considered "reality" and as a way, as critics might say, of pandering to viewers' antipathies toward American policies. Media savant Michael Wolff, writing from the Persian Gulf, would comment in *New York* magazine: "It's pretty hard to adequately describe the level of bloodiness during an average al-Jazeera newscast.

It's mesmerizing bloodiness. It's not just red but gooey. There's no cutaway. They hold the shot for the full viscous effect." The telegenic martyr had come of age.

If news programs were weeding out certain images in those first days after 9/11, I said to Sontag, then perhaps they had a motive: to scale back the peripheral ghoulishness and concentrate on the core horror. More to the point, I asked: How many news crews had actually taken what could be considered "graphic" pictures—beyond the horrific sequences of bodies in free fall? Did many with cameras manage to penetrate the security cordons? Had falling objects, including human beings, dissuaded those who might have moved closer? And once photographers arrived on site, how much carnage was there to shoot? The towers had buried almost everything in their vicinity.

"There was not a lot left of them," says *Time*'s director of photography, Michele Stephenson, solemnly, addressing the destruction's severity. "We saw pictures of the excavation where they came across body parts in the weeks following. There was [talk of a photo of] a bucket with fingers. In terms of seeing bodies: there weren't many." *Time*'s picture editor, MaryAnne Golon, says that when speaking before European audiences in the months following the attacks, she and her American peers would have to fend off charges that they had somehow softpeddled the gore. "They were sure we were censoring," she recalls. "They thought, There had to be arms and legs and hands. But there weren't. The FDNY photographer who worked with the forensics crews said the destruction was so complete there were times when you would not even see a whole telephone or a whole keypad. It had turned to dust." Kosner concurs: "There were so few pictures [of carnage]. I can't remember any that we put aside for taste reasons. I don't believe the photo editors edited them out before I saw them because there was no time to do that. [The videotaped sounds of] the thudding bodies were more horrifying than any photograph that I saw."

I told Sontag that I also attributed this general restraint to an American versus European sensibility. Separated by an ocean and a mind-set, television networks across the Atlantic would consistently air footage of "the jumpers." U.S. viewers, in contrast, would have been much less likely to have stood for coverage so potentially offensive. This was standard practice in time of conflict: American audiences, accustomed to the tastes and mores that guide commercial television and ad-supported publications (in which sponsors pay to have their products and services placed adjacent to *palatable* content), had never been an audience that could easily stomach such imagery—especially of murdered Americans—in its standard media outlets. While the United States may have experienced a rich tradition of gruff language and brutal violence dating back to the Wild West, its tastes when it came to public dissemination of images of bloodshed in the mainstream media remained positively Puritanical. Photojournalists knew the limits all too well. They continued to shoot pictures that might be deemed too graphic, and they sent them along to their editors knowing that they'd never see the light of day.

A few days after my exchanges with Sontag, however, I was nagged by her question and wondered if there wasn't a more plausible, even primal, explanation. I remembered the sentiment that had spread across the nation: many Americans felt united during those weeks after September 11. Their countrymen had been attacked, on their soil, for the first time since Pearl Harbor. As a result, amid the fury and the sorrow, the body politic seemed to exhibit an overwhelming sense of personal obligation, empathy, and civic duty. Perhaps this mood contributed to the self-censorship. Editors, to some degree, might have felt protective of *their own*, beholden to people they considered members of nothing less than an extended family—vast, grieving, and interconnected. These were not just photographs of combatants, slain during the first assault of a new sort of war. These were pictures of *their dead, their innocents*. They wanted to show them proper respect. In short, they just couldn't bear to have anyone see them this way.

By Thursday—the third day since the attacks—the calls and e-mails began to come in from my friends in Paris. (France was the birthplace of photography. Its capital, home base for many of my colleagues, remains one of the centers of the picture business.) They were reaching out to offer support and words of sympathy, realizing that Americans, especially those in New York, had yet to emerge from the shock.

And invariably, talk turned to "the jumpers." Each made the point of discussing the most grotesque aspect of the catastrophe: the sight of men and women plunging ninety or a hundred stories to their deaths.

According to a study conducted by *USA Today*, some two hundred employees, chiefly from the north tower, met their end in this manner. The paper noted that most of those who fell "came from the north tower's 101st to 105th floors, where the Cantor Fitzgerald bond firm had offices, and the 106th and 107th floors, where a conference was under way at the Windows on the World restaurant. Others leaped from the 93rd through 100th floor offices of Marsh & McLennan."

Ellen Borakove, speaking on behalf of the medical examiner's office, took issue with the term "jumpers," telling *USA Today*: "A 'jumper' is somebody who goes to the office in the morning knowing that they will commit suicide. These people were forced out by the smoke and flames or blown out." In an article for *The New York Times*, writers Jim Dwyer and Kevin Flynn made a further distinction: "Some commentators . . . remarked that those who had fallen had made one brave final decision to take control of how they would perish. Researchers say many people had no choice . . . 'This should not be really thought of as a choice,' said Louis Garcia, New York City's chief fire marshal. 'If you put people at a window and introduce that kind of heat, there's a good chance most people would feel compelled to jump.' "

The journalists would later track down Richard Smiouskas, a Fire Department lieutenant and photographer who took a camera with a long lens to the roof of a nearby building that day. What he witnessed, according to Dwyer and Flynn in their book *102 Minutes*, was what may have been a futile jockeying for position at many of the upper stories' ledges, as tenants, four and five at a time, "crowded into the same narrow window frame. [One] man pitched forward, nudged, it seemed to Smiouskas, by others crowding for a mouthful of air. As the desperation rose, it was impossible not to remember that a drowning person will push a lifeguard under water if it means one more gulp of air."

I soon realized why my Paris friends had seemed consumed with the subject. On French television during those first forty-eight hours, in contrast to the more sanitized Stateside coverage, videotaped scenes of plummeting people had been shown "repeatedly, constantly," one of them told me. In the tapes, men and women issued from the building alone, or in succession, one after another. Some tumbled. Some held hands, jumping in pairs, or three and four at a time.

Americans, in contrast, had watched fireballs, cyclones of debris, the valiant rescuers, but had been largely left to imagine the massacres at a remove—*inside* planes, *within* buildings, *hidden* beneath giant balls of dust and smoke, always beyond the range of the eye and the camera. Footage of the jumpers had isolated the instant just before certain death. And it brought the viewer of that instant, like the subject in the videos and photographs, to the very ledge of terror itself. Tom Flynn, a producer for CBS News at the time, was grateful that executives at his network decided not to air some of the scenes he had witnessed that day, even though he had almost died trying to get his partner's tape back to the broadcast center. "What's to be gained by showing these people killing themselves *at that moment*?" he asks, four years after that morning. "Either it becomes overly painful, gratuitously so—and you feel helpless watching it, or it becomes too ordinary. And a death like this shouldn't be [made into something] common. Those people did nothing wrong and they had to suffer so. I don't think people should have to relive that by seeing it."

The experience of watching a video of a man or woman about to die by force of gravity is far more mortifying than the experience of looking at a still image of a particular instant in that descent. A photograph can leave the viewer open to speculation. (She looks peaceful . . . At least he made a calculated choice . . .) A photograph can be consumed at one's own pace, then accepted or rejected or rationalized on one's own terms, largely because the experience has been decontextualized: terror, compartmentalized into pixels.

The corresponding ten-second video, on the other hand, is so vividly tendered in real time and space as to be practically insufferable. A viewer feels sickened while watching. The questions hurtle by at an unprocessable pace: Did she hesitate or not before she jumped? Are her eyes open or closed? What was she thinking? Was she praying? How could she have fallen so *quickly*? What would the falling, then the landing, *feel* like? "I just remember looking up," said firefighter Joe Cassalliggi, who worked out of the station closest to the Trade Center, "and thinking, How bad is it up there that the *better* option is to jump?" The videos allow the viewer to witness the horror whole.

Circumstances, of course, often determine whether a film clip or a photo best captures the emotional resonance of a historic moment. "In many cases," notes former *Life* magazine picture editor John Loengard, "the still is more moving than the moving picture. Eddie Adams's [1968] shot of a South Vietnamese officer executing a Viet Cong suspect with his revolver in the street is more 'moving' than the [television] image of the same moment. It's over so quickly you don't see it on film. The film taken while Joe Rosenthal took his [famous World War II flag-raising] shot [on] Iwo Jima has none of the emotional quality that the still photograph does. The film passes before the eye. [And yet] in China's [1989] Tiananmen Square confrontation between the protester and the tank, the television is riveting: he moves a little bit, the tank moves a little bit. They have a dance. That's what's extraordinary. The still photograph of the same situation is very dull.

"In [Evans Fairbanks's] video footage after the first tower's collapse," Loengard continues, "I remember being struck by papers simply floating in the air, back and forth, at random. They were so significant—papers from desks—and they wouldn't be floating there except for the destruction of those desks and the lives of the people at those desks. The movie was like a Chinese scroll unwinding. You knew what the event was, you knew inevitably what was going to happen, and you watched, in silence, to the end." But the corresponding photographs were just as breathtaking and sometimes "monumental," Loengard says. "The film—of the first and second planes going in, the buildings burning and collapsing—[is] equally as astonishing as the stills."

Few Americans were able to see many photographs *or* film clips of men and women in free fall, since neither were much in evidence in the American media after the week of September 11. That absence was readily apparent in the case of a picture that has come to be known as *The Falling Man*, the most iconic of such images *(Image 22)*.

Taken by veteran Associated Press photographer Richard Drew, the frame shows what appears to be a dark-skinned individual in a light jacket and black pants falling headfirst to his death, having leaped or been forced out of a window on one of the higher floors of the north tower. In the picture, the man's body, in upended profile, is positioned precisely at the juncture where the edge of one tower's facade eclipses the other's. His posture—eyes front, legs almost in a cyclist's mode, body erect and aligned with the buildings' striped cladding—seems to impart upon him a kind of "terrifying dignity," as the literary and culture critic Leon Wieseltier observed in *The New Republic*. "His physical integrity is extraordinary. He is standing in the world but the world is upside-down. He does not appear to be wounded. He seems composed, a stoic in the air . . . His hands are smartly at his side, his legs look as if they are marching . . . Turn this picture of the upside-down world upside-down, and . . . he looks like nothing so much as a soldier." Wieseltier even posits a degree of spiritual salvation inherent in the image. "When we are worthy," he wrote, "we ascend [to heaven]; when we are unworthy, we descend." By virtue of the Falling Man's inversion, Wieseltier implies, he rebukes gravity. By inference, the man's bearing and his being, like the "extravagantly . . . vertical" towers, are pointed heavenward.

Drew, it turns out, took a dozen shots of the man's descent—legs splayed, arms spread, jacket flapping. Only one asserts this hint of poise in the clutches of death. The man may actually have bequeathed a kind of nobility at this split second in his descent. And his salvation may indeed have been imminent all along. But any dignity derived from being forced to one's death in this way seems to be entirely a function of the viewer's mind-set—and Drew's eye as a photographer. He chose that single frame, he has said, "because of its verticality and symmetry . . . That picture just jumped off the [computer] screen."

The image is "the most famous picture nobody's ever seen," says Drew, regretfully, with the benefit of four years of hindsight. "We don't have any problem looking at Eddie Adams's photo of the police chief in Saigon shooting the victim or Nik Ut's [1972] picture of the [Vietnamese] girl after being napalmed, running down the road. They're powerful photographs and they keep getting shown over and over again. [But] my picture was either not used [by newspapers the week of September 11] or was used once and never used again." In fact, while the shot appeared in scores of papers on September 12, and was then republished in follow-up stories and year-end commemorative editions (because of its graphic power and because it seemed *less* exploitative than photos that showed individuals plummeting in groups or in contortions), it was generally kept out of circulation, as if by an unspoken compact among editors, art directors, and picture editors.

For its September 12 edition, *The Morning Call* of Allentown, Pennsylvania, decided to run Drew's shot on page A-28, the full length and breadth of a spread—"tip to stern on the broadsheet," in the words of the paper's photo editor, Naomi Halperin. David Erdman, the *Call*'s managing editor, had chosen the image because he considered it the first he had come across in his 9/11 picture search that, in Erdman's words, "conveyed what we felt we needed to do: show the loss of humanity." Halperin would note that prior to seeing Drew's image, "every photo was about twisted metal and broken buildings and people running . . . Without the photo, you cannot say visually that this [was an event entailing] a horrific loss of life. To hide that photo would be to hide that truth." On Wednesday, Halperin would recall in an e-mail, "I got in at 9 a.m., and had five v.m. [voicemail] message[s]. Four didn't leave numbers or names. They just screamed. For a while."

Drew, a Pulitzer Prize–winning news photographer, has never shied away from facing history from the front lines. At twenty-one he had stood so close to Robert F. Kennedy in the kitchen of the Ambassador Hotel in Los Angeles that when Kennedy was felled by an assassin's bullets, and five others were wounded, Drew's jacket was stained with blood. The pictures he took that day in 1968, he would write in a *Los Angeles Times* opinion column, were "shot through my tears. [It] still distresses me after 35 years. But nobody refused to print them, as they did the 9/11 photo. Nobody looked away."

Part of the reason the news media could shoulder such imagery back then was that the networks and the printed press viewed their institutions as beholden to the public interest: Kennedy's killing, after his brother John's and Martin Luther King, Jr.'s, was the third such act in five years. The truth, however indelicate, *had* to be shown, especially in times of national emergency. Nowadays, however, many of those same news organizations tend to play it safe, having been subsumed by media conglomerates that give less credence to exposing harsh realities than to turning a profit, entertaining mass audiences, and satisfying skittish advertisers.

Drew has noted that on September 11, as he stood at West and Vesey Streets, he mistook a series of loud smacks as "the sound of concrete debris striking the ground. But I was wrong. It was the sound of human beings hitting the pavement." He shot a dozen frames of the Falling Man through a 200-mm lens, along with sequences of about a dozen others who met a similar end. Then he kept on clicking his shutter as the north tower rained down upon him. (Drew's life was spared by the quick thinking of an EMT worker, who pulled him to safety.)

The photograph took on a dark power all its own, causing real-world aftershocks in the lives of those who, already reeling from their loss, saw in the Falling Man their own son or husband or brother or father. They were now doubly stricken—with new doubt, new denial, and with the even more hideous prospect that their relative—there, for all to see—had had to endure even this too.

Tom Junod would write the definitive article about Drew's picture, for *Esquire* magazine in 2003. (It would later inspire a documentary film.) He had examined Drew's outtakes and determined that the man in the picture was wearing an orange T-shirt under his white jacket. Junod approached the relatives of several people who might have been the man depicted. One family, that of Norberto Hernandez, a Windows on the World pastry chef from Queens, had for a time been divided into two camps by the photo, writes Junod: "Those who *knew*, right away, that the picture was not Norberto [and] those who [had] pondered the possibility." When Junod presented the evidence, Hernandez's wife, Eulogia, was vindicated. Not only had she dressed Norberto that morning, but her husband did not even *own* an orange shirt. The mother of another tower worker claimed the Falling Man was not her son because he had been "wearing a dark shirt and khaki pants." Then Junod located the brother and sister of a Windows worker whose physical description fit that of the man in Drew's shot. Moreover, they told Junod, their loved one habitually wore an orange T-shirt.

All the same, his family remained uncertain. There was no hard and fast proof that he was or wasn't the victim. The only certainty, Junod noted, was America's aversion to a picture that "went all around the world, and then disappeared, as if we willed it away." Junod writes:

> In the most photographed and videotaped day in the history of the world, the images of people jumping were the only images that became, by consensus, taboo—the only images from which Americans were proud to avert their eyes. All over the world, people saw the human stream debouch from the top of the North Tower, but here in the United States, we saw these images only until the networks decided not to allow such a harrowing view. [T]he jumpers—and their images—were relegated to the Internet underbelly, where they became the provenance of the shock sites . . . where it is impossible to look at them without attendant feelings of shame and guilt. [It was] as though the jumpers' experience, instead of being central to the horror, was tangential to it, a sideshow best forgotten.

Why did so many editors, who chose not to run images like Drew's, believe their readers would be repulsed—and repulsed on so many levels?

First, as Junod points out, visualizations of violent death—mass murder, random homicide, acts of torture—are the stuff of snuff films, torture videos, and sado-porn, in which the victims are decidedly nonfictional. (Those who did jump *had* been tortured: forced, by suicide hijackers, to choose between murder by fire and suicide by fatal descent.) The prurience inherent in witnessing such scenes is considered shameful in civilized societies. By not turning away, the viewer is thought to be "rubbernecking," as would a gaper at an auto accident—with the newspaper, magazine, Web site, or TV show serving as facilitator.

Second, news media decision makers felt loath to petrify. Jumping or falling from such a height is an incomparably terrifying act, laden with the prospect of certain, immediate death. That prospect was complicated by further terrors: the choice of whether or not to leap, the vertigo, the overlapping fears of the experience of free fall's lag time, the anticipated pain of the violent impact, and confrontation with the end just beyond.

Another factor was the issue of disrespect. In a conflict waged against noncombatants, one designed to inflict "anonymous" casualties, there was an impulse to censor the few faces of those who were not only caught in the act of dying but also recognizable. "One argument for censorship was humanitarian," historian Francis G. Couvares wrote about Drew's image. "The victim's loved ones would suffer horribly if they were forced to see, over and again, the sight of a father or son or wife or grandchild flailing desperately against the inevitable. The other argument was communal, protective of something far more elusive—culture, values, common decency."

Also entering the equation were the religious and social stigmas of suicide, which doubtless preyed on the minds of some of those who committed the act. "On the Internet," said the daughter of one man later proven *not* to have been the Falling Man, "they said my father was going to hell because he jumped." Some believed that their relatives would surely have proven more noble or brave had they chosen to remain in terror's trenches, so to speak (the act of jumping amounting to a betrayal, an outright choice of public self-annihilation that would not only bring *more* pain upon one's survivors, but possibly damnation).

Drew's photograph, to some, was even considered repulsive as a photograph. Many felt queasy about its picture-perfect artfulness. The composition was, well, too composed. Here was Life's Last Moment, made graphic, even operatic, as if the Falling Man had been projected onto a striated theater curtain. The buildings were a backdrop for The Fall. The End.

But most of all, as Drew puts it, *The Falling Man* was shunned because the viewer saw himself too clearly in the frame: a man who had been propelled to his death for having chosen to go to work that morning in an American office building. "I think that we just identify too much with this," says Drew. "Think about how many times you've seen a picture of someone who might have been attempting suicide, jumping from the

Brooklyn Bridge or some building. We have more curiosity than aversion. You know how you can't turn your face away from a car wreck? Well, we turn our face away from this. And the reason is because of the enormity of this act . . . This was the first time we've had any kind of an attack of this enormity on *our* soil. They were *more innocent* victims [than others photographed committing suicide]. They were forced to make choices.

"We might have to face that similar situation some time." Drew points out. "It could be us. My pure speculation is: It's hard for people to look at because they're thinking about what comes at the end of that, when he hits the ground, and that could be them . . . He is you and me."

Over time, raw imagery would lead to raw exploitation. The *New York Post* would register its own revulsion by running a front-page headline three weeks after 9/11: HOW SLEAZY SELLERS RAKE IN BIG BUCKS ON THE CITY'S SUFFERING. Its reporting team encountered vendors and photo-shop owners hawking "towers aflame" snaps for three dollars a print; two for five dollars. Within weeks, little flip-books of panoramas and shock shots, pirated from magazines, would go for ten dollars in Times Square and near Ground Zero.

Inevitably, such pictures, *qua* pictures, can do their share of harm. To those in mourning or attempting to work through their own trauma, the very act of glimpsing the collapse or the carnage can set them back. The American Red Cross would run full-page public service ads shortly after the attacks offering "helpful tips in dealing with the extreme mental and emotional stress caused by" September 11. The first item on the Red Cross checklist: "Avoid viewing repeated media coverage of the event."

"The value of photographs is incalculable [in the healing process]," says attorney Scott Gutterson. He concedes that there is virtue in the generosity of photojournalists and gallery owners who have donated the proceeds from their photo sales to assist those whose lives, families, or businesses were devastated by the terrorist acts. But since September 11, Gutterson has tended to avoid news pictures of the event. "I don't find any relief in looking. There are essay-books in bookstores, I don't pick them up. There's no comfort in seeing the towers hit, falling, knowing that I knew so many. And so many, thank God, that made it out. I cannot look one other time," he said—referring to photographer Stan Honda's much-published shot with a yellowish hue—"at that beautiful black woman covered in dust."

Indeed, September 11 coverage enveloped print publications. *The Wall Street Journal* noted that even small-circulation trade magazines—*Farm Journal*, *Ski Area Management*, and *Cheese Market News* among them—felt obliged to run 9/11-related features or special issues.

Given time, however, the most distinguished and lasting visual legacy of the events, beyond the countless videotapes made that day, may very well be the shelves of photographic books devoted to the attacks and their aftermath.

On Thursday, a patchwork of transparencies was laid out on a light table at the New York offices of Magnum Photos. Nearby were piles of contact sheets and work prints. Photographer Thomas Hoepker looked at the batch and was bowled over: Gilles Peress's shot of a soul-shaken fireman on his knees, flames roaring at his back; Susan Meiselas's image of a soot-covered sculpture—a businessman and his laptop—forlorn amid the refuse; and on and on. Hoepker realized that the agency had chronicled the September 11 attacks with enough variety and compassion to make a book of enormous power, if only they could crash-close it and get it to a publisher in days, not weeks. Hoepker and Magnum did just that. "Almost everybody in the office had a part in [creating] it," says Nathan Benn, the agency's New York director at the time. "[Even] photo interns took pictures on their own initiative," which became part of the tome. Indeed, at my family's annual Thanksgiving gathering, ten weeks after the attacks, guests spent much of the evening huddled over Magnum's compendium *New York, September 11*, a coffee-table book of the most distressing sort.

Out on the light table that first Thursday was one of Hoepker's 9/11 pictures that he had hesitated over, then cast aside. "It didn't live up to the drama of the other shots," he recalls. "It was too subtle for the news moment. At the time, you jumped to the obvious [photographs]." The image showed a disorientingly tranquil and schizophrenic scene: a handful of young people in Williamsburg, Brooklyn, as if on a lunch break or taking a breather from a bike ride. They seem to talk idly, turning their backs on the terror of a smoke-shrouded Manhattan *(Image 23)*.

"It's a kind of troubling picture," Hoepker says. "The sun was shining. They were totally relaxed like any normal afternoon. They were just chatting away. It's possible they lost people and cared, but they were not stirred by it."

It took Hoepker four years before he felt inclined to publish the shot widely. In effect, he had self-censored it. The picture seemed to capture and *invite* complacency. It lacked any sense of outrage, a response Hoepker believed the background ought to have elicited from any civilized person seated in the foreground. It didn't meet any of our standard expectations of what a September 11 photograph *should* look like. "The idyllic quality turned me off," he says. "It was too pretty. Maybe we didn't need to see that, then. Maybe I wasn't sure it would stir the wrong emotions [in the viewer].

"Over time, with perspective, it grew in importance. It's a very contemporary picture: the bright colors are up front [but] it has that touch of neutrality, a coolness, a bit of a distance to suffering and not trusting of emotions." Despite its postmodern cast, it reminded Hoepker of Pieter Bruegel's sixteenth-century painting *Landscape with the Fall of Icarus*, in which the subjects seem willfully immune to the epic calamity in their midst. Bruegel's work, says Hoepker, shows "a beautiful Flemish landscape and way in the sky this birdlike figure, Icarus, having flown too close to the Sun, [has] caught fire and is crashing down. [Similarly,] this is bucolic and in the background something [awful] is happening. I can only speculate [but they] didn't seem to care. It took a while for the news to sink in. It took a while to know how to react."

While certain moments like these were kept out of the image supply, a tide of others swept in. Photo books like Magnum's soon proliferated. *Life*'s editors published *One Nation: America Remembers September 11, 2001*, which remained on the *New York Times* bestseller list for weeks. In October, the FDNY put out *Brotherhood*, billed as a "pictoral tribute." Soon came *NewYorkSeptemberElevenTwoThousandOne* and *The September 11 Photo Project* and others, many with almost funereal all-black, all-type covers. By the following September, photographic volumes appeared by the dozen. Some bore respectful, poetic titles: *Empty Sky, Endure, As the Towers Fell, And No Bird Sang, Stepping Through the Ashes, United We Care, In the Line of Duty, Lamentation 9/11*. One was simply called *11*, a pair of ones eloquently signifying both the day and the towers. Some were slender, some thick as bricks, such as the monumental companion volume to the "here is new york" exhibition (864 pages in length)—which has become, without question, the definitive illustrated book dedicated to the subject.

Filmmakers, even more aggressively than publishers, pushed their images out into the world. Many directors, producers, and videographers had become discouraged by the political prudence, stridency, or hegemony of traditional television networks. So, in the first year or two after 9/11, they filled screening rooms, film festivals, and Web sites with documentaries, testimonies, and artistic statements, some of which would make their way onto cable (HBO, Discovery) or public TV (WNET's *Reel New York*).

There was *Underground Zero*, a medley of thirty-one short films "conceived as a means of counteracting the silencing of voices that was occurring in the mainstream media." There was *11′09″01*—eleven eleven-minute offerings from Claude Lelouch, Sean Penn, and directors in countries such as Iran and Burkina Faso. There was *7 Days in September*, which showcased the work of twenty-seven filmmakers, many of whom had recorded firsthand footage on 9/11. There were at least a dozen short documentaries about firefighters, and scores of other films, videos, and Web projects, including *Site, WTC Uncut, WTC: The First 24 Hours, Homeland Insecurity, First Person 911, 9 Views: 9/11, 9.11 Moments, Morning: September 11, Artist Response to 9.11, Telling Nicholas, Turning Tragedy into War, Voices for Peace, America Rebuilds, Aftermath*, and Invisibleinhabitants.com, a study of ghosts and the Trade Towers, begun a full year before the attacks.

Hollywood dramatizations of 9/11, such as Paul Greengrass's *United 93* and Oliver Stone's *World Trade Center*, would take five years to reach theaters. Early on, audiences were willing to accept documentaries, believing that the genre's more literal treatment of the tragedy would be inherently more faithful to the facts and, in turn, the memory of the departed. Acceptance of docudrama, with its overlay of an invented story line and what Greengrass has referred to as a "believable truth," became emotionally bearable or credible only with the passage of time.

Among the most compelling filmed documents connected to the events was *September 10 2001, Uno Nunca Muere La Víspera*, an elegy to the artist Michael Richards, who died in Tower One. Filmmaker Monika Bravo had shared a large studio space with Richards and a dozen other artists on the ninety-second floor of the building. On September 10, she spent more than six hours making time-lapse exposures of the boats below, the bridges, and an advancing storm that sent lightning through the night sky, illuminating Tower Two. Around midnight, Bravo gathered her tapes and bid Richards "Good night" as he watched the end of the Giants-Broncos game on *Monday Night Football*; he had chosen to remain there through morning. Her footage, shown in small venues and on the Internet, would be the last precious glimpse of how those who lived and worked and dreamed in the towers had regarded the city below them.

Newsstands stocked special, picture-rich editions of *Time* and *Newsweek* on September 13, sent to the printer within thirty-six hours of the attacks. The cover of each showed the same moment, shot from different perspectives: the south tower's upper floors crowned in an enormous fireball of orange, white, and black, the jet and its fuel having ignited upon impact like a detonated bomb.

Newsweek's headline read: EXTRA EDITION: AMERICA UNDER ATTACK. *Time*, its cover designed with a thin black frame (instead of the traditional *Time* red), preferred a more muted tone. The magazine dispensed with a headline and, instead, printed a caption-style phrase, in small type, at the bottom of the cover: SEPTEMBER 11, 2001 *(Figure B)*. The picture said it all. This was the raging apex of 9/11, and photographs of that moment became trademarks of the fury of the attacks, displayed in the media with such frequency that they would haunt victims' families for years.

The "explosion" shot, in time, became a convenient vehicle for conveying "Terror" or "The Horrors of 9/11"—the twin-towers-as-Roman-candle logo. TV news directors looking for a graphic shorthand for their upcoming September 11 stories would sometimes revert to the video footage or a frame from that sequence—weeks, months, sometimes a year or two later—without apparent concern for how such usage might trivialize the event. On September 12, in a similar vein, the *San Francisco Chronicle* used a tiny shot of the second plane sweeping in for the kill as part of a black banner—a photo decal leading into the phrase AMERICA UNDER ATTACK—that fit snugly above the paper's name. The edifice-in-flames and the streaking plane were being treated as instantly recognizable insignias. This compulsion to package an event by coupling a three-word theme with an eye-catching visual had its antecedents in product branding, campaign sloganeering, and the on-screen graphics of TV news and sports broadcasts.

On Thursday, though, none of this had yet come into play. The cover shots on *Time* and *Newsweek* were precisely what the historic moment required. The worst *had* happened, and had to be writ large for all to see, absorb, and comprehend.

Time's image was the work of Lyle Owerko, a commercial photographer who had brought a 400-mm zoom lens to the base of the towers. Owerko managed to take such detailed shots of the fires' progress—including a bright, circular burst of concentrated white light that shone briefly from the corner of the south tower—that for nearly a year afterward structural engineers and other experts referred to his pictures to understand precisely why the buildings had been compromised. "We had basically 8,000 photos and [Owerko's work] was one part of the puzzle," says William Pitts of the Building and Fire Research Laboratory of the National Institute of Standards and Technology. Owerko's pictures, says Pitts, "certainly were among the highest [resolution]."

The week before the attacks, Owerko had returned to New York from Tanzania, where he had been shooting documentary images and portraits of Masai tribesmen. Upon walking into his apartment on Franklin and Broadway, he had stowed his trusty Canon EOS 3 (with a long lens attached) and a Fuji 645zi medium-format camera in the front foyer. They remained there until the following Tuesday.

Upon hearing the screech of a jet engine, followed by an explosion, Owerko raced down the stairs, picked up his gear, and "sprinted down Broadway," he would recall in an e-mail, "making a sharp right at Chambers Street. Life was still oddly normal. People stood buying bagels and coffee [from] corner street vendors. Others strolled casually."

Turning a corner, he saw "the now-damaged W.T.C. for the first time. The complex stood tall and defiant except for the north tower, which was smeared with a gash of twisted metal. A trail of smoke emanated from what now had become a colossal smokestack." He ran closer and, because he had a long lens, decided to concentrate on the buildings instead of the onlookers. Suddenly, he says, the crowd around him emitted "a collective, piercing gasp. I looked up to see an object descending from the tower. I recognized it to be a person and stood frozen as the body flipped and turned in a slow, tragic ballet, down to the courtyard. People screamed and cried. I watched in shock as another human shape began falling to earth.

"Gravity dictates that objects drop to earth at 32-feet-per-second-squared," he says. "The towers were over 1,000 feet tall. Doing the math, you can sense how long a falling person's descent resonated with the observers below.* The next person who jumped I viewed through my fully-extended lens. I clicked away . . . with my heart shuddering as each human shape flailed against the modern steel-and-glass facade. I wasn't photographing death, it seemed to me. I felt, instead, that I was preserving the last moment of these individuals' conscious existence."

Soon, says Owerko, "I watched as a jet began a deliberate arc toward the south tower, at full throttle, though I seemed to be perceiving the twisting flight path in slow motion. I put my medium format camera up to my face as the plane hit the building with an incomparably concussive explosion. I clicked the shutter"—f8 at a surprisingly steady 1/250 of a

* Those who leaped or fell from the highest floors struck the ground in about ten seconds.

second—"producing the frame that would appear on the cover of *Time*. Heat from the explosion reached down with invisible fingers. Debris came an instant later and started raining around us. My ears were filled with the staccato of metal objects—plane parts and building parts—hitting the pavement. People were lying on the street screaming and crying. I seemed to be in the middle of a pack of bodies: observers on the street who had stumbled, fallen, and were [wedged] against one another in a panic to escape the falling debris. Clothes, purses, and shoes were scattered all over."

After eluding a policeman intent on confiscating his film, Owerko says he encountered a stranger "in a pink shirt [who] started small-talking with me. He said, 'This is jihad, you know?' as he looked me in the eyes. We stood in an almost absurd interlude, discussing our experiences in Africa." Owerko dropped off his film with his photo agency, Gamma, and was later told he might have a chance for a cover for one of the newsmagazines.

Over in Brooklyn, photographer Robert Clark snapped into action as well. Clark had been accustomed to landing covers. By his own count, he had shot seven *National Geographic* covers over the course of eighteen assignments in forty countries.* Within twenty-four hours, Clark, like Owerko, would have every reason to believe that he too had a shot at the cover of *Time*.

On the eleventh, Clark had been sitting in his apartment in the Williamsburg section of Brooklyn. His bags were packed with fifty rolls of Velvia 100 for a *National Geographic* assignment in Thailand—on dinosaur behavior—scheduled for later that week. "I was going to shoot elephants running," he says, noting that news "isn't my thing. I do sports, portraits, cultural stories, science." Working at his computer that morning, he had his back to the window, which looked out on the East River and the World Trade Center. His girlfriend (now his wife), Lai Ling Jew, a producer for NBC's *Dateline*, was in her apartment near Washington Square Park in Manhattan. She called him on the phone and said, simply, "Turn around."

* The covers Owerko had landed, in contrast, were mainly for music-industry trade magazines.

Ascending to his roof with a Canon EOS 1V and the equivalent of a 280-mm zoom, he began firing away. "I'm up there shooting," he says, "the smoke was heading downtown. And then the second plane came in. I didn't see it circle. Oddly enough, being a child of the '70s, I thought, Omigod, the Soviet Union—because [the angle and light made it look] like a *black* plane screaming in. My second thought was, This means Bush gets anything he wants." Clark shot the second attack in what turned out to be harrowing, flip-book fashion—all from the same vantage: the approach, the wing tilt before impact, the concussion, the explosion frozen in the sky like a gourd of glowing lava. After shooting four more rolls, he repaired to his apartment and called Alice Gabriner, a *Time* picture editor he knew, and said, "I got it. It looks like a postcard."

Even on September 11 Clark felt, as many journalists, politicians, and historians did, that the event signaled a sea change in American attitudes. "In regions of conflict all around the world, people had become accustomed to being bombed," says Clark. "They'd been fearful before, seeing planes or missiles in their skies. But for Americans, [9/11] was, 'Welcome to the rest of the world.' " (Clark's hunch has since been validated: his sequence has frequently been sold to publishers of history books. And it was with a sense of history, and journalistic pride, that he had heard through the grapevine that one of his images might well grace the front of *Time*.)

On Thursday morning Clark was at a US Color Lab on the West Side. Lyle Owerko, it so happens, was headed to a nearby photo lab on the same block, but stopped at a newsstand when he saw huge stacks of newly delivered *Time* magazines. "Framed in a black border was what appeared to be my picture on the cover," he says. "I picked it up to check the credit line. It was. Looking at the cover, I could hear the sounds beyond the frame, and smell the carnage in my nostrils, played back in real time."

With his friend Trevor Schoenfeld, a Toronto ad agency copywriter, Owerko started over toward his lab to drop off a new batch of film. As they walked along, flipping through the magazine, "a man runs out of a photo-lab doorway," says Owerko, "and asks me where I got the copy. He begins telling me his pictures are in the issue, grabbing the magazine from my hands. Landing on a double-page spread, he announces that these are his images. We see the four-shot sequence of the second plane hitting the south tower. We stand there uneasily with this stranger. Then my friend reaches over and plucks the issue from his hands. He leans forward and says, 'See this guy?'—pointing to me—'He shot this image'—pointing to the cover. Robert [Clark] looks at me and says, 'Ahh, you're the one who beat me out of the cover.' "

Clark now says that he recalls their conversation, "but quite a bit differently. I actually remember congratulating him on it . . . It was really an emotionally weird time. I didn't sleep much for weeks after that. That night, I'd [ridden] my bicycle up to Rockefeller Center and picked up [Lai Ling] and she rode home on my handlebars down Fifth Avenue and it was completely deserted. They wouldn't let cars into the city . . . I just remember *everything* at that point being kind of weird and awkward."

Clark insists that the last thing he wanted to do was gloat about or benefit from human tragedy. He says that the day before, in *Time*'s offices, a fellow photographer had congratulated him on his sequence; he didn't "take that [compliment] as dancing on other people's graves." Instead, he says, he understood that photojournalists make a "living off of these kinds of pictures, so you can't feel bad about it. Nurses nurse and reporters report. I started shooting pictures when I was fourteen years old in western Kansas. I'd rather the picture that I be remembered for be something along the lines of a [Margaret Bourke-White] Gandhi-at-the-spinning-wheel-type photo, as opposed to something like this.

"My reaction wasn't about competition," he says of his encounter with Owerko. "I was shocked that somebody was that close to it. I hadn't seen any of that. It's phenomenal. It's kind of an architectural beauty shot and then this news event happens in the middle of that. [I realized the event] was so well covered in so many ways that it was kind of stunning to see this split-second timing that everybody had on this."

Owerko, for his part, recalls being dumbfounded upon running into this stranger in the street: another person who had shot the same instant for the same issue of *Time*. "There is a moment of uncomfortable silence," he says. "I haven't slept in two nights from all of the adrenaline and painful imagery circulating through my body and my brain. I had plane and building parts rain down on me, from the sky, from the very plane he photographed . . . and this guy tells me I beat him for the cover? It makes no sense to me. I'd been drawn to photography to reveal, not to compete. I am torn, sad, and broken-hearted over all the death and destruction I've seen. I don't know how to respond."

"This came out of nowhere," recalls Schoenfeld, who was walking with Owerko at the time. "I didn't know this guy from Adam. How it became a scene of bragging rights—after one of the most horrific events in American history—was strange . . . A guy comes by and takes [the magazine] out of [our] hands to flip through it. 'Sorry guy. Let's figure this out. It's not about you.' "

"We bid one another goodbye," says Owerko, "and my friend and I walk[ed] away, heading toward Sixth Avenue."

The photo-laden edition of *Newsweek* also came out on Thursday, the magazine's white logo set in a band of black. Soon after it appeared, Cecilia Lillo's phone began to ring. Had she seen page 16?

There, standing just behind a woman covered in blood, was Cecilia's husband, Carlos, in an orange EMS helmet.

There was no mistaking Carlos Lillo. The man in the picture, slightly hunched over, was lugging a blue medical bag through the crowd. He wore Carlos's black watch. He had Carlos's walkie-talkie—radio number 170 clearly visible. And at his hip dangled Carlos's key chain, inset with a Puerto Rican flag.

It had been pictures, in fact, that had brought the couple together. Cecilia had become reacquainted with Carlos, an upperclassman from her high school, after she happened across his photograph. The pair reconnected, then dated, marrying in April 2001. That fall, they had hoped to start a family.

But all that changed on Tuesday. That morning, after the first plane hit, Cecilia left her Port Authority office, exiting the sixty-fourth floor of Tower One. As she was making her way down, Carlos, a Queens-based paramedic for the FDNY, was en route toward the scene. Carlos was presumed to have been lost in the collapse of Tower Two.

Three days later, *Newsweek* arrived. "While this has been an agonizing circumstance," says Richard Fox, of the EMS Command Memorial Foundation, "Carlos's widow has been able to gain some sense of abstract comfort. When you lose the love of one's life, you want to know every last second. A picture of a loved one showing trained professionalism in a time of grave danger verifies your instincts: I know my husband was there, doing what he does best."

For Fox, photographs have played another pivotal role: as evidence for determining who should receive survivor benefits. By relying on dozens of images collected by *Post* photographer and gallery curator Bolivar Arellano, Fox has identified EMS personnel in their final moments. "One of the reasons I've been able to assist survivors in obtaining benefits," he explains, "is by virtue of the photographs. There are charities out there that require 'due diligence.' Through pictures, I've been able to document the last activities of people operating in an EMS capacity.

"There was one case," he says, "of an emergency medical technician. I was able to locate him in [a] picture. By being able to trace his heroism, right there on film, I was able to get significant amounts [for] his family. A picture, in this instance, was worth thousands of dollars. In another case, there's a ten-year-old boy who's too young now. We've put aside a photo album for him, and years from now, when he's matured, he'll be able to see what his father did and understand it, and know that his father didn't die in vain."

Especially riveting among the many images in *Time*'s special issue were those taken by James Nachtwey, the most celebrated war photographer of his age, who has covered more conflicts more memorably than any photojournalist alive. Nachtwey, just the week before, had formally announced his affiliation with a new photo agency, called VII (pronounced "Seven").

First, some background. The week of September 4, many of the world's top photographers and picture editors had convened at Visa pour l'Image, the international conclave for photojournalists, held each summer in Perpignan, France. On the minds of many of those gathered was a perceived malaise in the industry. The previous few years had seen unprecedented consolidation in the news-and-feature side of the editorial photography business, and a mood of gloom had descended upon the photo community. Photojournalism seemed to be on the wane; celebrity magazines were ascendant. Many publications seemed to be sacrificing experience for expedience. And picture-industry titans such as Mark Getty (owner of Getty Images) and Bill Gates (who founded Getty's chief competitor, Corbis) had been buying up photo archives and agencies—grandly rewarding certain photographers while marginalizing others. It was shakeout time in the picture business.

And yet there was reason for hope on Saturday, September 8. That day, two independent photo agencies bucked this trend and formally opened their doors at the popular, low-key French festival. One agency—a completely digital operation, created by and for photographers and picture editors—was World Picture News (later christened World Picture Network), founded by photographers Seamus Conlan and Tara Farrell, and formally launched at a raucous Perpignan coming-out party. (I served on WPN's board of advisers at its inception.) The other start-up was VII, an agency of seven marquee-name photojournalists that announced its formation at a ragtag press conference earlier that day.

"We were inventing [VII] up as we went along," explains the agency's initial strategist, Gary Knight, "everyone cleaning out their ATM. We paid the lawyer in [photographic] prints. We paid the accountant and the Web master and the guy who designed the logo that way. That week was . . . the first time we had all met in the same room and had the opportunity to go through the business model together, face to face."

But the photo community, long starved for good news and a fresh approach, seemed to warm to their concept. "What we were doing was not a new idea," Knight admits, "but an old one in a new age." The notion behind VII was simple and counterintuitive. As picture agencies became more unwieldy and impersonal, why couldn't a septet of friends form their own collective—maintaining their ethical standards, photographic quality, camaraderie—and share their profits, all while transmitting their images digitally from their separate homes across the globe? And why couldn't more subtle, nuanced photographs make it into the journalistic pipeline? "For news pictures to break through the media clutter today, they have to be loud," says the photo agency savant Robert Pledge. "People who appreciate and defend serious still photography are like monks who appreciate silence in a noisy world." Knight was one of those monks. Somehow, he and his colleagues would try to elevate documentary photography—a silent, meditative, anachronistic medium in the light-speed realm of 24/7 news.

Knight was spurred on, he says, by the Magnum photographer Gilles Peress, who had been urging him to set out on his own and create something new. Knight felt something click one night, at 3:00 a.m. He happened to be visiting photographer John Stanmeyer on a trip to Hong Kong. "We were down in my studio," recalls Stanmeyer, "standing over an old [Macintosh] G-3. We were doing Web stuff, talking about how to market an archive. And Gary said, 'What about doing this together?' "

In the intervening six to nine months, via late-night rap sessions and countless e-mails, they banded together with other adventurous photographer friends—Ron Haviv, Antonin Kratochvil, Alexandra Boulat, and Christopher Morris—veterans of conflicts in Bosnia, Kosovo, and the West Bank. The photo business, explains Haviv, had become "dehumanizing. I found out about my agency being sold from a friend who called [my cell phone] while I was on a motorbike in East Timor."

And along for the ride came number seven—James Nachtwey, a photographer before whose viewfinder the woes of the whole planet seemed to pass. One imagines that in his dreams, or nightmares, he still sees the outstretched palm of a Somali woman curled up and starving in a wheelbarrow; the Romanian child abandoned and howling in a hospital's backward crib; the glare of death's lone eye peering out at him from the womb of a blanket's folds.

Grounded as a Zen master, cool as a jewel thief, Nachtwey seems to possess an invincibility under fire that borders on the mystical. On occasion, he has stood or crouched next to colleagues who themselves have then been wounded or killed. He has put down his cameras to help seek medical attention for citizens caught in the crossfire. He has been attacked by mobs and has felt the hot breath of bullets in Bosnia, Haiti, Indonesia, and South Africa. He once tore both Achilles tendons while sprinting away from snipers in the former Yugoslavia. He survived one nighttime attack in Iraq—sustaining shrapnel wounds that plague him to this day—when a grenade, tossed by insurgents hiding along the roadside, landed in the open compartment of the Jeep he was riding in. (His life and those of the three men traveling with him were spared when *Time* senior correspondent Michael Weisskopf reached to scoop up and toss out the grenade, only to have his body absorb the blow; Weisskopf lost his hand.)

According to one journalist who has worked with Nachtwey in Africa, the photographer, when in dire straits or under fire, sometimes "enters a zone" in which he acts as if he is shielded by a force field—"a protective circle. He told me one night that this power scared him." Nachtwey has said as much himself, admitting that when the bullets fly, he has been known to feel that a "guardian angel" guides his way.

Nachtwey, born in 1948, certainly looks the part of the combat shooter, with his marathoner's frame and George Peppard bearing. Six months before 9/11, as we talked at *Vanity Fair*'s Oscar party, Nachtwey—the subject of the Academy Award–nominated documentary *War Photographer* that year—was pulled aside to be introduced to the actor Adrien Brody, who wanted to meet *him*. Brody, the son of photojournalist Sylvia Plachy, had just completed filming *Harrison's Flowers*, in which he played a photojournalist in Yugoslavia. Upon shaking Nachtwey's hand, the actor gave a little bow. "Wow," he said. "The real deal."

That same month, Nachtwey had left Magnum, his photographic home of seventeen years. When he heard the early rumblings about VII, Nachtwey felt compelled to join his like-minded comrades, "a group of people," he says, "who all have worked with each other all around [the world] in adversity, in the kind of situation where strong friendships are made very quickly."

John Stanmeyer adds, "Someone did a study on the number of people who can coalesce in a group and not have factions form. And it was seven." "Even the name seven," says Nachtwey, "is a metaphysical number. The number that wins in a crap shoot. Seven also was Mickey Mantle's number. I'm a baseball fan."

And so, on September 8, VII was officially launched at a press conference in front of an appreciative, if skeptical, crowd of peers. The next morning, VII's Christopher Morris set out for home—Tampa, Florida—by way of Barcelona. A longtime White House photographer for *Time*, Morris was distinguished by his blond tresses and lean, leonine countenance. Along with Boulat, Haviv, and the photographer Luc Delahaye, Morris had been among the most accomplished war photographers throughout the protracted Balkan conflict of the 1990s.

On the morning of September 9, Morris was on a deadline. The magazine had assigned him to shoot a story on Internet gambling on the Caribbean island of Antigua. But he knew that after he completed that one-day shoot, he would have to quickly make his way back to Washington to cover his usual beat: dogging the trail of President Bush.

Driving to Barcelona in his rental car that morning, Morris made a pit stop at a supermarket in southern France. His wife, Vesna—born in Yugoslavia, raised in France, now living in the States—had a weakness for *sal de mar*, a special type of butter made with sea salt, which he knew he could find only in France. All week long, Morris recalls, Vesna had reminded him by phone "every day, 'Please, get that butter,' with me telling her I had bought the butter, but I hadn't bought the butter." That day, he dutifully purchased "five or six big bars," which he placed on the backseat. He pulled out of the parking lot and promptly lost his way. Then he hit a traffic jam. Morris finally made it to the airport, only to watch the plane take off without him. With no place to sleep, he decided to head back—120 miles—to Perpignan, butter in tow. As he drove, he realized he would never be able to make it to Antigua *and* keep his Washington assignment.

So, upon arriving, Morris turned to Nachtwey and persuaded him to take on the gambling shoot. "We buttered it up for Jim," Morris says, "telling him there were beautiful Chinese women who do the roulette tables." Nachtwey, half-jokingly, saw an opportunity at hand. Realizing that this was VII's first official assignment—on wagering and games of chance, no less—he beseeched the others: "Give me something to gamble with. [Photographer Robert] Capa used to go to the races with Magnum's money, hoping to raise some seed money." Each pitched in his share, and soon Nacthwey had a hundred-dollar bill to wager.

That night, remembers Morris, "We all met in this apartment in Perpignan and we opened the cube. They all had to taste this butter that I missed my plane over."

The next day, recalls Knight, "Jim leaves Perpignan one day early [than he had planned]. He pockets the hundred dollars. He hops on a train and airplane and arrives in New York on September ten, intending to go to Antigua to spend our hundred dollars.

"On the morning of September 11, *Time*'s messenger arrives with one hundred rolls of color-negative film, as he's packing his bags." Nachtwey lives downtown, near the South Street Seaport, just blocks from the twin towers. "And he hears a bang," Knight says.

Nacthwey quickly scrambled to his roof, exposed a few rolls of film, then dashed over to the World Trade Center, ten minutes away. He shot all morning, all afternoon, and came within steps of his own death, as he would recount on the *Digital Journalist* Web site in an interview with editors Peter Howe and Dirck Halstead:

> It seemed to me absolutely unbelievable that the World Trade Center could be lying in the street, and I felt very compelled to make an image of this. So I made my way through the smoke. It was virtually deserted, and it seemed like a movie set from a science fiction film. Very apocalyptic. A very strange ambiance of the sunlight filtering through the dust and the destroyed wreckage of this building lying in the street. As I was photographing . . . the second tower fell and I was standing right under it, literally under it. Fortunately for me, and unfortunately for people on the west side, it listed to the west. But I was still underneath this avalanche . . . of tons of material . . . falling directly down onto me. I realized that I had a few seconds to find cover or else I'd be killed.
>
> I dashed into the lobby of the Millennium Hotel, which was directly across the street from the North Tower, and I realized instantly that this hotel lobby was going to be taken out, that the debris would come flying straight through the plate glass and destroy the lobby. There was no protection at all. There was no other place to turn, and certainly no more time. It was about to happen any moment. I saw an open elevator and dashed inside. Put my back against the wall, thinking that it would afford

> some protection, which it did, and about a second later the lobby got taken out. There was a construction worker who dashed inside the elevator with me just as the debris swept through the lobby and it instantly became pitch black. [Later, once the darkness cleared,] together this other man and I crawled, groping . . . and then we made our way out.

Nachtwey would capture some of the most harrowing and memorable frames taken on 9/11: the south tower disintegrating above a steadfast cross (atop Trinity Church, *Image 24*); three ghostly figures, backlit and trudging through the haze of strewn debris; a single fireman perched on the pile, the sky churning above him in a Turneresque pinwheel of soot black and cindery gray.

He still can't help pondering the fate that befell those men and women standing on the *other* side of the tower that day. He had chronicled horror, and again he had survived. Yet the journalist in him had to move forward. Nachtwey believed in the new agency (he actually held on to the hundred-dollar bill as a keepsake, before misplacing it; Morris saved the *sal de mar* wrapper) and both photographers committed themselves to covering the broader conflict. "We launched on September 8, three days before the attacks," Nachtwey says of his agency's baptism by fire. "Then the world changed. And we've been following that story ever since." In due course, all but one of the VII team (later expanded to nine members) would cover the subsequent war in Afghanistan. Seven would do the same in Iraq, placing themselves directly on the front lines. Says Nachtwey, "We haven't let up."

(In 2005, in a case of art-imitates-life, filmmaker Oliver Stone would hire Nachtwey to come to Los Angeles to shoot photos on the set of his feature *World Trade Center*. On a Hollywood soundstage, Stone had fabricated a scene of sprawling devastation. And who better than Nachtwey to bring a wealth of firsthand experience to the site and to lend credibility to the endeavor? Stone, Nachtwey says, "re-created Ground Zero above ground and below ground, about fifty feet high and two hundred feet around, with twisted steel and concrete." By fashioning a faux September 12, just for the camera, the director could take his characters and his audience "to places we've never seen brfore," Nachtwey claims—

inside man-made caverns of death. In this way, moviegoers could approximate the experience of the horror of those rare individuals, pulled from the rubble, who had the courage to go on, and could sense the heroism of those who, despite the odds, had come to save them.)

Morris arrived in New York on Wednesday, September 12, having driven all night from Florida. He photographed on Wednesday and Thursday—or rather *tried* to photograph. "I got on the scene," he says, "got past the barricades, and was immediately seized upon by the police. It was impossible to shoot. Everybody hated photographers. We were like pariahs. Every time you lifted up your camera, you were whisked away. Everybody wanted to [lionize] the firefighters and the police. But photographers were despised. They treated you like you were the Antichrist.

"All those months later, they [would] want pictures" he says bitterly, as if imagining the moments he missed, beyond the police sawhorses. "But at the time, we were invaders. The historic importance of the aftermath and the rescue workers' [efforts] was not considered. They saw us as 'dirty photographers' [sullying] a crime scene."

In a galling irony, he says, he understood, firsthand, that there was no shortage of imagery to be had downtown in those first several days. Upon returning to the Time and Life Building in midtown, he says, he sat "in *Time* magazine['s office] and you'd have, constantly, guys with hard hats, Red Cross people, rescue workers—who were *allowed* to take as many pictures as they liked—walking in and trying to sell pictures."

"We took all comers," says *Time*'s picture editor, MaryAnne Golon. "For the three weeks post-nine-eleven, the most 'exciting' things to see, if you'd call them that, were [the photographs] from Fire Department workers and iron workers. We set up a system in the lobby where we were rotating picture editors to [handle] images from the general public. There would be guys in yellow slickers with dust on them in the twenty-fourth floor [waiting area] waiting their turn." Nevertheless, she fully understands Morris's resentment. "It was frustrating for *all* of us. *The New York Times*, as the newspaper of record, took the lead position, petitioning the city, saying this was a horrible [injustice that] there was no professional coverage of this national disaster, recovery effort, crime scene—whatever you want to call it—at Ground Zero."

Psychologist Richard Cohen walked over to the Associated Press offices in Rockefeller Center on the afternoon of September 11 with thirty rolls of photographs he had taken that morning. He sold seven pictures, right on the spot, including an image of three women in shock near the New York Stock Exchange. Then, passing through Times Square on the way home to his Greenwich Village apartment, he saw a sign for Reuters. He went in and sold several more, including one of a man, shot at an odd angle, pointing toward the smoking towers, which seemed to totter on a heaving horizon line. (Cohen says he took it after thinking, "Well, if this *was* going to be in a newspaper, how would they shoot this? So I walked up behind them, [stooped down,] and shot *up* at them.") His images ran on Web sites and were published in newspapers and books; the photo of the pointing man was enlarged, backlit, and placed in a glass display case in the Reuters lobby. In the course of several hours, Cohen, the chief of mental health services at New York's National Institute for People with Disabilities, had become a photojournalist.

Cohen, forty-nine, was a self-avowed street shooter who went through a daily "picture-taking ritual," he says, "to clear my head." He rarely went out and about without his Konica Hexar AF and Contax T3. That morning, he recalls, "I looked down and saw the towers 'lit,' so I ran down there." He shot the south tower as it fell, from twenty-five blocks away, then slipped through police lines to Chinatown and pushed on to Wall Street. He returned home to his wife, covered in dust, three hours later.

He had been hypnotized by the almost hallucinatory scenes he saw. "I'm shooting through the lens all the way through [the morning]. I had this thought in my head, My God, look, this person's running, screaming. So I just started shooting *them*. There was a kind of line I felt like I crossed at that point . . . to photojournalist. I found myself going, 'Look at this person's anguish right this minute,' and started taking pictures." He even photographed the north tower's collapse from behind a large, streetside flower pot, ducking down behind the barrier, and holding up his camera to shoot *into* the dust cloud, worried neither about his lenses nor his life. "I was not scared [that] I was going to die," he says, implying that he hadn't troubled himself over his personal safety or allowed himself more than a few moments' reflection on his remarkable good fortune, dumb luck, or blessed naïveté.

For the longest time Cohen felt guilty about the surge of adrenalin that had coursed through him all morning as he was transformed from Walter Mitty into the real, live photojournalist-for-a-day of his imaginings. "I couldn't stop," says Cohen, who ran through ten rolls of film, then bought twenty more at pharmacies he passed. "[A friend] said I had to take photographs to legitimize what I was witnessing. But I don't know if that was [the motive]. I had *never* seen this before: There was catastrophe, and every block was getting worse and worse . . . I had to [explore] what was going on."

Part of Cohen's heightened awareness of his surroundings, surely, was biochemical: a "fight or flight" response, medical experts say, that kicks in when one's survival is at stake, as the adrenal glands pump hormones into the bloodstream, causing the heart rate to ascend and the senses, even one's eyesight, to come into sharper focus. (Vietnam War correspondent Michael Herr described it best, perhaps, conveying the acute sensory convergence and clarity of the war zone. "In Vietnam," he would write in his classic war journal, *Dispatches*, one's "infatuation . . . with violence wouldn't go unrequited for very long, it would come and put its wild mouth all over you . . . Under Fire would take you out of your head and your body too, the space you'd seen a second ago between subject and object wasn't there anymore, it banged shut in a fast wash of adrenaline." There was a hyper-aliveness in the perpetual near-death experience, a "strobic wheel" surge, as Herr put it, "rolling all the way up until you were literally High on War [and] coming off a jag like that could really make a mess out of you.")

Cohen, however, was no Herr or Nachtwey. He felt distressingly out of step. The deaths he was witnessing didn't register with him, he now says, until he sat in front of the television set that evening and saw the annihilation in context—removed from the surreal fog of his day amid the ashes. The delayed imagery was more revelatory, in its way, than the reality he had seen with his own eyes. "There was a lot of denial," he admits. "When I was taking these pictures, I thought this terrible thing happened, but it just did not get into my soul. I couldn't *get* it. I'd see a shoe [in the street], and then it was, 'Where'd the shoe come from?' Then I saw these papers. Then I saw gay porno on the ground. Then I saw a pen and I saw a passport. I was, like, 'Oh, my God, this was somebody's desk and it blew out the window.'

"It did not hit me that there was death to such an extent until I got home," he says. "I'd been mostly shutting that off throughout the day. The question I ask myself: Had the camera [and] the experience of photographing forced me [not to feel]? Not until I saw the moving image of the plane that night and the bodies coming down did I really allow myself to go, Well, those floors were hitting one after another after another, and there were people in every one of those. It started hitting me and I starting getting depressed and anxious about it. I felt guilty that my . . . reactions were so detached. I'm a psychologist, and I couldn't feel. I was in denial the whole day, in effect, and afterwards I felt guilty. Then, I got over the guilt and started asking myself, Why is it? *How* is it you could not *feel* that? And why is it that when I saw those images it hit me so hard?"

For seven years Cohen had worked in the psychiatric hall of a Dallas hospital emergency room. "Maybe that numbed me," he says. What's more, he adds, "in order to be a psychologist, I'm observing, I'm listening, I'm having to feel but I have to remain at a distance [so as] not to muck up their experience. It explained to me why I could be a photographer that day, waiting [in the wings] to see what was happening." The act of taking pictures, however, did not delude him into thinking he had actually *become* a photojournalist. "Compared to mine," he says of the work of professionals who shot that day, "I couldn't *believe* how good their photographs were. My God, these guys are [so] much better than I am."

In certain ways, Cohen says, his experience in the street assisted him in his practice. "A lot of people [I treated] were having acute stress reactions and several had post-traumatic stress reactions [to the attacks]. They would have these images that would play themselves over and over in their head. Their sleep was disturbed. They would become anxious and panicked. They would become phobic when they'd come downtown. I understood that, too. But what helped me more with them was when they talked about how they had an absence of feeling, and that that was shameful for them. Having experienced that, I could understand."

4 FRIDAY, SEPTEMBER 14

At two in the morning on September 14, Gregg Brown was startled by the peal of his bedside phone. A representative from FEMA, the Federal Emergency Management Agency, was calling. He needed an aerial photographer. "FEMA has photographers," says Brown. "The Fire Department has photographers. So does the Navy and NYPD. But they needed someone *now*."

The city was in crisis mode and FEMA, as Brown understood it, had been so anxious to find a professional shooter before dawn that this man on the line had resorted to flipping through the Yellow Pages. He had stumbled across Brown's ad containing two oval-shaped images of a woman in nineteenth-century garb: PHOTO RESTORATION . . . DIGITAL IMAGING CENTER, PHOTOGRAPHICS UNLIMITED. "He asked me if I do aerial photos," recalls Brown, who had never even boarded a helicopter in his life. "I said, 'Yes.' So for the next forty-five days, I had a sheriff's department escort assigned to me [and I would] go up in the helicopter and [by the end of the day] drop off a hundred eight-by-twelves at the Duane Street fire station."

On his first day airborne Brown took roll after roll of the ravaged landscape below him. In the morning light, the smoke from underground fires gave the illusion of the haze of battle and conferred on the ruins the same gloom that might have hung upon the battlements of a sacked medieval castle. From certain angles, the north tower's facade looked as fragile as a shard of seashell thrust up in the sand; from others, it appeared as enduring as the Colosseum. As the weeks, then months, went on, the site beneath him transformed: smoking charnel, then steep crests ringed with cranes and earth movers, then a flat base of hallowed bedrock. Throughout, Brown's images helped officials survey the damage and chart the patterns of the fires that churned below the surface.

On his fifth day airborne, Brown inadvertently loaded his camera with a roll of film that he had partially exposed—during an architectural shoot the previous May. Believe it or not, the roll contained an image of the intact towers, thereby creating a double exposure: the buildings erect and resolute in a sunlit skyline, overlaid with the lattice of cataclysm—the hulking hull of the towers' outer walls. Says Brown, "I show this picture, I've seen people weep. It just captures the glory of the towers and the destruction, and the human effort."*

According to the receipt that she retains to this day, Tammy Klein's film was due to be picked up on September 11 at the US Color Lab on Bleecker Street. It was not until Friday, however, that she made it over to the West Village to retrieve it.

For the preceding two weeks, Klein, an Israeli student at the International Center of Photography, and her husband, Yossi Amossy, had collaborated on a self-generated photography project. The bedroom of

* In one of the most perplexing developments surrounding September 11–related imagery, the New York *Daily News* would report in 2006 that Brown, retaining the copyright to 30,000 photographs he took at FEMA's behest, had also taken video and "included part of the footage in a wacky documentary, 'Words,' surrounding scenes of Trade Center death and destruction with interviews of topless women talking about society's obsession with breasts and a group of New Yorkers traipsing around nude as part of a simulated Native American Ceremony." Brown defends his movie. "The premise of 'Words' comes from the idea of word association. The film moves from one topic to the next based on the connections between people, ideas, emotions. We began shooting 'Words' in 2000. Then, 9/11 happened . . . It would have been dishonest not to include [such imagery]."

their forty-fourth-floor apartment on Duane Street and Broadway had floor-to-ceiling wraparound windows, which, like a panoramic movie screen, looked out onto the World Trade Center, seven blocks to the south. "Everything is just glass," she says. "All you see is the twin towers." Whenever they were inspired by the way light played against the structures outside, they would walk over to a tripod-mounted Minolta and click the shutter. They shot the towers in moonlight and veiled in fog, at sunrise and at dusk. Over two weeks, they exposed two rolls, judiciously, then brought the film to the lab.

On September 10, Klein had a quiet dinner; her husband had left on a trip to Israel. Then, for some reason, she chose not to close the drapes in the bedroom before she went to sleep.

She awoke, alone, to see a plane heading toward, then hitting, the north tower.

"I went down in the elevator, in sweatclothes," she recalls, "to ask if it actually happened. No one knew in the elevator or the lobby. I shut up because I thought I was still dreaming. No one confirmed it. I was so confused."

Still haunted, she says, by the sight of the plane and "the noise [of the concussion], like someone shouting in your ear," she went back to her apartment, got some film from the refrigerator, where she stored it, and began shooting reflexively, shoving into the camera whichever roll she happened to pry from its canister—black-and-white, color negative, transparency. She ignored the telephone, which rang incessantly as worried friends tried to check up on her.

"After five, ten, minutes," she recalls, "I'm looking at the first one burning, but I'm waiting and I'm thinking, Something more can happen. As an Israeli, in our case we think maybe there's another bomb. We already are programmed to these catastrophes to think, This is a terrorist attack." (Over the past thirty years, bombings in Israel and on the West Bank have often been set to explode in staggered fashion so as to maximize the death toll, killing onlookers and rescue teams that arrive to treat those wounded in the first wave of an attack.)

Klein says she trusted her own instinct to stay put and "shoot until it was over." She felt safer in her bedroom anyway. "It was easier in a way to have a camera in front of my face," she explains. "On one hand you only see *that*—you can focus, you can zoom, so it's *more* scary. It draws you in. On the other hand, the minute you're the photographer, you're the viewer, so it's not happening to you. I'm only an observer. You're not *in* this reality. And that's where I wanted to be. I had no family [in New York]. I didn't have close friends—I'm here from Israel just a year. I gave myself an assignment: Stay there and photograph."

At one point, Klein composed a self-portrait with the smoke-shrouded buildings in the same frame by extending her arm and shooting inward. "I had to have a proof that it happened and I was there," she says. "I look horrible. It was so unreal that what the mind could not grasp, the film could."

Positioned south of the Trade Center, her view eclipsed by the south tower, Klein shot the tip of the second jet's right wing as the plane disappeared into the bulk of the building. She shot pockets of fire on one of the higher floors. She shot both towers as they caved in on themselves. She didn't leave until "all of the windows were covered with smoke" and her building was evacuated. She exposed twenty-six rolls, processed them at a "rush" rate in a West Village lab ("It was crazy in the labs and everyone wanted pictures, immediately, 'I need it now!' "), and, with the help of a friend, transmitted several shots to the Israeli daily *Yedioth Ahronoth*, where one appeared the next morning across the front page.

For the next few days, however, Klein was haunted by the pictures she and her husband had taken. She needed to reclaim the view that had vanished outside her bedroom windows. On Friday, she walked over to the lab and requested her prints.

She was taken aback when two men behind the counter looked at her warily, as if they had been waiting for her. "They didn't say anything," she recalls. "It was creepy. Even though it was so hectic [in the lab], they [had] stopped what they were doing, and they looked at the photos. They were suspicious that I must have *known* something.

"I felt like a serial killer," she says, "who takes pictures of the victims before he kills, who [then] comes and picks up the film after the murder."

"Tim Sherman spotted the photograph near the end of his first day of digging," Jim Dwyer would write in *The New York Times*, "on the Friday after that Tuesday."

Sherman, a New Jersey waterworks employee volunteering in the rescue effort, plucked the color three-by-five from a mound of ash. It was crinkled and torn. It showed three children, obviously siblings: two boys and a kid sister. Hoping it might find its way back to its rightful owner, he gave the picture to his local paper, the *Home News Tribune* of central New Jersey. The *Trib* ran it. And a reader named Brian Conroy, a bakery company sales manager, realized that he recognized the three: they were the kids of an old acquaintance, George Tabeek. Conroy traced Tabeek's last-known whereabouts to Brooklyn, placed a phone call, then waited nervously for the response.

George himself came on the line. Yes, he remembered his old colleague. And, yes, that photo of Steven, Georgie, and Dana—taken at a Sears store fifteen years previously—had been in his Port Authority office on 9/11. "It was on my credenza," Tabeek recalls, four years later. A week or two before the attacks, he had removed the shot from its frame and replaced it with a new image of his three kids, taken at Georgie's NYPD graduation. He then laid the snapshot up against the frame, which was fringed in *X*'s and *O*'s. "In my office on the thirty-fifth floor of Building Two," he says, "that picture was the closest thing to the windows."

Tabeek's story of his day of peril and valor is a remarkable one. Under his command as the Port Authority's manager of security and life safety, and within his circle of coworkers, Tabeek lost, by his own tally, thirty-two of his civilian staff, ten Port Authority officers assigned to the towers, and twenty-four Port Authority police officers, most of whom he knew well. He also helped rescue or begin the evacuation of scores of others that morning.

At a quarter to nine, he had stopped to grab a Krispy Kreme doughnut after a meeting outside Tower One. "That stuff'll kill you," said Robert Lynch, a Trade Center property manager. Tabeek took a bite, and a dollop of jelly squeezed out onto his gray suit. "We can't take you [any]where," said another companion, Joseph Amatuccio. (Neither Lynch nor Amatuccio, a manager of operations and maintenance for the twin towers, would survive that day.) "Just as he said that," Tabeek recalls, "we heard the engines roaring. The hit. Debris coming down, things as big as refrigerators. People were running for cover. Others lay on the ground hurt, including a man I saw get decapitated. I looked up and saw the building twisting violently, and saw rainbows caused by the shattered glass against the sun."

By radio, Tabeek ordered his team to set its evacuation plan in motion, and headed for the One World Trade Center promenade to assess the damage. "Bodies started coming down, following the rainbows," he says. "As the first person hit, the body exploded. All you saw was his brown pinstriped pants and his light brown shoes. I saw three, one right after the other." As Tabeek and his colleagues mobilized their teams, sending staffers to various locales—some never to return—Tabeek got word that three members of his security command center squad were trapped on the twenty-second floor of Tower One. An elevator, it seemed, had smashed through the ceiling and blocked a corridor wall.

Tabeek, Fire Department Lieutenant Andrew Desperito, and a small team climbed the twenty-two flights to find their three coworkers, passing exiting employees and redirecting them to a less congested stairwell. Tabeek's squad extracted the three men. Then, after looking out a window and watching the south tower collapse, Tabeek and Desperito decided to evacuate as well. Twenty-nine minutes later, after unlocking doors on fifteen floors on the way down (and shouting out to potential stragglers), Tabeek emerged, only to see the lieutenant, standing just to his right, get swept away in a gale as the building they had just descended crumbled around them. Though Tabeek was burned on his face and hand, and buried up to his shoulder blades in debris, he managed to stay alert enough to hear voices in the rubble. He helped locate six policemen, who made it out safely. To this day he is haunted by the fact that he was unable to save Desperito—and by the fact that fourteen of his colleagues had remained at their posts in Tower Two.

Tabeek, who comforted Port Authority families in the weeks that followed, still finds it hard to live with what he witnessed. "I keep lingering on the scenes," he says. "They play like pictures, picking away at you. It's funny how the mind tries to heal you by trying to block these things from your memory." But if he sees a lone ray of light, it is refracted through that snapshot of his children.

Tabeek, now retired at age fifty-five, keeps the picture, a little the worse for wear, on a shelf above his fireplace. "Inside the building, you never thought about your family. You thought about saving lives. But when the photo came up, this was a sign from God. He saved me for a reason. Was it for the sake of the six police officers I heard trapped after Building One [the north tower] collapsed and followed me out to safety? Was it for my children's sake? . . . That I'd be there for the sake of my kids growing up? . . . Or to help console the families who were looking to me [for guidance]? I'm Catholic. I didn't go to church before this. I now go every Sunday. My friends died; I was protected, by the grace of God."

Up from the detritus of that week, pictures continued to surface, pictures that had been displayed on workers' walls and desks and cubicles. They were mysterious artifacts of scattered humanity. Each buoyant face in each photograph was anonymous, as if the lifeblood had rushed from every cheek. Each depicted scene was shorn of any context, save the grand calamity. The salvaged shots emerged from unlikely nooks, just as dream fragments or repressed memories spout up from the unconscious.

Over the next three and a half years, many such photographs were plucked from oblivion, many of them from the Fresh Kills Landfill on Staten Island, where much of the material from Ground Zero—1.6 million tons of it, in fact—had been carted. "The pictures were water-soaked, burned, creased, filthy dirty, covered with concrete and dust," remembers Inspector James Luongo, who spent eleven months in charge of the Fresh Kills site. Most of the photographs were found by New York City police officers, hundreds of whom had combed the grounds in the year after the salvage effort began (along with members of twenty-eight government agencies, including the FBI, CIA, Secret Service, U.S. Customs Service, the Port Authority, and the Bureau of Alcohol, Tobacco and Firearms), adopting the extracurricular role of prospectors mining for the cherished relics of strangers.

Early on in the process Luongo had insisted that on-site personnel save any meaningful or potentially identifiable personal items. (Some 54,000 artifacts were put aside.) In particular, he insisted on singling out photographs and identity badges. "A lot of guys looked at me like I was nuts," he says. " 'Why are we keeping these photographs?' But I knew that based upon the devastation we saw, people were not going to be getting many things back, including bodies. I made the decision: Everything with an image on it—we had thousands of ID cards—or anything we felt would have personal value, like jewelry, we vouchered and safeguarded, put in clear police department envelopes, cleaned [them] to decontaminate them as best we could, then put [them] in plastic garbage bags, in drying cabinets, like ovens."

Eastman Kodak and NFL Films offered to take temporary possession of the photo cache, to provide the service of digital restoration—and redemption. Swatches of paper and chemical and faded color were slowly and systematically reanimated so that their inner worlds could begin to resonate again. According to Ronda Factor, who ran the project for Kodak, "We got the pictures that included people, and the NFL got the more landscape-type pictures. The pictures were damaged because they had been hosed down for hygiene reasons. We used chemicals and brushes, water and soap, to remove the ash from them. Then we digitally scanned them. Then we 'cloned' areas that looked not-too-bad and could match the shadings and color and contrast. It was largely to make the faces recognizable." Kodak also scanned any personal inscriptions and captions that appeared on the back of the photographs. What struck Factor was the diversity the images revealed: "People from different nationalities. Some pictures went back to World War II. One [showed] a soldier on a porch [at] an Army base. On the reverse there was a personal note from a young man, who was the soldier, to his girlfriend.

"On the one hand," she says, "you felt good because my team could take what we know best and help [those] affected by this tragedy. We could provide mementos—memories. On the other hand, it was a very eerie, sad feeling. You didn't know anything about what happened to these people."

In January 2005 the Port Authority of New York and New Jersey, having retrieved a batch of photo CDs from Kodak and the NFL, set up an online database, accessible to surviving World Trade Center employees and to families of those who had once occupied the towers. It contained an electronic archive of eight thousand photographs. Evacuees or victims' relatives could survey the pictures from the privacy of their own computers, and then, upon presenting proof that the images were their own (by showing a photo, say, with a similar likeness), could collect the specimens from the NYPD. A person clicking through the archive would have to spend an estimated four and a half hours just to view each image once for two seconds. And hundreds of people did just that.

In a curious coda, photographers who had been allowed access to Fresh Kills to document the workers, the wreckage, and the items there, organized an exhibition called "Recovery" that began touring the country in 2003. Among the images: a still life of police badges, a study of handcuffs, a 360-degree panorama of fire trucks from among the 1,300 vehicles brought to the site. Mixed in with the pictures were artifacts: a bolt-studded strip from one of the planes, a Trade tower elevator plaque labeled "78," and a tattered American flag.

On Friday, a relative of a friend (who wishes to remain anonymous) attended a company-sponsored meeting at which loved ones were asked to bring DNA samples and photographs to help authorities identify employees still unaccounted for. This woman had lost her husband and sat in the session with his picture in her lap.

Also attending the meeting were workers who had survived, having walked down dozens of flights of stairs to exit the Trade Center. Someone looked at the photo for a moment, then said to the wife of the man in the picture, "He was in front of me," in the stairwell. "He stopped to help me." (Because of the size of the firm, not everyone knew everyone else by name.) Another survivor described seeing this familiar man aiding others as well.

Without the photograph to prompt these recollections, the lost man's wife might never have had confirmation of what she already sensed, deep down: that her husband, ever the generous, hale, and self-sacrificing kind, had died trying to shepherd others to safety.

On 9/14, pictures of Osama bin Laden were put up on the Web site watch list of Interpol, the global law enforcement agency. Like the faces of the hijackers, the countenance of the al-Qaeda leader became ubiquitous. Within days, his image would be paraded through the streets of Peshwar, Jakarta, and Gaza, his likeness often cribbed from magazines or downloaded from the Internet; within weeks it would appear on everything from sheets of novelty toilet paper in New York (for $19 a roll, 10 percent of the profits earmarked for charity) to targets at U.S. rifle ranges.* In Pakistan's kiosks, bazaars, and open-air markets, Osama's face appeared on T-shirts, ballpoint pens, bottles of cologne, and candy wrappers.

Digital scanners had cribbed bin Laden's image from published sources. Digital printers allowed protesters to paste them hither and yon. Digital cameras had then photographed people holding posters with the pirated shots. The Internet then completed the cycle, zapping pictures of the pictures to the news shows, the wire services, and computer desktops everywhere.

Bin Laden was more than an idle beneficiary of this image traffic. He was a shrewd propagandist and spin doctor himself. During the 1990s he had conducted several sessions with Western reporters, TV crews, and photographers, who, at considerable personal risk, would travel to safehouses in Afghanistan and then wait to be summoned for some late-night conversation. "How can a man in a cave outcommunicate the world's leading communications society?" asked an incredulous Richard Holbrooke, the former U.S. State Department and UN powerbroker, confounded by bin Laden's facility at getting his post-9/11 message out, unfiltered, to his fundamentalist constituency and the Western world.

Though bin Laden was in league with the Taliban—whose camera-shy leader, Mullah Omar, was notorious for edicts banning any type of photography that depicted the human form—the al-Qaeda chief pos-

*Bush's photo would be similarly bandied about. At one Indonesian rally, mobs hefted a poster-board effigy of the president, replete with fangs, a "Big Satan" bandana, and a makeshift nameplate: Bush Dog.

sessed considerable media acumen and understood that any modern conflict, jihad notwithstanding, was best waged not only with troops, weaponry, and displays of force, but with a focused war of public image. Prior to bin Laden's rise, Islamist extremists had solidified their hold on their conscripts in part by exploiting an array of communications channels. Cassette tapes of fiery sermons delivered at radical mosques were copied, mass-produced, and circulated widely. Access to satellite television and, later, the Internet, turned various clerics into pan-Arab personalities in a manner not even Egypt's Gamal Abdel Nasser could have envisioned.

Soon bin Laden's story was as familiar as his visage. He had been an ally of the Afghan mujahideen in their successful campaign to expel the Soviet army from their land in the 1980s, channeling money from his powerful Saudi family (which ran a global business with interests in oil, energy, mining, construction, and media) into rebel coffers and establishing a toehold for long-term holy war. When he began to chastise the Saudi government in the early nineties for letting American forces use the kingdom as a staging ground in the first Gulf War, he became an outcast—expelled from Saudi Arabia, then eventually forced from the Sudan as well, moving his operations back to war-ravaged Afghanistan.

Placed on President Clinton's hit list in the 1990s because of his ever-more-potent terror organization, bin Laden began to find a horrified audience, by increments. He plotted terrorist acts (the 1998 African embassy bombings that claimed more than 220 lives and wounded or maimed thousands; the 2000 attack on the USS *Cole* in Yemen, which killed seventeen) designed to be bloody and daring enough to reverberate across the mass media. As a rule, he gave hints of impending strikes through warnings in the press, even releasing a lengthy videotaped screed just months before 9/11, in which he outlined his stepped-up war against America and Saudi Arabia.

Indeed, he was becoming so enamored of the camera that his Taliban protector, Mullah Omar, according to data intercepted from the hard drive of an al-Qaeda laptop, chastised bin Laden in 1999 (in an e-mail sent through an intermediary): "The strangest thing I have heard so far is Abu Abdullah [bin Laden]'s saying that he wouldn't listen to the Leader of the Faithful [Mullah Omar] when he asked him to stop giving interviews . . .

I think our brother [bin Laden] has caught the disease of screens, flashes, fans, and applause."

Bin Laden persisted, undaunted. And his minions continued utilizing the tools of the information age. "The grafting of modern techniques onto the most radical reading of holy war . . . is the hallmark of bin Laden's network," wrote terrorism expert Peter Bergen (who has interviewed bin Laden) in his book *Holy War, Inc.* "The Saudi militant's followers communicate by fax, satellite phone, and E-mail." The 9/11 hijackers synchronized their efforts through e-mail and, according to the Associated Press, mastermind Khalid Sheikh Mohammed [KSM], upon being apprehended by U.S. authorities in 2003, admitted that he had "communicated with [hijackers] al Hamzi and al-Mihdhar while they were in the United States by using Internet chat software." (Mark Hosenball, who covers intelligence matters for *Newsweek*, has reason to believe that the hijackers conversed by composing e-mails, which they never actually sent, but left sitting in joint Hotmail accounts. "Confederates with the password would log into the account," he says, "retrieve the messages, and delete them, making it almost impossible for government eavesdroppers to detect or recover the messages.")

Pictures, of course, always played a role in al-Qaeda's plans. In the early 1990s, for example, an al-Qaeda cell in Kenya established a darkroom for processing surveillance shots of terror targets. By 1997, KSM, in addition to hatching the attack plots, is believed to have been involved in monitoring news reports, updating computer systems, and laying the groundwork for what would later become bin Laden's "media committee," which would create al-Qaeda propaganda videos. In 1999, according to testimony supplied by a participant in the bombing of the USS *Cole*, the pre-9/11 training regimen entailed running through simulated in-flight computer programs and watching feature films that had hijacking scenes. Around that time—as would later be revealed on videotapes confiscated from an alleged Madrid-based al-Qaeda cell—what appeared to be advance teams, posing as tourists, took video cameras on scouting missions to potential U.S. targets, including a tour of the Trade Center's observation deck. Some investigators have even theorized that once missions were under way, al-Qaeda may very well have communicated by encrypting messages to one another, embedding them surreptitiously within photo files posted online.

Based on information gleaned by *The Wall Street Journal*'s Alan Cullison (who came into possession of two computers used by al-Qaeda's top operatives in Afghanistan), it is evident that bin Laden's men had devoted space on their hard drives to everything from scans of pilfered passports and ID cards to media coverage of the attacks to special interactive collages with faces of Islamist "martyrs." "[J]ust days after the attacks," Cullison would write in *The Atlantic Monthly*, an al-Qaeda conscript, presumably using video-editing software, created "a promotional video called 'The Big Job'—a montage of television footage of the attacks and their chaotic aftermath, all set to rousing victory music." (By 2005, bin Laden's man in Iraq, Abu Musab al-Zarqawi, whom U.S. forces would kill in a June 2006 raid, would set up a sophisticated "information wing," creating a spate of electronic offerings: from a monthly online magazine to videos in which Zarqawi himself would apparently behead Western hostages for the benefit of the camcorder. Video, in fact, would later backfire on Zarqawi when a tape of propaganda "outtakes" came to light, showing him, in American-brand gym shoes, fumbling with a machine gun, and requiring an aide's assistance to properly fire the weapon.)

Once bin Laden went into hiding after the September 11 attacks, he ceased to exist as a bona fide "public" figure and, instead, *became* his image. Just hours after the first U.S. aerial raids on Afghanistan, on October 7, he suddenly materialized on Qatar's al-Jazeera network, appearing for the first time since the September attacks. He had gone to great lengths to prerecord a defiant videotape in which he wore battle fatigues as he spoke of a planet irrevocably altered. "These events," he intoned, "have divided the whole world into two sides. The side of believers and the side of infidels." Bin Laden had made certain that once the U.S. bombing began, it would be *his* face and *his* message—direct and uncensored—that would play from Peshawar to Peoria, whether he was dead or alive.

On November 3 and December 26, he resurfaced on TV screens, both times in camouflage, though in the second session his limited gesturing and the placement of his gun—at his right side—caused analysts to wonder whether the left-handed militant might have been injured. In between these two tapes, an "unauthorized" homemade video emerged, recorded in November and shown on international television in mid-December. The tape, reported by *The Washington Post* to have been "obtained in Afghanistan during the search of a private home in Jalalabad," was made available not by al-Qaeda but by the U.S. government.

The footage—showing a seated bin Laden in what appears to be a private house, engaged in an animated, circuitous conversation with a Saudi sheikh—amounted to a self-incriminating deposition. As the sheikh speaks about jubilant Arab reaction to the attacks, bin Laden admits: "We calculated in advance the number of casualties from the enemy who would be killed based on the position of the tower. We calculated . . . three or four floors. I was the most optimistic of them all. Due to my experience in [the construction] field, I was thinking that the fire from the gas in the plane would melt the iron structure of the building and collapse the area where the plane hit and all the floors above it only. This is all that we had hoped for."

The clandestine nature of the tape—taken from across the room, at a low angle, with bargain-basement sound quality—left viewers and intelligence experts uncertain as to whether bin Laden knew or cared that he was being recorded, and whether the tape's release was somehow sanctioned by al-Qaeda. Some even wondered whether the video was a sophisticated bit of disinformation created or ginned up by American agents so as to prove, verbally and visually, that bin Laden was indeed behind the attacks. (On the tape, the normally reed-thin bin Laden seems fuller of face and at one point begins to write, uncharacteristically, with his right hand.)

The videos, of course, burnished bin Laden as man and as myth. Unlike still photographs, which could be doctored more convincingly—and with cheaper software—videos provided flesh-and-blood proof of his having survived, and their accompanying audio tracks made it possible to date them, since bin Laden would invariably refer to an event in the recent past. The tapes became the centerpiece of a concerted media campaign by al-Qaeda to convince the world that its leader—thought by some to have been killed, wounded, or cornered in the allied assaults on

Tora Bora, Afghanistan, in November and December—was still among the living and in command, even if he appeared weary, possibly recovering from recent war wounds. "After a month passed without another videotape," Jane Mayer pointed out in a 2003 piece in *The New Yorker*, "some experts began thinking that bin Laden was dead. Then came a stream of audio recordings, faxes, Internet postings, and other communications, all asserting, or implying, that bin Laden was alive."*

But videotape was always bin Laden's trump card. (Radio personality and humorist Don Imus would joke, comparing him to the recording artist: "Bin Laden's made more videos than Usher.") The tapes conveyed a measure of technical sophistication. They projected distinctive personality traits, and physical resilience, that still pictures could not. And they reinforced the extent of bin Laden's political reach. In the past, according to the old saw, all politics was local. Now, in the age of electronic connectivity, all political acts had the potential for worldwide impact, through the ripple effects afforded by global media. All that was required, bin Laden understood, was a leader with charisma, a cause, and access to a camera.

Bin Laden and his acolytes continued to disseminate dollops of video and audio during the five years after 9/11. On the attacks' second anniversary, al-Jazeera showed a clip depicting bin Laden making his way down a mountainside, prophetlike, walking stick in hand *(Figure G)*. "Intelligence analysts will no doubt scan the tape for every geographical clue they can find," wrote Philip Kennicott in *The Washington Post*. "But mountains are also mythic space . . . Mountains aren't just a place one retreats to, but a place of refuge, a place closer to God . . . Perhaps that's the intention. He is not on the run, he's out for a walk. He's not in a cave, but on top of the world.

"It's as if someone on his video production team," Kennicott reasoned, "has channeled the spirit of the old Nazi propaganda filmmaker, Leni Riefenstahl . . . straight from the annals of German romanticism: Show the old warrior looking like a young poet communing with nature . . . The tape shows not just that he's alive, but that he's alive and *in a better place*. If

*The Bush administration strongly cautioned U.S. media outlets against broadcasting lengthy excerpts from bin Laden's videos, warning that they might contain secret signals, possibly instructing his followers to initiate terror attacks.

you were carefully controlling your own mythology, this is precisely the kind of tape that would be inspiring right now. Osama in the clouds."

Then came the propaganda coup de grâce. In 2004, five days before Americans went to the polls to elect their next president, bin Laden appeared on camera, demon ex machina, addressing the U.S. voter in the language and manner he knew best: face-to-face and over the airwaves. In a new videotape he downplayed the significance of the two candidates and the political process. "Your safety," he declared, "is not in the hands of Bush, Kerry, or al-Qaeda. Your safety is in your own hands."

Whatever bin Laden's intentions, the video was cited as a linchpin in Bush's eventual triumph over Kerry: many on-the-fence voters, unnerved by the very propaganda they decried, decided to throw in their lot with the law-and-order candidate. Even John Kerry himself, interviewed in January 2005, contended that the video played a key role in his loss, even though he had been upended by many other factors. "I believe that 9/11 was the central deciding issue in this race," he said in his first postelection TV interview, with NBC's Tim Russert. "We were rising in the polls up until the last day when the [bin Laden] tape appeared. We flatlined [that] day . . . and went down on Monday." Kerry would tell Jeffrey Goldberg of *The New Yorker* that Americans felt "a visceral unwillingness to change Commander-in-Chief five days after the bin Laden tape."

If he weren't so diabolic a presence, the leader of al-Qaeda might well have been seen as irony incarnate. His appearance, in many ways, aped the famous antiwar ad created in 2002 by the progressive political activists at TomPaine.com (just as America was laying the groundwork for taking out Saddam). The ad, widely downloaded from the Web, shows bin Laden as Uncle Sam. He points toward the viewer, daring Americans to throw their support behind a war that could, as the ad copy reads, "distract [the U.S.] from fighting Al Qaeda . . . divide the international community . . . [and] destabilize the region." The picture's headline: "I WANT *YOU* TO INVADE IRAQ."

On September 14 Pakistani officials confirmed that the leader of Afghanistan's Northern Alliance, Ahmed Shah Massoud, had died five days earlier as a result of wounds inflicted when al-Qaeda operatives, posing as newsmen, assassinated him with booby-trapped camera equipment.

Massoud, the most visible and viable opponent of the Taliban regime, was known by his *pakul* hat, Lincolnesque beard, and appealing smile. He combined Che's mystique with Yasir Arafat's staying power. Even as his counterparts perished or slipped into obscurity, the charismatic Northern Alliance chieftain had persevered, fending off in turn the Soviet Army and the Taliban over a twenty-year span. In and around the peaks of the Hindu Kush, he had achieved the status of a warrior of the noblest mold.

Massoud's September 9 murder was particularly grisly. The bombers, disguised as journalists nominally employed by an Arabic news service, had commenced a prearranged interview with the guerrilla leader. As Massoud made himself comfortable in a chair, one of the men readied his camera. The supposed interviewer explained that he would be posing a series of questions, then asked: "What will you do with Osama [bin Laden] if you get him?" Massoud responded with a hearty laugh.

At that, the videographer triggered his bomb. He was blown to bits; only his legs were left intact. Massoud, too, was mortally wounded, dying within minutes of the explosion. The second assassin was shot dead by a Massoud bodyguard.

The killers had been enlisted by al-Qaeda as part of a plan to remove Massoud from the political and military stage on the eve of 9/11. Bin Laden had probably reasoned that were America to seek retribution for the pending attacks, Massoud would have been the only credible leader around whom the West and other Afghans could rally in their fight against al-Qaeda and the Taliban.

Bin Laden, tellingly, had always been wary of booby-trapped cameras. Christopher Isham, now chief of the investigative projects unit of ABC News, remembers that as long ago as 1998 bin Laden's minders had insisted that Western crews not videotape him unless they shot with gear provided by al-Qaeda. "His men insisted, repeatedly, on providing their own equipment and cameramen," says Isham. In a battle of wits, however, Isham managed to persuade bin Laden's minions that for authenticity's sake an ABC camera was far superior. "I said, 'With all due respect, I've seen your cameraman's work. You want your guy to look good, right?' Eventually, we were able to get a one-man crew in. Bin Laden's vanity had trumped his concerns for safety." Indeed, bin Laden and his team had possibly hatched their plot against Massoud as a ghoulish manifestation of this photo-paranoia.

"He lived and died by the media," explains journalist Sebastian Junger, who spent time in late 2000 covering Massoud for *National Geographic Adventure* magazine. Even so, Junger notes, the same could be said of "any other leader, including bin Laden, especially bin Laden." (The pair shared another attribute as well: Massoud's nom de guerre was "Lion of Panjshir"; "Osama," it so happens, means "lion.")

Massoud, Junger points out, had recruited his own internal press cadre. "He knew the power of the media," he says. "He trained six cameramen to document the war against the Soviets, realizing how difficult it was for journalists to get into Afghanistan and [then] get their film out into the world. Only one of those original six survived. They were very, very brave guys." When one young Afghan offered to fight with his troops, Massoud refused, says Junger. "You're too young," Massoud told the boy, "but here's a camera."

Junger says that he and Reza, the photographer who accompanied him on several trips to the region, learned about Massoud's last moments by talking with his closest bodyguard. "Massoud basically died in this guy's arms," recalls Junger. "He said Massoud had such respect for journalists—or understood their usefulness, depending on how you want to interpret it—that he [had a policy of asking] his bodyguards to step out of the room [in the presence of journalists]. He didn't want to show disrespect [or risk] being intimidating to them. He also ordered his bodyguards not to search reporters."

On the morning of his murder, Massoud expressed trepidations about the two journalists who had waited a week or two to meet him. Massoud's attackers, Junger believes, could not have "got as close to him with any other type of equipment." But the killing, he insists, was not the result of inattention. "It wasn't a sloppy naïveté at all," he says. "It seemed to be a sacrifice he was willing to make. He was trading security for the opportunity to reach out to the press. He realized he needed the press in a kind of way that bin Laden did too."

If Massoud's murder was inevitable, so might have been the weapon of choice: death by camera.

On Friday, I called my old friend Jean-Jacques Naudet, an editor at Hachette Filipacchi Magazines who specializes in photography. I had heard that on Tuesday the attacks had almost claimed his sons, Gedeon and Jules, both filmmakers, and both of whom I'd known since they were teenagers growing up in New York City, their adopted home. I wondered how the family was faring. Little did I realize how horrifying, and incomparable, their experience had been.

Jean-Jacques told me that on Tuesday he had been dining at the Voltaire, in Paris, with photographer Bettina Rheims. During the meal, the restaurant had begun to buzz. "New York has been attacked," he heard. "The World Trade Center . . ." Naudet excused himself and left for his apartment nearby. He was certain that his sons were in the twin towers.

The night before, at midnight Paris time, he had spoken by phone with "the boys," as we have always called them (even though Gedeon and Jules were then thirty-one and twenty-eight, respectively). For several months the pair had been making a documentary film about Engine 7, Ladder 1—the Duane Street firehouse in downtown New York, just seven blocks from the World Trade Center. That evening, Jules had cooked gigot—leg of lamb—for the thirteen men on duty, and had called his father to talk about the meal and the progress of the film; many nights Jules and his brother had checked in with their parents after finishing their station house dinner. "We knew they were up all night," said Naudet. "They were living there. They had been accepted [by the firefighters]. In their minds, they had *become* firemen."

That afternoon and evening (Paris time) Naudet and his wife, Shiva, watched it all play out on television, terrified for their sons. "I'm sitting five meters from her, in a corner across the living room," Naudet recalled. "We don't exchange one word for four hours. The telephone rings all the time. It's never the kids. I am extremely disagreeable to these callers. Finally, around seven p.m., we hear from a friend that both of them are at the firehouse alive. We both broke down, but still are separated by this huge living room."

Six months later, his sons' documentary, *9/11*—about the men of the Duane Street firehouse—would air for two hours, in prime time, on CBS. Directed by the Naudet brothers and their firefighter partner, James Hanlon, their film would be the only visual chronicle of the September 11 attacks from start to finish. Their footage (the brothers shot nine hours of tape that day) is the true Zapruder film of the New York terror attacks. With much of its narrative playing out in real time, the movie, including additional scenes distilled from more than 140 hours of reportage and interviews, is relentless, unflinching, and excruciatingly intimate. And yet at the same time it is inspirational in its portrayal of the valor of a tight knot of firefighters. "A monumental piece of history," in the words of the *Boston Herald*, "it could be the greatest, most intense TV movie ever made." Remarked *The New York Times*: "[It is] an important, firsthand piece of history . . . You may . . . find it impossible to take your eyes away [even] for a second." (I would have the opportunity to serve as an executive producer of the documentary, along with Graydon Carter, Susan Zirinsky, Hanlon, and the Naudets.)

The filmmakers' personal story is possibly the most chilling yet ultimately uplifting episode related to the visual representation of 9/11, a story that seems no less elemental in its way than the images they shot on the day that would forever alter their lives.

Gedeon and Jules Naudet were unusually devoted to one another, even as brothers go. Like many in their proudly bohemian circle, they were smitten with cinema and with New York City. They even possessed the smoky allure of film stars. Gedeon, compact, with the piercing eyes of a falcon, was Jean-Paul Belmondo; lanky Jules, three years younger, was a soft-featured Antonio Banderas. At boisterous parties and free-form dinners, they held forth on film and journalism and the meaning of existence with an intensity that often accompanies raw youth and perpetual sleep deprivation.

As boys growing up in Paris, and then on Manhattan's Upper East Side (where their father had resettled the family in 1989), Gedeon and Jules had a dark dynamic. Jules, looking up to his older brother, remembers him as "the cool kid. I wanted him to be my best friend. With his friends, he would avoid me at school. The lack of closeness with my brother was a very big factor in my [early] life." To make matters worse, Jules, on his sixteenth birthday, was diagnosed with severe curvature of the spine. He was consigned to a body cast, then a corset, for four years. "I would not date at all," he says. "I felt like a freak, everyone gawking. I turned inward and matured faster." Jules, over time, became more sensitive, self-effacing—and tough. At twenty-four, he sailed up the Amazon from Brazil to Peru. He took up fishing for marlin, competitively. He went scuba diving with sharks in the Indian Ocean.

Gedeon, on the surface, was the dark and brooding one. In fact, he possessed the wiles of a conjurer and a cheerleader's vim. He was quixotic, generous, fiercely principled—and amazingly resourceful. While directing his first film, at age twelve—with Jules serving as producer (filling in after one of Gedeon's classmates swiped their seed money to buy candy)—Gedeon duped his principal into giving him the run of their school for a week by insisting, falsely, that actor Gerard Depardieu had agreed to stop by for a cameo.

Gedeon was also endearingly impulsive. I remember an afternoon, several years before, when he and I were both attending the Arles photo festival in the south of France. After a long outdoor picnic on a ranch in the Camargue, Gedeon decided, on a whim, to try the local custom of dashing through the nearby bullring. He ended up bloodying his face in a scrape with a bull, requiring several stitches. In 2000, impetuous as ever, Gedeon proposed marriage to a childhood friend as they walked past New York's City Hall. She accepted, though five months later they divorced.

While growing up, the brothers had been spoon-fed movies by their father, formerly a film critic for French *Vogue*. As children, Jules remembers, "we watched a movie every night during dinner. Many evenings, if there was a classic on TV, we would watch that too, and my father would write a note to the teacher to explain, 'Sorry, the kids are tired, but they *had* to watch Hitchcock,' or Renoir."

In their twenties the brothers finally forged a lasting bond, through cinema. Gedeon took a full course load at New York University film school while Jules, pretending to be Gedeon but not actually enrolled, also attended classes. Soon they decided to make documentaries together: Jules became the fastidious producer, Gedeon the impassioned director. They believed that creating films—beginning with their first feature, *Hope, Gloves and Redemption*, about young boxers in Spanish Harlem—would allow them to indulge their affinity toward groups and social classes normally off-limits to outsiders. "We like to look on the other side of the mirror," Jules confesses, "and identify with people who live on the fringe of society. It's a French thing. We're definitely voyeurs." Adds Gedeon, "When we did our boxing movie"—which took grand-jury honors in 2000 at the New York International Independent Film and Video Festival—"we both almost joined the Golden Gloves tournament."

For years, firefighters had intrigued the Naudets. At a party in the mid-1990s, Gedeon, smoking a Gauloise, had met James Hanlon, a brash, cocksure fireman-in-training, smoking Luckys. They clicked at once, and the Naudets were soon palling around town with Hanlon, an occasional actor. (He has since left the FDNY to pursue his acting career.) They were taken with his French wife (a ballerina turned actress), his Bronx-Irish brogue (he narrated their boxing movie and, eventually, *9/11*), and his firehouse tales of camaraderie and peril. The more time they spent with him, the more determined they were to make a film with Hanlon that would explore the heroism and brotherhood among men such as those at his fire station.

In September of 2000 the three friends approached the Fire Department brass for permission to shoot their movie. By May 2001 the FDNY gave them carte blanche, the first such access granted since the 1970s. Their documentary would explore the closed world of Hanlon's post—Engine 7, Ladder 1, among New York City's oldest fire companies, founded in 1772. They would focus on a fresh-faced, twenty-one-year-old "probie," a rookie from the Bronx named Tony Benetatos, following him from his first day on the job and on through the summer and fall.

First, though, the Naudets and Hanlon needed financing. HBO, the Discovery Channel, and Vivendi Universal all turned them down. One network seemed intrigued, according to Hanlon, but "they wanted to turn it into *The Real World*: a Latin fireman, possibly a woman, a short, funny guy, and then a handsome guy. I said, 'I think we've come to the wrong meeting.' "

"Absolutely no one would produce the film," recalls the Naudets' father. "So they borrowed money from a friend. To pay back the loan, Gedeon took a job as a busboy on the Lower East Side." Jules, meanwhile, took a job assisting a Swiss film director on his first feature, a comedy called *Heartbreak Hospital*. (The brothers had one camera, which Gedeon would use; soon they decided to borrow more money to get a second, for Jules.) And almost every night they would repair to Duane Street. "I would sleep at the firehouse," says Jules, "do our film at night, go to work in the morning."

The Naudets spent weeks trying to win over the firehouse. "Half the guys would not talk to us for a month," says Gedeon. "They really hate cameramen and journalists. Hate their guts." Says Hanlon, "Firemen are a very rough, brazen bunch. The boys came in very polite and courteous. Some of the guys thought it was an act."

But over the months, the brothers earned their subjects' respect by virtually living at the ninety-six-year-old station house, absorbing the arcana of the fireman's craft, and placing themselves in harm's way. Soon, a new anxiety set in. "Fire duty downtown had been sporadic through the summer," Gedeon says. "It was making the guys very nervous. If there are no fires for a long period, you know something really tough is going to happen. As the weeks passed, we were nervous, too, spending so much money on film, and there was no action. We were desperate.

"But we're having the best time of our life," he continues. "We were so excited, expecting to have a fire. We couldn't sleep, drinking coffee, anticipating the moment. All summer we heard from firefighters, 'Be careful what you wish for.'

"This firehouse, like every one, has superstitions. We'd heard about the Midget Rule. When you see two little people anywhere in the street, both on the same day, then you know you're going to have a job. For two months, we had been searching, then on the evening of the tenth of September, Jules saw little people and I saw little people. In two different places. Insane." That same evening, Jules cooked his special leg of lamb for the men on that night's shift. "I only made one leg," Jules recalls, "not enough for the group. So they busted my balls for two hours, gnawing on the bones like hungry cavemen. And *then* they ordered a pizza." The ribbing, in fact, was a sign that the brothers had been accepted into the fold.

Still hoping to respond to their first big alarm, the Naudets, as usual, sat up most of the night, occasionally dozing on the firehouse couch.

On the morning of September 11, the station received word of a gas leak at Lispenard and Church, near the twin towers. Chief Joseph Pfeifer, head of the battalion that includes the Duane Street house, responded; Jules, camera rolling, joined him in the battalion car. Unflappable and taciturn, his mouth set firm beneath a graying mustache, Pfeifer, forty-nine, sped north, two fire trucks trailing. (Gedeon, who always stuck close to Benetatos, the young probie, remained back at the station house; Benetatos was just going off shift.)

The fire team arrived at the scene of the reported leak. The day was bright and cloudless, as if cast in lapis.

Jules—a producer who, at his brother's urging, had learned to shoot video only the month before—trained his Sony PD150 on Pfeifer and his men at work in the street. To get a gas reading, they dangled a handheld monitor above a street vent. Jules focused on their hands, the monitor—and then he heard a roar directly above him.

"I look up, and it's clearly an American Airlines jet," he says. "There is a pause of about two seconds before reality sinks in. Because I had seen it disappear behind a building, I turned the camera toward where it was going to go—the World Trade Center, directly down the block. I see it go in. I'm filming it go in. The jet enters and you actually hear a boom, delayed." (The Naudets allowed a ten-second clip of the first plane's attack to be distributed to news outlets, but in those first months, they held off showing any more videotape, in deference to the families of the lost firemen.)

"We rush downtown," he recalls, "and I'm filming. I see there's about five floors missing where the plane crashed, everything absorbed. We arrive at Tower One, and firefighters are entering through the broken windows of the lobby. I don't see any other companies." Pfeifer, the first battalion chief on the scene, took command and would continue to dispense orders to the nearly two hundred firemen who arrived at the north tower that morning.

"Entering the lobby," says Jules, "I saw two bodies burning on the floor. One was screaming, a woman's scream. The jet fuel had come down through the elevator shafts and had created a fireball in the lobby. Time stood still. It was the first time I had seen someone about to die. The windows had all been blown out. The marble had come off the walls." Then and there, Jules says, he made a conscious decision not to photograph the horror he saw just beyond the range of his camera lens. "I didn't think anyone should have to see this," he remembers thinking, suspending his role as uninvolved journalist and assuming that of a humane soul caught up in a tragedy.

Nonetheless, he continued shooting. "In about five, ten minutes," he says, "we hear what sounds like explosions. A firefighter immediately says, 'We got jumpers.' People were leaping from such a height that, as they touched the ground, they disintegrated. Right in front of us, outside the lobby windows. There was completely nothing left of them." Their descent was so swift, their impact so total, these deaths cannot be discerned in the footage, except through the sound and fury of the firemen's reactions—and the worried jerk of Jules's camera. "With each loud boom," he recalls, "every firefighter would shudder."

Gedeon, at that stage, had left the firehouse by himself and rushed down Church Street, having heard what he thought was a sonic boom. "I take the camera," he says, "arrive at the corner, and see a huge hole in the building. Every single person in the street has stopped. I'm thinking, My God, this is too big. For two months we're waiting for a job and all of a sudden the most incredible catastrophe is right in front of you. You want to report [the story]. And you think, You're not ready. I'm all by myself. The probie's at the firehouse, Jules is following the chief.

"The cameraman in me took over. I realize I am here to film. This is too important to fuck up. And so I film. I'm attuned to the faces in the street. I look through the lens and see people expressing just what I'm feeling. I'm doing a succession of pans and tilts: people's reactions . . . up to the buildings. And as I'm tilting up, I hear a gigantic explosion, and I get the second crash on tape as the plane goes in.

"You have this extreme sense of emergency going on all around you," he says. "It's not just panic in the crowds. You *are* in real danger." Gedeon doubled back toward the firehouse, hoping to reconnect with Benetatos. On the way, camera rolling, he videotaped the havoc around him—confounded crowds on street corners, a woman whimpering as she ran, expressions of shock uttered in a half dozen languages. Through his lens, he spied a smoking hulk in the street; it would turn out to be the engine of the second plane.

Jules, meanwhile, was still filming in the lobby of the north tower, careful to stick close to Chief Pfeifer. "He always kept an eye on me," says Jules, "like a guardian angel." Jules, for the past hour, had photographed teams of arriving firemen, laden with gear, receiving their assignments from Pfeifer, then departing for the stairwells. At one point Pfeifer's brother, Kevin, a lieutenant with Engine Company 33, appeared, awaiting instructions. The Pfeifer brothers nodded, exchanging a sentence or two. Then Kevin turned to ascend Tower One.

Jules began wondering about his own brother. Surely, he thought, Gedeon and Benetatos would have already arrived with the engine company and then would have followed the others upstairs. He was certain he must have missed them in the chaos. Suddenly, Jules noticed that his hands were trembling as he shot. He was unnerved, he realized, by the look on one fireman's face, then a second, and a third.

"When I saw firefighters worried," says Jules, "that's when I started to panic. I saw something I'd never, never seen in a firefighter's eyes: uncertainty, disbelief—*what's going on?!* The bodies are falling. The guys are going up. Hearing of the second plane, hearing the Pentagon was hit.

"Then I remember hearing a rumble, and everyone starts to run like crazy. The roar is getting louder and louder as I run. The light changes and everything becomes pitch-black. I definitely think the building is coming down. I was afraid of dying. I put my T-shirt over my nose. The air is full of dust. I stop, crouch down, just waiting for the ceiling to crash on me. There is a strange calm." At this point, Jules believed that Tower One had partially caved in above him; in fact, Tower Two had just collapsed, covering the Tower One lobby in debris.

By his on-camera light, Jules established that he was on an escalator adjacent to the lobby, having sprinted down a concourse. A half-dozen fire chiefs, disoriented and coughing, were with him, stumbling in the ashen haze. Using his camera's beam as a lantern, he helped them navigate through dust clouds and devastation. But his light—and his camera—also revealed another sight: the body of Father Mychal Judge. Minutes before, the Fire Department chaplain had been administering last rites to a fireman outside. Now Father Judge lay dead at Jules's feet. "It was probably a heart attack," says Jules. "Or it could have been marble that flew off the wall and snapped his neck."

With this, Chief Pfeifer gripped his handheld radio and gave an order: "Command Post from Tower One. All units. Evacuate the building." His words were received and acknowledged, and his men began descending the tower.

"In the smoke and frenzy," Gedeon now says, reviewing the footage, "you can hear all the other chiefs talking. They are in shock. But Pfeifer is alert enough to pick up the walkie-talkie and call for an evacuation order. The reason Pfeifer thought about it first is because he was thinking about his own brother, whom he had ordered to go as high as possible to extinguish the fire. That would be the natural instinct of a brother."

"It's the biggest disaster since Pearl Harbor," says Hanlon, "and [Chief Pfeifer] never wavered. They didn't know—they *couldn't* know—the extent of the south tower just falling. I know from personal experience with Maydays that maintaining your focus is extremely difficult. But quickly, instinctively, he makes a command decision that saves possibly dozens of lives. He gave them just enough time to get out before the north tower fell."

By this time, Gedeon had arrived back at the station, having worked his way through the throngs in the street. "People were screaming and crying," he remembers. "I'm only focusing on 'I just lost the probie [in the crowd].' I hate myself for that. At the firehouse, I learn that Tower Two has just collapsed. As I'm filming, I'm realizing that they're all dead, all our firefighters. And maybe Jules is dead."

Gedeon and three firemen jumped into a pickup truck and headed for the Trade Center. He was troubled by the fact that everyone else seemed to be fleeing past them, *away* from the towers. Suddenly Mayor Giuliani appeared, passing in front of his viewfinder. Even the mayor was heading in the *other* direction. "The people are all completely covered with dust," Gedeon says. "I don't understand why everybody is leaving. It's driving me crazy. I'm filming because it was very important for me not to lose it, not to go hysterical. I didn't want to think the worst about Jules.

"We park almost at the corner of Church and Vesey Streets," he continues. "As we walk we see wounded people. And then something strange happens. As we're walking past the Engine 21 fire truck, I stopped and froze. There is a kind of force field pulling me back but I want to go forward to the tower. I feel it clearly, clearly inside, this image in my heart of Jules. I'm sure he needs me. But, like in *Star Wars*, 'the force' was telling me not to leave."

As he stood, immobilized, the firefighters receded from view, treading ahead through the squalls of dust. Gedeon remained stock still, watching them dissolve into the dust like phantoms. "It was like being a wild animal on alert," he recalls, "looking up, down, everywhere in great, great, great danger. And I just felt safer closer to the fire truck, enveloped in this huge, catastrophic feeling that Jules might be dead."

Four minutes later, Gedeon says, "I look up and I see the other tower collapsing, literally above my head. I jumped into the belly of the fire truck. An FBI guy jumped in as well. Everything is falling down and falling hard. I could hear pieces of steel crashing. I remember coughing and putting myself in a fetal position. I left the camera filming. I can remember the truck windows shattering. You're certain you're going to die with a big piece crushing you. The anticipation is killing you.

"But strangely enough, I was not thinking about my funeral, my parents, my friends. I'm thinking only of Jules. I was the older brother, feeling responsible for him. I felt like I had put *him* in this mess by making this movie. At the beginning, I had the only camera. But we had borrowed more money to get Jules a camera. Before August, Jules never took a camera in his hand. It's *my* fault for insisting that he film down here."

In the darkness of the truck, Gedeon says, he made a vow. If Jules were to somehow survive, "I would never treat him as a little brother again. I realized how much I loved him and how I'd never really treated him as a person but as someone I had to take care of."

Jules, a half block away at that instant, had just exited the tower through a glass-enclosed walkway and was now on the street—still close enough to be endangered by the collapse. He had been filming continuously for almost two hours. "I never stopped my camera," he says. "Just eight seconds to reload tape."

Out of nowhere, he recalls, he heard "this familiar roar. I heard one guy screaming, 'It's coming down!' I start running like hell, and the roar is getting closer and closer. I jump in between a TV news van and a car. I feel someone jump on top of me—I have no idea who. I've put my camera down. I'm aware that it's still running. I'm thinking, Why stop filming *now*? And I feel that gush of air. The dust crosses in front of me like a wall. Once again, I put my T-shirt over my nose and mouth. There's paper flying all over. Then it's pitch dark. Strangely, I'm really pissed. My reaction is not fear. I'm feeling: I've just gotten out of that building, where I thought I was going to die—and *this* happens. I thought, Enough! Can't I get a break?!

"About 20 seconds later, the person on top of me asks, 'Are you O.K.?' Now I realize it was Chief Pfeifer. He had thrown himself on me, to protect me.

"I held on to his arm as we walked away, through the dust. I think he saved my life a few times that day."

Jules decided to take leave of Pfeifer and started to walk the streets "completely in a daze," he says. "My thought was that my brother and the probie were probably in the tower when it collapsed. From there, it goes downhill. I can't film anymore. For the next half hour, I'm crying my tears out, just going up and down the street, asking every firefighter I see, 'Have you seen anyone from Engine 7 and Ladder 1?' In my mind, I've lost my brother, I've lost James [Hanlon]—my best friend—and the entire company's gone. Suddenly, a lot of guys scream, 'We have a gas leak. Run! It might blow.' I'm feeling pissed again, as if I'm trapped in a terrorist version of that [Martin] Scorsese film, *After Hours*. When is this going to end?"

The Naudets, as they would later learn, were wandering less than a block from each other. "It's not a street anymore," Gedeon recalls. "It's like a nuclear winter. All the cars are on fire and there's steel beams everywhere." The three firemen who had gone ahead of Gedeon minutes earlier were all seriously injured.

Within a half hour of the second collapse, Gedeon arrived at the firehouse, covered in dust. Sometime before noon Jules walked in through the engine bay, his eyes locking on Gedeon's. "We jump in each other's arms and hug quite a long time," says Jules, "letting go all the pain. Then I got into the filmmaker's mode. I said, 'I got the first plane going into the tower. I filmed during the entire thing.' " One by one, every member of Engine 7, Ladder 1, including the young Benetatos, returned—shaken, but alive—as Gedeon shot each joyful reunion.

At one point, Jules, alone with Gedeon in the firehouse kitchen, was overcome with emotion and, covering his eyes, began to weep. Gedeon embraced him, wrapping his head in his arms. A camera, operated by a friend of theirs, captured the scene as Jules confided to Gedeon, in French, "It's not pretty to see burned people. I know now what it feels like when you're going to die. I know now what death looks like."

Many would come to refer to Engine 7 as Lucky 7. In Fire Department parlance, 100 Duane Street became the Miracle House: every one of its fifty-five firefighters—including the thirteen on duty that morning and the forty-two who rushed to assist them—escaped alive, thanks in no small measure to Joseph Pfeifer's decisiveness. Though Kevin Pfeifer, the chief's brother, was killed that day, survivors say they saw Kevin between the ninth and tenth floors of the north tower, redirecting firemen to the cleared C staircase, saving them vital minutes in their descent and, quite probably, their lives.

"The parallels between the chief and I are so strong," says Jules. "We both knew our brother was in that tower. We lived through that ordeal side by side. We felt the same panic, same fear of death, same sense of loss. Worrying for your own flesh and blood brings the sorrow and the doubt to an even more horrible level. For me, I'm completely in awe of him. He's my hero."

For three weeks after September 11, the Naudet brothers and James Hanlon shoveled and filmed and shoveled at the Ground Zero pile. "The worst was not the eleventh," says Gedeon, "but the weeks after: remaining at this huge, tottering place, full of smoke and the smell of death, realizing you just dug up a piece of someone that a fireman is putting into a bag." They would go on to shoot the rescue effort, the precarious caverns beneath the rubble, the memorial service for Kevin Pfeifer. And, always, they returned to their brothers back at the firehouse.

Through the winter, the Naudets, Hanlon, and their colleagues at CBS News rushed to finish *9/11* for its March 11 airdate. The two-hour documentary would attract more than 40 million viewers during its first showing, then millions more on the first anniversary of the attacks, airing in more than 140 countries, winning the Emmy as the year's outstanding nonfiction special, and raising more than $2 million for a scholarship fund for the families of New York City firefighters. "Reviewing the footage in the editing room," Jules noted during the process, "we relive that day, every day, over and over and over. I have nightmares quite a lot. I have a dream that I'm still in the lobby when Tower One comes down."

Jules also had another distraction as he finished the film. He was planning a June wedding—at the fire station—to Jacqueline Longa, a human-resources counselor from Brooklyn (with whom he has since had two children). Gedeon would serve as best man. And although they were still finalizing the wedding's details up to the last minute, one thing was certain from the start: the brothers insisted they would not be serving lamb.

"In November, the night before the American Airlines plane crashed in Queens, Jules cooked lamb," said Gedeon. "He will never cook a leg of lamb again."

"That's off the menu," said Jules.

Their father, in hindsight, is able to assess his sons' shared experience not only as a parent but also as a journalist. "Most of the material of that day is Jules's," he says. "On September 11, things rebalanced between them. Jules is no longer the little brother. He never stopped filming. And Gedeon stopped twice. [Gedeon shot] the second plane but [missed] the collapse of the first tower. When the last tower collapsed, he mistakenly put his camera on zoom as he jumps inside the fire truck. Yet five minutes after they are reunited, Jules breaks down, crying. Gedeon, once more, in this moment, is the older brother again, comforting him."

On September 11, Gedeon evolved as well. "I realized that day," he says, "that Jules didn't need me to treat him as a little brother, someone you have to nourish and help grow up. He didn't need me for that anymore—and probably never had. Ever since, I've been a better brother.

"On that day," Gedeon adds, "Jules progressed as a cameraman more than I had my entire career. I never had this gift. Jules has it."

The image had moved on the Associated Press wire. But the remarkable story behind the image—one of the few taken *in* the towers *during* the attacks—hadn't begun to circulate within the photo community until later that week.

John Labriola was a committed amateur photographer who would try to devote a stretch of time each week to documenting his workaday world with a digital camera. "The light was beautiful that morning," he remembers. "My inclination was, and still is, to capture the life going on around me." Around 7:45 a.m. he shot cartons of pears and grapes at an outdoor fruit stand, the Manhattan Bridge arching over the East River, a Greek Orthodox church. He stopped to take a few frames of the Trade Center's south tower jutting up into the morning. Then, like thousands of others, he entered an elevator and went up to his office—on the seventy-first floor of Tower One, where he worked as a technical consultant for the Port Authority.

Forty minutes later, while in a meeting in a windowless conference room, he felt the building wobble "five or six feet in each direction," he says. He heard a massive explosion above him, which seemed eerily out of sequence with the rocking that had preceded it. He tried to rise from his chair but couldn't; the entire structure was swaying.

He peered through the door toward a far window. Slightly disoriented, he saw what he thought was a rivulet of tickertape outside the glass, akin to the streamers he had seen one year when the Yankees had won the World Series. In fact, he was watching rafts of files and papers, seven stories above him, that had been propelled from the building. At that very instant, balls of flame roiled past his line of sight.

Labriola rushed to his cubicle, instinctively grabbed his knapsack, and with other coworkers began hustling down a tower stairwell already jammed with evacuees from higher floors. Halfway into his descent, which would take a full hour, he brought the camera out of his bag. And for the next thirty minutes he photographed his companions. He shot the huddled procession of workers going down; he caught the expressions of firefighters as they climbed toward him, then past him, some never to return.

"I saw firewalls falling," he says. "I saw people burned. We felt the second plane hit, then heard through a news-retrieval pager that the Pentagon had been hit. The firemen's faces told the tale. They were contemplating the unknown. They looked like they'd been climbing a mountain. You could see that they were scared, but resolved."

Labriola's pictures, 110 frames in all, are extraordinary. Some show the blur of firemen's jackets—passing inches from his lens—as the men scale the stairs. In several pictures, firefighters seem to swirl like dervishes, their figures made spectral and indistinct by their rapid climb, the camera's movement, and the relatively slow shutter speed. Other images contain the streaks of passing helmets flickering like flames: red ID markers, yellow reflective tape. Labriola's digital memory card, like some spirit medium with access to the shadows of another world, was there to catch mortals going up and down to meet their fates.

One image—showing the firefighter Mike Kehoe, of Engine Company 28, walking up the crowded twentieth-floor stairway *(Image 25)*—would soon be printed the world over. Kehoe's expression seems slightly startled. He appears short of breath, burdened by seventy-five pounds of heavy clothing and equipment (just off-camera, he carries an oxygen tank with an extra cylinder and a leather control bag containing fittings and wrenches needed for hooking up a hose to a standpipe). His face glistens with sweat, illuminated by the flash. In the darkened stairwell, the blast of light gives a shimmer to the numbers on the helmet: 28 and 12898. Cherubic and ruddy-faced, boyish for his thirty-three years, Kehoe seems to be facing his destiny head-on, his eyes wide.

Much of the photo's power comes from the fact that the viewer, when first encountering it, reacts with a rush of observations and queries, thereby spinning out a silent story line: *He is going* up *the stairs. Surely, this man must have died shortly after this shot was taken . . . My God, he seems so young . . . How many more were with him?* It is from such twists of plot and misperception that certain pictures, taken at key moments in history, become little parables in a frame, acquiring the traction of fables. Given the right mix—compelling narrative, arresting light, surprising composition—such images can germinate into icons.

In fact, Kehoe made it out alive. He would retrace his steps, running down twenty-eight stories after receiving the evacuation order. Once in the lobby of Tower One, he paused to catch his breath, then exited—with no more than a minute or two to spare, by his own estimation. "We looked up," he says, "and the floors were pancaking on top of one another. We started running north up West Street. I turned around to see this charcoal-gray-brown dust cloud gaining on us. It was like being in a cartoon, trying to outrun what I thought [were] big chunks of concrete [and] steel." He crouched behind a fire chief's van as the wave of wreckage passed over him. The cloud filled his lungs with grit—"like cake was stuffed in my mouth," he says.

Six of Kehoe's mates would not survive. And soon after the attacks, their portraits—those of Michael Cammarata, Edward Day, John Heffer-man, Richard Kelly, Jr., Michael Thomas Quilty, and Matt Rogan—would be displayed at the firehouse on the Lower East Side. "They had a memorial out on the sidewalk," says Kehoe. "There were pictures of them afterwards outside on the wall. And they placed part of the door to the ladder from their fire truck that [had been] recovered. And somebody stole it." Despite this one act of vandalism, hundreds came to give, not take. They shared their sorrow and their prayers with the survivors and the families of the lost. They paid homage to the fallen by standing in silence before their photographs.

Yet for those outside the circle of the firehouse, it was Kehoe's portrait that would be the one the world would flock to. "[E]veryone wanted a piece of him," wrote *Time* magazine's Jodie Morse. "There were 40 messages a day from reporters . . . One particularly aggressive fan, 'Judy C. from New Hampshire,' wrote almost daily on stationery with pink hearts and drove all the way to New York City . . . just to see him in the flesh. Mike's father taped the photograph to his refrigerator next to a laminated postcard of Jesus." Kehoe, blinking away the tears, would accept a Pride of Britain award (on behalf of "400 emergency services personnel killed on September 11 and their surviving colleagues"), receiving accolades from Prince Charles and Prime Minister Tony Blair.

Some of his colleagues began to resent it all. "Guys were ribbing me constantly," he recalls. "Every day there were reporters there at the firehouse. Even when I wasn't working. They were relentless. It was bothering [the others]. You're trying to deal with the loss of the six guys in the firehouse. You were seeing families of the people that were missing. And here's the press trying to come in and set up lights and cameras. It wears on you. It wasn't easy."

Time's editors, it turned out, included the photo of Kehoe in their Person of the Year issue (which honored Mayor Rudolph Giuliani). Kehoe had never been in contention for the title, but he might have made an intriguing choice: an otherwise anonymous man, in a spur-of-the-moment photograph, nominated to represent all "first responders" who had come to the aid of others.

Kehoe had not perished. Nor had he saved a single life on September 11. But this slight-of-build son and brother of a firefighter seemed to personify his profession. Unlike hundreds of firemen who were *not* caught on film that morning, unlike 343 who would not return from their labors, Kehoe was the one who had walked into the light and the lens as *if* he were mere minutes from staring death itself in the face. As such, Kehoe had become an inadvertent icon, The Fireman in the Stairwell.

Four years later, Kehoe is still reluctant to don the mantle of fame and eminence that the picture's public weight has imposed upon him. The photo, to Kehoe, is of only glancing consequence. "I don't think it's changed me at all," he says. "I still go to work every day"—he has moved to a Brooklyn firehouse—"I look at the picture and I don't think: Hero. I think: If I was in a fire tonight, in a three-story brownstone, that'd be me again. If John [Labriola] had been shooting two minutes before or after, you wouldn't know anything about me. If he was taking video, he would have taken [footage of] all five firemen with me.

"I can see how other people would think I kind of represent everybody who was there and those who didn't make it back. But I look at it: I was just doing my job. That's what firemen *do*."

While Kehoe has certainly had his share of dark days, and went on medical leave for a while in late 2001, he seems to have gained an inner strength from the experience. And the photographer, like Kehoe, has no regrets. But John Labriola has weathered what he calls "a sea of problems" in recent years, trying to balance his professional obligations (he was out of work for a time) with a new baby and the pressures of putting out a book of his pictures—all of this colored by the horrors of the day that won't go away.

"Most people had some shelter from the event," says Labriola, now forty-five. "[They] could move on and *away* from it. But having to be the caretaker of those images, while sometimes it felt like a gift, can be a tremendous responsibility and a burden. Maybe I looked a little harder and lingered longer than most—as a photographer looking, and as someone who *knew* that building and so many of the people in it."

Labriola had taken more photos up inside the burning towers than anyone else that day. He offered his images to the NYPD, FDNY, and other agencies. He gave them to the Associated Press to distribute. With the help of his brother-in-law, a computer specialist, he placed JPEGs of the shots on a personal Web site that night, then sent an e-mail out to his friends. "It wasn't more than twelve hours before the server crashed because so many people from around the world were trying to see them," he says. "It cascaded into hundreds of thousands of hits. The digital photograph, in this case, was [like] the pebble, thrown from those towers, and the ripple effects issued out everywhere."

Inevitably, he was sought out by victims' family members, with whom he willingly shared the pictures and any recollections he could. The process went on for months. "Someone's lost somebody and they want answers—maybe some clue," he says, four years later. "It was delicate to talk to them, and painful but beautiful to face them. Often, there wasn't an answer in the image: Was the side of the ear of *this* man the ear of their brother? How do you deal with the desperation of those reaching out to you when you have [only] the slimmest hope of helping them? Having had to tell the story over and over again and dealing with survivors, maybe my post-traumatic stress was delayed—to maybe this last year. In some ways I felt stronger *then* than I am today."

He felt conflicted, further, by competing forces of gratitude and guilt—for having been the man who had thought "to [pick up] a camera while . . . escaping just like everyone else." Though he had always been a self-described street photographer, his bread and butter had been his day job: helping to design safety and security systems for the transportation industry. "All of a sudden," he says, "taking pictures everyone wanted was just about the worst thing that could happen to me. It's the absolute alpha and omega of what one person could feel at one time."

Providence, Labriola believes, became personal on September 11, and continues to be. Once outside the towers that morning, Labriola headed toward Trinity Church, just steps from the Trade Center, realizing a prayer was in order. He felt blessed to be alive, and thankful to have had his camera. "My mother taught Sunday school, but I wouldn't qualify as a churchgoer by many people's standards. I passed the door of the church [and] I *had* to go in. If there was ever a time that one should say a prayer, that was the day. I'd seen a lot of people die. I saw people hurt severely in the stairwell. I saw objects hitting . . . the courtyard [that] I realized afterward were people. If ever there was a clarion call that there was evil and good in the world, 9/11 was it. It was a gut feeling—to say a prayer for the people up there.

"I walked through the [church] doors, knelt down, and the south tower fell. And it was as if a freight train had come down around the roof, like someone had dropped a black cloth over everything." Labriola remained inside during the north tower's subsequent collapse. Then he decided to venture out, and became once again a street photographer. He took pictures of the churchyard with its swirls of tan dust, dappled and murky as Monet's London. He photographed streets made desolate in an urban sandstorm, a squad car caked in ash, men in suits staggering home.

Through the years, he now says, the clamor and fear and carnage have receded, but not that sense of compassion he encountered up in the tower. "After going through what I did," he explains, "the one conclusion I came to on 9/11 is that people in the stairwell—and this is my Catholic upbringing talking—really were in 'a state of grace.' They helped each other. They didn't panic. Kehoe and others like him were reassuring—

going up, calmly, even though they must have been scared to death. And a lot of lives were saved because of that. And I knew it that day: that most people are basically good. I knew this, with certainty, because I had gone through the crucible. What a great example people left: be selfless, help the person around you, and get through it.

"And I photographed that."

On Friday evening, September 14, my wife and I celebrated her brother's birthday, if rather somberly, at Baldoria, our favorite Italian restaurant in midtown. At times like these a family gathering seemed a sane, fortifying antidote. What's more, we felt especially close to Baldoria's proprietor and host, Frank Pelligrino, Jr.

Frank Jr. and I spent many late evenings in the company of friends, acquaintances, and grappa, grappling with political and religious issues. Both a restaurateur and a graphic designer, he was inquisitive, compassionate, and deeply spiritual. We frequently talked about our faith (Frank a soul-searching Roman Catholic, myself a part-time practitioner of a wholly improvised Judaism Lite), about the meaning of life, the afterlife, and clairvoyance (on Thursdays Baldoria featured a tarot-card reader in the upstairs dining room). When pressed, he confessed to believing that the major crises of the modern age, which seemed inevitably entwined with religious strife in the Middle East, might very well foreshadow devastation of biblical proportion—to be followed thereafter by the arrival of a global savior.

Frank once told me about a friend who had had a profound influence on him: Father Gerard Critch, a Canadian priest who had been working in street ministries for many years and, according to an item in *Catholic World News*, had exhibited symptoms consistent with stigmata—visible wounds in the same spots where Christ had endured them during the Crucifixion. The report noted that local doctors in Canada claimed that in 1998 Critch had suffered "excruciating pains in his side, hands, and feet . . . with blood oozing from wrists and ankles . . . Parishioners who touched [him] at a Mass . . . said they were thrown to the floor by an invisible force, or felt injuries healed." (Shortly after 9/11, Father Gerard had come to New York and, according to a church communiqué, spent eleven days aiding "firefighters, emergency personnel and construction workers, whose feet were blistered by the intense heat at ground zero.")

On the Sunday after the attacks, I would later discover, Frank Pelligrino, Jr., had sat down at his computer. He says he had heard rumors via Italian television that certain Web sites contained "pictures representing all these different apparitions that showed the Devil's face in the clouds when the towers went down." He was dubious, of course. One program, to make its case, had resorted to superimposing arrows on unpersuasive pictures, pointing out subtle contours in the clouds. The Devil, clearly, was in the details.

Frank was intrigued. He went to CNN's Web site, clicked his mouse a few times, and brought up an image from the Associated Press, subsequently credited to the photographer Richard Drew. It showed the north tower, backlit, in the process of collapsing—erupting like some rectangular volcano dome spewing gray and white ash *(Figure H)*. With effort, Frank could make out an angel in the clouds. The shape seemed arboreal, as if a winged figure were suspended in the boughs of a tree above its trunk. He thought he could discern the outlines of a face. "I was skeptical," he says, four years later, standing over the computer in his restaurant's upstairs office. That Sunday in September, he says, as he pointed out the patterns to his wife, Carla, the restaurant's chef, she too was dismissive. Seconds later she was thunderstruck. "What are *you* looking at?" Carla asked him. "Don't you see *her*?"

There, in the center of the debris cloud, was the figure of a naked female, her head lifted toward the heavens, breasts bare, her body poised on one of the tower roof's corners. Frank was taken aback. "I saw in this picture the head and bust of a woman," he explains, "She's looking up and covering her loin[s]. Above her you see a cherub . . . the wing, his head, his legs, almost like he has a bow. To the left, in the clouds, there's a bin Laden character, a face with a beard and a turban. Over to the right, there's another silhouette that looks like a demon, and another guy with a beard. I looked at it and I saw in that picture that this was alluding to what I believe: that this is the beginning of the End of Days.

"If you go through the Book of Revelation," he says, "there's a passage that says that out of the towers there is a lady with her twins that have been sacrificed. Apparently this could be the beginning of the End Times . . . I printed out the photo on my home computer, brought it in to show everybody at the restaurant."

That Tuesday Carla had been attending classes at the French Culinary Institute, at Grand Street and Broadway, a few blocks from the towers. She had walked out of the building to confront survivors in the mayhem: a man missing an ear, another whose back was scored with burns. After seeing the picture several days later, Carla, who is Brazilian, says she went to her Portuguese Bible and showed Frank passages from Revelation that her mother used to read to her about "a woman with the moon under her feet, giving birth [in violence]. And I saw this in the picture."

Today, Frank acknowledges that he had been grasping for answers back then. Perhaps he and Carla, he says, had needed an explanation for the horrors she had witnessed. When a friend with connections at the Associated Press e-mailed him a copy of the original image file (that came directly from Drew's camera), the woman was still there in all her eerie shapeliness, her wings and torso even more hard-edged and distinct than they had seemed on the more suffused "Drew_5976167.jpg" that had originally run on the newswires. But with the passage of years and the alteration of the photo's resolution, it had lost some of its suffused, chimerical resonance. The figures, Frank now says, could have been "a function of the reduction of the image and the size of the pixels. Initially, because of the magnitude of what had taken place, it was a horrific time—it was startling and too detailed to be taken only as coincidence. Now, looking at the original . . . perhaps it is not as divine as I had originally expressed." Indeed, when Frank showed Father Gerard that same image on that same computer, the priest had his own interpretation. "Look at the dove," Frank remembers him saying, "rising from the ashes."

Even today, though, Frank, Jr., contends that "any rational human being looking at that photograph on the computer could come to the same conclusion we came to that weekend. Before that day, we thought it was a horrible experience. But after seeing the picture, I thought 9/11 could be an epiphany of some sort. Or an omen. It depends on which team you're on. I read in the Bible that the city would burn for three months, and it did." The concept of an apocalyptic conflagration, Frank says, seemed a viable prospect. "Horrors, trials, and tribulations," he contends, "just seemed so hard to dismiss after seeing the coincidences in that picture as a culmination of all the events, the shock, the fear—not knowing what was going to happen next."

The Internet was surely a party to all this. When Mark D. Phillips, a part-time photojournalist and Web consultant, snapped an image of the smoking towers and gave it to the Associated Press, many viewers first saw his photo in their newspapers or on news Web sites. By the Friday after September 11, several thousand strangers had sent Phillips e-mails describing their reaction to his "Devil" picture *(Figure I)*. Most saw Satan's countenance in the billows, spreading across the southeast face of the south pillar, like the turbid visage on the Shroud of Turin. Others saw bin Laden, or angels, wings, and halos. Here were hordes of Net denizens with fear in their hearts and time on their hands.

Phillips had shot the picture from his Brooklyn rooftop on a brand-new Olympus E-10. He exposed a digital card of twenty-three images and, on a second camera, shot one roll each of slide and color-negative film. He retreated to his apartment office, quickly downloaded his take, resized the first frame, and sent it off at 200 dpi to the wire service. Those at the AP picture desk, Phillips says, were looking at the same image he was, as a reduced "thumbnail." "None of us saw a face," he contends.

Then Phillips returned to his roof, only to see a new pall of smoke over lower Manhattan as the second tower collapsed. "I was all by myself," he recalls. "I sat down and started crying." As a photojournalist he had witnessed the explosion of the space shuttle *Challenger* in 1986. He had seen dead bodies at homicide scenes. But this was human loss at a level beyond all reason.

The next day, his photo agent called him, with urgency in his voice: "You have a face in your photograph." Phillips went to his computer, opened the picture file, and started trembling. "It's the Devil's face," he remembers thinking. "How did this get in here?" Newspapers ran his shot across their front pages. Charges of image tampering surfaced, which both Phillips and the AP were quick to discount. For authentication, he took his photo to the digital camera division at Olympus, where John Knaur, now the company's senior marketing manager for digital SLRs, helped vet the shot. "That's around the time Olympus first began to use hidden markers," Knaur says, "bits of text data within the picture files. We were able to determine that it was not doctored and was an original file."

For months, the e-mails continued to flow to Phillip's in-box, by the hundreds. "Three and a half years later," he says, "I still get about ten to fifteen a month on that one picture. People are still looking for a reason."

5 SATURDAY, SEPTEMBER 15

On Saturday *The New York Times* ran a page with twenty mini-obituaries. Seventeen of the short text blocks were accompanied by tiny headshots. A similar page appeared the next day, then the next. Saturday's page was labeled "Among the Missing"; on Sunday (when it was apparent that the missing had not survived) it was given the title "Portraits of Grief."

The feature delicately compressed the lives of the lost into one or two epiphanies, spun like fine silk within the fabric of 250 words. The writing style was spare, often idiosyncratic, verging on the conversational. The reader's empathy derived from his or her identification with the telling details of another's life, which came in small, understated bursts. ("Suria Clarke's first name means 'the shining one' or 'the sun' in Sanskrit . . . Clarin Siegel Schwartz . . . liked red cars, red dresses, jazz [and] jelly beans . . .") Each obituary was accompanied by a simple portrait, when available. And almost invariably the face in the photograph bore a smile.

It was through these faces, day after day, that many New Yorkers and others gauged the toll of the tragedy. For many whose friends and relatives and colleagues had been spared, or whose wider clique had been fortunate enough not to have sustained losses, these faces were their next-door neighbors' faces—parents and children and siblings—staring out from paper you could hold in your hands. And the name, "Portraits," reinforced the visual. *Behold . . . A lost man or woman is now present and accounted for; he or she must be seen and acknowledged.*

"I wanted readers to look into the eyes of the dead to remember them," explains Stella Kramer, who would serve as picture editor of the section for three months, phoning up and acquiring images from relatives of the deceased until, as she says, "I couldn't anymore. It broke my heart."

"Portraits of Grief" would become a morning fixture in the lives of *Times* readers. Weather and headlines. Coffee and bagel. "Portraits" and a morning cry. *Look how young she was . . . My God, they'd just been engaged . . . I wonder if they've profiled Russ today.* What truly counted, in human terms, was there in black and white: in the short stories of real lives told in words and pictures on a page.

One of the first twenty entries that first Saturday honored Calvin Gooding, thirty-eight, a Cantor Fitzgerald employee. It read, in part: "Whenever Calvin Gooding went to the barbershop, he would stare wistfully at the photo of the Broadway and television actress LaChanze hanging on the wall. He pleaded for an introduction, but the barber always refused. Then one night, Mr. Gooding spied LaChanze . . . in a Manhattan nightclub. He managed to introduce himself, and was instantly smitten. Two years later they were married . . . The Goodings had one daughter, Celia Rose, and Mrs. Sapp-Gooding is expecting another child in October."

Eventually, more than 2,400 Portraits of Grief would run in the *Times*. (Kramer was part of the editorial team that would win a Pulitzer Prize for public service for the section "A Nation Challenged," in which the Portraits page appeared. The *Times* would be awarded a record six Pulitzers for its coverage of September 11 and the war on terror, including two honors for photography.) They were journalistic haikus not just about people who had perished, but about people who had *lived*. People devoted to their mates, their hobbies, their pets, their volunteer jobs. People with newborns, fathers- and mothers-to-be, new immigrants and foreign workers just trying to make a go of it in a new world. And, not infrequently, people for whom photographs provided an outlet or a passion or a vital family bond.

People like Anthony Portillo, a Raytheon architect, who "considered himself a serious collector of calypso music . . . was also an amateur photographer. On weekends, he would take his family to places like the Brooklyn Botanic Gardens and set up his tripod." Leobardo Lopez Pascual, who worked in the kitchen at Windows on the World, had left four youngsters behind in Mexico, but would regularly receive "envelopes stuffed with photographs; it was how he watched his children grow up. He sent home a picture . . . too: He is sitting in a ferry on the way to see the Statue of Liberty." Avnish Patel, a globe-trotting research analyst, was "a talented photographer [who] pasted images from his travels (along with nuggets of wisdom culled from his favorite novels) . . . on [his] Web site." In his ninety-third-floor office in the north tower, Patel kept a black-and-white shot of the Statue of Liberty, "a proud dark silhouette across an expanse of glinting water [next to which he] had written: 'Freedom! Liberty! The ultimate symbol of the greatest city in the world.' " Salvatore F. Pepe, an assistant vice president at Marsh & McLennan, "kept [his] family connected [by putting] together a photo-filled calendar marking the birthdays and anniversaries of the 60-odd members of his, and his wife's and his six siblings' families and hand[ed] it out to everyone." Berry Berenson Perkins was "a photographer for *Life* and *Vogue*; a model with Vermeer-blue eyes and golden hair; an actress; the sister of Marisa Berenson; the wife of [actor] Anthony Perkins; the mother of their two handsome boys . . . Oz and Elvis. [S]he boarded American Airlines Flight 11 to see Elvis, a musician, perform in Hollywood."

And there was NYPD photographer Glen Pettit, mentioned earlier. Pettit's "Portraits of Grief" entry, headlined "The Smile Behind the Camera," would read in part:

> Glen Pettit took on a lot and never let it slow him down. In addition to being a New York City police officer, he was a TV news cameraman, a freelance photographer, a volunteer firefighter and a devotee of Irish tradition and music.
>
> . . . Officer Pettit, 30, had joined the [police] department's video production unit, which makes training and promotional videos. "His great-

est love was being behind a camera, composing a shot," said his partner, Officer Scott Nicholson. The video unit responded to the World Trade Center attack hoping to get footage for an annual promotional tape it makes called "Heroes."

"Glen was telling us, 'I'm gonna get in close; you stay and get the establishing shots, get the rescue workers responding,' " Officer Nicholson recalled. "I looked over and Glen was running past me, camera in hand, heading toward the towers."

And those entries were just from the *P*'s.

At Camp David, Maryland, on Saturday, George Bush's war council convened. They were presented with a briefing booklet entitled "Going to War," created by George Tenet's team at the Central Intelligence Agency. Every page of the classified document was stamped at the top with a small photograph of Osama bin Laden, his image used as clip-art, squeezed inside a circle with a hash mark. No caption necessary. The message was clear: This struggle was not against inchoate enemies (violent extremism, global terror), nor was it a showdown with Iraq's Saddam Hussein, whom some White House insiders had already hastily implicated as an accessory to the attacks. Instead, terror had a face. This was about routing al-Qaeda and Osama bin Laden.

Barbara Baker Burrows was working through the weekend. *Life* magazine's picture editor, Burrows, along with a small photo-research crew, was pulling together images for what would become a bestselling 9/11 photo book, *One Nation, America Remembers September 11, 2001*. In time, she would accumulate thousands of images related to the attacks, collected in a makeshift archive—on photo CDs, computer printouts, duplicate slides, laser copies, and photocopies.

As the months passed, Mayor Giuliani began to focus on preserving, for posterity, a lasting record of his administration's efforts. Soon, working alongside legendary documentary producer Sheila Nevins of HBO.

Giuliani fixed upon the notion of creating a visual and oral archive of the events of 9/11. Fanning out to find hidden gems among the city's photo trove of that day, HBO's team, headed by Brad Grey and Nevins, would hire TV documentary producer Peter Kunhardt. Nevins's and Kunhardt's teams tracked down nearly a thousand hours of footage from videographers and filmmakers, known and unknown. At the same time, Kunhardt turned to Burrows, who provided copies of her copies. (Kunhardt grew up in a virtual archive himself. His father, Phil, the ex-editor of *Life*—and my first boss—collected nineteenth-century photographs, and helped accumulate the Meserve-Kunhardt Collection, an extensive private archive of Civil War images, which includes the work of Lincoln's photographer, Mathew Brady.) The pictures that Burrows, Kunhardt, and HBO assembled would eventually be edited down, then copied into duplicate sets and donated to the New-York Historical Society and the Museum of the City of New York.

Their project would become an award-winning HBO documentary called *In Memoriam*, possibly the most unvarnished visual presentation of September 11 shown on U.S. television. At the public premiere of the film, in May 2002, Giuliani would make comparisons with Pearl Harbor and the Holocaust. He contended that viewing the so-called graphic images of the attacks would not numb us but embolden us, making certain that our memories of the horror—and, in turn, our resolve—would never fade. With pictures, Giuliani said, "comes truth"; through truth, he insisted, "we are bound together."

Among the artifacts gathered by Kunhardt's crew was an item that never made it into the documentary: a holiday card sent to friends and relatives of the Uman family, of Westport, Connecticut. The card contained three dozen small pictures of Jonathan Uman, an eSpeed managing director who had been lost on September 11. "[T]his holiday season," read the inscription, "I share with you some of my priceless, irreplaceable memories. I share with you a look at my last year with Jonathan . . . Celebrate this holiday season knowing that you are appreciated and loved. Cherish each other and enjoy each moment together. Take lots of pictures."

The greeting read:

HAPPY HANNUKAH, MERRY CHRISTMAS & HAPPY 2002

LOVE, JULIE, ALEXANDER AND ANNA UMAN

Giuliani's words and the Umans' pictures brought to mind the sentiments of editor and scholar Leon Wieseltier. In early 2001, he had written the foreword to *The Last Album*, a volume of family snapshots—formal portraits, group portraits, baby pictures, wedding pictures—taken from prisoners just prior to their extermination at the Auschwitz-Birkenau death camps, then collected in book form decades later by Ann Weiss. "These photographs," wrote Wieseltier, "were brought to Auschwitz because they represented what the martyrs wished to remember . . . We do not know the names of the people in these photographs, but we know something just as precious, just as binding: we know the objects of their devotion, who and what they loyally loved. We have been initiated by their deaths into their intimacies. We remember what they wished to remember; and in the memory of their memory, they live."

Ad agency chief David Lipman has a home on Murray Street, the first residential block north of the World Trade Center. For more than an hour and a half on September 11, he experienced the same frenzy as many of his neighbors: careening around downtown Manhattan in search of his loved ones. "I was looking for my wife, son, and daughter," Lipman remembers. "I found my son's stroller, empty. I didn't find my family until after the second tower came down." Fortunately, all four of the Lipmans returned home that day.

On Saturday (as he did for most of that first week, and as he would for the next), Lipman volunteered at Ground Zero. Some nights he stood on the assembly line, passing debris in buckets; at other times he dispensed water or hamburgers to workers. Throughout that first week Lipman noticed something that surprised him.

"On the hour or half hour," he says, "a break would come. And all of a sudden cameras would come out for just a few minutes. A Hasselblad, a Mamiya, a Pentax, a Rolleiflex. Everything from medium-format to disposable cameras. These firemen and E.M.S. workers took pictures. It seemed like every time you turned around there was a camera.

"There was definitely an unwritten code," he remembers, "that no one would know about it. It wasn't about glamorizing the event. It was very personal. I think they wanted to document this for themselves—for their own memory. I kept saying, 'I *feel* why they're doing it.' Everything was so emotional, my hands would have been trembling had I brought my Contax. I couldn't [bring myself to] bring it."

Lipman, a sometime photographer himself, believes that those pictures, taken from the firemen's perspective, hold the unseen story of the disaster: the eyewitness take, up close and intimate, by those at the tragedy's epicenter. "No movie set," says Lipman, "could ever re-create the way it was lit. It was so theatrical, so moving—you see these broken buildings and thousands and thousands of workers with a mission to find one person. Their pictures show the eyes, the emotions, the fear, the terror, the hopelessness, the emptiness, the loss. And yet they don't even begin to show how destitute it really was. When the second week of digging started, there was really no hope."

For six months, Lipman would linger over photos of the event. He went so far as to place a huge blowup of Ground Zero on his office wall—nine feet square, a print so large you could discern hundreds of individual workers on the pile. "I couldn't run away from it," says Lipman. The main reason he displayed the image so prominently, he says "was to recapture and face what happened. Flying two planes into a building is so beyond human comparison. We know war, we know conflict. But this sci-fi, *Die Hard 4* disaster movie coming to real life is beyond your worst nightmare. Watching the people fall. The screams of onlookers coming like a rolling wave. So I searched for something visual that would say: *That's* what I went through, *that's* what these people went through. The closest thing to capturing it was the firemen's pictures that are now stashed in homes and drawers and closets, unseen."

Tens of thousands of New Yorkers, drawn by the images as if by a force field, had to see the site with their own eyes. And even though the zone was closed to civilians, visitors got as close as they could—within a few blocks.

Officials firmly discouraged photographers from taking pictures of the devastation. But many amateurs and professionals found ways to document the street life that echoed out from the ruins. Photographers such as Kevin Bubriski turned their backs on Ground Zero and, instead, focused on the reactions of individuals and couples as they laid eyes on the killing fields for the first time. Bubriski's black-and-white Hasselblad portraits—square in format, blade-sharp at the center and progressively softer at the edges—are arresting studies of the stunned.

Shot from the waist up, each of his subjects has just encountered the destruction over the photographer's shoulder. And each seems anchored in the pavement, shocked into stasis. They are oblivious to his presence, some craning their necks or covering their mouths. A few clench their fists; others fold their arms. Each is mesmerized, engulfed in a hollow, pit-of-the-stomach dread. Their stillness is cocooned, in a way, since the narrow depth of field afforded by the 80-mm lens subtly blurs their immediate surroundings. They look up and out at the sprawling mangle and they remain immobilized by how moved they are. They take on the appearance of figures in nineteenth-century portraits who were forced into fixed positions, the picture-taking process, as the literary critic Walter Benjamin wrote three generations ago, the "procedure itself caus[ing] models to live, not *out of* the instant, but *into* it; during the long exposure they grew, as it were, into the image."

Why had these people been compelled to come and look? "Their motives were probably a confusion of the noble and the impure," visual arts critic and writer Richard B. Woodward would observe. Some, suspicious of televised terror, needed a firsthand glimpse of the annihilation. Some had to witness in order to tell others that they had witnessed. Many were aggrieved. Many were gawkers. Most however, were sincere.

On five occasions between September and December of 2001, Bubriski, who lives in Vermont, made the two-hundred-mile "pilgrimage," as he called it, to watch how bystanders "slowly approached the site, [then] came to a full stop, planting their feet firmly as if to keep themselves from wavering or falling," then settled into their own private "moment of reflection." In cloth coats, in suits and ties, in surgical or even gas masks. With eyes closed in prayer; with hands or chins pressed, to steady them, against a lover or a friend; with a child hoisted on a shoulder.

Each photograph has an overriding quietude. And yet they are, as Woodward noted, "among the most shattering pictures to come out of the event, and the quietest." He would liken Bubriski's images to Roger Fenton's scattered battlefield cannonballs during the Crimean War: post-combat shots that reduce war's horrors to its reverberations. In a hushed manner not altogether dissimilar to Fenton's, Bubriski chose to focus on war's ruin, refracted. He made the devastation more bearable, perhaps, by how it registered as sorrow and stoicism in the body language of passersby. Here was the body politic not as a citizenry terrorized but as a sequence of individual, living witnesses, enduring.

As time went on, however, an element of terror tourism crept in. Within the larger flock, some had come to sheepishly ogle at the "spectacle," to be able to say that they were there, and to come away with a 35-mm memento. The last week of 2001, a large "viewing stand" was set up to accommodate the throngs. Five months later, the cleanup was considered complete.

The absence of the towers would slowly become a fact of metropolitan life. When tourists would travel to New York, many would wend their way to the site, only to discover that there was little left to *see*. The expressions on the faces of out-of-towers would sometimes betray an inner disappointment. They had come because they felt they had to pay their respects, even if only to inhabit the space next to the space. Inevitably, they would take out their cameras, and, absent any remarkable vista, would photograph one another in front of a fence. Some three thousand died. Here. Now we are here too.

To some degree, observes journalist Regis Le Sommier, each edifice damaged in the attacks now stands in for its absent mates. "In order to see the wounds," says Le Sommier, five years later, "you've got to find them on [surrounding] buildings [that] look like ghost[s] of the missing towers. There is an old building right next to it that bears the scars. There are slight burns that are still visible in the underground parking lots.

"Aside from ritual ceremonies that are held every year on the site, where the names of the dead are proclaimed, the emptiness makes it hard all through the year to commemorate the powerful impact of those dead towers. All of this is to say that the towers had to be found somewhere else."

Though the skyline, and our cameras, have been deprived of the towers, they now appear phoenixlike on posters and maps and in painted renderings that have been mass-produced, suitable for framing. Gift shops teem with talismanic towers on key chains, statuettes, bumper stickers. Tourists, unable to tote home actual images from the site, can still stuff the pint-sized versions into their carry-on bags, regardless of whether or not profit from the sale of such items has gone to any cause that assists those affected by the attacks. The WTC icon has become a profitable marketing entity, and has survived unscathed.

This was nothing new, of course. "[P]roliferating images . . . rippled out from the trade center almost from the moment it was built," wrote WTC "biographer" Eric Darton in his 1999 book *Divided We Stand*. "From the great factory of consumer culture, millions of World Trade Centers emerged . . . New York television station WPIX used the twin towers as an emblem of its channel designation: the number 11. Over the years the trade towers made cameo appearances in the form of novelty license plates and on countless postcards . . . Rendered in silhouette form, the towers' symmetrical doubling has been used as a kind of visual shorthand signifying 'New York.' "

"You see more pictures and postcards sold in tourist shops with New York and 'The Twins,' " says Le Sommier, "than with the city as it appears now. For the first time in its history, New York, a city built upon the idea of perpetual transformation, is stuck in time."

In New York, this is true enough. But there *is* a place where the city exists and the towers rarely do. And that place is television. Immediately after 9/11, non-news-related images of the World Trade Center were "almost universally erased" from the screen, noted Marc Peyser in *Newsweek*, whether it be "from a scene in *Friends* or the opening credits of *Who Wants to Be a Millionaire* and *Law & Order: SVU*." During entertainment programming, any on-air sequence that showed the towers standing became pictorially non grata. Establishing shots showed midtown, never downtown—with neither the old twins nor their gaping absence. (Movie studios began cleansing their footage as well, removing the buildings from features such as *Zoolander* and *Serendipidity*.)

This across-the-board purge didn't stem from the fear that the towers might "date" a program or a film. Instead, it was supposed that the sight of them had become so potentially hurtful to so many viewers that even a hint of them would prompt phone calls, complaints, even protest campaigns. The logic went like this: the towers, shown on a television screen, would call to mind the structures' demise and the deaths of thousands, thereby handing another subtle victory to the terrorists. Therefore, when consuming our daily dose of entertainment, it was better to cleanse the programs of the images than to risk the anguish of confronting the reality that those images represented.

"Everywhere I look I see people with cameras," Ingrid Sischy thought. "Photography's got its job back."

Sischy, the photography and art critic and the editor of *Interview*, would immediately begin writing a piece for *Vanity Fair* entitled "Triumph of the Still." In it she observed: "Wherever one looked—in newspapers, in the weeklies, in the many special editions, which sold by the millions—there were photographs to make one gasp, to break one's heart, to inspire . . . Within days people were predicting the rebirth of photojournalism."

In fact, off and on throughout the week, former colleagues of mine from *Life*, where I had worked for nineteen years, would call or send e-mails, bemoaning the fact that the magazine had recently suspended publication. "Where is it now, when we need it?" one asked. Said another: "I haven't worked at the magazine for two years now, but I immediately had the impulse to come to the Time and Life Building [to pitch in]."

In her article, Sischy would compare the pictures of September 11 to canonical images in the news-picture repertoire, such as Sam Shere's shot of the *Hindenburg* zeppelin. Borrowing a phrase from the introduction to a collection of images taken by World War II servicemen, she noted: "It's all there, all shot basically in one 72-hour period 'by thousands of Mathew Bradys.' "

In the course of a day, a new breed was born: the man (or woman)-in-the-street photojournalist. And she was a precocious child, at that. By 2004, the world was able to witness the Pacific tsunami's calamitous path thanks to the proliferation of tourists at several beachfront resorts who scrambled to brandish their camcorders. A year later, when four al-Qaeda bombings rocked the London transit system, killing fifty-two civilians and wounding more than seven hundred others, passengers on the darkened underground fished out their camera-equipped mobile phones before the smoke had cleared. Their images (of fellow riders wedged in subway cars or making for the Tube station exits) were posted on Weblogs and at photo-sharing Web sites before press photographers could even get to the scene. The next morning, "history was made," according to journalism professor Dennis Dunleavy, an arbiter of technology's role in visual culture. "For the first time, both *The New York Times* and *The Washington Post* ran photos on their front pages made by citizen-journalists with camera phones."

The next month, a photo-syndication agency, Scoopt, would be launched out of Glasgow, Scotland, for the sole purpose of selling amateur picture-phone photos to digital and traditional media outlets. Indeed, cell phone picture-taking among the young and the wired had become almost de rigueur when one's daily circumstances suddenly took on a special or extraordinary blush. Alain Genestar, the editor of *Paris Match*, would insist in 2006, "If 9/11 had happened today, the people inside [the towers] would have taken photographs on their cell phones, from inside, and sent the pictures out [over the Internet]."

News stations, during this period, would also begin to see the virtue of tapping into this great, underutilized resource: lensmen who already lived in the field. When Hurricane Dennis bore down on the Alabama and Florida coasts in 2005, CNN, MSNBC, and various local channels solicited videos and stills from viewers who might be closer to the storm's path than the stations' own news crews. Such overtures made sense at a time when budgets and news bureaus continued to be pared back, even as the news cycle had been sped up. A deluge of problems, however, seemed to be looming on the horizon. Who would be considered at fault, the network or the citizen-photojournalist, when the stunning footage turned out to be doctored or swiped, or proved to be an invasion of privacy or a misrepresentation of what it purportedly depicted?

No matter—for the time being, at least. The cat was out of the camera bag. In 2005, India's Arko Datta, winner of the prestigious World Press Photo of the Year Award (for his image of a prostrate woman crying out in the immediate aftermath of the tsunami), would go so far as to say that he was heartened by the appearance of such enlightened newcomers. "I feel it's a welcome trend," he told *The New York Times*. "The line between professional photojournalists and amateurs is thinning. And with more and more non-professionals opting to use their cameras to capture socially relevant images, it can only make photojournalism more popular."

Such optimism was not universally shared. Far from it. Photography scholar and publisher Fred Ritchin, director of Temple University's Transmedia Center, would argue in *Aperture* magazine that photojournalism, regardless of the power of the images generated on September 11, had in recent years been devalued as a credible catalyst for social and political reform. Instead, news pictures and documentary images (taken in the humanist tradition of what photographer Cornell Capa termed "concerned photography") had an ever diminishing influence in a society whose empathies had been deadened by the "bleak, unrelentingly grim" news cycle, and in mainstream media in which "images have become disconnected from the events they depict, informed more by the manipulative strategies of those in power, whether governments or media corporations, than by any moral compass."

As Ritchin saw it:

> Our vocabulary of imagery in mass media has . . . shrunk as we have abandoned the interrogatory form for the knee-jerk affirmation and for quick resolutions to our dilemmas. The destruction of the Twin Towers made for riveting imagery, but resulted in a series of instant histories whose intent was to produce immediate icons of the event. These icons, revolving around an amalgam of the Christian cross and American flag-

raising, were provided to replace doubt with the reward of instantaneous resurrection. We barely had time to grieve.

The managers of mass media, terrified of photography's capacity for disquieting ambiguities and irresolvable questions, prefer to illustrate bromides . . . In the medium of the mass, at least for the moment, the photograph has started to closely resemble a caged bird.

An elite regiment of Mathew Bradys—or a lone bird in a cage? Which is it? The documentary photographer, and his precious photo trove, has always been at risk. But rumors of the death of the photojournalist have been exaggerated for quite a while now, at least since the rise of television in the 1950s.

For the moment, I suspect, the old shooter still has some life in him yet. Along with scads of digital memory and a few rolls of Tri-X, for good measure.

Amid all the horror and ruin and death, why all this talk of pictures?

I am drawn to this subject—this week, of all weeks—because so many of us are at the mercy of images when it comes to understanding the events of September 11. I am also drawn to pictures because I believe that photography is a medium that gives us the illusion of immortality. We somehow feel that once we leave this domain, slices of us will live on in pictures, like cell samples on a microscope slide.

Most of us hardly realize how pictures serve as a nourishing undergrowth in the recesses of our lives. The weather forecast that helped me choose what I would wear today was created by meteorologists interpreting sequences of still photographs. The security cameras in my office building, my local bank, the various public spaces I traverse each day, are recording me in a steady stream of surveillance shots. My computer stores images and exchanges them with other electronic devices. My cellular picture phone takes snapshots through a viewfinder on its flip-back (I walk around with sixty images of family and friends and favorite landscapes and one clandestine video taken at a Rolling Stones concert in Toronto). My wallet contains pictures of my kids and my nephews, along with my driver's license—a photo ID that allows state and federal agencies to keep tabs on me. When my wife began to have early contractions seven months into her pregnancy, a sonogram (an image created with sound waves) revealed we were going to have twins.

For the typical modern man or woman, the mural of daily life is a sweeping photomosaic. An urbanite absorbs several dozen publicly displayed pictures every twenty-four hours. At the turn of the millennium, *Life* magazine noted that every day some 46,575,343 photos were generated in the United States alone—on digital equipment and traditional SLRs and throwaway cameras. But in only five or six years, with the cell phone snapshot explosion and the proliferation of photo-sharing Web sites, that number seemed paltry. By the spring of 2006, the buzz among some of the Web developers at Microsoft's MIX conference in Las Vegas was that the picture-rich MySpace.com was experiencing traffic surges of 1.5 billion page views every *day*. (A 2003 study by the School of Information Management and Systems at the University of California at Berkeley estimated that there are 900 billion photographs in existence, 150 billion of them created in the two years leading up to the 9/11 attacks.) Still images are the lingua franca of billboards and posters, magazines and catalogs, diagnostic files and police dossiers. They comprise the graphic bedrock of film and video, newspapers and Web sites.

In the larger scheme, photographs are shared documents, sometimes globally so. Our validation of world events often comes from news photographs, a common currency of information exchange. Our understanding of microbiology and subatomic physics owes to the beckoning eyepieces of electron microscopes. Our understanding of universal forces, on the grandest of scales, is derived from observations that astronomers have made through the star-drenched lenses of their telescopes, tracking events suggested by signatures of light that have left their distant sources eons ago, back near the first stirrings of time itself.

One sign of the medium's vigor is that the picture *business* is thriving. Despite widespread tales of woe (photographers forced to reinvent themselves in the digital age; photo labs and traditional picture firms closing by the score; photo jobs and budgets being slashed everywhere), there has been an explosion elsewhere in the industry due to the mass migration to digital. "Photography has never been healthier in its history," says my friend Jean-Jacques Naudet. "The need for pictures and the reference to photographs are now absolutely everywhere. [Prices at photo] auctions escalate and escalate. Collections are selling for millions. The celebrity, paparazzi, and party-and-event photographers work every night. There are now 100 photographic galleries in New York [alone]. In London, Milan, Paris, Madrid, Moscow, and Rio de Janeiro they have photography galleries in every block in some neighborhoods, and festivals [too]. My friend [recently] lost everything, and now he's making a fortune selling pictures for your cellular phone."

Fashion photography has become a cultural engine, fueling social and consumer trends and, in the process, blurring the lines between celebrity, style, and public image. Fine-art photographers have become as celebrated as painters. Photographs hold increasing sway through advertising and product packaging, and across the pop-porn-shop-and-gossip Google-monger called the Internet. Teenagers celebrate themselves and contemplate their belly rings by posting digital self-portraits online, updating their profiles and archives nightly. And now anyone with access to a mobile phone can become, with a few swipes of the thumb, an amateur shutterbug. (Nextel peddled one of its recent models with an intriguing promise to turn its owner into one of the "pocket paparazzi.")

The *New York Times* culture critic Frank Rich has gone so far as to assert that media has now usurped nature as "America's backdrop." (The average American, in fact, spends 95 percent of his day indoors.) As media creatures in this dense thicket, we consume a hearty daily diet of news, information, and entertainment that is largely parsed out in pictures. As a society we've spent countless eye-years absorbing ads, flipping through photographically plenteous publications, and surfing or clicking through screens.* And we are doing all of this, of course, as we blithely

* The average U.S. household has 2.4 TVs. Fifty percent of Americans live in homes with a digital camera. Seventy-three percent live in homes with one computer or more, and the typical Internet user in those homes devotes the equivalent of four full days every month to online pursuits. As of 2006, 50 million working cell phones in the United States had cameras in them; 125 million were able to access the Web. Smartphones, handhelds, and iPods (which in 2006 sold at a rate of one per *second*, worldwide) also allow consumers to surf the Net or view videos. All told, there are 1 billion PCs, 1.5 billion televisions, and 2 billion mobile devices on the planet.

multitask: a recent study of the habits of American teens showed that they take in, on average, 8.5 hours of media a day—in 6.5 hours!

Some believe that today's photo deluge has served to devalue each individual image, espousing the mantra that "nothing shocks us anymore" (an argument successfully presented, and later amended, by Susan Sontag). But one can also argue that such oversaturation has also made us graphically astute and therefore better able to gauge the subtle messages inherent in the images that parade before us. Clicking our electronic magic wands—or, as they've been called, our digitalia (the mouse, the joystick, the remote control, the miniaturized keypad, the Treo, the digital camera's shutter release), leafing through the pages of our dog-eared stacks of analog catalogs-mags-and-papers, snapping and scanning and e-mailing our latest Priceless Moments, we have emerged as an army of casual photo connoisseurs—armchair photo editors, part-time scanners, compulsive printmakers, family archivists, and, yes, empowered, self-published photographers, who also happen to be rather savvy judges of what makes one picture more inherently engaging than another.

Just as everyone's a critic in this age of the blog—Everyman is now a cameraman. And it has ever been thus. The photographic pioneer Alfred Stieglitz, in 1899, wrote that the sheer ease of taking pictures was "a fatal facility" requiring "little labor and . . . less knowledge [that] has of necessity been followed by the production of millions of photographs [each of which has] invariably some measure of attraction . . . even extremely poor ones." The medium, in the words of anthropologist Robert Dannin, is "the most democratic art form since charcoal and ocher were applied to limestone caves about twenty-thousand years ago."

We are vain (overly concerned with our own appearance) and voyeuristic (stimulated by visual input, often sexual in nature). We are hedonists (who enjoy the immediate gratification that pictures provide) and skeptics, wary and demanding of evidence. As such, we sometimes require visual certification of reality: in many cases we need to see an actual *image* of an event before we will accept as truth an assertion or innuendo by a politician or a news anchor, a scandalmonger or a movie star.

The pictures that matter most, to most of us, are innocent snapshots. Quite frequently they become our only tangible links to those spaces and faces we have loved and lost. Their appeal partly resides in the perceptible breath of spontaneity within them, "the tiny spark of accident, the here and now," as Walter Benjamin put it in 1931. "That spark has, as it were, burned through the person in the image with reality," Benjamin observed, "finding the indiscernible place in the condition of that long past minute where the future is nesting, even today." It is as if trace elements of yesterday had been bottled in the camera, like port, to be siphoned, once matured, from the vintage print. "Even our simplest snapshots," says Tom Bentkowski, *Life*'s former art director, "are complex documents. They are records of the present, made for the purpose of showing, sometime in the future, what the past looked like."

For many of us, photos are the glue we use to hold in place the disjointed bits of fiction and fact that make up the stories of our lives. They are also receptacles of secret fantasies, aspirations, myth, and love that can become the most cherished or powerful objects in our possession. When I was falling in love with the woman who would become my wife, it was a black-and-white portrait that her sister had taken that I returned to again and again, to glimpse the gaze that had smitten me: Nancy, the mischievous sprite, wearing a playful bowler and a seductive, sidelong glance. Her picture, for me, became a confirmation of what I took to be her essence.

Our most private images of all are those that we record through the mechanics of memory—at times a pictorial process. While memories, of course, can be nonvisual (the ability to recollect words or sequences; to retain and retrieve complex concepts; to sense, as Proust did, the swoon induced by the scent of madeleines), a good many memories have some visual component. They come individually, customized and embedded in our psyches. They come en masse, seeping into the culture's collective unconscious (a mushroom cloud over a desert testing ground; earthrise over a moonscape). These remembered scenes are actually symbolic mental "stand-ins" for long-ago moments. They can be mundane or historic, real or imagined. They can seem vivid, as are many short-term memories, or vaporous, fading in detail the longer they remain with us. They become soured or sweetened in our minds by how they have been witnessed and then encoded in the cerebral equivalent of the freeze-frame. "Watch her carefully, every moment, every gesture," says Gar O'Donnell in Brian Friel's play *Philadelphia, Here I Come!* O'Donnell is thinking aloud as he takes one last gander at his housemaid, Madge, on the eve of his departure for America: "Keep the camera whirring; for this is a film you'll run over and over again—Madge Going to Bed on My Last Night At Home . . . That's all you have now—just the memory; and even now, even so soon, it's being distilled of all its coarseness; and what's left is going to be precious, precious gold."

We gain access to these golden, visualized experiences through the most fragile of membranes: a pinholed lattice called memory that tends to flutter across the brain not as a smooth scrim of moving pictures—not as Madge scurrying about the house—but as a flicker of discrete, still images. These virtual snatches of past events, actual or fanciful, reside in the lightning-swift firings of neural systems, electric nerve impulses traded between nerve cells in the brain. Our memory banks, full of faded smidgens of ocular experience, are filed away as a vast, cross-indexed picture archive, whose frames are ready to be called up at an instant. The act of recollecting scenes or encounters or individuals that were first experienced visually is the act of tripping the mind's shutter to set the search engine in motion. Many of our memories, then, are retrievable as stills. Even the word—"stills"—implies that our perceived relation to a time and space somehow *remains*, if only in the infinitesimal span of a synapse.

"It makes evolutionary sense that our visual memories seem to be encoded as still and somewhat faded images, rather than moving ones," says the psychiatrist Jeffrey Claman, a professor at the University of British Columbia. He believes that biology may explain why "the still photograph resonates with our subjective experience of visual memory." Our brains, he says, have "a system of neurons that inhibits the activation of the vividness of memory (that is itself inhibited during REM sleep). It would be maladaptive if the waking memory of a perception were as vivid and real as the actual perception. We would be unable to distinguish between them. Remembering a perception would be akin to hallucinating that perception."

We trust pictures. We are neurologically comfortable with what we can see. Even in this era of computer-manipulated imagery, in which we are duped every day by the transmogrification afforded by Photoshop, even as we wholeheartedly acknowledge that pictures are *subjective* representations—biased by the particularities of film stock, camera type, lens length, and shutter speed; by the method of printing or displaying the finished image; by the aesthetic or journalistic "perspective" of the photographer—we tend to trust what we see within the boundaries of the photographic frame, appearances notwithstanding. Photographers, though famously crafty spinners of myth, are often called *impartial* observers. Pictures, although often deliberately untruthful or misleading—and almost always electronically enhanced, airbrushed, or tidied and tarted up—are nonetheless considered reality's proof positive, a sort of indelible fingerprint of past experience.

At dawn on Saturday, on assignment for *Vanity Fair*, I surveyed Ground Zero with Harry Benson. A legendary photojournalist who has made portraits of every U.S. president since Eisenhower, Benson is probably best known for his quintessential pictures of the Beatles at their vertiginous pinnacle in 1964: engaged in a midnight pillow fight in John Lennon's room at the George V Hotel in Paris. For most of his career he has been as comfortable covering conflict as he has the Paris peace talks—or the Paris collections.

Among Benson's most haunting portraits is one of Omar Abdel Rahman, the blind sheikh who inspired the 1993 World Trade Center bombing. It shows the white-turbaned, smoky-eyed cleric looking ominous and oracular in front of a black-velvet backdrop. Harry and I have worked as a reporter-photographer team in Kuwait and Oman, Israel and the West Bank, Poland under martial law and Afghanistan under Soviet siege, a shock-trauma unit in Baltimore and drug dens in New York City.

On September 11, in fact, I left my office and headed for Harry's Upper East Side apartment while he was covering the events for *Newsweek*. In the early afternoon, his wife, Gigi, and I ventured out to pick him up, along with his film and gear. Four days later, Harry and I made our way downtown.

Standing on the ridge of the pile, I saw devastation without end: beams in mammoth heaps, gnarled steel like fields of tumbleweed. I felt a chill as emotions rolled over me in bracing waves: despair, awe, hopelessness. In the tangle in front of me, a galaxy of human life had been enveloped and consumed.

I stood there, letting the cold ache subside, then felt a second surge—an odd and reassuring warmth. It came from the swell of solidarity among men who, by the hundreds, walked the ruins with a common purpose. And I realized that rarely in American memory had so much dedication and cooperative spirit been concentrated in one dark place.

The photographs and the television coverage I had seen had only hinted at the scale. Ground Zero was not one site, but several, spread out in mounds of almost Incan magnitude. My field of vision seemed to expand to encompass the sweep of it. Across sixteen acres, a thousand thousand tons of matter, now in heaps before me, had collapsed in fire and physics.

I watched men navigate through the tortured metal and Sheetrock, steelworkers toiling in the thick pall, setting torches to I-beams. I watched search-and-rescue squads—many of them firefighters, whose brethren lay dead beneath them—clawing for the fallen in the rubble's chinks and caverns.

Though the place pulsed with urgency, uniformed men and women, at every turn, kept trespassers at bay. And with good reason: nearby buildings were in variously precarious conditions; this was a crime scene (around which officials hoped to keep disruption to a minimum); and terror-conscious police and military personnel seemed to regard any intruder as a potential threat. Consequently, outsiders with cameras were considered extraneous, their passage forbidden throughout most of the zone—a function of an acute resentment toward the press, and the red tape that can enmesh disaster sites.

There was also something else afoot: a deep, inviolate respect for the dead. In the view of these guardians, whose coworkers had died merely doing their jobs, *their* job was crystal clear: they were to brook no trivial intrusion. Journalists, one could argue, were interlopers, meddlers, couriers of disrespect. They were, by their nature, intrusive, distracting, and superfluous to any situation they covered. They brought to each scene an outsider's taint. To these men and women, this was sacred space. And cameras were there for no other reason than to make that space accessible to *any*one. Cameras witness. Their pictures allow others to judge. But on that hallowed ground, the guardians believed, only the Almighty could judge.

Despite such restrictions, Harry and I managed to make our way to the precipice abutting Ground Zero, where the tower's exterior columns resembled the hull of a battered ship bobbing up from an ocean's folds. Moaning earthmovers, fire trucks, and tractors crept like prehistoric creatures. Masked figures strode through clouds of dust. Armed men stood at checkpoints. "It's like Beirut," said a priest standing next to me. Father David Engo had recently arrived from his home in Fall River, Massachusetts, intending to pitch in. "We came down for this," he said. The Reverend James McManamy, from Toronto, stood beside him. "Our main job," explained McManamy, "is to support the firemen and the policemen and their grieving. And to bless the bodies."

Suddenly the clergymen were summoned. Harry and I walked along with them. They joined a cordon of silent men in hard hats bearing a bulky bag on a stretcher. We took in the grim faces. We took in the new odor. We straggled behind as they walked, quickly but deliberately, past others who seemed to stop, respectfully. The stretcher bearers entered a wide doorway—MORGUE, a sign read—that seemed to lead through a gutted Brooks Brothers shop, its street-front window wells having been shorn of their panes. We followed, passing a line of exhausted rescuers receiving massages. "No, over here!" a fireman shouted.

One or two in the procession complained and grunted; then, rerouting ourselves back out the door, we were directed toward a large tent where a dozen people stood ready to receive the remains. The tent's door flap was drawn open. We could see rows of men and women inside. The shelter, like a tabernacle on a hillock, had a distinctly religious air. The hushed solemnity reinforced this impression. I thought, naïvely, that this group was waiting primarily so that it could bear witness as the priests blessed the departed—before the body would then be transported offsite. Instead, we would discover much later, the gathering was forensic. This was the disaster mortuary team.

Working under the auspices of the medical examiner, the group inside the tent included members of the uniformed services (police, Fire Department, Port Authority, the National Guard, among others). The team's role was to triage and prepare any remains for further examination at the city morgue. "The idea was to get the remains packaged properly," the head of the medical examiner's DNA lab, Robert Shaler, now recounts, "and then get them back where the autopsy could be done so that things could be documented properly." Whatever the search-and-rescue squads recovered was "put in a log book," says Shiya Ribowsky, director of World Trade Center identification operations. "The whole site was gridded out. The GPS satellite position of where it was found was noted, as well as who found it. If they were remains, the remains were tagged, then placed in body bags. I doubt very highly that what they carried that Saturday was a corpse. In fact, I only saw one whole intact body in all my time there. Instead, it was probably a significant portion of a body."

We stood under the threshold. The men with the stretcher stopped at the tent door and stood for a moment, half in daylight, half in shadow. Harry took photographs of the priests, the escorts, the stretcher that they carried. And then the men inside the tent became agitated. A knot of faces closed in around us.

"Get the hell out of here," one said.

"You sick fucks," said another.

The mere presence of a camera in this sanctum was intolerable. Heads turned, faces reddened. Two men at the tent door seemed to move toward us. We felt certain that police would soon be summoned to escort us off the grounds.

As we walked, Harry pressed the automatic rewind on his camera. He slipped me his exposed roll, which I hid in a pocket of my knapsack. Silently, we took our leave and hustled away. We could still hear one of them swearing.

Our escort around Ground Zero's outskirts was Mike Carter, then vice president of the firefighters' union (now a financial planner). At first he rebuffed our attempts to gain entry to the site even though we explained our intention to photograph "the heroes" of Ground Zero. "The perimeter's in almost total lockdown," he explained, adding, "how on earth can you photograph heroes here? *These* are the heroes." He gestured, pointing to his unseen colleagues under the rubble.

After lengthy conversation, Carter acknowledged that our photographic mission might have some merit. Soon he was helping to spirit us past sentries at roadblocks. He looked the other way as we burrowed camera equipment in backpacks and bulky clothing. He led us to the site perimeter, introducing us to firefighters who would pose for Harry's camera.

Carter offered up his own Tuesday tale. "I was in my car when the south tower fell," he remembered. "I got there and was carrying equipment in and we were quickly approaching the north tower." But Carter and his crew were held back by a chief who insisted they wait a while before he deployed them. "Three more minutes, I would've been directly in front of it. I would've died." Several months later, photographer Todd Maisel, who covered 9/11 for the New York *Daily News*, would send Carter a CD with 560 photographs that showed the event unfolding, minute by minute. "I sat down with a couple of beers one night," Carter now recalls. "I watched one frame at a time, for hours. I had this *need* to have to know . . . What were the first two units doing? Where were the rigs parked? What were the expressions on their faces? It wasn't a morbid curiosity. It was literally looking at the history of the event *before* I got there. A good friend, Danny Suhr, was killed. My understanding is that he was hit by a jumper. Todd has pictures of the guys in the company dragging Danny away from the towers. I got an opportunity to see their faces."

Pictures served a deeper purpose too, as solemn proxies for the deceased. Says Carter: "I literally went to funerals—over a hundred—in a four-month period. It was sucking the life out of me. At the funerals, up in the front by the altar, they would have pictures. At all the line-of-duty funerals before that, I had never seen photographs displayed this way. So the pictures were standing in for the bodies they couldn't find. At the memorials, where there *is* no casket, they would set up a little table, normally put a helmet out, a folded American flag, and they would have photos of the firefighter."

In the firehouses, sometimes near the engine bay, shrines would rise. Often personal effects and regalia would be laid upon a table, surrounded by flags, bunting, fire axes, painted frescoes, flowers, candles, and photographs. "It reminds me of the months I spent in Belfast and Northern Ireland," says correspondent Regis Le Sommier, who visited many stations. "Wall paintings there proclaim heroic deeds and remember dead heroes in the same way. Street after street, it is roll of honor after roll of honor, a deep sense of martyrdom that runs through generations. A lot of firefighters in New York are of Irish descent and their way to commemorate [and] venerate [may have this] cultural element to it."

With new seasons came new funerals. "From my town, Suffern, New York," Carter recalls, "Charlie Anaya had just gotten on the FDNY. September 11 was the first fire he ever went to, poor guy. They found his remains [later that winter]. They had used DNA. They finally buried him in May. On the back of the funeral program they had pictures. In one of them, he's with his wife standing with his children, standing on a dock in Jersey City. Almost rising up right behind his head were the twin towers.

"Who would think," he says, exhaling deeply, remembering the ex-Marine who had re-upped during the Gulf War, "that such an evil thing was going to happen in the very building that was the backdrop to such a beautiful photograph? Who would've looked at his smiling face, [on] clearly a beautiful day, and said, 'Two years from now this building's gonna kill you?' "

In the days after 9/11, colleagues of Carter's in the FDNY's photo unit assembled a collection of headshots of the firefighters lost while responding to the emergency at the towers *(Image 28)*. In a matter of weeks, a poster bearing the faces of 343 men—in eighteen tidy, heart-rending rows, framed by a pair of American flags and two Fire Department shields—would grace the walls of homes and offices as well as scores of watering holes and restaurants throughout the five boroughs.

The men who had tried to banish Harry and me from Ground Zero that day would have seen no paradox in sanctioning these pictures of the dead. This grid of faces was a sign of tribute, not of trespass. Placed in this formal, authoritative context—each in department dress, each accounted for, each burnished by his proximity to symbols of brotherhood and country; all positioned under the headline "New York City Fire Department Members Who Made the Supreme Sacrifice"—the firefighters were being given their due, recognized as heroes in a manner that was graphically proper, incontrovertible, and permanent. Their images, like souls, would surely outlast them.

After ninety-three hours of uninterrupted news coverage, CBS television finally resumed its regular rotation of commercials on Saturday at 6:00 a.m. When the attacks began, says Sandra Genelius of CBS News, "we were on live with *The Early Show*. The network went on at 8:55 and officially went . . . straight through with not a single commercial. Unprecedented in [CBS] television history." The other networks ran similar, marathon coverage, withholding commercials until some time around the ninety-to-one-hundred-hour mark.

Clearly, TV had been the great connector that week. When photographer Andy Levin brought his early "take" of the attacks to the Sygma photo agency on West Twenty-fourth Street, with its ninth-floor view of the still-smoking towers, he was struck by the fact that "the entire staff was looking up at a TV in the center of the room, watching the replays of the second plane exploding into the tower [instead of watching the] actual disaster unfolding only a mile away, and visible from the windows."

Even those *without* televisions learned about the events through television. Luc Sante doesn't have a TV because his house is on a road with no cable hookup and is situated in a pocket valley in upstate New York that is resistant to aerial reception. But he got the news from a television viewer: his mother's cousin, calling from Belgium. "This was an old woman who lives in the country," he says. "She doesn't know we didn't live in the shadows of the towers. [After her call,] I stayed online almost continuously, trying to find footage and ground-level reports from lower Manhattan."

Likewise, Robert Pledge felt eerily out-of-sync with the day. The West Side office of his photo agency, Contact Press Images, had neither a TV nor a view of the towers. (His garment district building was not wired for cable.) Instead, he relied on television, secondhand, as friends and clients overseas vividly described the scenes on their screens. "Everything was in deferred time," he recalls. "The calls came in from Delhi, Paris, Berlin, London, Tokyo, California. I knew the world [had] changed that day, for the worst, because of the amplification. TV had magnified it for everyone, and immediately. I understood the event's importance by this bow shock from Europe. We actually saw it through other people's eyes."

David Grogan, a science editor, had the opposite reaction. He was only ten years old in 1963 when President John F. Kennedy was assassinated, but he retains distinct impressions of television's power, back then, to unite the nation. "I remember watching the initial news reports that day in the classroom," Grogan says, "and then huddling around the TV at home with my family during the next few days, while other families across the country huddled around their sets. Television helped draw people together and had a calming effect. It was as if we were all gathered in a giant circle, holding hands." But Grogan's television experience on September 11 was anything but calming.

On 9/11, he walked from his Brooklyn apartment across the Manhattan Bridge and *into* the city, against the tide of evacuees—to extract his daughter from school. When he returned home, he turned on the television, expecting an update. (Grogan's proximity to the twin towers' antennae had always given him such clear reception that he didn't need cable service.) Yet all he encountered was a dull gray on every channel but one: a public station, he recalls, broadcasting from outside the city. The smoking skyline was faintly visible through a flurry of white static. He watched what he calls "the loop-loop of the footage of the plane hitting the trade towers." Then the TV went dead.

"For me," Grogan says, "watching the same footage of the towers played over and over again—even during the short time we had reception—was mind-numbing. The more I saw it, the more unreal it seemed . . . Much of TV news these days is inherently unreal because of the way time is distorted . . . That's not hard news: it's just visual porn." For Gro-

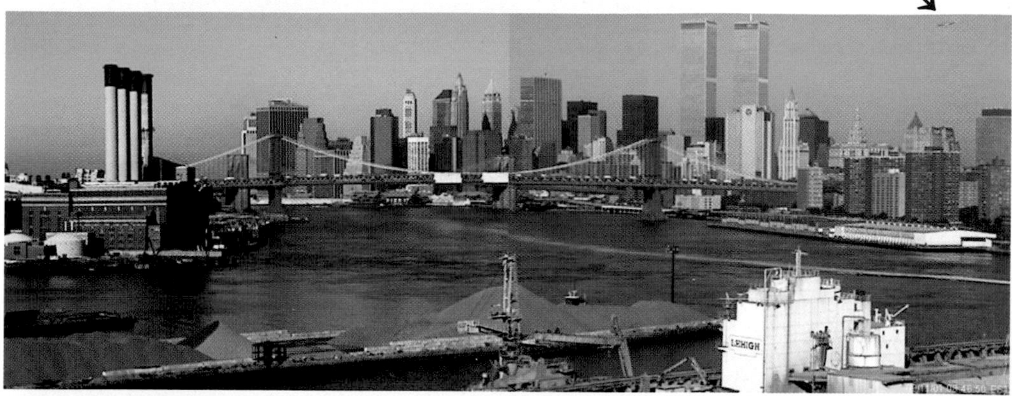

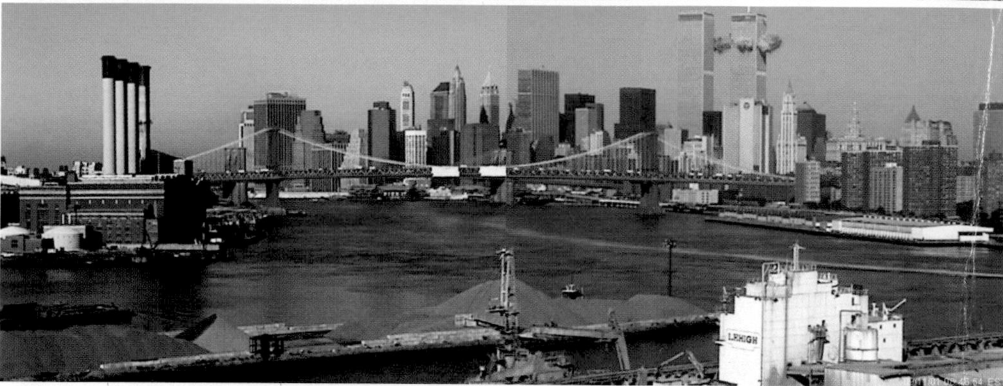

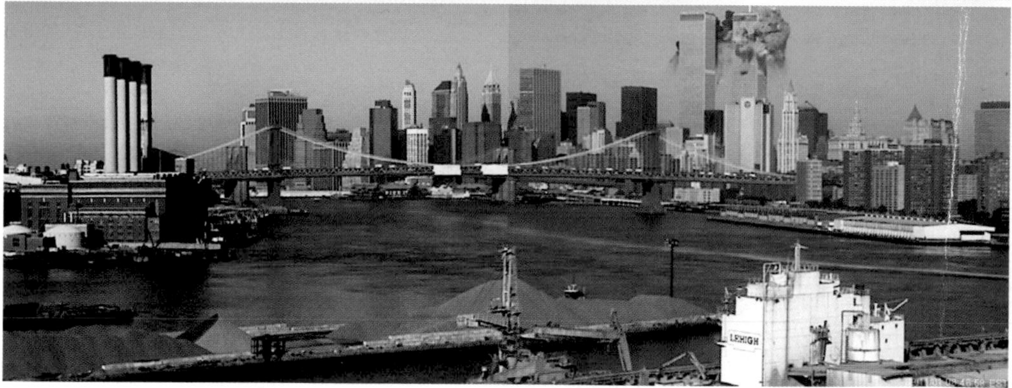

1. American Airlines Flight 11 (at arrow) approaches and penetrates the north tower of the World Trade Center on September 11, 2001. This largely unknown triptych, shot from a Brooklyn window, was part of an ongoing Internet art exhibition that displayed "updated" panoramas of downtown Manhattan every four seconds. (Photographs by Wolfgang Staehle, courtesy of the artist)

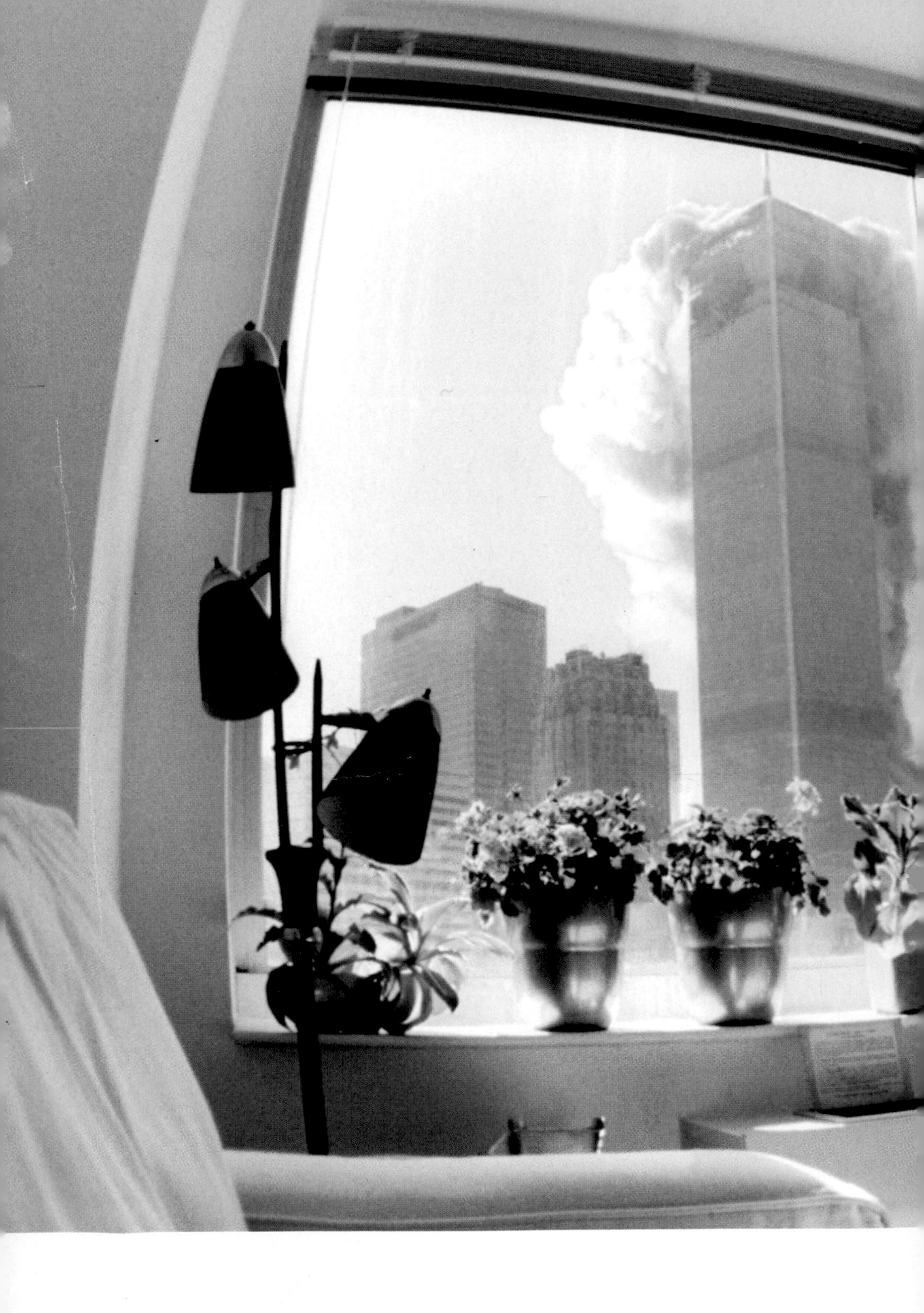

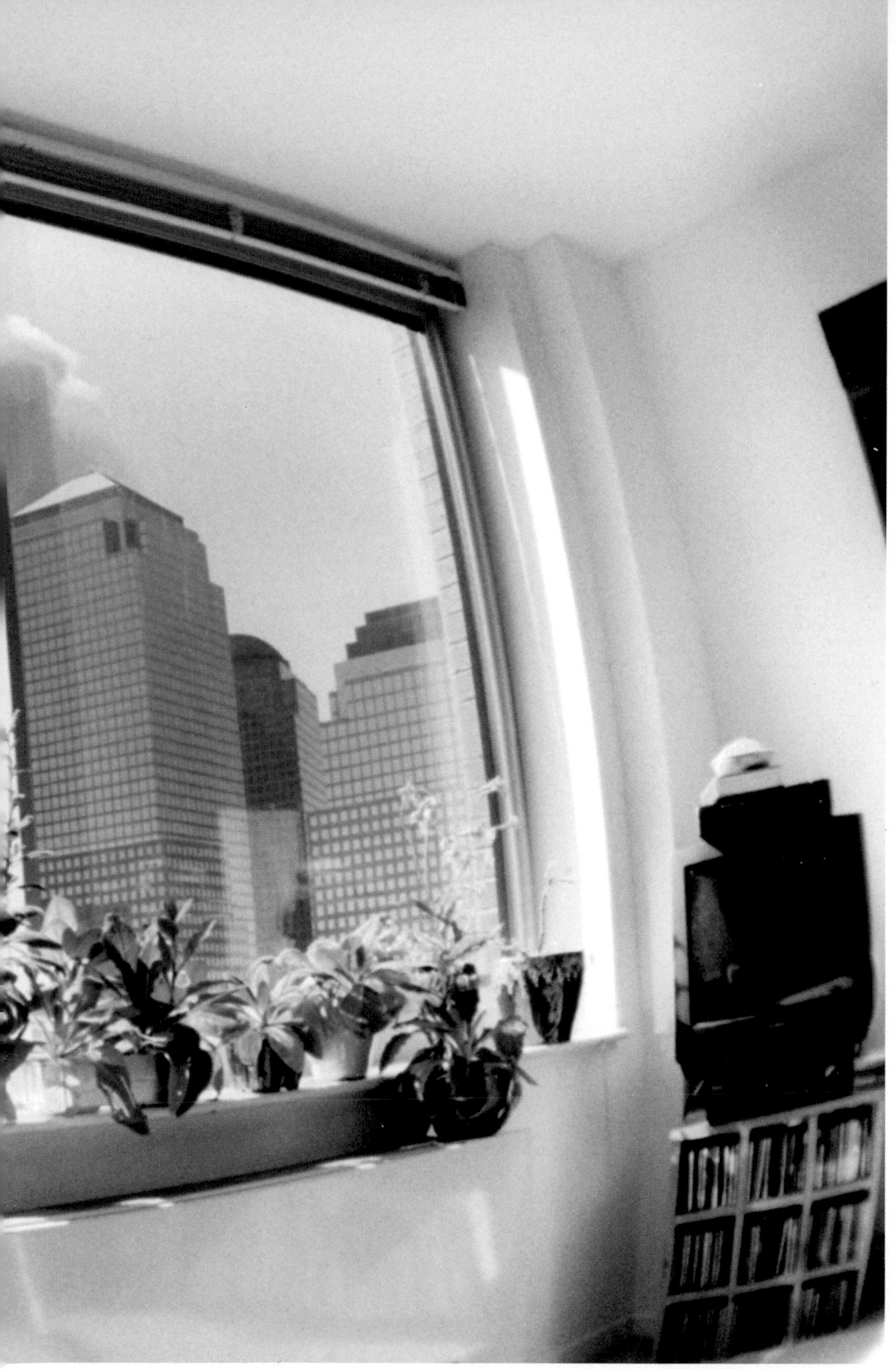

2. As seen through a fish-eye lens from an apartment four blocks away, smoke streams from the north tower within minutes of the first plane's attack. (Photograph by Patricia McDonough)

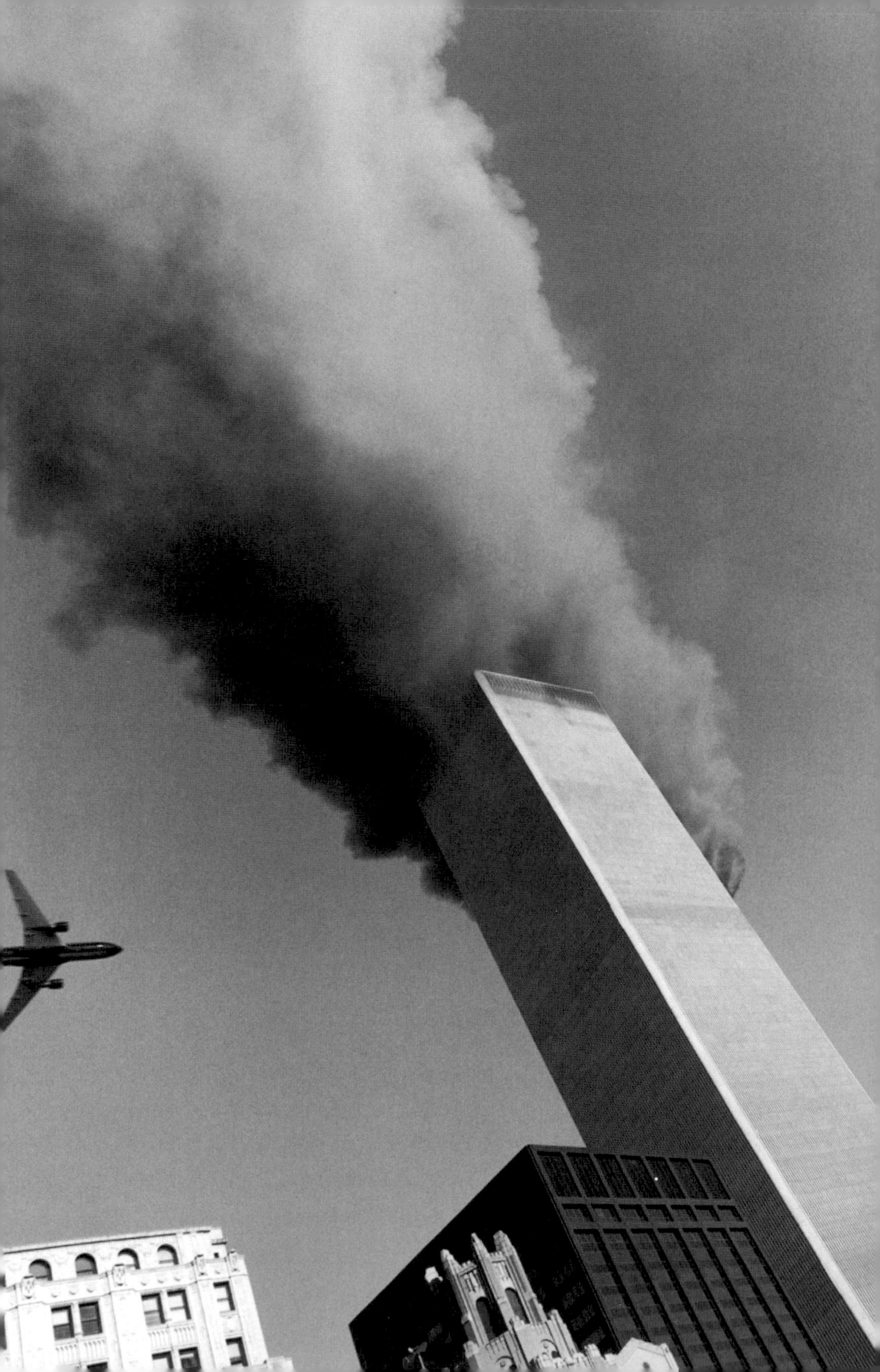

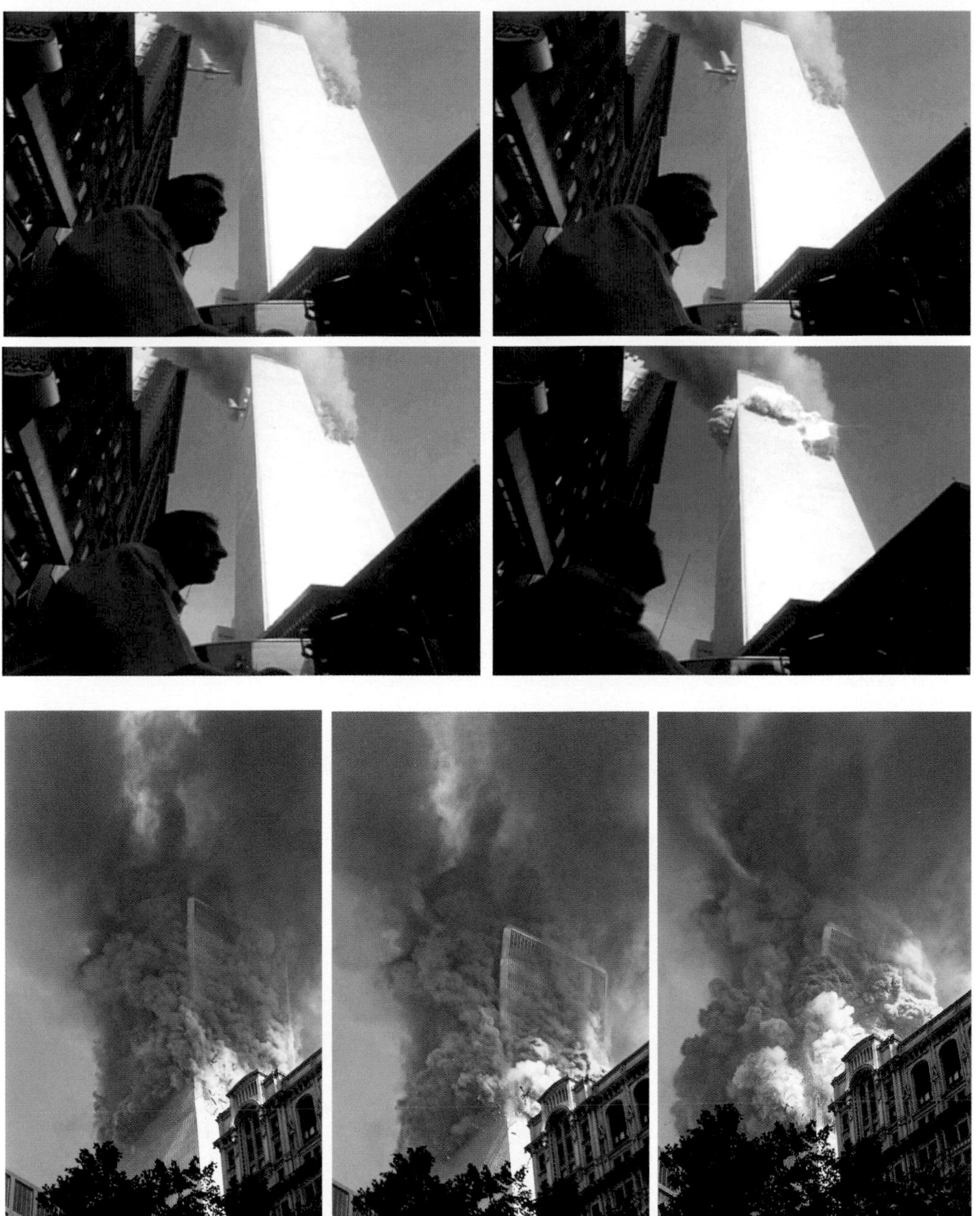

3. ABOVE A printing plant account manager emerged from the subway to shoot this harrowing sequence of the south tower's collapse. (Photographs by David Brondolo)
4. TOP Chaos in the street compelled a videographer to leave a meeting at Trinity Church. A few minutes later, he captured the second plane's strike as he stood at the foot of the south tower. (Copyright © 2006 Evan Fairbanks)
5. OPPOSITE At Rector Street and Broadway, a photographer leaned out his window with a medium-format camera and caught the moment before the second plane's impact. (Photograph by Rob Howard)

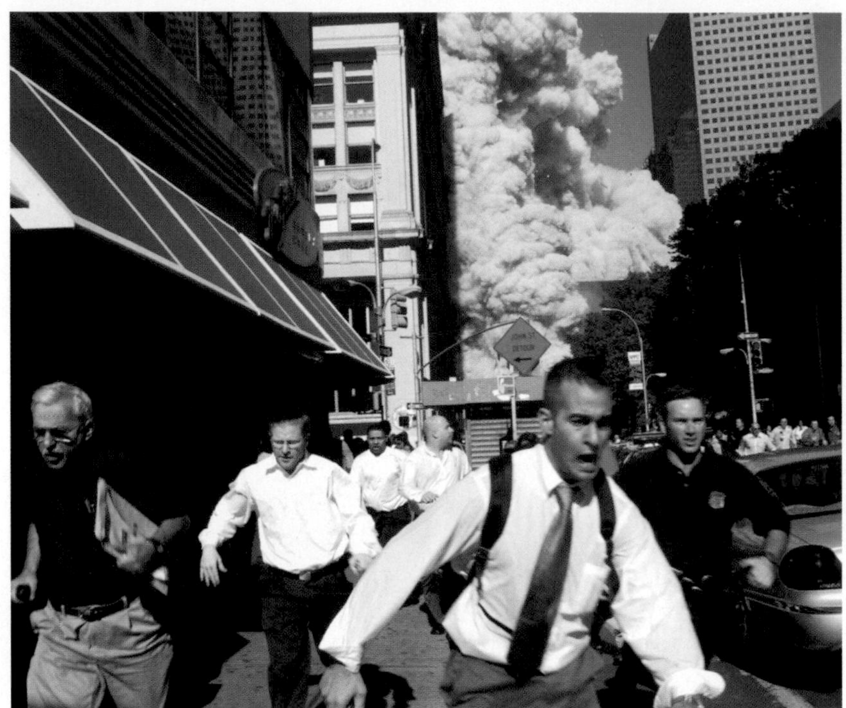

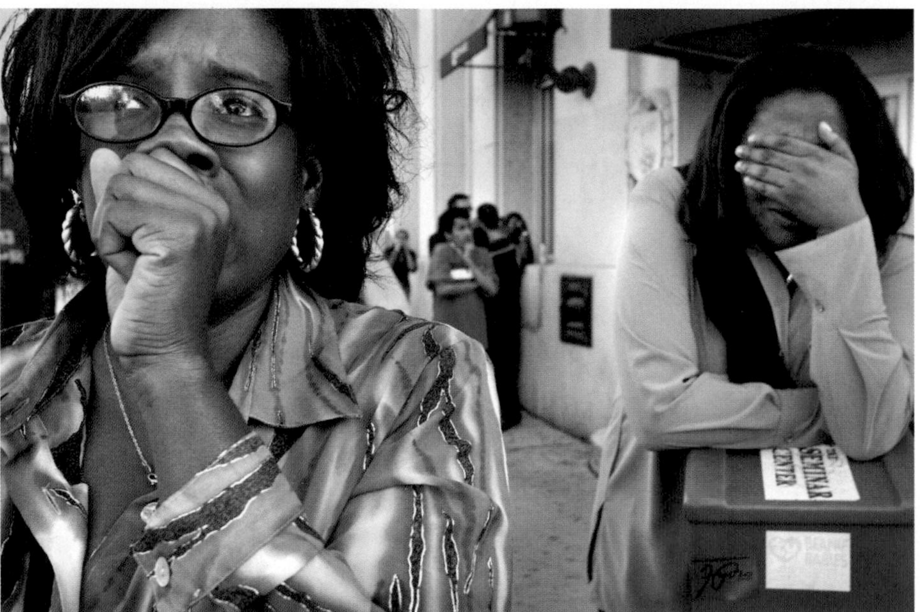

6. TOP Citizens flee for their lives as the south tower falls and fills nearby streets with debris. (AP Photo / Suzanne Plunkett)

7. Two agonized onlookers react to the horror. (Photograph by Angel Franco / *The New York Times*)

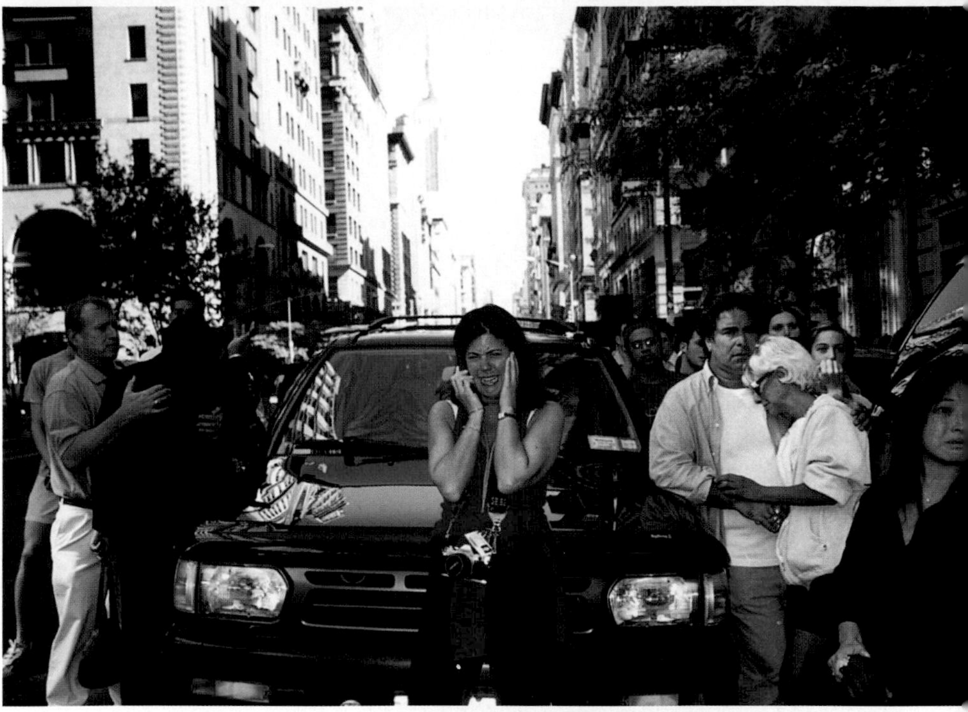

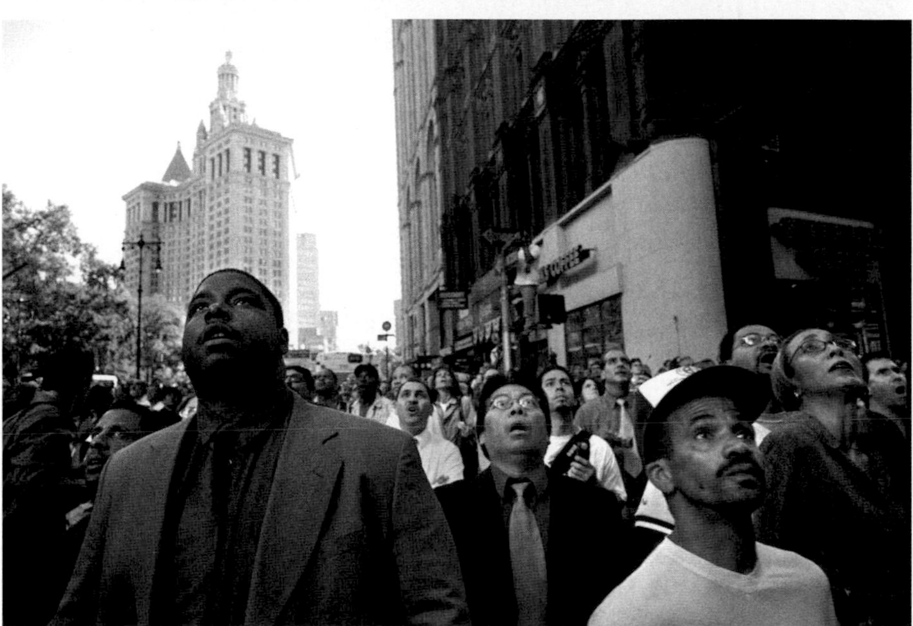

8. TOP News of the attacks sent many New Yorkers into the streets with cameras. Here, a photographer turns away from the disaster to capture a tearful stranger who has set her camera aside. (Photograph by Cynthia Colwell)

9. A knot of bystanders at Park Row and Beekman Street look up as the south tower begins to collapse. (Photograph by Patrick Witty)

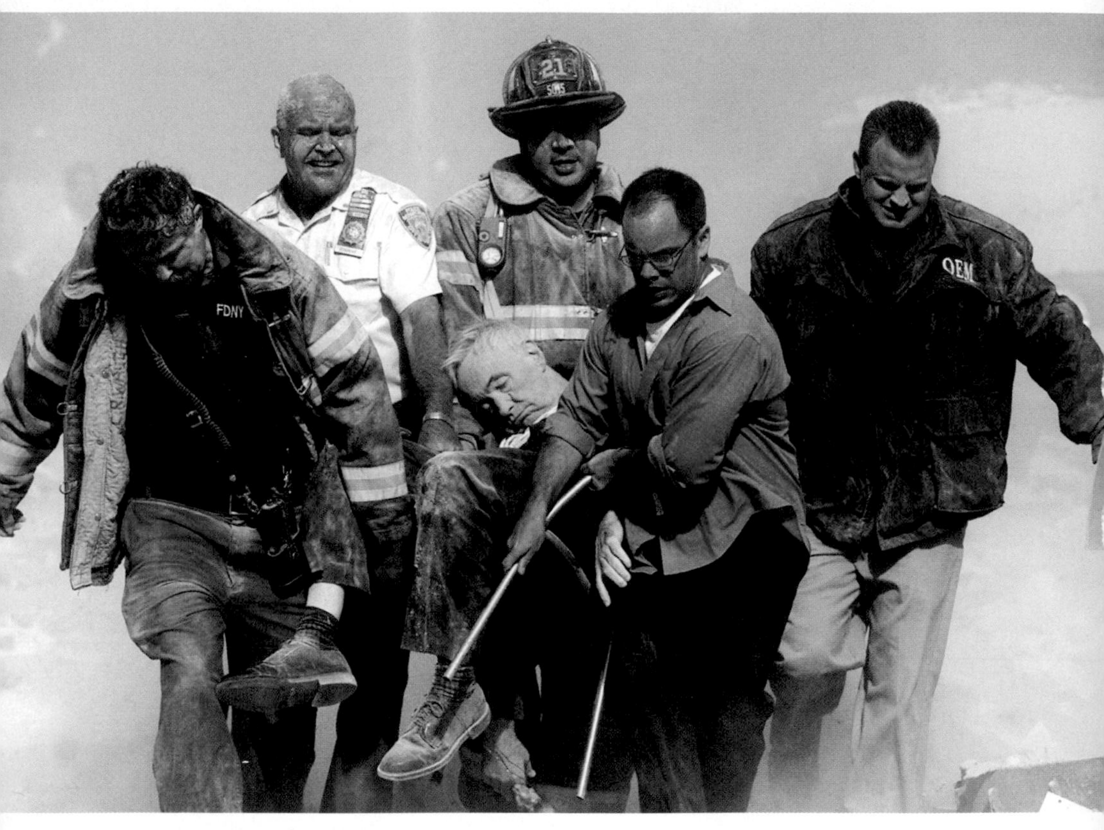

10. Out of the wreckage of the south tower, first responders carry the body of Father Mychal Judge, the FDNY chaplain, to St. Peter's Church. (Photograph by Shannon Stapleton / Reuters)

11. OPPOSITE TOP Not yet realizing a terrorist attack was in progress, architect Isabel Daser, eight months pregnant, asked a coworker to take her portrait as a record of the day. (Photograph courtesy of Isabel Daser Bessler)

12. OPPOSITE On a Brooklyn rooftop, shortly after the collapse of the twin towers, Jenna Piccirillo and three-month-old Vaughan embody innocence and resilience, according to the photographer: "Life continues in the face of disaster . . . despite the horrors we inflict on one another." (Photograph © Alex Webb / Magnum Photos)

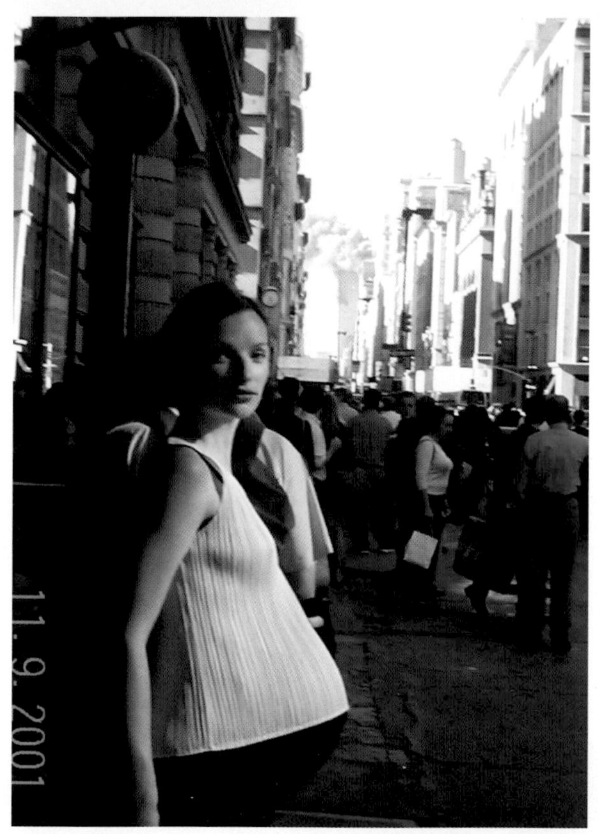
11.9.2001

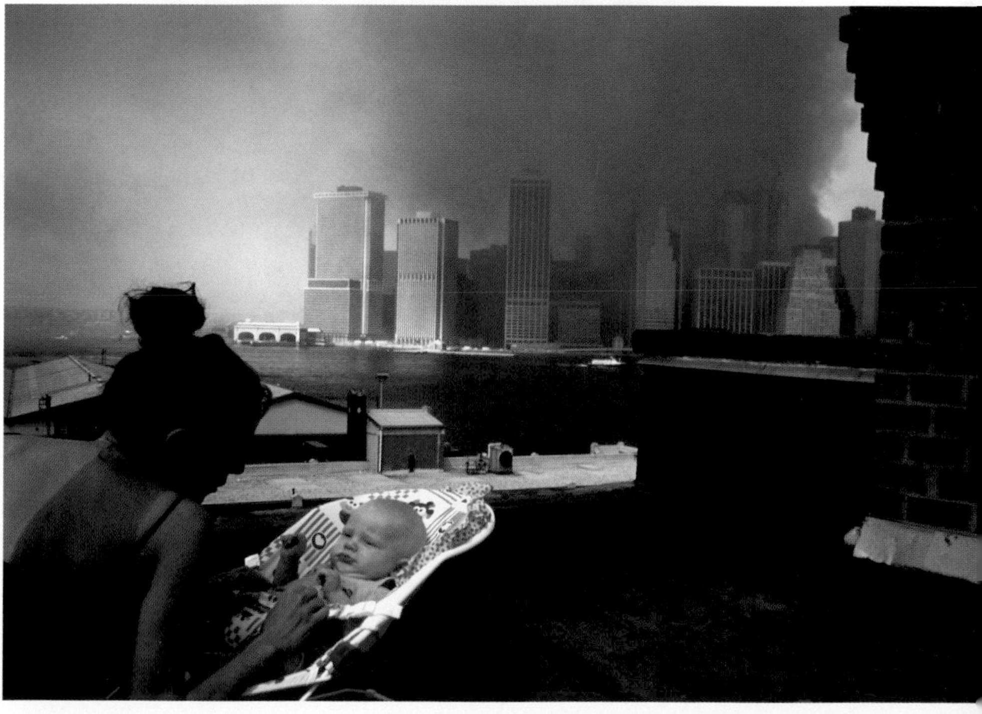

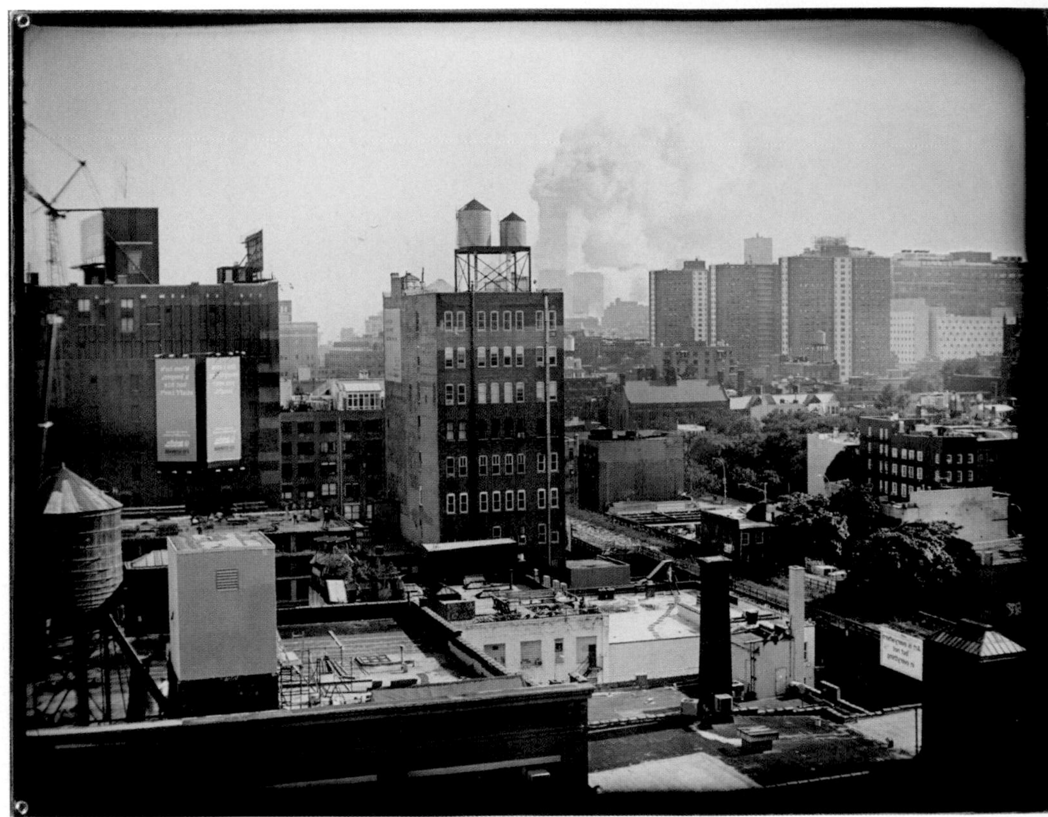

13. An expert in nineteenth-century photographic techniques brought a wooden view camera and a daguerreotype plate to his Chelsea rooftop, making a three-second exposure as the south tower disappeared on the horizon. (Photograph by Jerry Spagnoli)

14. OPPOSITE TOP Freelance photographer Bill Biggart was killed in the north tower's collapse. Crews recovered his battered equipment—and some three hundred pictures. (Photograph by Tom McKitterick)

15. OPPOSITE "Missing" posters bearing photos of the lost cover a Greenwich Village pizzeria. (Photograph by David Turnley)

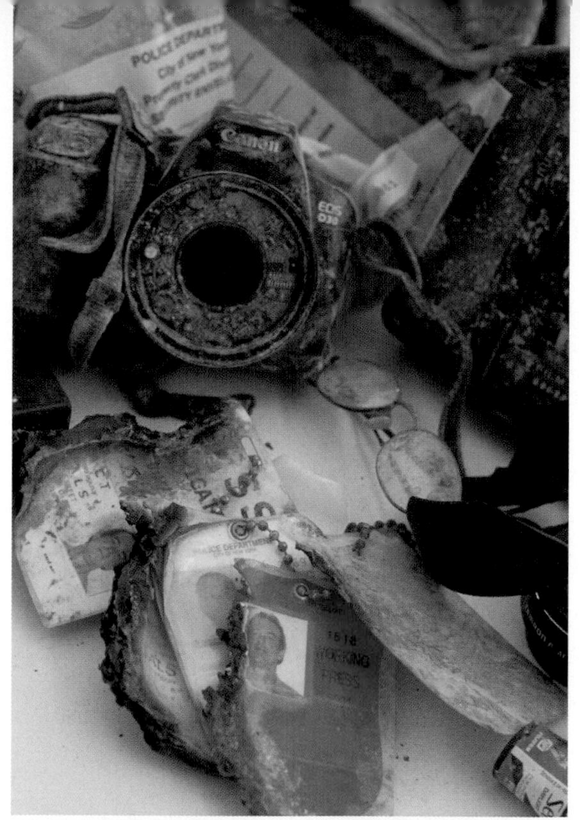
POLICE DEPARTMENT
City of New York
Canon
WORKING
PRESS

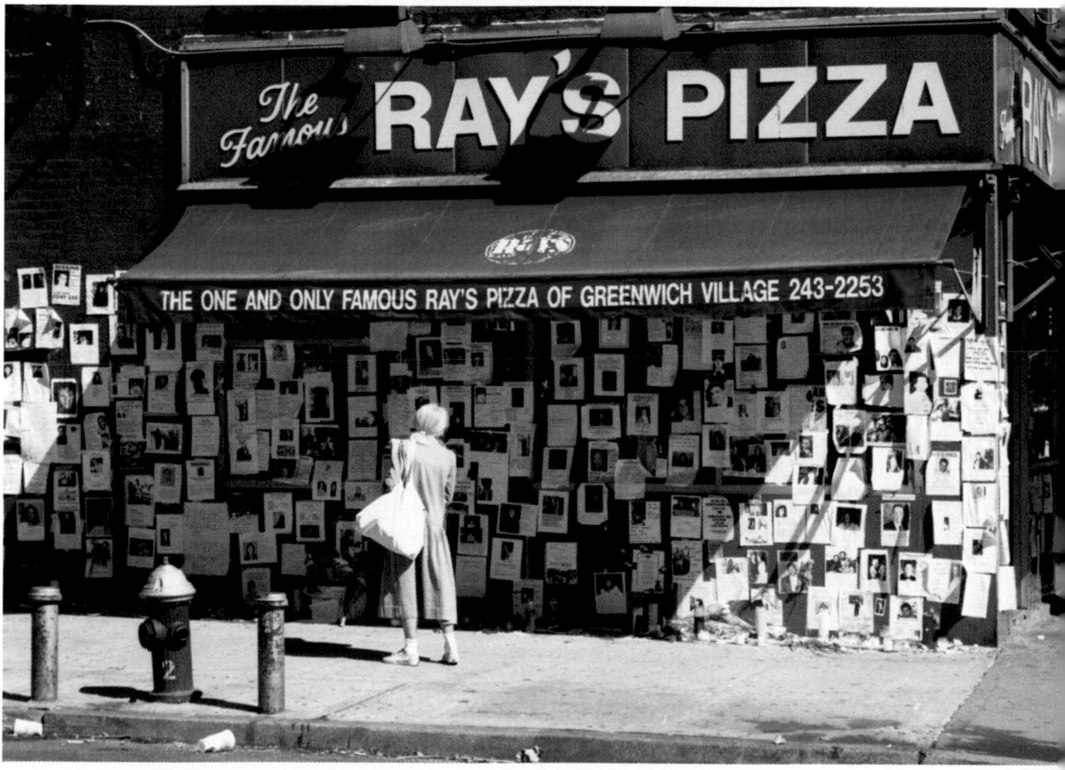

The Famous RAY'S PIZZA
THE ONE AND ONLY FAMOUS RAY'S PIZZA OF GREENWICH VILLAGE 243-2253

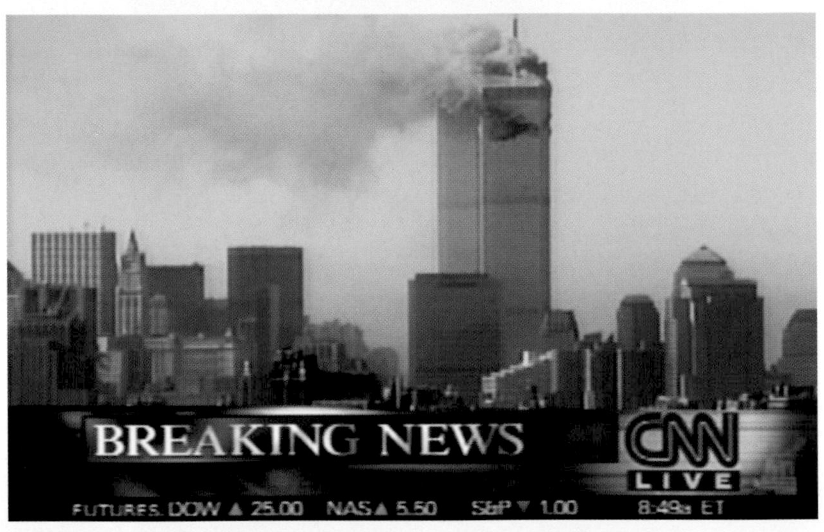

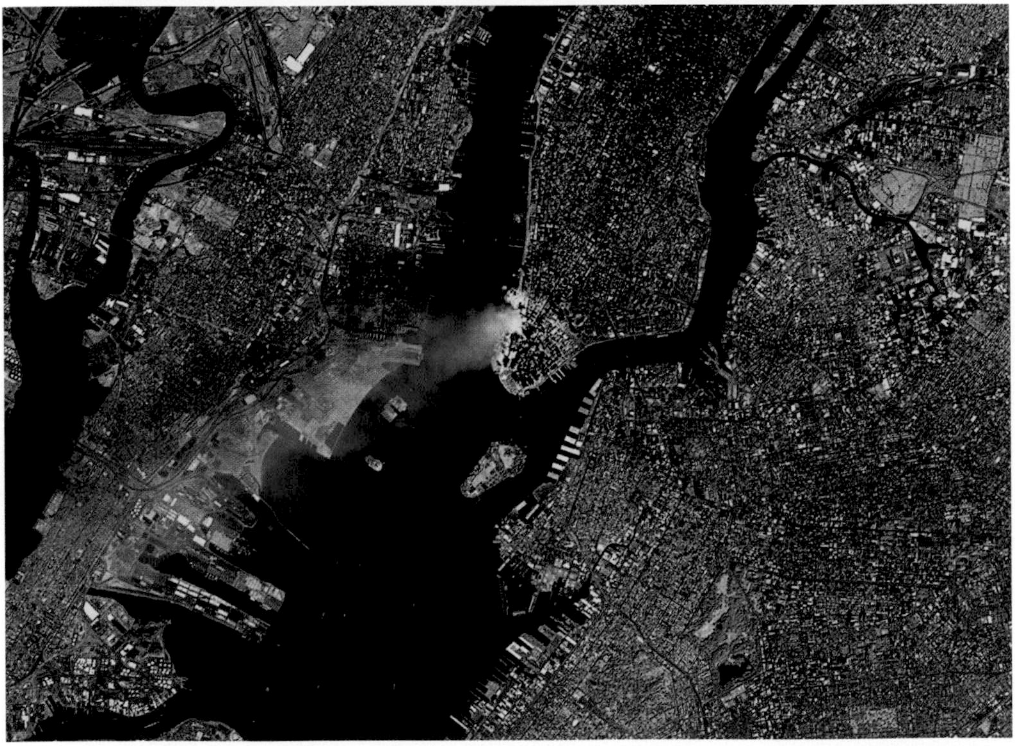

16. TOP New York City's WNYW (FOX 5) was the first station to air live footage of the attack, at 8:48, one minute after the first plane hit. CNN, at 8:49, would transmit images of the events of September 11 throughout the world. An estimated two billion people would view the scenes across hundreds of channels that day. (Courtesy of CNN)

17. Smoke plumes are clearly visible in this Landsat 7 satellite image of New York City, made early September 12. (Photograph courtesy of NASA)

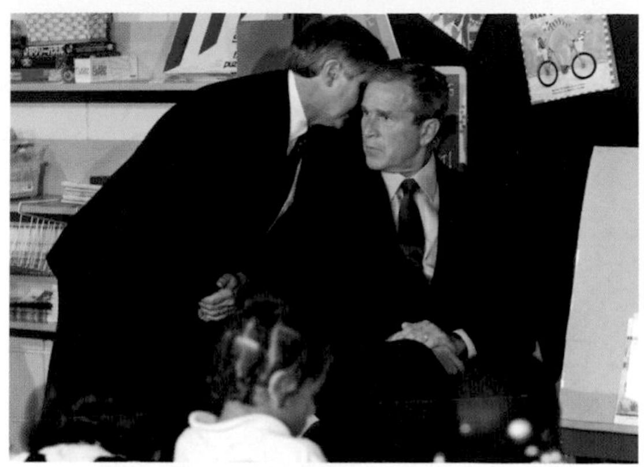

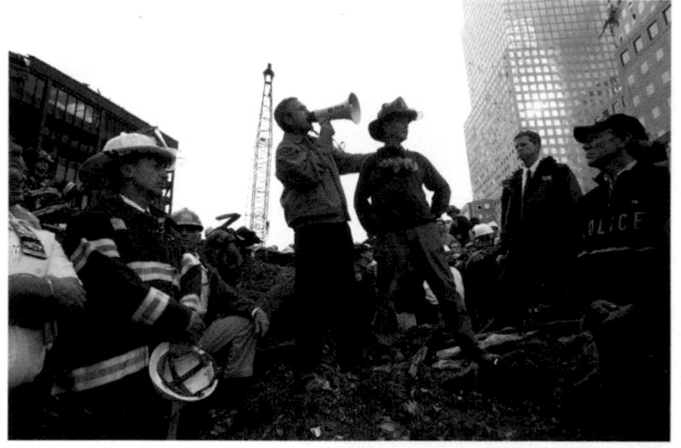

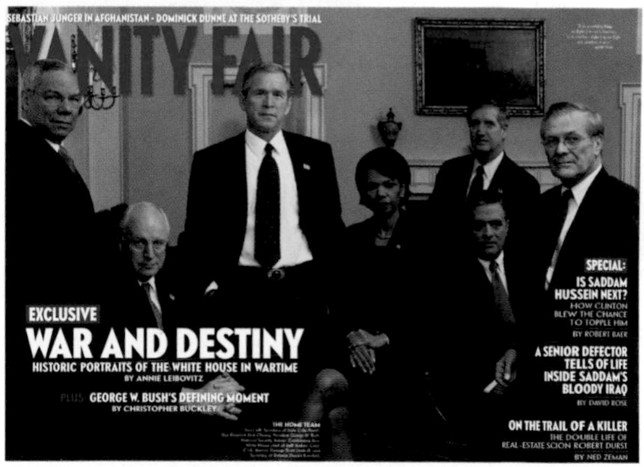

18. TOP During an event in a Florida classroom, Chief of Staff Andrew Card informs President George W. Bush, "A second plane hit the second tower. America is under attack." (Photograph by Win McNamee/Reuters)
19. CENTER On September 14, the president visits workers at Ground Zero, embracing retired firefighter Bob Beckwith. (White House Photo/Eric Draper)
20. BOTTOM As U.S. and allied troops battled Taliban forces in Afghanistan, President Bush and his war council posed for the February 2002 cover of *Vanity Fair*. (Photograph by Annie Leibovitz/Contact Press Images for *Vanity Fair*, copyright © 2002 Condé Nast Publications Inc. Reprinted by permission. All rights reserved)

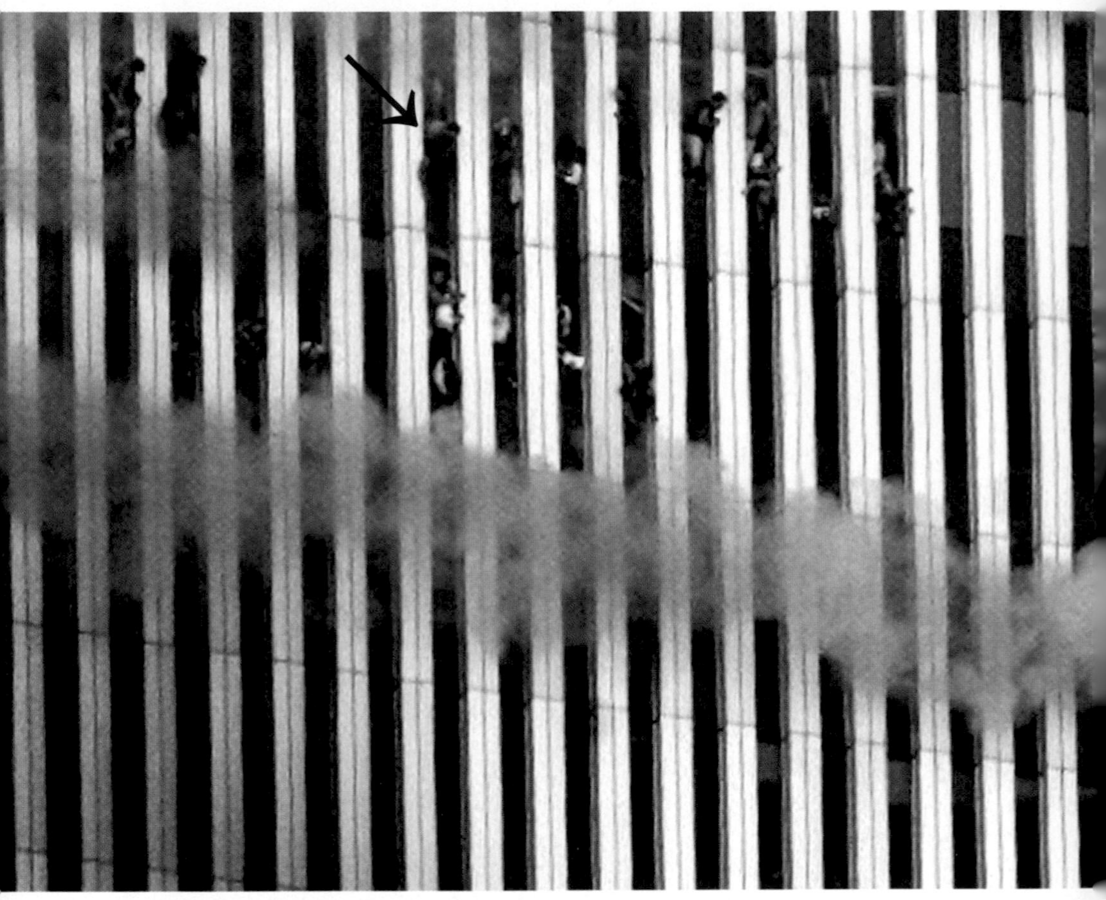

21. TOP Trapped workers gather in the windows of the upper reaches of the north tower fifteen minutes before its collapse. The arrow denotes a figure that Mike and Jindra Rambousek believe to be their son Luke. (Photograph by Jeff Christensen / Reuters)

22. A man plummets from the World Trade Center in an image that, while sent out over the AP wire, was not widely published in the American press. Many editors found it too disturbing to run. (AP Photo / Richard Drew)

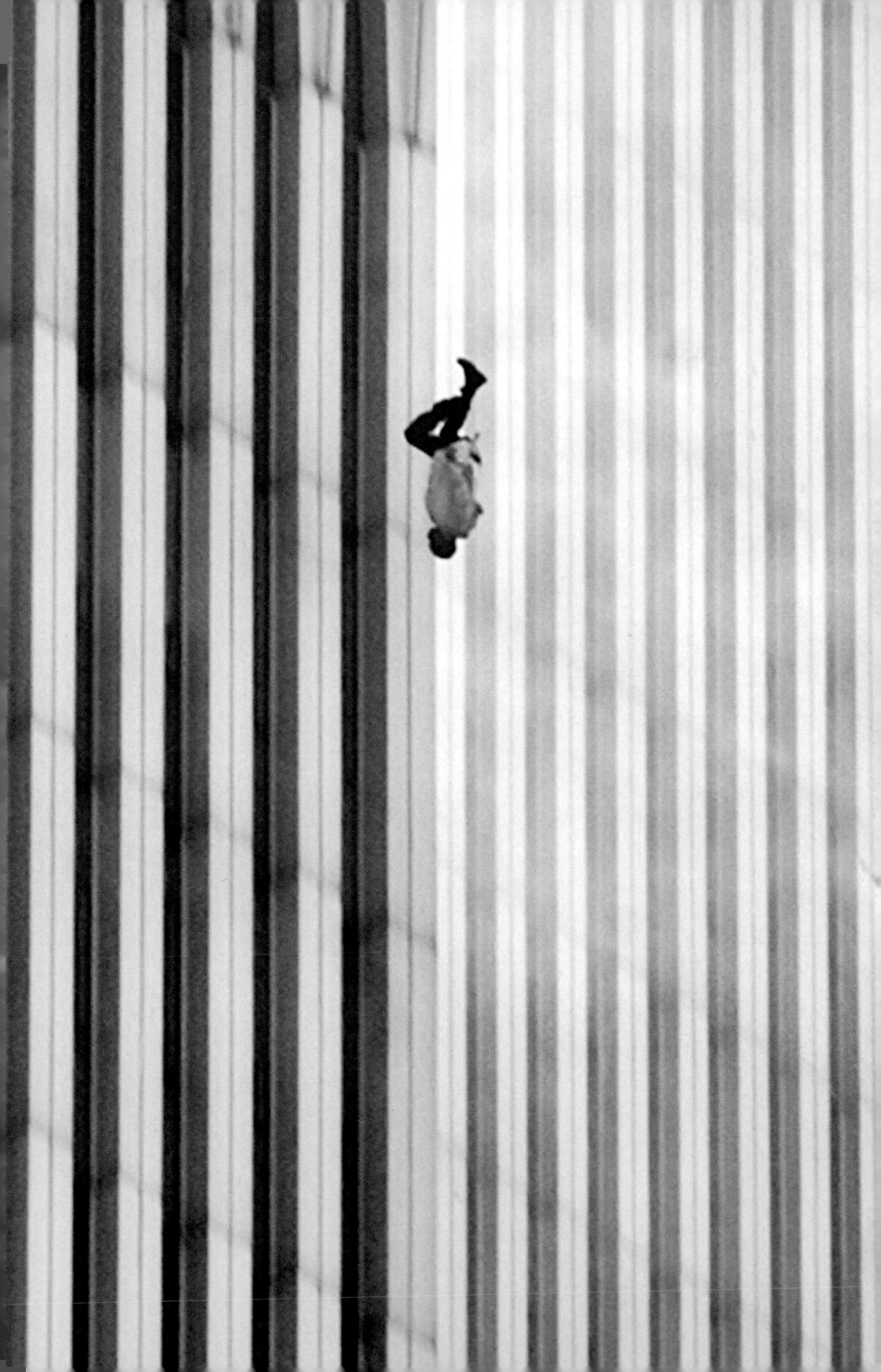

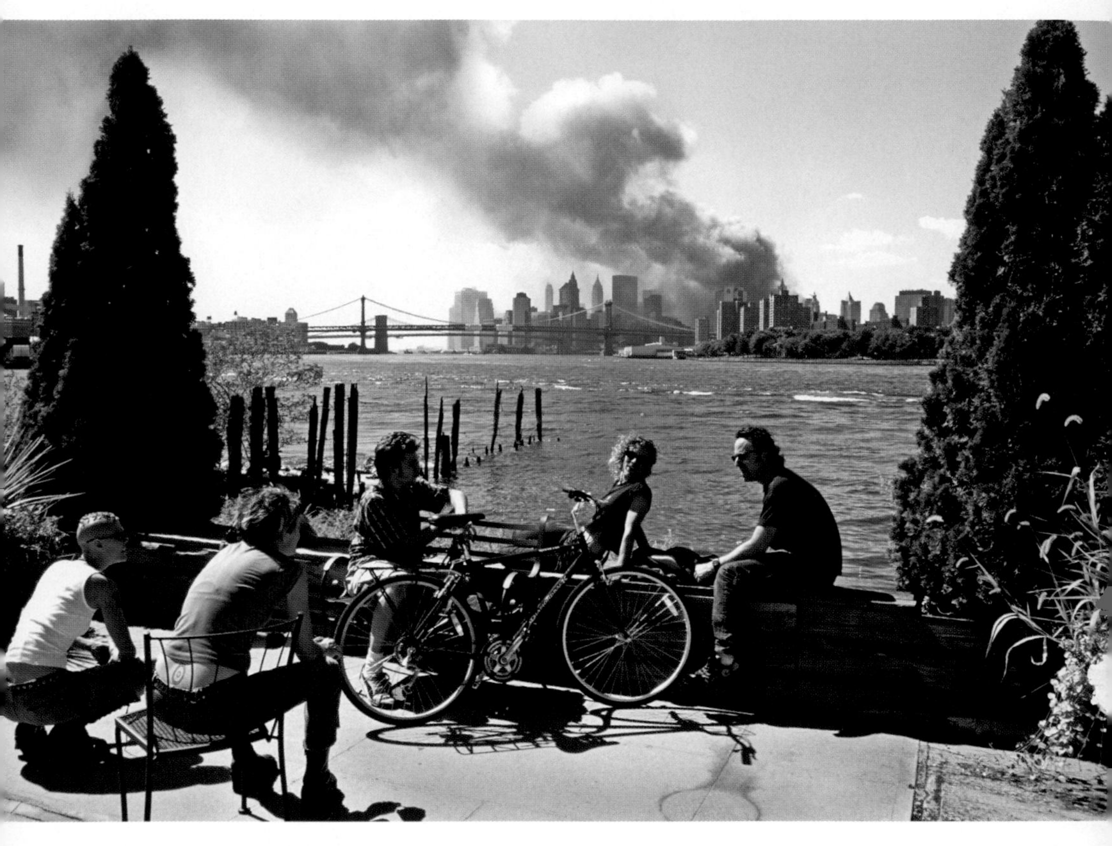

23. After taking this picture on 9/11 in Brooklyn, the photographer found it upsettingly tranquil, and decided not to publish the image widely until four years after the attacks. (Photograph © Thomas Hoepker/Magnum Photos)

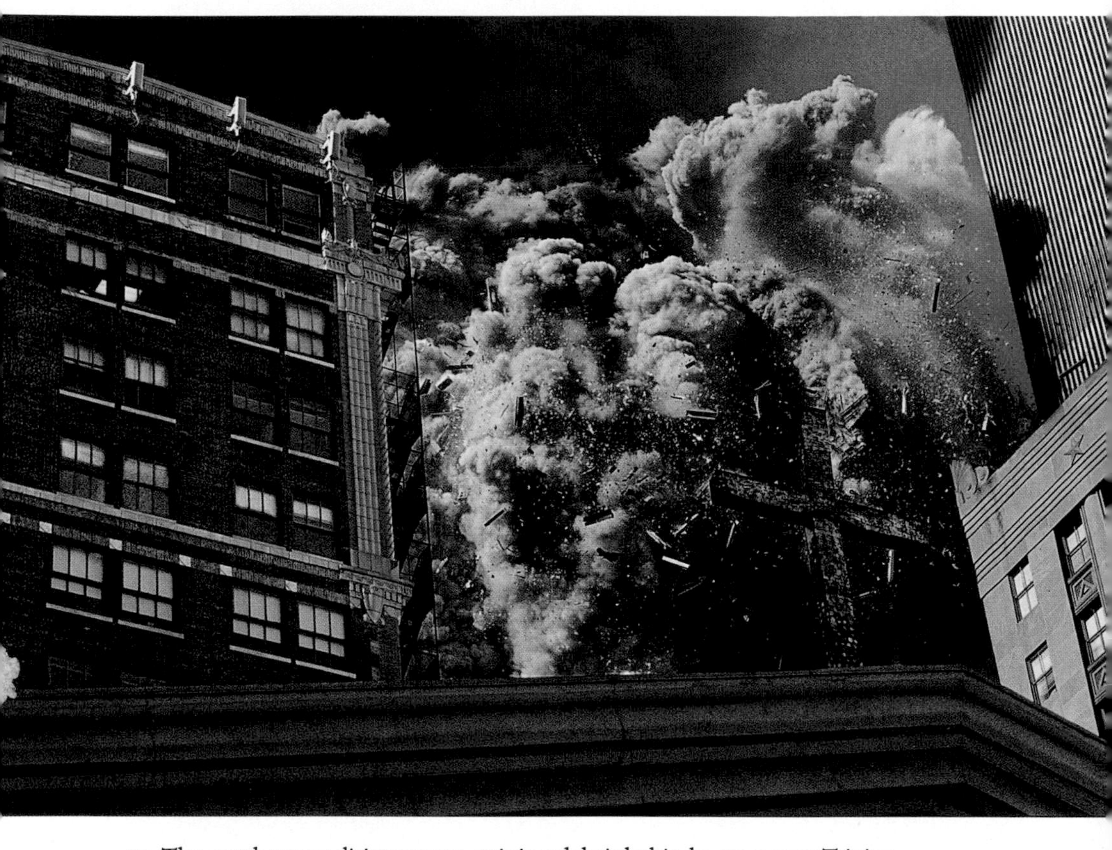

24. The south tower disintegrates, raining debris behind a cross atop Trinity Church. (Photograph by James Nachtwey / VII for *Time*)

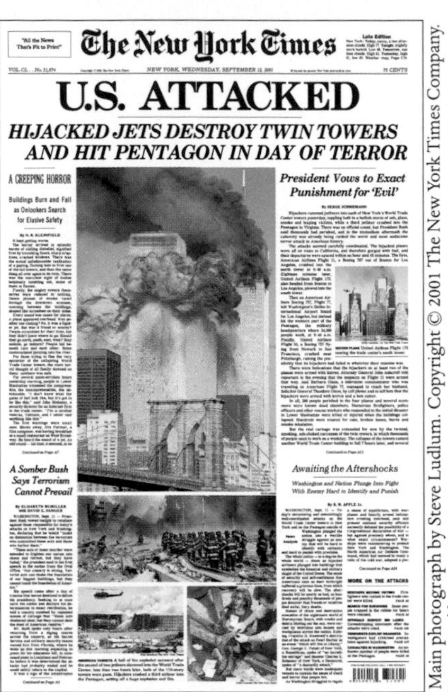

"All the News That's Fit to Print"

The New York Times

Late Edition

VOL. CL . . No. 51,874 — NEW YORK, WEDNESDAY, SEPTEMBER 12, 2001 — 75 CENTS

U.S. ATTACKED

HIJACKED JETS DESTROY TWIN TOWERS AND HIT PENTAGON IN DAY OF TERROR

A CREEPING HORROR

Buildings Burn and Fall as Onlookers Search for Elusive Safety

President Vows to Exact Punishment for 'Evil'

A Somber Bush Says Terrorism Cannot Prevail

Awaiting the Aftershocks

Washington and Nation Plunge Into Fight With Enemy Hard to Identify and Punish

MORE ON THE ATTACKS

Main photograph by Steve Ludlum. Copyright © 2001 The New York Times Company. Reprinted by permisson

A

Photograph by Lyle Owerko/Wonderlust. *Time*, © 2001 Time Inc. Reprinted by permission

B

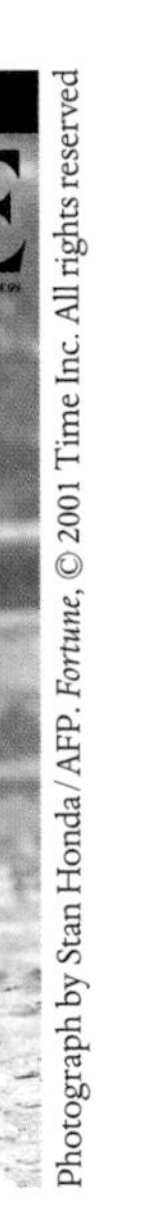

Photograph by Stan Honda/AFP. *Fortune*, © 2001 Time Inc. All rights reserved

C

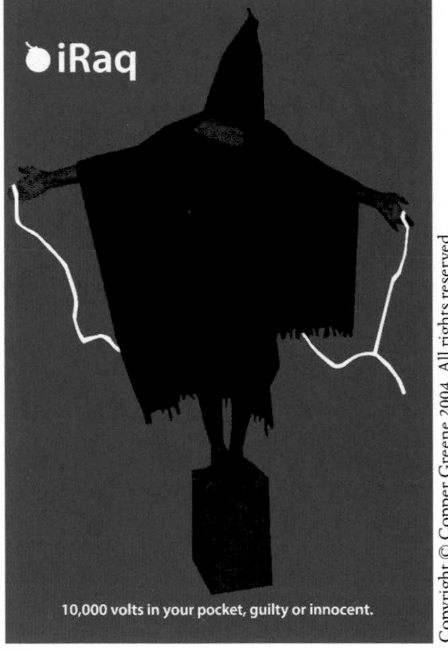

iRaq
10,000 volts in your pocket, guilty or innocent.

Copyright © Copper Greene 2004. All rights reserved

D

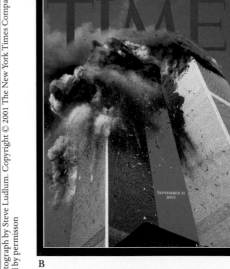

In the media, images of the attack and its aftermath became iconic literally overnight. A photograph of the second plane striking the south tower appeared on the front page of the next day's *New York Times* (*top left*) and, without a caption—none seemed necessary—on the special issue of *Time* that went on sale later that week (*top right*). On the cover of *Fortune* the next month, a man covered with ash and debris was made to represent the devastation of the financial services industry (*bottom left*), and in 2004 a poster (*bottom right*) used a visual allusion to Apple's iPod advertisements to express horror over the Abu Ghraib torture photographs and the U.S.-led war in Iraq.

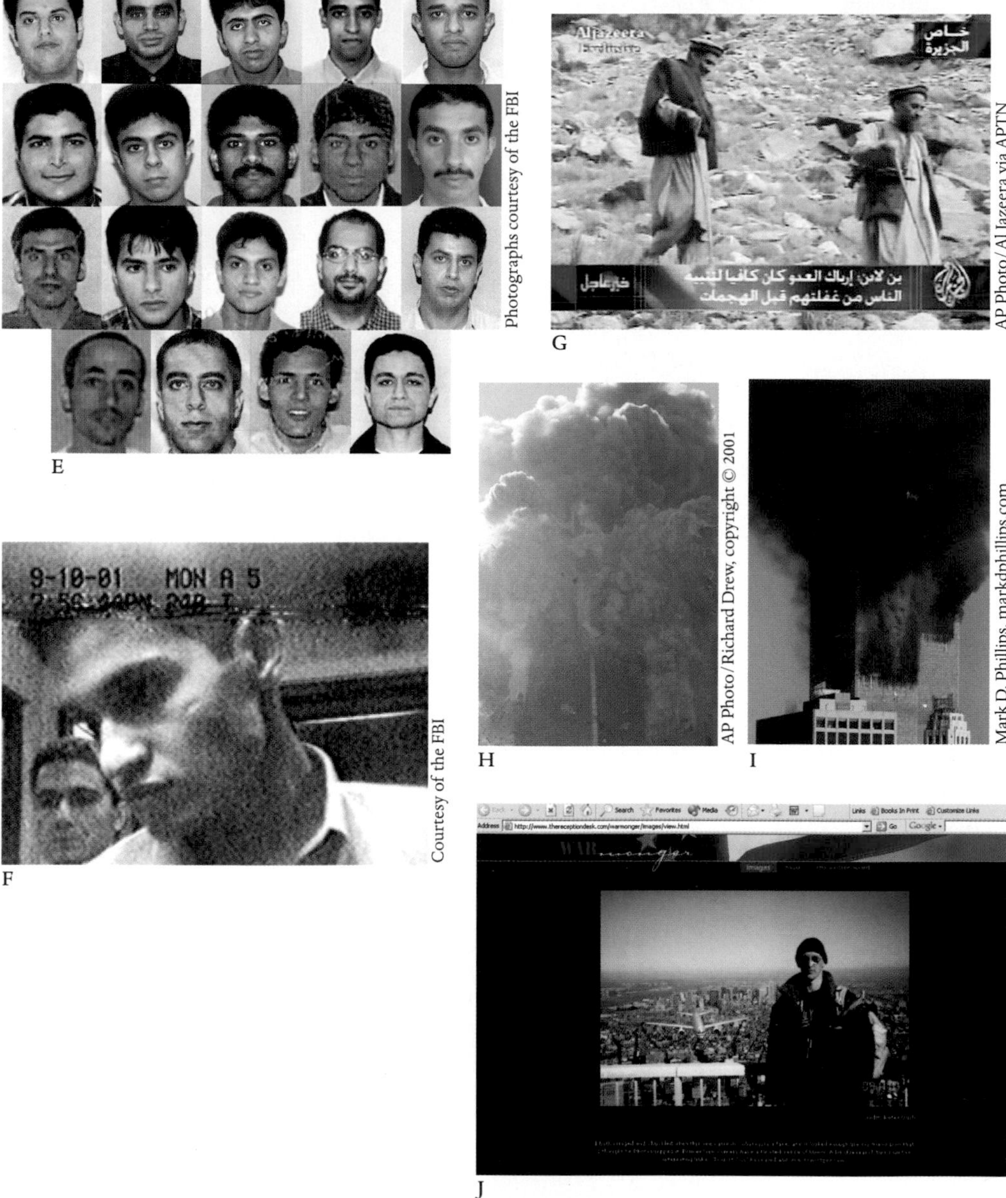

Photographs produced evidence, both real and imagined, of how the attacks had come about. The FBI released headshots of 19 suspected hijackers (*top left*), two of whom had been photographed by a surveillance camera at a bank in Maine on September 10 (*bottom left*). Videotape from 2003 showed Osama bin Laden and his deputy, Ayman Zawahiri, descending a mountainside (*top right*). On the Internet, people claimed to perceive odd shapes—a naked female figure (*middle left*), a demonic face (*middle right*)—in the smoke that engulfed the two towers. In the weeks to follow, Web sites displayed a phony photograph supposedly taken from the south tower's observation deck (*bottom*).

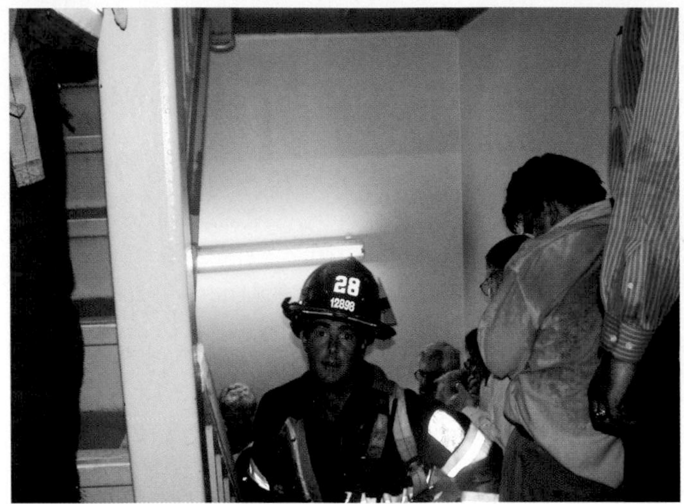

25. Firefighter Mike Kehoe climbs a north tower stairwell, passing the lens of an exiting Port Authority technical consultant. Kehoe would escape only a minute before the structure fell. (Photograph copyright © John Labriola, 2001)

26. BELOW As the wreckage was cleared, fires still burned in the recesses of the World Trade Center ruins. (Photograph by Sacha Waldman, copyright © Sacha Waldman)

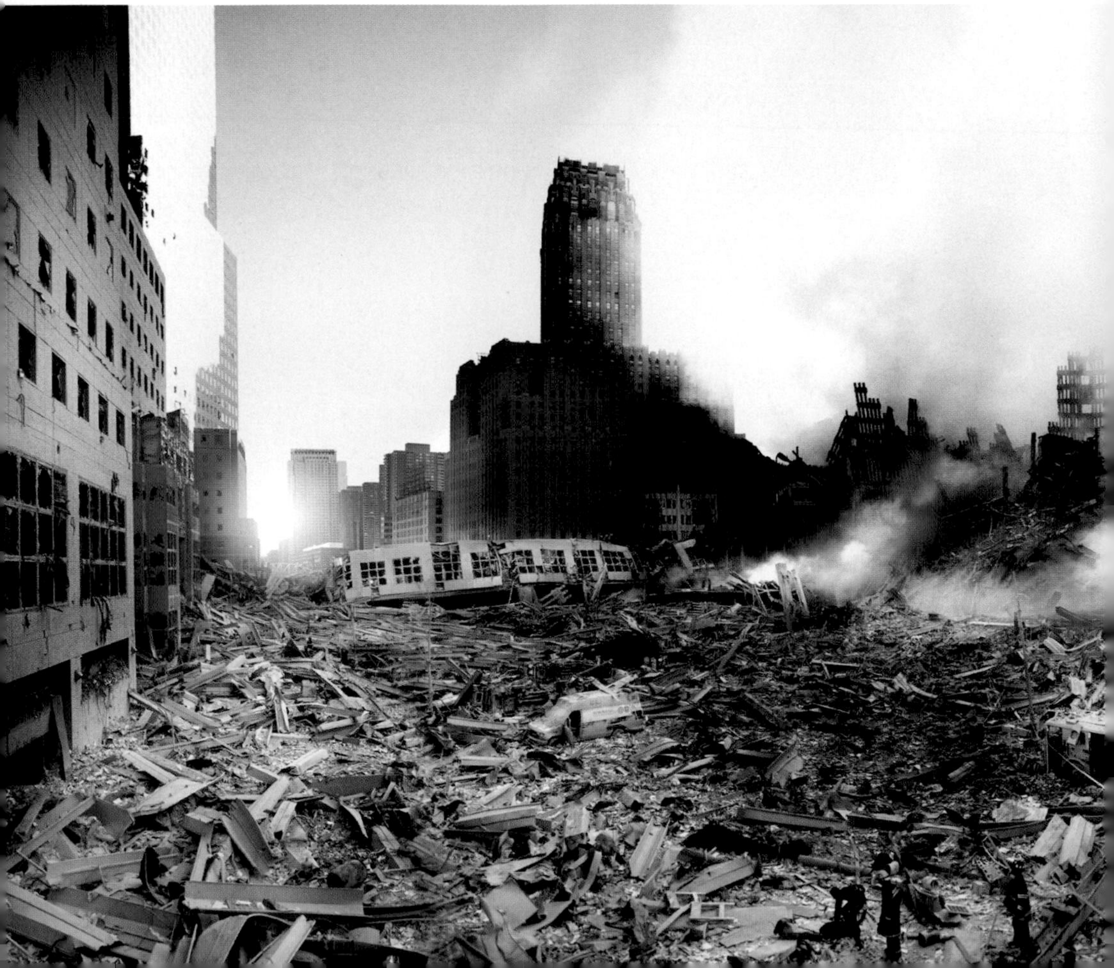

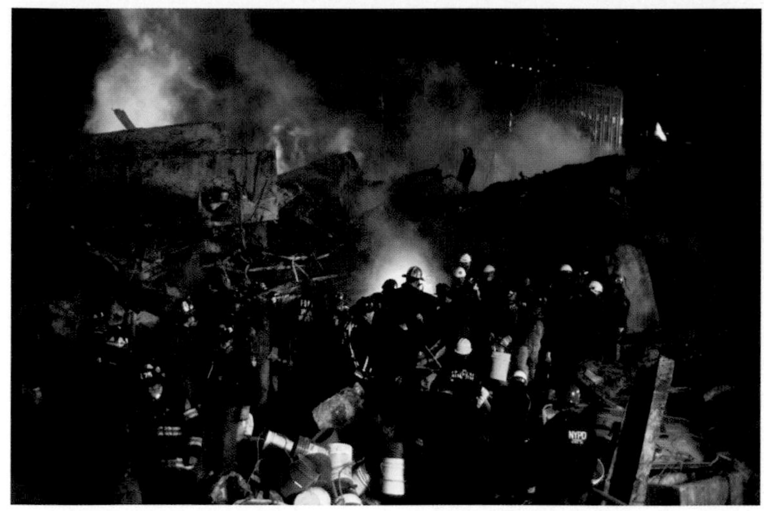

27. "October 26, 2001: Five More Found": The remains of five firefighters are discovered in the wreckage of the south tower. (Photograph copyright © Joel Meyerowitz, courtesy of the Edwynn Houk Gallery)

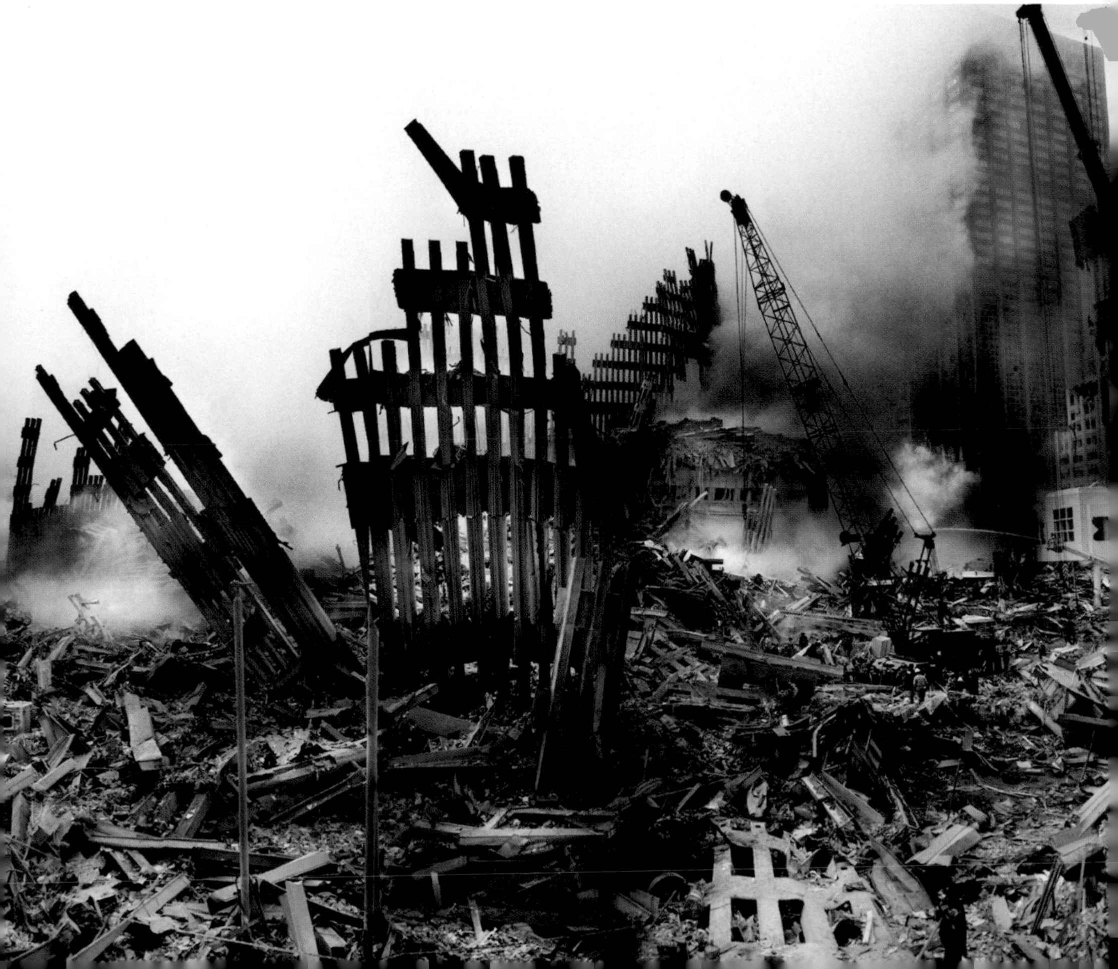

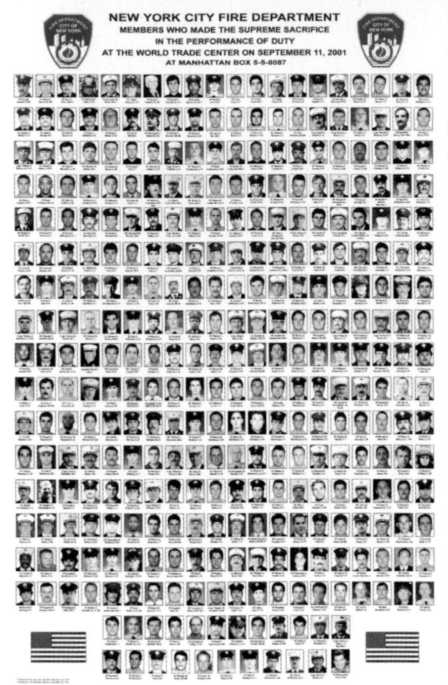
NEW YORK CITY FIRE DEPARTMENT
MEMBERS WHO MADE THE SUPREME SACRIFICE
IN THE PERFORMANCE OF DUTY
AT THE WORLD TRADE CENTER ON SEPTEMBER 11, 2001
AT MANHATTAN BOX 5-5-8087

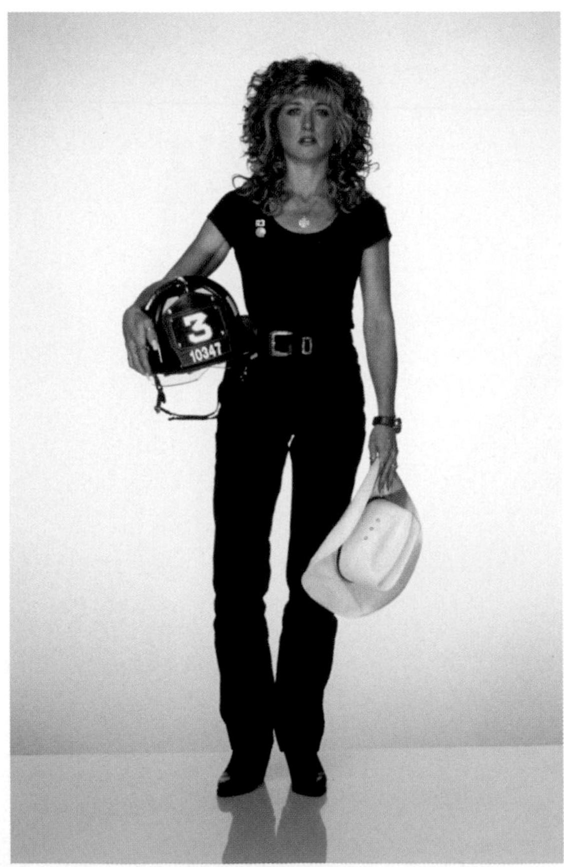
3
10347

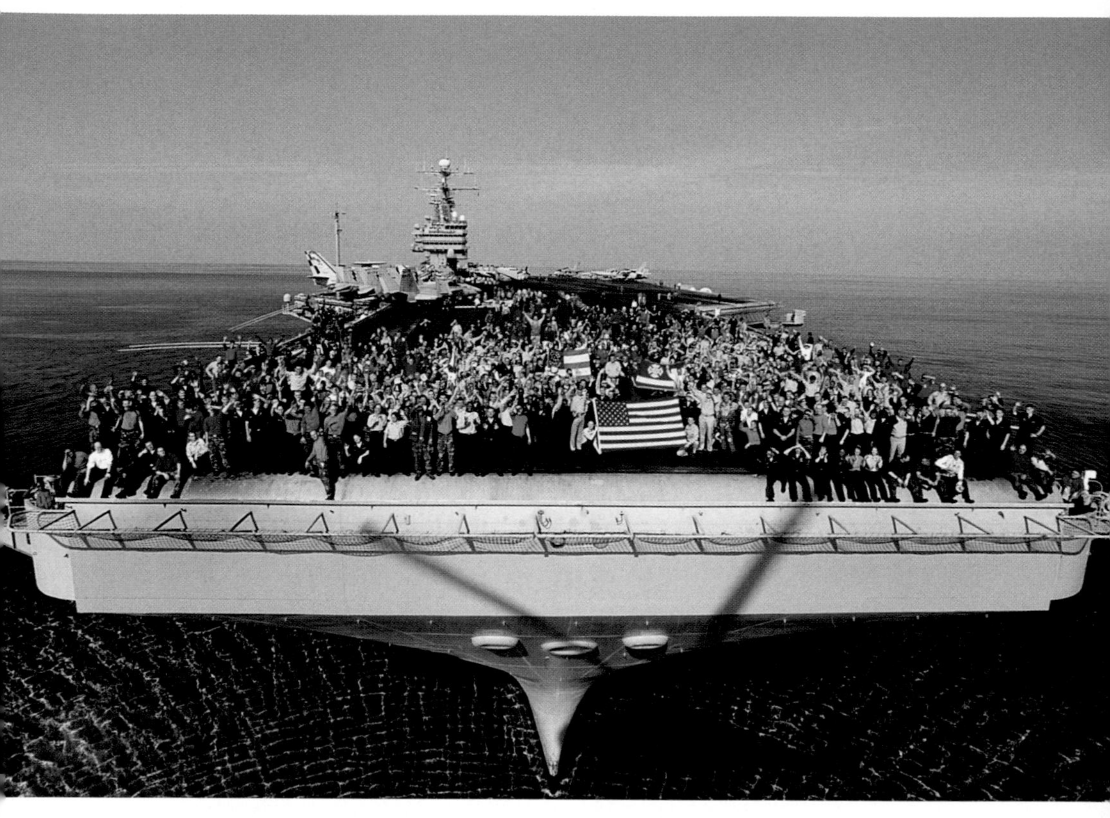

28. OPPOSITE, TOP A poster pays homage to the 343 members of the FDNY who lost their lives at the World Trade Center on September 11. (Courtesy of the FDNY)

29. OPPOSITE Joanne Foley Gross, who lost her brother Tommy Foley, agreed to pose for a portrait, one of three hundred larger-than-life-size Polaroids taken of people associated with the events of 9/11. (Photograph by Joe McNally for *Life*; © Joe McNally)

30. ABOVE The crew of the USS *Theodore Roosevelt* displays a Ground Zero flag while stationed in the Arabian Sea in December 2001. (Photograph by Harry Benson for *Vanity Fair*; © Harry Benson)

31. NEXT PAGE Three firefighters raise an American flag at Ground Zero on September 11. The image would become the most widely reproduced news photo of the new millennium. (Photograph by Thomas E. Franklin/*The Record*; © 2001 The Record [Bergen Co., N.J.]/Thomas E. Franklin)

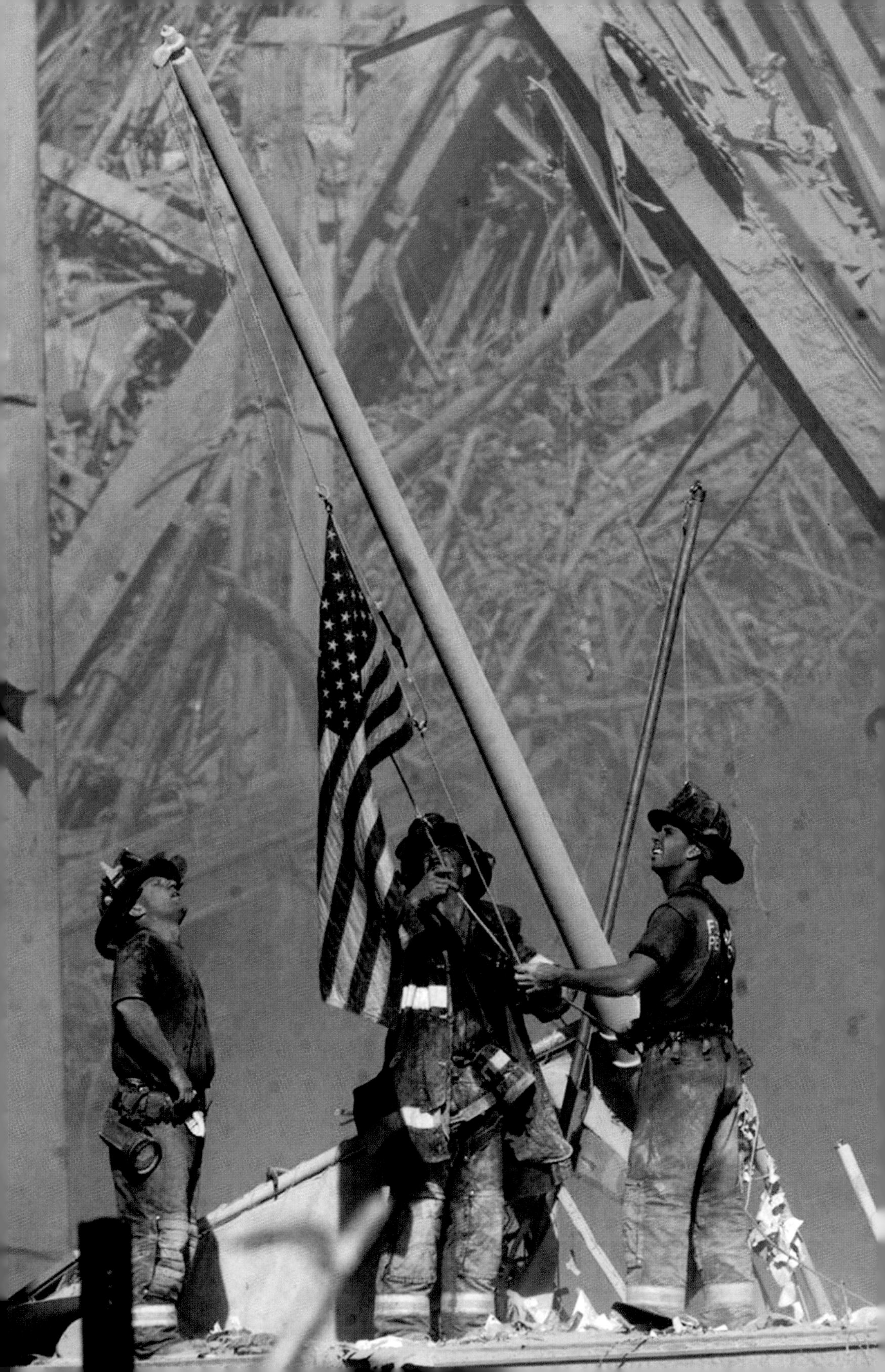

gan, TV deconstructed the event in a manner that made it, in an odd way, *too* palatable when compared to the view he could see plain as the blue day out his window: "I don't trust TV as a source of hard news in any sense . . . TV makes it easier for people to say, 'Let's go get 'em.' You see it in a box and you're at a remove. You can imagine responding like a cowboy.

"I don't discount the fact that people who watched the towers burning on TV might have experienced a similar shock to their systems. But I suspect it was of a qualitatively different nature. There was clearly a lot of fear and anger across the nation—which subsequent news coverage helped bring to a fever pitch. My impression is that New York in the weeks after 9/11 was not a place in the grips of fear and anger, but rather a place where tragedy triggered a remarkable outbreak of kindness among friends and strangers alike."

Anthony Liotti seems to suggest that television's shortcomings are merely a reflection of the nation's. A marketing executive at a large brokerage firm, he walked down sixty floors on September 11. Liotti says he understands the inherent limits of television in a culture as dispersed as ours. "We're the *United* States," he allows, "but this country's come to a point where if it doesn't happen in your backyard, it doesn't happen to you. Did the Oklahoma City bombing *directly* affect *me*, here in New York? Not really. Not until I went there on business and saw the memorial with these chairs representing all the people killed there, with little chairs for the kids. [To a New Yorker,] taking the Trade Center down was like taking the pinstripes off the Yankees. Here, it *affects* you. I saw two bodies obliterated before my eyes, just like that. TV [didn't] show that. It's superficial. TV doesn't connect us in a way that matters."

Television—American television at least—also took on the role of the Great Homogenizer, largely unwilling to address the larger political issues *behind* the attacks during that first week of sorrow and shock. The photographer Larry Towell recalls being interviewed with other photographers just after September 11 for a segment for CBS News. In Towell's view, it was a time of national reflection, not rage. "America was still questioning why this could have happened," he says. "The war drum hadn't yet been beaten. There were vigils in Union Square. There was a pensive attitude." Towell says that as the TV cameras rolled, he and his fellow journalists focused on: "What were they striking at? What were they saying to America? It was a sensitive thing." When the segment aired, however, the comments were reduced to a short clip about their experiences shooting pictures. "I remember feeling a little deceived. I remember a producer saying, 'Well, we're going to cut out all that anyway'—anything about questioning our previous actions as a country, [about] how this relate[s] to foreign policy and the Arab world in general."

The television audience remained all week long. And even though the commercials returned—and, with them, a small degree of normalcy—the face of television had been changed indelibly.

Behind the scenes, network news operations, post-9/11, instituted multiple fail-safe plans for dealing with breaking stories. More newsmen and women became proficient at using digital video cameras. (Once picture phones became popular, NBC News made sure that staff members, even nonjournalists, had mobile phones with cameras, just to have backup "coverage" if they happened to find themselves in the vicinity of a newsworthy event.) CBS News, as a direct result of the attacks, would start keeping "a reporter and producer [at the ready] with the necessary technical ability to go on the air at any time, should the need occur," says Susan Zirinsky, the executive producer of *48 Hours*. "We also have a series of alerts for various levels of management . . . that advise [us] if there's breaking news. Without giving away trade secrets, we have technically upgraded so that those that need to talk, instantly, to decide the next course of action are able to do that."

The on-screen palette would undergo a facelift as well. The "crawl line" that snakes along the bottom of many cable news programs (offering a whirligig of headlines, news nuggets, and corporate cross-promotions—"To vote, go to our Web site") certainly predates September 11. It is a product of the go-go 1980s, when financial and sports news junkies required real-time updates in the guise of the stock market ticker and the wire service "zipper" that once adorned heavily trafficked urban facades. The crawl (or loop or scroll) was later gussied up, like a garish hemline, becoming a convenient way to accommodate both breaking stories and prepackaged filler material, such as anniversary items and celebrity factoids.

But then came 9/11. "CNN, MSNBC, and FOX News Channel," according to *Entertainment Weekly*, "inserted the crawls on September 11 (FOX was first, at around 10:45)" and they've been up and running everywhere ever since. In these newsier times, viewers required facts, right then and there. What was the latest on the anthrax scare? Was the terror alert still at "orange"? How many casualties were reported overnight in the region where my nephew's unit is stationed? And so the recorded segments and the feel-good pieces and even the newscasters themselves became secondary. The networks were admirably taking on the public interest burden that they had shouldered since the medium's infancy.

Ever after, TV news directors stuck with the crawl, which would typically repeat its litany about six times an hour. The template was flexible enough to accommodate vital news (on September 12, CNN listed the names of the deceased aboard the doomed planes as soon as their identities became available) or divergent views ("The official Saudi news agency reports . . ."). But as the months went on, what began to matter, more and more, was the variety and richness (read: overload) of the news-watching experience. As the audience share fluctuated among TV-news consumers, eroded by competing and plentiful media options, the crawl became a way to help maximize a viewer's visual "points of entry," a lure for engaging those who might otherwise entertain the itch to switch elsewhere (especially the young, MTV-weaned, attention-deficit-prone). The crawl also allowed news desks to offer unsubstantiated items without guilt. "They can now run stories they haven't confirmed, with attribution to a wire service like Reuters," observed the *Times*'s Marshall Sella. "Zipping along at the bottom of the screen, it's a sly way to appropriate other news outlets' reporting."

Meanwhile, the on-screen smoke screen of ever splashier graphics projected the illusion that viewers had actual *choices*—just as they did on their home computers. The crawl was accompanied by other accoutrements siphoned from the Internet, video games, and sports shows:

stat boxes, drop shadows, logo bugs and Chyrons, and the Weblike arrows, overlays, borders, and dingbats that flooded the zone with color, trivia, texture, and movement. The screens at ESPN and Bloomberg can look as crammed as a nuclear reactor night watchman's—carrying with it the hidden message that there *is* no real news hierarchy (or objective reality), no matter what the talking heads might imply. "Multiple images" presented on a single screen, *New York Times* critic Caryn James has noted, "capture the fragmentation of our postmodern world, with its sense that truth is often subjective . . . [providing] dazzling immersions into many points of view at once."

Larger perceptual changes, attributable to 9/11, shook the industry as well. Because every channel had become consumed with the same scenes on September 11—and, soon, with rather indistinguishable coverage of the war on terror—American viewers began to wonder how it came to pass that these different networks had begun to speak with what sounded like a common voice. Audiences became more and more aware of the fact that multinational corporations—Disney (ABC), General Electric (NBC Universal), News Corporation (FOX), Time Warner (CNN), and Viacom (CBS)—owned the major TV-newsgathering operations and therefore controlled the slant of the stories they aired and the imagery that Americans watched. The viewing public began to recognize that most large news organizations were part of much larger entertainment-communications-and-information companies, businesses with vying allegiances and therefore potential conflicts of interest—and opportunities for editorial compromise. These were companies that, for their economic and political survival, needed to curry favor with the U.S. government, the FCC, their advertisers, and the newly empowered audience itself, one that didn't just "tune out" when turned off by controversial or offensive programming, but that knew how to use the Internet to organize protest campaigns against networks or advertisers if it took issue with questionable content.

News coverage of the ongoing conflict tended to be supportive of the U.S. government when America, Great Britain, and their allies retaliated against al-Qaeda and the Taliban (taking the war on terror into Afghanistan in late 2001) and then expanded the counterterror mandate to include Iraq as well. As a result, most outright criticism of the war in Iraq in the mainstream press was muted at best (at least through the fall of 2005, when a decline in Bush's approval ratings allowed dissenting voices to emerge). *Vanity Fair*'s James Wolcott was one of the early critics who came out and chastised his media colleagues, the White House press corps in particular, for their posture during the first stages of what he would refer to as Dubya Dubya III: "Since September 11, much of the press has dropped to both knees before George W. Bush to take dictation . . . The American press sniffs at the cult of personality that once plastered the walls and billboards of Iraq with portraits of Saddam Hussein while remaining oblivious to the cult of personality that has cowed most of them." Said the BBC's editorial chief, Greg Dyke, about the initial coverage of the Iraqi campaign: "I have been shocked by how unquestioning the American broadcast-news media has been . . . We can't afford to mix patriotism and journalism."

But mix the networks did. FOX News and MSNBC, which honed much of their vitriol and raison d'être during Clinton's rocky second term and the pitched battles surrounding the divisive 2000 presidential election, began to seem like house organs for the Bush administration. What had changed was the unabashed partisanship that colored much of the coverage across the board—and the fact that viewers seemed to get progressively cozier with the idea of using their remote controls to seek out the ballast that best matched their own political temperament. And the images on the screen, in turn, were often tailored, or suppressed, to fit the wartime agenda.

The nation had a long-standing aversion to pictures of American casualties in wartime. There were fewer taboos, of course, against showing the corpses of enemy combatants or the suffering of "outsiders." One cynical critic's formula for why the weekly *Life* magazine had been such a runaway success upon its launch in 1936 was the fact that the publication combined generous doses of "the decapitated Chinaman, the flogged Negro, the surgically explored peritoneum, and the rapidly slipping chemise." But come the 1940s, if a news organization as much as entertained the notion of transmitting a wire photo of a U.S. serviceman killed in action, the censors would immediately intercept the indignity. It wasn't until September 1943, twenty-one months after America entered World War II, that *Life* ran the conflict's first published picture of fallen GIs: photographer George Strock's shot of helmeted soldiers facedown in the sands at Buna Beach on New Guinea. Fifty years later, military censors during the Gulf War of 1991 forbade similar imagery. It took the *Detroit Free Press* shooter David Turnley days of cajoling the authorities at the Joint Information Bureau in Dhahran, Saudi Arabia ("You're denying these guys . . . their due right to heroism") before they would agree to release his pictures, including one that would become the most famous photo of the war: Sergeant Ken Kozakiewicz weeping in a helicopter's hold upon being told that the figure in the body bag to his right was that of his friend, Andy Alaniz.

Since 2001, such coverage, in the main, has been homogeneous, partisan, and sanitized, rarely depicting U.S. and allied casualties. "The government has blocked the press from soldiers' funerals at Arlington National Cemetery," Sydney Schanberg observed in *The Village Voice*. "The government has prevented the press from taking pictures of the caskets that arrived day after day at the Dover Air Force Base military mortuary in Delaware, the world's largest funeral home. And the government, by inferring that citizens who question its justifications for this war are disloyal Americans, has intimidated a compliant press from making full use of pictures of the dead and wounded."

The Pentagon has understood that one of the keys to maintaining the public's support for war has been the administration's ability to maintain control over the public's eye onto war's carnage. And so it has come to pass that this ongoing "war on terror," which has come to include the streets and villages of Iraq, has become a scrupulously unpublic matter, photographed at an extreme wide angle. Thousands of lives, as a consequence, have met their ends offscreen.

We were all watching, as they say, the world change. That a major shift in the tactics of terrorism was under way was evident in the scale of the carnage, in the sophistication of the attacks (coordinated, almost choreographed, against several targets), and in the enemy's unbridled presumption (striking America's centers and symbols of commercial, military, and governmental power, on American soil). But the question, then, became: What *was* the change that we were observing in the surfeit of photographs, and watching on our television sets?

The answer, of course, depended on the viewer's perspective. The world was spinning on a new axis that day. New York–Washington was the center of humankind's attention: magnetic north. And it was as though one of Earth's poles were supercharged by an opposing force—al-Qaeda—causing all compasses to point toward that new axis, now magnetized by radical Islam.

On one end of the spectrum, many believed they were watching the initial cannonade of Armageddon, or, at least, the clash of civilizations, epic and foreordained, between the Christian West and the Islamic East. On the other extreme, those sharing the sympathies of the perpetrators believed they were watching the beginning of the end of the West's global dominance, and the emergent voice, illegitimate or not, of the radical wing of the Islamic underclass (railing against Israel, the West, and those in power in wealthy, dictatorial Middle East regimes that were propped up by the West). Across that great divide, viewers believed they were watching any number of antithetical, irreconcilable messages: the infidel's demise; "freedom" under siege; the faith-splintered West imploding; the American ideal resilient, ready to rebound—and stronger still.

Nedjma, the Muslim feminist author, called it a collision of "two fundamentalisms." Social historian and cultural savant Christopher Hitchens called it "an unprecedented attack on modernity . . . the fatwa against [Salman] Rushdie, carried out on a city." German editor Ulf Poschardt called it "the moment the perceived savages became high-tech futurists—nihilists becoming one with the machine while dying, [bent on destruction and on] destroying their own religious culture." Don DeLillo, the novelist, called it an attack on "the white-hot future" and on "the thrust of our technology . . . our perceived godlessness . . . the blunt force of our foreign policy . . . the power of American culture to penetrate every wall, home, life, and mind."

French philosopher Alain Finkielkraut called it the moment the rest of us transformed into "soldiers of the disrespected civilization." *Newsweek*'s Fareed Zakaria cited Thomas Hobbes, calling it a harbinger of the resurrection of the State in the name of security: "We will see government become more powerful, more intrusive and more important." Noam Chomsky, who often appraises the role of language in international affairs, called it the emergence of "a new type of war [in which] the guns are now aimed in a different direction"—targeting the landmasses of Western, traditionally colonialist powers—"something quite new in the history of Europe and its offshoots." Photo editor and agent Gigi Benson called it, as many commentators did, the end of American innocence, the nation entering a new phase of distrust, fear, and insecurity. "Over There," she said, "became Over Here."

Depending on one's perspective, the images of planes, of towers tumbling, of Americans doomed were visions of

pure Evil finally establishing its beachhead
the fiery twilight of the era of oil dependency
democracy unbowed, to be defended at all costs
America's sins "come home to roost"
the enactment of the American lesson that "freedom is never free"
the ushering in of the new age of unilateralism
the slow run-up to World War III

We were watching the resilient, lone superpower, its cities attacked and its citizens slain, primed to retaliate with a force the world had never seen. (Two years later, on the eve of the U.S.-led invasion of Iraq, the conservative stalwart William Bennett insisted the campaign would "go down as one of the greatest military efforts of all time.") We were watching the United States of America, the impervious terra firma, now terrorized and burning as fiercely as Nero's Rome, suddenly vulnerable, perhaps ultimately and fatally so. We were watching the coming of age of sabotage as spectacle—orders of magnitude beyond that used to help establish the state of Israel in the 1940s, galvanize support for the Palestinian cause in the 1960s, or oust a superpower (the USSR) from

Afghanistan in the 1980s. Key features of Western progress* had been retrofitted as weapons and turned against innocent members of the society that created them. And, undeniably, we were watching the opening act of a blood-soaked revenge play, owing as much to Sophocles (with newsmen and politicians standing in for the ancient Greek chorus) as to Exodus (with its invocation of an eye for an eye), intended, this time, for the eyes of six billion.

If the fixed, focused cameras assured any sort of certainty, it was this: that history's revisionists would find it impossible to erase the event from civilization's conscience. We had the goods—millions of pictures and thousands of hours of videotape. If nothing else, this multiplicity of perspectives on an actual breaking news event provided, in reporters' parlance, "the best obtainable version of the truth" (the motto coined by *The Washington Post*'s Bob Woodward). September 11 had a set of bearings that were as objective as any observed event could be: established, historical facts that would make it much more difficult, in years to come, for the public record to be challenged.

The images mattered—the historical record mattered—because after a four-year gestation period, the conspiracy theories, bred of anger and desperation, and spread by the Web, had begun to metastasize. ("Google [the phrase] '911 conspiracy,'" *New York* magazine's Mark Jacobson has written, "and the bytes bury you.") Many in 9/11 conspiracy circles, already feeling marginalized by Bush's policies and pushed to the brink of reason by years of institutionalized government prevarication, had been taken in by the Net's net of half-baked plots. There was a kind of geek paranoia-chic that came from devoting hours to the fetishistic study of online photos or from conjuring hidden meanings within the stream of connections, benign or nefarious, generated by Web search engines.

By the thousands, otherwise sane individuals, sometimes gathering at conspiracy symposia and conclaves, would buy into the fiction that on September 11 the Pentagon was strafed not by a plane but by a missile. (This thesis, popularized by French writer Thierry Meyssan, rests in part

* Jumbo jets, oil (in the form of 60,000 gallons of jet fuel), and massive edifices (the Pentagon and Trade towers representing three of the planet's largest structures).

on the modest size of the gash in the building and on the absence of a plane in early security-camera video released by the Pentagon.) In similar fashion, many people used the footage of the twin towers' collapse—which seems like a series of mini-explosions—to support their contention that the buildings' destruction was the result of a "controlled demolition" orchestrated by everyone from big oil companies to stock and gold speculators, from the CIA to the Mossad, from Dick Cheney to Marvin Bush (the president's brother, whose firm was involved in W.T.C. security). This view held that agents may have pre-rigged dynamite charges on floor after floor—*without the knowledge of World Trade Center staffers*. Over time, these beams and joists of conspiracy and coincidence had begun to buttress one another, creating a sort of phantom credence.

While photos, in the short term, fanned these flames, it would be photos, in the end, that would create the foundation for the historical baseline. Tragically, the energy spent on theories of terror collusion would divert attention from the real war crimes: the barbaric jihad of al-Qaeda and the popular appeal and emboldened ranks of radical Islam. What's more, this reweaving of the 9/11 narrative would help cloak or excuse the unconscionable ineptitude of the Bush administration and the intelligence community in their failure to heed al-Qaeda's numerous warning signals. It would also mask the culpability of Congress, which, through its bipartisan 9/11 Commission, ended up letting the executive branch off the hook despite systemic, catastrophic lapses.

History, then, would show that the proof is in the visual. Men boarded planes and flew them into U.S. landmarks. There are images, indelible ones, that support these facts—countless digital photos and videos; images of terrorists on surveillance cameras, on visa applications, on the "martyr walls" of al-Qaeda Web sites. The written record would also reveal, alas, that previous U.S. administrations had not done enough to thwart bin Laden and that the Bush team, even though privy to hints of the 9/11 plot, was unable to connect the dots.

Considered in this way, September 11 was arguably unique as a historical moment. It was not the typical *Rashomon*-like mist of evidence, misperception, legend, and propaganda that coalesces into an accepted narrative or an out-and-out myth. Nor was history "a fable [or] set of lies agreed upon," as Voltaire and Napoleon posited. Instead, observers aplenty were able to offer so many firsthand accounts that the core event *can* be understood in a framework approaching consensus. With this aggregate objectivity, largely furnished by the camera, the historical essence of the events of 9/11 can remain relatively intact over time. And so the interpretation of the motives, causes, and effects, and their larger historical context, might be more clearly understood (or their understanding retained) as time goes on. History is less likely to be recast, even as the conspiracy theorists attempt to rewrite the present.

"In the modern way of knowing," Susan Sontag remarked, "there have to be images for something to become 'real.' Photographs identify events. Photographs confer importance on events and make them memorable . . . through the various systems (from television and the Internet to newspapers and magazines) that diffuse photographic images to millions."

The change that the world was watching, it so happens, was not just reflected in the level of violence or the unique visibility of the targets or the military prowess of the unsuspecting recipient of the attacks, but in the realization that the actions were conducted not behind a palace wall or in some Godforsaken trench or back alley. Instead, September 11 was enacted *for* the audience—an audience that would remember every nuance.

In some ways, the notion of the TV camera as an instrument of political accountability was forged in the revolutionary summer of 1968, as student dissent swept across Europe and North America, and as the emerging counterculture recognized the power that this emerging medium held over the established culture. As the Vietnam War escalated in the late sixties and as graphic TV footage of battle scenes made its way into the nightly news chain, leaders of the antiwar movement realized the huge, global impact of the small screen. Videotaped coverage of that afternoon's protest marches, like coverage of the war itself, could be witnessed that very evening on prime-time news broadcasts. TV, if not yet a tool of the revolution, was certainly a coconspirator, standing shoulder to shoulder with the youths in the streets and ensuring that their actions would be witnessed and their voices heard. In fact, at the very pinnacle of the U.S. student demonstrations in 1968—at the Democratic National Convention, held that August—organizers and protesters were so conscious of how their brutal treatment by police would be transmitted via TV cameras that the demonstrators' signature chant was not "Stop the War" or "Kill the Pigs" (that era's nickname for police), but "The Whole World Is Watching."

The whole world *was* watching. In a year when a war raged in Southeast Asia, the USSR invaded Czechoslovakia, and both Martin Luther King, Jr., and Robert F. Kennedy were assassinated, TV cameras had sprung open the political portholes. It was no surprise that within two months, when two African-American athletes won medals at the Olympics in Mexico City, they would choose to raise their clenched fists in a Black Power salute—during the American national anthem—knowing that the world's TV screens were tuned to the ceremony and that few activists had ever had a more visible platform for making a worldwide statement.

Shortly thereafter, when the singer-songwriter Gil Scott-Heron coined the famous 1970s slogan "The revolution will not be televised," his lyrics suggested that even the most discerning observers of the culture (and counterculture) had little inkling that in a single generation the medium would evolve, as the world's communication system evolved, into a porous, symbiotic web of electronic networks. The lines in Scott-Heron's song—

You will not be able to plug in turn on and cop out . . .
The revolution will not be brought to you by Xerox
In four parts without commercial interruptions . . .
There will be no pictures of pigs shooting down
brothers in the instant replay.
There will be no pictures of pigs shooting down
brothers in the instant replay . . .
The revolution will not be televised, will not be televised,

will not be televised, will not be televised.
The revolution will be no re-run brothers;
The revolution will be live

gave no indication that a rudimentary knowledge of round-the-clock TV-news manipulation would become an essential tool of any revolutionary hoping to mold world opinion—or that television would not only be the preferred means for verifying political change but the stage for staging it. ("If Hitler had had television," Nazi architect Albert Speer once surmised, in an interview with the art critic Robert Hughes, "there would have been no stopping him.")

Scott-Heron's world has now been upended. The technological advances that ushered in the visual age and "real-time" news have brought about a kind of global omniscience. The heinousness of these acts, seen the world over, may very well be destined to be retold for generations, thanks to digital storage technologies and the impulse of the modern-age data packrats who obsessively maintain the frayed strands of history, no matter how transcendent or trivial—in text and pixels.

If September 11 was the globally witnessed political atrocity, it manifests a hidden compact that, in the future, whatever one does in public life, for good and especially for ill, may very well be witnessed by a camera.

In this all-seeing age, beset with its crashing tide of digital cameras and videotape, contemporary society has been imposing, quite inadvertently, a layer of accountability on social interactions. Happenstance photography, quite literally, provides an oversight function. Do something untoward and there is a good chance that it might be observed, recorded and, given time, judged. (That phrase might as well have been lifted, in its entirety, from the Scriptures.)

The witness might well be a bystander with little or no connection to the action observed. The witness might be a hidden, closed-circuit monitor. But cameras, in the right hands—or at least in more and more hands of average citizens—may help create a culture in which the previously powerless have the welcome recourse of evidence against the culpable.

"We . . . are compassed about," says Hebrews 12:1, "with so great a cloud of witnesses."

Synchronized universal regard is not unique to the electronic epoch. From prehistory up through this morning, most living beings, every day of their lives, have observed or responded to the journey of the sun, moon, and stars. A given sunset or eclipse; a meteor shower; the steady march of the constellations, night after night, are events that are shared visually or biorhythmically by all who happen to reside in the same slice of hemisphere.

In early times, the sun, responsible for sustaining life and providing light, became justly revered by the ancients as a god, or as the god of all gods. Across generations, as deities emerged, so did idols and icons—visual representations of key figures in the stories of the faiths. These icons were graphic embodiments of gods, celestial objects, forces, or spiritual beings that ruled the lives of mortal beings, or they represented the heroes whose deeds inspired the faithful.

Together, then, we witnessed the cosmic or the divine through archetypes. The visual arts, from cave paintings on, channeled this act of witnessing, revering, interpreting, sharing. And nearer the modern age, aided by advances in mass communication such as the invention of the printing press (in the 1450s) and the photograph (1826–27), large numbers of us could visually share an archetype—an idealized, meaning-laden facsimile of a significant original—and witness it as if it were the thing itself.

In our time, the screen (the television, the computer, the handheld device) expanded the notion of common regard. Typically, the screen *disconnected* us from the flow of real life and from spiritual forces, offering a gray oasis of distraction. For certain exceptional events, however, the screen helped draw us together so that we were witnessing "as one."

While humanity still yearned for glimpses of the celestial or the divine, ours was the era of self-regard. Above all else, what modern culture seemed to desire was to witness the shifting tide of human events. What mattered were *our* deeds, our trivia, our tales of inspiration and pathos, our privileged celebrities and their falls from grace. The screen could now give global prominence to the individual human drama, whether grand or grave: from the first steps on the moon to the final leg of an Olympic race—to acts of mass murder by terrorists.

Then came 2001. When the planes hit and the buildings fell and the thousands died, our act of witnessing entwined our own stories with the bigger story, encrypting our personal reactions into the overarching horror. Vision made each witness something of a victim. Chant was met with response. Through the act of witnessing, the baffled, angered, civilized millions mattered as much as—or, arguably, even more than—the evil inherent in the acts they witnessed. The lone witness, realizing he was part of a society of witnesses, *each of whom had just seen what he had seen*, was obliged not only to watch but to take action. Even as terrorism demanded witnesses, the universal witness had become a player in the event itself.

The downside, of course, was that none of this escaped the attention of the terrorist. "If you think about the rise of terrorism *since* nine-eleven," says broadcast news consultant David Hazinski, "it's almost proof that terrorist[s] recognize this is a global village. Now, you have the potential to reach a two and a half billion audience for your act. That changes the dynamic. A young child you're trying to recruit as a terrorist, you don't have to spend a lot of time indoctrinating and explaining [the importance of] getting that global eye to turn on *them* [to publicize] Their Cause. They already *get* it. They got to see the act—*and* they got to see the shock. They saw the pictures."

All day long, visitors came to the Postmasters Gallery on West Nineteenth Street to see a new-media photography show called "2001." The exhibition, which had opened on September 6 and would be on view for a month, consisted of three "projections": a view of a Berlin TV transmitter, a Bavarian landscape with a medieval monastery, and a harborside shot of lower Manhattan, dominated by the World Trade towers.

Each of the projections was taken by a stationary, unmanned Webcam. The shots were sent over the Internet as live freeze-frames, then projected onto the gallery walls as huge twenty-four-by-nine-foot murals. On the walls, one could watch the bulbous communications tower, like some enormous Christmas ornament, glowing brighter as dusk advanced; the deepening shadows on the monastery's stone facade; the afternoon sun meandering across the New York City skyline and its apron of bridges.

Every four seconds, the image files would be refreshed, and the three scenes would alter slightly—a boat or a cloud would seem to twitch—while the digital clocks in the corner of each frame would advance by four digits. The work, by Wolfgang Staehle, explored "the dynamics, sensations and implications of connectivity," according to the gallery text. "[Staehle] takes the next logical step in the lineage of image making: painting, photography, film and video are now replaced by a real time digitally transmitted image." In fact, the installation was a shrewd hybrid of still photography, video, and electronic art—with a twist. By putting more or less objective slices of reality up on a museum wall (i.e., by replacing art with a real-time video version of reality), Staehle was deobjectifying these objects and moving our perceptions of our everyday terrain into a realm less tethered to traditional conventions of time and space.

"Seeing reality in real time in an art space," says Staehle, alters one's definition of art. It is no longer, in his view, "the thing on the wall, but something that happens in your head. It is more about a meditative attitude." In effect, the exhibition was asking: Wouldn't our lives be richer if we regarded every bend in the road as a perpetually replenished work of art? (A corollary question: Wouldn't such an attitude, by extension, take some of the onus off the camera—the great, all-seeing, ever-invasive lens of urban existence—and place it more in league with Buddha than with Big Brother?)

Staehle, a German-born New Yorker, was an Internet-art innovator who founded The Thing—thing.net/thingnyc—a Web-based clearinghouse for issues involving new media, contemporary art, and social activism. His installation was asking viewers to stop and revel in the planet's synchronicity. By watching three distinct points on the earth's surface (the high-tech spire, the spiritual retreat, the bustling metropolis), by watching the sky progressively darken on one wall and remain vibrant on another, one could gather that time was observer-dependent. The world, in effect, transcended our view of its smidgens as it went through its cycles, ruled by the dictates of celestial mechanics, climate, earth science—and the ravages of humanity.

"We return ourselves to slowness," Alexi Worth wrote in a review of the show in *ArtForum*, "to the world of micro-events. The wind shifts. A facade brightens . . . Its neutrality is vexing, an emblem of indifference but also of continuity." Through the camera and the Internet, an ocean had been crossed in the shimmer of a pixel. The wired world was forcing us to recognize, even if only in rudimentary ways, that everyone, everywhere, is part of a single entity.

Staehle also had other lessons in mind. He was presenting the omniscience of the surveillance camera as society's boon and burden. He was urging viewers to resist *interpretations* of the world (through media, culture, even art itself) so as to get at reality, the thing itself. And he was repudiating the modern-age construct of progress and precision for their own sake. At the entrance to the show, Staehle had hung a panel quoting philosopher Martin Heidegger's 1935 formulation about what would come to be known as "real time":

> When the farthest corner of the globe has been conquered technologically and can be exploited economically; . . . when you can simultaneously "experience" an assassination attempt against a king in France and a symphony concert in Tokyo; when time is nothing but speed, instantaneity, and simultaneity . . . there still looms like a specter over all this uproar the question: what for?—where to?—and what then?

In preparing the New York portion of the triptych, Staehle had gone to the Brooklyn apartment of his friend Walter Palmetshofer, an accomplished computer technician. Staehle took two Sony digital video cameras and aimed them out the tenth-floor window at lower Manhattan. By using twin cameras, he could "sandwich" their pictures to create a single sweeping panorama from across the East River. He decided to position the twin towers in the dead center of the right-hand frame *(Image 1)*.

Staehle and Palmetshofer then attached the cameras to two computers that contained video cards (to digitize the incoming analog signal) and a special video "frame-grab" program (to snatch a new "still" every few seconds). The two images were then turned into JPEGs (transmittable, viewable digital files), then sent online to the Manhattan gallery. In the exhibition space, the procedure was reversed. Two computers, hooked up to a cable modem with a Netscape browser, would receive the pictures, route them to two projectors, and splash them up on the wall.

In this way, Berlin, the Comburg monastery, and Manhattan could be displayed as real-time snapshots. "On three walls, static video images glowed in the darkness, like vast electronic postcards," wrote Worth. "Only a periodic shiver, like a transparent curtain stirring, indicated that they were live-feed webcam transmissions, updated every four seconds."

Three days after the exhibition opened, Staehle decided he wanted to retain a record of this evanescent endeavor. Instead of just capturing the shots, projecting them, and losing the files to oblivion, he and Palmetshofer began to archive the JPEGs by storing them locally on the hard drives of each camera's computer. In this way, he would have a permanent, sequential accounting of the show.

Even so, no one except Palmetshofer would have access to the URL (the Web address) to see the updated pictures. The only way to view them was to visit the gallery and watch the landscapes illuminate the walls. Palmetshofer began his archiving midday on September 9. And every four seconds the computers on South Eleventh Street in Williamsburg would automatically store a fresh panorama of the World Trade Center.

On September 11, at 08:46:50 EDT (as stated in the lower right-hand corner of the frame), Staehle's stationary camera recorded a smudge in the sky: a distinct though slightly blurred aircraft heading for the picture's right-hand tower. "There's one frame, you see a plane," says Staehle. "It's only a few pixels." At 8:46:54 the tower disgorges puffs of white-and-orange cloud from the three visible facades. At 8:46:58 the top half of the tower bursts in a halo of flame and smoke. The sequence, when viewed for the first time, is thoroughly startling.

Palmetshofer happened to be awake at the time, talking with European colleagues online. When he saw the buildings out his window, he realized that the camera across the room had captured the attack. "He was, like many programmers, constantly in their chat rooms," says Staehle, "because they're into open-sourcing, sharing information. [He told] his fellow programmers, Austrians and Germans, what was happening. And he gave them the URL. Then these five people in Europe looked at it and told their five friends. Within half an hour, you could see [that] the picture interval [between shots of the Trade Center had] slowed down to about nine or ten seconds because there were so many requests coming in. Everybody wanted to look at it. It spiraled a bit out of control." Among the first online views of the attacks, then, were those witnessed not in America, but across the Atlantic.

Palmetshofer alerted Staehle, who could see the towers out his window on Ludlow Street on the Lower East Side. Staehle alerted his dealer, Magda Sawon, the owner of the gallery, who was already at her desk that morning. "Turn on the projectors," he told her.

"One building was burning," she remembers. She had been alone in the as-yet-unopened exhibition space. "I saw it all on the walls. I saw it live [as part of] this artwork, not out the window, not through CNN. My picture was 24-feet long, double-projected on the main gallery wall, smoking and monumental. It was bizarre, unique, and *silent*. I saw it *only* in pictures.

"I watched both towers collapsing, by myself, in silence," she says. "I saw a series of still pictures but they were replacing each other so fast that it had a sense of jagged motion. The towers went down, but stopped in mid-air . . . The inevitable gravity of it—metaphysical gravity and the unstoppable physical gravity taking these buildings down—[was] emphasized by its choppiness. It's a completely perverse experience on some level. It was traumatizing for me. You don't understand [what you're observing] completely. It removed it from reality on some level. I didn't hear the newscast or the sound of the collapse. It *became* the picture.

"Then I put it in the context of what it ultimately meant," she says, hesitant even four years later to discuss the loss of so many friends she had known and lost that day.

By 11:00 a.m. or so, Staehle was standing in the gallery with two friends, watching, in effect, a lost horizon. His city in repose had become a high-tech *Guernica*. The towers fell, the city was consumed in cloud, and the darkened gallery became a space of anguish. Though he had hoped to fashion a more expansive view of the world, removed from the perpetual media cycle, the world had made other plans. His work suddenly became antithetical to its thesis: the Webcam was a sieve through which The News poured in, continuously, obliterating the long view in favor of the local and hurtling urgency of the now.

"I was there with two friends," he says, not wanting to demean the loss of life with talk of art, but compelled to do so by what he calls the "freak coincidence" of his having recorded the attack. "One said, '*Now* this is really an important piece. Now it has this historical significance.' I was a little upset about that. To me, it was important *before* that too. Then the other friend said, 'No, now it's destroyed your original artistic intention. It's overshadowed by this calamity.' "

Though Staehle had carefully chosen three landscapes, New York's had become the *only* one that mattered anywhere and everywhere. The whole world was WATCHING THIS SPACE. Staehle's wide window had instantly slammed shut. And yet the presence and persistence of the Berlin tower and the Bavarian monastery were more than distracting bookends to the carnage. That morning, and for the weeks that followed, they were windows onto the world beyond. One could almost feel, in standing there and seeing these two scenes re-re-replenish, that a great wound would slowly, eventually heal.

Even now, Staehle's pictures of that day remain relatively unknown. He has chosen to soft-pedal them, restricting their access over the Internet and publishing them intermittently, mainly in art journals and books. Nonetheless, critics far and wide have praised the impulse behind the exhibit. When portions of Staehle's "2001" were shown in Paris at the Cartier Foundation for Contemporary Art in 2002, as part of an exhibition called "Unknown Quantities," the philosopher Paul Virilio described the work as encompassing a dichotomy: twenty-first-century cataclysm has been the inevitable consequence of twentieth-century progress and rampant globalization. "You invent an airplane with six hundred seats," Staehle explains, "and you invent the accident with six hundred people dead." Virilio and Staehle both espouse the view that one way to escape this cycle is not to blindly pursue technology but to assume responsibility for those advances, and to be mindful of technology's underpinnings—the accumulated wisdom of science, reason, faith, and world culture over the centuries.

Most relevant and perceptive of all, perhaps, was artist, educator, and critic John Menick, who saw Staehle's austere cityscapes as scoffing at the modern "mania" for parsing the second. "Real time," according to Menick, became possible only with the invention of the atomic clock, in 1955. The utterly accurate second, in turn, would help "generate a more perfect metre, and thus all spatial standards, from the threading of screws to the size of cargo containers. Space travel, all scientific research . . . would rest upon the second's refinement." So what was the dark force behind this obsessive drive for accuracy? "When in doubt, look for the profit motive," said Menick. The culprit? "International capital's need for quicker transactions." Here, then, Staehle had it. Here was World Trade, slumbering, tamed, made part of a grander scheme.

The world, however, suddenly trumped the art. The work, in Menick's estimation, "could not anticipate a murderous attack. [It lacked any] protective irony to shield itself. The work waited for something to happen, and something unexpected did. If most real-time technology attempts to dominate the world, then Staehle's work was subsumed by the world. This is true openness, and it leaves little room for comfort."

Staehle's grand experiment used the ever-open eye of the camera to help transcend the quotidian, the material, the false front of "real time." But the most elegant theory we can concoct buckles under the weight of the actual. "Somebody put it very nicely," says Staehle. "History was coming on like a train. And I just walked onto the track, and history ran me over."

A still photograph isolates a fraction of time, one-sixtieth of a second, say. A film or video clip hints at the subtle actions and rhythms that transpire, instant by instant, as a minute elapses. "Motion pictures" use a sequence of still photographs to approximate an action's essence, an arc of virtual reality, in much the same way that calculus, measuring discrete limits below a curve, allows us to approximate the area under that curve.

But what about a sequence of images, taken at regular intervals, over an exceptionally long period? What about a time-lapse film, shot continuously for ten years, that follows the seasons and the process of rebuilding at Ground Zero? Could such a movie, deliberately played at "fast-forward" to compress ten years in the furnace of twenty minutes, help Americans heal?

That's what Los Angeles–based filmmaker Jim Whitaker had in mind when he first set foot on the site and walked along the fencing. "I thought of time-lapse, right there," he says of that visit a month after September 11. Whitaker (who works for the Hollywood production company Imagine Entertainment, cofounded by producer-partners Brian Grazer and Ron Howard) conceived of a film that would help move viewers beyond the gyre of "retrospect," and, instead, propel them *through* time itself to a place where they might acknowledge life's inevitable cycles of sacrifice, transition, and rebirth. He conceived of a movie focused on the future.

"As I was standing there," he says, "I could see the smoke, the debris. There was a kind of intensity: many people had masks, everyone and everything was moving. [Compared to TV footage] I had seen, the pile had seemed [to have gotten] smaller, and quickly. As I watched the rescuers and clean-up people I could see this great determination. In twenty minutes, literally, I went from feeling this dread and anxiety to this feeling of comfort that we're going to be O.K. We're going to rebuild."

Whitaker's epiphany became something of an obsession. Like many students of film, Whitaker had been enchanted at one time or another with time-lapse photographs. He vaguely knew of the landmark nineteenth-century work of Eadweard Muybridge, whose seminal stop-action sequences of horses in full gallop and men in various states of physical exertion had helped lay the groundwork for "the movies." He was familiar with Frank Percy Smith's 1910 time-lapse studies of hyacinths and lilies, of crocuses and roses doing their sunup-to-sundown dances, opening and closing their petals like ruffle-skirted chorines on a conga line. As a documentary filmmaker, before he moved to features (such as Eminem's *8 Mile*), Whitaker had even done some time-lapse work with the director of photography Thomas Lappin. But this endeavor was time-lapse at hyper-speed. And Whitaker was swept headlong into it.

Project Rebirth (funded by the Aon corporation, among others) has now been up and clicking, nonstop, since the six-month anniversary of the attacks. With a live digital Webcam (shooting a new image every minute) and between six and ten fixed cameras firing off 288 frames a day from separate spots in and around Ground Zero, Whitaker and his team are committed to providing a ten-year time capsule of the site's revitalization. The lenses are perched high (twenty-two and forty-seven stories up), low (one peeping up from the base of what once was the Trade Center; one from the grass in the graveyard at St. Paul's Chapel), and center (from other strategic locations). All cameras are equipped with an apparatus that automatically trips the shutter every five minutes and a computer-synced light meter that ensures correct exposures. In the footage (viewable at projectrebirth.org), construction workers seem to ricochet, vehicles flit and flutter, cranes swivel like weathervanes, and banks of office window lights come on like desert stars. All the while, clouds rush by like schools of plump salmon, the shadows and snowdrifts advance and recede, and the silent opera of resuscitation proceeds.

Eventually, Whitaker says, he hopes to display the parallel films simultaneously—on or near the area where the twin towers once stood—as part of "an in-the-round theatrical experience, so the buildings can literally rise up around people in twenty minutes." In this way, the public wound at Ground Zero will appear visibly mended through the suture of years.

Taking a cue from the British *Up* documentary series (in which the director-cum-sociologist Michael Apted films and reinterviews the same handful of British subjects every seven years—as they mature, age, and face life's dreams and hardships), Project Rebirth is also videotaping what Whitaker calls "human time-lapse subjects." The filmmakers are now in the process of chronicling ten years of human rejuvenation by recording testimonies and tracing significant rites of passage in the lives of ten individuals whose destinies were recast on September 11. (Thus far the raw, uncut "profiles" are revealing. One person close to the project says that while some of the subjects have clearly moved on with their lives, certain individuals show evidence of being stalled or stuck, their predicaments echoing the Ground Zero site itself, long mired in contentious politics over the future shape it will take.)

"I tend to think of the footage as a meditation," says Whitaker, echoing Staehle. "When you watch it for an extended period, it starts to put you in a sort of meditative state. While you are watching the progress of the building, you start to pay less attention to the actual physical building and more to the feeling of the progress and growth. I hope there is also a sense of regeneration one can feel. Closure is perhaps too strong a word." Also inherent, as the minutes click along, is the transitory nature of our days alive, and the eddies that ripple on in our wake. Whitaker's version, in effect, is the director's cut: as if the scene at Ground Zero is being witnessed not only from ten vantage points, but also from above.

In this virtual omniscience, we sense that decay and rebirth are inevitable, not incongruous, aspects of the same film.

6 SUNDAY, SEPTEMBER 16

Joel Meyerowitz still remembers every detail of that first Sunday. As he recounts his tale, four years later, he sounds, by turns, like a Zen master or a Broadway-bound comic working out the kinks in a one-man show.

"I went down to Ground Zero," he says. "You couldn't get anywhere near it. I got as close as Chambers and Greenwich and it was closed off with cyclone fences and tarping and I stood in the crowd and had this epiphany moment. I raised my Leica to my eye and behind me a cop gives me one of these nudges in my shoulder with her forefinger and she says, 'Hey, buddy. No photographs here. This is a crime scene.' She called me 'Buddy.'

"I said, 'Don't give me that crap. I'm standing here in a public thoroughfare.' She shouldn't have touched me.

"She said, 'I'm going to take that camera away from you.'

"And it is a New Yorker's birthright," Meyerowitz explains, "to argue when you know you're in the right. I said, 'What if I said I'm with the press?'

"She said, 'Press, huh?' And she points with her thumb. And there, about a half block back from me, are twelve people, press guys with videos and booms and tripods and they're tied up with yellow [police] tape in a cordoned-off area. There's a tree in the midst of them. They're stuck."

Meyerowitz remembers feeling queasy as he saw his fellow photographers, as if on some life raft, adrift. He continued to argue with the officer. "This is a crime scene," she repeated. "No photography allowed. I'm just doing my duty."

"That phrase," he says, "sends chills through you. I had this sudden recognition. Fuck them. I resented that. If they're not going to let people photograph here, then they're taking history away. So I thought what could *I* do? Make sandwiches for the workers? Give blood? That wasn't needed. I knew, then, I could make an archive that had a usefulness. I could go in there as a New Yorker and as a photographer and as someone who had just been told that history was going to be denied Americans."

As Meyerowitz stood there, steaming—a renowned photographer forbidden to photograph—he still felt the pernicious sting of her jab to his shoulder blade. "By poking me and getting me riled up, she gave me the incentive. That little poke was the hinge that sent me in a different direction. She gave me consciousness. She was my Buddhist teacher."

Meyerowitz's plan was simple—in theory. He would somehow force his way onto the site and chronicle the rescue, recovery, and reconstruction in color (his film eventually supplied by Fuji), using various photographic formats: a 4×5 Deardorff View Camera, a 6×7 Mamiya, and his trusty Leica. He understood the value of creating a systematic record of historically significant events, having spent weeks during the 1990s doing research in the archives of the Library of Congress and elsewhere for a book on the history of street photography. He also had a case of World Trade Center on the brain. For the previous two or three months, he'd been at his home on Cape Cod looking at four-foot-tall test strips of the twin towers (shot from his longtime photo studio on Nineteenth Street) for an exhibition, "Looking South: New York City Landscapes," set to be installed in October 2001. (Meyerowitz, now sixty-seven, with the bald pate and wry patter of the comedian Larry David, remembers the days *before* the towers' construction, when workmen were extending the riverbank with landfill, creating Battery Park City. "It was rustic," he says. "Periodically, I'd shoot the weather systems moving across when lower Manhattan looked like Big Sky Country. You'd have a sense of vastness. This spaciousness, this island quality.")

The next week he sent written proposals to various organizations; his entreaties were rebuffed or met with silence. He appealed to the mayor's office—knowing Rudolph Giuliani was an amateur photographer—with no results. Without any official backing, he parlayed a letter from the Museum of the City of New York into a "worker's badge" of red oaktag, which he then counterfeited on his computer to get around the system of colors and designs that would change every twenty-four hours. "I would [go down] and get thrown out every single day, [then] push around and find a weak link, flash my letter." He would continue sneaking around and noodging and exhausting security personnel, shooting for up to twelve hours a day, even as he was repeatedly ejected.

Then, as luck would have it, he fell in with a coterie of detectives on the NYPD's Arson and Explosion Squad. They immediately understood his vision, contending that their children needed to see the history of their colleagues' endeavors. Meyerowitz says, "I explained my problem with the mayor and they said, 'Fuck the mayor. We're going to help you. Anyone tries to move you, stand still and call us on *any* of our cell phones.' [After that,] I'd get stopped twice a day sometimes and they'd come around and ream out these cops or FBI guys or Port Authority. They invented language you never heard. And they said, 'He's with us.' "

After fifty days of shooting in this manner, Meyerowitz finally persuaded the powers-that-be to create a special badge for him: "Mayoral Photographer." For eight and a half months he continued, compiling an unparalleled body of work: the most complete record, in still photographs, of the efforts at Ground Zero—much of it in large format. (A few others were also granted special access, including Andrea Booher of FEMA, Sergeant Patrick Jennings of the National Guard, Stephen Delory, Gary Suson, and Sacha Waldman—who shot stunning panoramic composites *[Image 26]*. But none was more persistent, or better at marketing his work, than Meyerowitz.)

Meyerowitz would treat his images, unusually rich in color and crisp in resolution, more as art pieces than works of photojournalism. He would scan each frame, then run the output through a digital enlarger, printing them up thirty-by-forty inches on conventional photographic paper. He gave them titles one might bestow upon museum pieces: *Twi-*

light, Iron Workers, Bringing Out the Dead, Midnight. In his image *Smoke and Steel*, for example, white vapor rises from the nighttime ruins like steam above a thermal pool, so that Ground Zero appears to churn with spirits. In *A Bugler Plays Taps*, a trumpeter and four others in helmets cast portentous Four Horsemen shadows while, in the distance, the hull of the tower's obstinate columns stands tall. When discussing the images, Meyerowitz—no humble street-shooter he—sometimes refers to Rembrandt's *Night Watch* and to the nature photography of Ansel Adams.

Five More Found was taken one October night from inside the wreckage of the south tower *(Image 27)*. Meyerowitz explains: "I see a bunch of men start to run up into the pile through standing steel that looks like daggers coming up in the dark. I look into this gulley and there are about fifty men assembled. And I see this orange light and I make my picture, click, click, click. And there's a . . . collapsed space and a guy comes out from where the steel timbers had left a void. And he says, 'This is a stairwell. And there are five firemen in here. And they are all intact. This is the stairwell from the *north* tower.'

"When he said that, it was as if a hand pushed everybody back with the recognition as it sunk into them. That stairway had flown hundreds of yards—the markings on it were from the other tower—and comes to land inside the south tower with these guys. They were ejected and flew, intact, there."

The work, five thousand images strong, was collected for eventual residence at the Museum of the City of New York. Twenty-eight photographs were selected and printed, each thirty-five times, then packed and crated into thirty-five identical exhibitions. Under the auspices of the U.S. State Department, the show, entitled "After September 11: Images from Ground Zero," would travel to cultural centers in some three hundred cities in ninety countries. It is still traveling to this day and has been viewed by millions around the world. Its primary mission: to help "remind . . . audiences of the true dimensions of the attack and the response."

Its unstated secondary missions, surely, were to espouse American values as universal values and to deflect or soften negative public sentiment toward the United States in a post-9/11 world. In its own way, this comparatively modest installation, once embraced by the American government, professed to take on some of the lofty goals inherent in Edward Steichen's massive 1955 *The Family of Man* exhibition, which depicted the commonality of humankind through 503 pictures by 273 photographers depicting life in 68 nations. That show, after its opening at the Museum of Modern Art, was sent on a global tour (underwritten by the United States Information Agency) just as the cold war was heating up. "These pictures," wrote historian Eric Sandeen of the most widely viewed photo exhibition ever mounted, became "part of an American projection abroad that included both marketing and foreign-policy objectives."

Even if Meyerowitz's work had become a calling card of the Bush administration, a worthy photo project that had grown out of proportion (to be collected in a book of hundreds of photographs), and the ultimate State Department p.r. coup—Ground Zero and its nameless heroes, recast as an export—none of this mattered. Meyerowitz's purpose remained pure: he had gone where most others were forbidden and documented the humanity that, curiously enough, overshadowed the destruction.

"Everywhere we went," says the State Department's Brian Sexton, who organized the touring show, "firemen came in uniform. [They arrived] with candles in Central America. In Honduras all the guys with sniffer dogs came. We showed it outside of Topkapi Palace in Turkey in the same place that earthquake pictures had been shown the year before. People's reactions were: We never knew Americans pulled together and bled together and lit candles and prayed together. We thought Americans were all about consumption, opportunism, individualism. The collective spirit of volunteers and firemen, working for months on end, really resonated.

"Journalists in Kuwait asked, 'Isn't this just propaganda?' They stayed there and looked. Once they got past those questions, they felt, These are very powerful [pictures. The show] went to a shopping mall in Kuwait and thousands came. Same thing in the Mexico City subway system. We jumped over the government-to-government stuff to go people-to-people. We never 'spun' them. [The message] wasn't: Bad guys did this. [It was a] balance of human suffering, human resilience. Tragedy is universal."

Meyerowitz, looking back, says he wasn't sniping for instants of perfect reportage. He wasn't going after images that might fit handily into some editorial hole within a particular news cycle. The work, in fact, has been criticized as unexceptional or underwhelming by respected figures in the photojournalism community. But Meyerowitz claims he was seeking something else, something whole. By immersing himself in the totality of Ground Zero—its pathos, its sweep, and the interlocking needs and mind-set of its populace—his work would be *of* the site: photography not as document but as organic expression of a dominion experienced.

"Going there every day, it became part of me, within me," Meyerowitz contends. "I was with these people in this space, and one of them. I walked it every day, around and around. It was spiritual, submitting to a larger force. You realize your own insignificance and minuscule scale in the larger picture. You see yourself as being a part of an interconnectedness: millions of people, chairs, buildings . . . I tried to . . . leave the residue of the photographs as all. It was peripatetic: be spacious, be cool and calm down and let the event tell itself."

Meyerowitz says that he was after nothing less than replicating Ground Zero's potential to evoke "the sublime," using the term as it was applied in the eighteenth century: an almost unbearable awe that we experience upon confronting the boundless power of nature's grandeur. This concept of awe, it so happens, would later inform the work of the Hudson River painters, many of whom continue to inspire Meyerowitz. The sublime, as the writer John Updike has pointed out (in his assessment of Andrew Wilton and Tim Barringer's exhibition "American Sublime," on the Hudson River painters), was a "delightful horror, a sort of tranquility tinged with terror," so the philosopher Edmund Burke described it in 1757. In Immanuel Kant's view, the sublime was an energy or entity "transcending every standard sense . . . absolutely great . . . comparable to itself alone."

When Meyerowitz first saw the denuded Trade Center site, he says, he felt an enveloping humility toward a greater force, a sense that the breadth and depth of this profound chasm had somehow ripped him off his moorings. He was submitting to and paying homage to the unfathomable nature of the sight in front of his lens, but also to the unfathomable nature of the universe beyond. "Most people saw the horror" on September 11, Meyerowitz says. "But the aftermath of the event left this decay and destruction which is exactly what nature leaves behind. The sublime in nature painting has always been reckoned as the cataract, the waterfall, raging storms at sea. These immense forces of nature humble us. The awesome monumentalness of their upheaval makes mankind powerless.

"And so that's what I encountered in my first awestruck moments at Ground Zero. To stand in that space that had been hollowed out by 'the fall' and to see the city rising behind it to the northeast and the weather playing out across the empty sky, shook me with awe. You're standing down in the pile and you feel the forces of nature—the gravity that pulled the buildings down—even though a man flying a plane brought this down."

When Meyerowitz finally made it onto the site, on September 21—five days after his Sunday epiphany—he was overwhelmed. "I started shaking and crying that day. It was convulsive. I allowed myself to have those emotions, rather than covering them up and being functional and documentary and thinking about f-stops. I didn't want it professionalized and predigested for a newspaper and magazine audience. I stayed vulnerable to that experience.

"To be standing at the foot of this cascade of one hundred stories of steel, I saw a terrible beauty," he says. Meyerowitz compares the vista to one he might witness on a majestic mountainside as "a million trees, clouds, crags, snow, and the cumulative complexity of nature is displayed before you—this strewn-about quality."

"Terrible beauty," unfortunately, was not a phrase that would sit well with many of those whose lives had been tragically altered by the attacks. His vision was incommensurable to that of hundreds of firefighters, who viewed the space as purely horrific. Meyerowitz was criticized for making these sorts of statements in lectures and in newspaper articles, and for seeming to dwell on the artistic or philosophic aftermath—not on the root causes of the September 11 attacks or on the sacrifices made that day. But he was also heralded as well. Meyerowitz was familiar with the power of photography, not the power of politics or religion or ultimate judgment. The photograph, he believed, could be of service to the eye. It could help persuade some viewers to think about the response and cooperation *after* September 11, and it could help teach others to remain open, in every encounter of their lives, to subliminal layers of beauty, tragedy, chaos, and grace.

He recalls looking at the vast expanse—"the rebar, the wires, the I-beams. On a summer day, with smoke, the smell that first morning, I saw it. Geysers of water [from fire trucks] being poured into it and the tiny bodies of men calling to one another. It was theatrical beyond Hollywood.

"It was not that you saw tragedy or horror," he says. "You saw a fact."

There would be many others like Meyerowitz, whose photography—not spot-news coverage, but long-term documentary work—would come to light. Legendary portraitist and photojournalist Mary Ellen Mark photographed the facades of firehouses. Some of the stations in her pictures resemble mausoleums, their vast red doors yawning open, flanked with pictures of lost brothers in helmets set amid arrangements of roses, flags, religious icons, and candles of red, white, and blue. Joel Sternfeld and Mike and Doug Starn—three of the most accomplished fine-art photographers who were working downtown on September 11—made still lifes of singed and crumpled documents, letters, and spreadsheets that had floated down from above. "When the papers were falling all around the studio where I work," Mike Starn explained, "I had to pick them up: these were someone's things. They are somehow vicariously part of the people who died, we can't leave them just like trash." Jeff Mermelstein, the street photographer with New York's finest comic eye, shot misery at every corner he turned, once stopping to photograph a group portrait in the litter—Buddies in Tuxes—now defaced and anonymous.

David Turnley shot an extended photo essay on the community spirit that flowed at the 225-year-old St. Paul's Chapel—Ground Zero's "little church that could," spared in the upheaval all around it. Eugene Richards documented Manhattan's aftershock, then paired his contemplative black-and-white pictures with first-person narratives compiled by Janine

Altongy. Jonas Karlsson, for *Vanity Fair*, made formal portraits of search-and-rescue workers, medical teams, firefighters, families of the missing, and flight attendants from American, Delta, JetBlue, and United who had gathered at West and Canal Streets to join hands, pray, and pay tribute to their slain colleagues. Nathan Lyons photographed the panoply of flags (and posters and stickers and drawings of flags) that radiated across the urban and rural landscape. Several concentrated on the candlelight vigils that took place nightly across the city, others on memorial services or on communities that lost large numbers of citizens or on a single family coping, over months, even years. Others chose to document the reconstruction effort or the twin beams of light that, on anniversaries, radiated in the Trade Center's absence, piercing the night sky with shafts of blue.

Working at the invitation of *Life* magazine, Joe McNally borrowed a gargantuan Polaroid camera—physically the size of a one-car garage—to take what were actually larger-than-life-size portraits (forty by eighty inches) of three hundred people directly connected with the events of September 11. Six and a half feet tall, McNally's outsize images would bring the humanity of the tragedy into daunting relief, allowing viewers, made modest in the presence of the photographs, to begin to scale the heights and depths of emotion to which McNally's subjects had ventured.

McNally photographed twenty-year-old Peter Regan, who had left his Marine base at Camp Pendleton, California, to search the wreckage for his firefighter father, Donald. He photographed Michael Lomonaco, executive chef of Windows on the World restaurant, which lost seventy-three workers; Elizabeth McGovern, who made it out of the World Financial Center by descending forty flights that morning, but who lost her mother, Ann, who was thought to have been but one elevator load away from exiting as she waited in line on the seventy-second floor of the south tower.

The so-called Museum Camera, conveniently housed in a studio near the Trade Center site, was a one-of-a-kind creation—the most massive camera of its kind. (It had once been broken down, flown to Rome, then reassembled to photograph the artworks of the Vatican.) Two technicians would actually sit *inside* the camera booth, and McNally, outside in the studio and connected via radio link, would direct each shoot. McNally would position his subject in front of the open lens, coax him or her into a plane of focus, and place an intense light source "as close to the subject as he [could] bear it," he says. "Inside they are looking at the spectral highlights in the eyes. When those get pinpoint sharp, they call out on a radio from inside the box." McNally would then cap the lens and tell his subject to remain completely stationary as the two technicians, in the darkness of the interior chamber, would pull a massive roll of paper across a trapezelike bar and rest the Polaroid against a pressure plate. Just before each exposure, a vacuum would suck the paper evenly onto the plate. McNally would call for the studio lights to be extinguished, and then physically pull the cap off the lens. A second camera—a 6×7 Mamiya—would fire the strobe system, giving him duplicate exposures, one on the Mamiya, one on the giant Polaroid.

The camera assistants would then peel the film off the roller, place it on the floor inside the camera and, ninety seconds later, a Polaroid image would appear. "The people would come around back, *into* the camera," McNally recalls, "and we had tough guys, a lot of 'em. They'd see their picture emerge, and just fall to pieces. You'd have Joanne Foley Gross crying while I'm photographing her *(Image 29)*, holding her brother Tommy's ceremonial fire helmet and his cowboy hat three days after her brother Danny, a firefighter [with Engine Company 68] came in with Rescue 3 [from the Bronx]. Danny [had] promised his family, 'I'll go there and find Tommy.' Danny stood for his Polaroid a couple days after he found Tommy. He actually found his body—they knew roughly where the truck [had gone in].

"The studio was rife with emotion like this," says McNally, who sometimes found himself photographing through his tears. "The experiences they came in with into the studio were very raw. Everything was very fresh. Stories of loss, stories of recovery. We would get crews from the pit at three o'clock in the morning. I slept in the studio. You couldn't *not* be affected by it."

The large Polaroids would be mounted in Grand Central Station, in Boston, London, Chicago, San Francisco, Los Angeles. The images, now stored in twelve one-ton crates in a New Jersey warehouse, may in time be acquired, in whole or in part, by the Smithsonian, the Library of Congress, or the National Portrait Gallery. "The most satisfying thing for me," says McNally, "was the amount of emotional solace and relief it brought to many, many people. It was an ultimately hopeful project, about the living, about going forward."

On Sunday, Laura Greenstone was making final arrangements to go to a support center in northern New Jersey. A licensed professional counselor and board-certified art therapist, she sometimes worked in a battered women's shelter and was accustomed to treating families scarred by trauma and domestic violence. Now, her faculties and stamina would be pushed to the brink. Under contract to an insurance company that had lost dozens of employees on 9/11, she would spend the next week offering crisis counseling each day to twenty family members seeking connection with people like themselves and searching for guidance about everything from the whereabouts of relatives to the nuances of life insurance policies.

Two months later, recognizing the need for outreach, she and her fellow clinicians at Amanda's Easel Art Therapy Program offered bereavement and recovery services specifically tailored for 9/11 families in Monmouth County. In their program, youngsters, ages three to eight, and their parents, almost exclusively women, would work in parallel, the moms meeting in group sessions with Greenstone in an open art studio, the kids in their own sessions two doors down with Greenstone's partner, Cindi Westendorf. The parents would address how to manage their anxieties and feelings of loss; over time, they would begin to use different art materials (photography, watercolor, chalk pastels, magazine collage) to express themselves, to calm themselves, to cope. The children would explore their own emotions through art, working through their immediate reactions to the trauma. Some of Greenstone's participants would draw their spouse's portraits, based on photographs "as a way to dialogue with that lost person," as she puts it. Others would use their family pictures as tools for healing.

One 9/11 widow came to Greenstone harboring the fear that her children, ages five and seven, were not going to remember their father as time went on. The mother talked about a cache of photographs of her husband that seemed to overwhelm her. So Greenstone persuaded her to bring in her pictures and begin sorting through them as a way of putting her life in order. "She needed some kind of containment for them," Greenstone remembers. "I suggested that I could teach her how to bind her own album, if she would like to make one. I asked if there were some important material she would like to use. And she said she wanted to pick out shirts of her husband's. Her two children each chose a shirt that they liked of their dad's. She went into the closet and they did this as a kind of ritual together." The mother would then create two photo albums, each covered in fabric, front, spine, and back.

Greenstone understood that the soft, tactile nature of the clothing would be comforting. The woman then continued to work on her project at therapy sessions, off and on, for two and a half years, "systematically going through the photographs of her children with their dad, from birth until present. I've been subtly processing her memories with her. She's trying desperately to take these fragmented images and put them into some context—unconsciously—to help her make sense of this loss. Her life was just all in pieces. The photographs, strewn around, really highlighted that for her. This was a way for her to validate [for her children] that their dad was real in their lives."

"As art therapists working in trauma," she says, "we understand how images are much more powerful than the spoken word. Trauma memories are not stored in parts of the brain that are verbal. They get processed in areas that actually encode in images. That's why it's often difficult to talk about trauma, because we literally don't have the words to describe it. If someone is unable to process a catastrophic event, they may be experiencing nightmares, flashbacks, free-floating anxiety that they can't really describe. But in art therapy we use imagery, and we can help a person work through the trauma without reliving it, and come to some resolution . . . The 9/11 trauma is made more intense because it has been such a public event. [In Monmouth County,] we've had average families who've had media crews following them around for a year. It's never 'over.' Moreover, many children have been exposed to images that they never would have seen if it wasn't publicized on television. A lot of the children . . . thought *all* the buildings were coming down. And the fact that they saw it over and over again, they didn't realize it was just one incident. Some of the children actually saw the towers fall as it was happening, on television, and watched their [mothers] respond to seeing their husbands die."

The woman who bound her photo albums with her husband's shirts "cried for maybe the first two years that I worked with her," says Greenstone. Come 2005, she was "actually looking at these photographs with pleasure." Pictures, Greenstone believes, helped her patient "come to terms with how concrete [her husband's] life was, and how permanent his loss is. He's gone, and now she seems to accept that. Each photograph allows her to find a home for that particular memory, a past experience that won't get lost. The memories have some permanence. And so they validate that his life was meaningful."

I phoned a friend in London to see how he was coping, to offer support. He briefly explained his own saga, then elaborated, months later, in excruciating detail. As we spoke, I recalled the days I used to visit him in the lofty bower of the Cantor Fitzgerald offices at One World Trade Center, before he and his family moved to England. I remember admiring the massive sculptures in the foyer: Rodin's *Balzac* and *The Burghers of Calais*. (Much of Cantor's extensive Rodin collection was reduced to rubble in the collapse.) I remember marveling at the speed with which my friend and his sky-high partners, plugged into a network of other financial desk jockeys, would sap the phone lines of all the best new jokes of the day. They were modern humor's equivalent of an early warning system, in the days before the Internet linked up the rest of us.

On September 11, my friend, an executive at eSpeed (a Cantor subsidiary in London), had been on a conference call with his counterparts on the 103rd floor of Tower One. Over the course of his call, he had listened to what he remembers as the "turmoil over the squawk box," as colleagues spoke about some sort of explosion. Later came sounds that he now claims are too nightmarish to describe. Within hours, he had confirmed what he had already known: Cantor had lost more than 650 workers, a loss of life that would turn out to be greater than that of any other Trade Center firm.

For months, my friend and his wife, like so many others connected to Cantor, would help their peers and their families cope with their losses and try to get on with their lives. But everything, he says, "was overshadowed by the reality of having heard the harrowing cries of intimate colleagues at their last moments."

In the first weeks, he says, he was angered by the barrage of photos of the attacks. Wherever he looked, the towers followed. While he yearned for information about the event, it seemed to him that the media was after prurience, served straight up, flooding the culture with "stuff" about the massacre. "The images were absolutely repulsive initially," my friend would recall nine months later.

"The first week, the first two months," he says, "the shock and the horror you associate with pictures. Then, as your healing process begins, after the pity and the horror and the hate, you need something tangible to connect to, so you associate that feeling of healing with individual images: the raising of the flag or the stretchers bringing body parts out. You think: How is this helping me and how can I go on to live the rest of my life?

"One of the stumbling blocks to healing is the belief that this is about *you*. An image takes you out of yourself and gets you out of the 'poor me' syndrome. It's not about you. It's about how it affected *everybody*. The images reinforce that you have to come out of yourself to commiserate, to empathize. Pictures unblock your own pain.

"So the images assist you." he says. "This is only true with *still* images. The moving images pull you into the maelstrom again. The falling towers are too evocative of the horror. But you isolate a moment in a still image, and you make it your own. Once you get through the process of revulsion, you find a moment of serenity and then the image becomes positive. For me, the image[s] of the smoldering girders and debris are more healing than those of the empty hole. Because the scene was complete and not yet dismantled, it seemed as if those souls were still there."

The Cantor Fitzgerald Relief Fund would lend its support to a unique portraiture project. The concept: any family that lost a relative in the World Trade Center attacks would be able to send his or her photograph to artist Nancy Gawron, of Middletown, New Jersey (a community that suffered nearly fifty losses on 9/11), and she would create a colored-pencil sketch, free of charge. All told, Gawron would complete 335 portraits of men and women from Cantor and a number of companies and emergency services.

"At first," says Gawron, "it felt like an altruistic thing to do. But doing the portraits, and being a part of the healing process for these families, has turned it into something else. It has begun to be as important to my life as the gift is to theirs. [For me] the tragedy has a face with every portrait I do, and every set of eyes I look into."

Within nine months of September 11, 103 expectant mothers whose husbands had perished on 9/11 would bear children. For some of these women, Gawron would draw composite group portraits—a single sketch of the deceased, his wife, their newborn child, and any other children in the family. Sometimes Gawron would make sure the father's hand or arm was placed, just so, around the new child, who would never know the touch of his or her natural father.

In 2005, she would look back on the experience of creating the sketches as having been fraught with spiritual significance. Gawron says that she sees the living and the deceased as residing in a common dream state. "When we die we will awaken from this dream [the reality of everyday life] and it will seem no more real than the dreams we have when we are sleeping." Through the act of looking at the photographs and sketching the portraits, she was plumbing that realm, she contends, where life and death intersect. "I sometimes had a strong sense of [the subject in a drawing] looking over my shoulder when I was working. I did portraits that I should not have been able to do, given the [photographic] reference material that I had. One father called me in tears after receiving the portrait. He said when he opened it and looked into his son's face it was like he said, 'Hi, Dad, I'm home.' "

On Sunday, a prop plane swept the skies above Ground Zero. On board was a special spectrometer, an imaging device that could scan a path beneath it in various wavelengths, determine the landscape's chemical makeup, and thereby gather evidence of potentially toxic pockets within the rubble. The Airborne Visible Infrared Spectrometer (AVIRIS) had previously been deployed by NASA for probing the dense cloud tops of the outer planets. Now it would be put to more urgent, earthly use.

Based on AVIRIS data collected on September 16, scientists from the U.S. Geological Survey and NASA's Jet Propulsion Laboratory located thirty-four fires that still raged underground. Experts quickly generated maps, which, the *St. Louis Post-Dispatch* reported, were "shipped to emergency response teams in New York. Based on this information, firefighters redeployed their equipment and changed how they were attacking the fires." At the same time, geophysicists took AVIRIS evidence and ran a series of tests to ferret out traces of any hazardous materials that, according to *Chemical & Engineering News*, might have been present in "two different kinds of aerosols: pulverized dust from the collapse of the towers and smoke from the fires in the debris piles."

Five years later, even after extensive study, symposia, and debate (along with a Mount Sinai Medical Center screening and treatment program for some ten thousand workers and volunteers), medical professionals are only beginning to understand how harmful materials at Ground Zero have contributed to lung scarring, diminished lung capacity, and potentially fatal maladies among World Trade Center employees, emergency personnel, nearby residents, and on-site crews, many of whom worked for weeks or months on the pile.

Students at Stuyvesant High School, just a few blocks from the Trade Center, had been asked to remain in their building on September 11 after the school's principal received what he called an official assurance that the towers were not in danger of imminent collapse. The student body's shared experience of withstanding the shock waves from the south tower's disintegration, while devastating, was not enough to break its spirit. Not in the least.

On September 16, an estimated four hundred Stuy students assembled in Washington Square to paint giant "hope and unity" murals on two twelve-by-eighty-foot tarps. One hundred and sixty posed to commemorate the occasion in a group photograph, almost all of them sporting T-shirts, wide grins, and expressions of promise, not defeat. One of the murals, according to the fall edition of the school paper, *The Spectator*, was incorporated (along with the American flag) into the senior class photo.

On Sunday I channel-surfed, absorbing some of the television images of the events. As I watched NBC's coverage of the Ground Zero efforts, I heard anchor Tom Brokaw make the comment that, from a distance, the figures swarming atop the World Trade Center pile looked like something out of a "Sebastião Salgado photo."

Late Sunday morning, Lisa Palazzo was still in bed at her sister-in-law's home in New York's Westchester County. For five days she had not heard from her husband, Tommy, a broker for Cantor Fitzgerald. But she still believed he was safe somewhere, somehow. After all, a rumor had been circulating on Thursday that Tommy's name had appeared on a list of possible survivors.

One of her husband's childhood pals, George Morrell, had also worked at Cantor. He too was missing. George's wife, Robbie, a close friend of Lisa's, came over that Sunday and got right into the bed with her.

"I knew I had to talk to her," says Robbie. "She was lethargic. She was hiding, not just under the covers—hiding from life. I didn't think she'd been out of bed for a while." Robbie had decided to have a memorial for George the following week and she wanted Lisa to hear it from her own lips.

Robbie realized she had to move on. And her transformation had been swift and dramatic. On Thursday, she and Lisa, along with two others whose husbands had been Cantor employees, had been videotaped by two TV crews in Robbie's home in Bedford—one from the CBS newsmagazine *48 Hours*, another from NBC News. They were determined to get their photographs out to the viewing public.

"George had walked down from the 101st floor eleven years before," Robbie says. "I thought he could survive this one. Maybe there was a pocket in the basement. We went on TV to show pictures so that if anybody from Cantor made it out, [they could] get in touch with us." Someone had even heard that George had been spotted walking up the West Side Highway.

"Honestly, my feeling was: He's wandering the streets," Lisa now says, recalling how she held up Tommy's picture for the TV cameras. "If anybody can get out, it's Tommy Palazzo—and he's got six people on his back. I thought he was wandering, burnt. We didn't know."

Even by Friday, Lisa and Robbie had held out hope. When Robbie's brother-in-law suggested that she consider scheduling a memorial service, Robbie snapped, "Absolutely not." But the next day she heard that rescuers had recovered the remains of one of their coworkers. Robbie, becoming increasingly conflicted, thought about her sister Nancy, who had died many years before. She suddenly remembered a close relative who knew a psychic. Perhaps, Robbie thought, he could contact her sister—though Robbie had never previously spoken to a psychic in her life. That same night, she says, she called the medium, in Florida, and talked for more than an hour. "He didn't know me from Adam," she says. But, as Robbie describes it, the man on the other end of the phone was soon conveying messages—not from her sister, but from George.

"He was telling me things from my husband, like, 'Thanks for putting my picture on the table on the front porch,' which I had just done, with candles. 'I'm sending you roses for our anniversary,' which was coming up in fifteen days. He said, 'If you want to verify this, go up to my gray suit and check in my pocket.' " She did, and says she found an item of special significance to them. "He talked about different vacations we had: things nobody would know." Robbie Morrell was convinced. "Whether it was the placebo effect or not," she says, "it was enough for me to realize that I have four kids that have to go on."

As Lisa remembers it, "Robbie Morrell crawled in my bed [that] Sunday [and said,] 'We're going to have a memorial for George.' And it was scheduled for a Wednesday. I said, 'I'm not going to have one for Tommy. It's too soon.' She turned to me and said, '*You're* supposed to be the strong one.' She was *trying* to say, 'Lisa, they're gone.'

"We scheduled Tommy's [for] the following Saturday. George and Tommy were like brothers."

Lisa Palazzo, vibrant, trim, and strong-willed, now sits in her handsome house in Armonk, New York, avoiding the packing boxes. She is moving out, three and a half years after the attacks, to relocate to a nearby town. As her third and last daughter begins to look at colleges, Lisa explains, she fears the emptiest of empty nests. "I couldn't wake up in this house alone," she says.

While the home is full of bustle and light, a patina of mourning seems to have settled in, like a dew, upon the cheery interiors. Her hair a shimmering blond, offset by her black turtleneck, Lisa is tanned from a winter ski trip to Vermont, the kind she used to take with Tommy, her soul mate since she was seventeen. "We always had a camera flung around our shoulders," she says, her manner hesitant. "Tommy on vacation would be the one on Stratton Mountain to ask the [ski slope] photographers, 'C'mon, you take our picture? Two-thirty, top of the gondola.' We have a million of these."

We are here because the Palazzos' friend, Don Johnston, has told me that the house had been brimming with photographs of Tommy. And now, because of the pending move, Lisa has finally begun to stow them away. "It was literally a shrine," according to Johnston. "There were hundreds of pictures. Hundreds." And so there are. On her living room table, in the dining room, in the kitchen, on bookshelves, ledges, and sills, in frames of distressed wood, black metal, gold.

There is a large black-and-white portrait of Tommy, then forty-four, Lisa, forty-three, and their children, Kristin, Kerri, and Kate, taken on August 11, 2001—a gift for Tommy's parents' eightieth birthdays. On the coffee table there is an oval keepsake box with a painting of Tommy on the lacquered lid. There is a blowup of Tommy on the beach with his fishing rod, shots of him swimming, with the dog, in the clutches of golfing partners and children and brothers.

"He was everyone's favorite sibling, buddy, big Italian family of seven," says Johnston, who, along with his wife, Maryellen, sits reminiscing with Lisa, her daughter Kerri, and another friend, Elisa Foley. They relate how Lisa and Tommy were high school sweethearts, how they were devoted to each other. Tommy phoned Lisa frequently from the Trade Center throughout his workday. When he'd finish playing eighteen holes at Westchester Country Club he would break with customary foursome protocol and call Lisa to invite her to the grill room to join them. "He had the biggest heart in the world," says Lisa.

Out in the car there are pictures of Tommy. Out on the cutting board in the kitchen is Tommy's crinkled photo ID, retrieved from the Fresh Kills Landfill and sent to Lisa only weeks ago. Behind the kitchen sink, mass cards are propped against the window—one for Tommy, two for George.

"Pictures warmed my heart," Palazzo says. "I had [filled] every counter with pictures, every available space, practically . . . When I went to sell [the] house, my real estate agent said, 'You have to clean some of the counters off.' "

Johnston ribs her about the pictures. There were so many, he says, "You couldn't eat at the kitchen table."

"No way," Lisa says good-naturedly. "We could eat *around* his pictures."

"You had a hard time eating," explains Maryellen. "You had the plate in your lap."

Lisa describes how the pictures began to proliferate. "For the first Christmas, in 2001," she says, "I made a framed collage for each kid, and a scrapbook." She brings out a large framed collage chock with cutout figurines. Every torso in every snapshot has been neatly clipped from a photograph, paper-doll style, with a smidgen of outline bordering each body, like an aura. The edges and crescents of the photos overlap like shimmering fish scales. "I try each Valentine's or Easter to find a new picture of the girls with their dad."

Somehow, as the months went on, the pictures had seemed to fill a void. They were a deep well into which she could dip to get a swig of Tommy. The drink was soothing, slightly narcotic, with a bitter nip. "Sometimes I look at a picture and it kind of hurts," she says, "but I could not imagine our home not filled with all our memories. It keeps him with you and brings [it all] back."

Palazzo now realizes she had put herself on a strict no-media diet. For a year, she says, "I did not turn on a TV. I did not read a newspaper—anything to do with news. I didn't read a book. It was the concentration level." Instead, she started keeping a journal, beginning each entry "Dear Tommy." And she began sifting through her photo archive.

Pictures can bring solace, but they can also bring time to a standstill. I tell her about a newspaper reporter I know who became alarmed when she visited a firefighter's widow in the weeks after 9/11 and saw that every night the wife would set a table for three and sit down to dinner with her young daughter—and a poster of her husband, placed in his empty chair.

"You want to hear something?" Lisa responds, as if to say, You think *that's* strange? Her tears begin to flow. "I haven't slept under the sheets since [September 11]. I got new sheets and a new comforter, but I still haven't slept *under* the sheets. I slept in [my daughter] Kristin's room for the first year, when she went [away] to college."

Lisa Palazzo seems more comfortable discussing her images. Like a bird's nest, compiled resolutely from disparate scraps, her shrine was designed as a safe haven, a place where she and her family could reside, for a spell, suspended—even if only for a few moments in the day—in the time and space that existed before the irreversible occurred. It also evolved into a retreat, meant in both the physical and the spiritual senses, a cloister on a suburban street to which her spirit could recede or ascend and still reside with Tommy's. It preserved him. It protected her.

The flip books and collages and displays were not exalted nostalgia but a picture-lined comforter, soft as down, providing a warmth she couldn't quite find in any other quarter.

Tommy Palazzo (or TP, as old pals called him) was cut from the same cloth as many of his friends. Like Don Johnston and George Morrell, he was unquenchably social, full of brio and generosity. Always in a boyish baseball cap, he seemed to sparkle, as he does now in the photos under glass and plexi and Lucite—"I am the diamond glint on snow," so his mass card proclaims.

Because the Palazzos are moving, Johnston realizes that this may be his last chance to bask in TP's milieu. Tonight, he savors the images, a bittersweet elixir. Before the evening is out, Lisa shows him an electronic slideshow of Tommy on a portable DVD player and two videos on the living room TV—one from Tommy's fortieth birthday party, another from a golf outing that happened to have taken place on September 10, 2001.

Lisa stands next to the screen, arms folded, watching player after player, most from Palazzo's firm, as they tee up their drives. "He's gone," she says. "He is too. And all three," she says, pointing to a cluster of golfers at the edge of the first tee.

While sitting in Lisa Palazzo's home, I thought of my friend Carl Mydans, a pioneering photojournalist who had recently died at age ninety-seven, in August 2004. Many weekends, I would visit Carl at his home in Larchmont, New York, and see his desks, tabletops, and walls festooned with the bounty of a picture taker's life. I associated Carl, whom I'd known for twenty-five years, with the indomitable persistence of photographs.

As I talked with Lisa, I also thought of Carl's son, Seth, a foreign correspondent for *The New York Times* and *The International Herald Tribune*. Within weeks of Carl's death, Seth would be in Russia, covering the aftermath of the massacre in Beslan, where Chechen kidnappers had taken over a school, eventually killing 344 (including 172 children). "I was still in mourning for my father," he had told me. "Still grieving."

Yet his job required him to report on others' grief. And on the fortieth day of his mourning (a sacred day in the Russian Orthodox Church, denoting the time when the soul of the deceased is believed to leave this earth toward its final resting place), Seth met a man named Vova Tumayev.

Tumayev's wife, Zinaida, and their ten-year-old daughter, Madina, had been slaughtered in the schoolhouse attack. Tumayev was in such shock and denial that every morning since their death, so Seth noted in an article for the *Times*, Tumayev continued to get up and set the breakfast table for three: "Mr. Tumayev sits alone for a little while, then clears the table. There is nothing Mr. Tumayev can do—no ritual, no act of mourning that can begin to fill the emptiness their loss has left behind. At night, he said, he sleeps in his daughter's bed.

"Mr. Tumayev," the article continued, sounding somewhat like others written around the 2001 terror attacks, "is just one lonely mourner in a town where thousands of people are bereaved."

Seth concluded his article this way:

> He took a small album of photographs from a shelf and began turning its pages one by one, explaining each picture to a visitor as he went.
>
> "That's her," he said, showing a picture of a smiling girl in a red dress. "That's her, that's her, that's her at the beach; that's also her and here she is, here she is, here, here she is; there she is in the countryside, there also, and that's her, too."
>
> "Oof, this is difficult," he said, but he kept turning the pages.
>
> "There she is in Rostov, there she is, too; there she is with her mother; there she is, she was tall, almost as tall as me; that's her, too, and that's her, too, and that's her, and that's also her, also her, also her; there she is with her friends, that little girl died, too, there she is waving."
>
> "Everything in here is her," he said, handing the album to his visitor. "I don't want to look anymore."

At week's end, and on into the next several months, the nation's newspapers became a study in graphic self-restraint. I don't mean the editorial pages, where the news and feature photographs continued to be grim and plentiful. I mean the reserved and almost spartan look of the ads pages. Everywhere, advertisements—mainly public-service-oriented—began shedding photographs, replacing them with black-and-white text-only panels espousing sympathetic, respectful, patriotic themes.

With the country now at war, and a populace in torment and in mourning, the last message advertisers wanted to get across was: business as usual. So companies and their ad agencies ditched their fall campaigns and worked overtime to create new copy and art that de-emphasized products and services. Most expressed condolence, unity, ways to help. Many reached out to employees or to clients and their families. (There was no patience for the handful of firms that seemed to be touting their own role in raising funds or in assisting those affected by the tragedy.) Advertisers, with few exceptions, took pains not to capitalize on the tragedy or even to *appear* exploitative. To that end, they needed to produce tasteful, unambiguous ads, without any hint of irony. That meant, naturally: no photographs.

Part of the impact of photography, like the transporting power of music, comes from its interpretive nature. A viewer brings his own set of emotional associations to each image he views. By stripping ads of pictures, which might otherwise hold hidden or unanticipated signals, and replacing those pages with sober, precisely worded blocks of type (sometimes laid out in the shape of two towers, sometimes accompanied by corporate logos or newly created logos that incorporated twin vertical bars), advertisers knew they were less likely to offend and more likely to get across their intended message.

Neither publishers nor advertisers wanted to be in a position of creating the environment for an unseemly ad/edit face-off: an image of devastation, for instance, juxtaposed with a model in a new fox fur. So the subdued treatment ruled. One incidental benefit of this practice was that vital, groundbreaking journalism that week, especially in the form of photographs—unencumbered by the comparatively petty exigencies of commerce—seemed even more distinctive amid that sea of black letters and well-apportioned white space. News pictures ended up resonating with readers all the more.

When advertisers *did* resort to photographs, the pictures tended to be graphically spare. "There was a lot of visual imagery around the American flag, around symbols of hope and love—like the dove and heart," says Peggy Conlan, president of the Ad Council. One of her organization's ads for the International Fire Chiefs Association, for example, utilized an image of a firefighter shrouded in brown haze or smoke, as if he were a spectral presence, walking into the breach—or coming back from the beyond.

On television, the hardest of hard news has traditionally shoved commerce off the screen. And in the context of 9/11, ad spots would have seemed tasteless and irrelevant, exhibiting disrespect for the deceased, trivializing the atrocities, and risking a serious backlash against both the network and the sponsors. Therefore TV, as explained earlier, refrained from airing ads for much of the week. Conlan insists that the networks have no guidelines for decorum in national emergencies. "There wasn't a playbook," she says. "Everything that I know [tells me] that we as an industry were making this up as we went along. We were trying to be respectful and thoughtful. Part of it was that there wasn't any appetite [among] the major networks to put any commercial messages in."

Into this advertising void came one particularly effective public-service campaign. Early on, ad wizard Roy Spence and the Austin-based firm of GSD&M rose to the challenge. Together with the Ad Council—known for hatching many of the most persuasive public service spots in U.S. marketing lore (World War II's "Loose Lips Sink Ships" campaign, Smokey Bear, "A Mind Is a Terrible Thing to Waste," among many others)—Spence and his team set their minds to helping coordinate a PSA blitz dubbed "I Am an American." Their goal, in this fractured time, was to create a nationwide appeal for "tolerance." Hundreds of citizens—representing a young/old, rich/poor, ethnically and religiously diverse cross section of the country—were videotaped by dozens of creative teams around the continental United States. "I Am an American" was repeated as a statement of pride, as an assertion, as a rallying cry.

The footage was then shipped to Austin for a breakneck edit. And within ten days the spots hit the airwaves, eventually channeled to three thousand television outlets, generating $100 million in donated air time in 2001. By year's end, Chris Bailey, a traveler passing through an Atlanta airport, would recount his experience of viewing one of the spots on an overhead TV. "By the time [it] was over," he said, "there were at least 40 people gathered around just that one monitor. With smiles on our faces, we broke up and went about our business."

Imagery would not have been able to blanket the planet as it did had it not been for yet another late-twentieth-century breakthrough: the accelerating ubiquity, elasticity, and popularity of the Internet.

"Around the year 2000 we entered a whole new era," the foreign-affairs columnist Thomas L. Friedman has written in *The World Is Flat: A Brief History of the Twenty-first Century*. "[S]oftware . . . in conjunction with the creation of a global fiber-optic network . . . has made us all next-door neighbors." What Friedman has rhetorically termed the "flattening" of the planet—a process that has helped empower economic competitors anywhere on earth, making them theoretical equals—has had an undeniable impact on how images have been processed and absorbed in the aftermath of September 11.

To wit: Scott Heiferman and the e-mails he was fielding on September 16, five days after the attacks—responses, sent to him by total strangers, expressing intense gratitude tinged with conviction and consternation.

The Tuesday before, Heiferman had stood on his roof at Elizabeth and Houston Streets, and had taken out his tiny, two-megapixel Canon ELPH. He shot a single frame of the twin towers, gray smoke frothing against blue sky. At the time, he didn't quite understand what he was photographing, thinking in knee-jerk pop-culture terms. "Maybe they were filming a sequel to *Independence Day*," he surmised, as a mind in a dream-state might wonder, only capable of grasping this stranger-than-fiction vision through a recognizable template.

Heiferman then sat down at his computer and simply floated the picture onto the Internet. The photo showed a skyline view: the rooftop and water tower next door, and, above them, a billowing, ashen train sweeping out from the towers and across the city.

Never much of a writer ("I've got some kind of mild dyslexia and/or ADD," he says in an e-mail, "I like pictures"), he had decided to launch his own Weblog in April 2001, putting up a single photo every day (a sunset over a marsh, the weave in a cable-knit sweater, the shadow of a man behind a hardware-store counter). His online exercise, a "daily discipline," as he calls it, was among the first wave of photo blogs (a phenomenon started in 2000).

Scott Heiferman is a soft-spoken Iowan who had always stood out from the general gaggle of geeks. Back in 1995, he harbored dreams of harnessing the power of the Web to connect people in meaningful ways.

And so at twenty-two the self-described "net idealist" moved to New York and started a tiny company, iTraffic, out of his Astoria, Queens, apartment. Five years later, his firm had become a force in the online ad business, with more than one hundred employees on both coasts. It was gobbled up by Agency.com for $15 million, then by industry goliath Omnicom. After earning a handsome payday in the bargain (snatched just before the Internet bubble burst in 2000), Heiferman knocked around for a while, actually spending time peddling burgers and fries at his local McDonald's (as a learning experience). He saw himself as "a 20-something dethroned dotcom ceo," he writes on his Web site, where he likes to lapse into the lowercase first-person self-deprecation of e-mail-ese, "[and] went to work the counter at McDonald's . . . to get back in touch with the real world. Also, after 6 grueling years in the internet whirlwind, i wanted to experience a profitable, well-oiled multi-billion-dollar machine."

But Heiferman still felt unsatisfied. He realized that building "companies," he now says, was "a bit soulless. I decided that whatever I did next, I wanted to cut out the middleman and do something that directly help[ed] people."

The day of September 11, along with everything else it had wrought, also brought Scott Heiferman a Eureka moment. Still taken with the horror he had seen and posted on his blog, Heiferman and his then girlfriend, Cindy McBennett, a Wall Street lawyer, felt compelled to draft a flyer with a simple message, which they photocopied the next morning at their local Kinko's. On the streets of New York, while hundreds of others were pasting up "Missing" posters, they chose to distribute a sheet that urged people to go outside their apartments that night at 7:00 p.m. and light a single candle. "You have to understand," says Heiferman, then twenty-nine, "my hippie/New Age quotient was quite low. I'm part of the Kurt Cobain generation. Despite my Internet utopianism, I can't escape formative years as a Gen-X, disaffected cynic. And here I am being a vigil organizer. As we walked around, handing out flyers, we came across two groups of people handing out flyers with almost the exact same message, 'Unite Tonight.' I was terribly interested in this feeling of local community."

This cohesive spirit "was more powerful offline than online for me," he says. "Eye contact on the streets. Neighbors talking in elevators. A vague sense that the city was a neighborhood, less a city of strangers."

As a response to this public outpouring of goodwill, he began formulating what were to become two influential Internet businesses. The first was Fotolog.net, a Web-based community photo album that would allow bloggers to share pictures and picture stories with other bloggers. "Fotolog embraced the global-village idea," he says, "but brought people's local, private, real worlds to it. [It made] it easy for people to do what I was doing—[uploading a] photo of the day—and make it infinitely more interesting because it would be a community." (Today a million new images are uploaded to Fotolog.net each week from among a photoblogging network of one million amateur lensmen in more than fifty countries. A quick click through a random moment's deluge reveals a photo flood: teens playing dress-up in a dorm room in Lisbon, five men in kilts in the Australian outback, a blue Christmas tree in Aichi, Japan—just three treasures amid tens of thousands freshly minted that day.)

The second company Heiferman cofounded grew out of the mood he had felt in the streets of Manhattan in the weeks after 9/11, a mood that made him think that he could use the Internet to "spark community in new ways," he says. Not content to merely connect people PC to PC, he helped create an online town commons that would allow neighbors to seek out neighbors with concentric interests and then schedule group sessions in the here and now—a short walk or ride from their home or office—at a school, community center, conference hall, place of business or worship, or a convenient living room. "Meetup.com" took off almost immediately, then exponentially, mushrooming to two million adherents. And, in consort with the already established MoveOn.org, it would become an engine that would drive the grassroots mobilization and fundraising efforts for the Democratic Party during the 2004 presidential elections, propelling the Vermont governor Howard Dean to national prominence and forever recasting how individuals could network locally.

On September 11, the World Wide Web was a logical destination for those seeking urgent information—especially in New York, where phone lines were jammed and antenna-borne TV service was spotty. "CNN.com saw 162 million page views on the day of the attacks," observed the Poynter Institute's Steve Outing, in *Editor & Publisher*, who noted that typical traffic was in the 14 million range. Stuart Allan, in the book *Journalism After September 11*, pointed out that "between September 11 and 16 the online news category grew by 80 percent compared to the previous week in the U.S."

Despite these spikes in viewership, however, most sites spent the day playing catch-up with traditional news sources. Because of increased volume over taxed telephone networks, many news sites' servers crashed or slouched to a crawl. *Editor & Publisher*'s Wayne Robins wrote on September 17 that most newspaper Web sites covering the event lacked timely or original reporting, running borrowed videos or text alerts from sister news agencies and wire services. Two hours after the first plane struck, Robins noted, "the *New York Post*'s site . . . had a small 'This Just In . . . Planes Crash Into World Trade Center' item, an afterthought to a story on the Democratic mayoral candidate Mark Green. A click on the crash link led to a dry, early AP story under a sexy banner ad for MTV." A Pew Research Center study would soon find that 81 percent of those polled said they had first turned to television for their news updates; by comparison, a paltry 3 percent chose the Internet as their prime news venue.

In late 2001, news junkies had not yet become obsessed with checking the headlines by goosing their handhelds throughout the day, nor had broadband or Wi-Fi reached the levels of penetration that they would enjoy by mid-decade. Nonetheless, the Web triumphed in countless other ways, many of them photographic, in the days and weeks that followed.

First, as Heiferman understood, cyberspace had become a primary hub for connecting different spokes of the greater September 11 "community." That first week, the Web was an electronic philosopher's stone, an ultimately pliable medium for coordinating relief and emergency response, reaching out through message boards or chat rooms, posting company emergency bulletins and obituaries, linking passengers' families to data from airline manifests, raising relief funds, and outlining terms of compensation among government agencies, corporations, and insurance companies.

Second, over time, the Internet proved unmatched as a receptacle for posting and archiving stores of information, much of it visual. Space Imaging company, for instance, created a high-resolution satellite photochronology of the Pentagon and Ground Zero sites as viewed from beyond our atmosphere. Kodak and AOL created an online PhotoQuilt, a digital patchwork with images of the deceased, of volunteers, of community activists and supporters, interwoven with "uplifting" pictures, all uploaded by Web site visitors. Even more ambitious would be filmmaker Steven Rosenbaum's 7,000-gigabyte collection of 9/11 minutiae and visual material, as well as the September 11 Digital Archive project, funded by the Alfred P. Sloan Foundation in association with the Library of Congress and other institutions. The archive would eventually store a wealth of digital images, e-mails, and other electronic records for posterity.

Most comforting of all were the electronic memorials, scores of them, created by people sometimes armed with little more than a Web address, a few pictures, and a prayer. At one such site, dear friends and perfect strangers still gather to commemorate September 11 victim Cora Hidalgo Holland. At nancymorgensternmemorial.org, a photo gallery is posted along with reflections and testimonies about Cantor Fitzgerald's Nancy Morgenstern, whom the Web site calls "a serious biker and a devoted Jew [who] joyously blended those two apparently conflicting passions." Some sites, such as buildthememorial.org, are repositories for reflections and photos until a real-world memorial is established.

Other URLs have been compiled according to orientation or heritage (one dedicated to "Gay Victims and Heroes," another to those who were "Irish by birth or by descent who died in the attack on America"). Hundreds of photo-and-text profiles are accessible through databases of the deceased at sites like wallofamericans.com, CNN.com, and legacy.com, where visitors can click on a name, access a photo and obituary, or sign a guestbook to share memories or condolences. Several home pages offer a poster: a photo-mosaic of the twin towers composed of hundreds of tiny headshots of the deceased.

Just as these high-tech tributes provided individuals with a personal forum and a common ground, so the blogosphere offered universal access to more intimate, human facets of the tragedy, sometimes punctuated by imagery. September 11 helped move Weblogs from the murky cultural backwaters and, in short order, made sites devoted to online opinion and "news with attitude" (replete with their powerful investigative components and cross-reference links) possibly the most influential new format for written commentary and reportage since the New Journalism of the 1960s and '70s. Blogs, pre-9/11, were often burdened with riff and rant, the elevated cant of pajama-clad navel-gazers preaching niche to niche, and inviting dialogue with their own circle of acolytes. Pictures, as a rule, were mere crumbs on the blogger food chain.

The week of September 11, however, suddenly conflated blogs with urgency. Hype and hyperventilation evaporated, replaced by firsthand accounts of destruction and death. Tall tales and trite asides made way for genuine, heartfelt observations that read like pearls of folk wisdom. And pictures were posted to fill in where the words could not. Immediately after September 11, "many people put their photos online," says Jeff Jarvis, a coworker of mine at both Time Inc. and Condé Nast (and a blog eminence since 2001), who had been in the World Trade Center on 9/11. "This is when I discovered the power of Weblogs to spread news quickly. In no time, word of more photos, more perspectives, new views spread across the world of links. But it was more than just the photos. The images were attached to people who were there and to their stories; the photos could not have been more intensely personal and that made them spread even faster. When the ['here is new york'] gallery opened online, I pored over it. That surprised me. I would have thought that I could not bear to see these images again. But my reaction was exactly the opposite: I had to find the images that matched my memory. For I couldn't believe my memory still. I was incredibly relieved—overjoyed would be the wrong word for it, but the emotion was that intense—when I came upon a photo that showed just that moment when the tower tipped to the ground. Yes, I really had seen that happen. I kept coming back to photos of the dust-covered world and . . . the people running from the cloud of death, all my memories. I bought prints of many of them. I haven't hung them up and don't plan to. I just have them."

Bona fide independent Web reporters had hit the streets with digital tape recorders, digital cameras, and cell phones, and had come back to their PCs as a breed of muckrakers and online slide-show makers. The events helped legitimize an already ascendant brand of citizen journalists (operating what came to be termed "citJ" Web sites). "Another kind of reporting emerged during those appalling hours and days," noted Dan Gillmor, a journalist who monitors grassroots aspects of both old and new media. "Via e-mails, mailing lists, chat groups, personal web journals—all non-standard news sources—we received valuable context that the major American media couldn't, or wouldn't, provide. We were witnessing . . . the future of news."

According to Stuart Allan, an observer of media and culture, in his essay "Reweaving the Internet":

> Hundreds of refashioned websites began to appear over the course of September 11, making publicly available eyewitness accounts, personal photographs, and in some cases video footage of the unfolding disasters. Taken together, these websites resembled something of a first-person news network, a collective form of collaborative newsgathering. Ordinary people were transforming into "amateur newsies," to use a term frequently heard, or instant reporters, photojournalists, and opinion columnists. [Their] "citizen-produced coverage" appeared from diverse locations, so diverse as to make judgments about their accuracy difficult if not impossible. These types of personal news items were [often] forwarded via e-mail many times over by people who did not actually know the original writer or photographer. Presumably for those "personal journalists" giving sincere expression to their experiences . . . the sending of such messages had something of a cathartic effect.

The lack of "vetting" was partly the point. The unfiltered blogs and ragtag sites had more urgency, humanity, and street-cred to them than their mainstream news counterparts. This was heart-to-heart communication, one person at a monitor to another. And the many digital Samaritans who helped stitch together dispersed bits of data—contact numbers, hard-to-get snippets of news, unique photographic takes—were providing a service (informing and comforting) while fulfilling their own psychic needs as crisis traffic cops. In a powerless situation, the Internet empowered those predisposed to journalistic or humanitarian callings.

Jarvis began buzzmachine.com, a popular early blog, in response to the attacks. That morning, he had exited the complex just after the first plane struck (having taken the morning's last New Jersey PATH train into Manhattan's World Trade Center station). He had witnessed human beings in free fall; watched the second plane's assault, directly above him; slipped into his reporter mode and began interviewing witnesses. He then phoned in on-the-scene reports to NJ.com, one of the local news sites run by his employer, Advance.net. Then he survived the towers' dual collapse.

"I started a blog a few days after 9/11, thinking I would do it for a few weeks," he says. "It soon took over all available life." (Now a new media professor at City University of New York, he spends several hours each day plastering the Web with opinion and insight, drawing 150,000 visitors to his site every month.) "The day after I wrote my first blog posts, a few bloggers in L.A. who later became friends linked to and commented on what I'd written. It was then that I realized that this medium is a conversation and that news should be a conversation. That changed my career as 9/11 changed my life."

Today, Jarvis says, he travels with a camera at all times because he wishes he had been carrying one that September morning. "There are so many images I saw that are lost to anyone but me," he insists. "The image I remember most is [of] walking into a scene out of *The Day After*: the fallout covering everything in sight. A young couple walked by me, covered as I was all in white . . . except for the trail of a tear on the woman's face . . . , black on white. Like that man on the cover of *Fortune [Figure C]*, I was covered in stone and death and I never saw myself that way. As I walked [north,] the farther uptown [I] got the more people looked at me with shock, even fear. Bums came up to me to ask whether I was O.K."

As Jarvis sees it, one of the curious alterations in the Internet landscape, post-9/11, has been the blurring of moving and static imagery. In the 1990s, the Web had already begun to break down conceptual walls—

between the private moment and the public spectacle, between a protected, copyrighted photograph and one that was royalty-free and anyone's for the asking. Coincident with the events of September 11, Jarvis posits, all images on the Web have become all-purpose graphic commodities. Once placed upon a server, in a digital format, a photograph "is no longer presumed to be still," Jarvis says. "Video and photography merge online: an image, a sequence of images, a video, it's all a continuum. I don't think that was true when the processes were so different: one physical, one electronic. But once both became digital, there was no longer a line separating them." (Television, one could argue, had prompted similar blurring. People who "ran to their television sets and stayed there for hours on end," educator Barbie Zelizer has remarked, watched "an endless loop of reruns of the actual attack whose ordering began to look more like still photographs than moving images . . . repeating themselves so often that they [came] to have the quality of photography.")

As blogs became more abundant after September 11, photographs soon followed, slipped between wedges of type, either as self-contained stories or as ways of illustrating inert, blocky paragraphs. Web pages, due to new graphics software, became platforms upon which even the most inexperienced designer could mortise a square patch of picture—a still or video file that would break up the dreary and often fallow fields of HTML or XML text. Users would scroll down and either linger on an image, or click on it to enlarge it or to open a video window to queue up a clip. In terms of pure Web-page aesthetics, the differences between stationary and moving pictures had been rendered moot. Soon, bloggers were sampling one another's wares, cutting and pasting visuals from one site to the next. Pictures became pollen, borne by the broadband winds and spread like juicy gossip.

Within days of the attacks came the photo-scavenger sites, where images from other Web pages and sources were appropriated at will. The pictures on many sites, despite their later disclaimers to the contrary, were not treated as uniquely rendered representations of events—sometimes captured at extreme personal risk to the photographers—but as public artifacts, copious and ripe for the plucking regardless of their genesis, veracity, or copyright. Worst of all were the sites like the one that displayed or linked to horrific videoclips (including an obscene edit of Jules Naudet's footage of the first plane entering and entering and entering Tower One on a perpetual loop). One site, which I won't name here ("created on September 11, 2001 at 9:30 A.M.," so its home page reads) practices a brand of exploitative bait-and-switch of the most deceitful sort, stocking not only 9/11 imagery but all manner of terror porn—hostage-beheading videos, Abu Ghraib torture photos, sexually explicit snapshots taken by soldiers in Iraq—alongside ads touting "Herbal Smoke Shop" and "hot lesbian" videos. (The come-on: the respectful-sounding names of such sites, intended to appeal to the sticky tentacles of Web search engines.) Once drawn into the tent, those with already vulnerable psyches are inundated with lurid imagery, available digitally and delivered right to the desktop. Terror, in this way, is made not only consumable, but also irresistible. And it is created with little to no overhead—and, at times, sponsor-supported, to boot.

One of the ghoulish drawbacks of the medium, of course, is its knack for fueling prank and rumor. We have the Web's phalanx of race-baiters, conspiracy theorists, and misinformation mongers to blame, in some measure, for perpetuating the myths that Nostradamus prophesied these terror attacks half a millennium ago; that hundreds of Trade Center employees of Jewish descent were forewarned (advised not to come to work on September 11); that the collapse of the towers was an "inside job" secretly pulled off by demolition experts hired by the CIA or the Mossad; that a man had somehow surfed the rubble down eighty-odd stories and survived.

Among the most unsettling of these hoaxes came in the form of a Photoshopped image, stamped 09/11/01 in the corner, that surfaced within days of the attacks *(Figure J)*. It showed a tourist in a ski cap, rucksack on his back, standing on the World Trade Center observation deck—a Boeing 757 with American Airlines markings just over the railing behind him, presumably caught a split second before impact. The shot was on-passed virally via e-mail, accompanied by a message that read: "This was from a camera found in the wreckage of the W.T.C., developed by the F.B.I. for evidence and released on the net today . . . The guy still has no name and is missing."

No matter that the "tourist" was wearing winter clothing on a summer day or that the plane was the wrong model approaching the wrong tower from the wrong side. The photo fabrication, sent within two weeks of the attacks, alarmed thousands of those who came across it when opening their in-boxes. It wasn't until November that the perpetrator was finally revealed. According to reported accounts he was a Hungarian tourist who had asked a friend to snap his picture at the Trade Center pinnacle in 1997. Shortly after the attacks, he swiped a shot of a Boeing jet off a Web site, plopped it into the background, and sent his manipulated composite to a handful of friends, as a private joke. His friends, in turn, e-mailed it with abandon, setting off a wired wildfire. He quickly became known on the Net as the "Tourist Guy" and the "Tourist of Death," inadvertently achieving, as the U.K.'s *Guardian* put it, "his 15 megabytes of fame."

Visually, then, the Internet is Pandora-expulsive. All photographed actions—deeds and misdeeds alike—are potentially consigned to permanent public memory. Once an image or videoclip barnstorms across the Net, there's no way to return old Flicker to the paddock and shut the door. Web pages persist. Even if they are deactivated, they can be retrieved if someone has retained a link or has electronically bookmarked that page. This propulsion into the public domain, irrevocable and universal and unfungible, is one of the positive and negative features of the medium.

The positives have much to do with the truths that come from transparency. In 2004, for example, Internet editor Russ Kick (of TheMemory Hole.org) was able to publish an online archive of long-suppressed images of the coffins of deceased U.S. soldiers returning from Afghanistan and Iraq, when he persisted in acquiring the pictures through a Freedom of Information Act request. "The Pentagon," according to the industry publication *Photo District News*, "quickly said the granting of Kick's FOIA request was a mistake, but the images were out there and there was no taking them back."

The downside of Pandora expulsivity is sheer and steep. With a leer and a shrug, pirated pictures are often thrown up on a Web site—ownership, libel, and privacy considerations be damned. Pictures appear, quite frequently, without credits or accurate captions. They appear, as the culture critic George W. S. Trow once coined the phrase, "within the context of no context"—free-floating story fragments that lack rational connections with a bigger picture.

The day after the 2004 tsunami, Robert Calo, of Berkeley's graduate school of journalism, told David Carr of *The New York Times*, "If you think back, news gatherers would [traditionally] get the story and then commission a photographer to go and get the pictures. Now we have flipped it around to where reporters are chasing the pictures, trying to create some context for what viewers are seeing." Digital-journalism expert George Kindel observes, "What we have in this sped-up news cycle and this spread-out Internet is the preponderance of immediacy, often in pictures—and a dearth of understanding."

On Sunday afternoon the president stood on the South Lawn of the White House and insisted that "this crusade, this war on terrorism is going to take a while." Later that day, he convened a meeting in the Treaty Room with his national security adviser, Condoleezza Rice, and his chief media aides—Karen Hughes, Dan Bartlett, and Ari Fleischer. Six days after the attacks, it was time, said the president, to focus on how "we communicate this war" to the American people. "For nearly an hour," wrote Bob Woodward in *Bush at War*, "they talked about what the president expected of his communications team, [including plans for] how to explain the mission [and] ways to showcase all [nonclassified] elements of the war."

"No equivocation," the president warned.

But pictures did much more than convey policy or shape public opinion. Images, in and of themselves, would actually play vital roles in ousting the Taliban from power over the next three months—and in unseating Saddam Hussein's regime in Iraq two years later. In military terms alone, the value of photographs was incalculable.

During the first days after the terrorist attacks, U.S. aircraft (manned and unmanned), along with reconnaissance satellites, monitored the movements of Afghan troops and matériel. In the war's planning phase, images, many taken from unmanned aero vehicles (UAVs) such as the Predator, sought out ground targets in Afghanistan—and bin Laden's whereabouts. Once combat commenced, airborne imaging systems recorded before-and-after shots of the bombings.

GIs used night-vision gear (goggles that would amplify the available light in darkened settings; helmets fitted with video cameras) and thermal gunsites that could resolve enemies from as far away as a mile and a half. As temperatures dropped in the dead of the Afghan winter, planners relied on infrared sensors that could pick out "warm" targets (men in caves, tank exhaust) against the frigid landscape. In fact, the first night that U.S. Special Forces set foot on Afghan soil, troops videotaped their first covert op: the storming of one of Mullah Omar's redoubts. (Some critics considered the raid's success overblown and its coverage expressly managed for public consumption.)

Yet for all its reliance on the photograph, the Afghan campaign paled when compared with what followed. The conflict in Iraq, as none before it, was a war waged and wagered in images; virtually every aspect of the conflict—in terms of military, political, and media strategy—would be refracted, in some manner, through a lens.

During the battle phase of the war in the spring of 2003, eighty aircraft, according to *Newsweek*, took "42,000 pictures [and] transmitted 3,200 hours of videotape." Camera-laden UAVs with zoom lenses and special sensors hovered above Iraqi positions at altitudes ranging from 100 to 60,000 feet. The remote-controlled drones—maneuvered by virtual pilots within the vicinity or hunkered down at computer screens 7,500 miles away in a command center at Nevada's Nellis Air Force Base—transmitted their shots back to commanders and intelligence analysts stationed in Florida and Virginia. (By 2005, nearly eight hundred pilotless planes were available, providing twenty-four-hour image coverage of both the Afghan and Iraqi theaters of operation.)

Cameras aboard combat and so-called intelligence-surveillance-and reconaissance (ISR) craft documented air strikes or evaluated their aftershock. When the visual or infrared spectrums proved murky, airborne teams resorted to radar imaging to penetrate sand squalls or the smoky pall of oil fires. And high above these fleets, arrays of satellites took spy shots, provided data to help steer missiles, and sent weather updates to the waiting laptops of Yanks in tanks.*

Photography was considered central to the ground-force arsenal as well. Image-assisted weaponry was ever present. Human targets would appear on tank monitors like virtual prey in computer games. As in Afghanistan, soldiers donned night-vision scopes and photographed their Special Ops raids—such as the much-touted rescue of POW Jessica Lynch—the better to disseminate their story their way. (They even carried packs of playing cards bedecked with mugshots of America's Most Wanted Iraqis—a memory trick for acquainting GIs with their quarry.) By way of comparison, Vice President Dick Cheney told *The New York Times* that during the first Gulf War, in which he served as secretary of defense to President George H. W. Bush, military leaders had used "maps, grease pencils and radio reports" to monitor troop movements. "Now, even in combat vehicles," according to the *Times*, "they click with mouses, and watch the war unfold on video displays." It goes without saying that Afghan and Iraqi forces lacked even rudimentary imaging systems in the planning and execution phases of conflict and were ill-equipped to counter these advances.

In terms of photographic firepower, of course, the American military had nothing on the media. The 2003 invasion of Iraq, quite simply, was the most widely covered combat operation ever undertaken, and the most universally and immediately observed. The NBC anchor Tom Brokaw, making a distinction between a breaking news story, such as 9/11, and an anticipated proceeding, called the March 19 commencement of hostilities "probably the most televised event in the history of mankind." *New York Times* correspondent Todd Purdum said, unequivocally, "No war in human history has been chronicled more constantly in real time, with reporters and photographers as close to the shifting frontlines as they have ever been, with communications equipment they have never had."

During the early, explosive stages of the war, coverage was dramatic,

*Many of these soldiers' hometown papers, in fact, ran satellite pictures of Iraq right next to the local five-day forecast, linking readers visually and vicariously to the conditions affecting far-flung troops.

prodigious, and fearsome. Day and night, network and cable stations cut from rooftop views of luminous billows over Baghdad to neon-green night-vision scenes to stunning videophone reports, transmitted in real time from the blurry perches on advancing tanks. Some commentators, impressed by the raw power of such footage, referred to these herky-jerky glimpses of desolate towns and desert landscapes as "real reality TV." Combat was being broadcast live from the battlefield, directly to home entertainment centers, government corridors of power, and countless corners of the developing world.

At the beginning of the war, the key variable in the press equation was the process of "embedding" journalists inside military units, which ensured that correspondents, like the troops they covered, would saturate the region. (The Pentagon conducted frequent briefings for legions of reporters sequestered in a million-dollar media command center in isolated Doha, Qatar.) Keen worldwide interest in the confrontation also drew nonembedded newsmen, termed "unilaterals," to the war zone, chiefly to Baghdad. (With this elevated head count came increased risk; figures compiled by the Committee to Protect Journalists supported the contention that Gulf II was the most perilous conflict ever covered. For the one thousand reporters and photographers in the field—more than six hundred of them embedded—the fatality rate topped 1 percent, compared with 0.1 percent for allied forces. Fourteen correspondents died in the war's first few weeks, compared with seventeen in the three-year course of the Korean War. On May 29, Memorial Day, 2006, a woeful milestone was reached: the number of working cameramen, reporters, and photographers killed in Iraq—seventy-one, according to Reporters Without Borders—became equal to the number of accredited journalists who died during two decades of combat in Vietnam.)

Embedding, from the start, was roundly criticized. Among the objections were that too few correspondents had access to the action or to Iraqi citizens' points of view; that journalists, thus confined, were missing "the big picture"; and that the Pentagon was controlling the news and making photographers beholden to (and therefore unduly sympathetic toward) the troops in their viewfinders. And who could blame them? In order to take photographs, one had to play by the rules. Access, therefore, became indispensable but also a palliative, mimicking the principle of the campaign bus: give the journalists their snacks and their face time with the candidate, and they'll give you a fair shake. Familiarity would breed contentedness. "This is the danger of the embed," wrote Anthony Swofford, author of the Gulf War chronicle *Jarhead*. "War can't be that bad if they let us watch it."

"Somebody expressed 'being embedded' as being indentured," says Temple University's Fred Ritchin. "The Vietnam War was covered by photographers who would make up their own minds over a period of time, [sometimes] years. They would go deeper and make pictures reflecting that. Pictures were earned." In Iraq, Ritchin believes, embedded photographers played the role of photo-illustrators, purveyors of a preconceived vision of the war. "You could either illustrate the point of view of the government—or not. The price paid for being embedded was giving up one's independent judgment. If it were a movie, it would have been scripted as Good versus Evil—World War II, in color. Nuance was missed. Historians are going to be very, very critical of the coverage."

Nonetheless, the system was superior to the journalistic straitjacket applied in other recent U.S.-led campaigns such as those in Grenada, Panama, and Kuwait. "The military was shrewd enough," says *The New York Times*'s Mike Smith, deputy picture editor during the invasion, "to let photographers get close and do what they do best. They made friends with their subjects. They saw what really happened. I don't think [embedding was set up] for any noble reason. They did it to avoid the criticism they'd received in the first Gulf War [where] you had censors deciding whether or not your pictures could be seen. In this war, you could [transmit] just about any picture you shot, unless American soldiers were wounded or dead. In which case you had to wait two or three days for their families to be informed. Which is fair."

It should be pointed out that nonembedded photographers operated at the mercy of their Iraqi "minders." Despite these constraints, many lensmen were resourceful enough to return with remarkable views from the war's epicenter. One sensed shock, if not awe, in pictures of the allies' nighttime barrage of Baghdad, especially in the pyrotechnic tableaux caught by numerous video cameramen and photojournalists.

And yet it was the imagery of unremitting civilian anguish that resonated around the world in the battle for Baghdad. For millions, the brutality of the conflict was embodied in the image of twelve-year-old Ali Ismail Abbas, first photographed by Yuri Kozyrev for *Time*. Ali Ismail lost both arms—and his mother and stepfather—when a missile struck his house in April. Immobile, bandaged, and badly singed, he peered from front pages, across news wires, and on antiwar posters. CBS called him "a symbol of Iraqi suffering." Pictures of this innocent boy, unimaginably maimed, prompted outpourings of sorrow, anger, and compassion the world over. Within days, he was brought to Kuwait for surgery, followed by physical therapy. Observed John Fleming, editor of *The Anniston* (Alabama) *Star*: "That still photo . . . tells the difficult naked truth. This war has caused unimaginable pain to simple, ordinary people . . . Still photography in the right hands can define an event more accurately than days upon days of film footage and volumes of the written word."

As the war continued, the soon-to-be-toppled Iraqi government and, in time, the Iraqi insurgency adopted their own vile uses for videotape. Official Iraqi TV would show footage of the bodies of U.S. soldiers killed during raids. Hussein's troops would parade U.S. POWs in front of waiting cameras, in violation of the protocols of the Geneva Convention, which forbid mistreatment of captured combatants. Abductors would videotape their captives as they threatened and coerced them to make compromising statements (Western soldiers, journalists, contract employees, aid workers, and Iraqi-based diplomats among them). In several cases, abductees were beheaded while the cameras rolled so that shock and gristle would become part and parcel of the propaganda war.

Not to say that the other side didn't have its officially sanctioned flourishes. (I will discuss the Abu Ghraib photographs shortly.) When Hussein's sons Uday and Qusay were killed in an allied ambush in July 2003, it was pictures and pictures alone that provided proof of the brothers' demise. According to CNN, the Pentagon handed out images of their bullet-scarred cadavers, on convenient CD-ROM, "through the provisional authority in Baghdad . . . The CD also include[d] X-rays said to show wounds Uday Hussein suffered in a 1996 assassination attempt.

These X-rays helped U.S. forces identify [his remains]." When Saddam himself was caught that December—found hiding in an underground "spider hole"—he was photographed disheveled and disoriented for the world to see, captured by a "combat camera crew" armed with a four-thousand-dollar Sony PD150 digital video camera. (Snapshots were later taken of Hussein in captivity, fastidiously cleaning his own underwear.)

If a single picture or video clip served as the war's photographic Rorschach test in the first weeks of the war, it was the sequence taken on April 9, 2003, as a towering statue of Saddam tottered and fell in Baghdad's Firdos Square. That one event—actually a photo illustration of a fallen sculpture of a leader overthrown—signaled the end of Hussein's reign and prompted utterly antithetical reactions. Online commentator and illustrator Ted Rall was appalled after watching TV footage that showed that American Marines had actually used an armored vehicle and a thick cable to help protestors yank down the monument. "The stirring image of Saddam's statue being toppled," wrote Rall, "turns out to be fake, the product of a cheesy media op staged by the U.S. military for the benefit of cameramen." Photo editor and critic John Loengard also expresses skepticism. "It was telling," he says, that one of the key events "we remember the war by took place in front of the hotel in Baghdad where all the press was hunkered down. Statues fall. Some czar was toppled in St. Petersburg, George III in Bowling Green, many Stalins and Lenins bit the dust—and history forever onward. Unfortunately, things that are perfectly meaningful and symbolic [can be] something of a cliché."

Not exactly, said the preponderance of Western observers that day. The sight of a facsimile Saddam collapsing in chains, and the attendant street scenes of exultation, captured a deeper truth about standing up to despots, about the joys that burst forth once a long-fettered populace is unbound. The week of the Fall, the *New York Times* columnist William Safire published an editorial in which he charged the scene with his own political valence: "Just as video of human suffering understandably triggers demonstrations against any war, unforgettable images of the jubilation of enslaved people tasting liberty drive home the wisdom of just wars."

Whether epic or hyperbolic, the incident proved that at certain junctures in history, the image, resilient and universal, can be more eloquent than words. "Nothing can in any way at this moment get in the way of these dramatic pictures," proclaimed NBC's Tim Russert as events unfolded. *Newsweek*, in a splashy three-page gatefold meant to evoke the same stirrings of euphoria that erupted when the Berlin Wall fell in 1989, displayed Ilkka Uimonen's shot of a mallet-wielding man blasting away at the statue's pedestal. And the morning after the event, R. W. Apple, Jr.—who has reported for *The New York Times* from one hundred countries—was at such a loss for words that he too turned to pictures: "Not since [*Life*'s] Alfred Eisenstaedt documented the end of World War II with his iconic shot of a sailor locking a nurse in extravagant embrace in Times Square has the United States enjoyed a similar catharsis."

Here was the supremacy of the still photograph endowing a moment with historic consequence. One wonders: Would a regime have fallen in the desert that day if a camera had not been there to record it?

In many ways, the case for war had pivoted on faulty intelligence in the first place—bolstered by suspect images. When Secretary of State Colin Powell addressed the United Nations in February 2003 to present the nation's most comprehensive and compelling evidence of Iraq's attempt to procure or produce weapons of mass destruction (WMD), he knew that Saddam's regime had a history of stockpiling toxic agents and that Hussein had ordered the use of poisonous chemicals against his own people—killing thousands of Iraqi Kurds during a string of attacks in the late 1980s. What's more, Saddam had played a cat-and-mouse grudge match with weapons inspectors throughout the 1990s as UN teams searched for (or were impeded in their search for) traces of Iraq's supposed WMD program. But could Powell prove that Baghdad was still in pursuit of these weapons? For that, he would have to have persuasive, visual support.

As Powell faced a rapt, tense, and skeptical UN chamber, he first took time to praise the U.S. intelligence community's "imagery specialists . . . with years and years of experience poring for hours and hours over light tables." Next, Powell presented a series of satellite pictures purported to reveal Iraqi chemical munitions bunkers (along with nearby decontamination vehicles). He also provided artists' renderings of mobile trailers (supposedly equipped for making biological agents) and what he called "high-specification aluminum tubes" (which Saddam's regime had probably acquired, he said, to aid in the process of enriching uranium).

In time, the chemical bunker photos were widely debunked, even by the UN's chief weapons inspector. The mobile trailers, according to *The New York Times*, were determined by the Defense Intelligence Agency to be intended for use in "produc[ing] hydrogen for weather balloons used in artillery practice." And the special tubes, said American weapons experts, would never have worked in the requisite centrifuges; they were meant, in all likelihood, for conventional rocketry.

The visual confirmation, presented as incontrovertible, had in fact been highly suspect and open to various interpretations. Powell himself would later criticize the vetting structure that had allowed him to be handed dubiously sourced intelligence, going so far as to tell ABC's Barbara Walters that the incident had left "a blot" on his reputation. "I'm the one who presented [the case] on behalf of the United States to the world," he noted, "and [it] will always be a part of my record. It was painful . . . There were some people in the intelligence community who knew at that time that some of these sources were not good and shouldn't be relied upon, and they didn't speak up. That devastated me."

In some instances, members of the administration were predisposed to see what they wanted to see in the evidence—or, as the investigative reporter Seymour Hersh would characterize it in *The New Yorker*, to cherry-pick corroborating details from intelligence data that would best suit their objectives. Kenneth Pollack, a onetime White House expert on Iraq, told Hersh that by circumventing long-established vetting procedures, the Bush team had effectively dismantled "the existing filtering process that for fifty years had prevented the policymakers from getting bad information. They created stovepipes to get the information they wanted directly to the top leadership."

If the clamorous rumor of war had been advanced by the visuals, then why not the rumor of victory too? When White House image masters wanted to make the point on May 1, 2003, that "major combat operations in Iraq have ended," as the president would announce that day, it seemed only fitting that the commander in chief should slip into a flight suit and land on the deck of the USS *Abraham Lincoln*. The resulting Top Gun photo op showed Bush, helmet at his hip, posing in front of a huge banner stating MISSION ACCOMPLISHED. Some Democrats charged that the visit, at an estimated cost to taxpayers of $1.1 million, was staged with the express purpose of tripping photographers' shutters. Republicans rebuffed such criticism, contending that the president was merely expressing his gratitude to U.S. troops, and citing similar forays by photo-hungry Democrats.

The image, at first, caused a stir of a curious sort. The columnist Maureen Farrell, writing for Buzzflash.com, took the racing pulse of the pundits, some of whom seemed almost to hyperventilate at the sight of the president in full battle array. "George W. was a hottie in his flight suit," observed Suzanne Fields of *The Washington Times*. "The president has to meet a testosterone standard that appeals to women but does not offend men." Wrote Lisa Schiffren in *The Wall Street Journal*: "[T]here was the president . . . stepping out of a fighter jet in that amazing uniform, looking—how to put it?—really hot. Also presidential, of course . . . But mostly 'hot,' as in virile, sexy, and powerful." (*The Village Voice*'s Richard Goldstein couldn't help tossing in his own vote: "I can't prove they gave him a sock job [but] Bush's outfit gave him a very vivid basket. This was the first time a president literally showed his balls.")

Longtime editor Ed Kosner now calls it "the defining picture of his presidency. It connotes all the muscularity of the war. It was just the swagger of it, initially, that made it the picture." Nonetheless, he adds, "How things played out [over time] gives it a subtext that developed *after* the picture was developed."

Indeed, only five months later, *Time* would reprise the picture on its cover with the headline "Mission *Not* Accomplished." Combat operations, America would soon discover, were far from over. In the first two years *after* the photo op, more than two thousand U.S. servicemen would die in Iraq, thousands more would be seriously wounded (at a rate of sixteen soldiers a day), and, by 2006, by President Bush's own admission, an estimated thirty thousand Iraqi citizens would lose their lives. By the war's third anniversary, according to Ayad Allawi, the first Iraqi prime minister after Saddam's ouster, "as an average, fifty to sixty people through the country" were being killed each day. Although the newly established Iraqi government had made great strides in holding free elections and in advancing the cause of democratic self-governance, the insurgency was emboldened, its methods of sabotage and sequential suicide bombing increasingly effective and bloody. The conflict had become a nascent civil war and the United States seemed trapped in a military and political stalemate, with no clear American exit strategy.

A year after the president's carrier landing, it appeared to be almost foreordained when a batch of damning snapshots would emerge, dozens of them—all taken by GIs using digital cameras. They were as profane in their way as images of the charred corpses of four U.S. security men strung up above a bridge in Falluja in March 2004 by Iraqi insurgents who videotaped the desecration. In terms of global perception, the U.S. soldiers' snapshots would undermine American calls for "human rights" and would soon erode support for two of the main rationales for Western intervention in Iraq: to liberate the nation and to spread democracy.

In what came to be known as the Abu Ghraib prison scandal, Iraqi detainees at a U.S.-run holding facility near Baghdad were photographed by their American captors in a variety of humiliating poses: lying naked while wearing a makeshift collar and leash; cowering in the nude while being attacked by a guard dog; covered by a hooded shroud while having wires strung from their genitals; stripped naked and then handcuffed together or forced to simulate sex acts with other detainees or forced to assume positions in a makeshift human pyramid. In some of the shots, U.S. troops were shown with exultant expressions on their faces. In two frames, soldiers actually give thumbs-up signs while leaning over or crouching next to the corpse of a detainee. Servicemen seemed to delight in the abuse itself or in the act of posing for the photographer, as if they were clowning for a few vacation snapshots intended to be sent to friends back home: *Here I am in Iraq, wish you were here.*

"The pictures from Abu Ghraib are trophy shots," Luc Sante would remark. "The American soldiers included in them look exactly as if they were standing next to a gutted buck or a 10-foot marlin . . . There [is] something familiar about that jaunty insouciance, that unabashed triumph at having inflicted misery upon other humans . . . The last time I had seen that conjunction of elements was in photographs of lynchings [taken during] the first four decades of the 20th century . . . Often the spectators at lynchings of African-Americans are so effusive in their mugging that they all seem to be vying for credit. [T]he mood is giddy, often verging on hysterical, with a distinct sexual undercurrent." (Such battle porn was hardly confined to the war in Iraq. "There were hundreds of these [photo] albums in Vietnam, thousands, and they all seemed to contain the same pictures," writer and war correspondent Michael Herr would observe in *Dispatches*, "the severed-head shot, the head often . . . being held up by a smiling Marine, or a lot of heads arranged in a row, with a burning cigarette in each of the mouths . . . the VC [Viet Cong] suspect being dragged over the dust by a half track." In many modern conflicts since the introduction of portable cameras in the twenties and thirties, soldiers have used personal snuff snaps as talismans, the camera becoming a way of isolating the violence and madness in a dark box for buddies and loved ones and themselves—they'd seen this, done this, come close to this very same end—just as warriors for centuries had left the battlefield with specimens from the bodies of the enemies they'd vanquished.)

The Abu Ghraib pictures show Iraqi men who are terrorized, violated, and dehumanized on a number of levels: by being subjected to torture, pain, and the threat of death; by being treated like animals or slaves for the pleasure of others; by being forced to engage in or witness coerced sex acts that defy any measure of human decency; by being placed in the proximity of pornographic pantomimes that, as a *New York Times* editorial noted, "brutaliz[ed them] in exactly the manner most horrific to Muslims"; and by being forced to endure the dual humiliation of their own nakedness while in front of a camera. "The intent of the pictures," art and photography critic Michael Kimmelman would point out, "is precisely to compound the [subjects'] humiliation."

The images were kept secret until Specialist Joseph Darby learned of their existence and took matters into his own hands in January 2004: downloading them onto a CD-ROM, alerting his superiors, and setting off alarms within the army's Criminal Investigations Division. By late spring, the images would appear on *60 Minutes II*, in *The New Yorker* and *The Washington Post*, and on various Web sites.

In short order, the pictures were inflated at home and abroad into icons of American militarism gone mad. In world capitals, many would lose sight of the fact that the pictures conveyed a cruelty that was completely contrary to the nation's values and the coalition's mission. "Every American knows that the brutal and gruesome images [from Abu Ghraib] are the antithesis of the definition of an American soldier," writer and physician Hesham A. Hassaballa would note in the *Chicago Tribune*. "No doubt, the abuse of Iraqi prisoners by some U.S. soldiers has stained and shamed every American the world over. [T]o judge every American by these [images] is patently unfair and unjust." (Indeed, the setting for the photographs was not lost on many viewers: Abu Ghraib was the very facility where Saddam Hussein's minions had tortured and killed prisoners for years.)

But what became apparent in the months that followed was that torture of detainees, many of whom were held on minor charges, was not isolated to one prison or committed by a couple of wayward sadists. According to studies by the Red Cross and a U.S. government panel, the abuse was an offshoot of a practice that had been used in Guantánamo Bay, Cuba, during the incarceration or interrogation of prisoners of war captured in Afghanistan. While previous rumors of abuse at American-supervised compounds in Iraq had at first seemed unfounded, the photographic evidence made the accusations undeniable.

The pictures revealed how policy had led to the conditions that would allow such atrocities. By fighting a war against terror on numerous fronts—within our own borders, in Afghanistan, and then in Iraq—and by adopting comparably brutal methods for extracting information from detainees in entirely different circumstances, lines had been blurred.

Detainees caught in this wide-ranging war, even those with no ties to "terror" whatsoever, had become victims of counterterror methodologies and of misapplied rules and rhetoric.

Blowups of the photographs were reproduced overseas as part of what would become an anti-American propaganda blitz. The Cuban government, according to the Associated Press, went so far as to put up "a billboard emblazoned with photographs of American soldiers abusing Iraqi prisoners that included a huge swastika and a 'Made in U.S.A.' stamp [across from] the United States Interest Section's offices [in] Havana." In the States, the pictures served as the centerpiece of an underground campaign that would fuse "art, street culture and commercial design," according to critic Faye Hirsch in *Art in America*. A renegade artists' collective (using the pseudonym Copper Greene) dummied up a mock ad showing the hooded prisoner, in black silhouette, attached to white electrical wires—in the manner of Apple's popular ad showing an iPod user, with white earphone wires, against a Day-Glo-colored background *(Figure D)*. The parodists changed the accompanying logo from iPod to iRaq, and fly-posted copies of the mock ad onto walls and billboards throughout New York's SoHo.* "That hooded figure," said Carol Wells, of L.A.'s Center for the Study of Political Graphics, "is now as iconic as the woman holding her dead child in Picasso's *Guernica*, or the protester with her arms outstretched at Kent State." It became apparent that the clandestine snapshots were now viewed, at home and abroad, as symbols of the dark, dirty underside of an ill-defined war.

At the beginning of the scandal, Secretary Rumsfeld reportedly complained that the pictures had been disseminated in the first place without prior Defense Department sanction: "People are running around with digital cameras and taking these unbelievable photographs and then passing them off, against the law, to the media, to our surprise, when they had not even arrived in the Pentagon."† By the time the soldiers depicted in the images would face courts-martial, few would question the pictures' legal-

* Concurrently, and independently, a Los Angeles design team dubbed Forkscrew crafted similar protest posters, which were sniped across Hollywood.

† Photography historian and critic Vicki Goldberg noted that "once the scandal broke . . . Rumsfeld banned cell phone cameras on military bases in Iraq, [a] recognition that the military no longer had control of censorship in the digital era."

ity or belittle their provenance. Though the photographs had been taken, astonishingly enough, by the perpetrators themselves, it had been other soldiers, concerned citizens, and journalists—with Internet connections—who allowed the heinous evidence to reach a wider world. "Without [the Abu Ghraib photographs]," Luc Sante observes, "news of what happened within the walls of that prison would never have emerged from the fog of classified internal memos. We owe their circulation and perhaps their existence to the popular technology of our day, to digital cameras and JPEG files and e-mail."

Indelible or not, images will help historians judge the war, over time, as a liberation or a decimation, a triumph or a quagmire. Indeed, he who lives by the still may in time be done in by the still. "Perhaps," says Sante, "the digital camera will haunt the future career of George W. Bush the way the tape recorder sealed the fate of Richard Nixon."

My son, Sam, and I took our place in our den's large easy chair. In what would become our Sunday night ritual, we turned on the television and waited for that night's episode of HBO's World War II drama *Band of Brothers*. A week ago—on September 9—we had nestled into the same seat to watch the first two installments of the show. Sam, age thirteen, had been mesmerized by the program's graphic depiction of GIs rushing ashore on D-Day. When the telecast had ended, he had turned to me and asked, "Dad, will we ever go to war?"

"Not likely," I'd responded, thinking back to the last major U.S. conflict, in Vietnam, which had ended a generation ago, while I was still in college. "Let's hope not in your lifetime."

That was Sunday night. The war began on Tuesday morning, thirty-three hours later.

7 MONDAY, SEPTEMBER 17

A woman tacked a sign on a gate near Ground Zero:

> *ALL OF YOU TAKING PHOTOS*
>
> *I wonder if you really see whats here or if you're so concerned with getting that perfect shot that you've forgotten this is a tragedy site, not a tourist attraction. As I continually had to move "out of someone's way" as they carefully tried to frame this place [of] mourning. I kept wondering what makes us think we can capture the pain, the loss, the pride & the confusion—this complexity—onto a 4×5 glossy.*
>
> *I LOVE My City*
>
> —*Firegirl, NYC, 09-17-01*

President Bush declared, "I want justice. There's an old poster out West I recall, that said, 'Wanted, Dead or Alive.' "

Late in the day, the design team at the *New York Post* laid out a mock Wild West poster showing the face of Osama bin Laden, with the headline: WANTED, DEAD OR ALIVE. It would appear as a foldout in the next morning's paper, and would be plastered on walls and windows throughout the city.

Harry Benson and I returned downtown to witness the resumption of everyday life on the first new workweek after September 11. Many employees had stayed away until Monday, recovering from the initial shock, monitoring the fates of lost colleagues and friends, and spending time with their families. (Many had been unable to enter their buildings anyway, due to security concerns and lack of power; the markets had been closed all week, Monday being the first day that normal trading resumed.) We saw men and women of stern face, heads bowed or eyes set straight ahead, walking with briefcases through the dust-lined streets. The mood was mournful and tense. Most were clearly resentful of the press attention. They had lost friends, their lives and companies were in flux, their work world had been nearly obliterated. They had urgent, or mundane, matters to attend to. They did not consider themselves appropriate props for someone's pictures.

We saw Wall Street brokers with security passes who had dressed for the day: toting American flag placards or sporting American flag ties, loud and proud as they strode to their offices. We saw a huge flag banner that dominated the exterior of the New York Stock Exchange, which was bathed in TV floodlights for its first day of trading since the attacks. The message being telegraphed: despite the efforts to impede them, the engines of commerce would rev on.

Harry suggested we head south and take an early ride on the Staten Island Ferry, which would grant us a view of the crippled city. More important, once we made it to the far bank of New York Harbor, Harry would be able to photograph residents embarking on their first post-9/11 commute into Manhattan.

What we hadn't anticipated was how overpowering the scene would be through the viewfinder. We joined the passengers from Staten Island on the foredeck of the ferry, and stood speechless. Even six days after the attacks, the furnace beneath the rubble emitted so much smoke that a single photographic frame could not contain it. A long band of cloud curled up from a hole in the downtown skyline and was swept due west, like a gray ribbon, toward the Statue of Liberty. Manhattan seemed irreparably disfigured, a Brobdingnagian creature asleep on a distant shore with a limb or wing plucked away. The remaining buildings appeared off-kilter. A woman in a windbreaker stood next to us, and Harry, his back to the morning sun, photographed the streaks of her tears.

As I stood on the pier that morning, my gut told me that the story wasn't really here, in New York. The story, inevitably, would be *over there*, in Afghanistan. Six days before, the president had laid down the gauntlet: "We will make no distinction between the terrorists who committed these acts and those who harbor them." America and its allies were surely going to retaliate, and soon.

So I logged a cell-phone call, there on the dock, to the office of General Hugh Shelton, the chairman of the Joint Chiefs of Staff. I had been Harry's editor for stories on Shelton in 1994 (when he commanded U.S. troops in Haiti) and in 1999 (during the U.S. peacekeeping mission in the Balkans). Two days later, Harry was at the Pentagon photographing Shelton and his new successor, Richard Myers, for *Vanity Fair* and, several weeks later, General Tommy Franks, who would go on to command the Afghan campaign and the initial sweep into Iraq.

Though we couldn't have realized it then, that phone call from the pier would set the stage for an ambitious photo session. At year's end, Harry would spend a perilous twenty minutes suspended in a helicopter over the Arabian Sea, barking over his headset to officers on the bridge, convincing them to turn the USS *Theodore Roosevelt* into the sun a little bit more—to avoid harsh shadows in his shot. Harry's assignment: to render a group portrait of the 5,500-member crew of the aircraft carrier, posing on the ship's four-and-a-half-acre deck—holding up the American flag that had been hoisted at Ground Zero by three New York firemen *(Image 30)*.

As Benson shot roll after roll, the famous flag shimmered in the sun.

But was it, in fact, that famous flag?

There it was again. This time, on the cover of *Newsweek*. For six days the photo had been in print, on TV, online—the picture soon known as the Flag Photo, the Flag-raising Photo, the Shot Seen Round the World.

The photo showed three Brooklyn firefighters—George Johnson, Dan McWilliams, and Bill Eisengrein—standing at the rim of the World Trade Center ruins as they hoisted the American flag *(Image 31)*. Photographer Thomas Franklin, of New Jersey's Bergen *Record*, had taken the shot in the late afternoon on September 11. After midnight, it was released over the AP newswire.

The Flag Photo was instantly snapped up in newsrooms throughout the land and wedged into the next available edition. On Wednesday, it made the front page of newspapers from *The* (Appleton, Wis.) *Post-Crescent* to the Los Angeles *Daily News* to the *Bremerton* (Wash.) *Sun*. On Thursday, the *New York Post* ran it above an anthemlike headline: "*. . . gave proof through the night that our flag was still there.*" And so began the picture's viral surge through the cultural bloodstream.

People tore it from newspapers. They downloaded it from Web sites. They posted it in the windows of homes and schools, government and office buildings, buses and cars. They embossed it on medals and blew it up on billboards. Artists reinterpreted it, adding vibrant colors or new details in the background: a bald eagle, a crucifix, the towers miraculously upright.

In Texas, it was incorporated into a stained-glass window. In New York, Madame Tussauds turned it into a life-size waxwork. Citizens tattooed it on their biceps. Soldiers toted it into battle. Over the Internet, hucksters sold reconstituted versions of it—painted or lithographed or digitally rejiggered—framed or unframed, with matte or without. Americans wanted to *own* the image, have a piece of it, display it as an object that expressed their inner tangle of emotions: sorrow, defiance, fortitude, pride.

Of all the pictures from that day of pictures, this was the one that presented a semblance of hope. Standing on the mount where thousands had been killed, three men had thought to raise a flag "caked in crud," as one of them would put it, to rally the living and honor the dead.

In a matter of weeks the photograph had taken on iconic status. It became an emblem of America's unbroken will, of resilience and valor in the face of terror. Its impact derived, in part, from the fact that it eerily echoed another icon (one that had helped bolster the country at a turning point in World War II): the shot of six men, also poised atop rubble, raising the colors during a break in the battle for Iwo Jima, in 1945.

The Flag Photo would become the most widely reproduced news picture of the new century. It would grace a U.S. postage stamp, mistakenly touted as the first to depict living, identifiable human beings—reprinted 255 million times and used to raise more than $10 million on behalf of emergency workers and their families.

And yet, swirling just outside the frame was a tempest of contention and mystery. The frantic crush to embrace the image, and to wring revenue from it, would soon stand at odds with the picture's message of unity, endurance, and sacrifice. The photo's ubiquity would come to haunt the lives of the three firemen depicted. Legal wrangling surrounding the image would spur separate probes by the Fire Department and New York's attorney general. Even the flag itself would become ensnared in controversy—inexplicably misplaced, exchanged, hidden, or stolen (and still missing, to this day), somehow replaced by a larger flag, which was then shuttled around the world with a Navy escort.

"Anybody tells you they don't know where the [original] flag is," says a former high-ranking member of the NYPD, referring to his Fire Department counterparts, "they're full of shit. One of those three [firemen] *has* to know or somebody of authority [does]. Somebody has it and intentionally has not let it come [out]."

Such a notion is outrageous to Bill Eisengrein, one of the three flag raisers, who is quick to describe the chaos during that first week. "My fire helmet, a flashlight, and a pair of gloves," he says, were swiped from his fire truck in the morning hours of September 12. "So would I be surprised that a flag would be stolen, and maybe somebody has it in their closet somewhere? Not really, no."

The chaos argument doesn't sit well with Shirley Dreifus, the owner of the original flag, who tried to sue the city of New York to force them to find it. "The person who took it down knows he took it down and knows where it is," she says. (It was her chartered yacht, docked at a pier near Ground Zero, from which the flag had been removed by firefighter Dan McWilliams on the afternoon of 9/11.) "This was a guarded area. People were in charge of it. And you just don't take a flag down unless you know where it's going—or somebody *told* you to do it."

While the flag-raising picture would become America's photo—all Francis Scott Key and mournful bugles—the image, sub rosa, has lived out a fitful antilife, generating backstories myriad and strange, each more bizarre than the last. And the vignettes behind the photograph, many told here for the first time, speak volumes about what is truly decent, and what is rather despicable, in modern American life, media, and commerce.

Bagpipes played. Local notables gathered. The ceremony was solemn, decorous. It was Christmas week, three months after the attacks, and it would be the first sign that the photo, for all its healing properties, was also under the spell of the surreal.

At a Brooklyn podium stood the city's fire commissioner, Thomas Von Essen, his eyes moist. Fire captain James Graham was tearful too. "It wasn't a fire," he insisted. "It was an act of war." Yet there was an air of buoyancy as well. "[In] raising the flag," said Mayor Rudy Giuliani, three firefighters "have brought honor to the department, to their city . . . and in a way in which they probably never understood at the time, lifted immediately the spirits of an entire country."

Front and center, under a large sheet of cloth, rested an eighteen-foot-tall clay model. Plans called for a bronze monument—of three firemen and a flag, inspired by the famous picture—to be installed outside FDNY headquarters the following April.

Then came the money shot. The fabric was tugged away as the TV cameras rolled. Reporters moved closer. And it was soon apparent to everyone that this was no faithful rendering of the photo. The firefighters' arms, observed *Newsday*, "appear[ed] more sinewy" than those in the picture. Their poses had been altered, their bodies trimmed down. In fact, their faces bore little resemblance to the three Brooklyn firemen. Instead, one was African-American, another Latino, a third Caucasian.

The figures, explained a spokesman, were "composites, intended to symbolize the entire FDNY." Commenting on behalf of the Vulcan Society, an organization of black firefighters, Kevin James said he hoped that "the artistic expression of diversity [would] supersede any concern over factual correctness."

The decision to alter the firemen's races had been made jointly among the Fire Department, the project's underwriter (developer Bruce Ratner), and the design studio. "Somewhere along the line," says Ivan Schwartz, director of the Brooklyn studio that created the prototype, he phoned his FDNY contacts and stressed that "three hundred forty-three firefighters of all races had died on that day. I raised the point to bring [to light] the issue of the long-term impact of memorializing *all* the people who died."

Schwartz says he also warned about the consequences of erecting too literal a memorial. The statue would be derivative of not one but *two* famous images, both of them known for sparking intense emotions. Perhaps they wanted a more metaphorical statue. Perhaps they wanted to slow down the project and arrive at a more cautious consensus. ("The main Civil War memorials," he now reflects, "didn't [emerge] until roughly fifty years later, once the veterans were dying off.")

Instead, Schwartz says, passions prevailed. The FDNY chose to hew to the flag-raising theme. What's more, they had "decided we should represent one [fireman as] black, one white, and one Hispanic." Schwartz's studio complied.

No one, however, had received permission from the three flag raisers. Or the photographer. Or the newspaper that owned the copyright to the picture.

The faux firemen created a firestorm. Members of the public—and of engine and ladder companies across the city—called the monument an example of "political correctness run amok." A petition drive conscripted many of the FDNY's rank and file, who clamored for the project to be quashed. ("The . . . horrible events [must be] present[ed] accurately and truthfully," read one petition. "To depict [the flag raising] in any other manner sullies a historical and heroic act and desecrates hallowed ground.") Pundits joined the pile-on. Conservative commentator Jonah

Goldberg asked, "Why not [convert the figures into] a Muslim woman in a floor-length burqa, a Chinese guy in a wheelchair, and a whole passel of midgets of various hues and nationalities?"

Two weeks after the ceremony, Schwartz, sitting in his Brooklyn studio, noticed a snowdrift of e-mails, piling up by the thousands, he later estimated. He was inundated with notes of protest, he says, that were filled "with all kinds of invective. Many were personal, like, 'Fuck you. How dare you put the head of a nigger on one of these heroes?' "

The fact that the original picture incorporated so many patriotic touchstones (the flag, the towers' rubble, the dust-daubed firemen as if risen from the ashes, the figures posed in the manner of the GIs from Iwo Jima) made its emotional resonance almost combustible, an extract of pure political dynamite. The proposed statue was perceived as blasphemous, even seditious, an attempt to co-opt and transmute the American values engraved in the picture.

The Bergen *Record*, which had the right to authorize all commemorative uses of the image, considered filing an injunction to stop the project. The attorney for the three firefighters implored the statue's creators to cease and desist. Dan McWilliams—the fireman who had come up with the idea of lofting the flag in the first place—confessed in a statement, released by the law firm of McCarthy & Kelly, to being "disgusted by the controversy . . . because the flag-raising was supposed to promote harmony. It's just disgraceful that the country should be focusing on this. Guys are dying in Afghanistan and this is what we're fighting over?"

Plans for the statue were quietly scrapped. The model, which sat in the foundry for months, was destroyed: an ill-conceived prototype of a bronze replica of a photographic replica of a symbolic moment.

But the picture, from whence it sprang, pressed on.

Just before 9:00 a.m., a news editor had come running through the Bergen *Record* photo department, announcing that a plane had crashed into the Trade Center. Moments later, Thomas Franklin sped out the door with his digital camera gear, drove to Jersey City's riverside Exchange Place, and ditched his car. "It's absolute mayhem," he says. "People driving the wrong way down streets, people fleeing buildings. I'm like a fish swimming upstream." He scrambled on foot to the shore for a clear view of downtown Manhattan. From there, he would take pictures for more than two hours: of the towers' giant thunderheads, of boatloads of soot-cloaked workers, of injured firemen arriving from Manhattan by ferry.

During a testy encounter with a policeman, who kept insisting that bystanders evacuate the area, Franklin stood his ground, continuing to shoot. Suddenly, he says, the cop turned and shoved him against a lamppost, causing Franklin's Canon to jam and erasing all of his pictures. In an instant, every shot he had taken that morning had been electronically vaporized.

"I break down," Franklin says, remembering the tears. "I kneel on the ground, scrolling through my camera, trying to figure out what's wrong. I'm in despair, totally distraught. That's how my day began."

Franklin, thirty-five, sandy-haired and boyish, and a normally upbeat guy, felt out of his element. Though known for his resourcefulness, he wasn't a conflict photographer, by any means: the week before he had been in the Dominican Republic shooting a baseball story—about Danny Almonte, the twelve-year-old Bronx Little League star, originally from Santo Domingo, who turned out to be an imposing, fourteen-year-old pretender (with a seventy-mile-an-hour fastball).

Franklin managed to regain his composure and soldiered on, boarding a ferry and making his way to the smoke-shrouded city. He eventually maneuvered through security cordons to the heart of Ground Zero, where he would shoot all afternoon. With the day's light waning, Franklin stood near a first-aid station that had been set up at the corner of Liberty and West Streets. Dozens of firemen had gathered there, he says, stopping for water and receiving eyewashes to flush out the grit. Dust seemed to have settled on everything, even on the boats docked in the harbor at the nearby marina.

"It's approaching five o'clock," Franklin recalls. "The light's beautiful. But everything's gray from the pulverized debris in the air. I filled up virtually all my CompactFlash cards—my digital film. I have less than a hundred frames left and I'm thinking I need a game plan to get back to

Jersey"—to hitch a boat ride across the Hudson and transmit his pictures to the paper. (Many of Manhattan's phone lines were disabled.)

Suddenly, the firemen and workers were told to flee. Seven World Trade Center, the forty-seven-story building right in front of Franklin, was on the verge of collapse. Franklin was about to make his move for the harbor.

Dan McWilliams, a firefighter from Brooklyn, was walking past the North Cove marina. There, gracing the stern of a yacht, was an American flag. McWilliams caught a glimpse of it and had a moment of inspired bravado. According to a friend of McWilliams's, the firefighter approached a policeman, who had been standing near the 130-foot boat *Star of America*. "I'm going to take that flag," McWilliams said. Then he simply helped himself to the banner, aluminum pole and all, wrapping it into a tight cylinder and heading in the direction of the downed towers, careful not to let the flag scrape the dust-caked street.

Walking toward Ground Zero, McWilliams enlisted George Johnson, a friend from his Brooklyn ladder company. In his typically taciturn manner, McWilliams said to Johnson, "Gimme a hand, will ya, George?"

"I knew exactly what he was doing," Johnson would later remark.

The two men then filed past Billy Eisengrein, from Brooklyn's Rescue Company No. 2—an acquaintance of McWilliams's from their days growing up on Staten Island. Eisengrein asked, "You need a hand?" He fell in step with the others.

McWilliams realized that in order for the Ground Zero rescue crews to see it, the flag had to be placed on high ground. The men spied a large flagpole jutting up from the mangled steel, likely a vestige from the gutted Marriott Hotel. They walked onto an elevated platform, above the remains of a construction trailer, and converged on the pole. They detached a tattered green banner, damaged in the collapse. Then they removed the Stars and Stripes from the ship's staff and began securing the flag to the line.

Out of the corner of his eye, Franklin saw a flash of motion and color through the haze. "I see the three firemen fumbling with the flag," he remembers. He was standing across the street, a hundred feet away, talking to photographer James Nachtwey, of all people. "They look dusty and chalky. There's [supposedly] tens of thousands of people dead at this point. In this setting, at the time, my antennae are up: this is something I should be shooting."

He swiveled his 245-mm lens toward the action. "I almost missed the shot," he says. "I'm not quite sure whether the flag's going up or going down. They're not quite raising it. I'm anticipating."

Over the next minute and forty-five seconds, Franklin triggered twenty-four frames. In each shot the composition is confused, the figures clustered in odd ways. But in frame number fourteen, snapped at 5:01 p.m.—at a shutter speed of 1/640 of a second and an aperture of f9—the elements align. "They're fussing with the flag," says Franklin. "The flag going up casts a shadow on the firefighter in the middle. And then I shoot it." All three men look up, the flag unfurls. The glare of the late-day sun highlights their figures against a curtain of wreckage, which rises above and behind them, slightly out of focus.

Johnson, in that instant, steps back, hands on his hips. McWilliams, in the center, and Eisengrein, to the right, work the halyard, lofting the colors up the pole.

Also shooting the scene were a handful of others, including a Police Department videographer, at street level, and two still photographers, positioned on the Two World Financial Center promenade, *above* the firemen: Lori Grinker, on assignment for *People* (kneeling and leaning out a broken window), and Ricky Flores, from *The Journal News* (White Plains, N.Y.), literally straddling Grinker. Their images showed the firemen dwarfed by the wasteland around them. ("In some ways," acknowledges Franklin, their versions of the event were "very dramatic [and] more descriptive than mine.") But Franklin's shot rendered the men straight on, iconographically. As in the image from Iwo Jima, the flagpole slices across the frame like the barrel of a cannon.

"Just at that moment," says a confidant of the firemen, "came [word] that building Seven might collapse. So people began to evacuate. As they raised the flag, they saw people running away, in the periphery of their vision."

"Everybody just needed a shot in the arm," McWilliams would say two days later, overcome with emotion in a brief interview with writer Jeannine Clegg of *The Record* (in his only public comment about the moment). "Every pair of eyes that saw the flag got a little brighter."

The firefighters would later explain that they did not know they were being photographed, that they had not intended for their act to be chronicled. They had merely wanted to raise their compatriots' spirits. Johnson would even recall that "a few guys yelled out, 'Good job' and 'Way to go.' "

Then the firemen walked down from the precipice, and the flag remained, flying in the dying light of day.

Franklin almost missed the boat, quite literally.

He evacuated just minutes before Seven World Trade Center imploded. He spent twenty minutes arguing his way onto a police boat. Upon arriving at the park next to the Statue of Liberty, he disembarked, still wearing a surgical mask (a precaution many had taken to protect themselves from toxic particles in the air). Immediately, he saw evacuees from other vessels forming lines to be "decontaminated" by hazmat crews.

For Franklin, the clock was winding down. Over the past nine hours, hundreds of other photojournalists, jacked into iBooks and notebook PCs, had been sending wave upon wave of imagery to the waiting terminals of picture editors at the nation's newspapers and magazines, photo agencies and wire services. Most of his fellow photographers at *The Record*, in Hackensack, had already uploaded their caches. It was now 6:30, and Franklin feared he might miss the 9:00 p.m. deadline for the early-closing front page. (Press time had been moved up: the publisher, given the historic nature of the events, needed precious extra minutes to print more copies than usual.) The few remaining slots in the rest of the paper were quickly dwindling.

Franklin knew the drill. He had to locate his laptop in the trunk of his Honda Civic, three miles away. He had to find somewhere to cull through the nine hundred–plus pictures he'd taken that day. He had to winnow them down to a choice two or three dozen, then caption the lot, then secure a line to transmit his take of the day's devastation.

Upon seeing the long rows of passengers, Franklin bolted, with his mask still on. Cops called after him. He sprinted through a parking lot, made it to a roadway, and flagged a passing SUV. The driver (near tears as she related how she had barely escaped the south tower's collapse) dropped Franklin off at around 7:00 p.m. He got caught in a traffic jam, plowed over a highway median strip, and finally steered into a hotel lot. He darted into the Secaucus Radisson, covered in dust, and set up his laptop at the edge of the lobby bar.

A dozen hotel guests huddled behind him. They watched his screen fill up with scenes of ash and cataclysm. They stood in silence, occasionally gasping or murmuring as pictures pulsed across his laptop. As he edited his take, Franklin noticed the TV above the bar, seeing for the first time "the video image of planes crashing into the buildings." To make sure he didn't lose his cache of pictures yet again, Franklin saved his "selects" onto the desktop, adding short captions to each. Then, at 8:00 p.m., he began transmitting them, one by one, in the order he had shot them. At 8:37, his thirtieth frame arrived on the server at *The Record*.

Danielle Richards remembers "trying to decompress a little bit" from the horrors of the day. Richards, a *Record* photographer, was standing in the picture department's digital control center, looking over the shoulder of another shooter, Chris Pedota. He had docked his laptop into a workstation terminal, hoping to see what the wires were servicing and what other staffers had shot. Images of annihilation splashed across the monitor. The room seemed to surge and contract, the journalists caught in the undertow of an earth-churning news event. Mixed in with the exhilaration of a breaking story—and the perpetual present-tense tension of a cloistered newsroom—was an oppressive dread. Many colleagues had loved ones, friends, and neighbors who were still unaccounted for. Scores from among the paper's wide readership were missing.

"I was looking at a lot of other pictures and feeling worse and worse," says Richards. "Then Tom's came in."

Franklin's shot appeared on the screen within a grid of a dozen "thumbnails," each displayed horizontally. One caught Richards's eye. "Bring that one up," she said. Pedota rotated the frame, vertically. He double-clicked on the picture, enlarging and isolating it, then used an image-editing program to "give it a little pop" of brightness.

"Oh my God," she said, then looked over and summoned the paper's photo chief, Rich Gigli, and several others. "You guys, you have to see this picture. This is Iwo Jima."

They walked over and began to absorb the scene, their silence taking on weight and texture. "They were just speechless," says Richards. "Their mouths were all agape, literally [in] a trance."

The company president, Jon Markey, joined them.

"Once you looked, it sort of took hold," recalls Markey. "Particularly in the circumstances, I thought, This is historic. It was transcendent. From a human perspective, this was the one—in a collection of thousands—that was stunning, emotionally."

Richards broke the hush. "That's not a picture," Pedota remembers her saying. "It's a fucking icon."

Gigli thought, "My God, that's the classic shot . . . I've been waiting for. It hit a nerve." Knowing he was "right up against the deadline," he says, "nine o'clock sharp for the color front and back page," he took an H-P copy print and ran it out to Bob Townsend, the front-page designer. We couldn't change the front page, so we put it across the top of the back page, swap[ping] it for a vertical shot already in position in the layout. A couple of editors didn't want to change it. I insisted on it."

The Record's presses started rolling at 11:30 p.m. Gigli, a veteran journalist who knew how to protect an exclusive, watched the clock, waiting for midnight. He needed to make sure that Franklin's image, at least in the New York area, would run in *The Record*—and *The Record* alone. "I deliberately didn't move it to [the] AP [wire]," he says, "until about ten after twelve"—once the deadlines of the local broadsheets and tabloids had passed.

Once it went across the wire, newspapers felt the tremors. Journalists working the night shifts throughout the Western United States quickly remade their next day's front page. Their Web sites posted it too. "By the morning of the twelfth," Franklin remembers, the phones at *The Record* were "ringing off the hook. By the end of the day, there were hundreds of calls an hour. By the end of the week, they hired [freelancers] just to answer the phones."

"We were fielding calls from Chicago, Providence, Seattle, Texas," says Richards. "The calls weren't [only] for reprints, but for appreciation. 'My daughter's bringing it to school' . . . 'I just want to tell you guys how moved we were.' We never get that. In this business, usually we get hate mail."

In the first few weeks after the attacks, inquiries to reprint, license, or market the image came in "from Japan to Switzerland to Omaha," says Jennifer Borg, general counsel for *The Record*'s parent company, the North Jersey Media Group. "We received tens of thousands of e-mail requests. I had to hire temporary people to look at my e-mail box. The marketing department, the editors, the reporters—we couldn't get the paper out if we read all of these."

While Borg understood that the picture had the potential to raise millions for charity, many of those seeking permission didn't seem sensitive to the subject matter. "One person's trash is another person's treasure," she says. "We didn't want it on a T-shirt. We thought, My God, three thousand people died. [But] a lot of [the] public said, '*You* don't own it. The picture belongs to *everyone*. Why aren't you letting us use it?' "

The NFL wanted to print the image on tickets for January's Super Bowl. The rock group *NSYNC requested it for a concert backdrop, donating $25,000 to charity, unsolicited. On the other extreme were companies asking to place the scene on snowboards or to re-create it, in miniature, inside snow globes.

Mixed in were urgent, private pleas. Firefighters' families hoped to put the photo on mass cards at funerals and memorial services. Heartbreaking requests would come from those whose loved ones were missing, or who wanted their own personal copies. Borg remembers one widow who told her, "This is the only thing that's helping me get out of bed."

Over time, Franklin began compiling a slide show of various renderings and misappropriations of his picture. Opportunists had incorporated the image into candy wrappers, cigar box lids, jack-o'-lantern carvings, Christmas ornaments, light-switch cover plates, office chair seat cushions. The shot, swiftly slapped on canvas, was sold on eBay as "911 Rescue Firefighter Painting Print #2"—opening bid: $14.99. The image was plastered on the side of a Quonset hut at a Louisiana prison, a car dealership in Washington, a barn in upstate New York.

"The picture has this life of its own," explains Franklin. "At various points, I've felt tremendous pride—or disgust—when others have [used] my picture in different applications. I'm covering the 2001 World Series. Phoenix, Arizona. Game One. I'm in the first base photographers' box, singing the national anthem. And I look out on the field and see these three [local] firemen and a flag on a pole." To Franklin, the men seemed confoundingly out of time, like a group of Civil War reenactors. Even the pole had been set on an incline to replicate the one in the shot. "The national anthem ends," Franklin remembers, his eyes rolling. "They raise this flag. And *New York Post* photographer Charlie Wenzelberg goes, 'Tom, they should've had you go out and photograph the reenactment'—as part of the reenactment.

"You see something you've created—bigger than life," Franklin reflects. "In an odd way there's some flattery in that. It surprises me [that] a war and a half have transpired, but this is still happening. Soldiers in Afghanistan were using my picture as a morale thing. They were leaving [copies of] it as a 'calling card' after they went on raids." Crews were also said to have painted replicas of the photo onto the sides of bombs.

The use of the photo as a tool of battlefield propaganda helped it serve as a visual rebuke. Hurling the picture back at the Taliban and al-Qaeda implied: Take *this*, along with America's firepower. What's more, the image of men in uniform, hoisting a flag, would bridge the conceptual gap between the bravest and the brave GI. To many of those looking for potent symbols—as grist in the argument for expanding the fight against terror, to Iraq and elsewhere—the photo provided a pictorial validation that firefighter and terror fighter were kindred combatants in a single, seamless war.

In the main, though, the picture was used more for inspirational than for political ends. "If you scour the visual record," Richards contends, "there were so many different iconic images that came out of [this] defining moment of our generation. David Handschuh's picture of the [tumbling tower], looking straight up. That's tattooed in my brain. The AP shot of the people that looked like they were dipped in chalk. Father [Mychal] Judge being carried out. But Tom's image was the only one that gave people a sense of resurrection. After seeing the same loop on TV over and over, of the planes going in, Tom's tugs at your heartstrings in a positive way. Tom's picture said: Despite this horrible event, we're going to come out all right. I slept a little better that night after seeing it."

Even so, a backlash toward the image arose within the photo community. Franklin's shot, in many photojournalistic circles, was dismissed as flat, trite, and unimaginatively composed. While the picture aptly conveyed steadfastness and resilience, to photo purists it bore few of the hallmarks of Joe Rosenthal's classic scene at the summit of Mount Suribachi. Rosenthal's picture had nuance, stature, exquisite symmetry, and an almost propulsive force. The six men raising the flag were knotted together as one unit. Their dramatic gesture was compounded by the tension in their figures: the ground resisted their effort; their flag was wielded as one might thrust a bayonet. The rubble at their feet—actually the rocky surface of a volcanic crater—resembled a pile of bones.

In contrast, cynics considered Franklin's shot the made-for-TV version. Had Franklin not been there to fashion it, Madison or Pennsylvania Avenues might have dreamed up the "feel good" tableau out of whole cloth. And naysayers pointed out that other photographers had been shooting the same moment—from arguably better angles; Franklin's paper had merely been fortunate enough to get his shot up on the wire much faster. Indeed, the following spring, just weeks before the Pulitzer Prizes were to be awarded, one picture editor from a large daily confided to me: "We don't care what wins. As long as it's not the damn flag." (Franklin's shot did not win; instead, *The New York Times* swept, for its extensive breaking-news and feature coverage—from 9/11 and on through the war in Afghanistan—by its team of seventeen photographers.)

Much of the contempt, of course, was born of envy. Franklin's picture had become the instant insignia—precisely because it *lacked* poetry and nuance. The photograph had an almost irreducible simplicity, power, and balance—prerequisites for classic iconography. The three equidistant figures stand in piercing sunlight, which separates them from their surroundings, as if in bas-relief. They appear illuminated, statuesque, aggrandized. The flag, the ultimate symbol of the nation, centers the photograph. The towering rubble is a crushing presence, consuming every inch of the background. Just as Franklin's camera is angled up toward the firemen, the firemen squint up toward the flag and, by implication, the heavens. And high above them, some have noticed, broken beams form the shape of a cross.

Franklin's photograph, in short, was no less than the digital-age descendant of Rosenthal's Iwo Jima, 1945; of Apollo 11 astronaut Buzz Aldrin, in 1969, having just planted the star-spangled banner on the rocky lunar surface; of Emanuel Leutze's *Washington Crossing the Delaware* (in which three figures stand as a boat comes ashore on Christmas 1776: General Washington and two compatriots, brandishing an angled flag). Even if the Flag Photo seemed artistically deficient, the public ignored that, embracing it and reproducing it more than any other taken that day.

James Bradley, coauthor with Ron Powers of the definitive history of the Iwo Jima photo, *Flags of Our Fathers*, has pointed out the similarities between Franklin's and Rosenthal's shots: "Both sets of flag-raisers not aware of a nearby photographer, both shots offering hope . . . both flags from ships." (The 1945 flag was borrowed from the USS *Missoula* and hauled up the slopes of Suribachi to inspire the soldiers below.)

But Franklin's picture, it turns out, has more parallels with Rosenthal's than might immediately meet the eye. Both were taken on an outcropping above a killing field. (Seven thousand Americans perished over thirty-six days in the battle for Iwo Jima.) Both were taken in a conflict with unseen enemies. (The Japanese had assumed positions in a warren of island tunnels, pillboxes, and blockhouses; their airborne comrades were best known for their suicide-bombing runs.) Both incidents were also covered by others, whose efforts have largely escaped the public memory. (Rosenthal, Speed Graphic in hand, was accompanied by a private with a still camera and a sergeant who had a movie camera equipped with color film.) Both were destined for America's front pages, immediately recognized by picture editors as conveying an elevated human response at a low point in a bloody conflict. (Upon first seeing the Iwo Jima picture, AP's Guam photo chief, John Bodkin, picked up the glossy, whistled, and then shouted across the news bureau: "Here's one for all time!") Both became freshly minted American icons that helped buck up a wartime populace.

Both images would later be blemished by rumors of their having been staged, though neither was set up in any way. Indeed, Rosenthal almost missed the moment (the flag raising took all of four seconds), just managing to snag it in one shot, on sheet film. (He was actually photographing a *second* flag that had been carried to the summit, intended to replace a smaller one that had been hoisted earlier that morning by a different contingent of soldiers.)

One shot showed six men, the other showed three. One had men in fatigues, the other in firefighter's garb. One was taken at the end of a protracted conflict, the other on its very first day. But in both pictures, exposed fifty-six years apart, anonymous men in helmets, grasping at a flag, took it upon themselves to use their nation's most beloved symbol to turn a decimated landscape from a battleground into sacred ground in one fleeting, eloquent gesture.

It all began so sensibly and congenially—before the partnership and the esprit de corps frayed, unraveled, dissipated. To this day, it is hard to put one's finger on it. And even though the picture's mission continues, irreconcilable differences in how to display the image, and how to profit from it, have polarized those who control the photo and those inside the frame.

That first week, thousands clamored for permission to use the picture: schoolteachers and business leaders, fire chiefs and news directors. Someone had to take charge and stem the tide. And into the fray stepped

Jennifer Borg. Tack-sharp and stunning, Borg was a young attorney with printer's ink in her veins; her great-grandfather, in 1930, had purchased outright what would become *The Record* of Bergen County, N.J. It was Borg, the company's in-house counsel, who would come up with a Solomonic solution.

Within thirty-six hours of the attacks, *The Record*'s marketing department had wisely thought to seek advice from colleagues at *The Daily Oklahoman*, recalling the horrors of that city's terrorist bombing in 1995. As Borg remembers, they asked: "We're a newspaper whose neighbors have just suffered a terrorist act. What do you wish, in hindsight, that you had done differently? Oklahoma advised us that we really needed to be there for the long term." So *The Record*'s owners, intent on assisting local residents for years to come, set up the North Jersey Media Group Disaster Relief Fund the day after the attacks.

Next, Borg enlisted the actual *subjects* of the photo. "Ethically," she says, "we felt we should get the firefighters' consent before we went ahead and responded yea or nay to the multitude of requests." (*The Record* believed it was required by law to secure their permission for any commercial or publicity use of their likenesses.) So she suggested a meeting, hoping they would want to be a part of the process. "When you start with: What's the right thing to do?," she says, "it all falls into place."

Borg met the firemen over beers at Blondies, a West Side bar, two months after 9/11. "It was very bittersweet," she recalls. "The atmosphere was like going to a wake—as if you have something in common and you wish it wasn't *this* that brought you together. The last thing we were going to talk about was the photo. The photo was the untouchable." When she walked in, the three firemen were already assembled—reserved, weary, and grateful, she recalls.

Dan McWilliams, the one who had lifted the flag from the boat, is the son of a firefighter. According to intimates, he is the cryptic, quiet one who uses neither e-mail nor cell phone. "Dan's a doer," says his attorney, Bill Kelly. An FDNY lieutenant, McWilliams has an almost military bearing, says an acquaintance, calling him "tough, true grit, hard as nails. If I was in a burning building I'd want [him] running in to save me." Says a third associate, "He's sensitive. A lot of the toughest guys you meet are tough because they're sensitive. [He's also] an extremely principled guy—easily frustrated [by bureaucracy]."

George Johnson, from Queens, recently made captain. Like McWilliams, he comes from a firefighting family and is a rugby "sevens" player, who suits up for the FDNY team and the Rockaway Fisheads Rugby Club. (His nickname: "Rocket.") Johnson, says a colleague, "is an outdoors guy. He's a surfer. He comes across as a go-with-the-flow guy, but he deeply *cares*. He's secretively passionate about people, the world, the world outside the firehouse." Five years before 9/11, says Kelly, "George gave bone marrow and saved a kid's life in Kentucky because his marrow proved to be a one-in-sixty-million match."

Bill Eisengrein, the figure to the right in the picture, knew McWilliams as just another neighborhood kid on Staten Island. The two men, says a friend, "are polar opposites"; Eisengrein "is much more trusting, open, gregarious." A member of a Staten Island motorcycle club, Islanders M.C., his passion is his Harley. His forearm bears tattoos of the towers, the flag, a Harley Davidson. (Eisengrein dates an NYPD detective, Kathleen Malone; McWilliams and Johnson are married. All three were in their mid-thirties when the photo was taken.)

Jennifer Borg remembers her first encounter with the three men as "poignant, almost overwhelming. They probably went to five funerals a day. [They seemed] overworked, exhausted. They were a little bit embarrassed that the attention was on *them* and not on all the people who died or got maimed and hurt. All I could think of was: the temperament that prompted them to raise the flag is the same one that allowed them to go out of their way to meet me because they saw something good that could be done. There was just something noble about them."

And so the partnership began. The firefighters decided to set up their own fund, in tandem with *The Record*'s; all income from the licensing of the image would be split fifty-fifty between the two charities. Bill Kelly, a savvy, telegenic attorney with expertise in litigation, intellectual property, and personal injury cases, was chosen to represent the interests of both parties. (Johnson is now married to Kelly's sister.)

More than half a million dollars from the newspaper's fund—including profits from the editorial syndication of the picture—would go to New Jersey families affected by the tragedy. Grants from the firefighters' charity, the Bravest Fund (to date, they have dispensed around $300,000), would go to those who had fallen through the bureaucratic cracks: the group of retired firemen who set up a van service to shuttle injured colleagues to hospital visits; the fireman whose daughter's bacterial meningitis had resulted in a series of amputations, and who needed to adapt his home to accommodate her wheelchair and automatic chairlift.

"It was a beautiful thing," Franklin asserts. "*The Record* has chosen not to profit from the picture. [Nor have] the three firemen." (Franklin, since it is his photo, has earned what he calls "a very, very modest amount.")

One day Borg lugged four cartons, crammed with inquiries, from the trunk of her Volvo station wagon, and handed them over to Kelly. In time, he would field about sixty thousand entreaties—people wanting to use the picture on everything from bomber jackets to credit cards to mouse pads. One gun maker hoped to fashion the image into a rifle stock. (Request denied.)

At first, everything went smoothly. Both the paper and the firemen signed off on all major requests. "We prioritized," Borg recalls. "Bill and I realized we had no problem if a woman in Oklahoma wanted to put it on T-shirts to raise proceeds for her firehouse. But we *did* have a problem with a major company using it exclusively for their commercial gain." Moreover, *The Record*, mindful of the sensitivity of the subject and its own journalistic reputation, wanted to protect the integrity of the photo from tacky or demeaning exploitation. (Fire truck decals were in; beer can and wine labels were out.) The bulk of Kelly's time was taken up with hunting down unauthorized infringements—like the topless bar in upstate New York that plastered the image on a billboard. "We pulled in about two million dollars in settlements," Kelly recalls.

Little by little, though, tensions mounted. The firefighters, through Bill Kelly, began insisting on uses of the photo that *The Record* routinely vetoed. "They wanted to put the image on things that we, as a newspaper, didn't agree with," says Borg. "And that was the rub. I understood their point: 'How can you deny a family from getting money because you won't license it on snow globes, just because you don't think that's appropriate? Who cares about appropriateness? We're going to too many funerals.' But as a newspaper we are safeguarding the image, journalistically, through its context."

Borg felt the firefighters were somehow "typecasting us as big, bad business." Kelly told her, "You're too interested in getting a Pulitzer. I'm so sick and tired of going back to them and telling them your committee has rejected another licensing offer." Borg countered, "We're not rejecting these things to be assholes. We have valid concerns about how to display a photo that meant so much to so many people around the world and [depicted] such a horrible tragedy . . . From our perspective, we thought that certain uses were not dignified."

"The Pulitzer was the be all and end all for them," Kelly now insists. "Once the Pulitzer was lost, there was a cavalcade of approvals for commercial uses. All bets were off. The red light had become a green light." Borg insists this is not true.

Things deteriorated further. Borg says she began receiving "unusual and disproportionately high legal bills from Kelly's firm, with charges—to *The Record*—for non-legal items, such as the use of cell phones and the making of travel arrangements"—accusations which Kelly disputes. "Any law firm bills for its paralegals," he says. "Our bills were *way* below industry standard." Then, after "repeatedly demanding" that Kelly's firm provide financial statements for the accounts, she looked at the spreadsheets and found what she calls "little evidence that money from the Bravest Fund was going to recipients when the money was most needed, in 2001 and 2002." She says she was alarmed, as well, by the "shoddy bookkeeping. It wasn't malfeasance, but deposits meant to be split fifty-fifty between the funds were entered in ledgers with no indication of whether they had already been divided, or were about to be. We felt we were owed."

Not so, says Kelly. "In those first two years there was a lot of money out there, so [the firemen] sought to distribute to those people *outside* existing [channels]. Jennifer *requested* that we do the ledgers this way . . . to streamline operations so as not to use their existing [outside law firm] that was very expensive." Not exactly, says Borg. "He was retained to keep an accounting of revenues from the licensing of the photos. But we were not privy to *how* he was keeping those records."

It all came asunder in March 2004. Reporter Michele McPhee of the New York *Daily News*, investigating these issues, wrote two front-page stories: PROFITS OF DOOM and CASHING IN ON 9/11: "Lawyer for fire charities reaps 553G from funds." For the second article, McPhee sat down with Kelly and the firefighters in a closed-door session. The *Daily News* then printed a piece stating that his firm had "reaped more than $500,000 in legal fees while the charity has given just $73,000 to the needy." Kelly denied the charges but New York attorney general Eliot Spitzer's office swiftly opened an inquiry.

The firefighters, whose loyalty is virtually ironclad, took the articles as an affront and lined up in support of Kelly. McPhee, according to Eisengrein, "was basically given the opportunity to do the first interview, ever, with the three of us. And she was on her own personal agenda and decided, for whatever reason, to do her article *her* way."

McPhee says she wrote a thorough, newsworthy story, "taking pains to not attack the firefighters themselves" yet criticizing their charity for its sluggish dispersal of funds. Soon, however, she was harassed by letter and phone, she says, recalling one particularly graphic and abusive tirade from a firefighter. "I've covered the FDNY for years," she says, "and I'd never heard anything like this—even in my coverage of the Mafia." Another fireman, she recalls, went on a Web site and called her a bitch "and certain people added to it. It dominoed."

In the end, though, the IRS and an independent auditor were satisfied with how the funds had been handled, a contention also supported by Joe Pierpont, a philanthropy expert who was brought in to monitor the charities. Kelly's and his firm's names were cleared, even as Kelly stepped aside as joint representative for the funds. The attorney general's office concluded, in 2005, that it was satisfied that the Bravest Fund had "reorganized. They've dispensed between four and five times the money as they have in previous years. They've got new management in place. And we will continue to keep an eye on their activity, moving forward."

Nonetheless, the damage was done. "We arrived at the conclusion that it was best to go our separate ways," says the paper's president, Jon Markey. Borg took on the legal workload that Kelly had done for *The Record*'s charity. The firemen, in response to the state probe, had to divert six figures' worth of their fund's money "to hire an attorney," Pierpont contends, "and every dollar paid in legal fees to handle the attorney general's inquiry would have gone to uniformed members' families—and that's the real shame of it."

To this day, even though both sides continue to consult on every noneditorial sale or license, there are lingering issues and misunderstandings. "We just haven't been totally, a hundred percent satisfied with the relationship we've had with them," says Eisengrein, describing how things with Borg "soured over time." Borg insists, with a hint of sorrow in her voice, "What led to the firefighters and us having our 'divorce' was raising money. Money was the tragic flaw in all this. Some of it goes back to the widow who says how horrible it is that this is what you're making money off of—and another widow, who says, 'It's money the victims wouldn't have [had] otherwise.' "

The Flag Photo, Borg admits, "*has* raised *millions* of dollars. It's the American way, but it's also anti-American. [All along the way,] people's greed [emerged while they were] trying to make an Almighty buck off of it. It's like John Milton—*Paradise Lost*. From something so good, how could something so bad happen?"

"Barbara Walters would call every six months or so," says Bill Kelly. "Oprah called. Not their offices—Oprah herself . . . The NFL tried to get them to go to the Super Bowl and re-create the photo. NASCAR called. MTV . . . They said no to everybody. [Then] that *Daily News* story shut the door for life. They will not do anything, at any point, any time. They refuse to talk about the picture . . . There's zero reason for them to do anything. These guys *hate* the press. That's the nice way of putting it."

The firemen's reticence was somehow refreshing in these tell-all times. After the attacks—with so many of their colleagues deceased, and so many others busy digging through rubble or assisting the grieving—how, in good conscience, could they have entertained anything resembling self-regard? Ever since, they have adopted a media embargo (though Eisengrein agreed to break their code of silence for this book).

"They're scared to death of any spotlight whatsoever," says Pierpont.

"They're shy of even the positive recognition—of any potential for anything to backfire against them . . . They feel they did a good thing and they've been run through the ringer for it. Dan and George have become disillusioned . . . They feel they don't trust the outside world—not just the press. And that's sad because most of the outside world would like to shake their hands."

Their fiercely private stance had deeper roots as well. They were more than anonymous faces in a frame. They were characters in the most public news photo in American life. And while the message of that photo was a hopeful one, its subtext, of course, was terror. Any press attention, therefore, raised fears, whether realistic or not, of drawing the wrath of al-Qaeda. "Can you think of a better target than us?" one of the firefighters remarked during the first year after September 11, as if bin Laden or his minions might actually set their sights on the firefighters as a sort of "trophy for al-Qaeda." Eisengrein explains: "I remember hearing that the military was dropping copies of the picture [at sites in] Afghanistan or Iraq. This is just hearsay, possibly they were. And if they were, we viewed it as, 'Hey, cool,' y'know. But then on the other hand you can say, 'Well, as a big Fuck-You to America, if they took one or all three of us out, it would be, like, 'How 'bout *that*?' Is it a possibility? I doubt it. [But] a lot of things go through your mind."

The firefighters' intractable stoicism, in fact, was reminiscent of their World War II counterparts. Ira Hayes (at the extreme left in Rosenthal's Iwo Jima shot, his hands unable to reach the flagpole) would resist most accolades when he returned Stateside, remarking, "How can I feel like a hero, when I hit the beach with two hundred and fifty buddies and only twenty-seven of us walked off alive?" John "Doc" Bradley (the medic in the center of the picture) cultivated his own stony silence. Until his dying day, at age seventy, in 1994, he refused to share more than scant details about the war or the image, training his eight children, according to his son James, "to deflect the phone-call requests for media interviews that never diminished over the years." Even so, the trio of survivors from that long-ago photo (three had died in battle in the days after the shot was taken) made their public bows and scrapes to support the image over the years—at ceremonies for the postage stamp and the Marine Corps memorial; with President Truman in the Oval Office and John Wayne on the set of *The Sands of Iwo Jima*.

The firemen did the same—in Battery Park, for the roll-out of the stamp; aboard the USS *Theodore Roosevelt* off the coast of Virginia; at a City Hall event to hand over the flag to the new mayor, Michael Bloomberg; at Madame Tussauds, where their likenesses were rendered in wax. And through it all, the three stayed mum. "None of us want to have a microphone put in our face and [be asked,] 'Well, what were you feeling when you were doing it?' " Eisengrein admits. "The comparison has been made between our picture and the picture at Iwo Jima. [But] name one of those six guys. Nobody seems to know [them]. Why should our picture be any different? It doesn't matter *who* we are, *where* we came from. It was just three people, happened to be three firefighters, but it was basically three Americans that decided to do something. There's no reason for us to become a household name."

Instead, they've let the picture and their charitable gifts do the talking. What's more, says Pierpont, who has worked with major charities since the 1960s, "their personal involvement with the people they're helping is intimate—unlike any other client I've ever had. They're not the dispassionate philanthropist who never has to run into who he's helping at the [country] club. They *live* with these people [who] come up to them with requests that would tear your heart out. They *are* the people they're helping . . . They have done absolutely nothing to capitalize on this for themselves."

And yet, try as they might, the firemen have met with infuriating obstacles in their attempts to do good by the photograph. The "Heroes of 2001" postage stamp is a prime example. The stamp ostensibly raised $10.5 million to assist emergency workers and their families. But not until the spring of 2006 had a penny of these funds been dispensed. First, the money had to be channeled, by law, through FEMA, an agency tarnished by charges of bureaucratic ineptitude in the wake of Hurricane Katrina, which devastated New Orleans and the Gulf Coast.

"Bureaucrats," wrote the *New York Post*, have been "sitting on every dime." Adds Gary Ackerman, the Long Island congressman instrumental in bringing the stamp into being: "The people [at FEMA] have hog-tied themselves in their own red tape, [mired in] incoherent . . . irresponsible [and] half-assed bureaucratic bullshit."

"It's reprehensible," says Jennifer Borg. "Here was a picture that epitomized bravery, courage, and our American ideals. We were honored to have our government choose it as the image on a stamp—to represent those same values. And then to have that very same government *keep it*, in its pocket, flies in the face of the honesty and courage the photo represents."

In the tumultuous life of the photograph, the most bizarre chapter of all entails the untold mystery of the lost—or stolen—Stars and Stripes. The flag that the firemen raised at Ground Zero has, quite simply, disappeared.

When the flag first made its anointed, appointed rounds, the media reported its whereabouts as it would a priceless artwork in a traveling exhibit. The flag was lowered in mid-September and escorted up to the Bronx to put in an appearance at a memorial service in Yankee Stadium; it was signed by Mayor Giuliani, Governor Pataki, and the fire and police chiefs; it was ferried out to the Arabian Sea to serve as the "battle flag" aboard the *Roosevelt*, ceremoniously passed among the thirty-some vessels under the aircraft carrier's command. (That winter, says Franklin, "a sailor e-mails me, out of the blue [sending a] picture from the ship"—a shot of the flag rippling above the *Roosevelt*.)

That March, Congressman Ackerman, along with Johnson, Eisengrein, and a small delegation, flew out to meet the carrier as it was returning to its base in Norfolk. They made a dramatic shipboard landing, some three hundred miles from shore. Then, as the crew looked on, the neatly folded flag was officially surrendered to the two firemen. Three sailors made the handoff; a fourth delivered a rendition of the Navy Hymn. Johnson, in turn, offered a fire helmet to the ranking admiral, to the applause and cheers of five thousand sailors.

The flag next festooned City Hall, where Mayor Bloomberg added his signature to the others. It was escorted to outlying police stations and firehouses. And then, quite unexpectedly, it was proved to be an utter fraud.

In August 2002, the flag was borrowed for a few days by its original owners—the yacht-charter operators Shirley Dreifus and Spiros Kopelakis. A group of firemen had organized a sailboat race to honor two of their own, Arthur Barry and Eric Olsen, who had died on September 11. They wanted to raise the flag during the pre-regatta reception—on the same yacht from which McWilliams had removed it. So Dreifus and Kopelakis put in a request to take temporary possession, and the city readily agreed.

The only problem was that the flag was the wrong flag—and it had been the wrong flag *all along*. The moment the yacht owners removed it from its flag box, to pose for a *New York Times* photographer, they had a sinking feeling. Surely, it smelled of the smoke of Ground Zero (as did all of the many flags that were displayed there). It bore the same distinguished signatures. But this one was five by eight feet, the size of a bedspread.

The flag in the photo had measured between three by five feet and four by six, tops. (The firemen, in an affidavit, even attested to that fact.) Yet when the banner was unfurled the next morning, says Dreifus, "it blocked our entire view of the captain because it was so big it draped all the way down. It was pretty obvious it didn't come from our boat." Even some of the firemen on the yacht that day, she remembers, grumbled and voiced concerns that someone, somewhere, had made a switch.

There had been similar suspicions at a spring ceremony downtown. According to Bill Kelly, when McWilliams first laid eyes on what he thought was the banner, he remarked, "Something's wrong. This isn't the same flag. It's bigger. *Much* bigger." There had even been initial whispers aboard the *Roosevelt*, Ackerman says, among several guests "in the official party accompanying the firemen [that] somewhere along the line the flag got swapped."

But Dreifus and Kopelakis, it turned out, had more than a passing interest in the size and well-being of the flag. On the six-month anniversary of the attacks, the couple had stepped forward, convinced that the flag should be donated to a museum like the Smithsonian—and mindful that its provenance would be a critical factor in determining its authenticity. They requested an acknowledgment that the flag had come from *their* yacht. (McWilliams complied.) They claimed that their motive was simple: to ensure that the relic, once recovered, be given over to a respected institution. (There had been rumors that someone had acquired it and was quietly selling swatches of it.) Soon, a British newspaper was reporting that Kopelakis, his charter business reeling after 9/11, wanted the flag back so that he could donate it—and possibly get a tax break. Other accounts dubbed the couple opportunistic "millionaires."

Nothing seems to have been further from the truth. Since they had a negative income, says Dreifus, they were in no position to benefit from a tax write-off. "People had this image of us being these greedy, money-sucking [yacht owners]," she says. In fact, despite receiving disaster financing, she claims to have lost and borrowed a small fortune trying to keep the business going. "We felt kind of obligated . . . to continue. We would've left a lot of people unemployed. Giving up wasn't an option. This was terrorism. If everybody just gave up, then they've won."

After the unsettling shipboard discovery, Kopelakis and Dreifus insisted that the city find their flag. Mayor Bloomberg, in response, set the FDNY to the task. "The mayor recognizes the flag has become an iconic image of America's resilience," said a spokesman, "and has asked the Fire Department to see if it can track the chain of custody." An internal investigation commenced. Several weeks later, Bloomberg was asked by a reporter if he had any clue where the flag was. "None whatsoever," he remarked. "I don't know where Osama bin Laden is either."

Kopelakis was watching television at the time. "My husband got totally frosted with that," Dreifus recalls. "He said, 'They can't find it, and don't really care.' " The couple filed a notice of claim, the first step toward a lawsuit, figuring it might spur a legitimate, full-fledged investigation. When the flag still hadn't surfaced in the months that followed, they decided to sue the city. They asked for $525,000, a figure based on an appraiser's estimate. An FDNY official, apparently aghast, told the *Daily News*; "They paid ten dollars for a flag, and now they want a half-million?"

To this day, after more than three years of probing, the FDNY has yet to find the flag—or even divulge the name of a suspect who might have taken it.

At first, a logical conjecture was that it was filched on the Navy's watch. Retired firefighter Roddy Von Essen remembers being called into the office of his brother Thomas, the fire commissioner, the week of September 17. The aircraft carrier *Roosevelt* was going to be redeployed to support any retaliatory mission against the Taliban and al-Qaeda, and the Navy wanted to fly the firefighters' flag from the masts of the Atlantic fleet. "They were steaming away to the region," he recalls. "This got thrown in my lap."

But there were complications. "By then the picture had been all around and the flag had become its own monster, in a way," says Roddy Von Essen. "Knowing the [firefighters], we thought: Maybe they weren't going to give [up] *that* flag." What's more, the teams on the ground had other priorities. "Some chiefs were so inundated, they really got a little annoyed with stuff like this, like when senators came by. Sheikhs wanted to have a tour. None of this mattered to our guys."

With the approval of Deputy Fire Commissioner Frank Gribbon, Von Essen says he assigned the task of regaining the flag to one of the men who worked in Gribbon's office. As a high-ranking Navy contingent cooled its heels at City Hall, this firefighter, whose full name Von Essen does not remember, called Von Essen on his Nextel from Ground Zero to say, "Okay, I'm having a problem." "He couldn't just walk up and get the flag," Von Essen explains. "Guys would've lynched him. It took some maneuvering and persuading, he was telling me." Within an hour, though, the flag was turned over to its Navy caretakers. Whether someone had "swapped it right then," says Von Essen, "or whether they'd switched it before then, I don't know. The emmissary took what he said was the flag and gave it to the Navy." The FDNY, despite my repeated requests, has been unable or unwilling to make this firefighter available for comment.

Later that week, just before a memorial service at Yankee Stadium, the flag was presented to "the governor and the mayor to sign," says Admiral Robert Natter—at the time the commander of the Atlantic fleet—

who was there that night. "My recollection is it was the one the firefighters flew." A Navy official accompanying Natter distinctly remembers the flag being "about the size of the one in the firemen's picture. It was not a large, eight-foot flag. An eight-foot flag, folded, is different in feel than a smaller flag. I even recall unfolding it . . . before we sent it out [to sea]. It was enough to hold in my arms' length. [Anything larger] would've made an impression on us."

The FDNY's Frank Gribbon has a completely different impression. "I know a flag came down," says Gribbon, "the *second* flag. There's not a trace of the original." Gribbon thinks he has narrowed down the time of its disappearance *not* to that trip to Yankee Stadium, *not* to the overseas deployment, *not* to its tour of the firehouses and police stations—but to the now-murky first seventy-two hours after the attacks.

"They take it from a yacht," says Gribbon. "They hang it on the flagpole. Franklin takes the famous picture. What we understood to be that flag, three days later, or something like that, was taken down . . . As best as I can reconstruct it, at some point between Franklin's photograph [and] several days later, when there's a buzz about the flag and it becomes somewhat iconic and captures imaginations, someone may have—I don't want to say 'switched' flags, [but] there was an *exchange* of flags. And a *larger* flag was raised. The larger flag was subsequently lowered several days later . . . Flag Number Two was the one that's removed and goes on tour [with the Navy]." (This *larger* flag actually bears the dignitaries' signatures.)

As to who made the swap, Gribbon says, "All I have is cold trails." There are no leads among members of Giuliani's inner circle either, says Sunny Mindel, speaking on behalf of the former mayor.

The three-day time frame, though, jibes with Eisengrein's memory. While working at the site on Thursday or Friday morning, he says, he looked over and saw an empty pole. "Towards the end of the week, I noticed that it wasn't flying anymore, and I just said, 'Okay, whatever' and really didn't think about it again . . . Who took it down, I have no idea. It was just gone. If there [had been] another flag in its place, it probably wouldn't have struck me. At the time it wasn't such a big deal as it seems that it grew into. We got what turned out to be now three thousand people [who died]. I know somewhere in the neighborhood, personally, of a hundred people. My focus is trying to find these people and bring them home. I'm not worried about a flag." (Had he been given the opportunity to sign the genuine flag early on, he says with a hint of resentment, his handwriting might have conferred a means of identification. "If this is such an important flag, why weren't the three of *us* asked to sign it? Like Mayor Giuliani and Governor Pataki—what did they have to do with it? And it was: kinda nothing.")

"In hindsight," Gribbon says, "it was this world-famous photo and this world-famous flag, but at the time . . . it was fucking chaos—coordinated chaos . . . bringing in heavy equipment, cranes . . . This is the old needle in a haystack. For those three days, that's not what we were thinking about. Firefighters didn't see the *New York Post* the next day. They didn't see *Newsweek* later." Firefighter James Hanlon concurs. He spent the first four days after 9/11 putting out fires near the flag-raising site. "There was no sense of preserving," he says. "It was really about trying to find anybody alive or dead then. After the third or fourth day and it started to rain and the rats came out, we knew it was a futile effort . . . Maybe it just got lost in the shuffle."

Not a chance, says a high-ranking police official at the time, speaking anonymously so as not to provoke the Fire Department. That sector, at Liberty and West Streets, he says, was highly trafficked, but hardly chaotic. "You have Port Authority, police, emergency services guys there in that spot," he insists. "A fire chief [was in charge]. There was a chain of command. For somebody to take the flag down and nobody to know it? Impossible. There was no 'dead of night'—it was so well lit. If somebody was gonna take it down, somebody'd be paying attention."

He switches to detective mode. No one outside the Fire Department, he believes, would have even had "a motive to take down the flag. Because if somebody else would take it down, they'd get their ass whipped. Cops, firemen would give that guy the beating of his life. Somebody had to authorize it. The only people who'd change it without being told would be one of the three guys who put it up—*or* there was an order to take it down to protect it for safekeeping, to memorialize it.

"It was [also] a piece of evidence of the Trade Center," he continues, arguing that unauthorized individuals "wouldn't take that piece of evidence, that history. It was probably one of the most important pieces of material down there. It was the symbol of resistance that brought us all together."

Shirley Dreifus concurs. "Ground Zero was a fairly protected area," she says, recalling how she couldn't even return to her home that week. "People were in charge of it. I don't know who [removed the flag, but] it had to be somebody who was on the site legitimately. The person had permission to take the flag down."

Bernard Kerik, the former police commissioner, has no doubts that there was an official in charge. He remembers being ordered by the mayor, early on, to impose strict rules on the Ground Zero rescue (and then recovery) effort. An incident commander—a member of the Fire Department, says Kerik—"was established going into the night of the second day. I'm positive of that. Giuliani called me and Tommy [Von Essen, the fire commissioner] and said that the protocols for the [mayor's] Office of Emergency Management need to be in place."

Gribbon insists that while an overall incident commander had not yet been appointed, the *sector* commander on day three was Peter Hayden, a man who, in Gribbon's words, was "one of the highest-ranking people who was there that day"—now chief of department of the FDNY. Hayden declines to comment directly, but Gribbon asserts that Hayden, like most fire officials, was "oblivious" to the flag: "He had life and death on his mind, the safety of his men, rescues. We had numerous of our own [lost] there too. He was not fixated on any flag nor does he recall pausing . . . to pay homage to it."

Adding to the confusion, flags began sprouting up all around Ground Zero—on fire truck ladders, on the sides of buildings, on streetlamps. In the first few days, remembers Eisengrein, "Everybody and their brother was putting an American flag somewhere." And flags recovered from the wreckage soon assumed new significance. On day three, a giant, eight-by-twelve-foot Old Glory that once soared above the main plaza of the complex was unearthed from the ruins, badly damaged, but identifiable by its "Port Authority" tag; it would grace flagpoles during the World Series, the Super Bowl, the Olympics. Another tattered flag was discovered at the Staten Island recovery site and donated to the Smithsonian. A third was lowered by police and National Guardsmen, brought to Kerik's headquarters ("It was all burnt up," he recalls, "my office smelt of the stench"), then ended up flying on the space shuttle, along with specially made shields honoring the twenty-three members of the NYPD who perished on 9/11.

So who made off with the flag? And why? And why right then?

Even in the most peaceful of times, lowering a flag is an act laden with protocol and consequence. Moreover, to lower *this* piece of cloth, on the spot where thousands died, would have required an authorization or a motive. (The three firemen had taken care to attach it securely; it didn't simply blow off the pole.) One logical explanation could be that someone hoping to cash in on it had recognized its financial possibilities once it appeared on the front page of the September 13 *New York Post*—which upped its cultural value. Perhaps an official had sought to safeguard it, and ordered it stowed away. Perhaps someone in command perceived it as too modest a flag to be seen from a distance (the massive pole, after all, had once flown a much larger banner) and deliberately replaced it with a more commanding flag—five by eight feet—to better suit the setting and the historical moment.

Flags of Our Fathers, the book about the Iwo Jima image, seems to shed some light in this regard, since the circumstances surrounding that flag so closely parallel this one:

> The Secretary of the Navy, James Forrestal, had decided . . . he wanted to go ashore and witness the final stage of the fight for [Mount Suribachi]. Gazing upward at the red, white, and blue speck, Forrestal . . . was so taken with the fervor of the moment that he decided he wanted the Suribachi flag as a souvenir. The news of this wish did not sit well with [Marine colonel] Chandler Johnson . . . "The hell with that!" the colonel spat when that message reached him. The flag belonged to the battalion, as far as Johnson was concerned. He decided to secure it as soon as possible, and dispatched his assistant operations officer, Lieutenant Ted Tuttle, to the beach to scare up a replacement flag. As an afterthought, Johnson called after Tuttle: "And make it a bigger one."

One final option: "After the third or fourth day," Hanlon observed, "it started to rain." On Friday, in fact, nearly two inches of rain fell on lower Manhattan. It is possible that someone may have removed the flag simply to protect it from the elements.

But who? And where did they stow it?

"Want to make a wager?" asks a former NYPD official. "They got to get over the statute of limitations, five years from the act. Or five years from when they leave office. Then, [the person who now has it will] come up with the flag and sell it."

And, if that happens, Shirley Dreifus will be there to judge its authenticity. "There's something on it that distinguishes it," she says cryptically, refusing to divulge whether it bears a specific tear, discoloration, quirk, or blemish. "We could identify the flag if it ever were found." (Dreifus and her husband eventually dropped their suit.)

Eisengrein, meanwhile, knows that his existence goes on as before, flag or no flag. He resides not in some idealized scene in two dimensions, but in the messy material world. "I still have to work a second job to pay my bills," he says. "I do home construction on the side, home improvements. People get a little bit star-struck when they meet you and I have to tell 'em, 'Well, listen, this is all well and good, but you notice I'm still bangin' nails.'

"'The only ones *not* makin' any money on this picture is the three of us. Everybody else involved is . . . I don't resent it. The three of us are very proud, humbled, to be in the history books. But we're still struggling like everybody else in the world to make ends meet."

Photographer Thomas Franklin describes his life, post–Flag Photo, as creatively rewarding and civically gratifying. Through one click of the shutter he affected the lives of millions of people. Yet deep down swirls a well of disappointment. Watching his image ply its way through the culture, he admits, is "kind of an out-of-body experience. I look at my picture, but it isn't mine. It's owned by *The Record*. But even *The Record* can't control it. It's in snow globes. It's on colored charcoal drawings sold on the street. I sit back and see it passing by, but I'm removed from it. I see humor in it [all]. I see sadness in it. I see absurdity.

"It got complicated because of a lot of reasons," he says. "We live in the digital age: people could rip it off. It was perceived as a positive image in the middle of one of the most negative events in American history. And the business—the selling of the picture, *The Record's* willingness to include the subjects in the picture [in determining its reuse]—was very admirable. But it made . . . the commercialization of the picture . . . complex—for better or for worse."

Someday the Flag Photo will have its own authentic statue. Sculptor Stan Watts has been working on the monument for two years, in Salt Lake City, hoping to raise the requisite $4.5 million. The firefighters, in fact, have already approved his plans: McWilliams, Johnson, and Eisengrein will be cast in bronze, standing eighteen feet tall; their flag will soar thirty feet, ascending from a twelve-foot marble pedestal. "It's colossal," says Watts, who has crafted a model in clay with an armature of styrofoam and steel. "Iwo Jima's four times life-size; mine's three times."

Nonetheless, Watts's statue—like the Brooklyn monument doomed by the protest campaign—has been mired in its own political thicket. It was recently voted down by community leaders in its original host city, Colorado Springs. Plans to erect it in Washington, D.C., or New York City never got off the ground. Then the International Association of Fire Fighters backed out of the project in late 2005.

Watts says he will build it even so, having already plowed about $150,000 of his own money into the project. He contends that a statue, unlike a photograph, feels fixed, permanent, "of this world." A statue, especially of gargantuan proportion, seems immutable, a three-dimensional *fact* of history. A photograph, in contrast, is always open to a viewer's interpretation, its meaning and context as fluid as history itself. "Photographs burn," Watts says. "In civilizations, what we have are artifacts after hundreds and thousands of years. [The flag raising] was, at one point, on the front of all the newspapers, but those won't last. *This* will endure."

Which brings to mind the statue that the firefighters visited on the six-month anniversary of the attacks—the day their stamp was unveiled at a session with President Bush in the White House.

The day began auspiciously. On their flight down to Washington, the pilot acknowledged the firefighters' presence over the intercom. Passengers erupted in applause, then gave the three men a standing ovation as they left the plane. They had breakfast with Postmaster General John Potter, and learned that the president had personally chosen the design of the stamp. At around 2:45 p.m., the group was ushered into the Oval Office, joined by Potter, Franklin, Bill Kelly, and Congressman Ackerman.

Upon meeting the president, the firemen offered him a gift—a wooden flag box with an American flag on the cover, originally a present to George Johnson from the family of the bone marrow recipient whose life Johnson had saved. The president placed it on his desk, insisting it would stay there. Then he turned to them, Kelly remembers, "and the president said, 'You can tell the people back in New York we're going after these bastards and we're kicking their ass.' We're all laughing; the president said 'ass'—and '*kicking* ass' too." (Ackerman recalls Bush taking a card from his desk with a presidential seal and signing it for the lawmaker: "To Stamp Dude.")*

Before heading back to New York that day, McWilliams, Johnson, and Eisengrein made a point of stopping by the Marine Corps War Memorial in Arlington, Virginia, at dusk. There, they stood in silence and beheld the statue of six men, cast in bronze and four stories tall, frozen in the positions they had assumed a half century before. In their grasp was a sixty-foot flagpole. The firemen read the inscription: "Uncommon Valor was a Common Virtue."

"The sun was going down," Kelly remembers. "The statue was jet black against the sky. It was almost surreal. Just the four of us." A tourist with a camera, standing nearby, recognized them and walked over, remarking, "Say, you're the three firefighters . . . How about a picture?"

*At a short press event, the president told the firefighters: "I appreciate you all allowing the Postal Service to use you as a way to help our nation remember the terrible incident that took place six months ago." Bush's remarks were reminiscent of those made by a previous postmaster general upon introducing the Iwo Jima stamp: "In the glorious tradition of the Marine Corps, [these men] submerged their identities, giving themselves wholly to the United States of America." (As James Bradley, the son of the medic in the center of the shot, would later write, "I can only imagine the thoughts that must have coursed through my father's mind . . . listening to the news that his identity would never again be his own: that it would remain, in some irretrievable way, the property of the nation. He would not be able to leave the image. The image would not leave him. He was a figure in The Photograph.")

With a sense of the day's magic still in the air, the three men agreed to pose: three mortals having stepped out of an icon, gathering in front of an icon. "Somewhere in this country," jokes Bill Kelly, "there's a tourist with shots of the firefighters standing and smiling in front of the soldiers."

At sundown on Monday, September 17, Rosh Hashanah began. Approaching the Jewish New Year, many felt buffeted spiritually. They were burdened with the weight of bereavement, the call of obligation to assist and comfort others, the yearning for answers as to why so many had to suffer and die. For the first time ever, my family attended services at our local synagogue, and the resonance of the losses murmured in prayer after prayer.

Later, back at home, I picked up the prayer book I keep at my bedside and read the words of the Mourners' Kaddish, the Hebrew prayer for the dead. But how to say Kaddish for three thousand?

I stared at the framed photo beside the prayer book. It showed my sister, Janet, brown eyes twinkling, her young life gone in a single stroke, in a car crash, in 1997. Yet I felt through the photograph that her absence was somehow a presence, and that she must be busy. This nurse, who used to work on a children's bone marrow ward in Seattle, would have been swamped that week. Watching her smile on the nightstand, I thought: Janet must be ministering and offering guidance and compassion, now that heaven was packed.

By now, we know the cold statistics. It was the bloodiest day in U.S. history. It was the result of a stunning assault that claimed thousands of lives. It came on a clear September morning, when men and women wept openly, when a nation felt rent in two. And much of it was captured on film, relentlessly, by intrepid chroniclers with cameras.

I am referring, in fact, to September 17, 1862, the date of the Civil War's battle of Antietam, a battle that for 139 years had marked America's deadliest twenty-four hours. The one-day toll: four to five thousand fatalities and some 24,000 casualties among Union and Confederacy ranks. The photographers who descended upon the scene to record the carnage, Alexander Gardner and James Gibson, were working under the auspices of Mathew Brady, President Lincoln's portraitist. The men carted their darkroom in a horse-drawn carriage, etching images of slaughter on glass-plate negatives. Their pictures were curiously bucolic: next to farmhouses and alongside rural fences, soldier after fallen soldier appeared to grace fields like stoic boulders. The photographs of Antietam, made a generation after the medium's invention, were the first to show American war dead.

When the photos were displayed in the window of Brady's New York gallery in the fall of 1862, pedestrians "pressed up against the windows . . . to stare," according to historian Martha Sandweiss. "The pictures were as alluring as they were repellent." Oliver Wendell Holmes, Jr., would remark upon seeing the photographs: "It is so nearly like visiting the battlefield to look over these views that all the emotions excited by the actual sight of the stained and sordid scene . . . come back to us, and we buried them in the recesses of our cabinet as we would have buried the mutilated remains of the dead they too vividly represented." Indeed, the images still startle the eye and marrow a century and a half later.

Until recently, an American asked to single out the day that claimed the heaviest U.S. battle toll, might have thought of Antietam. Or he might have answered: Pearl Harbor, where 2,400 U.S. servicemen perished on December 7, 1941; or D-Day, which, according to the United Kingdom's D-Day Museum, resulted in 2,500 Allied deaths on June 6, 1944—1,465 of them American—and 10,000 total assault-force casualties. (Germany's D-Day toll is "estimated as being between 4,000 and 9,000 men.")

Such a response may be attributable, in part, to the power of imagery itself. Classic photographs of war have become ingrained in the national psyche, reinforcing the horrific impact of combat in an almost tactile way. At Pearl Harbor, some Navy cameramen responded to Japanese bombers by brandishing lenses instead of guns. Their images, later splashed across spreads of *Life* magazine, gave terror a face: a riot of black cloud engulfing the USS *Shaw*; the battleship *Arizona* a fireball on the horizon as sailors and planes stand paralyzed at a nearby Naval Air station. On D-Day, in the teeth of the German barrage, photojournalist Robert Capa managed to squeeze off four rolls of film, eleven frames of which survived. His depiction of a half-submerged private rushing ashore that morning at Omaha Beach came to symbolize the hellish blur of battle.

But now we are faced with a new day, one that defies all sense and proportion. The horror of the incidents of September 11 transcends their body count. The assaults were so diabolic that we seem to need proof, irrefutable evidence, to convince ourselves that the unthinkable—the destruction of the World Trade towers and the Pentagon, along with hundreds and hundreds of lives within them—could have actually happened. Not at distant Antietam but on a rather recent September morning.

Yes, we have sage voices to listen to—those of the reporter, the poet, the historian, the counselor, the cleric. We have been heartened, surely, by the generosity, sacrifice, and heroism of thousands. And yet at this pivotal juncture in history we have been forced to rely again on pictures. In some nagging hollow of the soul, we have taken a small measure of comfort in knowing that there were thousands among us who had the poise and wherewithal to pick up cameras so that the world might witness and respond.

It is a questionable assumption, surely, that any picture really mattered over those seven days. Not given how many men and women departed this life that Tuesday. But it is chiefly in their memory, and in the name of memory itself, that photography cast its long shadow over that longest of weeks.

NOTES

The sources for *Watching the World Change* follow here. Unless otherwise noted, all quotations in the book that appear in the present tense come from author interviews or correspondence with the subjects between 2002 and 2006.

Lengthier text excerpts and song lyrics are cited in the permissions acknowledgments on page 437.

INTRODUCTION

ix **At 8:46 a.m. on September 11:** *The 9/11 Commission Report: Final Report of the National Commission on Terrorist Attacks upon the United States* (New York: W. W. Norton, 2004), p. 7.

ix **There was the man who videotaped through the window:** *In Memoriam: New York City, 9/11/01*, Brad Grey Pictures and HBO, Brad Grey, Jonathan Liebman, Sheila Nevins, et al., prods., 2002.

ix **Bucky Turco, an arts editor and gallery owner:** Correspondence with Evan "Bucky" Turco; George Rush and Joanna Molloy, "Rush & Molloy," New York *Daily News*, March 7, 2002; posting by Turco on *Gothamist.com* Web site, July 29, 2005.

ix **Computer programmer Mike Cunga:** *7 Days in September*, CameraPlanet Pictures, Steven Rosenbaum, dir., Steve Carlis and Steven Rosenbaum, exec. prods., Arts & Entertainment, September 4, 2003.

x **Photojournalist Carolina Salguero:** Interviews with Salguero.

x **Jenny Merot Mannerheim, a graphic designer:** Interview with Mannerheim.

x **TV producer Mark Obenhaus:** Interview with Obenhaus, and ABC News videotape, September 14, 2001.

x **Journalist Jacques Menasche:** Interviews and correspondence with Menasche.

x **"one young woman, face puffed":** Jacques Menasche, untitled essay in *Eleven: Witnessing the World Trade Center 1974–2001*, Robert Pledge, ed. (New York: Universe, 2002), p. 24.

x **claiming 2,749 victims:** Official toll confirmed by Dr. Robert Shaler, the Office of the Medical Examiner, New York City, 2005.

x **taking 184 lives:** Timothy Dwyer, "Something Personal in Stainless Steel: Prototype Made of Benches to Honor 9/11 Victims," *The Washington Post*, March 8, 2005, p. B1.

x **killing 40:** Tom Gibb and James O'Toole, "Ceremony Lauds Spirit of Flight 93 Passengers," The *Pittsburgh Post-Gazette*, September 12, 2002 (www.post-gazette.com); Samantha Levine, "One Year After: Shanksville, Pa," *U.S. News & World Report*, September 2002.

x **Amid the horror, New Yorkers:** David Friend, "Two Towers, One Year Later," *Vanity Fair*, September 2002, p. 327; estimate by photo-agency chief Eliane Laffont and Vin Alabiso, executive photo editor of the Associated Press in 2001.

xi **"My very senses . . . reject their own evidence":** Edgar Allan Poe, "The Black Cat," *Edgar Allan Poe's Tales of Mystery and Madness* (New York: Atheneum, 2004), p. 1.

xi **Simultaneous attacks on U.S. and French military compounds:** "Significant Terrorist Incidents, 1961–2003: A Brief Chronology," Office of the Historian, Bureau of Public Affairs, U.S. Department of State, March 2004 (www.state.gov).

xi **killed 224:** Michael Grunwald and Vernon Loeb, "Charges Filed Against Bin Laden," *The Washington Post*, November 5, 1998, p. A17. While many sources estimate that 224 died in the 1998 African embassy bombings, two different State Department sources place the toll at 257 and 301, respectively. ("U.S. Embassy Bombings," U.S. Department of State Bureau of International Information Programs, *UsInfo.State.Gov*, 2005; "Significant Terrorist Incidents, 1961–2003: A Brief Chronology," Office of the Historian, Bureau of Public Affairs, U.S. Department of State, March 2004 [www.state.gov].)

xii **The "when" . . . a span of 102 minutes:** Jim Dwyer and Kevin Flynn, *102 Minutes: The Untold Story of the Fight to Survive Inside the Twin Towers* (New York: Times Books, 2005), p. xxi.

xiii **I helped edit the magazine's special edition:** "One Week in September," *Vanity Fair*, Special Edition, November 2001.

xiii **The CBS television documentary:** *9/11*, Goldfish Pictures and Silverstar Productions in association with Reveille, Jules Naudet, Gedeon Naudet; James Hanlon, dirs.; Jules Naudet, Gedeon Naudet, James Hanlon, Susan Zirinsky, Graydon Carter, David Friend, prods., CBS, March 2002.

xiii **Which aired in more than 140 countries:** Estimates by Mark Koops and Ben Silverman, Reveille.

xiv **In New York City, more than five hundred:** Interview with Fashion Week spokesperson Zach Eichman.

xiv **Fifteen photojournalists from Magnum:** Interview with Nathan Benn, then New York chief, Magnum Photos.

xiv **Some sixty photographers flocked:** Interview with MTV spokesperson. In fact, the prize bestowed upon each winner was a Moon Man statuette—based on the 1969 photo of astronaut Buzz Aldrin standing next to Old Glory on the lunar surface.

xiv **In and around Washington, D.C. . . . a curious streak:** "Trenton: Russian Rocket Vaporizes," *The New York Times*, September 7, 2001.

xiv **At a science conference, astronomers announced:** James Glanz, "Evidence Points to Black Hole at Center of the Milky Way," *The New York Times*, September 6, 2001.

xiv **And the administration . . . held its first-ever:** Richard A. Clarke, *Against All Enemies: Inside America's War on Terror* (New York: Free Press, 2004), pp. 237–38.

xv ***Popular Mechanics* touted VideoRay:** "TechWatch: Deep-Diving Robots," *Popular Mechanics*, September 2001, p. 22.

xv ***Wired* plugged the Casio:** Dave Schiff, "Dick Tracy's Photo Album," *Wired*, September 2001, p. 166.

xv **cover girl Carolyn Murphy:** Katherine Stroup, "Newsmakers: A Model Replacement," *Newsweek*, September 17, 2001.

xv **The week before September 11 began with the death:** Lawrence Van Gelder, "Pauline Kael, Provocative and Wildly Influential *New Yorker* Film Critic, Dies at 82," *The New York Times*, September 4, 2001.

xv **And as the week ended, the Afghan opposition leader:** Barry Bearak and James Risen, "Reports Disagree on Fate of Anti-Taliban Rebel Chief," *The New York Times*, September 11, 2001.

xvii **I recalled a 1963 shot by a photographer:** "Headlines: November 22, 1963," from Carl Mydans, *Carl Mydans: Photojournalist*, Philip B. Kunhardt, Jr., ed. (New York: Abrams, 1985), p. 187.

1. TUESDAY, SEPTEMBER 11

3 **French filmmaker Jules Naudet:** *9/11*, Goldfish Pictures and Silverstar Productions in association with Reveille, Jules Naudet, Gedeon Naudet; James Hanlon, dir.; Jules Naudet, Gedeon Naudet, James Hanlon, Susan Zirinsky, Graydon Carter, David Friend, prods., CBS, March 2002.

3 **At the same instant, across the East River:** James Glanz, "A Rare View of Sept. 11, Overlooked," *The New York Times*, September 7, 2003, p. 1.

3 **Also fixed on the twin towers:** Interview with Wolfgang Staehle; "2001," an exhibition of new works by Wolfgang Staehle, Postmasters Gallery, New York, N.Y., September 6–October 6, 2001.

4 **Moments later, artist Lawrence Heller:** Interview with Heller; *In Memoriam: New York City, 9/11/01*, Brad Grey Pictures and HBO, Brad Grey, Jonathan Liebman, Sheila Nevins, et al., prod., 2002.

5 **Patricia McDonough was jolted from sleep:** Interviews with McDonough.

6 **Her photos . . . would later run in *Esquire*:** Photograph by Patricia McDonough in "War Comes to America," *Esquire*, November 2001, pp. 106–107.

6 **Jonathan Torgovnik noticed that his hands:** Interview with Torgovnik.

7 **At one point he turned his camera vertically:** David Friend, "Two Towers, One Year Later," *Vanity Fair*, September 2002, p. 333.

7 **Dave Brondolo was a printing plant account manager:** Interviews and correspondence with Brondolo.

8 **Rockville Centre . . . lost thirty-eight people:** "Two Towers, One Year Later," p. 332.

8 **Also inside the church . . . was Evan Fairbanks:** Interviews with Fairbanks.

8 **Anglican Archbishop of Wales:** "Rowan Williams Confirmed As New Archbishop of Canterbury," *Guardian Unlimited*, July 23, 2002 (www.guardian.co.uk).

9 **"His videotape [recorded] 25 stunning, silent minutes":** Sarah Boxer, "Catching the World in the Act of Changing," *The New York Times*, November 22, 2001.

11 **Grant Peterson was in a quiet photo studio:** Interview with Peterson.

11 **The gash conferred proportion:** Eric Darton writes in *Divided We Stand*, his 1999 history of the twin towers: "With the World Trade Center, the skyscraper mutated. [Its] scale and form had exploded the structure beyond any relationship to its surroundings. Its proportions simply gave people nothing in which they could recognize a human referent." (Eric Darton, *Divided We Stand: A Biography of New York's World Trade Center* [New York: Basic Books, 1999], p. 129.)

12 **His work would be displayed:** *American Photo*'s Russell Hart would review the exhibition, calling Peterson's prints "epic landscapes that offer an astonishing level of detail—one we haven't seen in any other pictures of that black day. (As you study them more closely, you can see tiny human observers gathering . . . on the intervening rooftops.) They have a postmodern neutrality that, combined with their size, recreates their subject more powerfully even than the day's remarkable photojournalism, which seems melodramatic by comparison." (Russell Hart, "Technology & Vision," *American Photo*, March/April 2003, p. 73.)

12 **like the one in 1993 that had killed six:** "Significant Terrorist incidents," U.S. Department of State, 2004.

12 **at 9:03:** *The 9/11 Commission Report: Final Report of the National Commission on Terrorist Attacks upon the United States* (New York: W. W. Norton, 2004), p. 8.

12 **HBO would later show footage:** *In Memoriam.*

13 **Steve Ludlum, whose photo of the two towers:** *The New York Times*, September 12, 2001, p. A1.

13 **The power of Ludlum's image, says John Loengard:** Interview with Loengard.

13 **Bond analyst Will Nuñez:** *here is new york: a democracy of photographs*, Alice Rose George, Gilles Peress, Michael Shulan, Charles Traub, eds. (New York/Zurich: Scalo, 2002), p. 187; interview with Nuñez.

13 **Many people put off having their film processed:** "New pictures kept emerging," says Gary Fong, director of editorial graphics and technology at the *San Francisco Chronicle*. "Every day for a week it was like it was happening over again, tragically. Like we were covering the story anew. All the amateurs coming out with photos, shots from across the river, and from different angles, and the [news]wires would then carry them. You saw the explosion again. Then you had to re-experience it again." (Interview with Fong.)

14 **Rob Howard was at the window:** Interviews and correspondence with Howard.

14 **"The only way I could sort of reconcile":** The Newseum with Cathy Trost and Alicia C. Shepard, *Running Toward Danger: Stories Behind the Breaking News of 9/11* (Lanham, Md.: Rowman & Littlefield, 2002), p. 249.

14 **Fifty-six minutes . . . twenty-nine minutes:** *The 9/11 Commission Report*, p. 285.

14 **"To have them crumble [was] like ripping your heart out":** Steve McCurry, Susan Meiselas, et al., *New York September 11 by Magnum Photographers* (New York: powerHouse, 2001), p. 10.

14 **"the world was coming unglued":** Ingrid Sischy, "Triumph of the Still," *Vanity Fair*, December 2001, p. 193.

14 **Photo researcher Adam Woodward:** Interview with Woodward.

15 **Suzanne Plunkett was immovable:** *Newsweek* Extra Edition, September 13, 2001, pp. 10–11; *Time* Special Edition, September 13, 2001, pp. 6–7.

15 **Magnum's Susan Meiselas, who planted herself:** *New York September 11*, pp. 24–25.

15 **Kelly Price, a freelance photo editor:** Interviews with Price.

15 **Frank Hurley's haunting shots:** *South with Endurance: Shackleton's Antarctic Expedition 1914–1917: The Photographs of Frank Hurley* (New York: Simon & Schuster, 2001).

15 **W. Eugene Smith's 1945 image:** "Battle of Iwo Jima, 1945," from *W. Eugene Smith* (Paris: Centre National de la Photographie, 1986), p. 17.

15 **That man . . . then a senior writer for *TheStreet.com*:** George Mannes, "Code of Silence: The Unspeakable Horror," *TheStreet.com*, posted September 11, 2001, 10:12 p.m. EDT (www.TheStreet.com).

16 **At 8:47 . . . one of the Web site's message boards:** "*TheStreet.com*'s 9/11 Coverage: RealMoney Columnist Conversation—First Post on the attack at 8:47," *The Street.com*, September 11, 2001 (www.TheStreet.com).

16 **The fall of the towers would . . . take the life:** "Coming Back: *TheStreet.com*'s 9/11 Coverage," *TheStreet.com* (www.TheStreet.com); *Portraits 9/11/01: The Collected "Portraits of Grief" from* The New York Times (New York: Times Books, 2002) p. 331.

16 **As the sprinting figure in Price's picture:** To Kelly Price, Mannes has since become a metaphor—"in one breath histrionic [and] prophetic"—for what happened to the press immediately *after* the towers fell. "The Bush administration has used that day," she contends, "to take away so many of our liberties through the PATRIOT Act and through any number of obstacles placed upon our freedom of the press and freedom of speech. This photo is iconic—a reporter with a portable camera—being chased by a cloud, that ominous shadow representing the pressures that now dog the heels of journalists." (Interview with Price.)

16 **"If your pictures aren't good enough, you're not":** Richard Whelan, *Robert Capa: A Biography* (Lincoln: University of Nebraska Press, 1994), p. 211. In many other sources, Capa's dictum is recounted in slightly altered form: "If your pictures aren't good enough, you aren't close enough" (William Manchester, *In Our Time: The World As Seen by Magnum Photographers*, [New York: W. W. Norton, 1989], p. 424).

16 **"the world caved in":** Don Halasy, "The Earth Fell on Top of Me: Post Photog Tells of His Near-Death," *New York Post*, September 12, 2001, p. 17.

16 **"getting hit in the back by a wave":** Susan Markisz, "Seeing the Horror," *The Digital Journalist*, October 2001 (www.digitaljournalist.org).

16 **"Before September 11, all I did":** "How 9/11 Changed Us," *New York*, September 15, 2003, pp. 34–35.

17 **"It continues to be a long haul":** Handschuh admits that even today he is "battling chronic pain, breathing difficulties, and emotional issues left over from Septem-

ber 11." But he has turned his ordeal into something of a call to action. Two years *before* the attacks, he had covered the aftermath of Colorado's Columbine High School massacre, and decided to participate in a pilot program set up by the Dart Center for Journalism and Trauma, attending a seminar designed to provide journalists who cover conflict with ways to cope with the psychological impact of the violence they have witnessed. "I'd been to thousands of homicides," he now says, "and nobody opened up. Journalists were keeping stuff in. Photographers rarely discussed feeling guilty for sticking their cameras in people's faces. But with Columbine, it was like the sun and moon and stars lined up. Journalists started talking with each other about their emotions. It opened the floodgates.

"I remember seeing a photographer covering one of the [Columbine] memorials. He started crying inconsolably. He was deeply religious, had two smaller kids, and was just broken down. I said to him, 'Man, you need to get yourself together *now* to take pictures, but when you get home you've got to talk to someone.' " Soon thereafter, Handschuh, by then the president of the National Press Photographers Association, became instrumental in establishing stress and trauma counseling programs for colleagues, not fully realizing how such assistance would become vital to his own career and recovery. (Interviews and correspondence with Handschuh; Jimmie Briggs, "Trauma and Photojournalism: What Have We Learned?," *Photo District News*, December 2001, pp. 30–36.)

17 **Pettit told Handschuh that he had "unbelievable footage":** "Seeing the Horror."

17 **He was last seen by a fellow officer:** *Portraits 9/11/01*, p. 391.

17 **"He was Type A-plus-plus":** Interview with Wendy Doremus.

18 **"He's going to get killed":** Interview with Bolivar Arellano and from *Running Toward Danger*, p. 67.

20 **"One thing he always taught me":** Jerry Adler, "Shooting to the End," *Newsweek*, October 15, 2001, p. 74.

20 **The Smithsonian Institution would contact:** Interviews with Wendy Doremus and the Smithsonian's Michele Delaney.

20 **"I think it was the most photographed event":** Interviews and correspondence with Michael Shulan.

21 **There was the woman with a Canon around her neck:** Interviews with Cynthia Colwell.

21 **Patrick Witty, standing at Park Row:** Interview with Witty.

22 **"After emerging from the cloud":** Patrick Witty, "New York, September 2001," *Double Take*, Special Edition 2001, p. 115.

22 **Using a metal chair as a makeshift stretcher:** Whether by fate or by chance, the affiliations of the men gave the frame an added layer of nuance. In a fortuitous confluence, four actually wear uniforms that represent three of the key "first response" agencies that day: two firemen, one police officer, and one member of the Office of Emergency Management.

22 **A victim . . . listed . . . as Victim No. 00001:** Dan Barry, "At Morgue, Ceaselessly Sifting 9/11 Traces," *The New York Times*, July 14, 2002, p. 25.

22 **Father Judge had been blessing the deceased:** Interview with filmmaker Jules Naudet; Jennifer Senior, "The Fireman's Friar," *New York*, November 12, 2001, p. 74.

23 **With the towers belching white smoke:** Correspondence with Isabel Daser Bessler.

23 **Artist Michelle Chojecki:** Interview with Michelle Chojecki.

23 **In the moments after both towers had fallen:** Interview with photographer Alex Webb; Paul Maliszewski, "Brooklyn Rooftop, 9/11," *Smithsonian*, September 2003, p. 21.

24 **"What does the future hold?":** In writing about Webb's photograph a year after September 11, photographer and art historian Max Kozloff would observe: "[T]he mother and the baby . . . glow with a radiance enhanced because cataclysm happens in the background. Not for a moment do we overlook the distinction between what is crucial and what is incidental . . . No other medium but photography, as it holds both life and death in one view, can make this transformed state a visible object of reflection. What, more than anything else, was the 9/11 attack, if not a strike against innocent civilians? Well, here are the civilians, smiling for the camera." (Max Kozloff, "Terror and Photography," *Parnassus: Poetry in Review*, 2002, Vol. 26, Issue 2.)

24 **For months, he had been engaged in a photo documentation project:** Interviews with Jerry Spagnoli.

24 **using a photographic tool introduced in 1839:** Sarah Greenough, Joel Snyder, David Travis, and Colin Westerbeck, *On the Art of Fixing a Shadow: One Hundred Fifty Years of Photography* (Washington, D.C.: National Gallery of Art/Art Institute of Chicago, 1989), p. 10.

25 **"The events of September 11 were shaped":** Barbie Zelizer, "Photography, Journalism, and Trauma," from *Journalism after September 11*, Barbie Zelizer and Stuart Allan, eds. (London: Routledge, 2002), p. 50.

25 **"We couldn't take our eyes off the buildings":** Interviews and correspondence with George Kindel. "We congregated around the television set at school," says Deborah Minchin, a history and government teacher at New Rochelle (New York) High School. "I could see the replays of the second plane going in. I could see the smoke when the tower fell. I could read the words on the screen—'The first tower has collapsed'—but my mind still couldn't grasp it. The tower had *collapsed*? What did that mean?" (Interview with Deborah Minchin.)

25 **The initial televised footage of the attacks:** Interviews with sources at CNN, FOX News, and the Newseum.

25 **"He went off the air":** Interview with Joe Farrington.

26 **Cable News Network, in turn:** Interviews with Karen Curry, CNN, and Alicia C. Shepard, the Newseum.

26 **At exactly 8:49:36:** Interview with Lucy Erickson, CNN, while she reviewed archival 9/11 footage.

26 **"You are looking at obviously":** *Running Toward Danger*, p. 20.

26 **That footage was seen "broadly, nationally, first on CNN":** Interview with Karen Curry.

26 **CNN executives . . . wall to wall":** Interview with Carolyn Disbrow.

26 **According to Steve Pair . . . each of the city's stations:** Interview with Pair.

27 **CBS had a fixed camera:** Interviews with various CBS sources.

27 **Due to the location of the transmitters . . . six TV engineers:** *Running Toward Danger*, p. 25; *Portraits 9/11/01*, pp. 101, 128, 234, 422, 477.

27 **"I have never been in a control room":** Megan Larson, "Hard News Views," *Multimedia News*, September 18, 2001.

27 **"For the first forty-five minutes to an hour":** Interview with John Frazee.

28 **Ashleigh Banfield, of MSNBC:** David Bauder for the Associated Press, "Chaotic Scene Unfolds on National Television," *SFGate.com*, September 11, 2001 (www.sfgate.com).

28 **"I took off my high heels and ran":** Ibid.

28 **"I felt him cover me":** *Running Toward Danger*, p. 119.

28 **"It looked like a normal plane":** Mark K. Miller, "Three Hours That Shook America: A Chronology of Chaos," *Broadcasting & Cable*, August 26, 2002, p. 1.

28 **ABC went to . . . John Miller:** Transcript of ABC News Special Report/Newscast, September 11, 2001.

28n **"best-known suspect is Osama bin Laden":** NBC News videotape, September 11, 2001.

28n **"this is the work of Osama bin Laden":** CBS News videotape, September 11, 2001.

29 **Joseph McCarthy, a freelance videographer:** Interview with McCarthy.

29 **Joe Scurto often responds to fires:** Interview with Scurto.

30 **Tom Flynn and his wife:** Interviews with Flynn and personal writings, used with his permission.

31 **The first international station credited with having broadcast:** Interviews with CBS sources.

31 **"*This* is your story":** Interview with Amy Wall.

32 **In America alone . . . 80 million prime-time households:** "Selected News Events: Multi-Network Combined Audiences, 1969–2005," Nielsen Media Research.

32n **By comparison, 85.6 million tuned in:** Correspondence with Karen Gyimesi, vice president, communications, Nielsen Media Research.

32 **"Petty competition vanished":** *Running Toward Danger*, p. x.

32 **ABC piped . . . CBS . . . NBC:** Interviews with network public affairs representatives; Eric Deggans, "On TV, Mayhem Unfolded in Waves," *St. Petersburg Times*, September 12, 2001 (www.stpetersburgtimes.com).

32 **CNN's domestic coverage:** Interviews with CNN spokespeople.

32 **In all, more than two billion people:** Interview with David Hazinski.

33 **"The 1998 World Cup":** Interview with David Hazinski.

33n **When men first landed on the Moon:** "Selected News Events."

33n **The Super Bowl has been known to draw:** Ibid.

33 **In a world peopled by . . . one and a half billion television sets:** *The World Fact Book*, Central Intelligence Agency, 2003. Other estimates, depending on the sources, range from one to two billion TV sets, worldwide.

33 **Carl Bialik . . . refutes past claims that 2.5 billion watched:** Carl Bialik, "When It Comes to TV Stats, Viewer Discretion Is Advised," *The Wall Street Journal Online*, July 21, 2005 (www.wsj.com/NumbersGuy).

33 **It is certainly safe to assert, however, that "hundreds of millions":** Interviews with Nigel Pritchard.

34 **"It's probably the only period in a day":** Interviews with Robert Pledge.

35 **The "cool medium":** Marshall McLuhan, *Understanding Media: The Extensions of Man*, W. Terrence Gordon, ed. (Corte Madera, Calif.: Gingko Press, 2003), p. 39.

35 **The event, like the viewer, had been petrified:** This stasis was also a consequence

of the penchant, in many TV newsrooms, for live content, often at the expense of recap and context. On September 11, University of Georgia associate professor David Hazinski was watching both the on-air coverage and the back-channel satellite feeds being pulled in by his local CNN and CBS affiliates. In his estimation, "the networks appeared so fixated on 'live' [that they resisted] go[ing] back to videotape, even though it was literally walking in the door from a couple of blocks away, [and] even though [the tape sometimes] told a better story, which is a strange sort of irony. As a result, the majority of the coverage ended up as talking heads and tower-cams. There was some *great* footage that ended up being sent to affiliates that didn't get on actual air that day." (Interview and correspondence with Hazinski.)

36 **"If you didn't know better . . . you'd say":** Terry Jackson, *The Day That Changed America* Special Issue on 9/11, *American Media*, 2001, p. 72.

36 **"The way she ordered was very specific":** Interviews with Geraldine Davie.

36 **As they went about their rounds, Edward Ornelas:** Photograph by Edward Ornelas, *San Antonio Express-News*, September 12, 2001, via the Associated Press.

38 **The very first poster . . . was dashed off by the daughter:** Marshall Sella, "Missing: How a Grief Ritual Is Born," *The New York Times Magazine*, October 7, 2001, p. 49.

39 **They would dominate kiosk-style signboards:** Author observation; "One Week in September," *Vanity Fair* Special Edition, November 2001, pp. 38–39.

39 **"Please Find My Daddy!":** Descriptions of, or quotations from, "missing" posters come from examining press photographs of signs.

40 **Cell-phone networks were overloaded:** Henry Porter, "The Cell-Phone War," *Vanity Fair*, December 2001, p. 218.

40 **New York City's 911 lines couldn't handle the call volume:** *The 9/11 Commission Report*, pp. 286–87.

40 **"Amidst the horror":** Interview with Stephen Claypole.

40 **"Americans understand the divine":** Personal writings of Paul Elie, used with his permission.

42 **"like desperate ivy":** Amy Waldman, "Posters of the Missing Now Speak of Losses," *The New York Times*, September 29, 2001, p. 9.

42 **"For the first week, there were still nagging doubts":** Interview and correspondence with Don Johnston.

42 **"words of hope and desperation":** Personal writings of Steve Simon, used with his permission.

42 **Ambreen Qureshi took Polaroids:** Interviews with Ambreen Qureshi and Giorgio Baravalle.

44 **"I'd seen that stance before, that posturing with pictures":** Interview with Larry Towell.

44 **"We had no doubt":** Interview with Patty Lampert.

44 **Bobby Baierwalter was a forty-four-year-old father:** "Robert J. Baierwalter: A Man Who Took His Time," in "Portraits of Grief," *The New York Times*, June 16, 2002.

46 **"For this was how the language of grief":** "Missing," p. 50.

46 **"Our insides are now outside":** Remarks at a memorial tribute to the artist Gretchen Bender, The Kitchen, New York, N.Y. January 15, 2005.

47 **But on Friday, the skies opened:** "Actual vs. Average Precipitation Listings, New

York City," The Weather Underground, September 2001 (www.weather underground.com).

47 **Curator Louis Nevaer:** Glenn Collins, "Cataloging the 9/11 Archive," *The New York Times*, May 30, 2006, p. B6.

47 **"In Union Square . . . park workers":** "Missing," p. 51.

47 **"offered some small degree of immortality":** Malcolm Daniel in endnotes for Maria Morris Hambourg, Pierre Apraxine, Malcolm Daniel, Jeff L. Rosenheim, and Virginia Heckert, *The Waking Dream: Photography's First Century* (New York: Abrams, 1993), p. 281.

49 **Hale Gurland . . . calls "the confusion of that first afternoon":** Interview with Gurland.

49 **[Gurland's] images, chiseled in deep blacks:** *Eleven: Witnessing the World Trade Center 1974–2001*, Robert Pledge, ed. (New York: Universe, 2002), pp. 81–91.

49 **"From a historical perspective, some of his pictures":** Interview with MaryAnne Golon.

49 **"We went as welders":** Interview with Ira Sapir.

50 **Sapir's high-speed color-negative:** Mary Stephens, R.N., *United We Came: A Personal Account from Ground Zero* (Orlando: Longwood, 2002).

2. WEDNESDAY, SEPTEMBER 12

51 **On Wednesday morning, Detective David Fitzpatrick:** Interviews with Fitzpatrick; The New York City Police Department, *Above Hallowed Ground: A Photographic Record of September 11, 2001* (Viking Studio, 2002).

51 **The result . . . from a perch as high as 6,500 feet:** David Friend, "Two Towers, One Year Later," *Vanity Fair*, September 2002, p. 335.

52 **"A documenter, by nature":** *Above Hallowed Ground.*

52 **In his basement in Rockville Centre:** Interviews with David Fitzpatrick and Christopher Sweet.

52 **Orbiting Earth . . . some 250 miles:** Henry S. F. Cooper, Jr., *A House in Space* (New York: Holt, Rinehart and Winston, 1976), p. 2.

52 **"I was flabbergasted, then horrified":** Frank Culbertson, Letter from Expedition Three Commander, NASA, September 12, 2001 (http://spaceflight.nasa.gov).

52 **"We were about four hundred miles away from New York":** Interview with Frank Culbertson.

54 **a NASA photo expert says:** Interview with anonymous NASA source.

55 **one of his Naval Academy classmates:** Interview with Culbertson; Todd Halvorson, "Station Commander Knew Pilot of Hijacked Plane," *Space.com*, October 17, 2001 (www.space.com); William Harwood, "240 Miles Up, Seeing Tragedy," *The Washington Post*, October 11, 2001, p. A31.

56 **"Tears . . . don't flow the same in space":** Culbertson, Letter, September 12, 2001.

56 **U.S. ATTACKED:** *The Arizona Republic* Extra Edition, September 11, 2001, p. 1; *The Flint Journal* (Michigan), September 12, 2001, p. 1; *The Free Lance-Star* (Fredericksburg, Virginia), September 12, 2001, p. 1; *The New York Times*, September 12, 2001, p. A1.

56 **DAY OF TERROR:** *News & Record* (Greensboro, North Carolina) Extra Edition, September 11, 2001, p. 1; *The Times* (Munster, Indiana), September 12, 2001, p. 1.

56 **IT'S WAR:** New York *Daily News*, September 12, 2001, p. 1.

56 **UNTHINKABLE:** *Arizona Daily Star*, September 12, 2001, p. 1; *Courier Times* (Bucks County, Pennsylvania) Special Edition, September 11, 2001, p. 1; *The Register-Guard* (Eugene, Oregon), September 12, 2001, p. 1; *The Patriot-News* (Harrisburg, Pennsylvania), September 12, 2001, p. 1; *The Salt Lake Tribune*, September 12, 2001, p. 1.

56 **HORROR!:** Los Angeles *Daily News*, September 12, 2001, p. 1.

56 **OUR WORLD IS CHANGED:** *The Gamecock* (University of South Carolina, Columbia, South Carolina), September 12, 2001, p. 1.

57 **The Associated Press . . . transmitted 1,200 frames:** Interviews with sources at the Associated Press.

57 **In one especially curious photo-op:** "After the Attacks: Reaction from Around the World," *The New York Times*, September 13, 2001, p. A17.

57 **"Came the photograph of Yasir Arafat":** Deanne Stillman, "Arafat's Blood," *Rolling Stone*, October 25, 2001.

57 **Among the more widely remembered photos:** The Poynter Institute, *September 11, 2001: A Collection of Newspaper Front Pages Selected by the Poynter Institute* (Kansas City: Andrews McMeel, 2001).

57 **"A second plane hit the second tower":** *The 9/11 Commission Report: Final Report of the National Commission on Terrorist Attacks upon the United States* (New York: W. W. Norton, 2004), p. 38.

57 **The scene was shot by five photographers:** Interview with source in White House photo office.

57 **"A portrait . . . of a president":** David Shribman, "The Presidential Viewfinder, Scripted or Not: Memorable Photos Focus Attention on Image of Leadership," *The Boston Globe*, November 7, 2001, p. C1.

58 **After receiving Card's warning, the president remained:** Scot J. Paltrow, "Day of Crisis: Detailed Picture of U.S. Actions on Sept. 11 Remains Elusive," *The Wall Street Journal*, March 22, 2004, p. A1; *Fahrenheit 9/11*, Michael Moore, dir., Miramax Film Corp., Dog Eat Dog Films, Fellowship Adventure Group, Sony Pictures, 2004.

58 **He would tell the 9/11 commission that his instinct:** *The 9/11 Commission Report*, p. 38.

58 **Video footage of the same scene:** *Fahrenheit 9/11*.

58 **Several days later . . . this one taken on board Air Force One:** Interview with source in White House press office.

58 **"While most pictures are worth a thousand words":** Maureen Dowd, "Bush's Photo Op-Portunism," *The New York Times*, May 15, 2002, p. A23.

58 **The Bush team . . . contended that the Democrats:** Elisabeth Bumiller and Don Van Natta, Jr., "On Day of Big Fund-Raiser, White House Is Attacked as 9/11 Marketer," *The New York Times*, May 15, 2002, p. A18.

59 **"We are part of that punditry in the White House":** Interview with Ari Fleischer.

59 **"Two days in which Bush blinked":** Margaret Carlson, "A President Finds His Voice," *Time*, September 24, 2001, p. 50.

59 **"His performance was not reassuring":** Bob Woodward, *Bush at War* (New York: Simon & Schuster, 2002), p. 19.

60 **The president . . . followed TV coverage:** Interview with Mark KcKinnon: photos of Bush standing near TV set on 9/11.

60 **Richard Clarke . . . chaired a crisis management meeting:** Richard A. Clarke, *Against All Enemies: Inside America's War on Terror* (New York: Free Press, 2004), pp. 2–3.

60 **On a series of wall monitors (one always tuned to CNN):** *Against All Enemies*, p. 6.

60 **The president was patched in:** Paul Thompson and the Center for Cooperative Research, *The Terror Timeline* (New York: Regan Books/HarperCollins, 2004), p. 465.

60 **As Secretary of Defense Donald Rumsfeld . . . informed Clarke that smoke:** *Against All Enemies*, pp. 8–9.

60 **The Pentagon chief decamped to an alternate location:** In Clarke's book *Against All Enemies*, he notes that as the president was flying, Vice President Dick Cheney and his wife, Lynne, among others, were ensconced in the East Wing's "bunker." There, according to Clarke, "monitors were simultaneously blaring the coverage from five networks." Clarke recalled that at one point when he left his West Wing teleconference to confer with Cheney, an aide told him privately, "I can't hear the crisis conference because Mrs. Cheney keeps turning down the volume on you so she can hear CNN." (*Against All Enemies*, p. 18.)

60 **At 8:30 p.m.:** *The 9/11 Commission Report*, p. 326.

60 **He insisted, without equivocation:** George W. Bush, "Statement by the President in His Address to the Nation," The White House, September 11, 2001 (www.whitehouse.gov).

61 **When Bush's top aides repaired to Camp David:** Photograph by Brooks Craft/Gamma in an article by Evan Thomas and Mark Hosenball, "Bush: 'We're at War,' " *Newsweek*, September 24, 2001, p. 32.

61 **"our George":** Howard Fineman, "A President Finds His True Voice," *Newsweek*, September 24, 2001, p. 50.

61 **"I can hear you":** Videotape of President Bush's visit to Ground Zero, September 14, 2001, included on Bush-Cheney '04's "The Pitch," shown at the Republican National Convention, New York City, August 29–September 2, 2004.

62 **That photograph . . . "will be the most lasting":** Interview with Mark McKinnon.

62 **"I think it was unscripted":** Interview with Ed Kosner.

62 **"There were genuine reasons for the president":** Interview with Jonathan Adashek.

62 **"People wanted to see him climbing":** Interviews with Luc Sante.

63 **In March of 2004 . . . his campaign would recycle:** Richard W. Stevenson and Jim Rutenberg, "Bush Campaigns Amid a Furor Over Ads," *The New York Times*, March 5, 2004, p. A16.

63 **The International Association of Fire Fighters requested:** Ibid.

63 **"It's as sick as people who stole things":** Maggie Haberman and Thomas M. DeFrank, "Furor Over Bush's 9/11 Ad," New York *Daily News*, March 4, 2004, p. 5.

63 **"After three thousand people were murdered":** Ibid.

63 **Breitweiser . . . would soon be making public appearances:** Matthew Mosk, "Sept. 11 Widow Joins Campaign: Families of Victims Bring Their Passion and Grief to Partisan Fray," *The Washington Post*, September 29, 2004, p. A20.

63 **But six months later, at the Republican:** Bush-Cheney '04 convention video.

64 **Message-marshal Hughes set up a media "war room":** Interviews with Mark

McKinnon, Jim Wilkinson; Christopher Buckley, "War and Destiny: The White House in Wartime," *Vanity Fair*, February 2002, p. 85; Martha Brant, "Bush's New War Room," *Newsweek*, November 12, 2001, p. 29.

64 **the *Vanity Fair* story:** "War and Destiny," pp. 78–93.

65 **An 1873 oil showing:** Interview with spokesperson in White House curator's office.

65 **What should we convey?:** Author present at photo shoot.

65 **Throughout the day . . . the office . . . received bundles:** Dan Barry, "At Morgue, Ceaselessly Sifting 9/11 Traces," *The New York Times*, July 14, 2002, p. 25.

65 **In all, 19,915 body parts:** Interviews with Dr. Robert Shaler.

65 **From this sample . . . many [no] larger than a quarter:** Confirmation by Shaler; Joseph P. Fried, "The Grim Accounting of Sept. 11 Continues," *The New York Times*, January 16, 2005, p. 29.

66 **1,592 individuals:** Eric Lipton, "At Limits of Science, 9/11 ID Effort Comes to End," *The New York Times*, April 3, 2005, p. 29.

66 **The identifications were determined:** Correspondence with forensic science expert who requests anonymity.

66 **"Traditionally . . . DNA fingerprints are made":** Interviews and correspondence with Ariel Ruiz i Altaba.

66 **Without these murky but distinctive molecular glimpses:** The double-helix DNA code, in fact, was cracked via photographic sleuth-work in 1952. To come up with the famous first image—which showed up as a hazy double-X pattern set inside a circle—molecular biologist Rosalind Franklin bombarded a genetic sample with one hundred hours of intense X-rays. The resulting frame came to be known as Photo 51. "The instant I saw the picture my mouth fell open and my pulse began to race," pioneering geneticist James Watson would write in his memoir, *The Double Helix*, describing one of the key epiphanies in the history of medical science. Watson realized in an instant that "the black cross of reflections which dominated the picture could only arise from a helical structure."

In a cruel irony, the photo may have actually killed the photographer; overexposure to X-rays quite possibly triggered the ovarian cancer that in 1958 claimed Franklin, a genetic pioneer whom biographer Brenda Maddox called "The Dark Lady of DNA." (James Watson quoted in Horace Freeland Judson, *The Eighth Day of Creation: Makers of the Revolution in Biology* [New York: Simon & Schuster, 1979], p. 159; Brenda Maddox, *Rosalind Franklin: The Dark Lady of DNA* [New York: HarperCollins, 2002]; Life: *100 Photographs That Changed the World*, Robert Sullivan, ed. [New York: Life Books, 2003], p. 166.)

67 **"We knew what we were facing":** Interviews with Shiya Ribowsky.

67 **"If reinforced concrete was rendered into dust":** "At Morgue," p. 25.

67 **"I was never so happy to see somebody":** Interviews with Dr. Robert Shaler.

68 **A camera was always on hand:** Interview with police photographer who requests anonymity, and with Shiya Ribowsky.

68 **In one dramatic instance, fire captain Brian Hickey:** Confirmation by Shaler; Michele McPhee, "Sweat of His Heroism Helps ID Lost Captain," New York *Daily News*, May 20, 2002, p. 21.

69 **"You keep praying":** "Sweat of His Heroism," p. 21.

69 **On 9/12, MaryEllen Salamone was going:** Interviews with MaryEllen Salamone.

69 **She firmly believed . . . a preferred-stock broker:** *Portraits 9/11/01: The Collected "Portraits of Grief" from* The New York Times (New York: Times Books, 2002) p. 443.

70 **"You had to stand in line forever":** Interviews with MaryEllen Salamone.

71 **"I'm wondering why [a sports program]":** Interviews and correspondence with Nikki Stern.

72 **business analyst for . . . Marsh & McLennan:** *Portraits 9/11/01*, p. 397.

72 **To limit these sorts of episodes, Salamone:** In some settings, even warning labels are superfluous. In 2006, there were howls of protest when movie theaters ran the teaser for the Paul Greengrass docudrama *United 93*, which recounts the on-board saga of the flight on which passengers rallied to foil the hijackers. Audiences, as they took their seats to see other films, were literally forced to watch a horrifying re-creation with a title card written in the disconcerting tone of a Hollywood thriller: "The Day We Faced Fear." Unsettled viewers had no time to react, short of bolting out of the theater.

Such hype, to many, was cruel and unusual. "I see this trailer," wrote Slate.com's Michael Agger, "as an unwelcome and somewhat grotesque reminder of the great *Onion* headline published after 9/11: 'American Life Turns Into Bad Jerry Bruckheimer Movie' . . . Take another look at that trailer: I don't see catharsis, I see cash registers . . . The [in-theater promotion campaign] exists on a rotten foundation. We don't know what happened on that airplane, but whatever happened, it's not entertainment."

The only appropriate and respectful way to market the film at the multiplex would have been to create a minimalist trailer, with very little imagery, or, as Agger's colleague Dahlia Lithwick would suggest on *Slate*, to demand that theater owners place a placard at the door: "The previews will contain graphic images of 9/11." (Michael Agger, Dahlia Lithwick, Megan O'Rourke, and June Thomas, "*United 93*: A Brief *Slate* Debate About the Controversial New Movie," posted April 6, 2006 [www.slate.com]).

73 **He fiddles . . . and says he wants to show me the photograph:** Interview with Mike Rambousek.

74 **In the daytime, Luke, twenty-seven:** *Portraits 9/11/01*, p. 407.

74 **Mike . . . had been a computer system engineer:** Gregg Zoroya, "Strength Runs in the Family," *USA Today*, September 10, 2002.

74 **Ota, who took part in the Prague uprising:** Letter from Otakar Rambousek to William Casey, Director of the CIA, February 3, 1981.

74 **"for his outstanding patriotism":** Official commendation in possession of Mike Rambousek, 1983.

76 **"I didn't know I had that picture":** Interview with Jeff Christensen.

76 **"He had a gold heart":** Interview with Jindra Rambousek.

77 **She had lost two sons, Keith and Scott, both of whom worked:** *Portraits 9/11/01*, pp. 94–95.

77 **Keith . . . had moved back from London:** Interviews with Jean Coleman and anonymous eSpeed source.

79 **The blues . . . "is an impulse":** Ralph Ellison, "Richard Wright's Blues," *Shadow and Act* (New York: Vintage, 1995), p. 78.

80 **On Wednesday, Michael Shulan:** Interviews with Shulan.

80 **The passage, based on Edith Hamilton's translation:** Christopher S. Morrissey, Department of Humanities, Simon Fraser University, "In Our Own Despair: Robert Kennedy, Richard Nixon, and Aeschylus' *Agamemnon*," presented at the Classical Association of Canada annual meeting, May 12, 2002.

80 **"[Even] in our sleep, pain which cannot forget":** Correspondence with Michael Shulan on verbatim passage written on the newspaper.

80 **"A momentary stay against confusion":** Robert Frost, "The Figure a Poem Makes," *Poetry and Prose*, Edward Connery Lathem and Lawrance Thompson, eds., (New York: Holt, Rinehart and Winston, 1972), p. 394.

81 **Within two weeks, the impromptu display:** *here is new york: a democracy of photographs*, Alice Rose George, Gilles Peress, Michael Shulan, Charles Traub, eds. (New York/Zurich: Scalo, 2002), p. 7.

81 **"The city, for the first time in its long history":** E. B. White, *Here Is New York* (New York: The Little Bookroom, 1999), p. 54.

83 **"Part of it was participatory":** Interview with Carol Solomon Kiefer.

83 **In 2004 at Amherst College's Mead Art Museum:** *The Pain of War*, an exhibition curated by Carol Solomon Kiefer, Mead Art Museum, Amherst College, Amherst, Massachusetts, October–December 2004.

83 **"They took it upon themselves to scan pictures":** Michael Shulan, in the introduction to *here is new york: a democracy of photographs*, p. 8.

84 **"Photography . . . was the perfect medium":** Ibid., pp. 8–9.

84 **"September 11 was, in the most elemental way":** Notes written for a presentation by emcee David Halberstam, at the International Center of Photography's eighteenth annual Infinity Awards, at The Regent Wall Street, New York, N.Y., May 16, 2002.

84 **Ever since employees first started working:** *The 9/11 Commission Report*, p. 278.

84 **107th-floor observation deck:** Eric Darton, *Divided We Stand: A Biography of New York's World Trade Center* (New York: Basic Books, 1999), p. 149.

85 **fourteen TV stations:** *Running Toward Danger*, p. 25.

85 **in a basement bank vault at Five World Trade Center:** Interview with Jacques Lowe's representative, Woodfin Camp.

85 **Lost as well were 30,000:** "Broadway Digital Directly Affected by WTC Tragedy," Broadway Theatre Archive, *Broadway.com*, September 19, 2001 (www.broadwayarchive.com).

85 **"We were the house photographers up at Windows":** Interview with Sarah Merians.

86 **At 110 stories each:** *The 9/11 Commission Report*, p. 278.

86 **ten million square feet:** Jim Dwyer and Kevin Flynn, *102 Minutes: The Untold Story of the Fight to Survive Inside the Twin Towers* (New York: Times Books, 2005), p. 104.

86 **officially dedicated in 1973:** *Divided We Stand*, p. 142.

86 **They housed 50,000 workers:** *The 9/11 Commission Report*, p. 278.

86 **They weighed 1.5 million tons:** Life: *One Nation: America Remembers September 11, 2001*, Robert Sullivan, ed. (Boston/New York: Little, Brown, 2001), p. 16.

86 **43,600 windows:** Ibid.

86 **twin zip codes:** Queena Sook Kim, "What Becomes of Mail for Zip Codes 10047, 10048?," *The Wall Street Journal*, September 17, 2001, p. A10.

87 **"They pierced the skyline in arrogant confidence":** Vaira Vike-Freiberga, "Reflec-

tions: March 7, 2003," *Rethink: Cause and Consequences of September 11*, Giorgio Baravalle, ed. (Millbrook, N.Y.: de.MO, 2003), p. 94.

87 **"KSM reasoned he could best influence U.S. policy":** *The 9/11 Commission Report*, p. 153.

87 **New York is also "the cradle":** Interviews and correspondence with George Kindel.

87 **Well-heeled diners . . . were reportedly seen "celebrating":** Elisabetta Burba, "How Lebanon Reacted to the News," *The Wall Street Journal*, September 19, 2001; Bryan Appleyard, "Why Do They Hate America?," *The* (London) *Sunday Times*, September 23, 2001.

87 **Palestinians . . . took to the streets:** Lee Hockstader, "Palestinians Suppress Coverage of Crowds Celebrating Attacks," *WashingtonPost.com*, September 16, 2001 (www.washingtonpost.com); Hugh Dellios, "Reaction in Mideast Is Mixed," *ChicagoTribune.com*, September 11, 2001 (www.chicagotribune.com).

88 **The *New York Times* columnist Nicholas Kristof:** Nicholas D. Kristof, "The Chip on China's Shoulder," *The New York Times*, January 18, 2002.

89 **"world in a grain of sand":** William Blake, "Ideas of Good and Evil: Auguries of Innocence," *Collected Poems*, W. B. Yeats, ed. (London/New York: Routledge, 2002), p. 88.

89 **"global village":** Marshall McLuhan, *Understanding Media: The Extensions of Man*, W. Terrence Gordon, ed. (Corte Madera, Calif.: Gingko Press, 2003), p. 54.

89 **"Electric speed in bringing . . . functions together"** Ibid., pp. 6–7.

90 **"We were viewing together":** Interview with Robert Pledge.

90 **"For the Global Viewing Eye":** Interview with Luc Sante.

90 **"The implications from a television standpoint":** Interview with Roger Ailes.

92 **To get breaking stories into print . . . "you either went to a news bureau":** Interview and correspondence with Mark Greenberg.

93 **Derek Hudson, shooting for *Life*:** Interview with Derek Hudson.

93 **In this era before JPEGs, the image-transmission system:** Interviews with Peter Howe and Murray Goldwasser.

93 **Nonetheless, the first image that Hudson sent:** Photograph by Derek Hudson/Sygma in story by Lisa Grunwald, *Life: In Time of War* Special Edition, "Who the Enemy Was," March 11, 1991, pp. 34–35.

On another night, in Kuwait City, Hudson, with his compatriots Patrick Durand and Jacques Langevin, used a hotel service toilet as a developing tank (running the fetid water through a coffee filter), editing the negatives on a makeshift light table (a glass table with a lamp under it), checking the "pre-scan" image on the scanner's view screen, then transmitting the pictures via a satellite dish they had set up in the hotel parking lot. Several of the pictures were published with a muddy cast, due to the dirty developing water. (Interview with Hudson.)

94 **That day, Vin Alabiso:** Interview and correspondence with Alabiso.

95 **"On 9/11 we could not have met our deadline":** Interview with Regis Le Sommier.

96 **In 1905, the physicist altered humanity's sense:** Ronald W. Clark, *Einstein: The Life and Times* (New York: Avon, 1971), pp. 101, 133–34.

97 **This paradox . . . the *Hindenburg* dirigible collided:** John Loengard, Life: *Classic Photographs, A Personal Interpretation* (Boston: Little, Brown/New York Graphic Society, 1988), p. 24.

97 **"Oh, the humanity":** "Description of Hindenburg Crash, May 6, 1937," NAVAIR Lakehurst Web site, Naval Air Engineering Station, Lakehurst, New Jersey (www.lakehurst.navy.mil).

97 **"I call it the seven ages of satelliting":** Interviews and correspondence with Stephen Claypole.

97 **"All the world's a stage":** William Shakespeare, *As You Like It* (Act II, vii), *The Complete Works of William Shakespeare*, William Aldis Wright, ed. (Garden City, New York: Doubleday, 1936), p. 677.

98 **Since TV cameramen were allowed to rove:** "The real heroes were the cameramen," says Richard Pyle, former Saigon bureau chief of the Associated Press, even though he acknowledges numerous television correspondents whose distinguished battlefield reports made it into American living rooms—among them, NBC's Howard Tuckner. "Tuckner was well known for crouching during his on-camera 'stand-upper,' " Pyle recalls, "as if he were perpetually under fire. His stance became known as 'the Tuckner crouch.' One time, he *was* under fire and signed off saying, 'If you want to know if I'm scared, I'm *damn* scared. Howard Tuckner, NBC.' After the segment got to New York, he got a message back from NBC: Congratulations, Howard, they used the 'damn.' " (Interview with Pyle.)

98 **"By seeing television images of battle":** Interview with David Hazinksi.

99 **In Somalia . . . American foreign policy changed *overnight*:** In a similar vein, NPR's Daniel Schorr, a veteran of CBS News, recalled that pivotal dawn in August of 1961 when Soviet-backed East Germany erected the Berlin Wall. By eleven p.m. that evening, CBS was able to get hurriedly shot footage, taken on 16-mm film, onto American television screens. According to Schorr, President John F. Kennedy was "supposed to have seen our report from Berlin [and remarked]: 'We're going to live in a different world when America can see on the same day what's happening in Europe. We've lost our ability to sit, and have time, and have an explanation to go with events.' " (Todd Purdum, "The Message Mongers Rule Us, but Time Rules Them," *The New York Times*, November 6, 2005.)

99 **Peter Arnett and CNN's team:** Peter Arnett, *Live from the Battlefield: From Vietnam to Baghdad, 35 Years in the World's War Zones* (New York: Simon & Schuster, 1994), p. 361.

99 **Correspondents' dramatic accounts of nearby cloudbursts:** I was *Life* magazine's news editor at the time, my TV dial a compass needle locked on CNN. I recall hustling down to managing editor Jim Gaines's office that night of the first U.S. bombardment to tell him, "The war's started," as scenes of the night sky, the hue and texture of pea soup, showed Iraqi antiaircraft tracers traversing the screen like beams in the deadliest of video games.

99 **"The rush of watching all that eerie green":** Don DeLillo, "In the Ruins of the Future: Reflections on Terror and Loss in the Shadow of September," *Harper's Magazine*, December 2001, p. 38.

100 **Within two weeks, the network had been allowed to shuttle in:** The "uplink" was brought in with some help from a partner news agency, Worldwide Television News. (Interview with Stephen Claypole.)

100 **"[F]or the first time in history":** Robert Wiener, *Live from Baghdad: Making Journalism History Behind the Lines* (New York: St. Martin's Griffin, 2002), p. 293.

100 **"CIA director William Webster received word":** William A. Henry III, "History

As It Happens: Linking Leaders As Never Before, CNN Has Changed the Way the World Does Business," *Time* (1991 "Man of the Year" Issue), January 6, 1992, p. 24.

100 **To underscore . . . *Time* bestowed the title:** *Time*, January 6, 1992, cover.

101 **"Part of the transformation . . . was digital newsgathering":** Interview with Nigel Pritchard.

101 **Camera prices had also dropped . . . "totally eliminating":** Interview with Ben Silverman.

102 **"In the ten years . . . before September 11":** Interview with John Frazee.

102 **When hijackers took an Indian airliner:** Interview with Nigel Pritchard.

103 **Al-Jazeera . . . launched in 1996:** "About Al-Jazeera," *Aljazeera.Net*, 2006 (http://english.aljazeera.net).

103 **that serves a pan-Arab audience of 40 million:** Sebastian Usher, "Change of Image For Al-Jazeera TV," *BBC News Online*, June 16, 2005 (www.bbc.co.uk).

103 **having recently mobilized an international English-language service:** Anne Becker, "Marash to Anchor Al-Jazeera," *Broadcasting & Cable*, January 12, 2006 (www.broadcastingcable.com).

103 **Its influence has grown so . . . that in 2004 it was named:** Readers' Choice Awards, Brand Rankings by Impact, 2004, in Robin D. Rusch, "Readers Pick Apple in 2004," *Brandchannel.com*, January 31, 2005 (www.brandchannel.com).

103 **"Prior to 1991":** Interviews with Nigel Pritchard.

103 **"The driving force":** Interview with Roger Ailes.

104 **"It all comes back to Shakespeare":** Interviews and correspondence with Stephen Claypole.

104 **Poised 22,300 miles above:** Eric J. Chaisson, *The Hubble Wars* (New York: HarperCollins, 1994), p. 36; various sources, including Andrew C. Revkin, "Physical Effects of Sept. 11 Scrutinized from on High," *The New York Times*, September 17, 2002, p. F3.

104 **In 2002, when CNN surveyed respondents:** Fareed Zakaria, *The Future of Freedom: Illiberal Democracy at Home and Abroad* (New York: W. W. Norton, 2004), p. 121.

105 **John Doherty, the father of her friend:** *Portraits 9/11/01*, p. 132.

105 **one of 176 employees:** Transcript of "Patrick G. Ryan's October 23, 2001, Update," Ryan (chairman and CEO of Aon), Aon Web site (www.aon.com).

105 **Tamitha Freeman:** *Portraits 9/11/01*, p. 165.

105 **Freeman suddenly had second thoughts:** *102 Minutes*, p. 77.

105 **"I have my baby's pictures in it":** Martha T. Moore and Dennis Cauchon, "Delay Meant Death on 9/11," *USA Today*, September 3, 2002.

3. THURSDAY, SEPTEMBER 13

106 **On Thursday, U.S. agencies finalized their roster:** Press release listing "individuals who have been identified as hijackers aboard the four airliners that crashed on September 11, 2001," U.S. Department of Justice, Federal Bureau of Investigation, September 14, 2001 (www.fbi.gov).

106 **Working off passenger manifests . . . eighteen "probable":** CNN account cited in Paul Thompson and the Center for Cooperative Research, *The Terror Timeline* (New York: Regan Books, 2004), p. 461.

106 **On the morning of the attacks, communiqués:** Anonymous intelligence source.

106 **"Their entry into the U.S.":** Interview and correspondence with *Newsweek* national security expert Mark Hosenball.

107 **two of the hijackers . . . had attended:** Correspondence with Hosenball; *The 9/11 Commission Report: Final Report of the National Commission on Terrorist Attacks Upon the United States* (New York: W. W. Norton, 2004), pp. 181, 266.

107 **In response to the APB, the FBI:** Ibid., pp. 266–71.

107 **Most . . . in their twenties . . . typically around 5′6″:** Ibid., p. 231.

107 **Many had trained in al-Qaeda camps:** Ibid., p. 233–36.

107 **Thirteen had actually gone through:** Ibid., p. 231.

107 **Some of the hijackers . . . had their photos reshot:** Ibid., p. 243.

107 **sixty-three valid driver's licenses:** Becky Akers, "I.D. O.D.," *New York Post*, March 31, 2005, p. 29.

107 **though they usually traveled and made transactions:** Correspondence with Hosenball.

107 **And each of them . . . had sent off photocopies:** *The 9/11 Commission Report*, pp. 245–46.

107 **That first week . . . would help generate 36,000 leads:** Jason Burke, Julian Borger, and Kate Connolly, "Frantic Battle to Prevent Further Attacks," *The Observer* (U.K.), September 16, 2001.

108 **"If we get photographs out there":** Interview with Joe Valiquette.

108 **First, the agents scoured through "trash":** Interview with John Green.

108 **In all, Green's . . . lab amassed 311 cassettes:** Typically, says John Green, the security systems were about eight years old—the lenses dirty, the tapes physically degraded; venues would tend to use thirty tapes a month, rotating them daily, then recording over them. (Interview with Green.)

108 **Finally, teams of police officers:** Special forensic filters allowed the bureau to enhance individual frames to look for distinguishing scars, watches, and apparel. Due to the fact that Atta's suitcase had been recovered early on, John Green says, he personally photographed all of Atta's clothing, and then used pictures of the apparel to identify the hijacker in subsequent videos. (Interview with Green.)

108 **On the night of September 10, an ATM.:** Howell Raines and *The New York Times*, et al., *A Nation Challenged: A Visual History of 9/11 and Its Aftermath*, Nancy Lee, Mitchel Levitas, Howell Raines, Lonnie Schlein et al., eds. (New York: New York Times/Callaway, 2002), p. 133.

109 **The hijackers had been videotaped . . . there were no surveillance cameras:** *The 9/11 Commission Report*, p. 4.

109 **"Some of the most important images":** Interview with Dennis Murphy.

110 **"I look forward to visiting with you":** Transcript of telephone call, "Bush, Pataki, Giuliani: We Will Rebuild," *CNN.com*, September 13, 2001 (http://archives.cnn.com).

110 **"How should we be reacting to this?":** Interview with Smithsonian administrator who requests anonymity.

111 **"Within a couple of hours, I started thinking":** Interviews and correspondence with Michelle Delaney.

111 **Congress would eventually give the Smithsonian $5 million:** Fiscal Appropria-

tions Bill amendment signed into law by President Bush, January 10, 2002, as Section 601 of Public Law 107–17, cited in letter from U.S. Senator Christopher S. Bond to Lawrence Small, Secretary of the Smithsonian Institution, May 20, 2002; copy of draft of amendment, December 6, 2001.

111 **Since all commercial flights:** Andrew C. Revkin, "Physical Effects of Sept. 11 Scrutinized from on High," *The New York Times*, September 17, 2002, p. F3.

111 **Ever since 1960, when the first weather satellite:** "April 1 Marks 40th Anniversary of First Weather Satellite," press release, National Oceanic and Atmospheric Administration, March 30, 2000 (www.publicaffairs.noaa.gov).

111 **University of Wisconsin climatologist:** Dan McKinney, "9/11 Offered Rare Chance to Study Contrail-Free Sky," *San Jose Mercury News*, July 23, 2002.

112 **What this suggested to Travis:** "The big implication," David Travis told the *San Jose Mercury News*, "is that this is the first direct evidence that the global warming debate is complicated by jet contrails. [A]ny artificial temperature change isn't good for the environment." The visual evidence intuitively bolstered his findings: a satellite image, taken on the afternoon of September 11 and released by NASA's Langley Research Center a week after the attacks, reveals that the skies over much of the Midwest appeared relatively unsullied by contrails, save for three tiny streaks (like a scratch left by a cat's paw) just north of Peoria, Illinois: the signature of Air Force One, accompanied by two fighter jets, heading eastward from Omaha to Washington, D.C. (Photo credited to Peter Minnis, NASA Langley Research Center, in *The New York Times*, September 17, 2002, p. F3.)

112 **"unforeseen climatic effects of 9/11 suggest":** "Horizon Reveals Potential Huge Increase in Global Warming," press release for BBC Two's Horizon broadcast, "Horizon: Global Dimming," David Sington, prod., Matthew Barrett, ed., BBC Two, January 13, 2005 (www.bbc.co.uk).

112 ***Newsday*'s Thursday edition carried a photo:** "The Awful Toll," *Newsday*, September 13, 2001, p. 1.

112 **Michael Iken, thirty-seven, a bond broker:** Sean Gardiner, Margaret Ramirez, and John Moreno Gonzales, "Hope Beyond Hope," *Newsday*, September 13, 2001 (www.nynewsday.com).

112 **"I was one of the first ones out there":** Interview with Monica Iken.

113 **58,249 in all—are etched in black granite:** Vietnam Veterans Memorial Page, *TheWall-USA.com*.

114 **Though she hasn't yet chosen . . . site architect Michael Arad:** Errol A. Cockfield, Jr., "Arad's Vision Reshapes Lower Manhattan," *Newsday*, February 23, 2004 (www.nynewsday.com).

114 **As of this writing, the Lower Manhattan Development Corporation:** Interview with LMDC spokesperson.

114 **"Some of these become almost like wallpaper":** Interviews with Scott Gutterson.

115 **Security . . . had meant . . . getting 2,700 employees:** Remarks by Philip J. Purcell, "Morgan Stanley CEO Presentation to Employees," Morgan Stanley Web site, September 12, 2001 (www.morganstanley.com).

115 **Two days after the attacks, Eileen Hillock:** Interview with Hillock.

115 **Within moments . . . a decorated platoon leader who had served:** Michael Grunwald, "A Tower of Courage," *The Washington Post*, October 28, 2001, p. F1.

116 **Two of his security aides—Jorge Velazquez:** *Portraits 9/11/01: The Collected*

"Portraits of Grief" from The New York Times (New York: Times Books, 2002), p. 516.

116 **And Titus Davidson:** "A Nation Changed: In Memoriam," listing of deceased of September 11, *U.S. News & World Report* Web site, 2004 (www.usnews.com).

116 **For much of the 1990s, Rick Rescorla had insisted:** James B. Stewart, "The Real Heroes Are Dead: A Love Story," *The New Yorker*, February 11, 2002, p. 52.

116 **With years of combat experience (he was profiled in the book):** Harold G. Moore and Joseph L. Galloway, *We Were Soldiers Once . . . and Young: Ia Drang—The Battle That Changed the War in Vietnam* (New York: Random House, 1992).

116 **For an hour and a half . . . between floors ten:** "A Tower of Courage," p. F1.

116 **All 2,700 employees, and one thousand more:** David Friend, "Two Towers, One Year Later," *Vanity Fair*, September 2002, p. 339.

117 **Susan Rescorla would soon encourage author:** James B. Stewart, *Heart of a Soldier: A Story of Love, Heroism, and September 11th* (New York: Simon & Schuster, 2002).

117 **"When I first saw [the snapshot]":** Interview with Susan Rescorla.

117 **With Americans . . . the Pew Research Center:** Jane Black, "Don't Make Privacy the Next Victim of Terror," *BusinessWeek Online*, October 4, 2001 (www.business week.com).

118 **Among the initiatives soon put forward:** Matthew L. Wald, "U.S. Considers Requiring Cameras Providing Cabin Views," *The New York Times*, May 31, 2002, p. A21; Conrad De Aenlle, "An Extra Eye in Combat, and Maybe Aboard Airplanes," *The New York Times*, March 1, 2004, p. C3.

118 **By 2004, thousands of foreign visitors:** Abby Goodnough and Eric Lichtblau, "U.S. Institutes Fingerprinting at Entry Points," *The New York Times*, January 6, 2004, p. A1.

118 **For visitors from some two dozen nations:** Jennifer 8. Lee, "The Art and Craft of Security: Passports and Visas to Add High-Tech Identity Features," *The New York Times*, August 24, 2003, p. 26.

118 **"the use of data extracted from the body":** David Lyon, *Surveillance after September 11* (Cambridge, U.K.: Polity, 2003), p 68.

118 **One program, with the ominous overtones:** Ian Bishop, "Eye Flight: Iris Scan for JFK Passengers," *New York Post*, January 14, 2005, p. 2.

118 **more distinctive and singular than a fingerprint:** Bill Allen, "From the Editor," *National Geographic*, April 2002.

118 **Even though the concept sounded feasible . . . "false positives":** *Surveillance*, p. 78.

118 **Nonetheless, random-scanning programs:** Corey Kilgannon, "Cameras to Seek Faces of Terror in Visitors to the Statue of Liberty," *The New York Times*, May 25, 2002, p. B1.

119 **The plans soon began to sound like the much-touted:** Jack Manno, *Arming the Heavens: The Hidden Military Agenda for Space, 1945–1995* (New York: Dodd, Mead, 1984), pp. 4–5.

119 **"It was terribly dangerous . . . to let your thoughts wander":** George Orwell, *1984* (New York: Harcourt, Brace, 1961), p. 54.

119 **One winces to recall *1984*'s "Two Minutes Hate" sessions:** Ibid., pp. 13–14.

119 **In the spring of 2005 . . . Khalid Hakim:** Andrea Elliott, "In a Suspicious U.S., Muslim Converts Find Discrimination," *The New York Times*, April, 30, 2005, p. B1.

120 **Business Week would warn:** "Privacy in an Age of Terror," *Business Week*, November 5, 2001.

120 **Some months after 9/11, according to photo editor:** Interview with Gary Fong.

121 **For weeks, police would grant few exceptions:** Interviews with various photographers.

121 **For generations . . . from Walker Evans to . . . Camilo José Vergara:** Sewell Chan, "Want Shots Like These? Get a Permit: Ban of Subway Photography Would Defy a Tradition," *The New York Times*, January 7, 2005, p. B4.

121 **"to promote a vague public perception":** Matt Haber, "Forbidden Photos, Anyone?" *The Village Voice*, June 4, 2004.

121 **"We have been conditioned to accept":** Ibid.

121 **the decision was eventually reversed:** "New York Subway Photo Ban Rejected," *Photo District News*, July 2005, p. 16.

122 **From 1998 to 2004, according to a study:** Jennifer 8. Lee, "Caught on Tape, Then Just Caught: Private Cameras Transform Police Work," *The New York Times*, May 22, 2005, p. 36.

122 **A person out for a walk in the city of London:** Steve Stecklow, Jason Singer, and Aaron O. Patrick, "Watch on the Thames: Surveillance Cameras Monitor Much of Daily Life in London, May Help to Identify Bombers," *The Wall Street Journal Online*, July 8, 2005 (http: // online.wsj.com).

122 **"The distinction between private and government":** "Caught on Tape", p. 36.

122 **"the extent of CCTV coverage":** John Schwartz, "Cameras in Britain Record the Criminal and the Banal," *The New York Times*, July 23, 2005, p. A7.

122 **"the study suggested that low-tech measures":** Ibid.

122 **Sociologist and surveillance expert David Lyon . . . has noted:** *Surveillance*, p. 84.

123 **And so-called intelligent video systems:** Noah Shachtman, "The New Security: Cameras that Never Forget Your Face," *The New York Times*, January 25, 2006.

123 **"Traditionally, America has based its counterterror":** Interview and correspondence with John Levy.

123 **millions of cargo containers . . . only 4 percent:** Senator Susan Collins, "Cargo Containers: The Next Terrorist Target?," opening remarks, Committee on Governmental Affairs, March 20, 2003 (www.senate.gov).

123 **As Lyon has pointed out, it was ironic:** *Surveillance*, pp. 19–22. This principle—an isolated group keeping tabs on a larger population—has been termed *panopticon*, first espoused in the 1780s by political theorist Jeremy Bentham to describe a prison system with centralized guards positioned to monitor a large number of prisoners on their periphery. Lyon cites both Michel Foucault, who discussed panopticon in social terms, and Thomas Mathiesen, who coined *synopticon*, "the viewer society," in which the "many watch the few." (Jeremy Bentham, *The Panopticon Writings*, Miran Bozovic, ed. [London: Verso, 1995], pp. 29–95; Thomas Mathiesen, "The Viewer Society: Michel Foucault's 'Panopticon' Revisited," *Theoretical Criminology*, 1(2), 1997, pp. 215–34.)

124 **On October 9, 2001, a man with a camera:** Lisa W. Foderaro, "A 9/11 Lesson: Don't Photograph the Water," *The New York Times*, June 6, 2004.

124 **Mahmood, as luck would have it:** Rehan Ansari, "Detained to be Deported," *The* (Pakistan) *News* (Internet edition), April 3, 2005 (www.jang.com.pk); correspondence with Ansari.

124 **"It seemed too good to be true":** Ibid.

124 **That day in October, recalls Susan Davies:** Interview with Susan Davies.

124 **"the toppest place in the Hudson area":** Interview with Ansar Mahmood.

125 **Only three weeks before . . . "anthrax" letters:** "Amerithrax Press Briefing," November 9, 2001, Federal Bureau of Investigation, Major Investigations, Amerithrax, Evidence Description, Letter 1 (www.fbi.gov).

125 **Some two dozen people:** Tim Parsons, "Statistics Show Anthrax Outbreak Could Have Been Twice as Large," *The* [Johns Hopkins University] *Gazette Online*, March 18, 2002 (www.jhu.edu/~gazette); Senator Patrick Leahy, "Anthrax Victims Fund Fairness Act of 2003," statement introducing Senate bill to allow anthrax-attack victims' survivors compensation under the September 11 Victim Compensation Fund, October 16, 2003 (http://leahy.senate.gov/press).

125 **By the time Mahmood returned . . . two cops:** "A 9/11 Lesson"; interview with Susan Davies.

126 **He was rearrested, this time on felony charges:** Ibid.

126 **Their group . . . conscripted Senators:** Khalid Hasan, "U.S. Senator Regrets Pakistani Man's Deportation," *Daily* (Lahore, Pakistan) *Times*, September 2, 2004 (www.dailytimes.com.pk).

126 **"Mahmood wanted to be an ideal citizen":** Kirk Semple, "Man Arrested Over Photos After 9/11 is Deported," *The New York Times*, August 14, 2004, p. B2.

126 **By the end of 2001 . . . more than 1,100 detainees:** Statement by Kate Martin, Center for National Security Studies, before the Judiciary Committee of the U.S. Senate, 107th Congress, 1st Session, "Department of Justice Oversight: Preserving Our Freedoms While Defending Against Terrorism," November 28, 2001, via U.S. Commission on Civil Rights Web site (www.usccr.gov).

126 **"Between three and five thousand":** "Detention," ACLU's Safe and Free Page, American Civil Liberties Union, July 2005 (www.aclu.org).

126 **In time, the ACLU would contend that the FBI:** "ACLU Launches Nationwide Effort to Expose Illegal FBI Spying on Political and Religious Groups," ACLU press release, December 2, 2004 (www.aclu.org); "New Documents Show FBI Targeting Environmental and Animal Rights Group Activities as 'Domestic Terrorism,' " ACLU press release, December 20, 2005 (www.aclu.org).

126n **a *New York Times* probe would report that the National Security Agency:** Eric Lichtblau and James Risen, "Domestic Surveillance: The Program; Spy Agency Mined Vast Data Trove, Officials Report," *The New York Times*, December 24, 2005.

126n **In this Orwellian environment, wrote *Times* columnist:** Maureen Dowd, "Vice Axes *That 70's Show*," *The New York Times*, December 28, 2005, p. A19.

126n **whom Dowd is fond of calling . . . the Grim Peeper:** Maureen Dowd, "Googling Past the Graveyard," *The New York Times*, January 21, 2006, p. A13.

126n **"Vice . . . has [already] turned America into a camera obscura":** Dowd, "Vice Axes *That 70's Show*."

126 **"In the first nine weeks . . . over 700 violent incidents":** Hussein Ibish and Anne Stewart, "Report on Hate Crimes and Discrimination Against Arab Americans, September 11, 2001–October 11, 2002," American-Arab Anti-Discrimination Committee, 2003, p. 7.

127 **"Over 800 cases":** Ibid.

127 **"Everybody . . . thinks I have done something wrong":** "Detained to Be Deported"; correspondence with Rehan Ansari.

127 **On Thursday a magazine editor I know:** Encounter with editor who wishes to remain anonymous.

127 **The day before, New York *Daily News*:** Spokesperson for the New York *Daily News* confirms that the paper ran the image in its late edition and on a Web slide show on September 12, 2001.

128 **"You can't do the story without doing the story":** Jim Rutenberg and Felicity Barringer, "News Media Try to Sort out Policy on Graphic Images," *The New York Times*, September 13, 2001, p. A24.

128 **"That was the reality . . . I felt that it would be dishonest":** Interview with Ed Kosner.

128 **"I think we're going to have to remember September 11th in its reality":** *In Memoriam*. Giuliani would eventually live out this thesis in 2006 at the terror trial of Zacarias Moussaoui, the 9/11 conspirator arrested after taking lessons to pilot a plane. The mayor actually appeared at Moussaoui's sentencing hearing, and tried, unsuccessfully, to bolster the case for the death penalty by showing videotapes of the attacks and the devastation. (Kevin Johnson, "Horrors, Sorrow of 9/11 Fill Hearing," USAToday.com, April 6, 2006 [www.usatoday.com]).

129 **"Nine-eleven changed how newsrooms judged":** Interview with Naomi Halperin.

129 **Several weeks after . . . Susan Sontag, whose book *On Photography*:** Susan Sontag, *On Photography* (New York: Farrar, Straus and Giroux, 1977).

129 **she would publish *Regarding the Pain of Others*:** Susan Sontag, *Regarding the Pain of Others* (New York: Farrar, Straus and Giroux, 2002).

130 **Executives at ABC News:** "News Media Try to Sort"; Jim Rutenberg, "In TV News, Philosophies About Images of 9/11 Differ," *The New York Times*, August 30, 2004, p. P9.

130 **NBC had reportedly aired a single body:** "News Media Try to Sort."

130 **"Are we informing . . . or titillating":** Ibid.

130 **In 2005, the BBC would [place] time-delays:** Alan Cowell, "BBC to Use Time Delay Device to Weed Out Upsetting Images," *The New York Times*, June 24, 2005.

130 **When U.S. troops invaded Iraq that year, al-Jazeera:** James Poniewozik, "What You See vs. What They See," *Time*, April 7, 2003, p. 69.

130 **"It's pretty hard to adequately describe the . . . bloodiness":** Michael Wolff, "Al-Jazeera's Edge," *New York*, April 28, 2003, pp. 24–25.

131 **"There was not a lot left of them":** Interview with Michele Stephenson.

131 **"They were sure we were censoring":** Interview with MaryAnne Golon.

131 **"[The videotaped sounds of] the thudding bodies":** *9/11*, Goldfish Pictures and Silverstar Productions in association with Reveille, Jules Naudet, Gedeon Naudet; James Hanlon, dir.; Jules Naudet, Gedeon Naudet, James Hanlon, Susan Zirinsky, Graydon Carter, David Friend, prods., CBS, March 2002.

133 **According to a study conducted by *USA Today*:** Dennis Cauchon and Martha Moore, "Desperation Forced a Horrific Decision," *USA Today*, September 2, 2002 (www.usatoday.com).

133 **"A 'jumper' is somebody who goes to the office":** Ibid.

133 **"This should not be really thought of as a choice":** Kevin Flynn and Jim Dwyer,

"Falling Bodies: A 9/11 Image Etched in Pain," *The New York Times*, September 10, 2004, B8.

133 **[One] man pitched forward:** Jim Dwyer and Kevin Flynn, *102 Minutes: The Untold Story of the Fight to Survive Inside the Twin Towers* (New York: Times Books, 2005), p. 137.

134 **Some held hands, jumping . . . three and four at a time:** Interview with Peter Kunhardt, producer who viewed many videotapes.

134 **"What's to be gained by showing these people":** Interview with Tom Flynn.

135 **"I just remember looking up":** *9/11*.

135 **"In many cases . . . the still is more 'moving' ":** Interview with John Loengard.

136 **His posture . . . seems to impart . . . a kind of "terrifying dignity":** Leon Wieseltier, "The Fall," *The New Republic*, September 9–16, 2002, p. 46.

136 **Drew, it turns out, took a dozen shots:** Tom Junod, "The Falling Man," *Esquire*, September 2003, pp. 178–79.

136 **"because of its verticality and symmetry":** Ibid., p. 178.

136 **The image is "the most famous picture":** Interview with Richard Drew.

137 **"tip to stern on the broadsheet":** Interview with, and e-mail correspondence sent the week of September 11 by Naomi Halperin, used with her permission.

137 **"conveyed what we felt we needed to do":** David Erdman, editorial, *The* (Allentown, Pennsylvania) *Morning Call*, October 16, 2001.

137 **"To hide that photo would be":** Ironically, David Erdman and Naomi Halperin had first heard about the attacks as they walked into a classroom at Lehigh University on Tuesday morning to take part in a seminar entitled "Free Press and Decision-Making: Selection of Controversial Photos."

137 **"Shot through my tears":** Richard Drew, "The Horror of 9/11 That's All Too Familiar," *Los Angeles Times*, September 10, 2003, p. B13.

138 **"the sound of concrete debris":** Ibid.

138 **Tom Junod . . . determined [he] was wearing an orange T-shirt:** "The Falling Man," p. 198.

138 **"Those who *knew*, right away":** Ibid., p. 198.

139 **The only certainty . . . aversion to a picture that "went all around the world":** Ibid., p. 199.

139 **"In the most photographed and videotaped":** Ibid., p. 180.

139 **First, as Junod points out, visualizations of violent death:** "Part of the horror of 9/11," observed *Slate* culture editor Meghan O'Rourke, "was its protracted nature . . . [P]eople in the plane knew they were being hijacked, and, in the late moments, likely suspected that they were being flown into a building . . . To me this is excruciating to even begin to contemplate." The violation and cruelty of the attacks were amplified by the fact that loved ones and strangers had to witness them as they occurred. Workers were stuck in the towers, passengers were stuck on the planes, and onlookers were stuck watching as the minutes passed, doubly terrorized by knowing that the victims were terrorized and by imagining themselves as those victims. (Michael Agger, Dahlia Lithwick, Meghan O'Rourke, and June Thomas, "*United 93:* A Brief *Slate* Debate About the Controversial New Movie," posted April 6, 2006 (www.slate.com]).

140 **"One argument for censorship":** Francis G. Couvares, essay, "A Person Falls Head-

first from the North Tower of the New York World Trade Center, Sept. 11, 2001, by Richard Drew," in exhibition *The Pain of War*, curated by Carol Solomon Kiefer, Mead Art Museum, Amherst College, Amherst, Massachusetts, October–December 2004; text republished in "The Pain of War," *Amherst*, Winter 2005, p. 19.

140 **"On the Internet . . . they said my father":** "The Falling Man," p. 198.

141 **"We might have to face . . . He is you and me":** Interview with Richard Drew; "The Horror of 9/11."

141 **The *New York Post* would register:** Dan Kadison and Jessie Graham, "How Sleazy Sellers Rake in Big Bucks on the City's Suffering," *New York Post*, October 1, 2001, p. 1.

141 **The American Red Cross would run:** Print advertisement, the American Red Cross, Autumn 2001.

141 **"The value of photographs is incalculable":** Interview with Scott Gutterson.

142 ***The Wall Street Journal* noted that even:** Patricia Callahan, "What a Journal Called *Cheese Market News* Can Say About Sept. 11—Trade Magazines Are Compelled to Cover Biggest Story, Too," *The Wall Street Journal*, October 25, 2001, p. A1.

142 **Hoepker realized that the agency:** Steve McCurry, Susan Meiselas, et al., *New York September 11 by Magnum Photographers* (New York: powerHouse, 2001).

142 **"Almost everybody in the office had a part":** Interview with Nathan Benn.

142 **"It didn't live up to the drama of the other shots":** Interview with Thomas Hoepker.

143 **Pieter Bruegel's sixteenth-century painting:** *Landscape with the Fall of Icarus* in Keith Roberts, *Bruegel* (London: Phaidon, 1993), p. 33.

144 **"Conceived as a means of counteracting":** Jay Rosenblatt and Caveh Zahedi, Jay Rosenblatt Films producers' statement for *Underground Zero*, 2002 (www.jayrosenblatt films.com/undergroundzero).

144 **Hollywood dramatizations . . . "believable truth":** Jere Longman, "Filming Flight 93's Story, Trying to Define Heroics," *The New York Times*, April 24, 2006, p. E6.

145 ***September 10 2001* . . . an elegy:** Director's statement for *September 10 2001/Uno Nunca Muere La Víspera*, Monika Bravo, Brooklyn International Film Festival 2002, Brooklyn Museum, Brooklyn, N.Y. (www.wbff.org).

145 **Around midnight, Bravo gathered her tapes:** Carolyn Weaver, "Artists Respond to September 11," Voice of America TV, September 9, 2002.

145 **he watched the end of . . . *Monday Night Football*:** C. Carr, "The Witnessing Eye: Artists Document the World Trade Center's Demise," *The Village Voice*, June 5–11, 2002.

145 **Newsstands stocked special, picture-rich editions:** *Time* Special Edition, September 13, 2001; *Newsweek* Extra Edition, September 13, 2001.

146 **On September 12 . . . the *San Francisco Chronicle*:** "Nightmare," *San Francisco Chronicle*, September 12, 2001, p. 1.

146 **Owerko managed to take such detailed shots:** Archival photographs helped identify one of the weaknesses that may have hastened the collapse: gaps in the spray-on fireproofing that had been used to insulate sections of some buildings in the 1970s. (James Glanz, "Trade Center Fireproofing Tests Suggest a Wider Safety Problem," *The New York Times*, December 14, 2003, p. 59.)

146 **"We had basically 8,000 photos":** Interview with William Pitts.

147 **Owerko raced down the stairs . . . and "sprinted down Broadway":** Interviews and correspondence with Lyle Owerko, and personal writings, used with his permission.

147n **Those who leaped or fell . . . struck . . . in about ten seconds:** Author witnessing videos; "Desperation Forced a Horrific Decision."

148 **Over in Brooklyn, photographer Robert Clark:** Interview with Clark.

150 **Landing on a double-page spread:** Sequence of four photographs by Robert Clark/Aurora for *Time* Special Edition, September 13, 2001, pp. 2–3.

151 **"This came out of nowhere":** Interview with Trevor Schoenfeld.

151 **Had she seen page 16?:** Photograph by Jason Szenes/Corbis-Sygma, *Newsweek* Extra Edition, September 13, 2001, p. 16.

151 **Cecilia had become reacquainted with Carlos:** *Portraits 9/11/01*, p. 285.

151 **As she was making her way down:** Kristen Davis, "Paramedic Partners Buried While Saving Lives," *New York Post*, September 21, 2001, p. 17.

152 **"While this has been an agonizing circumstance":** Interview with Richard Fox.

153 **"We were inventing [VII] up as we went along":** Interview with Gary Knight.

154 **"For news pictures to break through the media clutter":** Interviews with Robert Pledge.

154 **"We were down in my studio":** Interview with John Stanmeyer.

154 **The photo business . . . had become "dehumanizing":** Interview with Ron Haviv.

154 **One imagines . . . the outstretched palm of a Somali woman:** James Nachtwey, *Inferno* (London: Phaidon, 1999).

155 **His life and those of the three men . . . were spared:** James Kelly, "From the Editor," *Time*, December 29, 2003.

155 **According to one journalist . . . "enters a zone":** David Friend, "The Black Slab: An Appreciation of James Nachtwey's *Inferno*," *The Digital Journalist*, July 2000 (www.digitaljournalist.org).

155 **Nachtwey has said as much:** Ann Gerhart, writing in *The Washington Post*, interviewed Nachtwey upon the publication of *Inferno*, and observed: "Cheating death seems to have been ordained . . . An eerie [video] clip shows him [in South Africa in 1994] bent over a South African photographer who has been shot and killed. Nachtwey's hair is jumping. Bullets are whizzing through it. Sometimes he thinks his survival 'is sheer luck,' he said, 'and sometimes I think I have a guardian angel looking over me.' " (Ann Gerhart, "War's Unblinking Eyewitness: The Worst of Humanity Has Brought Out the Best in Photographer James Nachtwey," *The Washington Post*, April 11, 2000, p. C1.)

155 **"a group of people . . . who all have worked with each other":** Interviews with James Nachtwey.

156 **The next morning, VII's Christopher Morris:** Interview with Morris.

157 **He shot all morning . . . as he would recount on the *Digital Journalist*:** Peter Howe and Dirck Halstead, "Seeing the Horror: James Nachtwey," *The Digital Journalist*, October 2001 (www.digitaljournalist.org).

158 **Seven would do the same in Iraq:** Giorgio Baravale, ed., *WAR* (Millbrook, N.Y.: de.MO, 2003).

159 **"We took all comers":** Interview with MaryAnne Golon.

160 **Psychologist Richard Cohen walked over to the Associated Press:** Interview with Cohen.

160 **His images ran on Web sites . . . the photo of the pointing man:** Photograph by Richard Cohen in Reuters, *September 11: A Testimony* (Upper Saddle River, N.J.: Prentice Hall, 2002), p. 9.

161 **Part of Cohen's heightened awareness . . . a "fight or flight" response:** Interview with Dr. Michael E. Mendelsohn.

161 **"In Vietnam . . . infatuation . . . with violence":** Michael Herr, *Dispatches* (New York: Avon, 1980), pp. 65–66.

4. FRIDAY, SEPTEMBER 14

164 **"FEMA has photographers":** Interview with Gregg Brown.

164 **the smoke from underground fires:** Life: *The American Spirit, Meeting the Challenge of September 11*, Robert Sullivan, ed. (New York: *Life* Books, 2002), pp. 28–43.

165 **Believe it or not, the roll contained . . . a double-exposure:** Ibid., endpapers.

165n **In one of the most perplexing developments:** Greg B. Smith, "Shameful Abuse of 9/11 Footage," New York *Daily News*, February 11, 2005; Greg B. Smith, "Families in Film Furor," New York *Daily News*, February 13, 2006.

165n **"The premise of 'Words' comes from the idea":** Interview and correspondence with Gregg Brown.

166 **"Everything is just glass . . . All you see is the twin towers":** Interview with Tammy Klein.

166 **Over the past thirty years, bombings in Israel:** David Friend and Robert Rosenberg, "Disarmers of Terror," *Life*, December 1984, p. 66.

168 **"Tim Sherman spotted the photograph":** Jim Dwyer, "From the Rubble, a Picture and a Friendship," *The New York Times*, October 23, 2001, p. B1.

168 **Sherman, a New Jersey waterworks employee:** Ibid.

168 **It was crinkled and torn:** Interviews with George Tabeek.

168 **And a reader named Brian Conroy:** Interviews with Conroy and Tabeek.

168 **"It was on my credenza":** Interviews with George Tabeek.

168 **"That stuff'll kill you":** Interviews with Tabeek.

168 **Robert Lynch:** *Portraits 9/11/01: The Collected "Portraits of Grief" from* The New York Times (New York: Times Books, 2002), p. 296.

168 **"We can't take you [any]where":** Interviews with Tabeek.

168 **Joseph Amatuccio:** *Portraits 9/11/01*, p. 13.

170 **Fresh Kills Landfill . . . where . . . 1.6 million tons:** "Expressing Gratitude for . . . Cleanup and Recovery Efforts at the Fresh Kills Landfill . . ." U.S. House of Representatives, *Congressional Record*, July 22, 2002, p. H5035; Amy Eddings, "WTC Recovery Subject of Historical Society Exhibit," WNYC, December 15, 2003 (www.publicbroadcasting.net/wnyc).

170 **"The pictures were water-soaked":** Interview with James Luongo.

170 **twenty-eight government agencies:** *Congressional Record*, p. H5035.

171 **Some 54,000 artifacts:** Ibid.

171 **Eastman Kodak and NFL Films:** Interview with Ronda Factor of Kodak.

171 **In January 2005 the Port Authority . . . set up an online database:** David W. Dunlap, "Victims' Relatives May Claim Photographs from 9/11 Ruins," *The New York Times*, January 8, 2005, p. B3.

172 **In a curious coda . . . an exhibition called "Recovery":** "Recovery: The World

Trade Center Recovery Operation at Fresh Kills," The New-York Historical Society, New York, N.Y., November 25, 2003–March 21, 2004, in conjunction with the New York State Museum (www.nyhistory.org/recovery); "Glimpse of a Tragedy," *Newsweek*, November 17, 2003, p. 10.

172 **On Friday, a relative of a friend:** Discussion with source who requests anonymity.

173 **On 9/14, pictures of Osama bin Laden:** David Friend, "Two Towers, One Year Later," *Vanity Fair*, September 2002, p. 338.

173 **Within weeks . . . sheets of novelty toilet paper:** Kevin Lynch, "Now You Can Wipe the Smile off Bin Laden's Face," *The National Enquirer*, October 16, 2001.

173 **targets at U.S. rifle ranges:** Fred Kaplan, "In NYC, More Take Up Arms," *The Boston Globe*, October 25, 2001.

173 **In Pakistan's kiosks . . . Osama's face appeared on T-shirts:** Howell Raines and *The New York Times* et al., *A Nation Challenged: A Visual History of 9/11 and Its Aftermath*, Nancy Lee, Mitchel Levitas, Howell Raines, Lonnie Schlein et al., eds. (New York: New York Times/Callaway, 2002), p. 149; photograph by Rafiqur Rahman/Reuters in *The Guardian* (U.K.), November 3, 2001.

173 **During the 1990s he had conducted several sessions:** Peter Bergen, "Terrorism's Dark Master," *Vanity Fair*, December 2001, p. 250; Robert Fisk, "My Days with Bin Laden," *GQ*, November 2001, p. 366; John Miller, "Greetings, America. My Name Is Osama Bin Laden," *Esquire*, February 1999.

173 **"How can a man in a cave outcommunicate":** *The 9/11 Commission Report: Final Report of the National Commission on Terrorist Attacks upon the United States* (New York: W. W. Norton, 2004), p. 377.

173 **Though bin Laden was in league . . . Mullah Omar, was notorious:** Ed Grazda, "Searching For Mullah Omar," *Vanity Fair*, February 2003, p. 138.

174 **He had been an ally of the Afghan mujahideen:** *The 9/11 Commission Report*, pp. 55–57.

174 **His powerful Saudi family (which ran a global business):** "Terrorism's Dark Master," p. 257.

174 **When he began to chastise the Saudi government:** David Rose, "The Osama Files," *Vanity Fair*, January 2002, p. 67.

174 **Placed on President Clinton's hit list:** Jane Mayer, "The Search for Osama," *The New Yorker*, August 4, 2003, p. 33; Richard A. Clarke, *Against All Enemies: Inside America's War on Terror* (New York: Free Press, 2004), p. 204; Bob Woodward, *Bush at War* (New York: Simon & Schuster, 2002), pp. 5–6, 34–35.

174 **He plotted . . . the 1998 African embassy bombings:** Michael Grunwald and Vernon Loeb, "Charges Filed Against Bin Laden," *The Washington Post*, November 5, 1998, p. A17. While many sources estimate that 224 died in the 1998 African embassy bombings, two different State Department sources place the toll at 257 and 301, respectively. ("U.S. Embassy Bombings," U.S. Department of State Bureau of International Information Programs, *UsInfo.State.Gov*, 2005; "Significant Terrorist Incidents, 1961–2003: A Brief Chronology," Office of the Historian, Bureau of Public Affairs, U.S. Department of State, March 2004 [www.state.gov].)

174 **2000 attack on the USS *Cole*:** William Branigin,"Two Sentenced to Die for USS Cole Attack," *WashingtonPost.com*, September 30, 2004 (www.washington post.com).

174 **As a rule, he gave hints:** Correspondence with Mark Hosenball; Michael Scheuer,

cited in Robert B. Bluey, "Bin Laden Expert: Muslim Tradition to Offer Truce Before Attack," *Human Events*, January 21, 2006 (www.humaneventsonline.com).

174 **"The strangest thing I have heard so far is Abu Abdullah":** Alan Cullison, "Inside Al-Qaeda's Hard Drive," *The Atlantic Monthly*, September 2004, p. 59.

175 **"The grafting of modern techniques":** "Terrorism's Dark Master," p. 254.

175 **"communicated . . . using Internet chat software":** John Solomon, "Terror Mastermind Reveals Sept. 11 Plot Included 10 Planes on 2 Coasts," *The Journal News* (White Plains, New York), September 22, 2003.

175 **In the early 1990s, for example, an al-Qaeda cell in Kenya:** *The 9/11 Commission Report*, p. 68.

175 **By 1997, KSM, in addition to hatching:** Ibid, pp. 149–50.

175 **In 1999 . . . the pre-9/11 training regimen entailed:** Ibid, pp. 157–58.

175 **Around that time . . . advance teams, posing as tourists:** Jose Martinez, "Videotape Cased Targets in City," New York *Daily News*, March 4, 2003, p. 6; Andy Soltis, "WTC Vid Reveals Planning of Attack," *New York Post*, March 4, 2003, p. 4.

176 **investigators have even theorized that . . . al-Qaeda . . . communicated by:** "Al Qaeda Hid Messages on Porn Websites," *The Times* (London), October 6, 2001, p. 11; Adam Cohen, "When Terror Hides Online," *Time*, November 12, 2001.

176 **Based on information gleaned by *The Wall Street Journal*'s Alan Cullison:** "Inside Al-Qaeda's Hard Drive," p. 68.

176 **Video . . . would later backfire on Zarqawi:** Niles Lathem, "Jihad Clod Zarqawi Couldn't Shoot Straight," *New York Post*, May 5, 2006, p. 6.

176 **By 2005, bin Laden's man in Iraq:** Susan B. Glasser and Steve Coll, "The Web As Weapon: Zarqawi Intertwines Acts on Ground in Iraq with Propaganda Campaign on the Internet," *The Washington Post*, August 9, 2005, p. A1.

176 **Just hours after the first . . . raids . . . he suddenly materialized:** Richard Bernstein, "Tape, Probably bin Laden's, Offers 'Truce' to Europe," *The New York Times*, April 16, 2004, p. A3.

176 **"These events . . . have divided the whole world":** "Bin Laden's Statement," *The Guardian* (U.K.), October 7, 2001 (www.guardian.co.uk).

176 **On November 3 and December 26, he resurfaced:** "Tape, Probably," p. A3; Neil MacFarquhar and Jim Rutenberg, "Bin Laden, in a Taped Speech, Says Attacks in Afghanistan Are a War Against Islam," *The New York Times*, November 4, 2001.

176 **though in the second session his limited gesturing:** "The Search for Osama," p. 28.

177 **The tape . . . "obtained in Afghanistan":** Walter Pincus and Karen DeYoung, "New Tape Points to Bin Laden," *The Washington Post*, December 9, 2001, p. A1.

177 **The footage—showing a . . . circuitous conversation with a Saudi sheikh:** Daren Fonda, "The Shadowy Sheik," *Time*, December 24, 2001, p. 49; Douglas Jehl and David Johnston, "In Video Message, Bin Laden Issues Warning to U.S.," *The New York Times*, October 30, 2004, pp. A1, A9.

177 **"We calculated in advance the number of casualties":** "Bin Laden Gives Chilling Account of Sept. 11," CBC Radio Canada Web site, December 13, 2001 (www.cbc.ca).

177 **The clandestine nature of the tape:** Steve LeVine, Jonathan Karp et al., "Import of bin Laden Video Is in Eye of Beholder," *The Wall Street Journal*, December 14, 2001, p. B1.

177 **Some even wondered whether the tape was . . . disinformation:** Ibid., p. B4.

178 **"After a month passed without another videotape":** "The Search for Osama," p. 28.

178 **"Bin Laden's made more videos than Usher":** Don Imus, "Imus in the Morning" radio broadcast, WFAN, fall 2005.

178 **And they reinforced the extent:** Starting in August 2005, al-Qaeda "spokesmen" began appearing in English-language videos in a bid by the movement to procure more airtime in the West.

178 **All that was required . . . was . . . access to a camera:** In 2005, mindful of being manipulated by terrorists, Public Broadcasters International, the global body that oversees the affairs of publicly funded television networks, began considering an initiative to adopt what TV executive Stephen Claypole calls a sort of "Geneva Convention" for dealing responsibly with audiovisual materials provided by groups like al-Qaeda. (Interviews and correspondence with Stephen Claypole; draft of Claypole speech given at PBI meeting in Oslo, 2005.)

178 **A clip depicting bin Laden . . . down a mountainside:** Philip Kennicott, "The Height of Myth-Making," *The Washington Post*, September 11, 2003, p. C10.

178 **"Intelligence analysts will . . . scan the tape":** Ibid.

179 **bin Laden appeared on camera, demon ex machina:** "Butt Out!" New York *Daily News*, October 30, 2004, p. 1.

179 **"Your safety . . . is not in the hands of Bush":** Corky Siemaszko, "In New Video [Bin Laden] Rips Bush, Threatens Another Attack," New York *Daily News*, October 30, 2004, p. 3; "In Video Message," pp. A1, A9.

179 **Whatever bin Laden's intentions:** In the tape, bin Laden expressed puzzlement over Bush's decision to linger in a Florida classroom after learning that the attacks were in progress. "It had never occurred to us," he claimed, "that the commander-in-chief of the American armed forces would leave 50,000 of his citizens in the two towers to face these horrors alone . . . It appeared [to President Bush] that a little girl's talk about her [pet] goat and its butting was more important than the planes and their butting of the skyscrapers." ("In Video Message," pp. A1, A9.)

179 **"I believe that 9/11 was the central deciding issue":** John Kerry, in an interview with Tim Russert, *Meet the Press*, NBC, January 30, 2005.

179 **"A visceral unwillingness to change Commander-in-Chief":** Jeffrey Goldberg, "The Unbranding: Can the Democrats Make Themselves Look Tough?" *The New Yorker*, March 21, 2005, p. 34.

179 **On September 14 . . . Massoud, had died five days before:** Sebastian Junger, "Postcript: Sebastian Junger on Afghanistan's Slain Rebel Leader," *National Geographic Adventure Online*, September 2001 (www.NationalGeographic.com/adventure).

180 **wounds inflicted when al-Qaeda operatives:** Interview with Junger; various other sources.

180 **The bombers, disguised as journalists . . . employed:** Sebastian Junger, "Massoud's Last Conquest," *Vanity Fair*, February 2002, p. 140.

180 **As Massoud made himself comfortable:** Ibid.

180 **"What will you do with Osama":** Ibid.

180 **He was blown to bits:** Ibid., p. 141.

181 **Massoud's nom de guerre:** Sebastian Junger, "The Lion in Winter," *National Geographic Adventure*, March/April 2001, p. 77.

182 **"New York has been attacked":** Interview with Jean-Jacques Naudet.

183 **Six months later, his sons' documentary, *9/11*:** *9/11*, Goldfish Pictures and Silverstar Productions in association with Reveille, Jules Naudet, Gedeon Naudet; James Hanlon, dir.; Jules Naudet, Gedeon Naudet, James Hanlon, Susan Zirinsky, Graydon Carter, David Friend, prods., CBS, March 2002.

183 **"it could be the greatest, most intense":** Monica Collins, " '9/11' Up Close and Painful: World Trade Center Footage May Be Too Tough for Many Viewers to Handle," *Boston Herald*, March 6, 2002.

183 **"an important firsthand piece of history":** Caryn James, "Experiencing the Cataclysm, from the Inside," *The New York Times*, March 6, 2002, p. E1.

184 **Jules . . . remembers him as "the cool kid":** Interviews with Jules Naudet.

184 **While directing his first film at age twelve:** Interviews with Gedeon Naudet; confirmation by family friend.

185 ***Hope, Gloves and Redemption*:** *Hope, Gloves and Redemption*, Jules and Gedeon Naudet, Lions Share Pictures, 2000.

185 **At a party in the mid-1990s, Gedeon, smoking a Gauloise:** Interviews with James Hanlon.

185 **among New York's oldest fire companies:** David Friend, "Bond of Brothers," *Vanity Fair*, March 2002, p. 184.

190 **Minutes before, the Fire Department chaplain:** Interview with Jules Naudet; press accounts.

193 **Many would come to refer to Engine 7 as Lucky 7:** "Bond of Brothers," p. 188.

193 **Though Kevin Pfeifer, the chief's brother:** Interviews with Jules Naudet and Joseph Pfeifer; *Portraits 9/11/01*, p. 392.

195 **"The light was beautiful that morning":** Interviews with John Labriola.

195 **He heard a massive explosion . . . eerily out of sequence:** John Labriola, *Walking Forward, Looking Back* (Irvington, N.Y.: Hyper Publishing, 2003), p. 22.

195 **He tried to rise from his chair:** Ibid.

196 **He appears . . . burdened by seventy-five pounds:** Interviews with Mike Kehoe.

197 **"We looked up . . . and the floors were pancaking":** Interviews with Kehoe.

197 **And soon after the attacks, their portraits:** Photo of six portraits in firehouse in "How Fireman Who Was Photographed Racing up Doomed Stairway Survived," *The National Enquirer*, October 16, 2001, p. 31; David Zucchino, "After the Attack: Heroic Firefighter Is Alive—and Still on the Job," *Los Angeles Times*, September 22, 2001, p. A1.

197 **"[E]veryone wanted a piece of him":** Jodie Morse, "Glory in the Glare," *Time*, December 31, 2001.

197 **Kehoe, blinking away the tears:** "British Award for New York Firefighters," *BBC News U.K.*, March 6, 2002 (http://news.bbc.co.uk).

199 **While Kehoe . . . went on medical leave:** "Glory in the Glare."

199 **"Most people had some shelter from the event":** Interviews with John Labriola.

200 **He took pictures of the churchyard:** *Walking Forward*, pp. 92, 94–97, 100–107.

201 **When pressed, he confessed to believing:** Interviews with Frank Pelligrino, Jr.

201 **Father Gerard Critch, a Canadian priest:** Interviews and correspondence with Critch.

201 **who . . . had exhibited symptoms:** "Antigua Priest Reported to Have Stigmata," *Catholic World News*, April 13, 1998 (www.cwnews.com); Tracy Barron, "Priest Receiving Treatment," *The Evening Telegram*, April 12, 1998; "RC Bishop Addresses

Reports of Unusual Events," *Montserrat Reporter*, April 1998 (www.montserrat reporter.org).

201 **"excruciating pains in his side, hands, and feet":** "Antigua Priest."

202 **spent eleven days aiding "firefighters":** "Walking Through the Valley of Death: Newfoundland Priest at Ground Zero," *The* (St. John's, Newfoundland, Archdiocese) *Monitor*, May 20, 2002 (www.stjohnsarchdiocese.nf.ca/monitor).

202 **"What are *you* looking at?":** Interview with Carla Pelligrino.

203 **"a woman with the moon under her feet":** *The New Testament*, Revelation XII: 1–5 (New York: American Bible Society, 1880), Vol. IV, p. 310.

203 **Drew__5976167.jpg:** Correspondence with Charles Zoeller, Associated Press.

203 **"perhaps it is not as divine":** Richard Drew himself admits that no one has ever made mention to him of any shapes in the clouds. When I asked if he sees "the figure of a woman, face upturned," he e-mails a response not atypical of the world-weary vagabonds who cover the news: "No. But I see a ducky and a pig." (Correspondence with Drew.)

203 **Even today, though, Frank, Jr., contends:** In Richard Drew's photograph, a female figure *does* appear in the clouds. And in so doing she stokes some of the earliest superstitions we have about photography. This image, like all photographic images, is part of what generations have regarded as a dark science, a medium with a spark of sorcery at its root. For more than 175 years, viewers have always been slightly awed by the camera's power to snatch a piece of reality and freeze it on a sheet.

The photograph has long been perceived as the centerpiece in an occult of the ocular. Photographers have been accused of stealing subjects' souls; portraitists slip their heads under black cloth to examine reversed, ghostly images on flat glass; images are first captured as negatives, then converted into positives; printers in cryptlike darkrooms quickly expose a piece of paper to light, then gaze into a pan of liquid as an apparition emerges from the depths; digital pictures are surreptitiously altered by the computer-magician's sleight of hand.

A woman in the clouds, then. Hadn't I often seen women in cloud formations—and sea horses and Old Man Winter, for that matter? Humans instinctively turn the pool of life into one wide reflecting pond of Narcissus, ascribing human attributes even to the heavens above. What's more, computers can amplify or distort these perceptions. Software, unabashedly, can have its way with virtually any photograph. And when images are displayed on monitors in a resolution lower than that with which they were initially created, their picture elements—the molecules of digital photographs—can pick up unintended anomalies.

I, too, saw the female figure as I stood in Frank, Jr.'s office. I knew, as he did, the tricks that digital images can play. Back in 2001, however, the photograph became a confirmation of a suspicion, a justification of a worldview: Be forewarned, for this is a sign, metaphoric or anthropomorphic, satanic or divine—or a sign of the unconscious stamped onto the event, courtesy of the mind's eye.

204 **By the Friday after September 11 . . . strangers:** Interview with Mark D. Phillips.

204 **Others saw bin Laden:** Rose DeWolf, "Demonic Image; Photog Didn't See It," Philadelphia *Daily News*, September 19, 2001, p. 16; Maggie Farley, "Hiding from What He Didn't See," *Los Angeles Times Magazine*, October 21, 2001, p. 11.

205 **"That's around the time Olympus":** Interview with John Knaur.

205 **For months, the e-mails continued:** Interview with Mark D. Phillips; Dave Lieber,

"Photograph Brings Unwanted Attention," *Fort Worth Star-Telegram*, October 21, 2001, p. 1.

5. SATURDAY, SEPTEMBER 15

206 **On Saturday . . . a page with twenty mini-obituaries:** "Among the Missing," *The New York Times*, September 15, 2001, p. A11.

206 **A similar page appeared the next day:** "Portraits of Grief," *The New York Times*, September 16, 2001.

206 **"Suria Clarke's first name means":** *Portraits 9/11/01: The Collected "Portraits of Grief" from* The New York Times (New York: Times Books, 2002), p. 91.

206 **"Clarin Siegel Schwartz . . . liked red cars":** Ibid., p. 453–54.

207 **"I wanted readers to look into the eyes":** Stella Kramer, remarks quoted at the International Center of Photography's eighteenth annual Infinity Awards, at the Regent Wall Street, New York, N.Y., May 16, 2002.

207 **"Whenever Calvin Gooding went to the barbershop":** "Among the Missing," p. A11.

207 **Eventually, more than 2,400:** Correspondence with *The New York Times* research department.

207 **Kramer was part of the editorial team that would win:** Howell Raines and *The New York Times* et al., *A Nation Challenged: A Visual History of 9/11 and Its Aftermath*, Nancy Lee, Mitchel Levitas, Howell Raines, Lonnie Schlein et al., eds.

208 **Anthony Portillo:** *Portraits 9/11/01*, p. 397.

208 **Leobardo Lopez Pascual:** Ibid., p. 383.

208 **Avnish Patel:** Ibid., p. 383–84.

208 **Salvatore F. Pepe:** Ibid., p. 387.

208 **Berry Berenson Perkins:** Ibid., p. 389.

208 **Glen Pettit:** Ibid., p. 391.

209 **At Camp David, Maryland, on Saturday:** Evan Thomas and Mark Hosenball, "Bush: 'We're At War,' " *Newsweek*, September 24, 2001, p. 32.

209 **Presented with a briefing booklet:** Bob Woodward, *Bush at War* (New York: Simon & Schuster, 2002), in text on ninth page of photographic insert (accompanying Illustration No. 13).

209 **Barbara Baker Burrows was working:** Interview with Russell Burrows.

209 ***Life* . . . was pulling together images:** Life: *One Nation, America Remembers September 11, 2001*, Robert Sullivan, ed. (Boston/New York: Little, Brown, 2001).

209 **As the months passed, Mayor Giuliani:** *In Memoriam: New York City, 9/11/01*, Brad Grey Pictures and HBO, Brad Grey, Jonathan Liebman, Sheila Nevins et al., prods., 2002.

210 **His father . . . collected nineteenth-century:** "The Story of the Remarkable Kunhardt Collaboration," ABC press release, December 1992, to accompany television program, *Lincoln*, Peter W. Kunhardt, Philip B. Kunhardt III, and Philip B. Kunhardt, Jr., prods., ABC Television Network, Capital Cities/ABC, Inc., December 26–27, 1992.

210 **With pictures, Giuliani said, "comes truth":** Remarks at the screening of *In Memoriam*, Ziegfeld Theater, New York, N.Y., May 2002.

210 **"[T]his holiday season . . . I share with you":** Holiday card sent by the Uman family, Westport, Connecticut, winter 2001; text reprinted by permission.

211 **"These photographs . . . were brought to Auschwitz":** Leon Wieseltier in foreword to Ann Weiss, *The Last Album: Eyes from the Ashes of Auschwitz-Birkenau* (New York: W. W. Norton, 2001), p. 15.

211 **"I was looking for my wife":** Interviews and correspondence with David Lipman.

213 **Photographers such as Kevin Bubriski:** Kevin Bubriski, *Pilgrimage: Looking at Ground Zero* (New York: powerHouse, 2002); "Pilgrimage," *Double Take* Special Edition 2001, pp. 52–59.

213 **the narrow depth of field afforded:** Interviews with Bubriski.

213 **"procedure itself caus[ing] models to live":** Walter Benjamin, "A Short History of Photography," from *Classic Essays on Photography*, Alan Trachtenberg, ed. (New Haven, Conn.: Leete's Island Books, 1980), p. 204.

213 **"Their motives were probably a confusion":** Richard B. Woodward, afterword to Bubriski, *Pilgrimage*, pp. 91–93.

213 **On five occasions:** Interviews with Kevin Bubriski.

213 **"slowly approached the site":** "Pilgrimage," p. 53.

214 **"among the most shattering pictures":** Ibid., pp. 91–93.

214 **Five months later, the cleanup:** Life: *The American Spirit, Meeting the Challenge of September 11*, Robert Sullivan, ed. (New York: *Life* Books, 2002), p. 43; interview with architect Kevin Kennon.

214 **"In order to see the wounds":** Interviews with Regis Le Sommier.

215 **"[P]roliferating images . . . rippled out":** Eric Darton, *Divided We Stand: A Biography of New York's World Trade Center* (New York: Basic Books, 1999), p. 185.

215 **Images . . . "almost universally erased":** Marc Peyser, "Anguish on the Airwaves," *Newsweek*, September 24, 2001, p. 64.

216 **Movie studios began cleansing their footage:** Benjamin Svetkey, "Hollywood Pulls the Trigger," *Entertainment Weekly*, December 2, 2005, p. 31.

216 **"Everywhere I look I see people with cameras":** Interview with Ingrid Sischy.

216 **"Wherever one looked—in newspapers":** Ingrid Sischy, "Triumph of the Still," *Vanity Fair*, December 2001, p. 186.

217 **"It's all there, all shot basically in one 72-hour period":** Ibid., p. 190.

217 **A year later . . . killing fifty-two civilians:** "Italy OK's London Bomb Suspect Move," CBS News, August 17, 2005 (www.cbsnews.com).

217 **The next morning, "history was made":** Dennis Dunleavy, "Camera Phones Prevail: Citizen Shutterbugs and the London Bombings," *The Digital Journalist*, July 2005 (www.digitaljournalist.org).

217 **The next month . . . Scoopt, would be launched:** Graham Holliday, "Citizen Scoops," *Guardian Online* (U.K.), August 4, 2005 (http://technology.guardian.co.uk).

217 **"If 9/11 had happened today":** Interview with Alain Genestar.

217 **When Hurricane Dennis bore down . . . CNN, MSNBC . . . solicited:** Joe Light, "Lessons of Internet Age: Citizen Journalism Shows How Firms Have Learned to Quickly Embrace New Technologies," *The Boston Globe*, July 16, 2005, p. A14.

218 **"I feel it's a welcome trend":** Douglas Heingartner, "Honoring News Photos As Picture-Taking Evolves," *The New York Times*, May 3, 2005, p. E3.

218 **Such optimism was not universally shared:** A lens that happens to be "first on the scene" is essential for recording the firing of that maiden historical synapse. Untrained citizens with digital cameras and cell phones now capture an increasing share of those moments, stoking the adrenal engine of the 24/7 news-headline

machine. But to provide a deeper awareness of the social, political, and human issues beneath the headlines demands images acquired over time, images acquired by trained eyes that know *how* to look for more nuanced scenes, fleshed-out stories, tales of individuals caught in history's storm surge.

According to Christian Caujolle, the chief of France's prestigious Agence Vu, "an immediate event captured by an amateur, who now has access to global markets," needs to be placed in balance with images "developed by professional[s] working in an auteur tradition . . . dedicated photojournalists who are still exploring, questioning and challenging the world." Only then, Caujolle believes, can the print press move away from its obsession with speed over depth and its current impulse to adopt the "televisual aesthetic—the frontal shots, the predilection for a supposedly neutral 'middle' distance."

Also required are skilled photographers from the developing world, not just well-intentioned Western interlopers who drop in for a few weeks to catch some lightning in a bottle, then depart for the next hot spot, the next awards banquet, the next incremental selection of images in a growing "body of work." This sentiment has been expressed time and again by champions of non-Western photojournalism such as Shahidul Alam, founder of the Drik Picture Library in Dhaka, Bangladesh. The developing world, says Alam, cannot be regarded "as fodder for disaster reporting, but as a vibrant source of human energy and a challenge to an exploitative global economic system . . . In media, there has to be a mechanism whereby other voices are heard. Media plurality is a very important concept. What happens today is that certain voices are left out of the dialogue." (Christian Caujolle, afterword to Mary Panzer, *Things As They Are: Photojournalism in Context Since 1955*, Chris Boot, ed. [New York: Aperture, 2006], pp. 377, 379; "Shahidul Alam on Third-World Disasters and First-World Media," *Photo District News*, December 2005, p. 23.)

218 **Photography scholar and publisher Fred Ritchin:** Fred Ritchin, "The Unbearable Relevance of Photography," *Aperture*, Vol. 171, Summer 2003, pp. 62–73.

218 **Cornell Capa termed "concerned photography":** *In Our Time: The World As Seen by Magnum Photographers*, William Manchester, Jean Lacouture, Fred Ritchin, eds. (New York: W. W. Norton, 1994), p. 446.

218 **"bleak, unrelentingly grim":** "The Unbearable Relevance," p. 64.

218 **"Our vocabulary of imagery in mass media":** Ibid, pp. 70, 72.

220 **An urbanite absorbs dozens of publicly displayed pictures:** Stuart Elliot, "Did You See That Sign? Advertisers Will Have Their Answer at Last," *The New York Times*, December 7, 2005, p. C5.

220 **At the turn of the millennium, *Life* . . . noted that every day:** *Life* statistic cited in Tom Bentkowski, monograph, "Thoughts on Magazine Design," 2003.

220 **By the spring of 2006, the buzz:** "Handling 1.5 Billion Page Views . . . ," *ScottGu's Blog*, March 25, 2006 (http://weblogs.asp.net/scottgu/archive); Vincent Bonfanti, "MySpace Handling 1.5 Billion Page Views . . . ," *Vince Bonfanti's Weblog*, March 27, 2006 (http://blog.newatlanta.com).

220 **A 2003 study . . . 900 billion photographs:** "How Much Information, 2003?" study by the School of Information Management and Systems, University of California at Berkeley, October 27, 2003 (www.sims.berkeley.edu).

221 **"Photography has never been healthier":** Interview with Jean-Jacques Naudet.

221 **Nextel peddled one of its recent models:** Billboard, sighted by author in Boston, 2005.

221 **The *New York Times* culture critic Frank Rich:** Frank Rich, "The 'Seinfeld' Hoax," *The New York Times*, May 13, 1998.

221 **As a society . . . flipping through . . . publications:** While Cassandras sound the digital death knell of print—forecasting the imminent demise of books, magazines, and newspapers—there has been a renaissance of sorts in image-based titles: catalogs; celebrity tabloids; product, shopping, and lifestyle titles.

221 **surfing or clicking through screens:** What's more, literally millions of new blog entries are posted each day—not counting entries of the estimated thirteen million people operating blogs in China. ("Measuring the Blogosphere," editorial, *The New York Times*, August 5, 2005; Howard W. French, "A Party Girl Leads China's Online Revolution," *The New York Times*, November 24, 2005, p. A1; Nicholas D. Kristof, "China's Cyberdissidents and the Yahoos at Yahoo," *The New York Times*, February 19, 2006, p. WK 13.)

221n **The average U.S. household has 2.4 TVs . . . All told, there are:** Various trade association sources; M: Metrics, Seattle (www.mmetrics.com); Mark Memmott, "Disaster Photos: Newsworthy or Irresponsible?" *USA Today*, August 4, 2005; Damon Darlin, "The iPod Ecosystem," *The New York Times*, February 3, 2006, p. C1; Jeffrey F. Rayport, "Competing in a World of Aggregators," Marketspáce lecture, Condé Nast Building, New York, N.Y., February 27, 2006.

222 **A recent study of the habits of American teens:** That same 2003 Berkeley study found that in the previous calendar year humans produced five exabytes—five billion gigabytes—of totally new information on "print, film, magnetic, and optical storage media," a twofold increase since the decade began. Five exabytes, according to the Berkeley number crunchers, "is equivalent in size to the information contained in 37,000 new libraries the size of the Library of Congress book collections." ("How Much Information, 2003?" Executive Summary, Summary of Findings, University of California at Berkeley, School of Information Management and Systems, October 27, 2003 [www.sims.berkeley.edu]; Verlyn Klinkenborg, "Trying to Measure the Amount of Information that Humans Create," *The New York Times*, November 12, 2003.)

222 **Some believe . . . "nothing shocks us anymore":** Susan Sontag, *On Photography* (New York: Farrar, Straus and Giroux, 1977); Susan Sontag, *Regarding the Pain of Others* (New York: Farrar, Straus and Giroux, 2002).

222 **"a fatal facility" requiring "little labor":** Alfred Stieglitz, "Pictorial Photography," in *Classic Essays on Photography*, p. 117.

222 **"the most democratic art form since charcoal":** Robert Dannin, "Defending the Passionate Observer," *Rethink: Cause and Consequences of September 11*, Giorgio Baravalle, ed. (Millbrook, N.Y.: de.MO, 2003), p. 237.

222 **We are hedonists . . . and skeptics:** "Skeptic," according to the *Oxford English Dictionary*, is derived from the Latin *scepticus* and the Greek *skeptikos*, meaning "thoughtful," and from *skeptesthai*, "to look, to consider."

222 **"the tiny spark of accident":** Walter Benjamin in *Classic Essays on Photography*, p. 202.

223 **"Even our simplest snapshots":** "Thoughts on Magazine Design."

224 **"Watch her carefully, every movement":** Brian Friel, *Philadelphia, Here I Come!* (London: Faber and Faber, 1965), pp. 79, 110.

224 **"It makes evolutionary sense":** Correspondence with Dr. Jeffrey Claman.

225 **A legendary photojournalist who has made:** Harry Benson, *First Families: An Intimate Portrait from the Kennedys to the Clintons*, Gigi Benson and David Friend, eds. (Boston/New York: Bulfinch, 1997).

225 **John Lennon's room at the George V:** Harry Benson, *Harry Benson: Fifty Years in Pictures* (New York: Abrams, 2001), pp. 28–29.

226 **Across sixteen acres:** *The 9/11 Commission Report: Final Report of the National Commission on Terrorist Attacks upon the United States* (New York: W. W. Norton, 2004), p. 278.

227 **"It's like Beirut":** Interview with David Engo.

227 **"Our main job":** Interview with James McManamy.

228 **This was the disaster mortuary team:** Interview with Shiya Ribowsky.

228 **"The idea was to get the remains packaged properly":** Interview with Dr. Robert Shaler.

229 **"The perimeter's in almost total lockdown":** Interview with Mike Carter.

229 **"Danny Suhr . . . hit by a jumper":** Interview with Mike Carter; *Portraits 9/11/01*, p. 484.

230 **"Charlie Anaya":** Ibid., p. 14.

231 **After ninety-three hours:** Interview and correspondence with Sandra M. Genelius, CBS News.

231 **Unprecedented in [CBS] television history:** By comparison, CBS ran four days of nonstop news when President John F. Kennedy was assassinated in 1963, but in that pre-24/7 era of test patterns, peacocks, and Ipana toothpaste, networks would sign off late in the evening, so the JFK reporting was not continuous, running slightly under fifty-five hours. (Ibid.)

231 **"the entire staff was looking up at a TV":** Interview with Andy Levin.

231 **"This was an old woman who lives in the country":** Interview with Luc Sante.

232 **"Everything was in deferred time":** Interview with Robert Pledge.

232 **"I remember watching the initial news reports":** Interview and correspondence with David Grogan.

233 **"We're the *United* States":** Interview with Anthony Liotti.

233 **"America was still questioning":** Interview with Larry Towell.

234 **NBC News made sure that staff members:** "Lessons of Internet Age."

234 **"a reporter and producer [at the ready]":** Correspondence with Susan Zirinsky.

234 **The "crawl line" . . . predates September 11:** Marshall Sella, "The Year in Ideas: The Crawl," *The New York Times Magazine*, December 9, 2001, p. 66.

235 **"CNN, MSNBC, and FOX . . . inserted the crawls":** Josh Wolk, "It's a Crawl World," *Entertainment Weekly*, November 23, 2001, p. 23.

235 **CNN listed the names of the deceased:** Confirmation from Carolyn Disbrow, CNN.

235 **"They can now run stories they haven't confirmed":** "The Year in Ideas."

236 **"Multiple images . . . capture the fragmentation":** On the other hand, the split screen has allowed for none-too-subtle propaganda, with one image serving as an ironic *commentary* on the other. When the Iraq War got under way in 2003, for instance, the Arab-language al-Jazeera used the split screen to juxtapose a press conference held by Defense Secretary Rumsfeld with a bedside shot of a hospitalized Iraqi girl. Nothing new there. This was just a more blatant use of the single screen

to exaggerate political differences and to infuse news events with a jolt of red-meat rage and irony. The trend toward expressing conflicting points of view in the same visual space has become increasingly popular since the mid-1990s, especially in U.S. cable television news, where FOX News has made its mark (and some say its fortune) through its point-counterpoint cockfights on roundtable and commentary programs. Television, the Internet, and a raft of new portable electronic devices, now capable of bifurcating any screen—and any viewer's attention span—have ushered in the electronic dialectic. (Caryn James, "Splitting. Screens. For Minds. Divided.," *The New York Times*, January 9, 2004, p. E7; Jonathan Alter, "The Other Air Battle: Al-Jazeera Rules the Waves—Whether the Pentagon Likes It or Not," *Newsweek*, April 7, 2003, p. 39.)

237 **"Since September 11, much of the press has dropped to both knees":** James Wolcott, "Round Up the Cattle!" *Vanity Fair*, June 2003, p. 86.

237 **"I have been shocked by how unquestioning":** Amanda Griscom, "Did We See the Real War?" *Rolling Stone*, June 12, 2003, p. 43.

237 **FOX News and MSNBC, which honed:** Alan B. Kreuger, "Fair? Balanced? A Study Finds It Does Not Matter," *The New York Times*, August 18, 2005, p. C2.

237 **"the decapitated Chinaman":** Bernard De Voto, "Report on Photography," *The Saturday Review of Literature*, January 29, 1938; Loudon Wainwright, *The Great American Magazine: An Inside History of* Life (New York, Knopf, 1986), p. 95.

238 **It wasn't until September 1943:** "60 Pictures That Changed Us Forever," *Life* 60th Anniversary Special Issue, October 1996, pp. 52–53.

238 **It took . . . David Turnley days of cajoling:** Ibid., p. 104.

238 **"You're denying these guys":** Ibid.

238 **"The government has blocked the press":** Sydney H. Schanberg, "Not a Pretty Picture: Looking This War in the Face Proves Difficult When the Press Itself Won't Even Put in an Appearance," *The Village Voice*, May 17, 2005.

239 **Nedjma . . . called it:** Alan Riding, "A Muslim Woman, a Story of Sex," *The New York Times*, June 20, 2005, p. E1.

239 **Christopher Hitchens called it:** Correspondence with Hitchens.

239 **Ulf Poschardt called it:** Interview with Poschardt.

239 **Don DeLillo . . . called it:** "In the Ruins of the Future: Reflections on Terror and Loss in the Shadow of September," *Harper's Magazine*, December 2001, p. 33–34.

240 **Alain Finkielkraut called it:** Alain Finkielkraut, "Dieser Feind bestimmt uns. Wir sind Soldaten der Zivilisation," *Frankfurter Allgemeine Zeitung*, September 27, 2001, p. 47.

240 **Fareed Zakaria cited Thomas Hobbes:** Fareed Zakaria, "The End of the End of History," *Newsweek*, September 24, 2001, p. 70.

240 **Noam Chomsky . . . called it:** Noam Chomsky, *9/11* (New York: Seven Stories Press, 2002), p. 21.

240 **Gigi Benson called it:** Interview with Benson.

240 **William Bennett insisted:** Christopher Marquis, "For Hawks, a Day to Sit Back and Say, 'I Told You So,' " *The New York Times*, April 11, 2003, p. B9.

241 **"the best obtainable version of the truth":** Carl Bernstein, "Watergate's Last Chapter," *Vanity Fair*, October 2005, p. 340.

241 **"Google [the phrase] '911 conspiracy' ":** Mark Jacobson, "The Ground Zero Grassy Knoll," *New York*, March 27, 2006, p. 32.

242 **This thesis, popularized by . . . Thierry Meyssan:** Ibid., p. 84.

242 **the absence of a plane:** Robert Burns, "Video of 9/11 Pentagon Attack Released," *The Journal News* (White Plains, N.Y.), May 17, 2006, p. 3B.

242 **In similar fashion . . . the twin towers' collapse [is called] a "controlled demolition":** "Charlie Sheen Doesn't Buy 9/11 Spin," *BostonHerald.com*, March 23, 2006 (http://thetrack.bostonherald.com); *Loose Change: 2nd Edition*, Dylan Avery, dir., Korey Rowe, prod., Louder Than Words, 2005.

243 **Nor was history "a fable [or] set of lies agreed upon":** Napoléon Bonaparte, *Napoleon on the Art of War*, Jay Luvaas, ed. (New York: Touchtone, 1999), p. 28.

243 **With this aggregate objectivity, furnished by the camera:** The avant-garde artist, photographer, and Bauhaus innovator László Moholy-Nagy in 1925 pointed out this underlying attribute of photography: "[I]n the photographic camera we have the most reliable aid to a beginning of objective vision. Everyone will be compelled to see that which is optically true, is explicable in its own terms, is objective, before he can arrive at any possible subjective position." (László Moholy-Nagy, "Photography," in *Classic Essays on Photography*, p. 166.)

243 **"In the modern way of knowing":** Susan Sontag, "On Photography (The Short Course)," *Los Angeles Times Book Review*, July 27, 2003, p. R16.

244 **At the very pinnacle of the U.S. student demonstrations:** Robbin Henderson, introduction to *The Whole World's Watching: Peace and Social Justice Movements of the 1960s & 1970s* (Berkeley, Calif.: Berkeley Art Center Association, 2001), p. 2.

245 **"If Hitler had had television":** Randy Kennedy, "Mr. Natural's Creator Visits the World of Art," *The New York Times*, April 16, 2005.

245 **If September 11 was the globally witnessed . . . whatever one does . . . may very well be witnessed:** When the 2005 bombings devastated the London transit system, and passengers immediately snapped pictures, they had crossed the Rubicon. The ever open-ended War on Terror—whose domain has been expanded by terrorists and politicians alike to encompass the entire planet—had conscripted unsuspecting citizens, as they went about their business, as nothing less than battlefield photographers, armed with cell phones, digital cameras, and camcorders.

And two months later, when Hurricane Katrina ravaged America's Gulf Coast—and as U.S. officials repeatedly assured the public that the feds had the crisis in hand—television footage exposed the government's dissembling and inaction, chronicling hour after hour of human suffering in living, heartbreaking color. Videotape revealed what many politicians, bureaucrats, and spinmeisters refused to acknowledge: 100,000 New Orleans citizens, largely African American and impoverished, had been left stranded in the Crescent City after several of the surrounding levees gave way, and floodwaters rose, killing hundreds.

In fact, it was President Bush's obstinate practice of *avoiding* television news (preferring, he claimed, to receive a digest of world events from his aides) that contributed to his administration's unconscionably dilatory response to what many consider the most devastating natural disaster in U.S. history. While the president learned about the escalating tragedy through third parties, the nation, in fury, watched scenes of mass starvation and displacement, and saw video images of street-side corpses and frantic rooftop rescues, right from their living rooms.

The first network correspondent on the scene, NBC's Brian Williams, later expressed bafflement at the president's TV-viewing patterns, echoing the stern rebuke that critics had leveled against Richard Nixon. Asked Williams: "What did [Bush] watch and when did he watch it?" During the height of the crisis, Williams even turned to his audience and said (underscoring the impact of television-as-arbiter in a time of national emergency): "Where is the help? The people inside the city of New Orleans are asking repeatedly to people in Washington, 'Are you watching? Are you listening?' " (Williams interview with Don Imus, "Imus in the Morning" radio broadcast, WFAN, fall 2005; "Hell and High Water," *Vanity Fair*, October 2005, p. 372).

245 **Happenstance photography . . . provides an oversight function:** True, the downside is that the amateur's cell phone snapshot of today's disaster or yesterday's compromised celebrity might very well be a fake—a digital hocus-focus concocted for kicks, financial gain, or character assassination. "The fabrication and manipulation of documents," photojournalism expert Christian Caujolle has noted, "has been employed by every totalitarian power, during purges and in the interests of propaganda. [Today's] digital technology facilitates such practices." But in the main these accidental artifacts—stolen moments in the street—have generally proven authentic and, at times, even invaluable. (Christian Caujolle, afterword to Mary Panzer, *Things As They Are: Photojournalism in Context Since 1955*, Chris Boot, ed. [New York: Aperture, 2005], p. 377.)

245 **The witness might well be a bystander:** Such voyeur vigilantism is a double-edged sword. Law enforcement agencies in towns such as Harlow, Essex, in England, have successfully persuaded scores of citizens to train their picture phones on evidence of vandalism and other acts of what local authorities call "anti-social behaviour" and then e-mail the images to the police. The downside: certain municipalities may eventually risk becoming digital Peyton Places where even a minor deviation from the social norm may be recorded for posterity, and possible prosecution, by the high-tech busybody next door. (Denise Harvey, "One Stop Cop Shop," *Essex Police* [Online] *Newsline*, January 31, 2006 [http://www.essex.police.uk/news]; "Together: Tackling Anti-Social Behavior," Together.Gov Web site, Office of the Deputy Prime Minister, 2006 [http://www.together.gov.uk]).

245 **"We . . . are compassed about":** *The New Testament*, Hebrews 12: 1 (New York: American Bible Society, 1880), vol. IV, p. 279.

246 **And nearer the modern age . . . the invention of the printing press:** *The New Encyclopaedia Britannica* (Chicago: Encyclopaedia Britannica, 1994), vol. 5, p. 581.

246 **the photograph (1826–27):** John Szarkowski, *Photography Until Now* (Boston: Bulfinch/Museum of Modern Art [New York], 1989), p. 22; "Photographer [Joseph-] Nicephore Niepce—History of Photography," Maison Nicephore Niepce: the reference site about the inventor of photography, Speos Photo School and Maison Nicephore Niepce (www.niepce.com).

246 **The screen could now give global prominence:** Imagine the lasting impact on human behavior had Mahatma Gandhi's 1940s hunger strikes and nonviolent protests against the British occupation of India been monitored in real time. Then again, Weblogs and 24/7 news would have been able to offer Gandhi's opponents more opportunities to undermine his cause through rumors, spin, and smears. ("India-hands want to know: Why do Gandhi and *Life* photo siren Margaret Bourke-White seem attached at the hip these days?")

247 **"If you think about the rise of terrorism":** Interview and correspondence with David Hazinksi.

248 **"the dynamics, sensations and implications":** Gallery text for *2001*, an exhibition

of new works by Wolfgang Staehle, Postmasters Gallery, New York, N.Y., September 6–October 6, 2001.

248 **"Seeing reality in real time in an art space":** Interview with Staehle.

249 **"We return ourselves to slowness":** Alexi Worth, review of *2001*, *ArtForum*, November 2001.

249 **When the farthest corner . . . has been conquered:** Martin Heidegger, "The Fundamental Question of Metaphysics," *Introduction to Metaphysics*, Gregory Fried and Richard Polt, trans. (New Haven/London: Yale University, 2000), p. 40.

250 **"On three walls, static video images glowed":** Worth.

251 **"One building was burning":** Interview with Magda Sawon.

252 **Nonetheless, critics far and wide:** Bill Jones would write in a review in late September 2001 that the work was "both of the Internet and divorced from it . . . In this installation, Staehle succeeded in pushing his medium beyond the basics of electronic communication . . . finding a level of poignancy that [the medium] has never before achieved. This is the purpose of art: to cut through the proliferation of pictures with an unwavering vision—a vision that stands apart from yet joins with all the images of the moment." (Bill Jones, "Art for a New World: Internet-art Pioneer Wolfgang Staehle Captures Our Moment," *TimeOutNY*, September 27–October 4, 2001.)

252 **When portions of Staehle's "2001" were shown in Paris:** *Unknown Quantity*, exhibition conceived by Paul Virilio, Fondation Cartier pour l'art contemporain, Paris, November 29, 2002–March 30, 2003.

252 **"You invent an airplane with six hundred seats":** Political theorist Hannah Arendt cautioned that "progress and catastrophe are the opposite faces of the same coin." (Ibid., Hannah Arendt, cited in Virilio introduction to catalog for exhibition, p. 3.)

253 **"Real time" . . . became possible:** John Menick, "Real-Time Futures: Five Notes on the Work of Wolfgang Staehle," *Parachute 113*, July 4, 2004 (www.johnmenick.com/archives).

253 **invention of the atomic clock:** "Atomic Ticker Clocks up 50 Years," BBC News, February 6, 2005 (www.bbcnews.co.uk).

254 **"I thought of time-lapse, right there":** Interviews and correspondence with Jim Whitaker.

254 **He vaguely knew of . . . Muybridge:** Rebecca Solnit, *River of Shadows: Eadweard Muybridge and the Technological Wild West* (New York: Viking, 2003), p. 4.

254 **He was familiar with Frank Percy Smith's 1910 . . . studies:** Byrony Dixon, "Percy Smith (1880–1945)," *screenonline*, British Film Institute; Jenny Hammerton, "The Birth of a Flower (1910)" *screenonline*, British Film Institute (www.screenonline.org.uk).

255 **the shadows and snowdrifts advance and recede:** Sarah Boxer, "Ground Zero, the Long View," *The New York Times*, September 8, 2004, pp. E1, E3.

6. SUNDAY, SEPTEMBER 16

257 **"I went down to Ground Zero":** Interviews with Joel Meyerowitz.

258 **He understood the value of creating a systematic record:** Colin Westerbeck and Joel Meyerowitz, *Bystander: A History of Street Photography* (Boston/New York: Bulfinch, 1994).

258 **For the previous two or three months . . . an exhibition:** Joel Meyerowitz, *Looking South: New York City Landscapes, 1981–2001*, Ariel Meyerowitz Gallery, New York, N.Y., November 3–December 15, 2001.

260 **When discussing the images, Meyerowitz . . . refers to Rembrandt's:** Sarah Boxer, "Even in a Moonscape of Tragedy, Beauty Is in the Eye," *The New York Times*, May 23, 2002, p. E1.

260 **The work, five thousand images strong:** Interviews with Meyerowitz.

260 **Under the auspices of the U.S. State Department:** Joel Meyerowitz, *After September 11: Images from Ground Zero*, U.S. Department of State Bureau of Educational and Cultural Affairs and the Museum of the City of New York (www.911exhibit .state.gov/about exhibit.cfm).

260 **three hundred cities in ninety countries:** Interviews and correspondence with Brian Sexton, U.S. Department of State.

260 **In its own way . . . through 503 pictures by 273 photographers:** Eric J. Sandeen, *Picturing an Exhibition:* The Family of Man *and 1950s America* (Albuquerque: University of New Mexico Press, 1995), p. 40.

261 **"These pictures" . . . became "part of an American projection abroad":** Ibid., p. 26.

261 **"Everywhere we went . . . firemen came in uniform":** Interviews with Brian Sexton.

262 **Andrew Wilton and Tim Barringer's exhibition:** *American Sublime: Landscape Painting in the United States, 1820–1880,*" exhibition of works by Andrew Wilton and Tim Barringer, Pennsylvania Academy of Fine Arts, Philadelphia, June 17–August 25, 2002.

262 **"delightful horror, a sort of tranquility":** John Updike, "O Beautiful for Spacious Skies," *The New York Review of Books*, August 15, 2002.

262 **"transcending every standard sense":** Ibid.

263 **"Terrible beauty," unfortunately, was not a phrase:** "Even in a Moonscape of Tragedy."

264 **Legendary portraitist . . . Mary Ellen Mark photographed:** *Brotherhood*, Tony Hendra, ed. (New York: American Express Publishing/Ogilvy & Mather, 2001).

264 **Joel Sternfeld . . . made still lifes:** Joel Sternfeld, "Parks Transformed," *Double Take*, Special Edition 2001, pp. 8–11.

264 **"When the papers were falling all around":** Mike Starn, quoted in Doug and Mike Starn, "Ashes to Ashes," *Double Take*, Special Edition 2001, p. 26.

264 **Jeff Mermelstein, the street photographer:** Jeff Mermelstein, *Jeff Mermelstein: Ground Zero, September 11, 2001*, exhibition at the International Center of Photography, New York, N.Y., September 13–December 1, 2002.

264 **David Turnley shot an extended photo essay:** David Turnley photo essay, "Sanctuary: At Ground Zero, a Church Survives, and Finds Its Mission," Life: *The American Spirit, Meeting the Challenge of September 11*, Robert Sullivan, ed. (New York: Life Books, 2002), pp. 56–65.

264 **Eugene Richards documented Manhattan's aftershock:** Eugene Richards and Janine Altongy, *Stepping Through the Ashes* (New York: Aperture, 2002).

265 **Jonas Karlsson . . . made formal portraits:** "One Week in September," *Vanity Fair* Special Edition, November 2001.

265 **Nathan Lyons photographed the panoply:** Lyons's photographs are symbols of a

symbol "spawned in war and revolution," in the words of Richard Benson, dean of the Yale University School of Art, that "has become our embracing shroud of grief and pride. [Lyons's] parade of flags [reveals] the diversity that the flag so boldly encompasses—it turns our many tribes into one." (Richard Benson, afterword to *After 9/11* [New Haven, Conn.: Yale University, 2003], p. 169.)

265 **Working at the invitation of *Life* magazine:** Joe McNally, "Faces of Ground Zero," Life: *One Nation—America Remembers September 11, 2001*, Robert Sullivan, ed. (Boston/New York: Little, Brown, 2001), pp. 142–67.

265 **Forty by eighty inches:** Ibid., p. 142.

265 **The so-called Museum Camera:** Ibid.

265 **Two technicians would actually sit *inside* the camera:** Interview with Joe McNally.

267 **On Sunday, Laura Greenstone was making final arrangements:** Interviews and correspondence with Greenstone.

267 **Two months later, recognizing the need:** A Web site for the county's September 11 memorial states that outside of Manhattan, Monmouth sustained the highest number of county-wide losses—146 residents, some of whom perished in the crash of United Flight 93 in Pennsylvania (http://mommouthcounty911memorial.com).

267 **Others would use their family pictures:** In counseling those dealing with grief, trauma, and mental or physical illness, colleagues of Laura Greenstone's such as PhotoTherapy pioneer Judy Weiser have long advocated the use of personal albums, picture-taking, and techniques for reacting to visual stimuli, as a way of helping clients probe their unconscious or arrive at a more objective sense of self-awareness. (Judy Weiser, *Photo Therapy Techniques: Exploring the Secrets of Personal Snapshots and Family Albums* [Vancouver: Photo Therapy Centre, 1999].)

269 **On September 11, my friend, an executive at eSpeed:** Interviews with source, who requests anonymity.

270 **Cantor had lost more than 650:** David Friend, "Two Towers, One Year Later," *Vanity Fair*, September 2002, p. 372.

271 **Middletown . . . a community that suffered:** Gail Sheehy, "September Widows," *Vanity Fair*, September 2002, p. 260.

271 **"At first . . . it felt like an altruistic thing to do":** Interview with Nancy Gawron.

271 **Within nine months of September 11, 103 expectant mothers:** "Infant Care Project," Initiatives Archives, Independent Women's Forum, 2004 (www.iwf.org).

272 **On board was a special spectrometer:** Andrew C. Revkin, "Physical Effects of Sept. 11 Scrutinized from on High," *The New York Times*, September 17, 2002, p. F3.

272 **Gather evidence of potentially toxic pockets:** Ibid.

272 **The . . . AVIRIS . . . had previously been deployed by NASA:** Andrew Schneider, "Roiling Cloud Filled USGS Scientists with a Sense of Urgency," *St. Louis Post-Dispatch*, February 10, 2002, p. A15.

272 **Based on AVIRIS data . . . scientists . . . located thirty-four fires:** Ibid.

272 **Experts . . . generated maps . . . "shipped to emergency response teams":** Ibid.

272 **"two different kinds of aerosols":** Louisa Dalton, "Chemical Analysis of a Disaster," *Chemical & Engineering News*, October 20, 2003, vol. 81, no. 42, CENEAR 81 42, pp. 26–30.

272 **Five years later, even after . . . a Mount Sinai Medicial Center . . . program:** "Red Cross Supports 9/11 Recovery with $50 Million in Grants," American Red Cross press release, June 30, 2004; Anthony DePalma, "Tracing Lung Ailments That Rose With 9/11 Dust," *The New York Times*, May 13, 2006, pp. A1, B5.

273 **On Sunday, an estimated four hundred:** Special commemorative edition of *The Spectator: The Stuyvesant High School Newspaper*, Fall 2001, p. 10.

273 **One hundred and sixty posed:** Ibid.

273 **Late Sunday morning, Lisa Palazzo was still in bed:** Interview with Palazzo.

273 **"I knew I had to talk to her":** Interview with Robbie Morrell.

273 **On Thursday, she and Lisa . . . videotaped by two TV crews:** Interview with spokespeople for NBC News; CBS newsmagazine *48 Hours*.

275 **"It was literally a shrine":** Interviews with Don Johnston.

275 **Tommy, then forty-four:** *Portraits 9/11/01: The Collected "Portraits of Grief" from* The New York Times (New York: Times Books, 2002), p. 379.

276 **"You had a hard time eating":** Interview with Maryellen Johnston.

277 **I tell her about a newspaper reporter:** Interview with anonymous source.

278 **Tonight, he savors the images, a bittersweet elixir:** The videos, to Johnston, are an unanticipated present. Reignited in a magic glass rectangle is that old spark, unextinguished. There's Tommy, just turned forty, dancing under a white party tent. Now someone is plopping a baseball cap on his head. Now Tommy has a microphone and he is on the back patio, looking across a crowd of family and friends, looking for Lisa, somewhere outside of the video frame. "I want to thank my best friend," he says, "my wife."

Sitting beside Maryellen later that night, Johnston drives home in the dark. He talks of his own TP "photo story," though he is quick to add a note of caution: "I'm not one of these guys out there looking for signs." (Indeed, as I've learned through ten years of friendship, he is levelheaded, benevolent, gregarious.) On an unseasonably windy morning—the second anniversary of 9/11—he decided, on impulse, to visit the graves of TP and George, despite the fact that he was pressed for time and due to rush off to a business meeting. On the way, TP's favorite songs began to play on the radio. Then Johnston's cell phone rang: the meeting had been fortuitously canceled. Upon arriving at the cemetery, he realized he couldn't locate their headstones, yet up pulled a caravan of cars and, unexpectedly, twenty of TP's and George's family members emerged, able to escort him to their graves.

Driving home, Johnston heard more TP tunes emanating from the dash. Then he arrived and walked up the back steps, only to find a photograph, he says, "in a Lucite frame, face up, and propped perfectly" on the landing. The rays of the afternoon sun seemed focused directly on the picture, illuminating it. The photo, according to Johnston, showed his son Dylan with TP's daughter Kerri, "faces pressed together," he says, "beaming, sun shining on the frame." It was the shot that Dylan had kept on his sill in the bedroom one floor above. "It had fallen out the window."

"For the first time ever," Maryellen explains, "the wind blew the [window's] screen latch open and the photo fell [down] onto the landing."

At first Johnston thought it was a snide joke: someone had known he'd gone to the cemetery and had placed it there to spook him (though he had told no one of his plans). But then he began to laugh, overtaken, he says, by "the intense emotions" and message-laden events of the morning. For fifteen minutes he stood there, infused with an overpowering bond to TP and George, reveling in what he calls the "wonder and funkiness [of this] sign" from above. Through this strange encounter, he believes, his friends were "conveying a connection to a world beyond us, where [they] may be in a safe and possibly better place."

278 **While sitting, I thought of . . . Carl Mydans:** Bill Foley, "Carl Mydans, 1907–2004," *The Digital Journalist*, September 2004 (www.digitaljournalist.org).

278 **Within weeks . . . eventually killing 344 (including 172 children):** Nabi Abdullaev, "Hostage Death Toll at 344," *The Moscow Times*, October 13, 2004, p. 4.

278 **"Mr. Tumayev sits alone for a little while":** Seth Mydans, "At a School in Russia, a World of Emptiness," *The New York Times*, September 28, 2004.

280 **"There was a lot of visual imagery around the American flag":** Interview with Peggy Conlan.

280 **One of her organization's ads:** "Your Support Has Touched Us More Than You Know," advertisement by the Ad Council on behalf of the International Fire Chiefs Association.

281 **Early on, ad wizard Roy Spence:** "Public Service Advertising That Changed a Nation," report, The Ad Council, New York, September 2004, pp. 27–28.

281 **the Ad Council—known for hatching:** "Ad Council Announces Crisis Response Team," Ad Council news release, October 4, 2001; "Ad Council's Coalition Against Terrorism Announces Communications Strategy," Ad Council news release, New York, October 30, 2001.

281 **Hundreds of citizens . . . were videotaped:** "Public Service Advertising That Changed a Nation," p. 28.

281 **eventually channeled to three thousand television outlets:** "Media Campaign Responds to Tragedy and Celebrates Diversity in America," Ad Council press advisory, September 20, 2001.

281 **"By the time [it] was over":** "Public Service Advertising That Changed a Nation," p. 29.

282 **"Around the year 2000":** Thomas L. Friedman, *The World Is Flat: A Brief History of the Twenty-first Century* (New York: Farrar, Straus and Giroux, 2005), p. 10.

282 **The Tuesday before, Heiferman had stood on his roof:** Interview with Scott Heiferman.

282 **Heiferman . . . simply floated the picture:** Scott Heiferman photo on "Scott Heiferman's Photo of the Day," 091101 (www.heiferman.com/photo/091101.htm).

282 **His online exercise . . . a phenomenon started in 2000:** Sarah Boxer, "Prospecting for Gold Among the Photo Blogs," *The New York Times*, May 25, 2003, p. B1.

283 **It was gobbled up by Agency.com:** Pamela Parker, "Agency.com Offers Direct Marketing Through Acquisition," *ClickZ* Network, December 15, 1999 (www.clickz.com).

283 **"20-something dethroned dotcom ceo":** www.heiferman.com.

283 **"As we walked . . . we came across two groups":** Scott Heiferman photo on "Scott Heiferman's Photo of the Day," 091301 (www.heiferman.com/photo/091301.htm).

283 **This cohesive spirit "was more powerful offline":** Interviews and correspondence with Scott Heiferman.

284 **Today a million new images:** Fotolog.net Web site (www.fotolog.net) and correspondence with Scott Heiferman.

284 **"Meetup.com" took off almost immediately:** "Meetup.com Forms Politics and Governance Advisory Council," Meetup.com press release, March 10, 2005 (http://press.meetup.com). As I discovered while poking around the Meetup.com Web site: on a single Wednesday in the spring of 2005, for example, in the city of San Diego, Meetup sessions were scheduled for local ex-patriot Germans (62 members), the San Diego Depression Meetup Group (53 members), fans of cable-TV host Bill O'Reilly (84 members), a local actors' collective (67 members), a San Diego–area faction of event planners (190 members), and San Diego entrepreneurs hoping to learn the "CAN SLIM investing method" (227 members). There are, in fact, no less than 200 Chihuahua-enthusiast Meetup cliques across the country. (The company's board includes investors such as high-tech seer Esther Dyson and eBay founder Pierre Omidyar.)

285 **"CNN.com saw 162 million page views":** Steve Outing, "Attack's Lessons for News Web Sites," *Editor & Publisher*, September 19, 2001.

285 **"between September 11 and 16":** Stuart Allan, "Reweaving the Internet: Online News of September 11," *Journalism After September 11*, Barbie Zelizer and Stuart Allan, eds. (London: Routledge, 2002), pp. 134–35.

285 **Because of increased volume . . . many news sites' servers crashed:** Wayne Robins, "The Web Fails Its First Big Test," *Editor & Publisher*, September 17, 2001.

285 **"the *New York Post*'s site":** Ibid.

285 **A Pew Research Center study:** "Attack's Lessons."

286 **Space Imaging . . . high-resolution . . . satellite:** "September 11: One Year Viewed from Space" (www.spaceimaging.com).

286 **Kodak and AOL created . . . PhotoQuilt:** Tribute to American Spirit Photo Quilt, presented by AOL and Kodak (http://photoquilt.kodak.com).

286 **Even more ambitious would be filmmaker Steven Rosenbaum's:** Glenn Collins, "Cataloging the 9/11 Archive," *The New York Times*, May 30, 2006, p. B1.

286 **the September 11 Digital Archive project:** Web sites for Library of Congress, www.911digitalarchive.org, and www.sloan.org.

286 **Hundreds of photo-and-text profiles . . . at sites like wallofamericans.com:** Amy Harmon, "Real Solace in a Virtual World: Memorials Take Root on the Web," *The New York Times*, September 11, 2002.

286 **Several home pages offer a poster:** Web site for Bolivar Arellano Gallery, 2006 (www.bollivararellanogallery.com).

287 **"many people put their photos online":** Interview and correspondence with Jeff Jarvis.

288 **operating what came to be termed "citJ" Web sites:** Steve Outing, "Can 'Citizen Journalists' Really Produce Readable Content?" *Editor & Publisher*, October 25, 2005.

288 **"Another kind of reporting emerged":** Dan Gillmor, *We the Media: Grassroots Journalism By the People, For the People* (Sebastopol, Calif.: O'Reilly, 2004), p. x.

288 **"Hundreds of refashioned websites began to appear":** "Reweaving the Internet," p. 127.

289 **"Like that man on the cover of *Fortune*":** Photograph by Stan Honda/Agence

France-Presse, "Up from the Ashes," *Fortune*, October 1, 2001, cover. The image shows Ed Fine, a fifty-nine-year-old entrepreneur from New Jersey, coated in dust and lugging his briefcase through the blighted city. Fine, clutching a towel to his mouth to fend off the air's debris, survived not only a seventy-eight-story descent of the north tower but, once outside, its thunderous collapse. (Peter Cheney, "Ed Fine Wants His Life Back," *The* (Toronto) *Globe and Mail*, March 11, 2002.)

289 **"Bums came up to me"**: This attraction to the visual was an evolutionary process. In fact, on September 11 he had been dismissive of a stranger who had requested that he photograph him. Jarvis wrote in his very first blog entry: "I wandered back up Liberty Street where a foreign businessman asked me to take his picture in front of the burning tower. I refused. I said this was a tragedy. He said, 'I know, I want to see myself and remember I am alive.' I still refused. I hope he still is alive. A minute later, the spreading fire high up in Two World Trade erupted into a mighty explosion and the building collapsed, sending its debris down and my mob running." (Jeff Jarvis, "The World Trade Center Tragedy: An Eyewitness Account," *NJ.com*, September 11, 2001, AdvanceNet [nj.com].)

290 **People who "ran to their television sets"**: Barbie Zelizer, "Photography, Journalism, and Trauma," in *Journalism After September 11*, p. 50.

291 **We have the Web's phalanx . . . perpetuating the myths:** Andrew B. Cohen, "Questions and Answers: Rumor-Busting," *Newsweek.com*, October 19, 2001; Maggie Farley, "Response to Terror: Hoaxes, Rumors and Wishful Thinking Spawned by Trauma," *Los Angeles Times*, September 28, 2001, p. A16.

291 **that the collapse . . . was an "inside job"**: Salman Rushdie, "Yes, This Is About Islam," *The New York Times*, November 2, 2001; Mark Jacobson, "The Ground Zero Grassy Knoll," *New York*, March 27, 2006, p. 31.

291 **that a man had somehow surfed the rubble:** This urban myth may have evolved from a story about a Port Authority officer rescued on September 12, 2001. It is referred to in a photo caption to a picture by Mary McLoughlin in the *New York Post*, September 13, 2001, p. 11: "SURVIVAL STORY: Nassau County cop Richard Doerler [Doyler] describes the 'miracle' rescue of a Port Authority officer identified as 'John,' who survived a fall from [the] 80th floor in the South Tower collapse."

291 **Among the most unsettling . . . a Photoshopped image:** New York *Daily News*, October 12, 2001.

291 **that surfaced within days of the attacks:** Randall E. Stross, "The Rumor Mail," *U.S. News & World Report*, November 12, 2001, p. 44.

292 **According to reported accounts:** Jeffrey Benner, "He's the Real Tourist Guy," Wired News, *Wired.com*, November 20, 2001; Leo Hickman, "Tracking Down the Tourist of Death," *The* (U.K.) *Guardian*, November 30, 2001.

292 **Web pages persist:** David Colker, "The Web Never Forgets," *Los Angeles Times*, November 27, 2001, pp. A1, A11.

292 **In 2004 . . . long-suppressed images of the coffins:** Sydney H. Schanberg, "Not a Pretty Picture," *The Village Voice*, May 17, 2005; Thom Shanker and Bill Carter, "Photos of Soldiers' Coffins Spark a Debate Over Access," *The New York Times*, April 24, 2004, p. A14.

292 **"The Pentagon . . . quickly said"**: "Abu Ghraib and Amateur Photos," *Photo District News*, May 2005, p. 29.

293 **"within the context of no context":** George W. S. Trow, *Within the Context of No Context* (Boston/New York: Atlantic Monthly, 1997).

293 **"If you think back, news gatherers":** David Carr, "With Thousands of Images from the Region, Broadcasters Struggle to Make Sense of a Disaster," *The New York Times*, December 28, 2004, p. A12.

293 **"this crusade, this war on terrorism":** Bob Woodward, *Bush at War* (New York: Simon & Schuster, 2002), p. 94.

293 **"For nearly an hour . . . they talked":** Ibid., pp. 95–96.

293 **In the war's planning phase, images:** Correspondence with ex–Air Force pilot Mark Brightman; Douglas Jehl, "Digital Links Are Giving Old Weapons New Power," *The New York Times*, April 7, 2003, p. B2.

294 **GIs used night-vision gear:** "Urban Warriors," *Time*, April 7, 2003, pp. 53–54.

294 **helmets fitted with video cameras:** Keith Naughton, "Lock and Download," *Newsweek*, October 22, 2001, p. 61.

294 **thermal gunsites that could resolve enemies:** Correspondence with Mark Brightman; Andrew C. Revkin, " 'I Know They're in There, I Can See Them Breathing,' " *The New York Times*, November 22, 2001, p. B4.

294 **As temperatures dropped . . . infrared sensors:** Ibid.

294 **The conflict in Iraq . . . was a war waged and wagered in images:** David Friend, "A War Waged in Images," *American Photo*, September/October 2003; David Friend, "A War Waged in Images: Of Embeds, Unilaterals, Sat Phones, Sandstorms, and a Divisive Conflict the World Has Had to See to Believe," *The Digital Journalist*, September 2003 (digitaljournalist.org).

294 **During the battle phase . . . eighty aircraft . . . took "42,000 pictures":** "War Costs: How Much? Well, How High Can You Count?" *Newsweek*, May 26, 2003, p. 10.

294 **Camera-laden UAVs with zoom lenses:** Eric Schmitt, "Remotely Controlled Aircraft Crowd Dangerous Iraqi and Afghan Skies," *The New York Times*, April 5, 2005, p. A9; Correspondence with Mark Brightman.

294 **The remote-controlled drones—maneuvered by virtual pilots:** "Remotely Controlled Aircraft."

294 **By 2005, nearly eight hundred pilotless planes:** "Remotely Controlled Aircraft."

294 **Providing twenty-four-hour image coverage:** Correspondence with Mark Brightman.

294 **Cameras aboard combat and . . . (ISR) craft:** Correspondence with Mark Brightman; Lt. Col. Randy Roberts interviewed on MSNBC, April 10, 2003.

294 **When the visual or infrared spectrums proved murky:** Correspondence with Mark Brightman; "Digital Links," p. B2.

295 **As in Afghanistan . . . the much-touted rescue:** Frank Rich, "Pfc. Jessica Lynch Isn't Rambo Anymore," *The New York Times*, November 9, 2003, pp. A1, 10.

295 **They even carried packs of playing cards:** "Following the Military's Hunt for Most-Wanted Iraqi Officials," *The New York Times*, April 14, 2003, p. B5.

295 **"maps, grease pencils and radio reports":** John H. Cushman, Jr., and Thom Shanker, "A War Like No Other Uses New 21st-Century Methods to Disable Enemy Forces," *The New York Times*, April 10, 2003, p. B5.

295 **"probably the most televised event":** Frank DiGiacomo, "Oscars at War," *New*

York Observer, March 26, 2003, p. 7; James Poniewozik, "Real Battles in Real Time," *Time*, March 31, 2003, p. 61.

295 **"No war in human history has been chronicled":** Todd Purdum, "Scenes That Linger: An Iraq Chronicle by the Witnesses to a War," *The New York Times*, April 20, 2003, p. B10.

296 **Some commentators . . . referred to these herky-jerky glimpses:** "Reality TV" (editorial), (Binghamton, New York) *Press & Sun-Bulletin*, March 23, 2003; Byron McCauley, "War Coverage—Real Reality TV," *The Cincinnati Enquirer*, April 11, 2003, p. 6B.

296 **Frequent briefings . . . in a million-dollar media command center:** Michael Wolff, "Live From Doha . . . ," *New York*, April 7–14, 2003, p. 28.

296 **Keen worldwide interest:** Howard Kurtz, "The Ups and Downs of Unembedded Reporters," *The Washington Post*, April 3, 2003, p. C9.

296 **with the elevated head count:** "A War Waged in Images." The Committee to Protect Journalists (CPJ) would later compare the death toll of newsmen in Iraq with casualties in modern-day war zones: "Conflicts in Algeria, Colombia, the Balkans, and the Philippines have resulted in similarly high rates of journalist deaths since CPJ was founded in 1981. In Algeria, at least 58 journalists were killed between 1993 and 1996 . . . In Colombia 51 journalists have been killed since 1986. In the Balkans, 36 died on duty from 1991 to 1995. In the Philippines, 36 were killed between 1983 and 1987." ("Iraq: Numbers Show Growing, Evolving Dangers in Covering Conflict," 2004 News Alert, Committee to Protect Journalists, October 19, 2004 [www.cpj.org]); Marc Santora and Bill Carter, "War in Iraq Becomes the Deadliest Assignment for Journalists in Modern Times," *The New York Times*, May 30, 2006, p. A10.

296 **For the one thousand reporters and photographers in the field:** Emily Nelson and Matthew Rose, "Media Reassess Risks to Reporters in Iraq," *The Wall Street Journal*, April 9, 2003, p. B1.

296 **the fatality rate topped 1 percent:** Ibid.

296 **Fourteen correspondents died:** "Media Casualties in Iraq," Committee to Protect Journalists, Special Report: War in the Gulf, Resources, Links and Information, May 28, 2003 (www.cpj.org).

296 **compared with seventeen:** "Media Reassess Risks to Reporters in Iraq," p. B1.

296 **On May 29 . . . 2006, a woeful milestone:** Figures based on Associated Press's accounting during the war in Southeast Asia, according to 2005 tally compiled during ceremonies marking the thirtieth anniversary of the fall of Saigon, per interview with AP's former Saigon bureau chief Richard Pyle.

296 **Among the objections . . . the Pentagon was . . . making photographers beholden:** David Carr, "Reporters' New Battlefield Access Has Its Risks As Well As Its Rewards," *The New York Times*, March 31, 2003, p. B2; Howard Kurtz, "Embedded, and Taking Flak," *The Washington Post*, March 31, 2003, pp. C1, C7.

297 **"This is the danger of the embed":** Anthony Swofford, "The Unknown Soldier," *The New York Times Magazine*, March 3, 2003, p. 19.

297 **"Somebody expressed 'being embedded' ":** Interview with Fred Ritchin.

297 **"The military was shrewd enough":** Interview with Mike Smith.

297 **One sensed shock . . . in the pyrotechnic tableaux:** cover, *Time*, March 31, 2003; "Baghdad Is Burning," *U.S. News & World Report*, March 31, 2003.

298 **For millions . . . the image of . . . Ali Ismail Abbas:** James Kelly, "The Boy in the Photograph," *Time*, April 21, 2003, p. 8.

298 **Ali Ismail lost both arms:** Ibid.

298 **CBS called him "a symbol of Iraqi suffering":** *CBSnews.com*, April 16, 2003.

298 **"That still photo . . . tells the difficult naked truth":** John Fleming, *Anniston Star* (Alabama), April 13, 2003.

298 **Official Iraqi TV would show footage of the bodies:** Helen Kennedy, "Horror Show: Iraqi TV Parades Terrified POWs," New York *Daily News*, March 24, 2003, p. 4.

298 **Hussein's troops . . . in violation of the protocols:** Bob Graham, Niles Lathem, and Gersh Kuntzman, "Ghouls Parade Our Prisoners," *New York Post*, March 24, 2003, p. 4.

298 **When Hussein's sons Uday and Qusay were killed:** Neil MacFarquhar and Neela Banerjee, "Army Is Reluctant to Flaunt Photos of Hussein's Sons," *The New York Times*, July 24, 2005, p. 1.

298 **According to CNN . . . their bullet-scarred cadavers:** Ryn Brahimi, David Ensor, Jamie McIntyre et al., "U.S. Releases Photos Said to Show Saddam's Sons' Bodies: Many Iraqis Want Proof That Uday, Qusay Were Killed," CNN, July 24, 2003 (www.cnn.com).

299 **When Saddam . . . was photographed disheveled and disoriented:** Corky Siemaszko, "A Bearded Bum Trapped Like a Rat," New York *Daily News*, December 15, 2003, p. 2; "We Got Him!" *Time*, December 22, 2003, cover, p. 17.

299 **"Combat camera crew" armed with a four-thousand-dollar Sony:** Virginia Heffernan, "Camera Down the Hole, and the World Follows It," *The New York Times*, December 16, 2003, pp. AR1, 10.

299 **Snapshots were later taken of Hussein:** "Butcher of Baghdad: Inside Saddam's Prison Cell," *New York Post*, May 20, 2005, front page, pp. 2–3; David E. Sanger and Alan Cowell, "Hussein Photos in Tabloids Prompt U.S. Call to Investigate," *The New York Times*, May 21, 2005, p. A3.

299 **If a single picture . . . it was . . . taken on April 9, 2003:** "Saddam Statue Toppled in Central Baghdad," CNN, April 9, 2003 (www.cnn.com).

299 **"The stirring image of Saddam's statue":** Ted Rall, "How We Lost the Victory," *AlterNet*, April 16, 2003 (www.alternet.org).

299 **"It was telling" . . . that . . . "we remember":** Interview with John Loengard.

299 **"Just as video of human suffering":** William Safire, "Jubilant V-I Day," *The New York Times*, April 10, 2003, p. A27.

300 **"Nothing can in any way at this moment":** Alessandra Stanley, "Amid the Scenes of Joy, a Sight Less Welcome," *The New York Times*, April 10, 2003, p. B12.

300 **"Not since [*Life*'s] Alfred Eisenstaedt":** R. W. Apple, Jr., "In Baghdad Statue's Fall, Vindication of a Strategy," *The New York Times*, April 10, 2003, p. B4.

300 **When Secretary of State . . . he knew . . . that Hussein had ordered:** Lisa Grunwald, "What Saddam Has Done," *Life* (Life *in Time of War*), March 4, 1991, pp. 48–49.

301 **"imagery specialists . . . with years and years":** White House news release of Colin Powell's address to U.N., 2003 (www.whitehouse.gov).

301 **the chemical bunker photos were widely debunked:** Charles J. Hanley/Associated Press, "U.S. Justification for War," *Seattle Times*, August 12, 2003; Fred Kaplan,

"Calling Out Colin," *Slate*, August 12, 2003 (slate.msn.com); Douglas Jehl, "Reading Satellite Photos, Then and Now," *The New York Times*, February 8, 2004.

301 **The mobile trailers . . . were . . . intended for use:** Douglas Jehl, "Iraqi Trailers Said to Make Hydrogen, Not Biological Arms," *The New York Times*, August 9, 2003, p. A1; Peter Beaumont, Antony Barnett, and Gaby Hinsliff, "Iraqi Mobile Labs [Had] Nothing to Do with Germ Warfare, Report Finds," *The* (U.K.) *Observer*, June 15, 2003; Michael Isikoff and Mark Hosenball, "Terror Watch: Bad Sourcing," *Newsweek* Web exclusive on *MSNBC.com*, February 11, 2004 (www.msnbc.msn.com).

301 **the special tubes . . . were meant:** "The Man Who Knew," *60 Minutes II*, CBS News, September 14, 2004 (www.cbsnews.com).

301 **the incident had left "a blot":** Interview with Barbara Walters cited in "Powell Calls U.N. Speech a 'Blot' on His Record," ABC News via *AOL News*, September 9, 2005 (http://aolsvc.news.aol.com/news).

301 **"I'm the one who presented [the case]":** Ibid.

301 **Kenneth Pollack . . . told Hersh . . . "the existing filtering process":** Seymour M. Hersh, "The Stovepipe," *The New Yorker*, October 27, 2003.

302 **"major combat operations in Iraq have ended":** President George W. Bush, "President Bush Announces Combat Operations in Iraq Have Ended," USS *Abraham Lincoln*, at Sea off the Coast of San Diego, California, May 1, 2003 (www.state.gov).

302 **The resulting Top Gun photo op:** A line of green-clad Aviator Bush action-figures, modeled after the photo, was actually released that August—for $39.99 a doll. (Tom Raum for the Associated Press, "Soldiers a Favorite Audience for Bush," *The* [White Plains] *Journal News*, June 29, 2005, p. 3A; Vincent Morris, "Dubya a Real Doll," *New York Post*, August 13, 2003, p. 3.)

302 **Some Democrats charged that the visit:** Sam Dealy, " 'Tailhook Scandal' Finds Congressmen in Same Boat," *The Hill*, May 13, 2003.

302 **Republicans rebuffed such criticism:** Ibid.

302 **Columnist Maureen Farrell . . . took the racing pulse of the pundits:** Maureen Farrell, "George W. Kowalski? Bush's Macho Facade Goes Limp," *BuzzFlash.com*, September 23, 2003 (www.buzzflash.com).

302 **"George W. was a hottie":** Suzanne Fields, "Norman Mailer, Down for the Count: Bush's Masculinity Wins the Day," *The Washington Times*, May 15, 2003, p. A19.

302 **"stepping out of a fighter jet":** Lisa Schiffren, "Hey, Flyboy: Women Voters Agree, President Is a Hottie!" *The Wall Street Journal*, May 9, 2001.

302 **"I can't prove they gave him a sock job":** Richard Goldstein, "Bush's Basket," *The Village Voice*, May 21–27, 2003.

302 **"the defining picture of his presidency":** Interview with Ed Kosner.

302 ***Time* would reprise the picture:** "Mission *Not* Accomplished," *Time*, October 6, 2003, cover.

302 **In the first two years . . . by President Bush's own admission:** David Greene, "Bush Puts Iraqi War Dead at More than 30,000," National Public Radio, *All Things Considered*, December 12, 2005 (www.npr.org); "Bearing the Scars of Battle," *Newsweek*, March 20, 2006, p. 37.

303 **By the war's third anniversary:** David E. Sanger and Thom Shanker, "On Anniversary, Bush and Cheney See Iraq Success," *The New York Times*, March 20, 2006, p. A1.

303 **A year after . . . a batch of damning snapshots would emerge:** Seymour M. Hersh, "Torture at Abu Ghraib," *The New Yorker*, May 10, 2004.

303 **They were as profane . . . as images of the charred:** "Private Warriors: The High-Risk Contracting Business," PBS *Frontline*, June 2005 (www.pbs.org/wgbh).

304 **"The pictures from Abu Ghraib are trophy shots":** Luc Sante, "Tourists and Torturers," *The New York Times*, May 11, 2004, p. A23.

304 **"There were hundreds of these [photo] albums":** Michael Herr, *Dispatches* (New York: Avon, 1980), pp. 211–12.

304 **In many modern conflicts since the introduction of portable cameras in the twenties and thirties:** David Friend, "Seeing Past 80," *Vanity Fair*, January 2001, p. 123.

304 **"Brutaliz[ed them] in exactly the manner most horrific":** "The Torture Photos" (editorial), *The New York Times*, May 5, 2004, p. A26.

304 **"The intent of the pictures":** Michael Kimmelman, "Abu Ghraib Photos Return, This Time as Art," *The New York Times*, October 10, 2004, p. AR 29.

305 **The images were kept secret until Specialist Joseph Darby:** Seymour M. Hersh, "The Gray Zone: How a Secret Pentagon Program Came to Abu Ghraib," *The New Yorker*, May 24, 2004.

305 **By late spring, the images would appear on *60 Minutes II*:** Thom Shanker and Jacques Steinberg, "Bush Voices 'Disgust' at Abuse of Iraqi Prisoners," *The New York Times*, May 1, 2004, p. A5.

305 **"Every American knows":** Hesham A. Hassaballa, "Defining Images: Prison Photographs Paint All Americans with the Same Brush," *Chicago Tribune*, May 23, 2004, Sec. 2, p. 1.

305 **Indeed, the setting . . . Abu Ghraib was the very facility:** Photographs by Ron Haviv/VII, "Images from Abu Ghraib," *VanityFair.com*, January 24, 2005 (www.vanityfair.com).

305 **According to studies by the Red Cross:** Mark Danner, "We Are All Torturers Now," *The New York Times*, January 6, 2005, p. A27.

305 **By fighting a war against terrorism:** As a matter of policy, President Bush has sought to blur the lines between the two campaigns: one against the Iraqi regime, the other against Islamist extremists. Columnist Paul Krugman of *The New York Times* has pointed out that during Bush's 2003 "Mission Accomplished" speech, he asserted that in toppling Saddam "we have removed an ally of Al-Qaeda." Krugman also noted that as early as the afternoon of 9/11, according to notes made by an aide during a session with top commanders, Rumsfeld reportedly issued the directive: "Judge whether good enough [to] hit S. H. [Saddam Hussein] @ same time—not only UBL [Osama bin Laden] . . . Sweep it all up. Things related and not." (Paul Krugman, "Weapons of Math Destruction," *The New York Times*, April 14, 2006; Paul Krugman, "Osama, Saddam and the Ports," *The New York Times*, February 24, 2006, p. A27.)

306 **The Cuban government . . . put up "a billboard":** Associated Press, "Cuba: Animosities on Display," *The New York Times*, December 18, 2004, p. A9.

306 **In the States . . . an underground campaign [of] "art, street culture":** Faye Hirsch, "Graphic Art in the Summer of Discontent," *Art in America*, October 2004.

306 **A renegade artists' collective:** Correspondence with Copper Greene.

306n **Concurrently . . . a Los Angeles design team dubbed Forkscrew:** Illustration used in the exhibition *The Pain of War*, curated by Carol Solomon Kiefer, Mead Art Museum, Amherst College, Amherst, Massachusetts, October–December 2004.

306 **"That hooded figure . . . is now as iconic":** "Graphic Art in the Summer of Discontent." Indeed, in March of 2006, *The New York Times* stated unequivocally that Ali Shalal Qaissi, an Iraqi human rights campaigner, was the man in the hood. Qaissi said or implied as much to the newspaper. PBS had reportedly endorsed this view; *Vanity Fair* had claimed in 2005 that "evidence suggests" they were one and the same, "although . . . it will likely remain impossible to say for certain who is pictured." Yet, within days of the *Times* story, the actual victim was revealed by Salon.com to be *another* tortured detainee, a man identified elsewhere as Abdou Hussain Saad Faleh.

So powerful was this picture, and so indicative of the widespread nature of the abuse, that two different men would adopt the public identity of the anonymous subject. The hooded man invoked, enraged, and literally *stood for* every detainee.

Certain images capture singular experiences so evocatively that people identify quite literally with the human figure inside the icon. I am reminded of the uproar at *Life* in 1980 when a reprint of a picture prompted ten sailors to write to the magazine, thirty-five years after the end of World War II, each one insisting, with convincing evidence—a distinctive hairline, a quirky vein on the right hand, a memory of a newly acquired Quartermaster 1st Class patch visible in the photograph—that he alone was the "kissing sailor" in Eisenstaedt's famous image of a Navy man embracing a nurse in Times Square on V-J Day. Three women wrote in and claimed to be the nurse. (Kate Zernike, "Cited as Symbol of Abu Ghraib, Man Admits He Is Not in Photo," *The New York Times*, March 18, 2006, p. A1; Donovan Webster, "The Man in the Hood," *Vanity Fair*, February 2005; Michael Scherer, "Identifying a Torture Icon," Salon.com, March 14, 2006 [www.salon.com]. Byron Calame, "The Wrong Man: Deception, Mistaken Identity and Journalistic Lapses," *The New York Times*, March 26, 2006; "Who Is the Kissing Sailor?," *Life*, October 1980, pp. 68–72.)

306 **"People are running around with digital cameras":** Maureen Dowd, "A World of Hurt," *The New York Times*, May 9, 2004, p. 13.

306n **"once the scandal broke . . . Rumsfeld banned":** Vicki Goldberg, "Truth and Atrocity," *American Photo*, March/April 2005, p. 91.

307 **"Without [the Abu Ghraib photographs]":** "Tourists and Torturers," p. A23.

308 **"Perhaps . . . the digital camera will haunt":** Ibid.

308 **That night's episode of HBO's World War II drama:** *Band of Brothers*, David Frankel and Tom Hanks, dirs., DreamWorks SKG, DreamWorks Television, HBO, Playtone, BBC, prods., first aired on HBO on September 9, 2001.

7. MONDAY, SEPTEMBER 17

308 **A woman tacked a sign:** *here is new york: a democracy of photographs*, Alice Rose George, Gilles Peress, Michael Shulan, Charles Traub, eds. (New York/Zurich: Scalo, 2002), p. 815.

308 **"I want justice. There's an old poster":** James Risen and Judith Miller, "Bin Laden's Trail Is Lost, but Officials Suspect He Is Alive," *The New York Times*, February 4, 2002.

308 **Late in the day . . . the *New York Post* laid out:** Poster in *New York Post*, September 18, 2001.

309 **the markets had been closed . . . Monday being the first day:** "Bush: Bin Laden 'Prime Suspect,' CNN.com, posted 8:01 p.m., September 17, 2001 (http://cnn.allpolitics.com).

310 **"We will make no distinction between the terrorists":** George W. Bush, "Statement by the President in His Address to the Nation," White House press release, Office of the Press Secretary, September 11, 2001 (www.whitehouse.gov).

310 **I had been Harry's editor . . . on Shelton in 1994:** Richard B. Stolley, "Our Man in Haiti," *Life*, November 1994, p. 56.

310 **And in 1999:** "Hall of Fame," *Vanity Fair*, December 1999, p. 322.

310 **Harry's assignment: to render a group portrait:** "The Big Guns," *Vanity Fair*, February 2002, pp. 94–97.

311 **This time, on the cover of *Newsweek*:** "God Bless America," *Newsweek*, September 24, 2001, cover.

311 **After midnight, it was released:** Interview with Rich Gigli.

311 **On Wednesday, it made the front page of newspapers:** *September 11, 2001: A Collection of Newspaper Front Pages Selected by The Poynter Institute* (Kansas City: Andrews McMeel, 2001).

311 **On Thursday, the *New York Post*:** ". . . gave proof through the night that our flag was still there," *New York Post*, September 13, 2001, p. 1.

311 **In Texas, it was incorporated:** Rick Hampson, "The Photo No One Will Forget," *USA Today*, December 27, 2001.

311 **Citizens tattooed it on their biceps:** Monica Davey, "Many Took Arms in Iraq with Images of Sept. 11 Etched in Their Memories," *The New York Times*, April 6, 2003, p. B7.

311 **Soldiers toted it into battle:** Interviews with Bill Eisengrein and Thomas Franklin.

311 **Standing on the mount . . . a flag "caked in crud":** Interview with associate of the firemen who requests anonymity.

312 **Its impact derived, in part, from . . . the shot of six men:** David Friend, "A Flag for Rosenthal," *The Digital Journalist*, January 2001 (www.digitaljournalist.org).

312 **It would grace a U.S. postage stamp, mistakenly:** According to philatelists, several previous U.S. stamps had done the same.

312 **Reprinted 255 million times:** Interview with United States Postal Service spokesperson Mark Saunders.

312 **Used to raise more than $10 million:** Ibid.

312 **"Anybody tells you they don't know":** Interview with former NYPD official who requests anonymity.

312 **"My fire helmet, a flashlight":** Interview with Bill Eisengrein.

312 **"The person who took it down":** Interviews with Shirley Dreifus.

313 **Bagpipes played. Local notables gathered:** "WTC Tribute Statue Unveiled to Public," Eyewitness News, WABC-TV, *7online.com*; December 21, 2001 (http://abclocal.go.com/wabc/news).

313 **"It wasn't a fire . . . It was an act of war":** Joshua Robin, " 'Flag-Raising' Statue Unveiled," *NYNewsday.com*, December 22, 2001 (www.nynewsday.com).

313 **"[In] raising the flag":** "WTC Tribute Statue Unveiled to Public."

313 **Front and center, under a large sheet:** Interview with Ivan Schwartz.

313 **The firefighters' arms . . . "appear[ed] more sinewy":** " 'Flag-Raising' Statue Unveiled."

314 **The figures . . . were "composites":** Vicki Goldberg, "Truth and Atrocity," *American Photo*, March/April 2005, p. 91.

314 **"The artistic expression of diversity":** "Multiracial Ground Zero Statue Offends Some NYC Firefighters and Families," Associated Press, *FoxNews.com*, January 11, 2002 (www.foxnews.com); "Ground Zero Statue Criticized for 'Political Correctness,' " Associated Press, *CNN.com*, January 12, 2002 (http://cnn.allpolitics.com).

314 **The decision . . . had been made jointly:** "Ground Zero Statue Criticized for 'Political Correctness' "; Stephanie Gaskell, "Flag-Raising Draws Criticism," Associated Press, January 10, 2002; Philip Messing and Andy Geller, "Monumental Change—Backer Scraps Plans for Altered FDNY Statue," *New York Post*, January 18, 2002; Gersh Kuntzman, "Memorial Chic," *Newsweek* Web exclusive, MSBNC.com, January 22, 2002 (http://msnbc.msn.com); interviews with Schwartz.

314 **"The main Civil War memorials":** Interviews with Schwartz.

314 **No one, however, had received permission:** Interviews with Thomas Franklin, Bill Kelly, and Jennifer Borg.

314 **Members . . . called the monument . . . "political correctness run amok":** Lynne Duke, "Red, White and Blue, for Starters," *The Washington Post*, January 18, 2002, p. C1.

314 **A petition drive conscripted many:** Gersh Kuntzman, "Memorial Chic: What to Do with Ground Zero?" *Newsweek Online* via *MSNBC.com*, January 22, 2002 (http://msnbc.msn.com); "To: New York City Council, New York City Fire Department," 2002 petition (www.petitiononline.com/flgraise/petition.html).

314 **"The . . . horrible events [must be] present[ed]":** "To: New York City Council."

315 **"Why not . . . a Muslim woman":** Jonah Goldberg, "Factual Correctness Supercedes Statue," *townhall.com*, January 18, 2002 (www.townhall.com/columnists).

315 **The (Bergen County, N.J.) *Record* . . . considered filing:** Interviews with Borg.

315 **The attorney for the three firefighters:** "Red, White and Blue, for Starters"; interviews with Bill Kelly.

315 **Dan McWilliams . . . confessed . . . to being "disgusted":** Philip Messing and Andy Geller, "Monumental Change," *New York Post*, January 18, 2002; January 2002 posting on Web site of McCarthy & Kelly (www.mccarthykelly.com).

315 **The model . . . was destroyed:** Interview with Schwartz.

315 **Just before nine a.m., a news editor:** Interviews and correspondence with Franklin.

315 **"It's absolute mayhem":** Interviews with Franklin.

316 **about Danny Almonte . . . Bronx Little League star:** "Almonte, Bronx Team Records Wiped Away," ESPN.com, August 31, 2001 (http://espn.go.com); "Almonte's Team Forfeits LLWS Victories," *Sports Illustrated* Web site, September 1, 2001 (www.cnnsi.com).

317 **Dan McWilliams . . . was walking past the North Cove marina:** Interviews with Franklin and Dreifus.

317 **the 130-foot boat *Star of America*:** Interviews with Dreifus; e-mailed photographs of boat from yacht charter offices.

317 **"I'm going to take that flag":** Interview with friend of Dan McWilliams who requests anonymity.

317 **Aluminum pole and all:** Interviews with Dreifus.
317 **"Gimme a hand, will ya, George?":** Jeannine Clegg, "Flag Raising Was 'Shot in the Arm,' " *The Record* (Bergen County, New Jersey), September 14, 2001.
317 **"I knew exactly what he was doing":** Ibid.
317 **an acquaintance . . . from . . . Staten Island:** Interview with Eisengrein.
317 **"You need a hand?":** "Flag Raising."
317 **The men spied a large flagpole, likely a vestige:** Interviews with Franklin and Lori Grinker.
317 **They walked onto an elevated platform:** Interviews with Franklin.
317 **They detached a tattered green banner:** Interview with and outtakes from the photographer Lori Grinker's take, Ground Zero, New York, September 11, 2001, courtesy of Grinker and Contact Press Images.
318 **"I see the three firemen fumbling":** Interviews with Franklin.
318 **He swiveled his 245-mm lens:** Interviews with Franklin.
318 **Over the next minute . . . Franklin triggered twenty-four frames:** Photographs from Franklin's take, Ground Zero, New York, September 11, 2001, courtesy of Franklin and *The Record*.
318 **But in frame number fourteen:** Correspondence with Franklin, reconfirming author view of photographs.
318 **Also shooting . . . positioned on the . . . promenade:** Interview with Grinker.
318 **And Ricky Flores:** Ricky Flores photograph, "A New Day of Infamy," *The Journal News* (White Plains, New York), September 12, 2001, p. 1.
318 **"Just at that moment":** Interview with anonymous source.
319 **"Everybody just needed a shot in the arm":** "Flag Raising."
319 **"a few guys yelled out, 'Good job' ":** Ibid.
319 **He evacuated just minutes before:** Interviews with Franklin.
319 **Most of his fellow photographers . . . had already uploaded:** Interviews with Franklin and Danielle Richards.
319 **It was now 6:30 . . . the 9:00 p.m. deadline:** Interviews with Gigli and Franklin.
319 **Press time had been moved up:** Interview with Gigli.
320 **At 8:37, his thirtieth frame arrived:** Interviews with Franklin and Richards.
320 **Danielle Richards remembers "trying to decompress":** Interview with Richards.
320 **He had docked his laptop into a work-station:** Danielle Richards, photographing in Weehawken, had made pictures of the south tower, she says, as it "filled up the entire sky with mushroom cloud—an absolutely beautiful day that someone had imposed . . . Hiroshima on." Chris Pedota had covered prayer services in Englewood and an altercation in Paterson—in one of the neighborhoods, it turned out, where several of the hijackers had lived for a time. (Interviews with Richards and Pedota.)
321 **"I was looking at a lot of other pictures":** Interview with Richards.
321 **He double-clicked . . . to "give it a little pop":** Interview with Pedota.
321 **"Once you looked, it sort of took hold":** Interview with Jon Markey.
321 **"That's not a picture . . . It's a fucking icon":** Interviews with Gigli, Franklin, Markey, Pedota, and Richards.
321 **"My God, that's the classic shot":** Interview with Gigli.
321 ***The Record*'s presses started rolling:** Interview with Gigli.
322 **"By the morning of the twelfth":** Interviews with Franklin.
322 **"We were fielding calls":** Interview with Richards.

322 **In the first few weeks . . . "from Japan to Switzerland":** Interviews and correspondence with Jennifer Borg.

322 **The NFL wanted to print the image:** Letter from Borg to Eisengrein, Johnson, and McWilliams, October 22, 2001; Interviews with Borg and Kelly.

322 **The rock group *NSYNC:** Interviews with Borg.

322 **On the other extreme . . . the scene on snowboards:** Interviews with Franklin; Michele McPhee, "Charity Begins at Home," New York *Daily News*, March 15, 2004.

322 **Firefighters' families hoped to put the photo on mass cards:** Interviews with Borg.

322 **"This is the only thing that's helping":** Interviews with Borg.

323 **Opportunists had incorporated the image:** Photographs collected by Franklin and made into PowerBook slide show, 2005.

323 **The shot . . . was sold on eBay:** "911 Rescue Firefighter Painting Print #2," among various offerings on *eBay*, February 2005 (http://cgiebay.com).

323 **The image was plastered:** Images collected by Franklin.

323 **"The picture has this life of its own":** Interviews with Franklin.

323 **Crews were also said to have painted:** "How 9/11 Changed Us," *New York*, September 15, 2003, p. 36.

324 **"If you scour the visual record":** Interview with Richards.

324 **Franklin's shot . . . was dismissed as flat:** Interviews with various sources for David Friend, "Two Towers, One Year Later," *Vanity Fair*, September 2002, p. 373.

324 **While the picture . . . bore few of the hallmarks of Joe Rosenthal's:** Frederick S. Voss, *Reporting the War: The Journalistic Coverage of World War II* (Washington: Smithsonian Institution/National Portrait Gallery, 1994), p. 79.

324 **The rubble at their feet . . . a volcanic crater:** James Bradley and Ron Powers, *Flags of Our Fathers* (New York: Bantam Books, 2000), p. 9.

324 **"We don't care what wins":** Interview with a picture editor, who requests anonymity, then coordinating the Pulitzer Prize nominations from his office at a daily newspaper in the Northeast.

324 **Franklin's shot did not win; instead, *The New York Times*:** Howell Raines and *The New York Times* et al., *A Nation Challenged: A Visual History of 9/11 and Its Aftermath* (New York: New York Times/Callaway, 2002), p. 238.

325 **Franklin's photograph . . . digital-age descendant of . . . Apollo 11:** NASA photo caption on image "Flight Day Six: Historic Lunar Launch, July 21, 1969," account of first manned lunar-landing mission, *Space.com*, June 30, 2005 (www.space.com).

325 **Of Emanuel Leutze's . . . General Washington:** Jonathan Jones, "Washington Crossing the Delaware, Emmanuel *[sic]* Gottlieb Leutze, 1851," *The Guardian* (U.K.), March 8, 2003.

325 **"Both sets of flag-raisers not aware":** James Bradley, "Remembrance and Reflection," Life: *One Nation: America Remembers September 11, 2001*, Robert Sullivan, ed. (Boston/New York: Little, Brown, 2001), p. 169.

325 **The 1945 flag was borrowed from the USS *Missoula*:** *Flags of Our Fathers*, p. 202.

325 **Seven thousand Americans perished:** Ibid., p. 10.

325 **The Japanese had assumed positions:** Ibid., p. 7.

326 **Rosenthal, Speed Graphic in hand, was accompanied:** Ibid., pp. 208–10.

326 **"Here's one for all time!":** Ibid., p. 220.

326 **Both became freshly minted American icons:** Joe Rosenthal's film took a circuitous route from the battlefield to the front page. "First it was tossed into a mail plane . . . headed for the base at Guam, a thousand miles south across the Pacific. There the film would pass through many hands, any of which could consign it to the wastebasket. Technicians from a 'pool' lab would develop it . . . Then censors would scrutinize it; and finally the 'pool' chief would look at each print to decide which was worth transmitting back to the United States via radiophoto." (*Flags of Our Fathers*, p. 215.)

326 **Rosenthal almost missed the moment:** Interview with Rosenthal, for David Friend, "Shooting Past 80," *Vanity Fair*, January 2001.

326 **He was actually photographing a *second* flag:** *Reporting the War*, p. 79.

326 **That first week, thousands clamored for permission:** Interviews with Borg, Franklin, and Richards.

327 **her great-grandfather, in 1930:** Correspondence with Borg; "Corporate History," North Jersey Media Group Web site, Bergen County, New Jersey, 2005 (www.njmg.com).

327 **So *The Record*'s owners . . . set up:** Interviews with Borg.

327 **"Ethically . . . we felt we should get the firefighters' consent":** Interviews with Borg.

327 **"It was very bittersweet":** Interviews with Borg.

327 **"Dan's a doer":** Interviews with Kelly.

327 **An FDNY lieutenant:** Interview with Joe Pierpont.

327 **McWilliams has an almost military bearing:** Interview with McWilliams acquaintance who requests anonymity.

327 **"He's sensitive":** Interview with source who requests anonymity.

328 **George Johnson . . . recently made captain:** Interview with Pierpont.

328 **Like McWilliams . . . a rugby "sevens" player:** Interview with rugby league player; "Player Profile: George 'Rocket' Johnson," Web site for Rockaway Rugby Club, October 2005 (www.rockawayrugby.com).

328 **His nickname: "Rocket":** "Player Profile."

328 **Johnson, says a colleague, "is an outdoors guy":** Interview with Johnson colleague; e-mail correspondence with a confidant of Johnson's.

328 **"George gave bone marrow":** Interviews with Kelly; Rick Hampson, "The Photo No One Will Forget," *USA Today*, December 27, 2001.

328 **Bill Eisengrein . . . neighborhood kid on Staten Island:** Interview with Eisengrein; description on Web site of the three firefighters' charity, the Bravest Fund, 2005 (www.bravestfund.com).

328 **The two men . . . "are polar opposites":** Interview with a friend of both men who requests anonymity.

328 **A member of a Staten Island motorcycle club:** Interview with Eisengrein.

328 **His forearm bears tattoos:** Interview with acquaintance of Eisengrein's.

328 **Eisengrein dates a detective:** Interview with Eisengrein.

328 **"poignant, almost overwhelming":** Interviews with Borg.

328 **The firefighters decided to set up their own fund:** Interviews with Borg and Kelly.

328 **Johnson is now married to Kelly's sister:** Interviews with Kelly.

328 **More than half a million dollars:** Correspondence with Borg.

328 **Would go to New Jersey families affected:** "*The Record*'s Now Famous Photo of 9/11 Heroes Makes Philatelic History," press release from *The* (Bergen) *Record*, June 10, 2002, posted on the Web site for New Jersey Media Group's September 11 charity, *GroundZeroSpirit.org* (www.groundzerospirit.org).

329 **Grants from the firefighter's charity . . . $300,000:** Correspondence and interviews with Pierpont.

329 **the group of retired firemen . . . fireman whose daughter:** Correspondence and interviews with Pierpont.

329 **"It was a beautiful thing":** Interviews with Franklin.

329 **One day Borg lugged four cartons:** Interviews with Borg and Kelly.

329 **In time, he would field about sixty thousand:** Interviews with Kelly.

329 **One gun maker hoped:** Interviews with Borg; "How 9/11 Changed Us," p. 36.

329 **"We prioritized . . . Bill and I":** Interviews with Borg and Kelly.

329 **Fire truck decals were in:** Interviews with Borg.

329 **The bulk of Kelly's time:** Interviews with Kelly.

329 **like the topless bar:** Interviews with Kelly; "How 9/11 Changed Us," p. 36.

329 **"We pulled in about two million":** Interviews with Kelly.

329 **The firefighters . . . began insisting:** Interviews with Borg and Kelly.

329 **"They wanted to put the image on things":** Interviews with Borg.

330 **"You're too interested in getting a Pulitzer":** Interviews with Borg and Kelly.

330 **"We're not rejecting these things":** Interviews with Borg and Kelly.

330 **"The Pulitzer was the be all and end all":** Interviews with Kelly.

330 **Borg insists this is not true:** Interviews with Borg.

330 **Borg says she began receiving "unusual":** Correspondence and interviews with Borg.

330 **"Any law firm bills for its paralegals":** Interviews with Kelly.

330 **Then, after "repeatedly demanding":** Correspondence and interviews with Borg; interviews with Kelly.

330 **She says she was alarmed:** Correspondence and interviews with Borg.

330 **"In those first two years there was a lot of money":** Interviews with Kelly.

330 **"He was retained to keep an accounting":** Interviews with Borg.

331 **Reporter Michele McPhee . . . wrote two front-page stories:** Michele McPhee, "Profits of Doom," New York *Daily News*, March 5, 2004, p. 1; "Cashing in on 9/11," New York *Daily News*, March 15, 2004, p. 1.

332 **"reaped more than $500,000 in legal fees":** McPhee, "Cashing in on 9/11"; "Fees to 9/11 Fund's Lawyer Are Called into Question," Associated Press, *NorthJersey.com*, March 16, 2004 (www.northjersey.com).

332 **Kelly denied the charges:** Interviews with Kelly.

332 **New York attorney general . . . opened an inquiry:** Interviews with attorney general's charities bureau spokesperson Brad Maione; Interviews with Pierpont and Eliot Green; "Cashing in on 9/11."

332 **The firefighters . . . lined up in support of Kelly:** Interviews with Kelly, McPhee, Pierpont, and anonymous source; "Cashing in on 9/11."

332 **McPhee . . . "was basically given . . . the first interview":** Interview with Eisengrein.

332 **"taking pains to not attack the firefighters":** Interviews with McPhee.
332 **Soon, however, she was harassed:** Correspondence and interviews with McPhee.
332 **In the end, though, the IRS:** Letter to Eliot Green from R. C. Johnson, Director, EO Examinations, Department of the Treasury, Internal Revenue Service, May 27, 2005; Interviews with Kelly and Pierpont.
332 **Kelly and his firm's names were cleared:** Interviews with Pierpont and Maione.
332 **even as Kelly stepped aside as joint representative:** Interviews with Borg and Kelly.
332 **The attorney general's office concluded . . . Bravest Fund had "re-organized":** Interview with Maione.
332 **"We arrived at the conclusion":** Interview with Markey.
332 **Borg took on the legal workload:** Interviews with Borg.
331 **The firemen . . . "hire an attorney":** Interview with Pierpont.
332 **To this day . . . both sides continue:** Interviews with Borg, Eisengrein, Kelly, and Pierpont.
332 **"We just haven't been totally . . . satisfied":** Interview with Eisengrein.
332 **"What led to the firefighters and us having our 'divorce' ":** Correspondence and interviews with Borg.
332 **"Barbara Walters would call":** Interviews with Kelly.
332 **"They're scared to death of any spotlight":** Interview with Pierpont.
333 **"Can you think of a better target than us?":** Interview with a source who wishes to remain anonymous; "How 9/11 Changed Us," p. 36.
333 **"I remember hearing that the military":** Interview with Eisengrein.
333 **"How can I feel like a hero":** *Flags of Our Fathers*, p. 12.
333 **John "Doc" Bradley . . . "to deflect the phone-call requests":** Ibid., p. 4.
333 **three had died in battle:** Ibid., p. 4.
333 **Made their public bows and scrapes:** *Flags of Our Fathers*, photographic folio following p. 280.
334 **"None of us want to have a microphone":** Interview with Eisengrein.
334 **"their personal involvement with the people":** Interview with Pierpont.
334 **The stamp ostensibly raised $10.5 million:** "Assistance Program under the 9/11 Heroes Stamp Act of 2001," notice from the Department of Homeland Security, U.S. Fire Administration, December 2005, Federal Emergency Management Agency Web site (www.usfa.fema.gov/heroesstamp/).
334 **But not until the spring of 2006 had a penny:** Ibid.
334 **"Bureaucrats . . . sitting on every dime":** Bill Hoffman and Susan Edelman, "Sticky Mess in 9/11 Aid—Stamp Rules Bungled," *New York Post*, July 30, 2005.
335 **"The people [at FEMA] have hog-tied themselves":** Interview with Congressman Gary Ackerman; "Ackerman Blasts FEMA's Plan for Distribution of Funds to 9/11 Emergency Workers," press release from Congressman Gary Ackerman, 5th District, New York, July 29, 2005; Bill McAllister, "Ackerman Fumes Over Rules for Semipostal," *Linn's Stamp News*, August 29, 2005.
335 **"It's reprehensible":** Interview with Borg.
335 **The flag that the firemen raised . . . has, quite simply, disappeared:** Adam Lisberg, "Flag That 3 Firemen Raised at WTC Has Disappeared," NorthJersey.com, September 5, 2002 (www.northjersey.com).

335 **The flag was lowered in mid-September and escorted:** Interviews with Roddy Von Essen and Admiral Robert Natter; Yankee Stadium prayer service transcript, September 23, 2001.

335 **it was signed by Mayor Giuliani:** Interview with Sunny Mindel.

335 **it was ferried . . . to serve as the "battle flag":** "The Photo No One Will Forget"; interview with anonymous military source.

335 **ceremoniously passed among the thirty:** "The Big Guns," pp. 94–95.

335 **"a sailor e-mails me":** Interviews with Franklin.

335 **That March . . . Ackerman . . . flew out:** Interviews with Ackerman and Eisengrein.

335 **They made a dramatic shipboard landing:** Interview with Ackerman.

335 **some three hundred miles from shore:** Sonja Barisic, Associated Press, "WTC Flag Returned to NYC Delegation," *Firehouse.com*, March 26, 2002 (www.firehouse.com).

335 **Three sailors made the handoff:** Ibid.

335 **The flag next festooned City Hall:** David W. Chen, "Three Firefighters Say Flag Came from Yacht," *The New York Times*, April 2, 2002, p. B3.

336 **In August 2002, the flag was borrowed:** David W. Chen, "With 9/11 Flag, a Mystery Unfurls," *The New York Times*, September 4, 2002, p. B3.

336 **A group of firemen had organized:** Invitation to FDNY Viking Association's 1st Annual Sailboat Regatta, *Star of America* charter cruise event, August 10, 2002.

336 **Arthur Barry:** *Portraits 9/11/01: The Collected "Portraits of Grief" from* The New York Times (New York: Times Books, 2002), p. 29.

336 **Eric Olsen:** Invitation to FDNY Regatta.

336 **The moment the yacht owners removed it:** Interview with Dreifus.

336 **But this one was five by eight:** Interview with Dreifus.

336 **The flag in the photo had measured:** Interview with Dreifus; Stephanie Gaskell/Associated Press, "Couple Claims September 11 Flag Missing," *Dockwalk.com*, March 2002 (www.dockwalk.com).

336 **"it blocked our entire view":** Interview with Dreifus.

336 **"Something's wrong":** Interviews with Kelly.

336 **There had even been initial whispers:** Interview with Ackerman.

336 **On the six-month anniversary:** "Flag Raised Over WTC Wreckage Missing," CNN.com, September 5, 2002 (http://cnn.usnews.com).

337 **McWilliams complied:** Interviews with Kelly.

337 **Soon, a British newspaper was reporting:** Toby Harnden, "Twin Towers Flag Pair Seek Tax Aid," *The* (U.K.) *Telegraph*, March 5, 2002; "With 9/11 Flag," p. B3.

337 **Other accounts dubbed the couple opportunistic "millionaires":** "Millionaires . . . Ask for Tax Break for Donating 'Ground Zero' Flag," *What the Papers Say* Web site, United Kingdom, March 5, 2002 (www.wtps.co.uk).

337 **"People had this image of us":** Interview with Dreifus.

337 **"If everybody just gave up":** The twin towers had been such an integral part of their lives that a proper accounting of this symbol of the day became something of a mission. The pair had gone on their first date in the Trade Center's Sky Lobby. They operated their business out of the eighty-ninth floor of the north tower—four floors below the impact "on the side of the direct hit," according to Shirley

Dreifus, who had chosen to sleep in on September 11. (That morning, all five of her employees were located in what proved to be a protected section of the floor; they escaped as the offices burned around them.)

337 **Mayor Bloomberg . . . set the FDNY to the task:** Interview with Frank Gribbon; "September 11 Flag Missing," *BBC News Online*, September 5, 2002 (www.bbc news.co.uk).

337 **"The mayor recognizes the flag":** "With 9/11 Flag," p. B3.

337 **"I don't know where Osama bin Laden is either":** "Flag Raised Over WTC Wreckage Missing"; Wayne Barrett, "Mayor Mute," TheVillageVoice.com, October 18, 2005 (www.villagevoice.com).

337 **"My husband got totally frosted with that":** Interview with Dreifus.

337 **The couple filed a notice of claim . . . they decided to sue:** Interview with Dreifus.

337 **They asked for $525,000:** Michele McPhee, "Sue City in 9/11 Flag Flap," New York *Daily News*, March 6, 2004.

338 **"They paid ten dollars for a flag":** Ibid.

338 **To this day . . . the FDNY has yet to:** Interviews with Gribbon.

338 **the Navy wanted to fly the firefighters' flag:** Interviews with Natter and a military source who requests anonymity.

338 **"They were steaming away to the region":** Correspondence and interview with Roddy Von Essen.

338 **With the approval of Deputy Fire Commissioner:** Interview with Von Essen.

338 **Later that week, just before a memorial service:** Interviews with Natter.

339 **"about the size of the one in the fireman's picture":** Interview with military source who requests anonymity.

339 **"I know a flag came down . . . the *second flag*":** Interviews with Gribbon.

339 **There are no leads among . . . Giuliani's inner circle:** Interview with Sunny Mindel.

339 **"Towards the end of the week":** Interview with Eisengrein.

340 **"In hindsight . . . it was this world-famous photo":** Interviews with Gribbon.

340 **"There was no sense of preserving":** Interview with James Hanlon.

340 **"You have Port Authority, police":** Interview with anonymous high-ranking NYPD source.

341 **"Ground Zero was a fairly protected area":** Interview with Dreifus.

341 **An incident commander . . . says Kerik:** Interviews with Bernard Kerik.

341 **Gribbon insists . . . the *sector* commander:** Interviews with Gribbon.

341 **"He had life and death on his mind":** Interviews with Gribbon.

341 **"Everybody and their brother":** Interview with Eisengrein.

341 **On day three, a giant, eight-by-twelve:** David W. Dunlap, "Architect Finds Spot for Flag Found in Ruins of 9/11 Site," *The New York Times*, July 29, 2005, p. B8; "Long May She Wave: Emblem of 9/11 to Appear at Bush Museum," press release from George (H. W.) Bush Presidential Library and Museum, September 2002 (http://bushlibrary.tamu.ed).

341 **Another tattered flag was discovered at the Staten Island:** Correspondence with Michelle Delaney and Marilyn Zoidis, National Museum of American History, Smithsonian Institution, Washington, D.C.

342 **A third was . . . brought to Kerik's:** Interview with Kerik.

342 **then ended up flying on the space shuttle:** "Members of the FDNY and NYPD Represent New York at Memorial Service in Houston for Columbia Astronauts," press release from New York City Fire Department, February 4, 2003 (www.nyc.gov/html/fdny).

342 **"The three firemen had taken care to attach it securely":** Examination of outtakes of photographs by Franklin and Grinker.

342 **One logical explanation . . . once it appeared on the front page:** ". . . gave proof through the night that our flag was still there," *New York Post*, September 13, 2001, p. 1.

342 **"The Secretary of the Navy, James Forrestal":** *Flags of Our Fathers*, p. 207.

343 **"After the third or fourth day":** Interview with Hanlon.

343 **On Friday, in fact, nearly two inches of rain fell:** Interview with the National Climatic Data center; "History for Central Park, New York, on Friday, September 14, 2001," National Weather Service Daily Summary, *wunderground.com* (www.weatherunderground.com); Thomas Von Essen, *Strong of Heart: Life and Death in the Fire Department of New York*, (New York: ReganBooks, 2002), describing rain in September 14 entry of "From the Pages of My Notebooks" section, following p. 208.

343 **"Want to make a wager?":** Interview with former NYPD official.

343 **"There's something on it that distinguishes it":** Interview with Dreifus.

343 **"I still have to work a second job":** Interview with Eisengrein.

344 **Sculptor Stan Watts has been working:** Interviews with Kelly and Watts.

344 **hoping to raise the requisite $4.5 million:** Interview with Watts; Ed Sealover, "Firefighters Give Up 9/11 Statue Plans," *The* (Colorado Springs) *Gazette*, September 27, 2005.

344 **The firefighters, in fact, have . . . approved:** Interviews with Kelly.

344 **"It's colossal":** Interview with Watts.

344 **It was recently voted down:** "Firefighters Give Up."

344 **Plans to erect it in Washington, D.C.:** Interview with Watts.

344 **Then the International Association of Fire Fighters backed out:** "Firefighters Give Up."

344 **Watts . . . already plowed about $150,000:** Interview with Watts.

345 **On their flight down to Washington:** Interviews with Kelly.

345 **They had breakfast:** Interviews with Eisengrein and Kelly.

345 **learned that the president had personally chosen:** Interview with Ackerman.

345 **At around 2:45 p.m.:** "Bush Unveils September 11 Commemorative Postage Stamp," press release from the White House, Office of the Press Secretary, March 11, 2002.

345 **Upon meeting . . . firemen offered him a gift:** Interviews with Eisengrein, Franklin, and Kelly.

345n **"I appreciate you all allowing the Postal Service":** "Bush Unveils September 11 Commemorative Postage Stamp."

345n **"In the glorious tradition of the Marine Corps":** *Flags of Our Fathers*, p. 295.

345 **Before heading back to New York that day:** Interviews with Eisengrein and Kelly.

345 **There, they . . . beheld the statue of six men . . . four stories tall:** "U.S.M.C. War Memorial" description, National Park Service Web site, 2005 (www.nps.gov).

345 **"The sun was going down":** Interviews with Eisengrein and Kelly.

346 **It showed my sister, Janet . . . her young life gone:** Jay Lovinger, "Celebrating Janet," *Life*, October 1997, p. 10.

346 **It was the bloodiest day in U.S. history:** David Friend, "America's Darkest Day," *The Digital Journalist*, October 2001 (www.digitaljournalist.org).

346 **I am referring . . . to September 17, 1862:** William A. Frassanito, *Antietam: The Photographic Legacy of America's Bloodiest Day* (New York: Scribner, 1978), p. 17.

346 **The one-day toll: four to five thousand fatalities:** Shelby Foote, *The Civil War: A Narrative—Volume II: Fort Sumter to Perryville* (New York: Random House, 1958), p. 702; David J. Eicher, *The Longest Night: A Military History of the Civil War* (New York: Simon & Schuster, 2001), p. 363.

347 **The photographers . . . Alexander Gardner and James Gibson:** *Antietam*, pp. 18, 51.

347 **Working under the auspices of Mathew Brady:** Ibid., pp. 53–54.

347 **The photographs . . . the first to show American war dead:** Ibid., pp. 19–20.

347 **When displayed . . . pedestrians "pressed up against the windows":** Martha A. Sandweiss, "Death on the Front Page," *The New York Times*, April 4, 2002, p. D13.

347 **"It is so nearly like visiting the battlefield":** Joel Snyder, "Inventing Photography," in Sarah Greenough, Joel Snyder, David Travis, and Colin Westerbeck, *On the Art of Fixing a Shadow: One Hundred Fifty Years of Photography* (Washington, D.C.: National Gallery of Art/Art Institute of Chicago, 1989), p. 27.

347 **Pearl Harbor, where 2,400 U.S. servicemen perished:** Nathan Miller, *War at Sea: A Naval History of World War II* (New York: Scribner, 1995), p. 206; Gordon W. Prange, Donald M. Goldstein, and Katherine V. Dillon, *Pearl Harbor: The Verdict of History* (New York: McGraw-Hill, 1986), p. xxxii.

347 **2,500 Allied deaths . . . 1,465 of them American:** "D-Day and the Battle of Normandy: Your Questions Answered," D-Day Museum, Portsmouth, United Kingdom (www.ddaymuseum.co.uk).

347 **10,000 total assault-force casualties . . . [German toll]:** Ibid.

347 **Their images, later splashed across spreads of *Life*:** Life's *Picture History of World War II*, Arthur B. Tourtellot, ed. (New York: Time, 1950), p. 84.

348 **Capa managed to squeeze off four rolls:** John G. Morris, *Get the Picture: A Personal History of Photojournalism* (New York: Random House, 1998), p. 6.

348 **eleven frames of which survived:** Ibid., p. 7.

ACKNOWLEDGMENTS

This book exists because of a horrific national tragedy and unparalleled loss of life. I would like to express my gratitude to all of those who, having lost loved ones, shared with me some of the most painful stories of their lives. My thanks, as well, go to the photographers, videographers, and filmmakers who cooperated with this project, each one unwaveringly obliging with insight, time, and spirit.

Graydon Carter encouraged my efforts on this book from its first glimmer in 2002. He has been generous and gracious and a guiding light. Paul Elie, of Farrar, Straus and Giroux, championed the project, shaped it, and challenged me to provide greater depth and clarity. Kevin Doughten and Maisie Todd were invaluable and unflappable. Chris Garrett and Stuart Krichevsky helped in myriad ways, as did Jeff Seroy, Sarita Varma, and Elizabeth Garriga at FSG. Jessica Flint, without fail, was at the ready, assisting with research and attempting to meet stringent standards of accuracy. She graced the project with astute attention to detail, equanimity, and dedication.

For help above and beyond the call, I'm beholden to Harry and Gigi Benson, Sarah Crichton, Thomas Franklin, Jonathan Galassi, David Hajdu, Jeffrey Hogan, Don Johnston, Peter Kunhardt, Jennifer Massoni, Mimi Park, Ann Paulsen, Joann and Michael Rooney, and Michael Shulan. I cannot sufficiently thank the Naudet family, along with James Hanlon, Mark Koops, Les Moonves, Ben Silverman, and Susan Zirinsky.

For reading portions of the book and offering criticism, expertise, and support, I'm grateful to Marc Kravitz (my editor since childhood), James Balog, Stephen Claypole, Tom Flynn, Mark Greenberg, Bruce Handy, Mark Hosenball, Jo Imeson, George Kindel, Scott Rubins, and Robert Walsh. Harriet Seitler, as always, inspires me and spurs me on.

The following people were valued contributors: Kim Akhtar, Anne Beagan, Jonathan Bender, Gary Berntsen, Jennifer Borg, Jimmie Briggs, Mark Brightman, Doug Brinkley, Sue Brisk, Rinker Buck, Bobbi Baker Burrows and Russell Burrows, Danny Callaro, Mike Carter, Jeffrey Claman, Tom Dallal, Gwen Davis, Andrew Eichner, Lucy Erickson, Jay and Kathy Reilly Fallon (and the Heavenly Lullabies initiative), Laury Frieber, Don Garber, Liz Garland, Chris George, Jeremy Gilley, Nancy Glowinski, Jordan Goldes, MaryAnne Golon, Mark Gompertz, Ed Grazda, Frank Gribbon, Khalid Hadi, Ann and Sandy Halstead, Dirck Halstead, David Harris, Willis Hartshorn, Hope Hening, Dan Higgins, Daisy Ho, Bill Hooper, Peter Howe, Holly Hughes, Bill Hunt, Martha Hurley, Masood Kamandy, Elaine Kaufman, Bill Kelly, Jim Kelly, Kevin Kennon, David Kirsch, Mark Kotfila, Nicholas Kristof, Beth Kseniak, John Labriola, Eliane Laffont, Andre Lambertson, Betsy Lembeck, Brian Lewis, Harlan Levy, John Levy, Laurent Lunetta, Jay Manis, Michele McNally, Michele McPhee, Nardi McWilliams, Danielle Menasche, Jacques Menasche, Michael Mendelsohn, Sunny Mindel, David Moore, Alison Morley, Amy and Bert Nalle, Cynthia O'Neill and Friends in Deed, Marybeth O'Neill, Mary Panzer, J. P. Pappis, Brad and Cathy Paulsen, Carla and Frank Pelligrino, Jr., Robert Pledge, Henry Porter, Ambreen Querishi, Ken Regan, Frank Rich, Steve Robinson, Ira Sapir, Bob Sauer, Aaron Schindler, David Schonauer, Henry Schuster, Lester Schwalb, Elliot Schwartz, Gil Schwartz, Ivan Schwartz, Carrie Seifer, Alicia Shepard, Tala Skari, Jeffrey Smith, Sreenath Sreenivasan, Michele Stephenson, Robert Stevens, Robert Sullivan, Christopher Sweet, Scott Thode, Helene Veret, Shelley Waln, Judy Weiser and PhotoTherapy Centre, Chris Whipple, Michael Wolff, Charles Zoeller, and Turning Lives Around (of Hazlet, New Jersey). I would also like to thank the Adashek, Berman, and Silverman families.

I'm indebted to mentors Ben Aronin, Eunice Borman, Paul Casey, G. Armour Craig, Mary Kerner, John Frook, Jonathan Larsen, John Loengard, Cullen Murphy, Carl Mydans, Doris O'Neill, Kay Rosenberg Simons, and Robert Stone, along with the managing editors of *Life*, who taught me key lessons about how to respect and harness the power of photojournalism: Phil Kunhardt, Dick Stolley, Judy Daniels, Pat Ryan, Jim Gaines, Dan Okrent, and Jay Lovinger.

The spirit of my sister, Janet, is ever present in my life, and for that I feel blessed. It is my good fortune to be able to gain strength from my brother, Richard, and my nephews Eliot and Jake.

My wife, Nancy Paulsen, possesses a saintly patience. A marvelous editor, she has always understood this writer's need for prolonged suspension of sanity. Throughout the writing of this book and throughout our lives together, her love has been unconditional, her wit undimmed, her understanding fathomless, always allowing a wide berth for journalistic and literary obsessions. Our children, Sam and Molly, have offered love, encouragement, and insight beyond their years.

For more information on the two charities that receive a portion of the proceeds from the sale of this book, please visit:

The Uniformed Firefighters Association Scholarship Fund
http://ufalocal94.org/ufa_funds/scholarship_fund/scholarship_fund.html

The Dart Center for Journalism and Trauma
http://www.dartcenter.org

DAVID FRIEND
May 2006

INDEX

G

K

L

M

N

O

P

S

Y

Z

PERMISSIONS ACKNOWLEDGMENTS

Grateful acknowledgment is made for permission to reprint the following previously published material:

Excerpts from David Friend, "Bond of Brothers," *Vanity Fair*, March 2002, p. 182, and David Friend, "Two Towers, One Year Later," *Vanity Fair*, September 2002, p. 326. Copyright © 2002 Condé Nast Publications. All rights reserved. Originally published in *Vanity Fair*. Reprinted by permission.

Excerpts from David Friend, "A War Waged in Images," first appeared in *American Photo*, September/October 2003. Copyright © David Friend. Courtesy Hachette Filipacchi Media.

Excerpts from David Friend, "America's Darkest Day," *The Digital Journalist*, October 2001. Copyright © David Friend.

Excerpts from "Portraits of Grief" for Calvin Gooding and Glen Pettit copyright © 2001 by The New York Times Co. Reprinted with permission of *The New York Times* and of the victims' families.

Excerpt from "At a School in Russia, a World of Emptiness," by Seth Mydans, copyright © 2004 by The New York Times Co. Reprinted with permission.

Excerpt from "The Falling Man," by Tom Junod, used with permission of the author. Originally published in *Esquire*.

Excerpt from "Seeing the Horror: James Nachtwey," *The Digital Journalist*, October 2001, used with permission from Peter Howe and Dirck Halstead, *The Digital Journalist*.

Excerpt from "The Unbearable Relevance of Photography," by Fred Ritchin, used with permission of the author. Originally published in *Aperture* #171, Summer 2003, copyright © Fred Ritchin 2003.

Lyrics from "The Revolution Will Not Be Televised," by Gil Scott Heron, copyright © 1971 Binestock Publishing Company. Used by permission. All rights reserved.

Excerpt from "The Height of Myth-Making," by Philip Kennicott, copyright © 2003 The Washington Post Company. Excerpted with permission.